What the Bible teaches

JOB

D. J. Newell

EDITOR   W. S. STEVELY

SERIES EDITORS

W. S. STEVELY   **D. E. WEST**

RITCHIE

John Ritchie Publishing

ISBN-13: 978 1 912522 25 5

WHAT THE BIBLE TEACHES
© 2018 John Ritchie Ltd.
40 Beansburn, Kilmarnock, Scotland

www.ritchiechristianmedia.co.uk

Typeset by John Ritchie Ltd., Kilmarnock
Printed by Bell & Bain Ltd., Glasgow

PREFACE

The publishers have commissioned this Old Testament series of commentaries to complement the completed set of New Testament commentaries issued under the general title "What the Bible Teaches". Together they seek to provide an accessible and useful tool for the study of, and meditation on, Scripture.

While there is no shortage of commentaries currently available on the various books of the Old Testament it was felt that there was no complete series that sought simply to apply the message of Genesis through to Malachi to the concerns of believers today.

The authors of these volumes are not scholars of the original languages and rely on others for guidance on the best modern views of word meanings and similar matters. However, all the authors share the conviction that the Bible in its entirety is the Word of God. They believe it to be reliable, accurate, and intended "for our learning" (Rom 15.4). This view has been explained further by Mr W. S. Stevely in a short series of articles that appeared in "The Believer's Magazine", also published by John Ritchie Ltd., in 1999.

The two Testaments fit together so that principles and illustrations from the Old are brought to bear on issues that arise on nearly every page of the New. Knowledge of the Old is therefore an indispensable aid to the proper understanding of the New. In particular the Lord Jesus can be seen in prophecy and picture again and again. He, Himself, as described in the Gospels, is an exemplar of this approach to the Old Testament through His constant reference to people and incidents whose histories are recorded for us, and to those prophetic statements that applied to Him.

Given this understanding of the nature and purpose of the Scriptures, the main lessons of the books are considered and applied to our circumstances today by authors experienced in preaching and teaching the Word of God.

Since no attempt is being made to produce an academic series the technical apparatus has been kept to a minimum. Where authors have judged it of value attention is drawn to linguistic and other issues. Transliteration, where appropriate, is accompanied by reference to the numerical system devised by Strong to allow the reader without knowledge of the original languages to gain access to the various lexical aids which have adopted this system. For clarity, numerical references to New Testament words only are given in italics, following the practice used in Strong's Concordance.

The system of transliteration generally used is that adopted by the Theological Wordbook of the Old Testament (TWOT), edited by Harris, Archer and Waltke, and published by Moody Press, Chicago, 1980. However, there are occasions when account has been taken of the commonly recognised English spelling of some Hebrew words.

References to Scripture without attribution are taken from the Authorised (King James) Version. Where other translations are quoted the source is indicated.

Biblical measurements are usually given in cubits. For ease of calculation the general assumption has been adopted that 1 cubit = 18 inches/46cms.

Since the commentaries do not necessarily follow a verse-by-verse approach, and to save space and cost, in general the text of Scripture is not included. It is assumed that all readers have available a copy of the Bible.

With the publication of this volume on Job the series "What the Bible Teaches" is complete. The earlier work on the New Testament ended with the commentary on Romans by Mr Fred Stallan in 1998. We, who have been the editors for the Old Testament, are grateful to the Lord for His help in enabling us to bring the task to a conclusion.

We wish to express our indebtedness to the many authors who have written for us. They have freely given the time, skill and effort involved, and we trust that the commentaries will continue to be profitable, practical and challenging to believers interested in the study of the Word of God.

W. S. STEVELY
D. E. WEST

CONTRIBUTOR

DAVID J NEWELL

David Newell, originally from St Albans, moved to Glasgow in 1974 where he was involved in education until his retirement in 2012. Since 1975 he has been in fellowship with the assembly at Eastpark Gospel Hall.

ABBREVIATIONS

ASV   The American Standard Version (the American variant of the RV).

AV   The Authorised Version (also known as The King James Version - KJV).

BBE   The Bible in Basic English.

CEV   The Contemporary English Version.

CHM   C H Mackintosh.

ESV   The English Standard Version.

ISV   The International Standard Version.

JND (also Darby)   J N Darby's New Translation.

JPS   The Jewish Publication Society Bible.

KJV   The King James Version (also known as The Authorised Version - AV).

LXX   The Septuagint: the ancient translation of the Old Testament into Greek. Often quoted in the New Testament.

MKJV   The Modern King James Version.

NT   New Testament.

OT   Old Testament.

RV   The Revised Version.

TWOT   *Theological Word Book of the Old Testament*, edited
                      by Harris, Archer & Waltke.

YLT   Young's Literal Translation.

JOB

D. J. Newell

CONTENTS

BIBLIOGRAPHY

(i) Bible Versions

Unless otherwise indicated, Bible quotations are taken from the King James Version of 1611 (KJV). Hebrew words are identified using the numbers provided in Strong's Concordance.

Other versions consulted and quoted are as follows, in each case the text being taken from the e-Sword electronic Bible:

The Revised Version (RV)
J N Darby's New Translation (JND)
The American Standard Version (ASV)
Young's Literal Translation (YLT)
The Jewish Publication Society Bible (JPS)
The Bible in Basic English (BBE)
The English Standard Version (ESV)
The International Standard Version (ISV)
The Contemporary English Version (CEV)
The Modern King James Version (MKJV).

(ii) Books

The following authorities are cited in the text from the electronic editions available with e-Sword:

Albert Barnes, *Notes on the Bible*
Brown-Driver-Briggs' Hebrew Definitions
John Gill, *Exposition of the Entire Bible*
International Standard Bible Encyclopedia
Jamieson, Fausset and Brown Commentary (where the Job commentary is by Fausset)
F B Meyer, *Through the Bible Day by Day*
Strong's Hebrew and Greek Dictionaries.

Readers wanting the bare minimum of aids to Job are directed to Delitzsch's commentary in the superb Keil and Delitzsch *Commentary on the Old Testament*, and Thomas Robinson's *Homiletical Commentary on Job*. The former provides an indispensable technical exposition of the text, while at the same time untangling the book's prolonged argument; the latter offers rich and heart-warming applications for the believer. Little else is needed.

Andersen, Francis I. *Job*. InterVarsity Press, 1976.
Archer, Gleason L. Jr. *A Survey of Old Testament Introduction*. Moody Press, 1964.
Barfield, Kenny. *Why the Bible is Number 1*. Baker, 1988.
Baxter, J. Sidlow. *Explore the Book*. Oliphants, 1960.
    A superbly incisive general overview.

Blanchard, John. *The Complete Gathered Gold.* Evangelical Press, 2006.

Bullard, Roger A. *Messiah: The Gospel according to Handel's Oratorio.* Hodder, 1995.

Bullock, C. Hassell. *An Introduction to the Old Testament Poetic Books.* Moody Press, 1988.
> *Another fine introduction.*

Bunyan, John. *The Whole Works.* Ed George Offor, reprinted Baker, 1971.

Cansdale, G. S. *Animals of Bible Lands.* Paternoster Press, 1970.
> *Illuminating on the zoology of Job.*

Constable, Thomas. *Notes on Job,* 2014, www.soniclight.com/constable/notes.htm.
> *Informed by recent scholarship but conservative in its approach.*

Culver, Robert Duncan. *Systematic Theology.* Mentor, 2005.

Darby, J. N. *Synopsis of the Books of the Bible.* Stow Hill Bible and Tract Depot, 1965.

Davidson, A. B. *The Book of Job.* Cambridge, 1951.
> *A liberal view of Scripture, but very useful in explaining the text.*

Davis, Dale Ralph. *1 Kings: The Wisdom and the Folly.* Christian Focus, 2002.

Davis, Dale Ralph. *Slogging Along in the Paths of Righteousness.* Christian Focus, 2014.

Davis, Dale Ralph. *Faith of our Father.* Christian Focus, 2015.

Delitzsch, F. *The Book of Job.* 1866.
> *Despite the advocacy of Solomonic authorship, this exposition, which forms part of the great Keil and Delitzsch "Old Testament Commentary", is an expert and wholly indispensable unfolding of the book's argument and development.*

Ellison, H. L. *Tragedy to Triumph.* Paternoster, 1958.
> *Brief but full of insights.*

Fausset, A. R. *Fausset's Bible Dictionary.* Zondervan, 1949.

Finlay, M. H. *The Arrows of the Almighty.* Moody Press, 1963; reprinted Ritchie, 2013.
> *One of the best short introductions, warm and devotional.*

Ford, Yannick. *The Gospel in Job.* Scripture Truth Publications, 2007.
> *Uses Job very helpfully as a launching pad into gospel truth.*

Fuller, Thomas. *The Worthies of England.* Folio Society, 1987.

Gesenius, Wilhelm. *Hebrew-Chaldee Lexicon to the Old Testament.* Baker, 1979.

Hall, Joseph. *Contemplations on the Historical Passages of the Old and New Testament.* Soli Deo Gloria, 1995.

Hammond, T. C. *In Understanding Be Men.* IVP, 1951.

Harris, Archer, Waltke (eds). *Theological Wordbook of the Old Testament,* 2 vols. Moody Press, 1980.

Harrison, R. K. *Introduction to the Old Testament.* Tyndale Press, 1970.

Harrison, R. K. & Pfeiffer (eds). *Wycliffe Bible Commentary.* Oliphants, 1960.

Hartley, John E. *The Book of Job.* (NICOT), Eerdmans, 1988.
> *An in-depth technical and scholarly analysis, but rather dry and very short on application.*

Hastings, Max. *Catastrophe: Europe Goes to War, 1914.* Collins, 2013.

Henry, Matthew. *Commentary on the Whole Bible;* Volume 3. Macdonald, nd.
> *Some excellent spiritual insight and practical applications.*

Hewlett, H. C. *The Companion of the Way*. Ritchie, 2014.

Jensen, I. L. *Survey of the Old Testament*. Moody Press, 1978.
Ideal introduction for students, with structural chart and questions.

Keil, C. F. *The Pentateuch*, 1866 (volume 1 of the Keil and Delitzsch *Old Testament Commentary*).

Kelly, William. *Notes on the Book of Job*, 1879.

Kelly, William. *Three Lectures on the Book of Job*. 1909.
The best of Kelly's accounts of Job.

Kelly, William. *Eleven Lectures on the Book of Job*. 1919.
Each of Kelly's three commentaries originally appeared in "The Bible Treasury".

Lewis, C. S. *Poems*. Collins, 1964.

Lightner, Robert P. *Handbook of Evangelical Theology*. Kregel, 1995.

Lutzer, Erwin W. *Ten Lies about God*. Word Publishing, 2000.

MacArthur, John (ed). *MacArthur Study Bible*. Word, 1997.

Mackintosh, C. H. *Job and his Friends*, reprinted in *The Mackintosh Treasury*. Loizeaux, 1976.

Mangalwadi, Vishal. *The Book that Made your World*. Thomas Nelson, 2011.

Morris, Henry M. *The Remarkable Record of Job*. Master Books, 2000.
Conservative overview with an overemphasis on creation truth and some eccentric exegesis, but contains useful comments.

Morris, Henry M. *The Defender's Study Bible*. World Publishing, 1995.

Parsons, Percy. *Studies in the Book of Job*. Duplicated notes, 1961.

Ramm, Bernard. *Protestant Biblical Interpretation*. 3rd edition, Baker, 1970.

Robinson, Thomas. *Homiletical Commentary on the Book of Job*. Richard D Dickenson, 1876.
An outstanding combination of careful exegesis and devotional application.

Sarfati, Jonathan. *The Genesis Account*. CMI, 2015.

Schaper, Robert N. *Why Me God?* Regal Books, 1974.

Scherman, Nosson (ed). *The English Tanach*. Mesorah Publications Ltd, 2011.

Scroggie, W. G. *Know Your Bible*. Pickering & Inglis, 1940.

Scott, Walter. *Bible Handbook: Old Testament*. Morrish, nd.

Sharp, D. & Bergman, Jerry (eds). *Transformed by the Evidence*. Leafcutter Press, 2014.

Shedd, W. G. T. *Dogmatic Theology*. 3 vols, reprinted Thomas Nelson, 1980.

Smick, Elmer B. *Job*, in *The Expositors' Bible Commentary*, ed Frank E Gabelein, vol 4. Zondervan, 1988.
A technical account, but encouragingly alert to some of the book's anticipations of New Testament revelation.

Spurgeon, C. H. *The Suffering of Man and the Sovereignty of God*. Fox River Press, 2001.
A collection of sermons on selected verses from the book, always practical and evangelical.

Spurgeon, C. H. *Autobiography; The Early Years*. Banner of Truth, 1962.

Strong, A. H. *Systematic Theology*. 1907, reprinted Pickering & Inglis, 1987.

Thomas, I. D. E. (ed). *The Golden Treasury of Puritan Quotations*. Moody Press, 1975.

Thiessen, Henry C. *Lectures in Systematic Theology*. Eerdmans, 1949.

Walvoord & Zuck (eds). *Bible Knowledge Commentary*. Victor Press, 1985.
  Includes an abridged version of Zuck's Moody commentary.

Wiersbe, Warren W. *The Wiersbe Bible Commentary: Old Testament*, David C. Cook, 2007.
  One of the most readable conservative accounts, combining paragraph analysis with constant spiritual application.

Wilson, Douglas. *Letter from a Christian Citizen*. American Vision, 2007.

Wood, G. Harding. *Bird's-Eye view of the Bible*. Marshall, Morgan & Scott, 1957.

Zuck, Roy B. *Everyman's Bible Commentary: Job*. Moody Press, 1978.
  A compact commentary by a Dallas professor skilfully joining conservative theology with recent scholarship.

Zuck, Roy B. (ed). *A Biblical Theology of the Old Testament*. Moody Press, 1991.

Zuck, Roy B. (ed). *Sitting with Job*. Baker, 1992.
  A collection of articles culled from a range of sources and theological standpoints, many of which articles are highly illuminating.

FOREWORD

One of the many lessons taught in Job is the value of honest speaking. If I had been asked which book of the Bible I should least like to write about, Job would probably have been at the top of the list, second only to Song of Solomon. Its particular difficulties, noted in the introduction, set it apart from every other volume in the remarkable library which makes up the Scriptures of truth. Teasing out its message for today has often come down to a wearisome struggle to get to grips with the sometimes obscure meaning of the text, the tortuous logic of the argument, and the complex interaction between five fractious speakers.

That said, the book has been nothing if not relevant. Almost at the exact moment that this attempt at exposition was started, a dear friend was struck down with leukaemia, while another went through some of those dizzying ups and downs of spiritual experience which bring the heart to the mouth and an ache to the stomach. Yet another friend found himself and his young child suddenly abandoned by his wife. Those of us who find cause to complain about our health, our workplace, our family or our assembly, will discover that a careful reading of Job sobers the mind by putting our own trivial problems into perspective. No one suffered like Job. No one, that is, apart from the Lord Jesus Christ, the uniquely innocent victim, whose trials on earth are faintly adumbrated in the pathway of this Old Testament saint. The book is therefore eminently practical. From the very outset, in company with Satan – a disturbing association! – the reader is invited to consider or, more literally, to set his heart on "my servant Job" (1.8). In so doing, we meet a man of outstanding piety, of astonishing self-restraint, of profound intelligence, and of frank outspokenness. Yet even such a man was not perfect. One of the great lessons of the book is to expose the failure of the best of men and, implicitly, highlight the contrast with the one impeccable man. To consider Job is, in the final analysis, to be confronted with human failure; on the other hand, to "consider him that endured such contradiction of sinners against himself" is the divine antidote to becoming "wearied and faint in [our] minds" (Heb 12.3).

David Newell
August 2016

SECTION 1
Introduction

It cannot be accidental that so many commentators freely acknowledge the extreme difficulties in this part of God's Word. Comments Ellison, "there are few books more difficult to write on than Job",[1] while Robinson calls it "one of the most difficult books of the Bible".[2] And the problems are considerable. There are, for example, passages which are notoriously hard to translate. Should a well-loved verse like Job 19.26 read, as in the King James Version, "yet in my flesh shall I see God", or "without my flesh shall I see God" (ASV)? Both translations bear testimony to Job's certainty of seeing God in an afterlife, but is he thinking specifically of bodily resurrection, or of the intermediate state? Again, the KJV rendering of the first paragraph of chapter 28 obliterates what more recent versions see as a remarkable description of underground mining for precious metals, placed there to contrast man's insatiable and risky quest for wealth with his failure to discover the source of wisdom. Then again there are occasional uncertainties about the tone of the argument. In chapter 27 Job suddenly appears to concede what he has hitherto been at pains to deny – that the wicked face indisputable and inescapable judgment in this life. Is he now being ironic, and parodying the argument of his friends? How are we to view his sudden change of approach?

Not surprisingly, the more liberal expositors take delight in dissecting and adjusting the text according to their own presuppositions, reallocating speeches willy-nilly to harmonise with their speculative theories. They, of course, have no prior commitment to the authority and inspiration of Scripture. Sadly, even a moderately conservative writer like Hartley feels the need to dispose of the problems of chapter 27 by crediting part of the speech to Bildad instead of Job.[3] But once started, there is no end to such editorial interference with what is, after all, the inspired Word. Davis offers an illustration to make the point:

> Reading the Bible may be like staying in someone else's house … During your tenure in their home you may think that – if it were your place – you would have arranged it differently. Perhaps you'd prefer a lighter color on the walls, a different style of furniture … but it's not your place – it's theirs. They have arranged items as they, presumably, want them and as a temporary guest you must simply accept their arrangement. So with the Bible: we may prefer another arrangement but our task is to work with what we have been given.[4]

This commentary therefore will accept the general text of Job as it stands in the King James Version of the Bible, while suggesting occasional translation emendations where the KJV is particularly obscure or has been shown to be in error.

Another fundamental problem faced by every commentator is the need to expound the book in a manner which is at the same time accurate and spiritually edifying. Few believers, I suspect, will have experienced a ministry series taking them systematically through the entire book. The reason is not hard to seek.

Job, by its very nature, does not lend itself to normal verse by verse platform exposition. It is not a biblical history like Genesis, packed with practical lessons, nor is it a series of prophetic messages from the mouth of the Lord like Isaiah. It does not consist of a collection of instructive poems or proverbial utterances which may profitably be dipped into at random without any danger of violating their context. Rather, what we have is a lengthy controversy between men of radically different viewpoints, none of whom will back down. Much of the dialogue seems to consist of tetchy bickering, and frequently wrong-headed or wrongly applied human opinions. Not surprisingly, then, the book rarely features in an assembly teaching programme. And yet it has not always been so. Kelly printed three different expositions of Job in his *Bible Treasury*, one in 1877-8, a second in 1908 (which is perhaps the best), and a third in 1919. This at least raises the probability that he engaged in consecutive oral ministry on the topic. But few have followed in his steps. It is both, I suspect, the intractability of the material, and perhaps the additional anxiety that he who writes or speaks about Job may be called upon to suffer something of what Job endured, which discourage the teacher. Wiersbe tells us, with disarming honesty, that when he started to pen his popular exposition of Job, entitled *Be Patient*, he said to his wife, "I wonder how much suffering we'll have to go through so I can write this book".[5]

At this stage, then, it is only proper that the book's distinctive problems be honestly foregrounded, so that a clear trail can be blazed through its forty-two chapters, allowing any reader who may for the first time be looking seriously at this part of Scripture to enter into something of the book's unquestionable riches. For rich it undoubtedly is. According to Robinson, it is "one of the grandest portions of inspired Scripture", a "storehouse of comfort and instruction".[6] Kelly calls it "a book full of interest and of great practical profit",[7] while Scroggie goes so far as to name it "a key to the whole Bible".[8] Many who have passed through serious affliction can testify to the blessing found in its pages, and those of us who have thus far been spared from extreme trials are humbled as we read about a man who endured far more than we can imagine and yet retained his confidence in God. There's nothing like reading Job to put our own trivial discomforts into perspective.

But first let us briefly enumerate the major obstacles confronting the first-time reader. Job is a unique and challenging book in at least six ways.

In sheer **size** it is one of the longest in the canon of Scripture, containing forty-two chapters which, apart from the bookends (the prologue and epilogue), require minute and painstaking investigation so as to be able to tease out the twists and turns of the tricky argument. Simply reading the book through is no easy task.

In **style** it combines a slender prose framework of deceptively simple vocabulary and narrative with a huge poetic body (chapters 3-42) which is both complex and sometimes obscure in its linguistic details. The Psalms are, of course, also written in Hebrew poetic form, but they are free-standing hymns of petition and praise, not contributions to a tortuous verbal debate, expressing different and increasingly exaggerated points of view as the two sides in the argument become more fractious and polarised. The psalmist, in his supplication and worship, attracts our sympathy and admiration; the human combatants in Job more frequently annoy or frustrate the reader.

The **setting** of the story lies outside Israel's time and culture zone, and contains no clear allusions to any Israelite distinctives, nor can the events be locked securely into any particular moment of Old Testament history. The clear timeline established by the genealogies carefully recorded in Genesis and 1 Chronicles, a timeline which helps us make sense of so much of Old Testament scripture, simply does not apply here. Indeed, the book seems to exist in what might be called a geographical and historical no-man's-land in which Job stands alone as a suffering saint representative of all eras.

Doctrinally, the **subject matter** is extensive, and covers a wide range of interests. These include the reason men worship God (which is the basis of Satan's initial challenge), the apparently capricious afflictions which befall a righteous man – the terrible personal experience which provokes the entire debate – and the cosmic grandeur of God's creatorial and providential majesty as revealed in Jehovah's concluding intervention. But many other meaty topics emerge to stretch our minds as the book proceeds: Satan's access into the heavenly court, the source of pre-Israelite information about God, the early understanding of what happens at death, the exclusively earthly focus of Job's final blessings. Reading this book raises questions.

The book's **strategy** is unusual in the context of the Scriptures as a whole. Because (apart from its narrative bookends) it is constructed as a drama, it is able to pose awkward questions, and then offer a variety of unsatisfactory human responses as Job and his friends debate the issues. Yet precisely because of its dramatic genre, it withholds any authoritative commentary to help distinguish between the truth and error which pervade the speeches of the disputants. Here it is necessary to make a vital and sometimes misunderstood point about the meaning of divine inspiration. Although "all scripture is given by inspiration of God" (2 Tim 3.16), not all its statements are therefore automatically correct. We need a keen eye for context. The Bible faithfully records human and devilish errors, starting with Satan's pernicious lie to Eve, "Ye shall not surely die" (Gen 3.4). And thereafter, as it traces a pathway through fallen human history, the Bible accurately and candidly records the mistakes and misunderstandings of sinful men. We must distinguish carefully between what it reports (in its astonishingly uncensored narrative of human history) and what it asserts. The only sections in the book of Job which may be taken as indisputably infallible are the framework chapters, which set the scene and relate the conclusion, and the two long speeches of Jehovah at the close.

How much easier the book would be were it to include inspired interjections or footnotes to lead the perplexed reader by the hand through the potential maze of misunderstanding! The poet Milton negotiated this problem when writing *Paradise Lost* by undercutting long speeches with crisp narrative asides. For example, when the newly-fallen Satan has expressed, with compellingly theatrical verve, the resolution to continue his war against heaven, the poet comments:

So spake the apostate angel, though in pain,
Vaunting aloud, but racked with deep despair.[9]

Satan may sound scintillating and self-assured but he is feeling rotten.
Sometimes Scripture does something similar. When the old prophet from Bethel
invited the man of God from Judah back to his home, he constructed a plausible
tale of divine guidance to attract his victim, but the narrator helpfully exposes its
falsity: "He said unto him, I am a prophet also as thou art; and an angel spake
unto me by the word of the Lord, saying, Bring him back with thee into thine
house, that he may eat bread and drink water. But he lied unto him" (1 Kings
13.18-19). How important are those final five words! Alas, there are no such
useful comments to guide us through the book of Job.

Only at the very end does God step in directly to terminate the contest. But
even then there are things to disconcert us. This **solution** is unexpected, not
because God speaks (for that has been Job's burning desire throughout), but
because Job's essential questions remain unanswered. Far from explaining to the
suffering patriarch the reason for his painful experience, the Lord confronts him
with a whirlwind of questions about the management of the universe which he is
utterly incapable of answering. Never does he learn what is revealed to the reader
at the very start - why he suffered as he did.

It is essential to keep in mind constantly that this book dates from the earliest
stages of divine revelation. Many areas of truth remain obscure and uncertain
until New Testament times, when revelation reached its climax and completion
with the coming of Christ, for "God, who at sundry times and in divers manners
spake in time past unto the fathers by the prophets, Hath in these last days spoken
unto us by his Son" (Heb 1.1-2). Only there do we find, for example, full teaching
about bodily resurrection, "made manifest by the appearing of our Saviour Jesus
Christ, who hath abolished death, and hath brought life and immortality to light
through the gospel" (2 Tim 1.10). There again, with the arrival on earth of the
ultimate innocent victim, the Lord Jesus, we meet the One whose sufferings,
unlike Job's, are borne with unwavering confidence in God, but which also have
unique atoning value. And in the final pages of the New Testament there is an
unfolding of God's eternal purpose in a new heaven and earth "wherein dwelleth
righteousness" (2 Pet 3.13), when "the tabernacle of God is with men, and he
will dwell with them, and they shall be his people, and God himself shall be with
them, and be their God" (Rev 21.3). That is the grand goal of universal blessing
towards which God's gracious self-disclosure moves.

Delitzsch concludes his commentary with this point:

A New Testament poet would have closed the book of Job differently.
He would have shown us how, becoming free from his inward conflict of
temptation, and being divinely comforted, Job succumbs to his disease,
but waves his palm of victory before the throne of God among the
innumerable hosts of those who have washed their robes and made them

white in the blood of the Lamb ... The view of heaven which a Christian
poet would have been able to give at the close of the book is only rendered
possible by the resurrection and ascension of Christ.[10]

And he is right. An unavoidable prerequisite for the right reading of this book
is to recognise its primitive position in the progress of revelation. We must first
take it at its face value, accepting its restricted disclosure of the divine purpose,
and then secondly come to it in the reflected glow of the New Testament. The
patriarch's agonised questions can only truly be answered in the light of the person
and work of the Lord Jesus Christ. The Christian believer approaches the story
of Job, then, privileged in knowing God's final word on the matter of human
suffering.

With this general preamble, we can now investigate in greater depth some of
the more important features of the book.

Setting
(i) The Period
The book's details suggest a patriarchal world, situating the events roughly in
the time of Abraham. If the final doubling of his material blessings applies also to
his years, Job's total age (42.16) was of patriarchal duration, for we may assume
he was 70 at the beginning, and therefore, with twice that number added after his
ordeal, lived until he was 210. Certainly he died "old and full of days" (42.17) or,
as Young's Literal Translation puts it, "aged and satisfied with days". The words
of Eliphaz are ironically proved true: "Thou shalt come to thy grave in a full age,
like as a shock of corn cometh in in his season" (5.26). His wealth is measured in
livestock rather than money (1.3; 42.12), just as was the prosperity of Abraham
and Lot (Gen 13.2,5-6). His function as family priest (1.4-5) also reminds us
of Abraham the worshipper with his four altars (Gen 12.7-8; 13.18; 22.9). At
the close, his three daughters are counted as heirs along with their brethren
(42.15), which was only the case under Jewish law if there were no sons to inherit
(Num 27.8). Some of the personal and place names also have early Pentateuchal
connections, names such as Eliphaz (Gen 36.4) and Uz (Gen 22.21). The only
form of idolatry mentioned is of a simple kind, worship of the sun and the host of
heaven (31.26-28). Fausset notes that the language bears traces of a primitive era:

> Lastly, the language is Hebrew with an Arabic and Syriac infusion found
> in no other sacred book, answering to an age when Hebrew still retained
> many of the elements of the original common Semitic, from which in time
> branched off Hebrew, Syriac, and Arabic, carrying with them severally
> fragments of the common stock. The obscurity of several phrases, the
> obsolete words and forgotten traditions (e.g. that of the bushmen, 30.4-
> 7), all mark a remote antiquity.[11]

Perhaps most significantly, the name of God as *Shaddai*, the all-sufficient One
(used thirty-one times in Job and nine times in the Pentateuch), was a name

familiar to the patriarchs (Gen 17.1). The God with whom Job has to do is the Almighty, the all-powerful, all-sufficient Creator of the universe. All this we may call positive evidence indicating that the book is set early in history. It appears to be one of the oldest books, if not the oldest, in our Bible.

On the negative side, there is total silence in the text about, for example, the Abrahamic covenant, the exodus from Egypt, the nation of Israel, and the Mosaic Law, matters which are central to the rest of the Old Testament. Such omissions place the book during the time shortly after Babel (Genesis 11) and either before or contemporaneous with Abraham (Genesis 12). Job certainly knew about Adam (31.33) and the global flood of Noah's day (12.15; 22.15-16), but he lacked any clear revelation of a future life (14.14) or a firm doctrine of resurrection. Interestingly, God is thirty-two times referred to as the "LORD" (*Jehovah*), but (apart from 12.9) only in the prose framework. The God of creation in Genesis 1 is *Elohim*; the term used in Genesis 2, which focusses on God's gracious interactions with man, is *Jehovah Elohim*, introducing a name later used to emphasise His special relationship with the elect nation of Israel (Ex 3.13-15; 6.2-3). That the God who so honours Job as His faithful servant and worshipper is described as *Jehovah* underlines His intimate involvement with those whom His hand has created in His image. Job is a book which forefronts the mysterious yet kindly dealings of God with men, and with one man in particular. The unprecedented focus of forty-two chapters upon a single individual shows, in the words of Kelly, "that God interests Himself most deeply about a soul".[12] In that truth every believer may take comfort.

(ii) The Place

The precise location of Uz is unknown, but two areas are usually suggested. Because Aram had a son called Uz (Gen 10.23), some place the land of Uz north-east of Israel in what was once called Aram but is now modern Syria. And it is true that Job is described as "the greatest of all the men of the east" (1.3). On the other hand, there is evidence associating Uz with Idumea (Gen 36.1,28; Lam 4.21). Eliphaz, Job's friend, came from Teman (2.11), a city of Edom (Gen 36.11; Jer 49.7,20). The geographical setting of the book therefore appears to be either the land of Edom or perhaps the area of Northern Arabia. The Jewish Talmud notes eight different opinions as to precisely where Job lived.[13]

Yet this broadly unspecific, timeless quality has a positive value, for it renders the book of unrestricted appeal and application. Job may have been unique in his uprightness but he is universal in his suffering. Says Scroggie, "The value of the writing is quite independent of date, and is indeed, as to its great message, dateless".[14] This of course is not to suggest that the book is fictional. The Bible insists upon Job's historicity, listing him with Noah and Daniel as a man of outstanding righteousness (Ezek 14.14,20), and citing him as the great exemplar of endurance (James 5.11). Further, the New Testament several times quotes from or alludes to the book as an unquestionably reliable source of truth. Eliphaz's words in 4.8 ("According as I have seen, they that plow iniquity, And sow trouble, reap the same") are repeated in Galatians 6.7-8 ("Be not deceived; God is not mocked: for whatsoever a man soweth, that shall he also reap. For he that soweth to his flesh shall of the flesh reap corruption"), and his remark in 5.13 ("He taketh the wise in their own craftiness") reappears in 1 Corinthians 3.19 ("For the wisdom of this world is foolishness with God. For it is written, He taketh the wise in their own craftiness"). His comment in 5.17 ("Behold, happy is the man whom God correcteth: Therefore despise not thou the chastening of the Almighty") is picked up in Hebrews 12.5-6 ("And ye have forgotten the exhortation which speaketh unto you as unto children, My son, despise not thou the chastening of the Lord, nor faint when thou art rebuked of him: For whom the Lord loveth he chasteneth, and scourgeth every son whom he receiveth"), a significant passage about the value of divine discipline in the believer's life. These citations are important in that they demonstrate that Job's friends, who are later rebuked by the Lord for their faulty words, could at times utter valuable truth even if, as so often, it was irrelevant to Job's immediate situation. Jehovah's question to Job in 41.11, "Who hath first given to me, that I should repay him? Whatsoever is under the whole heaven is mine" (JND), appears in Romans 11.35 ("… who hath first given to him, and it shall be recompensed unto him again?"), at the close of Paul's great argument for divine sovereignty over the affairs of men. Certainly, then, the writers of the New Testament see the book as a reliable source of truth, from which they can quote without fear of challenge. This commentary adopts a similar standpoint, and the reader will find frequent references to verses from such passages as Romans 8, Romans 11 and the epistle of James.

The author is unknown. Job may well have been written in the patriarchal era shortly after the historical events took place, although of course the date of a narrative is not necessarily to be identified with the date of its writing. One Jewish tradition attributes the book to Moses, whereas some more recent commentators date it in the time of Solomon (the heyday of wisdom literature) or even later. It is, however, wisest to respect the book's Spirit-inspired anonymity. Because all Scripture is God-breathed, we accept its clear attributions without reservation (therefore 2 Peter was written by Peter, and Ecclesiastes by Solomon, whatever critical scholars may say), but if there is no such ascription in the text (as for example in the Hebrew letter) we bow to its reticence and see past the unnamed human instrument to honour the divine Author. Morris credits the book to Job himself,[15] but though this is an attractive theory it damages the book's testimony to a faith which perseveres even in the darkness, for it requires that the protagonist eventually learned before his death the reason for his trials. Nowhere does the text support this.

Subject

Not for nothing is Job at the heart of our English Bible, for what we normally call the poetic books of the Old Testament deal with matters of the heart. The book of Psalms constitutes Israel's inspired hymnbook of praise and petition; Proverbs offers sage and pithy guidelines for living safely in God's world; Ecclesiastes exposes the ultimate emptiness of all worldly delights; and the Song of Solomon highlights a love relationship which can satisfy the soul. But Job, the first and earliest of these remarkable books, confronts head on the inescapable reality of human suffering. The key topic is the question of why, in this world, the bad often prosper and the good often suffer. It is a fact of human experience with which Psalms 37 and 73 famously seek to grapple. The problem, of course, was not new even in Job's day, although he and his friends seem to have forgotten the fate of righteous Abel. At the very outset of human history there lived a man whose faithful worship and divine commendation were rewarded with murder. The damaged state of the world and the fallen condition of mankind must never be forgotten.

The answer that the book of Job offers to the problem of suffering, perhaps surprisingly, is what might be expressed as an elaboration of Deuteronomy 29.29: "The secret things belong unto the Lord our God: but those things which are revealed belong unto us and to our children for ever, that we may do all the words of this law". That is to say, some of God's purposes will never be disclosed down here, but the absence of explanation is not a justifiable reason for human rebellion. The responsibility of man is always to obey what God in grace has revealed, and submit to what He lays upon us. In the prophet's words, "He hath shewed thee, O man, what is good; and what doth the Lord require of thee, but to do justly, and to love mercy, and to walk humbly with thy God?" (Micah 6.8). As Baxter puts it, in the Bible "enough is revealed to make faith intelligent. Enough is reserved to give faith scope for development".[16]

We learn through Job that "in adversity God may have other purposes besides retribution for wrongdoing",[17] a lesson which provides the believer with a light to illuminate many of the hard passages of Scripture and personal experience. The Bible as a whole teaches that good men may suffer for a variety of reasons: as punishment for particular sins (1 Cor 11.31-32), as an education in righteousness (Heb 12.6), or because God in infinite wisdom wills it (Ps 119.75), or indeed as a combination of all three. The Lord Jesus made it clear that one man's blindness was not the consequence of human wickedness (Jn 9.1-3), nor were the victims of two recent catastrophes guilty of more than usual sinfulness (Lk 13.1-5). But He spoke as the omniscient Son of God.

Even if we are theoretically aware of the possible explanations for an affliction, it is rarely easy in practice for onlookers to tick the correct box. It ill befits us to pronounce dogmatically on the reasons why a particular believer may go through extreme distress. In the vital ministry of consolation and encouragement, so necessary in this life yet so difficult, much wisdom and humility are required, qualities which were notably absent from Job's comforters. Although they rightly recognised that affliction may be the outworking of divine punishment for personal sins (22.9-10), and that it may act as a positive means of correction (5.17; 34.3-32), they remained oblivious to the real cause behind Job's circumstances.

Other major practical issues raised in the book include the following:

(i) The reality and limitations of Satan

Although the book dates from an early period of divine revelation it leaves no doubt as to the existence and activity of Satan. He lives up to his description, one not revealed until Revelation 12.10, as "the accuser of our brethren … which accused them before our God day and night". But even in the Old Testament his name unfolds his activity, for Satan means "opponent" or "adversary", and his malice is exposed in Zechariah where we find him in the process of accusing the post-exilic high priest Joshua. The passage is worth quoting because it demonstrates the essential link between name and nature. "And he shewed me Joshua the high priest standing before the angel of the Lord, and Satan standing at his right hand to resist him" (Zech 3.1). Young's Literal Translation usefully brings out the close relationship between the name Satan and the verb "to resist": "the Adversary standing at his right hand, to be an adversary to him". Satan takes delight in finding fault with God's people. It is a shame that so many believers follow his example. But Job also demonstrates – much to the encouragement of the child of God – that Satan cannot make a move without divine permission. The first two chapters are beautifully clear on this. It is also important to notice that after chapter 2 Satan completely disappears from the scene. He is but a bit-player in the drama.

(ii) The way in which the heavenly affects the earthly

The entire book works on the premise that what goes on in heaven has a direct impact upon the earth. Just as Daniel pulls back the curtain to unveil the heavenly antagonisms lying behind the political affairs of the nations (Dan 10.13), so the book of Job teaches us that there may be unseen purposes behind the temporal conditions of individuals down here. Only rarely is the screen lifted so that the spirit world can be glimpsed. Elisha's fearful servant was given such an insight when he awoke to discover his master's house surrounded by the Syrian army:

> And when the servant of the man of God was risen early, and gone forth, behold, an host compassed the city both with horses and chariots. And his servant said unto him, Alas, my master! how shall we do? And he answered, Fear not: for they that be with us are more than they that be with them. And Elisha prayed, and said, Lord, I pray thee, open his eyes, that he may see. And the Lord opened the eyes of the young man; and he saw: and, behold, the mountain was full of horses and chariots of fire round about Elisha (2 Kings 6.15-17).

But normally the believer walks by faith, not by sight. And Job, just like us, had to be content with trusting in God despite incomprehensible circumstances.

(iii) How tribulation can work patience

The concept is formulated by the apostle Paul in Romans 5, as he analyses the practical consequences of justification by faith.

> Therefore being justified by faith, we have peace with God through our Lord Jesus Christ: By whom also we have access by faith into this grace

wherein we stand, and rejoice in hope of the glory of God. And not only
so, but we glory in tribulations also: knowing that tribulation worketh
patience; And patience, experience; and experience, hope (Rom 5.1-4).

Those declared right with God are granted, amongst other benefits, the ability
to endure. But though Paul expresses it in doctrinal words, Job exemplifies it in
personal experience. Under the multiple blows of the disasters which befall him
in the first two chapters, he does nothing amiss and utters no word out of place.
And it is worth bearing in mind that his resigned demeanour in the prologue,
rather than his fraught verbal outpourings in the debate, is what lingers most
fixedly in the reader's mind. We are more affected by his concrete example than
by his abstract theorising.

(iv) The reason for worshipping God

Satan's challenge follows God's initiative in directing his attention to Job's
outstanding piety: "Then Satan answered the Lord, and said, Doth Job fear God
for nought? Hast not thou made an hedge about him, and about his house, and
about all that he hath on every side? thou hast blessed the work of his hands,
and his substance is increased in the land" (1.9-10). Why do men worship and
serve the Lord? Is it because they enjoy material blessing? Satan's focus, we might
notice, is purely on the temporal. He is the first propagator of prosperity theology,
that lopsided notion that the saints of God are always to expect material wealth
and health in this world. Job's outward benefits are therefore removed so that it
might be shown that "God is worthy of love even apart from the blessings He
bestows".[18] Of course, God's dealings with Old Testament Israel had a distinctly
material aspect, for they were given a land and promised both health and wealth,
conditional upon their obedience to God's law. But no such guarantee is offered
to believers of the church age. On the contrary, we are promised tribulation in
the world and glory with Christ in heaven. Remarkably, then, we have in a pre-
Israelite saint a partial pattern of our own condition, partial because Job's final
blessings, as far as the book is concerned, are still located on the earth.

(v) The sovereignty of God in all circumstances

Satan's absolute subservience to God is established from the start. But one of
the great strengths of Job's faith is that he sees past second causes, whether they
be human enemies, extreme weather conditions, or even Satan himself (although
there is no direct evidence in the book that Job knows about Satan), to the hand
of God in everything that befalls him. This truth is reinforced at the end when
the Lord gives Job an oral examination in the wonders of creation. Such a God,
who can create and control monsters like behemoth and leviathan, is supreme
over all. The teaching is made unambiguously clear in Jehovah's challenge: "None
is so fierce that dare stir him [leviathan] up: who then is able to stand before me?"
(41.10). Christians take delight in knowing that their God is in total control of
His universe. In contrast to the impotent idols of man's imagination, "our God is
in the heavens: he hath done whatsoever he hath pleased" (Ps 115.3).

(vi) The danger of judging by outward appearances

When Job's three friends arrived on their visit of condolence they were dumbfounded at what they saw. "And when they lifted up their eyes afar off, and knew him not, they lifted up their voice, and wept; and they rent every one his mantle, and sprinkled dust upon their heads toward heaven" (2.12). Clearly, Job was scarcely recognisable as the esteemed and influential man they once knew, so disfiguring were the effects of his disease. Instead of an honoured position in the city gate he was sitting alone on the rubbish heap, covered in suppurating sores. But in a fallen world appearances can be deceptive: external success does not guarantee spirituality, nor does deprivation prove depravity. Our senses are not adequately tuned to assess the invisible for, as Samuel had to learn, "man looketh on the outward appearance, but the Lord looketh on the heart" (1 Sam 16.7). Job's friends saw the collapse of his outward fortunes, the terrible deterioration of his bodily health, the ruin of his reputation, but they were not able correctly to deduce from these data either the condition of his soul or the reason for his afflictions. It is an all-too-common human failing that we quickly jump to conclusions instead of waiting on the Lord.

(vii) The insufficiency of human wisdom

Job is counted among the wisdom books of the Bible, and there are some striking similarities with the language and imagery of Proverbs and Ecclesiastes. Both Job and his friends are reckoned among the sages of their world. But as the discussion proceeds Job becomes more and more exasperated at a rigid wisdom which simply cannot do justice to the facts of experience. The problem is this. Eliphaz and his wise companions hold to a neat mathematical formula: great suffering in this world proves great sin, just as outward prosperity infallibly signals inner piety. Here, right at the start of the debate, the theory is articulated:

> Remember, I pray thee, who ever perished, being innocent? or where were the righteous cut off? Even as I have seen, they that plow iniquity, and sow wickedness, reap the same (4.7-8).

But Job is (rightly) convinced of his innocence. The theory therefore is false. His comments, not without reason, become increasingly sarcastic and bitter: "No doubt but ye are the people, and wisdom shall die with you" (12.2); "O that ye would altogether hold your peace! and it should be your wisdom" (13.5); "But as for you all, do ye return, and come now: for I cannot find one wise man among you" (17.10); "How hast thou counselled him that hath no wisdom? and how hast thou plentifully declared the thing as it is?" (26.3) Even as he discovers the limitations of traditional human philosophy Job begins to seek for something greater. Chapter 28 constitutes a marvellous poem about the quest for wisdom: "But where shall wisdom be found? and where is the place of understanding?" (28.12). The answer, that God alone "understandeth the way thereof, and he knoweth the place thereof" (28.23), may remind us of the great personification of wisdom in Proverbs chapter 8, a passage which makes us think of the person of Christ Himself, who is God's wisdom incarnate. Human thought processes can never fathom God's ways. The only way we can get the right perspective on our circumstances is laid down in the final verse: "And unto man he said, Behold, the fear of the Lord, that is wisdom; and to depart from evil is understanding" (28.28).

(viii) The way (not) to counsel those in distress

In one sense the book of Job is a practical counselling manual or, more accurately, a model of how *not* to bring comfort to believers who are going through times of affliction. To his moralizing friends Job responds, "miserable comforters are ye all. Shall vain words have an end? or what provoketh thee that thou answerest? I also could speak as ye do; if your soul were in my soul's stead, I could join words together against you, And shake my head at you. But I would strengthen you with my mouth, and the solace of my lips would assuage your grief" (16.2-5). Had their situations been reversed, in place of their abrasive comments and unsympathetic disdain Job would have offered genuine solace. If we cannot say what is upbuilding and helpful it is better not to speak at all. As Baxter remarks, "Far better be silent in the presence of suffering than say what is wrong".[19]

> Job's friends, who came to mourn with him,
> And comfort his dismay,
> Appalled by his appearance, found
> They had no words to say.
> They lifted up their voice and wept,
> Their garments they did tear,
> They sprinkled dust upon their heads
> And sat down with him there.
> His loss they could not comprehend,
> His body dare not touch;
> What consolation could they give
> To one who hurt so much?
> When of wise words we are bereft
> Then silent sympathy is left.
> On Job less anguish would have come
> Had his three friends continued dumb!

(ix) Submission as the true response to God's ways with us

Asked what he considered the greatest mission in the world, Hudson Taylor is said to have replied in the one word, "Submission". It is certainly the most difficult. Confessing personal ignorance and impotence does not come easily to proud man. But because we are finite creatures whose entire thinking process has been damaged by sin, it should not be surprising that there is much, even in this world, we shall never comprehend. As the Lord says through Isaiah, "my thoughts are not your thoughts, neither are your ways my ways, saith the Lord. For as the heavens are higher than the earth, so are my ways higher than your ways, and my thoughts than your thoughts" (Is 55.8-9). However, such lowliness of spirit is wholly inimical to men who boast in their intelligence and understanding. To accept the joint limitations of creaturehood and sinfulness requires the grace of God. It is only as Job turns from a concentration upon himself (his lost esteem and his present misery), and becomes aware of the immeasurable greatness of God, that his strivings cease.

(x) The universe as a testimony to God's magnificence

The divine greatness that produces submission of heart is best seen in the created universe, so vast, so beautiful, so various, so complex. Although this is the special emphasis of Jehovah's intervention at the close of the book, it has in fact been touched upon throughout the debate. As early as chapter 9 Job raises the matter of God's infinite majesty:

> He is wise in heart, and mighty in strength: who hath hardened himself against him, and hath prospered? Which removeth the mountains, and they know not: which overturneth them in his anger. Which shaketh the earth out of her place, and the pillars thereof tremble. Which commandeth the sun, and it riseth not; and sealeth up the stars. Which alone spreadeth out the heavens, and treadeth upon the waves of the sea. Which maketh Arcturus, Orion, and Pleiades, and the chambers of the south. Which doeth great things past finding out; yea, and wonders without number (9.4-11).

He returns to this theme in chapter 26, which commences his long final speech of self-defence:

> He stretcheth out the north over the empty place, and hangeth the earth upon nothing. He bindeth up the waters in his thick clouds; and the cloud is not rent under them. He holdeth back the face of his throne, and spreadeth his cloud upon it. He hath compassed the waters with bounds, until the day and night come to an end. The pillars of heaven tremble and are astonished at his reproof. He divideth the sea with his power, and by his understanding he smiteth through the proud. By his spirit he hath garnished the heavens; his hand hath formed the crooked serpent. Lo, these are parts of his ways: but how little a portion is heard of him? but the thunder of his power who can understand? (26.7-14).

As if in unconscious anticipation of Jehovah's voice, Elihu also adduces the doctrine of divine creation as a reason for submission and surrender:

> Hear attentively the noise of his voice, and the sound that goeth out of his mouth. He directeth it under the whole heaven, and his lightning unto the ends of the earth. After it a voice roareth: he thundereth with the voice of his excellency; and he will not stay them when his voice is heard. God thundereth marvellously with his voice; great things doeth he, which we cannot comprehend. For he saith to the snow, Be thou on the earth;

likewise to the small rain, and to the great rain of his strength. He sealeth up the hand of every man; that all men may know his work (37.2-7).

However, the difference between Job's earlier words and his final response to the divine awesomeness is that between textbook learning and personal experience. As he says, "I have heard of thee by the hearing of the ear: but now mine eye seeth thee" (42.5). It is one thing to know the truth in theory, but quite another to fall, overwhelmed and silenced, in the presence of the Lord of creation. All believers know how easy it is to have correct doctrine at our fingers' ends without a deep appreciation of the God we claim to know.

(xi) The worthlessness of the flesh even in the best of men

This final principle forms in one sense the most significant and the least easily assimilated of all Job's lessons. It is a feature of the book which has been particularly highlighted by teachers from an assembly background. Scott summarises it as well as anyone, when he describes Job as

> a book written upon the moral government of God in this world, not with a nation such as Israel, but with a God-fearing, prosperous man, yet one whose conscience had not been searched in the presence of God and in the light of His holiness. It carefully details the process by which a man learns the utter worthlessness of the flesh in its best estate.[20]

The man who becomes so satisfied with his own integrity has to learn that in the presence of the Lord not even the best of mere men has anything in which to boast. Chapter 4 of M H Finlay's magnificent introduction to Job is significantly entitled, "The Revelation of the 'Flesh' in a Godly Man". He comments, "It was not until Job, the upright, began to justify himself to his friends that he opened the door to his inmost being and brought to light the truly monstrous 'I' which dwelt within".

But happily that is not the end of the story. Confronted finally with the majesty of Jehovah, Job prostrates himself in the dust. And never does he rise higher spiritually than when down in these depths. The book which commences with an affirmation of Job's righteousness (1.1) ends with his repentance (42.6). Finlay again puts it so well:

> Of what did he repent? No mention is made of any specific sin: no evil deeds are suggested over which he need distress his soul in deep contrition. No, Job was a just man, a justified man, but seeing himself now in the light of God,s holiness, he repents of all the carnal thoughts which had passed through his mind while he had been occupied with self.[21]

Structure

As "a dramatic poem framed in an epic story",[22] the book ironically contrasts the ignorance of its human protagonists with the special knowledge afforded to its readers. From the very beginning, we are in on the secret of Job's trials, but neither Job nor anyone else on earth is. Part of the nature of Job's test is that he cannot even be told that it *is* a test. Had he been informed that God was using him as a demonstration to Satan of how a saint deprived of his earthly blessings will still continue to trust in the Lord, the purpose would have been lost. Job has to remain in the dark, clinging to what he knows of God. "To explain a trial [to this examinee] would be to destroy its object, which is that of calling forth simple faith and implicit obedience".[23] In the same way, Abraham was not to know that the order to offer up Isaac was a trial of his faith, and that God would countermand the instruction the moment he lifted the knife to slay his son. Had he known, the test would not have been a test.

This irony colours everything Job and his friends say, for none of them knows about the heavenly council of the first two chapters. It is therefore vital to remember that the lengthy speeches recorded between chapter 3 and chapter 37 are all, to a greater or lesser extent, somewhat off the point. And before we lambast either Job or his friends for their mistakes, we would be wise to remember that it is only by grace that we know more than they.

The book is constructed in three major sections which are outlined on the structural diagram on pages 654 and 655: a brief prose prologue and epilogue sandwich an extended poetic debate between Job and his visitors. The debate itself divides into what might be called three rounds of a verbal contest in which Job is urged to confess the hidden sins which have caused his current misery. These rounds are marked by the increasingly acrimonious dogmatism with which Job's friends assert his guilt, for to their mind only dreadful sin could merit such dreadful suffering. Job, by contrast, consistently avows his personal innocence. We must note that he never claims to be sinless, but only blameless: that is to say, he knows of nothing in his life to justify the extreme pain to which he is being subjected. Hence his frequent expostulations: "he breaketh me with a tempest, and multiplieth my wounds without cause" (9.17); "My face is foul with weeping, and on my eyelids is the shadow of death; Not for any injustice in mine hands: also my prayer is pure" (16.16-17); "the counsel of the wicked is far from me" (21.16); "My foot hath held his steps, his way have I kept, and not declined. Neither have I gone back from the commandment of his lips; I have esteemed the words of his mouth more than my necessary food" (23.11-12). It all comes to a head in his great avowal of innocence which constitutes chapter 31.

Now it is essential to a proper understanding of the book that we recognise he is correct in this self-assessment. Both the narrator (1.1) and the Lord Himself (1.8) testify unambiguously to Job's uprightness. And after his first trial, the Lord restates his innocence even more emphatically: "And the Lord said unto Satan, Hast thou considered my servant Job? that there is none like him in the earth, a perfect and an upright man, one that feareth God, and escheweth evil: and still he holdeth fast his integrity, although thou movedst me against him, to destroy him without cause" (2.3). "Without cause", language used by Job himself (9.17), is the key phrase: there was nothing in Job to deserve such treatment.

After the prolonged and inconclusive debate between Job and his peers, the young man Elihu puts himself forward to inject some new ideas into the discussion which, along with his references to an approaching storm, pave the way for God Himself to address Job directly out of the tempest. This climactic intervention brings the contest to a sudden halt, although Job's questions remain unanswered.

The book's unusual structure poses real problems for the would-be expositor. Unlike a doctrinal epistle, which normally progresses logically through its subject matter, or an historical narrative, which leads the reader chronologically or topically through a sequence of key events, the greater part of Job consists of an extended discussion between the protagonist and his friends. While Job's own thinking shifts and modulates under the pressure of outside stimuli, the three friends persistently tread for more than twenty chapters what is essentially the same ground.

One of my favourite childhood stories is about Winnie the Pooh on a snowy day. As Pooh and his chum Piglet make their way around a small copse they discover what they assume are the tracks of creatures walking in front of them, tracks which Pooh confidently identifies as those of savage Woozles. The intelligent reader will quickly spot his mistake. But the two friends press on:

> There was a small spinney of larch-trees just here, and it seemed as if the two Woozles, if that is what they were, had been going round this spinney; so round this spinney went Pooh and Piglet after them.[24]

Naturally, as Pooh and his friend follow the imaginary creatures ahead of them, the tracks in the snow multiply until it appears they are on the trail of an increasingly numerous pack of animals. But in reality they are in pursuit of an illusion.

In some ways Job's three friends are engaged in a similar enterprise. They traipse solemnly around poor Job to little purpose, constantly treading on their own tracks but getting nowhere. They say much, they become very excited and, towards the end, very cross, but – like Pooh and Piglet – they are merely going round in circles. And here is the problem: just as the would-be comforters keep repeating themselves, so the commentator finds himself forced to do much the same. Revisiting and responding to old ideas and tired arguments is therefore almost unavoidable in an exposition of Job. The reader must expect a good deal of repetition in what follows. Be forewarned, then: the exposition will refer regularly to certain inescapable key verses (Deut 29.29; Ps 55.22; Is 55.8-9; Rom 8.28; Heb 12.5-11; James 5.10-11).

Speakers

The nature of the dramatic genre is that it records different points of view without offering definitive guidance as to who is right and who is wrong. As a drama, then, the book contains much dialogue but little authoritative commentary or insight into motivation or feeling. We are given Job's words, but we are not, for example, informed of the precise way in which he spoke, his body language, or the visual and audible responses of the crowd who, we may assume, has gathered to listen. The speakers in the book may be divided into two groups.

Antagonists in heaven (God and Satan)

Allowed privileged insight into a heavenly council which determines Job's test, we learn that Satan, though powerful, can do nothing without divine permission. The parallel with Peter's experience at the Lord's trial is striking (Lk 22.31-32). It is also essential to realise that not Satan but God Himself initiated the entire trial for the glory of His name and for Job's ultimate good (James 5.11). Satan's challenge (that Job served God for gain) is in fact completely refuted by the end of chapter 2. But what Satan could not do through extreme physical affliction, Job's friends then nearly succeed in accomplishing through uncharitable speculation.

Antagonists on earth (Job and his challengers)

Although his friends travel a distance to see him for a very laudable purpose, "to mourn with him and to comfort him" (2.11), their arrival seems to cause an outburst of despair (chapter 3) which immediately provokes not so much comfort as criticism. Job, solitary in his misery, is faced with the wisest of his contemporaries (Eliphaz, Bildad, Zophar), men who claim to be "grayheaded and very aged men, much elder than thy father" (15.10), and after them the young and rather voluble Elihu. Each "comforter" has a distinct character and approach:

- Eliphaz – relies largely on experience (4.8; 5.3; 15.17). His characteristic formula foregrounds his personal insight: "as I have seen", "that which I have seen I will declare". His approach is initially sympathetic but thereafter, not meeting with the submissive repentance he expects, he becomes increasingly hostile, eventually accusing Job of gross sin and hypocrisy.
- Bildad – relies primarily on tradition (8.8-10), affirming the value of research into conventional wisdom: "inquire, I pray thee, of the former age, and prepare thyself to the search of their fathers". His words are generally cold and severe.
- Zophar – leans on simple dogmatism (11.6). The least attractive and most abrupt of the speakers, he boldly asserts, without any evidence, that Job is not being punished sufficiently: "Know therefore that God exacteth of thee less than thine iniquity deserveth".
- Elihu – boldly offers to be the mediator Job wants (33.6-7). Much of what he says is pertinent and potentially helpful, but he has the common youthful failing of self-important volubility. This has caused some commentators to dismiss him as a buffoon, but such an assessment hardly does justice to his important structural function in offering a criticism of Job quite different from that of the three friends. Whereas the friends have asserted that Job's woes are a proof of past sins, Elihu sounds a new note, arguing that Job's present words betray self-righteousness. Further, he acts, albeit unknowingly, as an appropriate overture to Jehovah's dramatic intervention.

Nevertheless, whatever truth may be contained in the various contributions, each speaker reasons on the basis of incomplete information. The book therefore consists largely of an inspired record of men's misunderstandings. Job's speeches especially must be read in the light of his unimaginable anguish, which accounts for their exaggeration, inconsistency, and occasional irreverence. Physical and emotional torment do not allow for cool, objective reasoning or dispassionate theology. But whereas his friends talk constantly *about* God, Job, for all his apparent impertinence and candour, regularly speaks *to* God in what amounts to earnest soliloquy or prayer (7.11-21; 9.27-31; 10.2-18; 13.20-28; 30.20-23). Loss of fellowship with the living God means more to him than loss of wealth, health, and honour (23.9).

Style

Most of the book consists of poetry, which has the particular effect of emphasising the strength of the speakers' feelings. This pitches the debate at the highest emotional level, although we should bear in mind that great heat does not automatically generate great light. A brief word about the nature of poetry may be useful, since few readers of the Bible feel instinctively at home with it. All poetry in whatever language involves, as its structural principle, regular repetition, whether of sounds (rhyme), rhythmic pulse (metre), or ideas (parallelism). The last is the distinguishing characteristic of Hebrew poetry, which means that unlike, say, English verse, biblical poetry can be translated into other tongues without losing its essential poetic character. As in the Psalms and Proverbs, parallelism in Job falls into three categories.

Synonymous parallelism (by far the most common) involves the repetition of an idea in different words. For example, "Shall mortal man be more just than God? shall a man be more pure than his maker?" (4.17). Or again, "Deck thyself now with majesty and excellency; and array thyself with glory and beauty" (40.10). In each of these examples, the first phrase in the verse is reiterated in the second, in the process clarifying and reinforcing the thought. In the first, we can almost hear Eliphaz's pious indignation as he confronts Job: "Is it possible for mortals to be more upright than God? Come now, Job, do you really think that a mere creature like you can be purer than his Creator?" Identifying this technique has a very practical value for students of the Bible, because it provides an aid to interpretation: if, when reading Hebrew poetry, we cannot make sense of a particular phrase, we may well find that its parallel will give us a clue.

The second form of parallelism is **antithetical**, which sets up a contrast between ideas. Thus, for example, "Though thy beginning was small, yet thy latter end should greatly increase" (8.7). Eliphaz's promise neatly contrasts a meagre beginning with a magnificent finish, holding out to Job the hope of future blessing, as long as he will confess his sins and repent. Another verse sets human suffering against apparent divine indifference: "Men groan from out of the city, and the soul of the wounded crieth out: yet God layeth not folly to them" (24.12). In both examples the connective "yet" signals the contrast.

The third form is **synthetic**, in which there is an accumulation or build-up of related ideas. When Job says, "I know that my redeemer liveth, and that he shall stand at the latter day upon the earth" (19.25), he asserts his confidence in a vindicator who lives, and – more – will one day stand upon the very earth itself to acquit him of all the false charges of his opponents. The testimony to his faith expands in detail and conviction as he utters it.

That most of Job is written in verse by no means undermines the accuracy or the truth of what is being stated; rather, poetry brings a level of passionate power to the written word. It has two effects. First of all, **memorability**: poetry sticks in the mind. Listen to Job describing the symptoms of his ailment:

> So am I made to possess months of vanity, and wearisome nights are appointed to me. When I lie down, I say, When shall I arise, and the night be gone? and I am full of tossings to and fro unto the dawning of the day. My flesh is clothed with worms and clods of dust; my skin is broken, and become loathsome. My days are swifter than a weaver's shuttle, and are spent without hope (7.3-6).

The tediousness of his painful existence, the lack of sleep, the unsightliness and extreme discomfort of his physical condition, the absence of light at the end of the tunnel – all this is described in language both graphic and gripping. Hebrew seems able to express itself so vividly in pictorial terms.

Secondly, poetry has the effect of adding personal **intensity** to writing. A deliberately heightened form of language captures our attention more vividly than plain prose. Sometimes the Bible juxtaposes a prose and a poetic account of the same event, allowing us to register the difference. The Red Sea crossing narrated in Exodus 14 is poeticised in Exodus 15. Similarly, in the book of Judges the historical description of the death of Sisera in chapter 4 is followed by Deborah's Song in chapter 5. Here is the historical record: "Then Jael Heber's wife took a nail of the tent, and took an hammer in her hand, and went softly unto him, and smote the nail into his temples, and fastened it into the ground: for he was fast asleep and weary. So he died" (Judg 4.21). The language is clear, unimpassioned, matter of fact, direct. But the following chapter translates cold historical narrative into the energy of a poetry that celebrates a divinely provided victory over Israel's enemy. In its expanded synonymous parallelism, Deborah's Song visualises Sisera's death at the hand of Jael with the precision of a slow-motion camera: "At her feet he bowed, he fell, he lay down: at her feet he bowed, he fell: where he bowed, there he fell down dead" (Judg 5.27). We see him collapsing slowly to the earth. In reality Sisera never fell down at all, because he was slain by a tent peg while lying on the ground. But Deborah's inspired poetry creates a dramatic scene of monumental decline and fall: the proud Canaanite general is brought low.

Job contains a rich vocabulary (five words for lion are used in 4.10-11), employing around one hundred words not found elsewhere. But the greatest appeal and also the challenge of reading Job is its urgent poetic energy.

Spotlights

Despite the toughness of the text and the convoluted nature of the argument, the book includes some remarkably clear moments of spiritual insight. Every reader stumbles upon verses and passages that stand out from the surrounding gloom as if suddenly illuminated by a divine spotlight. For all his perplexity, Job learns eventually to rest in God Himself rather than in intellectual answers. It is the nature of faith to bow to God despite apparent contradictions and the lack of explanations. As CHM puts it, "God must have the upper hand in the end; and it is the path of true wisdom to give Him the upper hand now". But for Job, it is his very distress which becomes an unexpected highway to new understanding, for "it is from the low place that we get the very best view of God and His salvation".[25] These intuitions provide the high ground of the book, as the patriarch rises from the mists of the valley of humiliation and suffering to occasional breath-taking peaks of sunlit elevation. Job's great pinnacles of faith include the following statements.

> Naked came I out of my mother's womb, and naked shall I return thither: the Lord gave, and the Lord hath taken away; blessed be the name of the Lord (1.21).

This is his matchless response to the devastating loss of temporal blessings in chapter 1. Far from cursing God as Satan predicted, he worships.

> But he said unto her, Thou speakest as one of the foolish women speaketh. What? shall we receive good at the hand of God, and shall we not receive evil? In all this did not Job sin with his lips (2.10).

In chapter 2 Job is suddenly plagued with the most painful and distressing of ailments. Yet he goes one stage further than his earlier confession, acknowledging now that God not only has the right to remove the good He has given (as stated in 1.21), but also the right to award calamity as He pleases. Even the loss of his wife's support will not shake his constancy.

> Though he slay me, yet will I trust in him: but I will maintain mine own ways before him (13.15).

Convinced that he is fast approaching death, Job combines a statement of absolute faith in God with a conviction of his own integrity.

> If a man die, shall he live again? all the days of my appointed time will I wait, till my change come. Thou shalt call, and I will answer thee: thou wilt have a desire to the work of thine hands (14.14-15).

Although possessed of no certainty about resurrection, Job has a deep confidence that, even if he dies, God has not finished with him. The God of the universe retains a deep and tender compassion for the creatures of His hand.

> Also now, behold, my witness is in heaven, and my record is on high (16.19).

Alone as he appears to be on earth, where even his wife and friends have turned their back on him, Job knows there is One in heaven who will undertake his cause.

> For I know that my redeemer liveth, and that he shall stand at the latter day upon the earth (19.25).

This, perhaps the grandest of Job's affirmations, made famous to a wider world through its sublime setting in Handel's oratorio *Messiah*, insists that, though all seems to be against him, he has a living Redeemer and Vindicator, One who will take up his case and come to his rescue. Whatever Job may have had in mind in the immediate context, it is both natural and proper for Christians to read this verse in the light of the New Testament revelation that "there is one God, and one mediator between God and men, the man Christ Jesus; Who gave himself a ransom for all, to be testified in due time" (1 Tim 2.5-6). He is the believer's Redeemer, Vindicator, Surety, and Saviour. But when Job lived, in the early patriarchal era, that "due time" had not yet arrived. It is therefore all the more astonishing that he should be able to peer beyond his immediate sufferings and perplexities to a divine provision still to be revealed.

> But he knoweth the way that I take: when he hath tried me, I shall come forth as gold (23.10).

Building on his earlier confidence in a heavenly champion, Job now testifies to his faith that, despite all appearances to the contrary, God is not against him but has a mysterious purpose, the end product of which will be to bring him out of the furnace of affliction like refined gold. Again, the New Testament expands on this concept by relating it to the believer's glorification at the Lord's return. Peter, writing to saints under singular trial, encourages them with the knowledge that they are

> kept by the power of God through faith unto salvation ready to be revealed in the last time. Wherein ye greatly rejoice, though now for a season, if need be, ye are in heaviness through manifold temptations: That the trial of your faith, being much more precious than of gold that perisheth, though it be tried with fire, might be found unto praise and honour and glory at the appearing of Jesus Christ: Whom having not seen, ye love; in whom, though now ye see him not, yet believing, ye rejoice with joy unspeakable and full of glory (1 Pet 1.5-8).

That Job should anticipate such a purpose in affliction before ever the Son of God entered this world is an amazing testimony to his faith. It is as if he stands on a mountain peak looking forward with what we must recognise as a Spirit-given desire to a faint glory on the horizon, still far beyond his clear vision.

And unto man he said, Behold, the fear of the Lord, that is wisdom; and
to depart from evil is understanding (28.28).

This final nugget of truth looks both forwards and backwards. It looks ahead
to Job's concluding expression of reverential awe in the presence of God ("I have
heard of thee by the hearing of the ear: but now mine eye seeth thee. Wherefore
I abhor myself, and repent in dust and ashes", 42.5-6) and back to his initial
description in the narrative as "one that feared God and eschewed evil" (1.1). To
continue to fear the Lord in the darkest of circumstances and to shrink from what
is dishonouring to Him is the mark of true and tried wisdom.

Solution

Although Job eventually finds his satisfaction in a renewed appreciation of and
fellowship with God, and though his material blessings are restored twofold, he
is never informed of the reason behind his trial. But it is noteworthy that this
omission by no means perturbs him. As one writer puts it, "he does not find the
answer he was seeking, but he loses the question he was asking".[26] Overwhelmed
by the infinite majesty of God, Job is both silenced and satisfied, discovering that
God Himself is greater than any of His gifts. When we cannot understand we can
trust. As already indicated, his questions can really only be answered in the light
of the New Testament. There we meet the truly sinless sufferer, whose atoning
death rendered to God a fit sacrifice which enables Him justly to pardon the worst
of sinners as well as the most pious of worshippers.

We naturally expect the Old Testament to anticipate the New. Its unfulfilled
prophecies, its unexplained rituals, and its unsatisfied desires all point ahead to
the coming of God's Son. The book of Job thus looks forward to Christ in two
distinct ways. He is the ultimate innocent victim whose sufferings are faintly
foreshadowed in Job's agonizing experience (16.9-11; 30.9-11), and the divine
vindicator (*goel*, "redeemer") for whom Job so earnestly longed (9.32-33; 19.25-
27; 31.35). As Kelly says somewhere (and his words are an excellent general
guideline for reading the Bible as a whole), "God is always first of all thinking of
His Son". Therefore, while Job can testify that "I know that my redeemer liveth",
the Christian reader, living in the good of Calvary, is privileged to know that very
Redeemer's name, and the exact nature of the work by which He has become His
people's deliverer. Indeed, from one of the earliest books in the canon of Scripture
we can turn to the last, and hear the Redeemer's voice: "I am he that liveth, and
was dead; and, behold, I am alive for evermore, Amen; and have the keys of hell
and of death" (Rev 1.18). It is only as we bring in the Lord Jesus Christ, raised
and exalted at God's right hand, and give Him the prime place, that Scripture and
human life make sense.

Suffering – for whatever reason – is a perennial feature of fallen human
experience. That is why the book of Job, with its honest and outspoken
investigation of one man's intense sorrow, will never become outdated. It offers
no simple answers; it provides no neat formulae; but it leaves us in the presence
of a God of such immeasurable majesty that all we can do is bow in worship

and wonderment. Many believers confess to having problems with the biblical doctrine of the sovereignty of God, which is sad, because in reality it is the sweetest of comforts. Whatever may be the deficiencies of their words, Job and his friends do not fall into the modern trap of reducing the all-glorious God of the universe to a cosy, diminutive deity of fallible knowledge, limited power, and uncertain wisdom. Christians never need apologise for One who "worketh all things after the counsel of his own will" (Eph 1.11), for this is the God who in free grace saved us from our sins.

A lovely moment in *The Lion, the Witch and the Wardrobe* illustrates the combination of the terrifying and the tender in God's awesomeness. The children have for the first time been told about Aslan. Susan and Lucy are understandably worried about meeting a great lion:

> "Ooh!" said Susan, "I'd thought he was a man. Is he – quite safe? I shall feel rather nervous about meeting a lion."
> "That you will, dearie, and no mistake," said Mrs Beaver; "if there's anyone who can appear before Aslan without their knees knocking, they're either braver than most or else just silly."
> "Then he isn't safe?" said Lucy.
> "Safe?" said Mr Beaver; "don't you hear what Mrs Beaver tells you? Who said anything about safe? Course he isn't safe. But he's good. He's the King, I tell you."[27]

Reading Jehovah's spine-tingling speeches at the end of Job we have to admit that the God of the Bible is certainly not safe; but He is wonderfully and gloriously good. As Elihu says, "God is greater than man. Why dost thou strive against him? for he giveth not account of any of his matters" (33.12-13). Yes, our God is infinitely great, and is under no obligation to explain all the mysteries of His dealings with His people. After all, who among us could take it in? But encountering the story of Job in the shadow of the cross we can be all the more certain that ultimately "all things work together for good to them that love God, to them who are the called according to his purpose" (Rom 8.28). William Cowper's marvellous hymn, originally entitled "Light shining out of darkness", might have been written as a commentary on Job:

> God moves in a mysterious way
> His wonders to perform;
> He plants His footsteps in the sea
> And rides upon the storm.
>
> Deep in unfathomable mines
> Of never failing skill
> He treasures up His bright designs
> And works His sov'reign will.

Ye fearful saints, fresh courage take;
The clouds ye so much dread
Are big with mercy and shall break
In blessings on your head.

Judge not the Lord by feeble sense,
But trust Him for His grace;
Behind a frowning providence
He hides a smiling face.

His purposes will ripen fast,
Unfolding every hour;
The bud may have a bitter taste,
But sweet will be the flower.

Blind unbelief is sure to err
And scan His work in vain;
God is His own interpreter,
And He will make it plain.[28]

SECTION 2
Prologue
Job 1 and 2

The narrative introduction to Job is crucial. "Without this prologue the Job of the dialogues and monologues might justly be considered a man with an insufferable self-righteousness".[29] Further, the reader needs this privileged perspective on the story in order to be able to understand the grand purpose of the book. The prologue divides into six main sections:

1. The Context: 1.1-5
2. The Challenge (i): 1.6-12
3. The Calamity (i): 1.13-22
4. The Challenge (ii): 2.1-6
5. The Calamity (ii): 2.7-10
6. The Companions: 2.11-13.

The fast-moving prelude to the debate which follows is written in a Hebrew prose that is both spare in its vocabulary and yet patently stylised in its presentation. It gives us a series of tableaux or vignettes which provide glimpses of Job on earth in his domestic felicity and then in his adversity, and insights into heaven to unveil the divine strategy behind his trials. Further, there is a crafted repetition of events and linguistic formulae to highlight the awesome solemnity of the scene. Job's initial disasters come hard on one another's heels, with increasing intensity (starting with the theft of his cattle and ending with the death of his children), and are announced in each case by one solitary surviving servant (1.13-18). The two heavenly scenes are introduced in almost identical manner, and involve a dialogue between God and Satan which uses the same patterned language (1.6-8; 2.1-3). Job responds orally to his two periods of trial with similar brevity and submission (1.21; 2.10).

The Context: 1.1-5

Our first encounter with Job sets the scene. There is no suggestion in the text that we are reading anything other than an historical record, for Job's **reality** (1.1a) is underlined by his geographical location and his personal name. Uz we may presume to be "a land somewhere east of Canaan on the edge of the desert".[30] Job's name is potentially interesting because its possible meanings can be seen to hint at the development of the story. "If the word be Hebrew it might mean the "assailed" or "persecuted" . In Arabic ... the name might mean the 'returning', that is, penitent".[31] This unites the beginning and the end of Job's history. At the start he is the persecuted man, the innocent victim of satanic malice, but at the close he is the penitent man. As the Lord says to Satan, "thou movedst me against him, to destroy him without cause" (2.3), but after his exposure to the divine majesty Job confesses, "I abhor myself, and repent in dust and ashes" (42.6). The man initially presented as a pattern of righteousness and resignation under terrible affliction becomes at the close a model of repentance.

Yet though Job has a personal name he is given no genealogy, which is unusual in patriarchal times, if we bear in mind the extensive genealogical listings which fill the book of Genesis. Even the youthful Elihu is introduced to us complete with family tree: "Then was kindled the wrath of Elihu the son of Barachel the Buzite, of the kindred of Ram" (32.2). Whatever the reason for the omission, it has the effect of setting Job apart as universal man, representative of the godly of all ages in his sufferings. More interesting still is that the Holy Spirit chooses to present a non-Israelite – indeed, possibly an Edomite – as the grand model of patience in adversity. Even the Old Testament, with its sharp focus on God's programme for Israel, provides evidence of divine mercy extending beyond the elect nation. To make his point about the trials of the saints, the apostle Paul quotes from the Psalms, although he could as easily have cited Job: "Who shall separate us from the love of Christ? shall tribulation, or distress, or persecution, or famine, or nakedness, or peril, or sword? As it is written, For thy sake we are killed all the day long; we are accounted as sheep for the slaughter" (Rom 8.35-36). The story of Job, then, is real, but stands as a pattern offering encouragement in trial to all God's people at all times. As Robinson puts it, "After Job, no saint need be staggered at his suffering."[32]

The historicity of Job is largely assumed in the text, but his personal **righteousness** (1.1b) is strongly documented. Four unqualified statements are made about him, designed to build up a remarkable picture of a man who was outstanding in his goodness. First, he is said to be "perfect" (8535)[33], a word which describes one who is complete and without moral blemish. It is used of Jacob (the "plain man") to distinguish him from his more ferocious and temperamentally explosive brother Esau. The idea is that of "personal integrity, not sinless perfection".[34] Second, he is "upright" (3477), that is to say, straightforward and righteous in his conduct, a man who faithfully observed God's revealed requirements. Similar language is used to describe godly people in early New Testament times like Zacharias and Elizabeth, who "were both righteous before God, walking in all the commandments and ordinances of the Lord blameless" (Lk 1.6). Third, he "feared God", which involved an outward manifestation of deep reverence for the Creator. And finally he "abstained from evil" (JND): Job steered away from all that was wrong. Chapter 31, which climaxes his long concluding speech, is a formal avowal of innocence, specifying the extent of his integrity, personal, domestic, and social. As Zuck puts it, "Job was no ordinary man".[35] So notable is his righteousness that he is linked with Noah and Daniel as a man who stood out in his generation (Ezek 14.14,20).

It is important to note that this initial commendation of Job does not stand alone. It is endorsed by the Lord Himself in the presence of the accuser (1.8; 2.3), and some of its terminology returns at the close of Job's great hymn in praise of wisdom: "And unto man he said, Behold, the fear of the Lord, that is wisdom; and to depart from evil is understanding" (28.28). From the very start of the book Job is the great exemplar of true wisdom, a man who feared the Lord and departed from evil.

What the book of Job does not directly explain is how it was that Job, a descendant of rebellious Adam, came to be such an upright man. Paul's analysis of fallen humanity, drawing on the language of the Old Testament, makes it clear that

> There is none righteous, no, not one: There is none that understandeth, there is none that seeketh after God. They are all gone out of the way, they are together become unprofitable; there is none that doeth good, no, not one. Their throat is an open sepulchre; with their tongues they have used deceit; the poison of asps is under their lips: Whose mouth is full of cursing and bitterness: Their feet are swift to shed blood: Destruction and misery are in their ways: And the way of peace have they not known: There is no fear of God before their eyes (Rom 3.10-18).

Uprightness, God-fearingness, goodness – all these qualities are totally impossible to men born in sin. How then could Job be so good? And was it this personal righteousness which made him acceptable to God? Is it possible to be saved by one's own good works? The answer is found in the following chapter of Romans, which deals with the central biblical doctrine of justification by faith, significantly citing the examples of the early patriarch, Abraham, and the Jewish monarch, David. Abraham, we learn, was declared right with God not because of any personal merit or religious ritual but on the basis of simple faith in His word:

> For if Abraham were justified by works, he hath whereof to glory; but not before God. For what saith the scripture? Abraham believed God, and it was counted unto him for righteousness (Rom 4.2-3).

From this example comes the invariable rule which comprehends the whole of human history: no man has ever been declared right with God on the ground of his own works. Abraham came into the blessing of justification by simple trust in God's promise. The exact moment is recorded in Genesis 15.6, where the word "believe" occurs for the first time in Scripture:

> And, behold, the word of the Lord came unto him, saying, This shall not be thine heir; but he that shall come forth out of thine own bowels shall be thine heir. And he brought him forth abroad, and said, Look now toward heaven, and tell the stars, if thou be able to number them: and he said unto him, So shall thy seed be. And he believed in the Lord; and he counted it to him for righteousness (Gen 15.4-6).

We may go further. If it is personal faith which brings one into a right standing with God, it is an accepted sacrifice which provides the divine foundation for this blessing. Back in the Garden of Eden, Adam, who sought initially to hide his sin, as Job knew full well (31.33), was clothed by God with an animal skin (Gen 3.21). To cover him in the presence of divine holiness a death had to take place. What we have there is one of the earliest typical anticipations of the work of Calvary, whereby all God's righteous demands have been met in the once for all sinless sacrifice of the Lord Jesus Christ. But because in Old Testament times that work was still future, the prescribed blood offerings acted as temporary stopgaps, while individual men and women came into the blessing of pardon by exercising faith in a God who could be counted upon to deal righteously with their sins. Again, it is Paul's gospel exposition in Romans which makes the point:

> God hath set forth [Christ] to be a propitiation through faith in his blood, to declare his righteousness for the remission of sins that are past, through the forbearance of God; To declare, I say, at this time his righteousness: that he might be just, and the justifier of him which believeth in Jesus (Rom 3.25-26).

The death of Christ is of such infinite value to God that it is gloriously retroactive: it meets the needs of Old Testament believers as well as those of us who live on this side of the cross. One of those believers was Job. Just like Zacharias and Elizabeth, his upright lifestyle was not the cause but the consequence of his salvation.

The principle is still the same. On the basis of faith in the all-sufficient work of Calvary, the believer is judicially acquitted of all charges against him, and declared eternally right with God (Rom 5.1). That is our unchangeable standing. However, built into God's gracious provision of salvation is an internal spiritual transformation which means that the justified sinner will want to live in a manner worthy of his Saviour (2 Tim 2.19). Those with a righteous standing will aspire daily to a righteous state, although in practice that will never be attained until the Lord's return, when we finally receive the redemption of our bodies. There is always therefore a tension between positional and practical righteousness, between my unchanging standing in Christ and my daily walk. That said, it has to be admitted that this extraordinary Old Testament believer, Job, as far outstrips us in his practical saintliness as he does in his sufferings. We, of course, know more than he did simply because we have access to the complete canon of Scripture; nevertheless, Job's genuine piety remains astonishing.

Of course, it also has to be remembered that, in Scripture, language like "righteous" and "perfect", when used of men, is only relative. God alone is absolutely and immutably righteous. The only man of whom it could be truly said, without any qualification, that He was "perfect and upright" was the incarnate Son of God.

We next learn about Job's **riches** (1.2-3). It cannot be accidental that the description of his godly lifestyle precedes the account of his material and familial prosperity. What counts most with God is placed first. Nevertheless God gave him a substantial progeny: seven sons and three daughters. Our secular society has brainwashed us into thinking that a sizeable family constitutes an encumbrance, but the Bible presents it as a blessing, for "children are an heritage of the Lord: and the fruit of the womb is his reward. As arrows are in the hand of a mighty man; so are children of the youth. Happy is the man that hath his quiver full of them" (Ps 127.3-5). Clearly, the possession of a large family was no impediment to Job's piety. But he was also the owner of considerable property. As one writer says, "Job's wealth was staggering. Though he apparently resided in a city, he owned and cultivated land nearby and employed numerous shepherds."[36] Obviously he was an eastern sheik of immense stature, with his 7,000 sheep, 3,000 camels, 500 yoke of oxen, and 500 female asses. Like Abraham, his affluence is measured primarily in terms of livestock and servants, serving to demonstrate that there is nothing intrinsically evil about being materially well-to-do. It is, we should always remember, not money itself but "the love of money" which is "the root of all evil" (1 Tim 6.10). Money-love remains a temptation open to rich and poor alike.

The rest of the book alerts us to yet another possession, that intangible wealth of public esteem and an honourable name, features which Job obviously valued as a great treasure. As he later tells us, looking back to his prosperous past:

> When I went out to the gate through the city, when I prepared my seat in the street! The young men saw me, and hid themselves: and the aged arose, and stood up. The princes refrained talking, and laid their hand on their mouth. The nobles held their peace, and their tongue cleaved to the roof of their mouth (29.7-10).

Job was a man of vast consequence in his city, one to whom others deferred and to whom they instinctively looked for wise guidance. Public reputation can often be of even greater value than material wealth, for "A good name is rather to be chosen than great riches, and loving favour rather than silver and gold" (Prov 22.1). But Job had it all. He enjoyed children, property and dignity. It is therefore not surprising that the narrator tells us he was "the greatest of all the men of the east" (1.3).

Finally we have a close-up illustrating how practical and persistent was his **reverence** for God (1.4-5). What was listed briefly as but one of his characteristics in verse 1 is now elaborated. It seems that his seven sons held regular feasts to which they invited their sisters. These may have been birthday celebrations, but some consider that the language suggests something much more frequent:

> The text, understood simply as it stands, speaks of a weekly round ... The seven sons took it in turn to dine with one another the week round, and did not forget their sisters in the loneliness of the parental home, but added them to their number. There existed among them a family peace and union which had been uninterruptedly cherished; but early on the morning of every eighth day, Job instituted a solemn service for his family, and offered sacrifices for his ten children, that they might obtain forgiveness for any sins of frivolity into which they might have fallen in the midst of the mirth of their family gatherings.[37]

So concerned was Job for the inner state of soul of his children that he acted as family priest to offer sacrifices on their behalf. Clearly he believed that his responsibility towards his children did not cease with their coming of age. Though his sons ran their own independent establishments, their father continued to care about their spiritual well-being, offering those blood sacrifices which, throughout the Old Testament, are foreviews of Calvary. The equivalent for the Christian is prayer. To intercede faithfully for family and friends is often the very best we can do for them. Job, we notice, was not satisfied with mere outward propriety, "for Job said, It may be that my sons have sinned, and renounced God in their hearts" (1.5, RV). To bring it up to date, it was not enough that they attended assembly gatherings wearing dark suits and carrying the largest Bibles. This earnest concern about the inside is a testimony to the genuineness of Job's own relationship with God, for it is the heart which is the mainspring of the life. Wisely does the writer of the Proverbs counsel his son to "Keep thy heart with all diligence; for out of it are the issues of life" (Prov 4.23). It is easy to conform externally and yet be spiritually cold as ice and dark as night within. There is, we should observe, an irony here: Job's particular anxiety lest any of his sons curse the Lord paves the way for the very ordeal through which Satan's malice is going to put him. Writes Davidson, "It is curious that the sin which Job feared in his children as the consequence of drinking too deeply of the joys of life was the sin to which he himself was almost driven by the acuteness of his misery".[38] In joy and in sorrow alike we need to be conscious of our responsibility to God. In case the reader suspect Job of only occasional and irregular spiritual exercise, the narrator puts us right: "Thus did Job continually" (1.5). Steadfast continuance in godliness is the mark of a real relationship with God.

The Challenge (i): 1.6-12

The scene having been set and the main human player introduced ("There was a man"), the perspective suddenly and startlingly alters, drawing us up into what we must assume is a heavenly realm ("… there was a day") where, we discover, "everything that is done on earth has its unseen roots, its final cause."[39] Whatever men may boast in their ignorant pride, "events on earth turn on the springs of heaven".[40]

But first we need to identify the **persons** in this new scene (1.6-7). Verse 6 mentions "the sons of God". For all the debate about the meaning of the identical phrase in Genesis 6.2 and 4, in Job it seems remarkably unambiguous.[41] It occurs only three times in the book (1.6; 2.1; 38.7) and describes those magnificent beings who, unlike Job, were present when the Lord "laid the foundations of the earth" (38.4), and who rejoiced in His creative handiwork. Such beings, we learn, are responsible to "present themselves before the Lord". It would seem that they appear before Him on a regular basis to give an account of their service. The verb "present themselves" (3320) means to stand (as in Exodus 2.4), and occurs again in Job referring to the impossibility of puny mortals opposing God: "None is so fierce that dare stir him [leviathan] up: who then is able to stand [3320] before me?" (41.10). These sons of God, then, are angelic beings who attend God as His ministers (Heb 1.14). They are elsewhere called "watchers" and "holy ones" (Dan 4.17), being entrusted with the supervision of national and international affairs. The New Testament gives us an extra glimpse into their function. In local assembly gatherings they look to observe godly order rather than rebellion among the saints (1 Cor 11.10), and in relation to the universal church they receive an education as they witness God's wisdom in saving a vast company of both Jews and Gentiles (Eph 3.6-11). We may assume that they gazed in amazement at Job's demeanour under trial, although the book remains silent about their response.

Then there is the Lord. Thus far we have read about *Elohim* (1.1,5), but now comes that special divine name (*Jehovah*, or *Yahweh*) which in the rest of the Old Testament is particularly linked with the covenant nation Israel. Yet here it appears outside any Israelite context, emphasising God as the One who is sovereign, self-existent, self-sufficient and eternal. Exodus 3.14 expounds the meaning of the name. Moses asked how he should introduce God to the down-trodden Hebrews in Egypt:

> And Moses said unto God, Behold, when I come unto the children of Israel, and shall say unto them, The God of your fathers hath sent me unto you; and they shall say to me, What is his name? what shall I say unto them? And God said unto Moses, I AM THAT I AM: and he said, Thus shalt thou say unto the children of Israel, I AM hath sent me unto you. And God said moreover unto Moses, Thus shalt thou say unto the children of Israel, The Lord God of your fathers, the God of Abraham, the God of Isaac, and the God of Jacob, hath sent me unto you: this is my name for ever, and this is my memorial unto all generations (Ex 3.13-15).

The meaning of the name LORD is therefore the unchanging, eternal, self-existent God, the God who remembers and keeps His covenants. Although this may appear foreign to the immediate context of Job, it serves to underline the faithfulness and eternal excellence of the One who puts Job to the test.

Finally there is Satan. The word appears with the definite article, which suggests it is more of a description ("the satan") than a personal name. Satan is the great adversary, the challenger, the accuser. In the progress of revelation, Scripture gradually unveils more and more of his character and conduct, finally locating his eternal destiny in the lake of fire: "And the devil that deceived them was cast into the lake of fire and brimstone, where the beast and the false prophet are; and shall be tormented day and night for ever and ever" (Rev 20.10). But between Genesis 3 and Revelation he remains insidiously at work in world affairs, opposing the people of God and deceiving the nations. His self-confessed roaming activity ("going to and fro in the earth, and ... walking up and down in it", 1.7) anticipates Peter's warning to New Testament saints facing persecution: "Be sober, be vigilant; because your adversary the devil, as a roaring lion, walketh about, seeking whom he may devour" (1 Pet 5.8). Dangerous he may be, but all-powerful he is not. That he appears before the Lord to report his doings indicates both his total subservience to God and his limited role in the divine programme, for God is simply going to use Satan as a tool to bring out the reality of Job's heart.

This is important to keep in mind lest we lose our perspective on the events of the book, or indeed on the happenings in world history. Satan is still accountable to God, required to report on his activities, and granted power only as God permits. His access to the presence of God will be finally terminated during the brief period leading up to the establishment of the millennial Kingdom, when he will be "cast out into the earth", and heaven will rejoice that "the accuser of our brethren is cast down, which accused them before our God day and night" (Rev 12.9-10). God and Satan are not equal and opposite forces of light and darkness who constantly battle it out, the advantage going sometimes one way, sometimes the other. Such a notion is totally pagan, and bears no relation to the clear testimony of Scripture that God is unrivalled in His autonomous sovereignty.

Verse 8 is critical to the entire book because it formally records Jehovah's unstinting **praise** of Job, praise which directly stirs up Satan's cynicism. The Lord endorses the exact description offered by the narrator in verse 1, but goes even further, acknowledging Job as "my servant", and highlighting his uniqueness. It is good to know that, even if men remain ignorant or unappreciative, God is always aware of the loyalty of His servants. Paul confessed he had no fellow worker quite like Timothy (Phil 2.20), but that was just a human assessment, whereas Jehovah's commendation authoritatively places Job on a pinnacle of spiritual attainment. Job himself never heard this testimony, any more than John the Baptist was there when the Lord Jesus gave him the highest of honours, informing the crowd that "among them that are born of women there hath not risen a greater than John the Baptist" (Mt 11.11). Down here praise too quickly goes to our heads and causes us to stumble. Only when we are glorified will we be equipped to handle both praise and rebuke in the right spirit. But Satan heard and bitterly resented God's approval. After all, he had been openly instructed specially to consider Job. Despite the unwillingness of some writers to acknowledge God as the originator of Job's testing, this verse could hardly be plainer. Kelly's comments are direct: "It is never Satan who begins the movement but God Himself … God is at the helm, and God alone gives the word … God, and not Satan … began the whole transaction".[42] It remains the same throughout human history: God takes the initiative in everything.

Challenged by the uprightness of Job, Satan moots his **proposal** (1.9-11). We should note that he makes no attempt to deny Job's piety. Nor does he fail to recognise that everything Job enjoyed came from God. It is not a man's superior skills which make him successful in this world, but God's blessing and gracious preservation. Rather, Satan's question unmasks his own state of heart; he cannot conceive of creatures worshipping and serving God for any reason other than material gain. As Robinson puts it, "bad men judge others by themselves",[43] for the thought of service out of love never crosses his mind. Nor of course can he enter into the spiritual blessings of a salvation which brings the self-confessed sinner into a living and joyful relationship with the God of heaven. Instead, he catalogues only what he sees as the quantifiable financial and domestic advantages of being an obedient worshipper. And it is true that in Old Testament times, especially in His dealings with Israel, God rewarded fidelity with wealth. Built into the Ten Commandments was a direct link between familial obedience and safe continuance in the land of promise (Ex 20.12), for though ownership of Canaan was God's free grace gift to Israel, her actual occupation of the land depended on each generation keeping the law. Nevertheless, even in the Old Testament the piety/prosperity connection was never absolutely invariable. Francis Bacon famously summed up the situation in this way:

> Prosperity is the blessing of the Old Testament; adversity is the blessing of the New; which carrieth the greater benediction, and the clearer revelation of God's favour. Yet even in the Old Testament, if you listen to David's harp, you shall hear as many hearse-like airs as carols; and the pencil of the Holy Ghost hath laboured more in describing the afflictions of Job, than the felicities of Solomon.[44]

Believers in the Lord Jesus today are never promised material prosperity in this world; instead, they enjoy something far better. They are instantaneously granted the immeasurable benefits of forgiveness (Eph 1.7), a treasury of spiritual blessings in the heavenlies in Christ (Eph 1.3), and the pledge of more to come with the redemption of the body (Eph 1.14). In response to Peter's inquiry about the benefits of following Him, the Lord replied:

> Verily I say unto you, that ye which have followed me, in the regeneration when the Son of man shall sit in the throne of his glory, ye also shall sit upon twelve thrones, judging the twelve tribes of Israel. And every one that hath forsaken houses, or brethren, or sisters, or father, or mother, or wife, or children, or lands, for my name's sake, shall receive an hundredfold, and shall inherit everlasting life (Mt 19.28-30).

In an era when Israel's promised kingdom was still being proclaimed as potentially imminent, the Lord indicated that devoted loyalty to the king would be eventually recompensed in the perfect enjoyment of what He called "the regeneration", and what Peter would later call "the restitution of all things" (Acts 3.21). Costly service for God is always rewarded, but not necessarily straight away. The Upper Room Ministry makes a similar point. Although persecuted in this world, the Lord's disciples would enjoy present tranquillity of soul in the confidence that their Master was in supreme control: "These things I have spoken unto you, that in me ye might have peace. In the world ye shall have tribulation: but be of good cheer; I have overcome the world" (Jn 16.33). Since the Christian's true wealth is inextricably bound up with the person of Christ, we gladly await His coming.

Satan's proposal is based on an over-simplified correlation between worship and wealth: remove the latter and the former will cease. "But put forth thine hand now, and touch all that he hath, and he will curse thee to thy face" (1.11). That is the test, and, we must remember, it is one which God has invited.

Although God grants Satan power over Job's possessions, the wording of the

permission (1.12) clearly spells out the limitations of his authority. First of all, Satan has to ask before he can touch a child of God. The truth is reiterated in Luke 22.31: "Simon, Simon, behold, Satan hath desired ["demanded", JND; "asked", RV] to have you, that he may sift you as wheat". He cannot even move without God's say-so. Second, God lays down the boundaries of Satan's zone of influence: "all that he hath is in thy power; only upon himself put not forth thine hand" (1.12). It is of incalculable encouragement to all distressed believers to know that our God never lets go of the reins. Like dogs on those long, extending leashes, Satan may at first glance appear to be at liberty to do as he will, but in reality he is not. He can only move within the permit of divine sovereignty. In verses 10-12 the word "hand" (3027) is used in relation to Job, God, and Satan. God has blessed the works of Job's hand; Satan urges God to put forth His hand on Job in affliction; and God gives Job's goods into Satan's "power (3027)". Behind the blessings of men we trace the hand of God (1.10); behind the distresses of men we may detect the hand of Satan, and yet always behind Satan there stands the living God (1.12), "who worketh all things after the counsel of his own will" (Eph 1.11).

Granted leave, Satan goes his way to put into effect his scheme of mischief. And still he remains unaware that he is, in the words of John Trapp, merely "God's scullion for scouring the vessels of his household". God can use the unlikeliest instruments in the accomplishment of His gracious purposes for His children.

The Calamity (i): 1.13-22

The cascade of calamities which befalls Job comes in two distinct waves, separated by another scene in heaven. In the first wave Job loses his property and his progeny, but not his piety.

The devastating sequence of disasters by means of which Job is deprived of all his **property** (1.13-17) seems to have taken place in one day. Tragedy can strike out of a clear blue sky. We are oftentimes at our most vulnerable when confronted with wholly unexpected catastrophes. "And there was a day when his sons and his daughters were eating and drinking wine in their eldest brother's house" (1.13-14). The description of his children's mutual happiness and innocent pleasure makes the sudden calamities that follow all the more shocking. Each blow seems to come from a different source, and each is heavier than the one before.

First, Job loses his oxen and asses to the marauding Sabeans. These were "a Semitic people living in a fertile district of the southwestern corner of the Arabian peninsula",[45] the area of modern Yemen.

Next, his sheep and their attendants are all destroyed by "the fire of God", language which appears to describe "that wind of the desert which often so suddenly destroys man and beast",[46] here accompanied by a violent storm of lightning. The International Standard Version translates "fire of God" as "a lightning storm [which] struck and incinerated the flock and the servants while they were eating" (1.16). Although this may correctly explain the weather conditions, it dilutes the testimony to divine involvement. It is true that "the fire of God" may be an Hebraic idiom for a mighty fire (just as the "goodly cedars" in Psalm 80.10 are, literally, "cedars of God"), but it is difficult to avoid the thought that Job would have seen, in this supernaturally devastating blow, the hand of the Almighty going out against him. After all, back in verse 3 the sheep are listed at the head of his possessions as his greatest asset, and would, we may presume, have been used for his regular burnt offerings to the Lord. Their loss signalled his inability to continue acting as family priest. He could have had no doubt that the Lord who had given them in the first place had now removed His blessings.

Finally, the Chaldeans suddenly plunder his camel herd, slaughtering the servants in the process. These people are not to be confused with the great Babylonian-based empire of later Old Testament times, but rather were early Chaldeans who had settled "in the south, towards the confluence of the Tigris and Euphrates".[47] Unlike the raiding Sabeans, they approached Job's territory using skilled military tactics, dividing themselves into three companies to seize Job's 3,000 camels, much as Abraham had split his forces when rescuing Lot from his captors (Gen 14.15).

But Satan is not content to deprive Job of his physical possessions; he means also to take his **posterity** (1.18-19). His children, engaged as usual in that domestic pleasure and mutual festivity which marked a happy and united family, are suddenly killed by "a great wind from the wilderness". This final "act of God" completes the first wave of Job's catastrophes.

Hartley draws our attention to the way in which Job's sufferings originate from every point of the compass:

> These four plagues revealed to Job that all the forces of heaven and earth
> had turned hostile toward him … Sabeans from the south, lightning from
> a storm out of the west, the Chaldeans from the north, and the treacherous
> sirocco blowing off the desert to the east.[48]

The hedge that Satan had observed as protecting Job's goods had been removed. We might note that Satan made sure that one survivor was left from each of his attacks to bring home to Job the enormity of the damage. A loss which goes unnoticed or unfelt is no loss at all.

Amazingly, despite this relentless assault on cattle and children, Job retains his **piety** (1.20-22), expressing his continued faith in God in a remarkable exhibition of worship. This is the climax of the chapter, and stands as a complete refutation of Satan's original contention. Outward blessings he can shatter, but he cannot shake the spiritual confidence of Job's heart. The patriarch's response is worth close investigation.

> Then Job arose, and rent his mantle, and shaved his head, and fell down
> upon the ground, and worshipped, And said, Naked came I out of my
> mother's womb, and naked shall I return thither: the Lord gave, and the
> Lord hath taken away; blessed be the name of the Lord (1.20-21).

Davidson suggests that "as became a man of his rank, Job had received the messengers sitting. When the full extent of his misery came home to him, he arose and gave way to the liveliest expressions of grief".[49] As a result we see an outward display of eastern emotion, for "Job [was] neither too insensible to feel grief, nor too proud to acknowledge it".[50] Reuben and Jacob both rent their clothes on the supposed death of Joseph (Gen 37.29,34), and Ezra tells us that he tore both his garments and his hair when he learned of the unholy alliances contracted by the returned exiles in Jerusalem (Ezra 9.3). But Job had lost everything. Spirituality does not involve the unnatural suppression of genuine sorrow, or the repudiation of legitimate cultural customs.

Nevertheless, as the mind of God is more fully disclosed, Scripture encourages a moderation in what might otherwise involve inappropriately extravagant or self-indulgent demonstrations of heartbreak. The New Testament – God's final word – gives the believer every reason for peaceful confidence in the face of bereavement. We know that the Lord Jesus has tasted death, defeated it, and guaranteed His people the glad hope of an eternity with Him in resurrected and glorified bodies. On that basis Paul can say to saints who have lost believing loved ones, "I would not have you to be ignorant, brethren, concerning them which are asleep, that ye sorrow not, even as others which have no hope" (1 Thess 4.13). And that is the Christian position: not that we do not sorrow at all, which would be akin to an insensible pagan stoicism, but that we do not sorrow in the same way as unsaved people. That is why there is all the difference in the world between the funeral of a believer and that of an unbeliever. The latter may be marked by numbed stillness, or feverish festivity, or even outbursts of uncontrollable grief, while the former will combine a genuine feeling of loss with a serene and triumphant confidence in God.

But though Job fell down to the earth, this must not be interpreted as the effect of unrestrained sorrow. Rather, he bowed in worship. This is far more than paralysed stupor or silent resignation in the face of disaster. It is the active response of personal faith in a God who is over all. More, Job had the capacity to put his trust into memorably incisive words, all the more striking because in the later dialogue with his friends he becomes a man of prolonged speech. But here his brevity is strength, for "In the multitude of words there wanteth not sin: but he that refraineth his lips is wise" (Prov 10.19). In the next few chapters Job will be accused of volubility: "Should not the multitude of words be answered? and should a man full of talk be justified?" (11.2). But here he utters not a word out of place.

What may we learn from his terse comment? Job recognised his innate poverty. This cannot have been the easiest thing for the greatest man of his day to grasp, but he did it. We enter the world with nothing of our own; we leave it the same way, for death strips us of wealth and poverty alike. Job uses the word "womb" to describe the source of life, whether it be the original creation of man from the dust of the ground, or the continuance of the generations in natural birth. David seems to use similar imagery in Psalm 139.15: "My substance was not hid from thee, when I was made in secret, and curiously wrought in the lowest parts of the earth". We come from the womb of the earth and return to it in death. Paul's words to Timothy are the New Testament expression of Job's understanding: "we brought nothing into this world, and it is certain we can carry nothing out" (1 Tim 6.7). A world accustomed to demanding its rights and downplaying its responsibilities would be perplexed by such an attitude, but Job knew that he had no intrinsic right to any of the God-given blessings he enjoyed. All we have – whether material or spiritual – is of God's free grace, for He is under no obligation to any man. It is that spirit which encourages worship and thanksgiving.

But, more, Job traces everything in his life, be it good or ill, directly to God's hand. He might have lamented, quite legitimately, that God had given him his cattle, and now the Sabeans, or unusually extreme weather conditions, or the animosity of Satan, had snatched them away. But he does not. He sees past all second causes to the first cause of all, God. Frances Ridley Havergal puts it so well:

> Every joy or trial falleth from above,
> Traced upon our dial by the Sun of Love;
> We may trust Him fully all for us to do;
> They who trust Him wholly find Him wholly true.

The theology, though unpopular, is correct. Here is Hannah's astute summary of the situation, which beautifully illustrates the reverent Hebrew habit of mind, so evident in the Psalms, of attributing everything to God:

> The Lord killeth, and maketh alive: he bringeth down to the grave, and bringeth up. The Lord maketh poor, and maketh rich: he bringeth low, and lifteth up (1 Sam 2.6-7).

And here is an example of the psalmist's poetic formulation of the same truth:

> O bless our God, ye people, and make the voice of his praise to be heard: Which holdeth our soul in life, and suffereth not our feet to be moved. For thou, O God, hast proved us: thou hast tried us, as silver is tried. Thou broughtest us into the net; thou laidst affliction upon our loins. Thou hast caused men to ride over our heads; we went through fire and through water: but thou broughtest us out into a wealthy place (Ps 66.8-13).

God is to be praised because He "holdeth our soul in life, and suffereth not our feet to be moved", which all sounds very positive and comforting. We can happily praise Him for such kindly acts. But that is not the end. The same God also tests and refines His people like silver, bringing them into the net, laying affliction upon them, causing them to be defeated by their enemies and to pass through the trials of fire and water. This does not sound quite so attractive. Yet it is just as much the hand of God at work accomplishing His purpose.

Even though he could not comprehend the reasons for his immediate distresses, Job had an unshakeable confidence in the reality of divine sovereignty. Having traced all his circumstances directly to God, he concludes with an ascription of unqualified praise: "blessed be the name of the Lord". Praise is often hard enough in days of prosperity, because we can easily become obsessed with and smug about our blessings, but in days of darkness it is well-nigh impossible. But then Job was God's special test case. And he passed the test: "In all this Job sinned not, nor charged God foolishly" (1.22). Not only did he say what was right, he refrained from charging God with acting improperly. The word "foolishly" (8604) only appears three times in the Bible (Job 1.22; 24.12; Jer 23.13) and seems to describe "any unseemly or vengeful act".[51] If, as Robinson puts it, "to misconstrue God"s character and conduct [is] the great sin to be guarded against under heavy trials",[52] Job was here triumphant. He avoided any utterance which might appear to criticise God in His dealings with His creatures.

In 1869 Spurgeon preached a sermon on this verse in which he directed the attention of his congregation to two chief points:

> The first is the exhortation drawn from the text – *learn to see the Lord's hand in everything*, in giving and in taking; and, secondly – and this is a harder lesson – *learn to bless the Lord's name in everything*, in giving and in taking.[53]

To see the Lord in all, and to bless the Lord in all – these are the great challenges of Job to every generation of believers.

When we suffer as a consequence of our own sins or follies, or endure persecution from the world because of a faithful testimony, we are often aware of the reason behind our adverse circumstances. It is rather like having a medical condition diagnosed by the physician; to name it is in one sense to understand it. But Job did not know why he was suffering as he did, and this must have caused him terrible agony of soul. Nevertheless he clung on to what he did know of God. Someone has said that believers should not doubt in the darkness what God has taught them in the light. Job stands as the grand example.

In many ways, Job's statement in 1.21 is a capsule summary of the believer's experience in a fallen world. Family, friends, gifts and blessings all come our way (as gracious provisions from God) and then go (as the Lord is pleased to remove them) – but the Lord Himself endures for ever as the immutable rock of His people. Though He gives and He takes, He alone steadfastly remains. We might notice the simple fact that "the Lord" begins and ends Job's comment: our lives are circumscribed by the Almighty. Jeremiah grasped this when, with aching heart and moistened eyes, he contemplated the appalling devastation of Jerusalem:

> The joy of our heart is ceased; our dance is turned into mourning. The crown is fallen from our head: woe unto us, that we have sinned! For this our heart is faint; for these things our eyes are dim. Because of the mountain of Zion, which is desolate, the foxes walk upon it. Thou, O Lord, remainest for ever; thy throne from generation to generation (Lam 5.15-19).

Job could have said the same. In blessing the name of the Lord he was implicitly bearing testimony to the truth that "Thou, O Lord, remainest for ever".

The Challenge (ii): 2.1-6

The second wave of Job's calamities begins with a repetition of the heavenly scene. Satan's first challenge has failed because it is evident that Job has passed the test. He lost his possessions yet retained his integrity, keeping perfect control over his words. The Lord therefore pronounces His **verdict** (2.1-3). Although the language of the first two and one half verses is almost identical to that of the previous chapter, Jehovah's additional comments about Job to Satan are highly significant:

> … still he holdeth fast his integrity, although thou movedst me against him, to destroy him without cause (2.3).

The word translated "integrity" (8538) appears only five times in the Old Testament as a whole and only once outside the book of Job. There its meaning is elaborated: "The integrity of the upright shall guide them: but the perverseness of transgressors shall destroy them" (Prov 11.3). Integrity is therefore a moral uprightness which sustains its possessor, in contrast to the self-destructive wickedness of those who defy God's law. A related adjective is used in the opening verse of the book to describe Job's character: he was "perfect" (8535). The word "integrity" in Job 2.3 is related to another more common term (8537) which first appears in Genesis 20.5-6 and many times in the Psalms:

> The Lord shall judge the people: judge me, O Lord, according to my righteousness, and according to mine integrity that is in me (Ps 7.8).

> Let integrity and uprightness preserve me; for I wait on thee (Ps 25.21).

> Judge me, O Lord; for I have walked in mine integrity: I have trusted also in the Lord; therefore I shall not slide (Ps 26.1).

> But as for me, I will walk in mine integrity: redeem me, and be merciful unto me (Ps 26.11).

> And as for me, thou upholdest me in mine integrity, and settest me before thy face for ever (Ps 41.12).

These are just a few examples, but they make the point that integrity is that moral and spiritual quality of uprightness which marks out the godly man. Most of the verses above could be put into the mouth of Job without any distortion of their meaning.

God, without any irony whatever, completely endorses Job's faithfully maintained integrity under terrible duress. His estimate of His servants is not in the slightest diminished because of their sufferings – on the contrary, it is enhanced. Further, it is God who takes full responsibility for what has happened to Job. Satan may be the instrument, but God is the final authority: "thou movedst me against him, to destroy him". And, of critical importance, God affirms that there is no disciplinary requirement for this suffering, for it is all "without cause". Job has done nothing to deserve such treatment. This completely undermines the basic assumption underpinning the arguments and expostulations of Job's friends as recorded in chapters 4 to 37. His pains are causeless. That Job himself is fully convinced of this is evident in his lament to Bildad: "he breaketh me with a tempest, and multiplieth my wounds without cause" (9.17).

Jonathan uses identical language when seeking to assuage his father's irrational hatred for David: "he did put his life in his hand, and slew the Philistine, and the Lord wrought a great salvation for all Israel: thou sawest it, and didst rejoice: wherefore then wilt thou sin against innocent blood, to slay David without a cause?" (1 Sam 19.5). Similarly Abigail pleads that David might spare her foolish husband, so that "this shall be no grief unto thee, nor offence of heart unto my lord, either that thou hast shed blood causeless" (1 Sam 25.31). In one of the great messianic psalms we hear the voice of the Lord Jesus Himself using the word in anticipation of His earthly experience: "They that hate me without a cause are more than the hairs of mine head" (Ps 69.4). The term does Job the greatest honour.

But Job's remarkable endurance and Jehovah's glowing testimony carry no weight with Satan, determined as he is to break down a faithful worshipper and prove that all piety is at root self-interest. His **vendetta** (2.4-6) is continued as he applies for authorisation to ratchet up the testing to the highest possible level. Job's outstanding faithfulness thus far he dismisses contemptuously with what is probably a proverbial expression: "Skin for skin". According to Smick, its meaning is explained in the rest of the verse: "Job was willing to give the life of another to save his own".[54] That is to say, though he had lost his animals, his servants and his children, his own life remained untouched. In Satan's view, a man will relinquish anything to spare himself excruciating physical pain in "his bone and his flesh". That is the challenge; and the Lord grants Satan the permission to go ahead, while once again placing clear limits on his power: "Behold, he is in thine hand; but save his life" (2.6). Even when the world appears to be in a state of chaos and moral confusion abounds, the believer must never forget that God remains in charge of His creation. He has never abdicated responsibility. Nothing can happen to His saints against His sovereign will. Indeed, as we shall see in the unfolding of the book, His purpose for Job was both to exhibit the reality of his faith and also to mature his appreciation of the Lord.

The Calamity (ii): 2.7-10

What has Job left to lose? His property has been devastated and his children slaughtered, but he still retains his health, and we may presume that, as a patriarchal figure, he was in the prime of life at the age of 70 or thereabouts. But now Satan smote him with an intense outbreak of boils. He thus lost his **physical wellbeing** (2.7-8).

This sickness is attributed to Satan, but once again we must remind ourselves of the big picture. Even the devil recognised that God was the final authority, for his words in 2.5 credit God with the real power: "But put forth thine hand now, and touch his bone and his flesh, and he will curse thee to thy face". Always behind Satan's hand is God's. Moses learned that physical ability and disability alike ultimately come from the Lord, for "the Lord said unto him, Who hath made man's mouth? or who maketh the dumb, or deaf, or the seeing, or the blind? have not I the Lord?" (Ex 4.11). At the same time it is true that illness can be a satanic affliction, for the Lord Jesus said of a poor woman who had long been bent double, "ought not this woman, being a daughter of Abraham, whom Satan hath bound, lo, these eighteen years, be loosed from this bond on the sabbath day?" (Lk 13.16). Death, disease and distress in the human race are all traceable to Adam's sin and to the penalty God as a consequence inflicted upon mankind, and they can be mediated through satanic instrumentality. Because we live in a fallen world such miseries are an unavoidable feature of life, although they do not necessarily signal punishment for personal sin. The Lord's response to the disciples' question about a blind man makes that clear:

> And as Jesus passed by, he saw a man which was blind from his birth. And his disciples asked him, saying, Master, who did sin, this man, or his parents, that he was born blind? Jesus answered, Neither hath this man sinned, nor his parents: but that the works of God should be made manifest in him (Jn 9.1-3).

How such an episode sheds light on our reading of Job, and what a help it would have been for him to know of such an example! The realisation that God may have gracious designs in our suffering is a wonderful fortifier of faith. But though Job had no such Scripture to which to turn he still retained his integrity. If ever a man trusted God in the dark, it was Job.

The text focuses upon the most evident outward symptom of Job's ailment, his enflamed and repulsive boils. Commentators have long speculated on the precise nature of his illness and its technical description, suggesting, among other diagnoses, elephantiasis, smallpox, and leprosy. Delitzsch, for example, comments that "The description of this disease calls to mind Deut 28.35 with Deut 28.27, and is, according to the symptoms mentioned further on in the book, *elephantiasis*, so called because the limbs become jointless lumps like elephants' legs".[55] But it is perhaps best to view the detailed account of Job's sickness which the book as a whole provides as a combination of many different maladies. We must allow for the fact that the language is not that of the western clinical physician but rather, in chapters 3 to 41, the intensely graphic imagery of Hebrew poetry. Nevertheless, the symptoms mentioned seem to include the following: unsightly boils (2.7), an excessively irritating skin condition (2.8), bodily disfiguration so extreme that old friends could scarcely recognise him (2.12), suppurating sores that scab and crack and become infested with worms (7.5), sleeplessness and nightmares (7.3-4,13-14), the sensation of choking (7.15), eyes red and swollen (16.16), foetid breath (19.17), emaciation (19.20), alternating fever and chills (21.6; 30.30), an ugly shrivelling of the skin (30.30), diarrhoea or dysentery (30.27), and the most acute bodily anguish (30.17). Furthermore, although we have no clear indication of a time-frame in the book, Job's condition seems to have lasted for months (7.3; 29.2).

He scraped his itching flesh with bits of broken pottery in an attempt to relieve his discomfort, and sat down alone on the heap of ashes, that spot "outside the Arabic towns where ... the dung and other rubbish of the place is thrown".[56] It would be for Job a place of exclusion from the community, and also "perhaps the most sterile place a man with sores could sit".[57] And it is on this ash-pile that Job sits for most of the book.

At this point the man who has lost so much loses even more: the sympathy and support of his **wife** (2.9). Her advice, to abandon his faith and curse God (what Satan wanted in the first place), is not said to be a direct result of devilish influence, but it certainly added to Job's grief, so that "she who should have been a comforter now becomes a tormentor".[58] Of the virtuous woman it is written, "The heart of her husband doth safely trust in her, so that he shall have no need of spoil. She will do him good and not evil all the days of her life" (Prov 31.11-12). Scripture offers us, among others, the sterling example of Manoah's wife, whose voice of common sense alleviated her husband's terror at the visit of the angel of the Lord (Judg 13.22-23). A good wife can be a mainstay for her husband. But not all wives are so worthy.

Historically, expositors have not been kind to Mrs Job. Delitzsch summarises the general opinion:

> Job has lost his children, but this wife he has retained, for he needed not to be tried by losing her: he was proved sufficiently by having her. She is further on once referred to, but even then not to her advantage. Why, asks Chrysostom, did the devil leave him this wife? Because he thought her a good scourge, by which to plague him more acutely than by any other means. Moreover, the thought is not far distant, that God left her to him in order that when, in the glorious issue of his sufferings, he receives everything doubled, he might not have this thorn in the flesh also doubled.[59]

Perhaps, however, we ought at least to try to enter into her distraught condition. She has seen her goods pillaged, her family destroyed, her husband plagued with the most hideous sickness and effectively ostracised by the community which once revered him. Should we be so surprised that, in her frenzy of mind, she virtually counsels suicide as the only way out of such misery? She was, of course, wrong. And Job's gentle rebuke at least hints that she was not normally like this. To say, "Thou speakest as one of the foolish women speaketh" (2.10), indicates that this was some terrible mental aberration which paralysed her normal senses, reducing her to the level of those who were godless in their attitude (Ps 14.1). In Scripture, foolishness is not so much an intellectual as a moral and spiritual quality: it is the opposite of the wisdom displayed in fearing the Lord and departing from evil (28.28). We have only to read through the book of Proverbs to see this contrast in operation. It may be reasonable, then, to assume that Job's wife spoke as she did simply because she buckled under the load. Later we learn that she was physically alienated from her husband by his trials (19.17). Under strain the wisest of men may utter unguarded and ungracious words. It was the case with Moses who, "because they provoked his spirit ... spake unadvisedly with his lips" (Ps 106.33). We shall discover later that it will be the case with Job himself, who at the close of the story is accused by the Lord of speaking "words without knowledge" (38.2).

But even the defection of his wife could not make Job give way. His answer to her is not only a model of gracious correction but an expression of submissive surrender. Job has not lost his capacity for intelligent **worship**: "What? shall we receive good at the hand of God, and shall we not receive evil?" (2.10). Davidson usefully expands Job's words like this: "We receive good from God, not due to us, but in which we see the gift of His sovereign hand; shall we not also do homage to His absoluteness when He brings evil upon us?"[60] Hitherto he has acknowledged the Lord's right to remove His benefits (1.21); now he assents to His right to inflict new calamity. Robinson sums up the spiritual progress in the verse: "thankfully to accept of good is merely human, thankfully to accept of evil is divine".[61] The Christian position is enshrined in Paul's instruction, "In every thing give thanks: for this is the will of God in Christ Jesus concerning you" (1 Thess 5.18). We may not be able to give thanks *for* everything, but *in* all circumstances, good or bad, we shall find something for which we can be grateful.

To continue to bow before the ways of God, despite pain and perplexity, shows a faith that endures. Many years later, Isaiah spoke about a day when the faithful remnant in Israel had no miraculous interventions to vindicate their zeal and no light to illumine their darkness. In such bleak conditions what should they do? They should simply plod on in faith:

Who is among you that feareth the Lord, that obeyeth the voice of his servant, that walketh in darkness, and hath no light? let him trust in the name of the Lord, and stay upon his God (Is 50.10).

That is what Job did. Few of us will know anything of his trials, but we can at least stand in awe and admire his patience. Despite every provocation, "In all this did not Job sin with his lips" (2.10). The added qualifier ("with his lips"), which is absent from 1.22 (although it may be implied in the phrase, "nor charged God foolishly"), possibly betrays a discrepancy between Job's words and thoughts. According to Delitzsch, "the Targum [traditional rabbinical paraphrase and explanation of Old Testament scripture] adds: but in his thoughts he already cherished sinful words ... The temptation to murmur was now already at work within him, but he was its master, so that no murmur escaped him".[62] If this is the case, then it is to his credit that he suppressed such views. It is the function of the rest of the book to bring out, through the provocation of his friends, what simmered deep down in his heart.

It ought to be noted that, after this point, Satan is nowhere directly mentioned again, although the gigantic monsters of chapter 40 and 41 may offer a disguised reminder of his immense power. However, just as behemoth and leviathan are constantly under divine control, so too is Satan. By the close of chapter 2, however, he has been conclusively defeated and retires, silenced, from the scene. But the object of the Spirit of God in the book of Job goes far beyond the defeat of Satan.

The Companions: 2.11-13

The news of Job's unprecedented calamities must have travelled abroad and reached the ears of his three particular friends, friends whom we may assume were men of similar piety and social eminence. Their response was both charitable and prompt. They arranged to journey together and visit him in his distress. There is no suggestion at this stage that their **sympathy** is anything but genuine (2.11). Nevertheless, Delitzsch proposes that, following the six terrible blows which have befallen Job (the loss of his oxen and asses, sheep, camels, and children, his sudden illness, and the collapse of his wife), the arrival of the three friends constitutes a seventh and final test for the patriarch. There is something to be said for his analysis of the situation, as it is their entrance onto the scene and their ill-advised counselling which stretch Job to breaking point, so that where Satan failed they almost succeed. But this negative impact does not begin to be felt until chapter 4.

Since this is our first introduction to any individuals outside of Job's immediate family, and since these men will play a prominent role in the rest of the book, their places of origin are specified. For the modern reader they are not easy to identify, but were doubtless in the general area of Edom.

Eliphaz the Temanite came "from Teman, 'the south land', a principal site in the northern region of Edom (Ezek 25.13). His identification with Edom fits his role in the speeches as a wise man of reputation, for Edom was well known for its excellence in wisdom".[63] In Genesis, Eliphaz is listed as a son of Esau (Gen 36.4), while Teman is a son of Eliphaz (Gen 36.11). Bildad the Shuhite originated in Shuah, a name "we know only from Gen 25 [referring to] the son of Abraham and Keturah, who settled in the east country. Accordingly it must be a district of Arabia lying not very far from Idumaea".[64] Zophar the Naamathite's dwelling place cannot be located with any certainty. Naamah (presumably what his city was called) only appears in Genesis 4.22 as the name of Tubal-cain's sister, in Joshua 15.41 in a list of the cities of Judah, and as the name of an Ammonitess whom Solomon married (1 Kings 14.21).

These personal names and places of abode tell us remarkably little of any value about Job's visitors, but their later words to him will tell us a great deal. What proceeds from our mouths (rather than the simple fact of where we were raised or who our parents were) is the best guide to our hearts, for "a good man out of the good treasure of his heart bringeth forth that which is good; and an evil man out of the evil treasure of his heart bringeth forth that which is evil: for of the abundance of the heart his mouth speaketh" (Lk 6.45). Too often a man is spiritually pigeon-holed on the basis of the assembly from which he comes or the family to whom he belongs.

Their agreed purpose was "to mourn with him and to comfort him". The verb "to mourn" translates a Hebrew word (5110) expressing a physical action signifying, according to Gesenius, "to be agitated … used of a reed shaken by the wind … to pity, to commiserate (as signalled by a motion of the head)".[65] Hartley summarises its meaning as "to shake the head or to rock the body back and forth",[66] as a sign of shared grief. The verb "to comfort" translates a word (5162) meaning (again Gesenius) "to lament, to grieve … because of the misery of others … [or] because of one's own actions; whence, to repent".[67] It is used in Job to describe, with some irony, the efforts of the friends (16.2; 21.34), Job's own counselling activities in the days of his prosperity (29.25), and – interestingly – his final self-humbling before the Lord when he confesses "I abhor myself, and repent [5162] in dust and ashes" (42.6). Its last occurrence in the book recounts the consolation provided by all his old friends and relatives once his blessings are restored:

> Then came there unto him all his brethren, and all his sisters, and all they that had been of his acquaintance before, and did eat bread with him in his house: and they bemoaned him, and comforted [5162] him over all the evil that the Lord had brought upon him: every man also gave him a piece of money, and every one an earring of gold (42.11).

Better late than never, perhaps, but this sudden and effusive outflow of pity seems curiously ill-timed. These fair-weather friends were conspicuously absent during his trials. "A friend loveth at all times, and a brother is born for adversity" (Prov 17.17), but it is the adversity which generally brings out the reality.

The **sorrow** (2.12) of the three visitors as they stared at Job's unrecognisable appearance is both touching, because it is a token of their genuineness, and chilling, because it graphically implies the appalling state of Job's body, ravaged with disease. The reader cannot easily comprehend how hideous Job must have looked, covered from head to foot with oozing sores. His friends naturally expressed their profound sadness in a typical eastern way, with audible and physical exhibitions of misery. Barnes informs us that "the ancients gave vent to their sorrows aloud. They even hired persons to aid them in their lamentations; and it became a professional business of women to devote themselves to the office of making an outcry on occasions of mourning. The same thing prevails in the East at present. Friends sit around the grave of the dead, or go there at different times, and give a long and doleful shriek or howl, as expressive of their grief". An example of this cultural phenomenon appears in the Gospels, when the Lord Jesus came to raise Jairus's daughter from the dead:

> And he cometh to the house of the ruler of the synagogue, and seeth the tumult, and them that wept and wailed greatly. And when he was come in, he saith unto them, Why make ye this ado, and weep? the damsel is not dead, but sleepeth. And they laughed him to scorn. But when he had put them all out, he taketh the father and the mother of the damsel, and them that were with him, and entereth in where the damsel was lying (Mk 5.38-40).

Such a startling shift from lamentation to laughter rips the veneer of authenticity from the orthodox mask of sorrow. Obviously these professional mourners were not in a state of inconsolable grief, for the sudden change of mood betrays their superficiality. If the little girl were not really dead they would presumably lose part of their fee.

But there is no hint in the text of Job that his friends – who, after all, were not hired mourners – were insincere. They wept loudly, tore their clothes, and sprinkled dust on their heads. Of the last action, Delitzsch remarks, "The casting up of dust on high is the outward sign of intense suffering … of that which causes [a man] to cry to heaven".[68] However, although in this action they testified to their oneness with Job in his anguished supplications to God, they are never recorded as interceding on his behalf. Yet intercession is today one of the most practical ways in which we can spiritually support one another. Paul's testimony to Epaphras highlights the value of continual prayer: "Epaphras, who is one of you, a servant of Christ, saluteth you, always labouring fervently for you in prayers, that ye may stand perfect and complete in all the will of God" (Col 4.12). To attempt spiritual consolation without earnest prayer is to reduce the ministry of encouragement to the level of mere psychological counselling.

There follows a period of intense quietness. This grief-stricken **silence** (2.13) for an entire week is in keeping with the culture of the time. When Jacob's family brought his body out of Egypt to Canaan for burial they engaged in a similar extensive period of mourning:

> And they came to the threshingfloor of Atad, which is beyond Jordan, and there they mourned with a great and very sore lamentation: and he [Joseph] made a mourning for his father seven days (Gen 50.10).

As Robinson says, "true sympathy [is] expressed by silence as well as tears".[69] It may be, as Zuck holds, that the friends' silence also betrayed a nagging anxiety about Job's state of soul. Surely only a bad man could suffer such terrible reverses? Was their old colleague nothing more than a hypocrite who for years had been pulling the wool over their eyes? The suggestion has its attractions, but one has to admit that there is nothing in the text so far to hint at it. On the contrary, the only reason the narrative offers for their quietness is this: "none spake a word unto him: for they saw that his grief was very great" (2.13). At this stage it was pure sympathy, not tacit suspicion, which governed their actions.

The term "Job's comforter" has engraved itself on the English language as shorthand for "a person who tries to console or help someone and not only fails but ends up making the other feel worse".[70] In the extended debate which fills the chapters that follow, Job's three friends certainly live up to that reputation. Nevertheless, their initial presentation in chapter 2 is wholly positive, so that all who seek to offer comfort to the distressed can learn much about thoughtful sympathy and practical concern from their behaviour.

First, their preparedness to take the trouble of making a personal visit is a clear token of the esteem in which they held their friend. Living as we do in days dominated by easy electronic communication, we sometimes forget that nothing can substitute for the personal touch. The simple physical presence in the flesh of real friends can bring incalculable blessing and warm cheer to the needy. The Lord's words to believing Gentiles at the close of the Great Tribulation have more than mere eschatological meaning, for they enshrine a basic principle: "I was an hungred, and ye gave me meat: I was thirsty, and ye gave me drink: I was a stranger, and ye took me in: Naked, and ye clothed me: I was sick, and ye visited me: I was in prison, and ye came unto me" (Mt 25.35-36). Paul tells us that, during his detention, he enjoyed the encouragement of a personal visit from Onesiphorus, who "was not ashamed of my chain: But, when he was in Rome, he sought me out very diligently, and found me" (2 Tim 1.16-17). It obviously took Onesiphorus both effort and courage to get to the apostle, but nothing would deter him from his errand of sympathetic support. The apostle John is equally emphatic about the value of intimate fellowship expressed through personal contact. Having written a brief letter to "the elect lady" and her children about matters requiring urgent attention, he concludes by saying that, though he had "many things to write unto you, I would not write with paper and ink: but I trust to come unto you, and speak face to face, that our joy may be full" (2 Jn v.12). When our fellow saints are in distress, the text message, the email, the card of sympathy, even the phone or Skype call, are no replacement for the human warmth of a personal visit.

Second, their ministry of comfort was strengthened by mutual fellowship; believers who seek to serve the Lord in harmony will find their labours, whether in worship or in solace, greatly enhanced. Paul writes glowingly of the enthusiasm with which the Macedonian believers prayed "with much intreaty that we would receive the gift, and take upon us the fellowship of the ministering to the saints" (2 Cor 8.4). This was in connection with the raising of financial aid for Christians living in a famine-stricken region, but the principle applies to all acts of spiritual service. What we seek to do for the Lord can be enriched when we do it in fellowship with the like-minded.

Third, they came, with the best of intentions, "to mourn with him and to comfort him" (2.11). They did not come as busybodies, to probe, snoop or gloat, or pick up shreds of gossip about Job with which they could satisfy the curiosity of people back at home. Their visit was designed to alleviate, not to intensify, his grief. It is proper that our acts of service for the Lord and His people have a clearly positive goal in view.

Fourth, they felt no embarrassment about displaying that outward compassion which was the cultural expectation of their time: they "lifted up their voice, and wept; and they rent everyone his mantle, and sprinkled dust upon their heads toward heaven" (2.12). In a similar manner David showed generous pity for those who had done nothing but return him evil for good: "But as for me, when they were sick, my clothing was sackcloth: I humbled my soul with fasting; and my prayer returned into mine own bosom. I behaved myself as though he had been my friend or brother: I bowed down heavily, as one that mourneth for his mother" (Ps 35.13-14). Though western mourning customs are different, it is still the responsibility of believers to "Rejoice with them that do rejoice, and weep with them that weep" (Rom 12.15). This is the way Job himself behaved in relation to the distressed: "Did not I weep for him that was in trouble? was not my soul grieved for the poor?" (30.25). Perhaps a stiff upper-lip culture needs to remind itself that there is nothing unspiritual about tears.

Finally, they knew the value of solemn quietness. Too often we seek to offer snap answers without even having done our afflicted brethren the courtesy of listening carefully to their problems and anxieties. Local assembly shepherds who would live up to the high standard Jehovah expected of Israel's spiritual leaders (as evidenced in Ezekiel 34) must learn the importance of an open ear. Sometimes feelings can be too deep for words, and hearts can be too distracted to be appeased by trite answers. Asaph had to confess that "I am so troubled that I cannot speak" (Ps 77.4), and this was Job's condition for seven days. As Solomon says, there is "a time to keep silence, and a time to speak" (Eccl 3.7), but to know which is the right time is no easy task.

> It's sometimes best to hold our peace
> When saints for answers seek:
> The greater part of wisdom is
> To know when *not* to speak.

For a whole week they sat in silence alongside their afflicted friend. At the close of that period Job could restrain himself no longer, and burst out in a complaint which articulated the pain and perplexity which had been building up within his heart. All this is compressed into the great lamentation recorded in chapter 3.

SECTION 3
Monologue
Job 3

The chapter devoted to Job's bitter complaint, which forms the necessary bridge between the prologue and the debate, breaks up into three short paragraphs:

1. Job's Imprecation: 3.1-10
2. Job's Aspiration: 3.11-19
3. Job's Lamentation: 3.20-26.

His friends wisely allowed Job to make the first utterance. After the prolonged silence came the storm, but it was not perhaps the storm that might have been expected. Job opened his mouth and cursed, not his God, as Satan had fondly hoped, but his birthday. For each of the sons of whom he was now bereaved, their "day" (be it their birthday or, more likely, some more regular occasion of communal feasting) had been one of joyful celebration (1.4); for Job, his own day was one of execration. He could only look back with bitterness to his entrance into a world which seemed, at that moment, to be one of unalleviated and unexplained misery.

Job's monologue does not take long to read aloud, but it leaves a strong aftertaste in the mouth. That being so, it is imperative for us to remember that his words are those of a man undergoing unimaginable stress, tormented both in body and in mind. To expect a structured platform address on the meaning of suffering, or a coolly reasoned account of the ways of providence, or a detached analysis of his personal experience, would be absurd in the extreme. What we have instead is a testimony to the devastating honesty of God's Word, which records the uncensored utterances of a godly man at the end of his tether.

Even in the New Testament we meet people who say what they do not mean. The heat of the moment can produce the strangest of statements. Peter's reaction to the Lord's miraculous power over the Galilean fish stocks is a case in point:

> When Simon Peter saw it, he fell down at Jesus' knees, saying, Depart from me; for I am a sinful man, O Lord. For he was astonished, and all that were with him, at the draught of the fishes which they had taken (Lk 5.8-9).

Utterly overwhelmed by the miracle and deeply conscious of his own unfitness even to be in the presence of so glorious a person, Peter actually asked the Lord to go away. In reality, of course, he longed more than ever for the companionship of such a Master, but was stunned by a stabbing awareness of his own sin. The Lord Jesus, however, who reads the heart rather than the spoken words, graciously refused his befuddled request. As Hall puts it, "No man ever fared the worse for abasing himself to his God … Simon could not devise how to hold Christ faster, than by thus suing to him to be gone, than by thus pleading his unworthiness".[71] The same Peter on the mount of transfiguration, again overcome by the amazing spectacle before him, spoke out of turn, "not knowing what he said" (Lk 9.33). A man should never be judged by his fellow men purely on the basis of unguarded words.

Delitzsch pertinently comments that there is "a great difference between a man who has in general no trust in God, and in whom suffering makes this manifest in a terrible manner, and the man with whom trust in God is a habit of his soul, and is only momentarily repressed, and, as it were, paralysed".[72] The second is the case with Job, for even in the saintliest of men faith and patience may suffer temporary eclipse without being completely extinguished.

Job's Imprecation: 3.1-10

The striking language of imprecation comes over very clearly in the first section of the chapter, exploding into Job's double use of the word "curse" (3.8). The imperative mood is expressed by the reiterated "let" of verses 3-9, a grammatical construction which catalogues the terrible ruin that Job, had he the power, would unleash upon his day of birth. This is climaxed by his explanation of the reason why this day deserved such treatment: "Because it shut not up the doors of my mother's womb, nor hid sorrow from mine eyes" (3.10). The noun "sorrow" (5999) almost becomes a key word summarising Job's appalling plight. Eight times it appears in the book, translated in the KJV by a range of terms expressive of its meaning: "sorrow" (3.10), "wickedness" (4.8), "trouble" (5.6-7), "wearisome" (7.3), "misery" (11.16), "mischief" (15.35), and "miserable" (16.2). It first appears in Genesis 41.51 to describe Joseph's "toil" in Egypt during his exile and slavery. Strong's Concordance sums up its significance: "*toil*, that is, *wearing effort*; hence *worry*, whether of body or mind". And it is this all-absorbing sorrow which provokes Job into what may be called, in the words of Smick, "a sizzling malediction".[73]

But what exactly does Job say? There is no evidence of incoherence here. His words, as befits a dignified eastern sage, are formally structured into a careful pattern, as he systematically curses both the day of his birth and the night of his conception. A summary statement (3.3) is followed by a detailed elaboration of the curse, first on the daylight hours of his birthday (3.4-5), and then on the night-time in which he was conceived (3.6-9). The language is dense with reiterated synonyms of obscurity ("darkness . shadow of death ... cloud ...blackness"), exclusion ("let it not be joined unto the days of the year, let it not come into the number of the months. Lo, let that night be solitary") and sheer misery ("terrify ... no joyful voice"). It is as if Job is attempting to reverse the great creative command of Genesis, "Let there be light" (Gen 1.3). It all reflects, by means of poetic hyperbole, Job's utterly dismal view of his current condition. Instead of bright hopes of future good, family solidarity, and the emotional gladness normally associated with the arrival of a new life, Job, by contrast, is surrounded by impenetrable darkness, has become a social outcast, and is overtaken by sorrow upon sorrow. This ceremonial curse on the date of his conception and birth puts into words all the dreadful confusion he feels about himself.

In his utter despondency, he even rhetorically invokes the professional necromancers of the ancient Middle East who, like Balaam, claimed to be able to pronounce blessings or curses upon their victims: "Let them curse it that curse the day, who are ready to rouse Leviathan" (3.8, JND). According to John Gill, "some understand this of astrologers, magicians, and enchanters, raising spirits, and particularly the devil, who they think is meant by Leviathan". This certainly fits the context. Even in the Jehovah speeches at the end of the book, where the monstrous creature leviathan appears as an example of God's immeasurable creative power, there is at least a hint that he may also stand as a type of Satan. The God who made and masters the natural world is in charge of the supernatural as well. We must, of course, understand that Job is by no means endorsing the supposed powers of pagan magicians, but simply saying that, if it were possible for such people to dispense maledictions, he would be glad for them to blot out his birthday from the calendar.

Nevertheless, he is not in denial of fundamental truth. This is important. Though Job's anguish of body and soul may cause him to say some things which might be better left unsaid, he still retains a godly intelligence. There is no incipient Alzheimer's about Job's words. Associating birth and conception makes the powerful point that conception brings into existence a genuine human being: "Let the day perish wherein I was born, and the night in which it was said, There is a man child conceived" (3.3). What is conceived is not reduced to a mere foetus or appendage but is identified as a "man child" (1397), literally a valiant warrior, a strong man. We have a testimony here to the value of human life from the womb. As the psalmist says, "My substance was not hid from thee, when I was made in secret, and curiously wrought in the lowest parts of the earth. Thine eyes did see my substance, yet being unperfect; and in thy book all my members were written, which in continuance were fashioned, when as yet there was none of them" (Ps 139.15-16). The Bible offers no support for the wicked practice of abortion.

The other place in Scripture where we meet similar language is in the prophecy of Jeremiah. There the faithful but persecuted messenger of Jehovah blurts out a desire never to have been born:

> Cursed be the day wherein I was born: let not the day wherein my mother bare me be blessed. Cursed be the man who brought tidings to my father, saying, A man child is born unto thee; making him very glad. And let that man be as the cities which the Lord overthrew, and repented not: and let him hear the cry in the morning, and the shouting at noontide; Because he slew me not from the womb; or that my mother might have been my grave, and her womb to be always great with me. Wherefore came I forth out of the womb to see labour and sorrow, that my days should be consumed with shame? (Jer 20.14-18).

This is all the more remarkable when we consider its immediately preceding context (Jer 20.11-13), which is a hymn of praise to God for deliverance. To read the entire chapter is to witness a man of God so thoroughly exhausted by heartache and discouragement that his moods waver erratically and irrationally. Is it possible for a genuine believer's emotions to swing so wildly, so unpredictably, between hope and dejection? God's Word and personal experience join to affirm that it is. The heroes of Scripture were not supernaturally immunised against distress or invulnerable to doubt. Indeed, the very fact that they were "subject to like passions as we are" (James 5.17) makes them such breathtakingly relevant patterns for saints in difficulties today.

Jeremiah 20 is a chapter of passionate intensity. And, as with Job, we are given the historical background to explain the prophet's dejection. Jeremiah's inflexible testimony to the approaching judgment upon apostate Jerusalem has not been heeded; on the contrary, he has become an object of scorn and opprobrium, a traitor to his people and a threat to the government. His enemies have been plotting against him. The constant strain of living under such vilification and peril has caused a momentary mental breakdown; hence his explosive language. Nevertheless, Keil warns against a simple identification of these two cases:

> The curse uttered … against the day of his birth, while it reminds us of the verses … in which Job curses the day of his conception and of his birth, is markedly distinguished in form and substance from that dreadful utterance of Job's. Job's words are much more violent and passionate, and are turned directly against God, who has given life to him, to a man whose way is hid, whom God hath hedged round.[74]

It is true that Job speaks at greater length, implicitly challenging God's dealings with him. But what both men have markedly in common is what they do *not* say. Neither Job nor Jeremiah contemplates suicide. Just as life from the womb is a gift from God, so too death is His unique prerogative. Hannah's words are right on target:

> The Lord killeth, and maketh alive: he bringeth down to the grave, and bringeth up. The Lord maketh poor, and maketh rich: he bringeth low, and lifteth up (1 Sam 2.6-7).

Whatever the strains under which the believer finds himself, self-murder is not an option.

Nonetheless, Job solemnly wishes he had never been born, and to do that is essentially to question the wisdom and rightness of God's ways. Darby helpfully notes that, though Job had passed the test of chapters 1 and 2, he here begins to unveil what is in his heart:

> The uprightness and even the patience of Job had been manifested, and Satan had no more to say. But God alone can search out what the heart really is before Him; and the absence of all self-will, perfect agreement with the will of God, absolute submission like that of Christ, these things God alone could test, and thus lay bare the nothingness of man's heart before Him.[75]

Job's Aspiration: 3.11-19

After the outspoken curse pronounced on the day of his birth, Job shifts into the language of wistful aspiration. Because life has become so intolerable, he longs for the release offered by the grave, where the oppressed and distressed are at least freed from troubles. Four questions head this section, crystallising a desire to have been still-born, deprived of all the natural provisions of care and succour. Had his father's knees not supported him as a baby, had his mother or nurse not supplied necessary nourishment, he would have slipped easily into the release of death. Job twice announces his desire (3.11-12,16), each time following it with a list of the beneficial results which would ensue. He contemplates the way death links the extremes of human life, uniting both the wealthy and the weary. Famous kings and counsellors may have devised great building programmes for their personal honour, but all their palaces are now heaps of ruins. Princes may have amassed for themselves gold and silver, but in death they leave it all behind (3.13-15). At the other extreme, both villain and victim find in death an escape from life's trials, for captives are discharged and slaves emancipated (3.17-19).

The melancholy language of this paragraph depicts the restful landscape of death. Job's thought seems to combine the grave (where the body sleeps, freed from the pains of living) with some kind of intermediate condition where the soul exists unencumbered by earthly sorrows. His vocabulary is not that of extinction or non-being, so it is hard to take this simply as a yearning for the physical dissolution of the tomb. Although he does not use it here, the word sheol (7585) appears eight times in Job as a whole, translated in the KJV by "grave" (7.9; 14.13; 17.13; 21.13; 24.19), "pit" (17.16), and "hell" (11.8; 26.6). Seven of these eight times it is Job who employs the word. It is the Old Testament equivalent of the New Testament term *hades*, the place of departed spirits.

Job appears to view the state of the soul after death as an experience of release for all, regardless of their social position or moral conduct in the world. It is a blessed liberation from the miseries of life: "There the wicked cease from troubling; and there the weary be at rest" (3.17). So compelling is the idea of repose that he employs four synonyms in verse 13 to drive it home: "lain still ... quiet ... slept ... at rest". As Wiersbe puts it, Job looks ahead to "a shadowy place where the small and great rested together, away from the burdens and sufferings of life on earth".[76] The quietness of the grave must have seemed an attractive alternative to a life dominated by "sighing" and "roarings" (3.24).

The Old Testament offers no clear information about the intermediate state which exists between death and resurrection, any more than it fully discloses the doctrine of bodily resurrection itself. In the progress of revelation this truth was only made known gradually, reaching its climax with the coming of the incarnate Son, who concludes God's gracious self-disclosure. But there are passages even in the Old Testament which challenge Job's simple notion of the grave as a place of indiscriminate respite. Ezekiel 32.17-32 records a lengthy funeral dirge or lamentation for the land of Egypt, giving us a glimpse into the state of powerful men after death:

Son of man, wail for the multitude of Egypt, and cast them down, even her, and the daughters of the famous nations, unto the nether parts of the earth, with them that go down into the pit. Whom dost thou pass in beauty? go down, and be thou laid with the uncircumcised. They shall fall in the midst of them that are slain by the sword: she is delivered to the sword: draw her and all her multitudes. The strong among the mighty shall speak to him out of the midst of hell with them that help him: they are gone down, they lie uncircumcised, slain by the sword. Asshur is there and all her company: his graves are about him: all of them slain, fallen by the sword: Whose graves are set in the sides of the pit, and her company is round about her grave: all of them slain, fallen by the sword, which caused terror in the land of the living (Ezek 32.18-23).

Several words and phrases in this passage speak of the intermediate condition. It is described as being located in the "the nether parts of the earth" (v.18), the "pit" (v.18), and "hell" (v.21). The first term (8482) suggests great depth, and is combined with *sheol* (7585) in the Song of Moses: "For a fire is kindled in mine anger, and shall burn unto the lowest [8482] hell [7585], and shall consume the earth with her increase, and set on fire the foundations of the mountains" (Deut 32.22). The second word (953) refers to a cistern or well, such as that into which Joseph was cast by his brothers (Gen 37.20). The third (7585) is the familiar *sheol*, often translated "hell" or "grave" in the KJV, although more recent versions prefer simply to retain the transliterated Hebrew term itself. It is normally defined as referring to the unseen world of departed spirits. Put together, the language describes a place of immeasurable depth in the earth, a place of conscious confinement, where the spirits of men are kept until final judgment.

Egypt, thus consigned to *sheol*, is put on a par with other fallen nations – Elam, Assyria, Meshech, Tubal, Edom, Zidon. Death is indeed the great leveller. Pharaoh's only comfort in the afterlife, and it is a cold one, will be that he and his defeated armies are not alone – the great world powers of the past are there too (Ezek 32.31). However, the scene, we may note, is not so much one of repose but rather one of ruination and desolation. Job's notion of universal release from misery is oversimplified. Of course, he is not offering a carefully worded doctrinal statement but pouring out the longings of a bruised heart for some kind of ultimate relief from his agony. And none can deny that the ills of this life are terminated at death. Nevertheless, "it is appointed unto men once to die, but after this the judgment" (Heb 9.27). Death ends life's pains, but it also brings man into a sphere of direct divine judgment.

Only with the incarnation comes a definitive glimpse into the world of the departed. In Luke 16 the Lord Jesus pulled back the curtain to relate the distinct and different destinies of the rich man in *hades* (the Greek equivalent of the Hebrew *sheol*) and Lazarus the beggar in Abraham's bosom. His words, spoken before the start of the church age, describe the situation as it existed in the Old Testament era. *Hades* may be described as the unseen realm of the spirit world. In Old Testament times the soul and spirit of every person went there after death. But there appear to have been two compartments: the righteous were separated from the wicked by the "great gulf" referred to in Luke 16.25-26. Since the time of Christ's resurrection, however, paradise or "Abraham's bosom" has been transferred to the "third heaven" (Lk 23.43; 2 Cor 12.1-4). This is in the immediate presence of God, for we are told that the Christian believer at death is instantaneously "absent from the body, and … at home with the Lord" (2 Cor 5.8, ASV). On the other hand, all the unsaved (both before and after Christ's resurrection) still go to *hades* where they suffer conscious torment in anticipation of their final destiny. At the judgment of the Great White Throne, which preludes the eternal state (Rev 20.11-15), the wicked will be raised for formal assessment. At that point *hades* will for ever become part of *gehenna*, the eternal hell. This everlasting and inescapable destiny is called, chillingly, "the second death".

For the Christian believer, however, death means "to depart, and to be with Christ; which is far better" (Phil 1.23), although, for the spiritual wellbeing of the saints, the apostle Paul was selflessly willing to forgo that immediate bliss. But Paul lived in the light of the cross. He knew exactly where he was headed, while knowing also that he had been commissioned to preach the gospel and instruct the people of God. Job had neither that knowledge nor that special entrustment. We should not be too surprised that, in his ignorance, he came to the conclusion that even death must be better than a life of misery.

Job's Lamentation: 3.20-26

Having expressed a longing for release, Job finally moves into direct lamentation, asking why the miserable should be permitted to live when all they wish is to die. His word choice reveals the desperation of his soul. People like him are "in misery, and … bitter in soul", they "long for death … and dig for it more than for hid treasures", they "rejoice exceedingly … when they can find the grave" (3.20-22). In these verses he refers to a general class of men who crave death, but in the next verses (3.23-26) he narrows his focus to speak directly about himself, changing from the plural to the singular and finally to the first person:

> To the man whose way is hidden, and whom God hath hedged in? For my sighing cometh before my bread, and my groanings are poured out like the waters. For I feared a fear, and it hath come upon me, and that which I dreaded hath come to me. I was not in safety, neither had I quietness, neither was I at rest, and trouble came (3.23-26, JND).

This is a significant passage. Job complains that his pathway is "hid". The word (5641) is translated "secret" in Deuteronomy 29.29, where we learn that "The secret things belong unto the Lord our God: but those things which are revealed belong unto us and to our children for ever, that we may do all the words of this law". This verse, in many ways a key to the entire book, hints at the concealed heavenly plan behind Job's suffering. But Job cannot comprehend: he cannot see the road God is taking him. He has been "hedged in", by which he implies not that he has been protected from harm but rather hindered from receiving help.

It is the very opposite of the idea expressed by Satan in the prologue (1.10). With painful detail he describes his current physical and emotional misery: he can hardly eat because of his unremitting grief, and gives voice to wails of distress with the regularity of a flowing torrent. The language of the KJV and Darby makes it easy to misread the final verses of the chapter. Job is not saying that, even in the midst of his earlier prosperity, he was living in perpetual dread of some terrible reversal. This would completely destroy the positive picture of godly contentment and blessedness presented at the start of chapter 1. Rather, he is speaking about his current situation in which the possibility of yet more disaster to come is a constant terror. Other translations bring this home by rendering the verse in the present instead of the past tense. Here is the Revised Version of 1881: "the thing which I fear cometh upon me, and that which I am afraid of cometh unto me. I am not at ease, neither am I quiet, neither have I rest; but trouble cometh" (3.25-26, RV).

One of the effects of present pain is to obliterate all memory of past joys. Job is so obsessed with his current condition that it is almost as though there is and never has been anything else. But there is always God. Probably the bleakest of all the Psalms is 88, in which the writer pours out his black distress without intermission, without any apparent hope of relief. But even in a poem consisting of eighteen verses of unmitigated gloom, beginning with "troubles" (v.3) and ending with "darkness" (v.18), we may detect seeds of comfort. For all his present misery the psalmist acknowledges God's salvation ("O Lord God of my salvation", v.1), His controlling sovereignty over all his currently adverse circumstances ("Thou hast laid me in the lowest pit, in darkness, in the deeps. Thy wrath lieth hard upon me, and thou hast afflicted me with all thy waves", vv.6-7), and His positive response to supplication ("I have cried day and night before thee: Let my prayer come before thee: incline thine ear unto my cry", vv.1-2). Throughout Job's speech we look in vain for parallel glimmerings of light. Job just could not understand why he had to live on and endure such meaningless suffering.

The Lord's disciples once asked a question similar to Job's. They saw a man who had been born blind, and they wondered why this had happened (Jn 9.1-3). The Saviour's answer indicated that God has strategies in suffering which transcend our neat theories. That particular man was born blind that he might become a standing trophy of the Saviour's grace and power. This memorable incident offers one answer to the question of why Job was born. Another is located in the letter of James. Encouraging saints under persecution and stress, he writes as follows:

> Take, my brethren, the prophets, who have spoken in the name of the Lord, for an example of suffering affliction, and of patience. Behold, we count them happy which endure. Ye have heard of the patience of Job, and have seen the end of the Lord; that the Lord is very pitiful, and of tender mercy (James 5.10-11).

James mentions the Old Testament prophets in general as faithful men grievously afflicted, who nevertheless bore up under the pressure. Then he turns to Job as the outstanding example of human endurance under strain. It is through his unparalleled sufferings that Job has become the divine model of fortitude for everyone under trial. Out of Job's desolation have come strength and encouragement for untold generations of believers. Because he was miserable Job has become memorable.

For all his blistering protests, Job is not silent about God. Although it may seem as though He is mentioned only in passing, God significantly appears twice in the chapter. He is named in connection with Job's distraught curse (3.4), and later in his ironic comment about being hemmed in by an impregnable wall of grief and pain (3.23). Neither allusion convinces us that, at this stage in the story, Job is particularly conscious of the presence of God in his agony. Yet his words suggest more than he may realise.

The first reference implicitly testifies to the truth that God **observes**: "Let that day be darkness; let not God regard it from above, neither let the light shine upon it" (3.4). The word "regard" (1875) means to require (as in Genesis 9.5) or enquire (as in Genesis 25.22). In his torment of soul Job wishes God had neither seen nor interested Himself in the day of his birth – but such a desire only makes sense if it is assumed that the gloriously omniscient God is in reality always deeply concerned about His creatures. His knowledge is not that of a detached onlooker, but that of one who cares deeply for the individual. As Hagar learned to say in her extremity, "Thou God seest me" (Gen 16.13). Whatever his current trials, the believer in the Lord Jesus may look back, not only to his entrance into earthly life as an event supervised by divine grace, but further back into eternity, rejoicing that God chose him in Christ "before the foundation of the world" (Eph 1.4). John Kent's hymn puts this truth into superb words:

> Before Thy hands had made
> The sun to rule the day,
> Or earth's foundation laid,
> Or fashioned Adam's clay,
> What thoughts of peace and mercy flowed
> In Thy great heart of love, O God.

The second allusion notes that God **preserves**: "Why is light given to a man whose way is hid, and whom God hath hedged in?" (3.23). Thoroughly embittered, Job can only feel that he has been singled out for suffering. And truly he has been, though not for the reasons he may think. Nevertheless his words, unbeknown to him, are an echo of Satan's initial grumble that God supernaturally protected Job and his property: "Hast not thou made an hedge about him, and about his house, and about all that he hath on every side? thou hast blessed the work of his hands, and his substance is increased in the land" (1.10). The Hebrew words are different but the idea is the same. The hedge of preservation has been withdrawn to expose Job to the icy blasts of Satan's animosity. But the linguistic echo cannot help but remind us of the reality that the Lord tenderly shelters His people. The God of the Bible is always in total control, whether He brings us into distress or whether He leads us out, for He "maketh poor, and maketh rich: he bringeth low, and lifteth up" (1 Sam 2.7).

God observes and God preserves. Job will come to a greater understanding of this truth as the book unfolds, but believers today have every reason to rejoice that the God and Father of our Lord Jesus Christ both watches over and sustains them in all their circumstances. In an era of limited revelation "faith committed itself blindfold to the guidance of God",[77] but today the light shining out from the completed canon of Scripture is steady and sure. In trial and distress the believer can retreat for spiritual nourishment to Romans 8, encouraged to know that "all things work together for good to them that love God, to them who are the called according to his purpose" (Rom 8.28). And that purpose? "To be conformed to the image of his Son, that he might be the firstborn among many brethren" (Rom 8.29). Because Job knew nothing of that, we may sympathise with and understand his perplexity; because we are privileged to be aware of a divine goal beyond his ken we have the greater responsibility to live in the good of that knowledge.

To wish one had never been born, to long for death, to question the purpose of one's life – such confused thoughts are not as remote from Christian experience as might be imagined. Pain, whether physical, emotional, or psychological, puts all kinds of pressures on people, and sometimes we crack under the strain. But there is only one man in Scripture of whom it is said "good were it for that man if he had never been born" (Mk 14.21). The God who grants life and salvation has for His people a purpose of eternal blessing which vastly outweighs all the afflictions they may have to endure down here. Paul's inspired summary cannot be bettered:

> For our light affliction, which is but for a moment, worketh for us a far more exceeding and eternal weight of glory; While we look not at the things which are seen, but at the things which are not seen: for the things which are seen are temporal; but the things which are not seen are eternal (2 Cor 4.17-18).

SECTION 4
Dialogue: Job 4 – 42.6
Contest: Round 1: Job 4-14
Eliphaz's 1st Speech: Job 4-5

Eliphaz, who appears to be the oldest of Job's friends, appropriately takes the lead in responding to the patriarch's anguished complaint. He originated from Teman, a place associated with the wise men of ancient Edom, of whom Jeremiah would later ask, "Is wisdom no more in Teman? is counsel perished from the prudent? is their wisdom vanished?" (Jer 49.7). He must have observed his friend's physical and emotional sufferings with deep distress, and listened with increasing alarm to his unconstrained lament. His lengthy answer divides into six paragraphs:

   1. The Preamble: 4.1-6
   2. The Premise: 4.7-11
   3. The Pretension: 4.12-21
   4. The Plight: 5.1-7
   5. The Proposal: 5.8-16
   6. The Prospect: 5.17-27.

He starts by congratulating Job on his past ministrations to the needy, but moves quickly into criticism: Job can give advice to the afflicted, but he cannot take it when touched by suffering himself. He then states his basic premise – that in this world the innocent are always blessed while the wicked are judged. This is the theological principle underlying all the arguments of the three friends: that great suffering invariably proves great sin. They allow for no exceptions in the ways of God with men (always a dangerous position to take), and assume that *in this life* there is a simple correlation between piety and prosperity. But this is to overlook the fact that we inhabit a fallen world where things will be out of kilter until the Lord takes up His righteous reign. Then, and not before, there will be a perfect correspondence between the spiritual and the material, between character and condition. Eliphaz goes on to support his idea by relating a personal (and, one feels, rather pretentious) experience in which he claims to have received some kind of supernatural revelation. On the basis of this, he urges Job to repent and turn to the Lord, committing his cause to heaven. That, undoubtedly, will lead to his restoration and renewed material blessing.

Before looking in detail at what Eliphaz says, a few points need to be made about the contribution of Job's three friends in general. First, their comments are all based on **ignorance** of the facts. Only the reader is privy to the council in heaven and the real reason behind Job's trials. Just as his often extreme words have to be read in the light of his excruciating distress, so their responses must be seen as perfectly sincere advice offered without any actual knowledge of the true situation. Much of what they say, taken as traditional maxims, is often both spiritual and sensible. The problem is that it is generally irrelevant to Job's case. As Kelly writes about one of the later speeches in the book, "There is a great deal of what is very beautiful in what Bildad said, only it had no bearing on the matter at all".[78] His words might accurately describe the kind of platform ministry that regales the saints with indisputable scriptural truths which, alas, have no relation to the Bible passage under consideration. Like some preachers, Job's friends are determined to sing their favourite song, however immaterial it may be.

Second, we ought to bear in mind that, again like Job, they had no written revelation from God to which to refer. Their theological understanding will presumably have been handed down from Adam (who lived long enough to give generations of his descendants a detailed oral account of the fall and its consequences), but it did not include God's call of Abraham or His covenant with Israel. As a result there is an inevitable **incompleteness** about their grasp of God's programme. They talk much about judgment, little about grace; much about divine loftiness, little about divine love. Our situation is incomparably superior for, possessing the completed canon of Scripture, we now have access to the fullness of God's declared mind on matters which concern life down here. All the principles we need to know are contained in the Word. The reader only has to ask himself to what biblical passages he might turn if confronted with a case similar to Job's. There is an abundance of material. The Psalms, with their memorable insights into the trials of the godly, the Gospels, with their inspired narrative of the earthly sufferings of the sinless Son of God, and the letters, with their counsel to believers under strain, are all packed with valuable truths to soothe the fevered soul. But Eliphaz and his companions had no access to any of this. That, of course, was no fault of theirs. But they do give the unfortunate impression that there is no flaw in their understanding, no possible gap in their knowledge. Comments Kelly, with some acerbity, "that is generally the case with people who know very little; they fancy they know everything".[79] Or, as William Osler has put it, "the greater the ignorance the greater the dogmatism".[80] This intolerably smug self-satisfaction eventually provokes Job's satirical riposte, "No doubt but ye are the people, and wisdom shall die with you" (12.2). Modesty and humility best become those who seek to offer spiritual counsel.

Third, their whole attitude displays a disturbing **insensitivity**. They are, after all, addressing a man who has in an instant lost everything - his property, his beloved children, and his health. He now wonders, not surprisingly, why he was ever born. Instead of attempting to pacify his grief they apportion blame, joining forces to badger him into a confession of some specific misdemeanours for which he is now being punished. Blinkered by their rigid preconceptions, all they can do over twenty-seven chapters or so is tread the same ground with increasing asperity. The New Testament instruction, to those dealing with a believer clearly guilty of some particular offence (which Job was not), is very different:

> Brethren, if a man be overtaken in a fault, ye which are spiritual, restore such an one in the spirit of meekness; considering thyself, lest thou also be tempted. Bear ye one another's burdens, and so fulfil the law of Christ (Gal 6.1-2).

The apostle requires that those who seek to recover an erring believer be marked by spirituality, meekness, and the sympathetic grace that can identify with the brother in his slip. Those in distress, whatever the cause, need the practical love that offers assistance in bearing the load. That kind of counsel lifts the spirits of the hearer. As says the proverb, "Ointment and perfume rejoice the heart: so doth the sweetness of a man's friend by hearty counsel" (Prov 27.9). Sadly, Job's friends could only offer him the kind of solace that he describes as "miserable" (16.2). Far from pouring oil into his wounds, they rubbed them with salt, intensifying his sorrow. "There are times", writes Robinson, "when the believer's faith is scarcely able to keep head above water".[81] It is at times like those that the grieving saint needs tender sympathy, not theological censure.

The Preamble: 4.1-6

Like most of the speakers in the debate, Eliphaz **commences** his argument with a formal introduction (4.1-2). Perhaps he is being diplomatic: "if we speak to you, Job, would you find it unbearable?" This intimates at least some willingness to enter into Job'"s terrible trauma, and a due wariness about adding to his grief. But perhaps it is simply the customary and often redundant courtesy of the east. In any case, Eliphaz is primarily leading up to a declaration of his own inability to keep silent in the face of Job's outrageous remarks. "Who can withhold himself from speaking?" (4.2) is the rhetorical signal that Eliphaz feels compelled to talk. Trouble is, the desire to say something is not to be confused with having something to say.

Shrewdly, he first of all **commends** Job's past life (4.3-4), finding something in his old friend to praise. And it is right that those who have to correct others should take time to acknowledge what is good. That was the pattern for Paul's letters of rebuke: he first praises the Corinthians for the fact that "ye remember me in all things, and keep the ordinances, as I delivered them to you" (1 Cor 11.2), before embarking upon his corrective ministry. Eliphaz concedes that Job is well known as one who has offered valued support and wisdom to those in need. In his final speech Job himself sums up his reputation for sage counsel:

> Unto me men gave ear, and waited, and kept silence at my counsel. After my words they spake not again; and my speech dropped upon them. And they waited for me as for the rain; and they opened their mouth wide as for the latter rain (29.21-23).

Eliphaz chooses four words to describe the scope of Job's benevolence. He has "instructed many". The word (3256) means primarily to correct, chasten or chastise, and is, for example, used of both domestic and divine discipline, for "as a man chasteneth his son, so the Lord thy God chasteneth thee" (Deut 8.5). He has "strengthened" the weak. This term (2388) is translated variously in the KJV as, for example, "lay hold of" or "encourage", and is first used of the two angels who "laid hold [2388] upon [Lot's] hand, and upon the hand of his wife, and upon the hand of his two daughters; the Lord being merciful unto him: and they brought him forth, and set him without the city" (Gen 19.16). His counsel has "upholden" the falling. This very common Old Testament word (6965) carries the idea of rising up or establishing, and is used of Moses rearing up the tabernacle (Ex 40.18). He has "strengthened" (553) the feeble. This is translated "good courage" in the Lord's exhortation to Joshua (Josh 1.6). Put together, Eliphaz's vocabulary testifies to Job's remarkable effectiveness as a corrector of error, a positive support and encouragement to those tottering under the pressures of life.

It is no surprise, then, that the New Testament borrows Eliphaz's description of Job when it urges believers to perseverance: "Wherefore lift up the hands which hang down, and the feeble knees; And make straight paths for your feet, lest that which is lame be turned out of the way; but let it rather be healed" (Heb 12.12-13). How much we need to urge both ourselves and our fellow saints to keep going in the race! Many are worn down by the strain of living, downcast by personal failure, and disheartened by the lack of visible fruit for their labours. They require sympathetic and spiritual support. Job stands as the model of a faithful and tender instructor in godliness.

But after the praise comes the blame, for Eliphaz, having commended what he can, now **corrects** (4.5-6). Although Job has ministered to many, he is unable to take his own medicine. It appears that his hitherto untarnished reputation for piety is beginning to crumble, for what use is godliness if it does not see us through the ups and downs of life? "Hath not thy piety been thy confidence, and the perfection of thy ways thy hope?" (4.6, JND). Job's notable uprightness sustained him in the past, but now it seems to be lacking. Undoubtedly those who attempt to teach the Lord's people should by grace seek to live in the practical good of their own instruction. All talk and no walk only encourages self-delusion.

> How easily we say what's true,
> And yet how hard it is to do!
> Lord, grant this grace to those who teach,
> To practise always what we preach!

On the other hand, it has to be admitted that in his earlier days Job never had to counsel anyone who was going through a trial like his, for it is presented in the book, and in Scripture generally, as utterly unprecedented in its severity. Eliphaz is therefore both inaccurate and inconsiderate in his rebuke. A much better pattern is found in Bunyan's Hopeful, who lifts the downcast spirits of his fellow-pilgrim Christian by reminding him of past blessings and deliverances. When his friend starts sinking as he crosses the river, Hopeful says,

> These troubles and distresses that you go through in these waters are no sign that God hath forsaken you; but are sent to try you, whether you will call to mind that which heretofore you have received of His goodness, and live upon Him in your distresses.[82]

And that, we shall see, without any encouragement from his friends, is exactly what Job learns to do. Although pained and perplexed in the extreme, he endeavours increasingly in his distresses to live upon the Lord and cast himself upon his God.

The Premise: 4.7-11

Eliphaz now introduces his crucial thesis, the principle underlying everything he and his colleagues argue in the course of the debate. It is essential that we get a firm grasp of this, for otherwise we shall find ourselves at sea during much of the following dialogue. If we lose sight of the three friends' basic misconception about Job we may begin to feel that they were guilty of nothing more serious than long-windedness. But this is the critical keynote of their position. Positively, it asserts that the "innocent" and "righteous" are preserved (4.7); negatively, that the wicked are punished (4.8). As far as Eliphaz is concerned, bad things only happen to bad people. This fundamental dogma is backed up by his own experience, for it is "Even as I have seen" (4.8), and validated by the power of God to destroy even the most formidable of earthly evildoers, of whom the lion family stands as a type (4.9-11).

In many ways, Eliphaz's doctrine is perfectly sound. The Old Testament teaches with no uncertain voice that the wicked will "perish" (Eliphaz's key word, used in 4.7,9,11,20), just as Egypt was destroyed at the time of Israel's exodus because of its refusal to heed Jehovah's word (Ex 10.7). Here is a sample of the combined testimony of the law, psalms, and prophets:

> And it shall be, if thou do at all forget the Lord thy God, and walk after other gods, and serve them, and worship them, I testify against you this day that ye shall surely perish (Deut 8.19).

> But the wicked shall perish, and the enemies of the Lord shall be as the fat of lambs: they shall consume; into smoke shall they consume away (Ps 37.20).

> For, lo, they that are far from thee shall perish: thou hast destroyed all them that go a whoring from thee (Ps 73.27).

> The hope of the righteous shall be gladness: but the expectation of the wicked shall perish (Prov 10.28).

> But if they will not obey, I will utterly pluck up and destroy that nation, saith the Lord (Jer 12.17).

But we should take careful note that these passages offer no indication as to the precise timing or location of divine retribution. It is neither necessarily immediate, nor is it to be assumed that it will take place in the present age. The total weight of biblical testimony must be considered. For a start, Solomon's view was not the same as Eliphaz's: "All things have I seen in the days of my vanity:

there is a just man that perisheth in his righteousness, and there is a wicked man that prolongeth his life in his wickedness" (Eccl 7.15). The same apparent and disturbing discrepancy between the principle of God's moral rule in the world and the observed facts of life is the subject matter of Psalm 73:

> For I was envious at the foolish, when I saw the prosperity of the wicked. For there are no bands in their death: but their strength is firm. They are not in trouble as other men; neither are they plagued like other men. Therefore pride compasseth them about as a chain; violence covereth them as a garment. Their eyes stand out with fatness: they have more than heart could wish. They are corrupt, and speak wickedly concerning oppression: they speak loftily (Ps 73.3-8).

Job is not alone in his contention that the godly often suffer and the wicked prosper.

Eliphaz's neat expression of the sowing and reaping principle (4.8) is quoted by Paul in Galatians 6.7-8 to demonstrate that God is not mocked. What we sow, we reap. Evil will eventually be judged by the God of perfect justice, as indeed Paul argues in his great doctrinal explanation of the gospel:

> And thinkest thou this, O man, that judgest them which do such things, and doest the same, that thou shalt escape the judgment of God? Or despisest thou the riches of his goodness and forbearance and longsuffering; not knowing that the goodness of God leadeth thee to repentance? But after thy hardness and impenitent heart treasurest up unto thyself wrath against the day of wrath and revelation of the righteous judgment of God; Who will render to every man according to his deeds (Rom 2.3-6).

Yes, says Paul, God's judgment is sure and inescapable, but at the moment He exercises "forbearance and longsuffering". That makes the all-important point – overlooked by Eliphaz – that heaven's judgment is rarely instantaneous, for God mercifully allows a space for grace. Even wicked Nineveh was given forty days' warning (Jonah 3.4), while the world before the flood seems to have had a period of 120 years' respite before judgment fell (Gen 6.3). Divine longsuffering in the present age provides an opportunity for repentance. This explains why blasphemers and idolaters and – let's face it – human beings generally are rarely cut off the minute they sin. If they were, who could be saved? God graciously withholds judgment so that men might have the opportunity to call on Him. This truth informs Peter's inspired answer to the mocking challenge, "Where is the promise of his coming?"

> The Lord is not slack concerning his promise, as some men count slackness; but is longsuffering to us-ward, not willing that any should perish, but that all should come to repentance (2 Pet 3.9).

But if God does not always intervene immediately in direct judgment on the ungodly, it is equally the case that He does not invariably preserve the godly from physical disaster. In His wisdom, God allocates degrees of suffering to His people in this world so that they might have the opportunity to mature intelligently in their faith. In other words, though it is correct in principle to say that God judges the wicked and blesses the righteous, it is a mistake to reduce this to a rigid dogma which insists that all misery in the present era is evidence of divine displeasure, and all earthly success a token of divine approval. God's ways with His creatures break out of the compound of our tidy theories.

Eliphaz, however, is anxious to demonstrate God's terrifying ability to deal with the wicked, however powerful they may seem. Perhaps he is thinking of the way Job's hitherto unchallenged security has suddenly been shattered. When God moves in wrath, there is no escape. Poor vulnerable man is instantly consumed simply by the breath of His nostrils, a metaphor for divine anger (4.9). The language echoes the creative process of Genesis 2.7: God is both author of life and dispenser of death. To illustrate His supreme power over the toughest of earthly adversaries, Eliphaz cites the lion family, using five different Hebrew words to suggest something of the amazing variety built into just one animal kind. "The lion", "the fierce lion", "the young lions", "the old lion", and "the stout lion" all render distinct words (4.10-11). In the light of the New Testament we may detect a coded hint of the savagery and yet the ultimate defeat of the greatest of enemies, Satan, that roaring lion who goes about "seeking whom he may devour" (1 Pet 5.8). For all his rapaciousness he will finally be broken and perish, his forces scattered when the Lord Jesus intervenes in glory. Every believer should be daily grateful for the omnipotence of his Lord; this it is that assures the absolute triumph of all His sovereign purposes.

The Pretension: 4.12-21

This paragraph, without doubt, is the most bewildering part of Eliphaz's speech, for it recounts a bizarre experience in which, so he claims, he received a supernatural vision. It is difficult to resist the conclusion that he is deliberately pulling out all the stops to impress Job with the solemn authority of his words. He spends five verses building up the **atmosphere** (4.12-16) and only another five verses reporting the actual **announcement** he heard (4.17-21). The language of terror ("fear ... trembling, which made all my bones to shake ... the hair of my flesh stood up"), the unearthly ("a spirit passed before my face ... It stood still, but I could not discern the form thereof: an image was before mine eyes"), and the mysteriously stealthy ("a thing was secretly brought to me ... when deep sleep falleth on men") dominates the passage. As the Fat Boy says in Dickens's *Pickwick Papers*, "I wants to make your flesh creep".[83] In this, Eliphaz certainly succeeds.

It all smacks somewhat of the odour of sanctity. It does not cost much to claim a divine visitation, and it may be that Eliphaz counted on a response like that of the New Testament Pharisees who said (of Paul), "We find no evil in this man: but if a spirit or an angel hath spoken to him, let us not fight against God" (Acts 23.9). The notion of an angelic messenger appealed to their theological presuppositions.

But was Eliphaz's vision a genuine revelation from God? The New Testament caution offered by John ought to be heeded: "Beloved, believe not every spirit, but try the spirits whether they are of God: because many false prophets are gone out into the world" (1 Jn 4.1). John was writing primarily about pedlars of false doctrine, but if the mouthpieces are to be distrusted how much more their demonic sources! Certainly, Eliphaz's night time encounter is strikingly unlike any other recorded in the Scriptures, being so ostentatiously theatrical in its accompaniments and disappointingly banal in its actual revelation. One has only to contrast it with the glorious manifestations of God found in Genesis, or the great vision in Isaiah 6, to see how impoverished Eliphaz's story is. There is, I think, no need to take the extreme view of Morris, who credits the whole thing to direct satanic deception, for what Eliphaz is doing is in fact not uncommon. He is seeking to add authority to his words by injecting special divine endorsement. It is not unlike the fashionable but ill-advised expression used among some believers, "the Lord led me", a phrase designed to give human actions the instant gloss of heavenly approval. Sometimes one hears a platform speaker announce that "the Lord gave me tonight's message", or words to that effect. Since there are no apostles or prophets functioning today (apart from false ones), all he presumably means is that he has studied the Scriptures and believes that what he has to say is both biblical and relevant. That should be sufficient. There is no need for any pretentious or pseudo-pious signals. The preacher of the word will get down to his business without such padding.

What, we might ask, did Eliphaz learn from his midnight visitor? First, there is an emphasis on the reality of human **iniquity**: it is impossible for man to be more righteous than his Creator (4.17). Two words for man are used, the first (582) meaning man in all his frailty, the second (1397) emphasising man's dignity and might. As the *Jamieson, Fausset and Brown Commentary* puts it, "Whether feeble or strong, man is not righteous before God". Agreed, but is not this self-evident? Eliphaz is telling Job nothing he does not already know. Second, there is a testimony to human **fragility**: since God's angelic servants fall short of His ineffable excellence, how much more does feeble man (4.18-21)? The passage underlines the brevity ("They are destroyed from morning to evening") and the precariousness of human life: man is "crushed" and "destroyed", people "perish" and "die". Man, made out of clay, is trampled as easily as the moth, his flimsy body dismantled like a tent: "Is not their tent-cord torn away in them? they die, and without wisdom" (4.21, JND). The language echoes the creation account in Genesis, but again the truth was well-known, handed down by Adam and his descendants. Further, and most significantly, it conspicuously omits important teaching about man's intrinsic worth. Genesis reveals that he was uniquely created to have rule over the earth and relate to God in a way unlike all others:

> And God said, Let us make man in our image, after our likeness: and let
> them have dominion over the fish of the sea, and over the fowl of the air,

and over the cattle, and over all the earth, and over every creeping thing that creepeth upon the earth. So God created man in his own image, in the image of God created he him; male and female created he them (Gen 1.26-27).

Man is far more than an insect. Made in the image of God, he was invested originally with tremendous dignity and responsibility. That this dignity has not been completely erased by sin is the clear testimony of Psalm 8, which raises and answers its own question:

What is man, that thou art mindful of him? and the son of man, that thou visitest him? For thou hast made him a little lower than the angels, and hast crowned him with glory and honour. Thou madest him to have dominion over the works of thy hands; thou hast put all things under his feet (Ps 8.4-6).

Unlike Eliphaz, Job never impugns man's majesty as the pinnacle of creation. Later in the book he speaks about God having "a desire to the work of thine hands" (14.15), which assumes a divine longing for fellowship with His creature. Nor does he ever deny man's acquired mortality, a condition brought about by Adam's sin. On the contrary, he later alludes directly to the creation and fall when appealing to God to "Remember, I beseech thee, that thou hast made me as the clay; and wilt thou bring me into dust again?" (10.9). No, Job knows all about man's origin and his destiny because of disobedience. He does not require any instruction from Eliphaz's bogus vision.

Eliphaz is simply (but portentously) reaffirming orthodoxy. Nevertheless, his narrow view of humanity falls short of the breadth of the biblical position, which teaches both man's dignity by creation alongside his depravity by sin. According to Eliphaz, men die constantly "without any regarding it" (4.20). Yet God regards it, for "precious in the sight of the Lord is the death of his saints" (Ps 116.15). The entire book of Job bears witness to His gracious interest in the individual. The New Testament goes further, revealing His paternal concern for even the lowliest of His creatures:

Are not two sparrows sold for a farthing? and one of them shall not fall on the ground without your Father. But the very hairs of your head are all numbered. Fear ye not therefore, ye are of more value than many sparrows (Mt 10.29-31).

The Lord's teaching argues from the lesser to the greater: if the glorious God of the universe takes an interest in sparrows, how much more does He understand and watch over those who are His children by faith?

Men may indeed die "without wisdom" (4.21), but it is possible for the man who humbly confesses his ignorance to "ask [wisdom] of God, that giveth to all men liberally, and upbraideth not; and it shall be given him" (James 1.5). Job is himself the great example, introduced as one who "feared God, and eschewed evil" (1.1). And that, as we know, is evidence of true wisdom (28.28).

The Plight: 5.1-7

Eliphaz now applies his visionary message to Job's situation, and especially to that impassioned outburst of grief recorded in chapter 3. He aims to place emphasis on Job's peril in rebelling against God's punishment of his sin. In the light of what he has just heard about man's depravity and vulnerability, how can Job, of all people, hope to get any answer from God, or even from an angel? (5.1) His appalling suffering proves he must have sinned, and refusal to confess and repent will only prolong his misery. Has he not been guilty of unguarded wrath in his bitter complaint, and envy in his longing for the peace that comes with death? Those who whine against God's ways tread on dangerous ground, "For he is a fool who is destroyed by complaining, and envy slays the simple one" (5.2, Delitzsch).[84]

It is worth remembering that in the Bible folly is a moral, not a mental defect. The fool (191) is the man in spiritual and moral rebellion against God, for "Fools make a mock at sin: but among the righteous there is favour" (Prov 14.9). A different Hebrew word (5036), the one Job used earlier of his wife (2.10), has much the same meaning, best summed up in the psalmist's description of wilful impiety: "the fool [5036] hath said in his heart, There is no God. They are corrupt, they have done abominable works, there is none that doeth good" (Ps 14.1). Eliphaz is painting in broad, sweeping brush strokes, but his target is obvious – Job. To solidify his case, he offers an example (perhaps imaginary) of a foolish man who seemed to thrive for a while, but then, victim of the divine curse on his folly, plunged into disaster (5.3-5). The specifications of this man's ruin are chillingly, and we may assume, deliberately, chosen to parallel Job's case. Initially he seemed to "take root", settled and secure in outward prosperity, but then the blow suddenly fell on his children, who were "crushed in the gate". The language indicates that they suffered formal judicial condemnation, excluded from any hope of deliverance. Their end was sadly like that of the insignificant moth (4.19). Eliphaz is not claiming to have uttered some prophetic curse over the man to invoke such devastation; rather, he traces in his fate the outworking of God's stern government. The foolish man's sin and discontent brought about his destruction, so that Eliphaz perceived the hand of divine judgment in his ruined habitation. His children were killed (we are meant to think of Job's family), and his harvest filched by robbers (again we think of the theft of Job's goods).

Since Job has already experienced such suffering in his own life, he must surely have committed similar folly. This is the constant theme of the friends – Job is guilty of sin that merits severe punishment, and to protest his innocence is mere hypocrisy. The real source of affliction, so prevalent in this world, is not the dust of the earth or the ground we tread upon, though that is indeed under a curse, but man himself. The very creature made out of the dust possesses, in consequence of Adam's fall, a heart at enmity with God (5.6-7). Our prime problem therefore is not our surroundings but our nature. As a result, man is "born unto trouble, as the sparks fly upward" (5.7). Eliphaz is right. This is the common lot of humanity in a sin-damaged world. The physical planet is under God's judgment, "For we know that the whole creation groaneth and travaileth in pain together until now" (Rom 8.22). Because of Adam's rebellion all mankind has been placed under the death penalty, for "as through one man sin entered into the world, and death through sin … so death passed unto all men, for that all sinned" (Rom 5.12, RV). That final death sentence includes all the lesser ills which draw us irresistibly towards it – sickness, sorrow, and suffering. Both the environment and the inhabitants have been fatally damaged by man's first act of disobedience. As David says of himself, "I was shapen in iniquity; and in sin did my mother conceive me" (Ps 51.5).

Eliphaz is not simply reminding Job of the inescapable fact of inherited sin which affects everybody; he is accusing him, albeit indirectly as yet, of specific and serious disobedience to God.

The Proposal: 5.8-16

The imagery of the sparks flying upward with which verse 7 closes (the same Hebrew word is used in Psalm 113.5 to describe God"s dwelling "on high") lifts the thoughts heavenwards, leading Eliphaz smoothly into his proposal – that Job, in humble penitence, should seek God. This is now the more kindly language of the sympathetic counsellor: "But as for me, I would seek unto God, and unto God would I commit my cause" (5.8, RV). Says Eliphaz, "If I were in your shoes, Job, I'd get down on my knees and ask forgiveness".

To encourage Job's repentance, he reminds him of God's total control over His world. The sovereign God is beneficent to the needy, but hostile to the unashamedly wicked. The verses that follow constitute what might be called a psalm of praise, packed with an intelligent and reverent rehearsal of God's majesty (5.9-16). Though we may not agree with Eliphaz's attitude to Job, we must give him due credit for a high view of God.

After a summary statement which underlines the greatness, immeasurability, and mystery of God's work (5.9), Eliphaz speaks of two aspects of divine activity. The passage is structured like a sandwich in that it begins and ends with God's **mercy towards the needy** (5.10-11, 15-16), while in the middle recounting His **justice on the wicked** (5.12-14). This chiastic pattern places special emphasis upon the goodness of God as the One whom Job ought to approach in quest of forgiveness. But first Eliphaz summarises God's infinite splendour. He "doeth great things and unsearchable; marvellous things without number" (5.9). The language anticipates David's great poem of worship: "Great is the Lord, and greatly to be praised; and his greatness is unsearchable" (Ps 145.3). Despite the development of human technology facilitating greater exploration of the created universe, the fact remains that God's works are still beyond our ability to measure, for "there is no searching of his understanding" (Is 40.28). How much more unfathomable are His saving dealings with His people! Paul's outburst of praise at the close of Romans 11 is in response to His redemptive mercy towards Jews and Gentiles:

O the depth of the riches both of the wisdom and knowledge of God! how unsearchable are his judgments, and his ways past finding out! For who hath known the mind of the Lord? or who hath been his counsellor? Or who hath first given to him, and it shall be recompensed unto him again? For of him, and through him, and to him, are all things: to whom be glory for ever. Amen (Rom 11.33-36).

The more we learn of such a God, the more we realise our own limitations. Eliphaz's design in all this is to convince Job of the fittingness of appealing to a God of infinite power.

The body of Eliphaz's psalm concentrates upon what God does in His kindness. His example is the provision of rain for the benefit of His creatures (5.10). The gift of water is in Sscripture one of the tokens of God's providential mercy:

Thou visitest the earth, and waterest it: thou greatly enrichest it with the river of God, which is full of water: thou preparest them corn, when thou hast so provided for it. Thou waterest the ridges thereof abundantly: thou settlest the furrows thereof: thou makest it soft with showers: thou blessest the springing thereof. Thou crownest the year with thy goodness; and thy paths drop fatness (Ps 65.9-11).

This early in the book we have a testimony to God's creatorial benevolence, a truth which, unbeknown to Eliphaz or Job, paves the way for Jehovah's grand intervention at the close. There we shall learn that He even bestows His bounty where there is no human requirement, bringing "rain on the earth, where no man is; on the wilderness, wherein there is no man; To satisfy the desolate and waste ground; and to cause the bud of the tender herb to spring forth" (38.26-27). As Eliphaz progresses in his speech, the focus shifts from God's ways in nature to His ways with people. A God of such astonishing benevolence deals in special thoughtfulness with the helpless, lifting "up on high those that be low; that those which mourn may be exalted to safety" (5.11). The relevance to Job is obvious. This fundamental truth, such an encouragement to humble faith, is reiterated by both Hannah (1 Sam 2.7-8) and Mary (Lk 1.52-53). As Eliphaz says at the close of his paean of praise, "he saveth the poor from the sword, from their mouth, and from the hand of the mighty. So the poor hath hope, and iniquity stoppeth her mouth" (5.15-16). God has the power to rescue the oppressed from their tormentors, restoring them to blessing while silencing their foes. The believer in the Lord Jesus will particularly rejoice that, though poor in himself, in Christ he has both present salvation and future hope (1 Thess 5.8).

But what about the wicked? "He frustrateth the devices of the crafty, so that their hands cannot perform their enterprise. He taketh the wise in their own craftiness: and the counsel of the froward is carried headlong. They meet with darkness in the daytime, and grope at noonday as in the night" (5.12-14, RV). This is an accurate précis of aspects of God's ways in providence. When it pleases Him, His hand stretches out to thwart the plans of wicked men. We have only to think back to those satanically-inspired plots to annihilate the nation of Israel, whether by Pharaoh or Haman. The king who ordered the drowning of Israel's baby boys lost the pride of his army in the sea; the politician who planned to hang Mordecai ended up swinging on his own gallows. It is the principle of ironic reversal. As David says of his enemy, Cush the Benjamite, "He made a pit, and digged it, and is fallen into the ditch which he made. His mischief shall return upon his own head, and his violent dealing shall come down upon his own pate" (Ps 7.15-16). Those who cunningly oppose the Lord are apt to find themselves hoist with their own petard.

So memorable is this description of the divine ability to overturn human schemes that Paul seems to pick it up when exhorting the Corinthians to distrust human wisdom: "it is written, I will destroy the wisdom of the wise, and will bring to nothing the understanding of the prudent" (1 Cor 1.19). But where exactly is it written? The margin of a reference Bible will list a number of possible Old Testament sources (for example, Isaiah 29.14 and Jeremiah 8.9), but Eliphaz must be the earliest. God subverts human pride and wisdom, especially when it comes to the matter of eternal redemption. In His grace He saves, not the great and the good, but the nobodies. And He does it by a salvation which, in its surpassing rightness, transcends the combined wisdom of the universities.

But once again it has to be said that, in this current age, God does not customarily interfere overtly in the affairs of men. Generally speaking, men manage to pursue their goals without reference to God, often achieving their ends without undue difficulty. Only in the final analysis will it be seen that human power and wisdom were futile. The full picture will not be unveiled until the coming of the King.

That is the kind of God to whom Eliphaz would direct the stricken Job. The description is sound, the intention sincere, but the understanding of Job's situation is simplistic. He is not a sinner who needs to repent in order to be restored.

The Prospect: 5.17-27

As he began with generous words looking back to Job's earlier days of spiritual service (4.3-4), so Eliphaz closes his speech holding out the prospect of a glad restoration consequent upon repentance. It has to be admitted that in verses 19-26 he paints an attractive and inviting picture.

His foundational statement stands right at the start of the section:

Behold, happy is the man whom God correcteth: therefore despise not thou the chastening of the Almighty: For he maketh sore, and bindeth up: he woundeth, and his hands make whole (5.17-18).

God disciplines His people with a view to recovery, and such an outcome makes His chastening, though bitter at the time, a matter of profound thankfulness. This is the first of over thirty appearances in the book of the name *Shaddai*, a name that foregrounds God's sufficiency for every emergency. The reason Job should not repine against God's ways with him is that this all-sufficient God only hurts that He might heal. He is the great physician whose scalpel enters the flesh to excise what needs to be removed in order to promote better spiritual wellbeing. The astonishing exactness of the words, "his hands make whole", is seen most fully in the earthly ministry of the Lord Jesus Christ.

Something of this basic principle is enunciated through Moses and reiterated by Hannah:

> See now that I, even I, am he, and there is no god with me: I kill, and I make alive; I wound, and I heal: neither is there any that can deliver out of my hand (Deut 32.39).

> The Lord killeth, and maketh alive: he bringeth down to the grave, and bringeth up. The Lord maketh poor, and maketh rich: he bringeth low, and lifteth up (1 Sam 2.6-7).

To do Eliphaz justice, he offers an accurate description of God. He is responsible for the bad things as well as the good things that befall His people, and Job, of all men, knew that full well (1.21; 2.10). But the principle can be advanced a stage further. God deliberately brings His people into grief that they might be the more cast upon Him. Asaph surveys a period of Israel's history like this:

> For all this they sinned still, and believed not for his wondrous works. Therefore their days did he consume in vanity, and their years in trouble. When he slew them, then they sought him: and they returned and enquired early after God. And they remembered that God was their rock, and the high God their redeemer (Ps 78.32-35).

The progression is underlined: they sinned, He slew, they sought. This is the aim of divine chastisement – to draw us back to the God from whom we have drifted. The seventeenth century poet John Donne concludes his "Hymn to God, My God, in My Sickness" with this tightly paradoxical line: "Therefore that He may raise, the Lord throws down". Sometimes we have to be laid flat on our backs so that the only direction we can look is upwards. Saul of Tarsus was knocked to the ground that he might be lifted into salvation. But the Hebrew writer deserves the final word because he joins together several Old Testament sources, Job included, to formulate a classic statement of God's fatherly purpose:

> And ye have forgotten the exhortation which speaketh unto you as unto children, My son, despise not thou the chastening of the Lord, nor faint when thou art rebuked of him: For whom the Lord loveth he chasteneth, and scourgeth every son whom he receiveth. If ye endure chastening, God dealeth with you as with sons; for what son is he whom the father chasteneth not? But if ye be without chastisement, whereof all are partakers, then are ye bastards, and not sons. Furthermore we have had fathers of our flesh which corrected us, and we gave them reverence: shall we not much rather be in subjection unto the Father of spirits, and live? For they verily for a

few days chastened us after their own pleasure; but he for our profit, that we might be partakers of his holiness. Now no chastening for the present seemeth to be joyous, but grievous: nevertheless afterward it yieldeth the peaceable fruit of righteousness unto them which are exercised thereby (Heb 12.5-11).

No believer can afford to be ignorant of this vital passage, which explains so much of God's educational programme for His people. However, the great difference between all these examples and the specific case of Job is that ancient Israel, as is often the case with believers today, deserved God's chastisement and needed His correction because of their failures, whereas Job was a model of rectitude. He was not being corrected for disobedience. For Eliphaz to assume gross error on Job's part, and then, in the context of his unprecedented misery, speak so blithely about happiness on the horizon, is more than a little unfeeling.

Two other of Eliphaz's words deserve notice. "Correcteth" (3198) becomes a significant term running through the entire book. It appears seventeen times and means, according to Brown, Driver and Briggs, "to prove, decide, judge, rebuke, reprove, correct, be right". It is translated "daysman" in 9.33, and occurs finally when the Lord Himself ironically accuses Job of rebuking *Him*: "Shall he that contendeth with the Almighty instruct *him*? he that reproveth [3198] God, let him answer it" (40.2). Its parallel word, "chastening" (4148), focusses attention on God's disciplinary dealings, and is commonly used in the book of Proverbs where it is generally translated "instruction" or "correction". The God of the Bible is constantly in the business of teaching, instructing, coaching and correcting His people.

The other word is "happy" (835). This is especially characteristic of the book of Psalms, where we learn about the happiness (or blessedness) of the man who practises separation (Ps 1.1), who trusts the Son (Ps 2.12), whose transgression is forgiven (Ps 32.1), who considers the poor (Ps 41.1), who is chosen to approach the Lord (Ps 65.4), whose strength is in the Lord (Ps 84.5), who fears the Lord (Ps 112.1), who is blest with many children (Ps 127.5), who has the God of Jacob for his help (Ps 146.5). This is merely a selection of examples. The important parallel with Job spells out the blessing of receiving God's educational correction:

Blessed [835] is the man whom thou chastenest, O Lord, and teachest him out of thy law; That thou mayest give him rest from the days of adversity, until the pit be digged for the wicked (Ps 94.12-13).

Unlike Job, the psalmist lived after the law was given, and therefore drew encouragement from its instruction. The believer today finds daily counsel and sustenance in the Scriptures as a whole. Nevertheless, though possessing no written revelation of God's mind, by the end of his story Job is convinced that the living God moves for His people's good, granting them "rest from the days of adversity". At the end of the journey is blessing.

What specific benefits lie ahead for the man who admits his fault and surrenders to God's corrective discipline? Eliphaz lists four. He can look forward to earthly security (5.19-23), material prosperity (5.24), a large family (5.25), and a contentedly long life (5.26). It is noticeable that these advantages are all material rather than spiritual, and earthly rather than heavenly. But then, of course, that was the particular outlook of the Old Testament. Israel's blessings were centred on the land God promised Abraham, and concentrated upon material well-being – cattle, children, long life, and victory over their enemies. The rewards held out to obedient Israel in Deuteronomy 28.1-14 make that clear. This perspective dominates the Old Testament, looking forward to a perfect fulfilment in the Kingdom age. Only in the New Testament, without in any sense cancelling God's earthly pledges to Israel, is the believer's gaze lifted to the heavenlies, where reside all our spiritual blessings in Christ (Eph 1.3). The current era of God's dealings with men, the church age, is an extraordinary hiatus between Old Testament expectation and millennial fulfilment.

A word of clarification is needed, lest the reader assume that the blessing of Old Testament saints was entirely restricted to the physical. Yes, their advantages were often earth-centred; but, no, that was by no means the sum total of their privileges. Simply to read the book of Psalms is to enter into the soul of men like David and Asaph who had a profound relationship with God which transcended the material. How else can we make sense of spiritual aspirations like those expressed in Psalm 42?

> As the hart panteth after the water brooks, so panteth my soul after thee, O God. My soul thirsteth for God, for the living God: when shall I come and appear before God? (Ps 42.1-2).

The story of Daniel confronts us with a godly young Jew who, snatched from the land of promise, found himself in an alien culture, yet faithfully retained his deep affection for and fellowship with Jehovah. A deep longing for communion with God is the hallmark of true godliness in both Testaments.

Nevertheless, Eliphaz seems here to be thinking primarily in terms of outward advantages. A chastened Job would enjoy **earthly security** (5.19-23). Whatever kind of trouble might be imagined (which is the meaning of the Hebrew idiom, "in six … yea, in seven"), the now penitent and restored Job would be spared from it (5.19). He would, for example, be safe from death and war (5.20), and protected against the spitefulness of slander and oppression (5.21). Indeed, he would be able to laugh in derision at the failure of any peril to touch him, whether it were famine or the depredations of wild animals (5.22), for the soil of his fields would be fruitful and wild beasts would not damage his crops (5.23). His **material prosperity** is condensed into one verse, better read in a translation other than the KJV: "And thou shalt know that thy tent is in peace; and thou wilt survey thy fold, and miss nothing" (5.24, JND). In other words, he would live in security, suffering no loss of livestock. The contrast with chapter 1 is obvious. More, he would be enriched with a **large family** (5.25) and a **contented longevity** (5.26). The language hints at more than mere length of days, which all too often are "labour and sorrow" (Ps 90.10), instead suggesting a rich fullness of life; he would die at a ripe age, having attained the blissful wholeness of mature experience. This, says Eliphaz, is what he and his associates have discovered, and Job ought to take it to heart for his own good (5.27).

One only has to read Paul's description of his own career as a faithful apostle of the Lord Jesus Christ to see the stark dispensational difference. Here is Paul:

> Giving no offence in any thing, that the ministry be not blamed: But in all things approving ourselves as the ministers of God, in much patience, in afflictions, in necessities, in distresses, In stripes, in imprisonments, in tumults, in labours, in watchings, in fastings; By pureness, by knowledge, by longsuffering, by kindness, by the Holy Ghost, by love unfeigned, By the word of truth, by the power of God, by the armour of righteousness on the right hand and on the left, By honour and dishonour, by evil report and good report: as deceivers, and yet true; As unknown, and yet well known; as dying, and, behold, we live; as chastened, and not killed; As sorrowful, yet alway rejoicing; as poor, yet making many rich; as having nothing, and yet possessing all things (2 Cor 6.3-10).

The believer of this dispensation has no guarantee of present earthly ease; in the wisdom of God, it is fitting that those whose real home is in heaven should be discouraged from putting their roots down here. The pattern of suffering followed by glory, typified by Joseph and displayed in the Lord Jesus, is the Christian's grand incentive to faithful life and service in this world. As Peter wrote to saints under trial:

> Beloved, think it not strange concerning the fiery trial which is to try you, as though some strange thing happened unto you: But rejoice, inasmuch as ye are partakers of Christ's sufferings; that, when his glory shall be revealed, ye may be glad also with exceeding joy (1 Pet 4.12-13).

Nevertheless, Eliphaz holds out to Job the promise of a blessed end in this world – and he is not incorrect. Everything he said eventually came to pass (42.10-17). Yet at its very root Eliphaz's analysis of Job's situation was wrong.

Let us pause to consider Eliphaz's advice. For all his pomposity and prolixity, he has touched on valuable truths which deserve to be acknowledged and enjoyed by believers. There follows a list of some lessons to be drawn from his argument:

- Faithful service should be encouraged and commended (4.3-4)
- Teachers must expect to be tested on their teaching (4.5)
- God has the power to punish the wicked (4.9)
- By nature man is both sinful and feeble (4.17-19)
- God can intervene in sudden judgment (5.3)
- Adam's sin means that man is bound to suffer earthly affliction (5.7)
- It is never wrong to commit our cause to God (5.8)

- Praise involves rehearsing God's attributes and actions (5.9-15)
- God can lift up the lowly (5.11)
- Divine correction is a blessing not to be despised (5.17-18)
- God preserves His people (5.19-20)
- Among God's earthly blessings are possessions, children, and longevity (5.24-26)
- It is possible to say the right thing at the wrong time and in the wrong way.

That last point highlights the pervasive problem with the book of Job. Much of what is said by all the human speakers is true and instructive, and yet in context it is often wholly inappropriate. Delitzsch, as usual, puts his finger on it:

Thus delicately and profoundly commences the dramatical entanglement. The skill of the poet is proved by the difficulty which the expositor has in detecting that which is false in the speech of Eliphaz. The idea of the book does not float on the surface.[85]

It certainly does not. We have to read and ponder with great care. It is sad that so much of Eliphaz's advice is offered under the delusion that Job is a man suffering the earthly consequences of unconfessed sin. The example of the Lord Jesus ministering tenderly to the bereaved forms a salutary contrast. In the wake of Lazarus's death, Martha and Mary approached the Lord with identical words ("Lord, if thou hadst been here, my brother had not died", Jn 11.21,32), yet how different was His response to each. To Martha He gave reassuring teaching about resurrection; to Mary He showed the depths of His sympathy with tears. Sometimes the best we can do for our afflicted brethren is to weep with them.

SECTION 5
Dialogue: Job 4 – 42.6
Contest: Round 1: Job 4-14
Job's 1st Speech: Job 6-7

After Eliphaz's lengthy, laboured attempt at consolation, Job's anguished response immediately indicates how far he has fallen short of his objective. The patriarch's speech breaks down into five main paragraphs:

> 1. The Arrows of the Almighty: 6.1-7
> 2. The Request for Release: 6.8-13
> 3. The Failure of Friends: 6.14-30
> 4. The Labour of Living: 7.1-6
> 5. The Desire for Death: 7.7-21.

Just as Eliphaz's first address lays down the parameters for the argument of the three friends, from which they will not depart in their succeeding contributions to the debate, so Job's reply establishes his own defensive position of injured innocence. While his complaint in chapter 3 was almost a kind of soliloquy in which, without reference to any particular audience, he aired his innermost thoughts, he now addresses his friends directly, not confining himself to Eliphaz but including all three in his plural pronouns (6.21-29). More important, though, is the fact that he subsequently turns away from his friends to God, so that the latter part of his speech, with its shift into the second person singular, partakes of the nature of prayer (7.7-21). Confidence can only safely rest in the Lord, for the best of earthly friends will let us down. As the psalmist says,

> Put not your trust in princes, nor in the son of man, in whom there is no help. His breath goeth forth, he returneth to his earth; in that very day his thoughts perish. Happy is he that hath the God of Jacob for his help, whose hope is in the Lord his God (Ps 146.3-5).

Job, of course, knew nothing of the God of Jacob, but he did know and trust the Almighty, finding in Him the refuge and resource that his peers could not provide. And this is Job's great strength, one of the conclusive evidences that he enjoyed a genuine relationship with God. Despite his sorrows, despite his ignorance of God's purpose, despite the unsympathetic attitude of his friends, he never, never turns away from the Lord. Rather, he casts himself the more wholeheartedly upon his God. Although Job lived long before the writing of Psalm 55, he is implicitly following its advice: "Cast thy burden upon the Lord, and he shall sustain thee: he shall never suffer the righteous to be moved" (Ps 55.22). Young's Literal Translation brings out the implication of the unusual Hebrew word for "burden": "Cast on Jehovah that which He hath given thee, And He doth sustain thee, He doth not suffer for ever the moving of the righteous". We are to roll upon the Lord that which He has placed upon us, for every burden, like every blessing, is ultimately of His bestowal. The former are sent with a view to drawing us closer to the only One who can meet our needs. As another Hebrew poet puts it, "I know, O Lord, that thy judgments are right, and that thou in faithfulness hast afflicted me" (Ps 119.75). The robustly God-centred world-view of the Old Testament has no qualms about giving God full credit for being in total control of His universe. All comes from His hand. The book of Job is the great testimony to His dealings, in blessing and in affliction, with the individual believer.

Let us summarise Job's response to Eliphaz. First of all he explains that his startling explosion of rash words in chapter 3 was the result of unbearable distress of body and mind. Echoing his earlier longing for death, he wishes God would grant that request, releasing him from what has become a life of intolerable misery. But he then rounds on his friends, accusing them of failing to offer practical support in his hour of need. They have, in the representative figure of Eliphaz, criticised his words but have been unable to point out any errors in his life which might account for his suffering. Lamenting the weariness of his present existence, he describes some of the physical and mental symptoms of his sickness. But finally his attention moves away from the friends sitting beside him to the God who has afflicted him, so that the last part of his speech becomes an urgent prayer for compassion, asking God why He has suddenly chosen to torment His servant.

The speech begins and ends with Job seeing himself as the hapless target of God's poisoned arrows:

> For the arrows of the Almighty are within me, the poison whereof drinketh up my spirit: the terrors of God do set themselves in array against me (6.4).

> If I have sinned, what do I unto thee, O thou watcher of men? why hast thou set me as a mark for thee, so that I am a burden to myself? (7.20, RV).

This is critical for our understanding of Job. Consistently the patriarch traces his circumstances to the God who, for no apparent reason, has turned against him. Job's greatest distress, we notice, is not his material and personal losses, devastating as they are, but his estrangement from the God he has long worshipped and served. Matthew Henry gets to the heart of the matter:

> It was not so much the troubles themselves he was under that put him into this confusion, his poverty, disgrace, and bodily pain; but that which cut him to the heart and put him into this agitation, was to think that the God he loved and served had brought all this upon him and laid him under these marks of his displeasure.[86]

And it is into the arms of the God who has chastised him that he runs. Ellison remarks that "much that he says in his anguish is false and exaggerated, and some of it is virtually blasphemous, but what matters is that he turns to God".[87] There can be no better course of action for saints under stress. Even when we cannot understand God's ways with us it is always right to pour out our hearts frankly, to confess all our doubts and fears to Him, to bare the turmoil of our soul in His presence. We might hesitate to use similar language in public at the Prayer Meeting, but we have to acknowledge that Job, like the psalmist, teaches us a lesson in the importance of absolute honesty in all our conversations with God.

The Arrows of the Almighty: 6.1-7

Bringing together the language of weights and measures, military assault, and food, Job speaks of the immensity of his **calamity** (6.2-3), its **cause** (6.4), and its **consequences** (6.5-7).

It is obvious that Job's venerable friends have been stunned by his initial outburst. He therefore starts by seeking to justify his blistering outspokenness. For all his terrible distress of mind and body, Job has been listening carefully to what Eliphaz has said. In fact, he picks up a word his friend used in his assertion that "wrath killeth the foolish man, and envy slayeth the silly one" (5.2). The word rendered "wrath" (3708) means, according to Brown, Driver and Briggs, "anger, vexation, provocation, grief". According to Ellison, the Hebrew term describes "our natural reaction of vexation, impatience, grief and even anger, when faced with injustice and offence".[88] "Oh that my vexation [3708] were but weighed, and my calamity laid in the balances together!" (6.2, RV), exclaims Job. "You presume to rebuke what you consider outrageously irreverent language, but you have no idea of what I am going through. I wish my grief could be placed on the scales of a balance and assessed so that outsiders would get some faint conception of its enormity". Eliphaz has implied that Job's words are absurdly disproportionate. Job, in reply, wants his pain measured to prove that his extravagant complaint only equals the heavy weight of his calamity. Great pain justifies great protest. And Job's pains are beyond the range of human assessment, "heavier than the sand of the seas: therefore have my words been rash" (6.3, RV).

For Job, the comparison with the ocean sands testified to incalculable sorrow; for another patriarch, informed of a unique divine promise, it illustrated the profusion of his future seed. As God says to Abram, "in blessing I will bless thee, and in multiplying I will multiply thy seed as the stars of the heaven, and as the sand which is upon the sea shore; and thy seed shall possess the gate of his enemies" (Gen 22.17).

For one, the simile spoke of suffering; for the other, blessing. But let's go forward in time. The New Testament reveals that our sins, heavy as they are, are vastly outweighed by the sheer overflowing lavishness of God's grace, for "where sin abounded, grace did much more abound" (Rom 5.20). Job wanted to demonstrate that his groanings matched his grief, but Christians rejoice that their innumerable iniquities are more than met by the fullness of the work of Christ. Indeed, although the apostle prays that we "May be able to comprehend with all saints what is the breadth, and length, and depth, and height; And to know the love of Christ", he goes on to admit, paradoxically, that what he wants us to grasp actually "passeth knowledge" (Eph 3.18-19). Divine love cannot be reduced to a neat mathematical formula.

Nevertheless, if Job's distresses could be properly calculated, people might at least understand why he spoke as he did. The specific **cause** of his grief (6.4) – and he has no doubts about this – is God's arrows. He is the guiltless victim of a divine archer, pierced through with poisoned shafts which spread deadly venom throughout his body. This key verse demonstrates that Job remains fully aware that his steps are supervised by God. He has not abandoned the theological position expressed so clearly in 1.21 and 2.10. Nevertheless, trust is mingled with dread, for he feels himself a defenceless prey to divine persecution, with God's terrors setting themselves in full military array against him, just as five local kings "joined battle" (same Hebrew word) with the invading coalition in Genesis 14.8. God has declared war on him, and he does not know why. But, as Robinson comments, "God's choicest saints often appear to be the butt of his sharpest arrows."[89]

The Christian reader is almost bound to think of another sufferer who bore far more than Job, for the incarnate Son received in His own body the punishment that was due to His people. And unlike Job, Christ was absolutely sinless. The idea of a unique sacrificial victim upon whom God pours out His anger threads through the Old Testament:

Deep calleth unto deep at the noise of thy waterspouts: all thy waves and thy billows are gone over me (Ps 42.7).

Yet it pleased the Lord to bruise him; he hath put him to grief: when thou shalt make his soul an offering for sin, he shall see his seed, he shall prolong his days, and the pleasure of the Lord shall prosper in his hand (Is 53.10).

Awake, O sword, against my shepherd, and against the man that is my fellow, saith the Lord of hosts: smite the shepherd, and the sheep shall be scattered: and I will turn mine hand upon the little ones (Zech 13.7).

Only in the work of Calvary does such language find its fulfilment and explanation. One of the many things of which Job was unaware was that, in his distress, he was privileged to become a faint foreshadowing of the ultimate innocent victim.

The outward **consequences** of Job's suffering (6.5-7) are the groans and sighs to which he gave voice in the terrible lament of chapter 3. How can he explain his misery to outsiders? He turns to the animal kingdom, drawing on a wild and a domesticated beast to make his point: do the feral ass and the tame ox bellow in distress if they have access to plenty of food? Of course not. We shall meet the wild ass again in Jehovah's intervention (39.5), where it is used to illustrate God's overruling control of His universe; here, however, it represents a state of simple, primitive contentment which Job lacks. He wants his friends to realise he is not complaining without reason. Continuing the imagery of eating, he asks if they expect him to smack his lips with pleasure at the insipid, tasteless food that God is serving up to him. This bitter understatement only highlights the mind-wracking intensity of his pain. One of the accompaniments of his many maladies would doubtless be a literal loss of appetite and a deterioration of taste. But he uses metaphorical language here to describe a much deeper, inner misery. What he would naturally shrink from – the desolation of loss, the tragedy of bereavement, the humiliation of being an outcast from society because of his offensive sickness, the sense of alienation from his God – all these loathsome things have now become his compulsory diet, his "sorrowful meat".

The Request for Release: 6.8-13

Job now expresses his great **wish** (6.8-10), while simultaneously confessing his bodily **weakness** (6.11-13).

The pain, physical, mental and spiritual, is so great that he would willingly die, yet he knows life and death are God's prerogative. Self-murder is categorically ruled out. He therefore expresses his **wish** (6.8-10) as a kind of wistful petition – to be destroyed and cut off in death. In doing so, he picks up another of Eliphaz's words. Twice the latter spoke glibly of "hope" (4.6; 5.16), but now, using the same Hebrew term (8615), Job names the specific blessing he "longs for [8615]" (6.8): removal from an unbearable existence. The word "hope" is used thirteen times in the book, usually in a negative context (7.6; 14.19; 17.15; 19.10). How different is the position of the New Testament believer, who, privileged to live in the good of Christ's death and resurrection, is eagerly "Looking for that blessed hope, and the glorious appearing of the great God and our Saviour Jesus Christ" (Titus 2.13)! For us, the future is secure because it rests on what God has done historically in the person of His Son:

> But I would not have you to be ignorant, brethren, concerning them which are asleep, that ye sorrow not, even as others which have no hope. For if we believe that Jesus died and rose again, even so them also which sleep in Jesus will God bring with him (1 Thess 4.13-14).

Believing in a Saviour who died and rose, we can be certain of His return. A sure past guarantees a glad prospect. Such a hope cannot fail.

Job's pitiable yearning for release is not surprising. It is not uncommon for believers of all eras to aspire to blessings which are not in God's purpose for them. Even the most unexceptionable of requests may not be granted, because God reserves the right to overrule our prayers and "do exceeding abundantly above all that we ask or think" (Eph 3.20). For example, the newly delivered Gadarene ex-demoniac was not permitted to join the band of disciples and accompany the Lord Jesus across Galilee; rather, he was instructed to stay at home as the Saviour's representative in a district that had rejected Him (Mk 5.18-19). But it is to his honour that he obeyed without rancour. The results of his faithful testimony have yet to be revealed, for the wisdom of God's plan for His people is often best seen in retrospect.

What Job desired is what King Hezekiah, in his terminal sickness, dreaded. The king uses similar language but the mood is wholly different: "Mine age is departed, and is removed from me as a shepherd's tent: I have cut off like a weaver my life: he will cut me off with pining sickness: from day even to night wilt thou make an end of me" (Is 38.12). Hezekiah pleaded to be allowed to live; Job prayed to die. The first request was granted (but was it ultimately for Hezekiah"s good?), the second refused, for "the Lord is very pitiful, and of tender mercy" (James 5.11). God's great end was Job's ultimate blessing, but he must endure the painful process by which this goal would be attained. Extreme and chronic ill-health frequently causes such lowness of spirits that we cry out for what we know, in our calmer moments, is not in accord with the Lord's will. Writes Smick, "that a man who had experienced such faith should speak from the depth of his being such words of anguish can only strengthen those in anguish".[90] Scripture records the example of a godly man like Job driven to distraction and bewilderment of soul as a consolation to believers going through their own private ordeals. We are never alone or unique in our sufferings.

But Job is so intent on escaping from God's animosity that he can see no other way out. Nevertheless, though assuming death is the inevitable end of his sickness, he still insists that he is guiltless of any specific error. He is ready to die, but he will not abandon his integrity, for "this consciousness of innocence is indeed throughout the whole book Job's shield and defence".[91] His great comfort and joy in pain is that he has not concealed or "denied [3582] the words of the Holy One" (6.10, JND). Psalm 40 employs the same language to affirm a faithful testimony before men: "I have not concealed [S3582] thy lovingkindness and thy truth from the great congregation" (Ps 40.10). David – and, of course, beyond him, the Messiah – faithfully bore witness to God's truth and mercy in a world with little time for godliness. Although Job had no authoritative written revelation from God, he did have, in common with others of his age, the handed-down memories of Adam and his immediate descendants. Those memories must have included not only an account of the first sin and its results, but also the promise of deliverance through the woman's seed. That he was well instructed in God's greatness is evident in his careful use of divine names. He knows God not only as *El Shaddai*, "the Almighty" (6.4), in His infinite power and majesty, and *Eloah*, "God" (6.4), in the reverence He inspires, but as "the Holy One" (6.10) in His ineffable purity. That knowledge was not simple intellectual awareness. Rather, it resulted in a practical godliness endorsed by the Lord when referring to "my servant Job … a perfect and an upright man, one that feareth God, and escheweth evil" (1.8). Job knew God and bore unbending witness to His magnificence.

The consciousness of his own innocence despite adverse circumstances was his "comfort" (5165). The psalmist (in the only other use of this word in the Old Testament) enjoyed a similar relief in distress:

> Remember the word unto thy servant, upon which thou hast caused me to hope. This is my comfort [5165] in my affliction: for thy word hath quickened me (Ps 119.49-50).

Unlike Job, the psalmist could turn for encouragement to the promises built into Israel's scriptures. When, for example, in Psalm 89 Ethan the Ezrahite was confronted with Israel's defeat in battle, he immersed himself in the sure covenant promises which God had made to David and his descendants. In days of darkness, there is always light and warmth in the Word. But believers of the present age are in a better position still, for we possess the complete canon of Scripture, "the faith which was once for all delivered unto the saints" (Jude v.3, RV). There can be no shortage of spiritual nourishment for those who have access to the revealed mind of God. Nonetheless, for all his lack of Christian revelation and privilege, Job retained an unshakable confidence in God. He had not denied "the words of the Holy One": that is, he knew of nothing in his life which flew in the face of those divine instructions handed down from his forefathers. The practical uprightness of his public and private lifestyle is yet to be recounted in chapters 29 and 31; his awareness of the need for sacrifice has already been demonstrated in chapter 1. And of course the Lord's wholly positive assessment was recorded in heaven (1.8). So when Job says, "Then should I yet have comfort; yea, I would exult in pain that spareth not: for I have not denied the words of the Holy One" (6.10, RV), what may sound like insufferable self-righteousness is in fact simple truth.

Notwithstanding, Job admits his human **weakness** (6.11-13). Although convinced of personal blamelessness, he is well aware that his current physical and emotional fragility must seem, to outsiders at least, to call this into question. Because of his debilitating illnesses he feels his disease-ravaged body cannot last much longer. What hope has he? After all, man is made of flesh and blood, not stones and bronze. Isn't it obvious, he asks, that he has neither resource nor strength left? "Is it not that there is no help in me, and soundness is driven away from me?" (6.13, JND). We are never allowed to forget Job's grievous suffering in body and mind. In spite of that, perhaps one of the most astonishing features of the book as a whole is that these troubles have not impaired his ability to think or speak with intelligence, astuteness and spiritual insight. Physically weak he may be, but his mind is fully alert. Which, one might ask, is worse; to be deprived of bodily vigour yet retain a sharp intelligence, or to remain physically strong while suffering dementia? For Job, the ability to comprehend his terrible condition without flinching is an essential aspect of his trial.

The Failure of Friends: 6.14-30

Such a man, pious yet afflicted by God with the most appalling sicknesses, expects from his friends not condemnation but comfort. They, sadly, have proved themselves a broken reed. A local **illustration** (6.14-20) expresses his disillusionment at their failure to offer real support. He describes their evident **consternation** at his condition (6.21-23), and then pleads for the kind of **ministration** (6.24-30) real friendship ought to provide.

Verse 14 is not entirely clear. Delitzsch's rendering offers one interpretation: "To him who is consumed gentleness is due from his friend, otherwise he might forsake the fear of the Almighty".[92] This urges kindly, loving treatment of the needy lest the poor man under pressure crack with the strain, abandoning his confidence in God. The sickroom is the place for loving sympathy, for the arm round the shoulder, not the cold theological discourse. But others translate differently: "He who withholds kindness from a friend forsakes the fear of the Almighty" (6.14, ESV). Here it is the would-be comforter who is in danger of impiety because he holds back from ministering tenderly and graciously to the sufferer. Either translation is practically instructive. Repeated blows of affliction may drive any man to breaking point. How much we all need loving care and support from the saints! But more, to fail in our duty to our brethren is to be guilty of sin against the Lord. That is how Samuel felt when he said to backsliding Israel, "as for me, God forbid that I should sin against the Lord in ceasing to pray for you: but I will teach you the good and the right way" (1 Sam 12.23). As Paul learned on the Damascus Road, what we do to the brethren we do to the Lord Jesus Himself (Acts 9.4-5).

The detailed **illustration** that follows is topical, relating to eastern travellers searching for water to sustain them on their journey. Job's friends, travelling to visit him, doubtless knew the practical value of stumbling on such refreshing streams in the desert. But these water sources are not always reliable, varying with the season. In winter they may be hidden under snow and ice; in summer they evaporate (6.16-17). Ironically, at the time they are most needed they tend to dry up. "Job's comparison of his friends to the brook is graphic and telling. In winter these brooks are full, but in summer when the thirsty caravan needs them and looks for them, they are found to have disappeared before the heat".[93] The frustration experienced by men journeying from Arabian locations like Tema and Sheba is vividly depicted (6.19-20), and Fausset explains the meaning:

> "the troops of Tema" are the caravans on the direct road anxiously "looking for" the return of their companions gone to look for water; the failure of it in the wady and the disappointment depict Job's disappointment at not finding comfort from his friends whose professions promised so much.[94]

His friends have proved a let-down. Job looked for refreshment for his beleaguered soul, but received nothing save criticism and insinuations of wrong-doing.

Job uses a common experience (the dried up water course) to illustrate the failure of a spiritual ministry (offering life-supporting consolation). But when the prophet Isaiah speaks of "streams in the desert", he is quite literally describing that great day when Messiah will reign in righteousness and peace. No streams then will fail. In that era of global blessing, the entire face of the earth will be transformed, the waste places removed, and human disability banished:

> Then the eyes of the blind shall be opened, and the ears of the deaf shall be unstopped. Then shall the lame man leap as an hart, and the tongue of the dumb sing: for in the wilderness shall waters break out, and streams in the desert. And the parched ground shall become a pool, and the thirsty land springs of water: in the habitation of dragons, where each lay, shall be grass with reeds and rushes (Is 35.5-7).

Something of this was briefly glimpsed during the earthly ministry of the Lord Jesus, for His messianic miracles proved His power to bring about such predicted Kingdom conditions. But its grand reality has yet to break upon the world. Those who look forward with joy to that glad millennial day should at least seek to live out its metaphorical truth in the present, providing their thirsty brethren with spiritual refreshment. For so many saints, the way has become wearisome. Only in the Scriptures is there a trustworthy source of revitalising nourishment which will never run dry. When our "soul melteth for heaviness", then the Lord will strengthen us according to His Word (Ps 119.28).

Job is not oblivious to the **consternation** his visitors feel (6.21-23). "So now ye are nothing; ye see a terrible object and are afraid" (6.21, JND). Like a dried up brook they could offer him nothing of value. But why exactly were they so frightened? The hideous, barely-recognisable, disease-racked figure before them was their old associate in wisdom and piety. His reputation for godliness had been second to none, but now he was struck down by God's hand. Was it perhaps that the thought flashed uncomfortably through their minds – "If this can happen to someone like Job, might it happen to me?" Or did they feel that to offer him support or commiseration might subject them to similar divine displeasure? Aghast at the possibilities, they shrank back in fear. Yet Job has not asked for money or material gifts. He has not pleaded for physical rescue from an enemy (6.22-23). All he entreats is simple kindness and understanding.

To explain what appears to us as a strange lack of sympathy and support we have to understand that Job's calamity fired a broadside into their philosophy of life. His situation was a standing challenge to a simplistic theology that judged everything by outward appearance. Like the natives of Malta, his friends assumed that physical circumstances were an infallible token of God's disapproval (Paul bitten by a snake must be a murderer experiencing punishment) or endorsement (Paul's immunity to the snake's poison proved he was a god). Like the Maltese, they were wrong on both counts (Acts 28.3-6).

> As the Maltese barbarians gazed upon Paul
> While he laboured to stoke up the fire,
> They saw a snake bite him. "Aha!", said they all,
> "He's a villain, and soon he'll expire!"
>
> But when he continued without any pain,
> They thought it exceedingly odd.
> His survival they found they could only explain
> By acknowledging he was a god.
>
> They were doubly mistaken; and people have erred
> When they've judged on the basis of sight;
> Job claimed he was guiltless, his friends all demurred -
> But in fact they were wrong, he was right!

There are people who think that what happens down here
Is a mirror of heaven's esteem:
If you prosper, you're good; if you suffer, it's clear
That you can't be as nice as you seem.

This prosperity gospel is fatally flawed,
For appearances often deceive;
Till the world is put right by our soon-coming Lord
What we see, let's be slow to believe!

Job now outlines the kind of spiritual **ministration** which should be offered
to one in desperate need (6.24-30). It is sad when the patient has to instruct
the physician, but these comforters had no notion of how to console a man in
distress. Job, we remember, had been a master in this kind of ministry (4.3-4).
He encourages them directly to point out his supposed errors. He is willing to
remain silent while they talk. After all, if (as their theory dictated) he was being
punished for wrong-doing, they ought to be able to specify the wrong-doing.
Hartley observes that "Job never denies the possibility that he has sinned; rather,
he denies having sinned as grievously as his suffering would seem to indicate".[95] If
he is to blame for his circumstances, what precisely were his transgressions?

Right words have their own built-in punch, as can be seen from the shocked
way people responded to the Saviour's teaching, but Job's friends talked away to
no purpose. In fact, all they were doing was censuring the emotional outburst of a
man under intense strain, when one can hardly take such words as representative
(6.24-26). As Delitzsch writes,

> The words of one in despair belong to the wind, that they may be carried
> away by it, not to the judgment which retains and analyses them, without
> considering the mood of which they are the hasty expression.[96]

It is sometimes necessary to look past the words that are spoken to the passions
that provoke them. Job's friends were tut-tutting over his murmuring when they
should have been binding up his wounds. They were acting as counsel for the
prosecution instead of tenderly ministering to the sick. All they were doing was to
"overwhelm the fatherless, and dig a pit for your friend" (6.27, JND). The losses
which had befallen Job made him feel orphaned, destitute and friendless, but his
so-called companions were making matters worse by rubbing raw his sorrows,
almost as if they were setting traps for him.

Instead, they should take a long, hard gaze at him. It appears they can scarcely
look him in the face, so disgusted are they by his physical repulsiveness, and
embarrassed by his (to their way of thinking) undoubted backsliding. If you
would only look me in the eye, says Job, you will surely be able to detect whether I
am lying or not when I protest my innocence. This, it has to be said, is not always
the case. Many a practised deceiver has been able to prevaricate smoothly without
batting an eyelid. As Duncan says in *Macbeth*, "there's no art/To find the mind's

construction in the face". Religious hypocrites are not easy to detect, so slick is their use of biblical phraseology and so plausible their outward demeanour. That is why Peter and Jude urge us in their letters to be on our guard against those who would cunningly mislead and exploit the saints. Only the omniscient God can read the heart and, for example, enable the apostle Peter to penetrate the veneer of Ananias and Sapphira's glib professions of generosity (Acts 5.1-10). But, as we know from the prologue, Job was no Ananias.

His friends should look him in the face and generously turn back in his support: "Return, I pray you, let there be no injustice; yea, return again, my cause is righteous" (6.29, RV). How could they abandon him, having made such unjust accusations of wrongdoing? They must relent and withdraw their unfair charges. It is noteworthy that Job will not surrender his personal convictions in order to appease his friends. Throughout the entire book he steadfastly maintains his innocence of any significant sin. And, he insists, he is not lying. For all his misery, his taste is still able to "discern mischievous things" (6.30, JND); that is, he can still differentiate between truth and falsehood. Tragedy has not robbed him of his moral discernment any more than it has deprived him of intelligent speech.

The Labour of Living: 7.1-6

Now Job speaks in greater detail about the sufferings lying behind his death wish. Life for him has become no more than miserable **servitude** (7.1-2) and **sorrow** (7.3-6).

The concept of **servitude** (7.1-2) is brought out in Darby's translation: "Hath not man a life of labour upon earth? and are not his days like the days of a hireling?" (7.1). The KJV' "appointed time" renders a common Hebrew word (6635) referring to warfare or service. The RV directly translates it as "warfare", but Darby's "life of labour" also makes good sense. The life of fallen man in a sinful world is hard. It is like military service, where the constant stress of battle makes the soldier long for his discharge; it is like the term of duty for a hired labourer, who keeps a close look out for the approach of the evening shadows which herald both his rest and his reward.

Job paints a bleak picture. But we must remember that this is the result of his current distress. In days of prosperous ease he would have expressed himself very differently. Present pains always tend to distort our memories of the past, creating an unbalanced cast of mind. The psalmist confessed to saying some things "in my haste" (Ps 31.22; 116.11), for it is easy to blurt out words unadvisedly. But both Job's comparisons (warfare and service) reappear in the New Testament. The first is used to describe believers as soldiers on active service:

> Thou therefore endure hardness, as a good soldier of Jesus Christ. No man that warreth entangleth himself with the affairs of this life; that he may please him who hath chosen him to be a soldier (2 Tim 2.3-4).

The true soldier faces up to the tough demands of his vocation, scrupulously avoiding anything that would hinder his military efficiency. In the same way, the believer must be prepared for a difficult pathway in this world, seeking as his prime aim the pleasure of his Master. The second comparison appears in John 10, where the hired servant stands in contrast to the good shepherd, whose ministry for His sheep is constant, faithful, and costly:

> I am the good shepherd: the good shepherd giveth his life for the sheep. But he that is an hireling, and not the shepherd, whose own the sheep are not, seeth the wolf coming, and leaveth the sheep, and fleeth: and the wolf catcheth them, and scattereth the sheep (Jn 10.11-12).

Those who seek to serve as shepherds in the local assembly should model themselves on the Lord, not on the hirelings.

Although Job's picture breathes weariness of living, his intimation of the respite and payment following the day's labour makes us look ahead. It anticipates some of the parables of the Lord Jesus, and hints at New Testament revelation of the blessings awaiting the believer at the Lord's return. There all His saints will truly enter into lasting "rest" (2 Thess 1.7) and "reward" (Rev 22.12), which will make worthwhile all the trials of the way.

In graphic detail Job spells out his **sorrow** (7.3-6). We have no clear idea how long he has been suffering, but he mentions "months of vanity, and wearisome nights" (7.3) which have been allotted to him. They were not his choice but God's appointment. Time drags when one is in perplexity or pain, and all that stretched out emptiness seems pointless. Nights in particular are frustratingly restless, while days are dominated by the nagging consciousness of physical discomfort. The further we read into Job, the greater our insight into his terrible ailments. The picture presented by the narrative in chapter 2 is bland compared with this. Indeed, Darby does not shrink from drawing attention to the distasteful reality of the symptoms: "My flesh is clothed with worms and clods of dust; my skin is broken, and suppurates" (7.5). Davidson tells us that "the allusion is to the alternate gathering and running of his sores, which went on continually".[97] His experience in this chapter may be summed up as one of "fever, sleeplessness, delirium, skin ulcers, and running sores infested with worms".[98]

But though nights may be long and his sleep impaired, in another sense Job sees his time as passing rapidly, "swifter than a weaver's shuttle" (7.6). The weaver's shuttle flies back and forth across the loom as the piece of cloth is formed. Once the cloth is finished, the thread is cut to separate it from the loom. The image is both traditional and telling. Barnes comments as follows:

> It was common to compare life with a web, which was filled up by the successive days. The ancient Classical writers spoke of it as a web woven by the Fates. We can all feel the force of the comparison used here by Job, that the days which we live fly swift away. How rapidly is one after another added to the web of life! How soon will the whole web be filled up, and life be closed! A few more shoots of the shuttle and all will be over, and our

life will be cut off, as the weaver removes one web from the loom to make way for another.

Job is meditating upon the approaching end of his life. All the evidence – his illness, his losses, his sense of divine animosity – cries out that it must be drawing near. The book, we should notice, is packed with references to the brevity of human life, which is likened to a wind or breath (7.7), a shadow (8.9), a runner (9.25), a fading blossom (14.2), and a vanishing dream (20.8). Man's time on earth is comparatively short, although it often takes ill-health to bring its transience home to us. That being the case, how important it is to follow the exhortation of Moses. Using similar images of evanescence, he first of all underlines life's fleetingness before pointing out the lesson:

> Thou carriest them away as with a flood; they are as a sleep: in the morning they are like grass which groweth up. In the morning it flourisheth, and groweth up; in the evening it is cut down, and withereth … So teach us to number our days, that we may apply our hearts unto wisdom (Ps 90.5-6,12).

To "number our days" does not mean we can calculate how many we shall enjoy; rather, it urges us to keep in mind how few and feeble they are and, as a result, live in the light of eternity.

Job claims his passing days are lived "without hope", that is, without the likelihood of miraculous recovery from his ailments, or the possibility of a rerun of life on earth. However much or little Job may have known about a future resurrection, this much he understood: death terminates our present condition. The New Testament agrees, although it does not stop with the certainty of death and judgment:

> And as it is appointed unto men once to die, but after this the judgment: So Christ was once offered to bear the sins of many; and unto them that look for him shall he appear the second time without sin unto salvation (Heb 9.27-28).

The Hebrew writer offers the believer the joyful expectation of the return of a once-sacrificed Messiah, a truth of which Job had no knowledge.

The Desire for Death: 7.7-21

Although still pondering the shortness of life, it is at this point in his speech that Job starts addressing God directly. Darby, in his translation, helpfully draws attention to the second personal singular imperative: "Remember thou that my life is wind; mine eye shall no more see good" (7.7, JND). Other singular pronouns are evident in verses 8,12,14,17-21.

In talking with God, Job frankly pours out his anxieties about the **brevity** of his life (7.7-10), its **misery** (7.11-16) and its **perplexity** (7.17-21).

The **brevity** of life is still weighing heavily on his mind (7.7-10). The imagery is compact and compelling. Human life on planet earth is like the merest breath of wind, like a cloud in the sky, swiftly and completely dispersed. No more will he see "good". The word (2896) refers to prosperity and wealth, and first appears when Job rebukes his wife: "shall we receive good at the hand of God, and shall we not receive evil?" (2.10). It alludes therefore to Job's past experiences – those blessings he once enjoyed but expects never to see again. The reason this good is for ever out of his grasp is his imminent departure from the world. Anyone who bothers to glance at him – and he has recently pleaded with his friends at least to look him in the face – will see him no longer, because God's eye is fixed upon him in punishment: "thine eyes are upon me, and I am not" (7.8). No man can survive the hostile gaze of Jehovah, so Job will shortly be removed from the scene and taken "down to the grave", from which there is no return (7.9-10). This is the first of the book's eight references to *sheol* (here translated "grave"), that place best defined as the abode of departed spirits. According to the *International Standard Bible Encyclopaedia*, "in its darkness, stillness, powerlessness, lack of knowledge and inactivity, it is a true abode of death; hence, is regarded by the living with shrinking, horror and dismay". Job has already spoken of the potential rest he believes it will afford (3.13-19); now he names the place directly.

Job's agony of mind frequently leads him into apparent inconsistency of speech. He has been longing to die, to escape the pain of earthly existence (3.13; 6.8-9), but at the same time he detests the speed with which his life hastes away. He wants to die and yet regrets life's brevity. The contradiction is understandable. The life of public honour and domestic felicity he once enjoyed has been cut short by sudden calamities. That contented life, in retrospect, appears to have been all too fleeting, and it is this that he bitterly laments. His present condition of misery, on the other hand, he would willingly surrender for the release of death.

And how overwhelming is his **misery** (7.11-16)! It is so intense, and death so close, that Job feels excused for launching into an unmuzzled outburst: "Therefore I will not restrain my mouth: I will speak in the anguish of my spirit; I will complain in the bitterness of my soul" (7.11, JND).

His complaint is that he does not understand the reason for his suffering. Why has he become the object of divine displeasure? He resorts to hyperbole. Is he a raging, tempestuous sea which requires God's constant supervision to keep its waves in check? Is he some hideous sea-monster to be held under restraint? In the Old Testament the sea sometimes typifies that mad rebellion against God's power which is the characteristic of fallen angels and sinful men. In particular it often represents the angry nations (Is 57.20; Ezek 26.3), those who war "against the Lord, and against his anointed, saying, Let us break their bands asunder, and cast away their cords from us" (Ps 2.2-3). Jeremiah uses God's supreme authority over the sea as a testimony to His majesty:

> Fear ye not me? saith the Lord: will ye not tremble at my presence, which
> have placed the sand for the bound of the sea by a perpetual decree, that it

cannot pass it: and though the waves thereof toss themselves, yet can they not prevail; though they roar, yet can they not pass over it? (Jer 5.22).

What hope can wicked men have in pitting themselves against such a God? "O Lord God of hosts, who is a strong Lord like unto thee? or to thy faithfulness round about thee? Thou rulest the raging of the sea: when the waves thereof arise, thou stillest them" (Ps 89.8-9).

In a similar way, the word here translated "whale" (8577), which first appears in Genesis 1.21, is used figuratively in the prophets to describe arrogant nations who oppose God, such as Egypt (Is 51.9; Ezek 32.2), Babylon (Jer 51.34), or Gentiles in general (Is 27.1). Job uses the word again in 30.29 to describe his personal desolation and solitariness.

Whether he is as savage as a foaming sea or a marine monster, Job feels that God is behaving towards him like a grim prison warder. "Watch" (4929) translates a word used of Joseph put "in ward" in the Egyptian prison (Gen 40.3-4). Once again, Job feels uncomfortably hedged in so that he cannot evade God's anger. His inability to find any exit is poignantly illustrated by the vain hope of experiencing relief in sleep. We have already learned of his insomnia (7.3-4), but now we are given an insight into what happens when he finally slips into the sleep of physical exhaustion. With all the emphasis of synonymous parallelism, verse 13 ironically lays out his wish, only to be followed by the disillusionment of verse 14:

When I say, My bed shall comfort me, my couch shall ease my complaint; Then thou scarest me with dreams, and terrifiest me through visions (7.13-14).

The inviting "bed" and "couch" are replaced by nightmarish "dreams" and "visions"; the possibilities of "comfort" and "ease" by the dreadful realities suggested in the verbs "scarest" and "terrifiest".

Job sought to sleep away his "complaint" (7989), the same word used by Hannah to explain to Eli why she seems so disturbed. It was not drink but distress that caused her sorrows: "out of the abundance of my complaint and grief have I spoken hitherto" (1 Sam 1.16). Job could have sympathised, for he too is misunderstood. The term is used by the psalmist in the superscription of Psalm 102, and by David on pouring out his soul before Jehovah in Psalm 142:

A Prayer of the afflicted, when he is overwhelmed, and poureth out his complaint before the Lord. Hear my prayer, O Lord, and let my cry come unto thee (Ps 102.1).

I poured out my complaint before him; I shewed before him my trouble (Ps 142.2).

Sleep can be a great healer, but Job lacked restful sleep. So disturbing were his nights that he confesses he would prefer death by strangling to a continuation of this loathsome life. Literally, he says, "my soul chooseth strangling, Death rather than my bones" (7.15, YLT), for his multiple afflictions have reduced him to a skeleton. In this condition he has no appetite for life. For Job, the idea of existing "for ever" conjures up a life of perpetual misery and decrepitude.

In his fantasy tale *Gulliver's Travels*, Jonathan Swift writes about a people who are born without the ability to die, whom he calls Struldbrugs. Gulliver the traveller is initially delighted to learn that some men possess the benefits of immortality.

> I cried out, as in a rapture, "Happy nation, where every child hath at least a chance for being immortal! Happy people, who enjoy so many living examples of ancient virtue, and have masters ready to instruct them in the wisdom of all former ages! but happiest, beyond all comparison, are those excellent STRULDBRUGS, who, being born exempt from that universal calamity of human nature, have their minds free and disengaged, without the weight and depression of spirits caused by the continual apprehensions of death!"

But when he meets them, Gulliver discovers that, far from being a boon, their unending existence is a burden. They simply grow older and older, prey to all the diseases and drawbacks of ageing, but without any hope of release:

> When they came to fourscore years, which is reckoned the extremity of living in this country, they had not only all the follies and infirmities of other old men, but many more which arose from the dreadful prospect of never dying. They were not only opinionative, peevish, covetous, morose, vain, talkative, but incapable of friendship, and dead to all natural affection, which never descended below their grandchildren. Envy and impotent desires are their prevailing passions.[99]

Job shrinks from the thought of an unending existence in his current misery: "I would not live forever" (7.16, ESV). But, for the child of God, the prospect of a glad eternity in the presence of the Lord Jesus, blessed with a body suited to that everlasting bliss, is the brightest of hopes. Eternal life in Christ is not endless deterioration in a sin-damaged body but unfading freshness and vitality, for the Lord will "transform our body of humiliation into conformity to his body of glory, according to the working of the power which he has even to subdue all things to himself" (Phil 3.21, JND).

Finally comes what the whole chapter has been moving towards – the explosion of Job's **perplexity** (7.17-21). This section is packed with questions which have long been simmering below the surface: what is man? how long must he suffer? why is he the object of divine assault? Why, supposing he has sinned, can he not be pardoned?

The first question picks up his earlier suggestion that God has been treating him like a turbulent ocean or a sea monster. The waters were gathered together into seas in day three of the creation week (Gen 1.10), while "great whales" were made in day five (Gen 1.21). But the climax of God's creative activities was the making of man in the divine image on day six (Gen 1.27). Job knows that he is neither a sea nor a sea monster, but a lineal descendant of Adam. He moves from picture language to plain speech. But that only raises another problem: what then is man, formed of mere flesh and blood, that he should be subjected, like Job, to such savage harassment by God? Two verses set out, first, the positive and then the negative:

> What is man, that thou makest much of him? and that thou settest thy heart upon him? And that thou visitest him every morning, triest him every moment? (7.17-18, JND).

True, Genesis teaches that man is greatly privileged, given dominion over the works of God's hands, and created so as to enjoy a unique relationship with His Creator. He has been selected as the special object of heaven's attention (7.17). Why, then, is man constantly visited for assessment and tested without relief? In the words of Delitzsch, "instead of ignoring him, [God] makes too much of him, by selecting him, perishable as he is, as the object of ever new and ceaseless sufferings".[100]

Poor Job is scarcely in the state of mind to appreciate the biblical doctrine of anthropology, which teaches that man is immeasurably honoured by his special creation but also damaged by sin. David's later psalm raises exactly the same question as Job, but offers a very different answer:

> What is man, that thou art mindful of him? and the son of man, that thou visitest him? For thou hast made him a little lower than the angels, and hast crowned him with glory and honour. Thou madest him to have dominion over the works of thy hands; thou hast put all things under his feet: All sheep and oxen, yea, and the beasts of the field; The fowl of the air, and the fish of the sea, and whatsoever passeth through the paths of the seas (Ps 8.4-8).

Man is amazingly dignified in his unique position as God's vice-regent over the created earth. And if anyone asks why, in the present world order, this is not as evident as it ought to be, the reply comes in Hebrews 2:

> Thou hast put all things in subjection under his feet. For in that he put all in subjection under him, he left nothing that is not put under him. But now we see not yet all things put under him. But we see Jesus, who was made a little lower than the angels for the suffering of death, crowned with glory and honour; that he by the grace of God should taste death for every man (Heb 2.8-9).

In the person of the Lord Jesus Christ, the incarnate Son, we shall see the fulfilment of all God's grand purposes for man. Where Adam, and all his descendants, failed, the Lord Jesus has triumphed; when He returns in glory He will take up the reins of righteous government in the mediatorial Kingdom on earth. When God created Adam, He always had His Son in view.

Job's suffering prompted him to ask the question, but we have to wait for the coming of the Son of God to learn the answer. Chronologically, Job was the first to pose the problem; David picked it up, leaving the fulfilment obscure; but in the New Testament we find the perfect execution rests with Christ. He alone puts into effect in its entirety the Father's will. We can only imagine with what joy and amazement Old Testament saints like Job will react to seeing, in the glorious Kingdom age to come, the answer to all their aspirations in the person of the Son.

But at this stage Job's only response to what he considers a divine attack on him is to plead for respite: "How long wilt thou not look away from me, nor let me alone till I swallow down my spittle?" (7.19, JND). "Let me alone", cries Job (he has already said this in verse 16), "and give me breathing space from incessant harrying". All the time, despite his disrespectful words, the fact that he persists in speaking to and arguing with God demonstrates that the very last thing he really craves is separation from the Lord's presence.

The final verses constitute the chapter's climax, a climax which touches significantly on the matter of sin and forgiveness. The Revised Version usefully brings out the hypothetical nature of Job's initial question:

> If I have sinned, what do I unto thee, O thou watcher of men? why hast thou set me as a mark for thee, so that I am a burden to myself? And why dost thou not pardon my transgression, and take away mine iniquity? for now shall I lie down in the dust; and thou shall seek me diligently, but I shall not be (7.20-21, RV).

The argument in verse 20 seems to go something like this. "Suppose I have sinned in some specific way which is beyond my present knowledge (because, as far as I am aware, I have done nothing to deserve my misery), how could that sin have any impact on such a great God? My failures cannot detract from the majesty and joy of the Creator. Why have I become what amounts to a divine punch bag? Why does God bother Himself with me?"

According to the commentators, the end of verse 20 should not read, "a burden to myself", but, "a burden to thee". This is because it forms one of eighteen traditional scribal changes in the text of the Old Testament. Writes Hartley, "these were changes the scribes made to ease a reading viewed as portraying God in a too human or negative manner".[101] More recent Bible versions certainly take this line and translate accordingly. One can see why pious Jews might recoil from language which credits one man with being burdensome to a God of infinite power and glory. But it is all in keeping with Job's current mood of uncensored protest. That Scripture records it is yet another testimony to the astonishing candour of God's word: it tells the truth about man and the truth about God with no holds barred.

Job uses three distinct terms to describe human failure. "Sinned" (7.20) has the idea of missing the mark, "transgression" indicates rebellion, while "iniquity" speaks of perverseness (7.21). Sin means, then, that we fall short of God's standard, rebel against His rule, and deviate from moral uprightness. It makes man culpable before God. Essentially the same three words for sin appear in David's great psalm of personal thanksgiving for divine forgiveness:

> Blessed is he whose transgression is forgiven, whose sin is covered. Blessed is the man unto whom the Lord imputeth not iniquity, and in whose spirit there is no guile (Ps 32.1-2).

The difference is this. David wrote as a man who had been graciously pardoned for definite sins (adultery and murder being the most obvious), while Job has been heralded from the start of his story as a man of unimpeachable uprightness.

Nevertheless, if Job is guilty of some specific sins of which he is as yet unaware, why can he not be forgiven? He must know that God promised in Genesis 3 to send a deliverer who would crush the enemy. He certainly knows about the need for sacrifice that God might be appeased, because he took the lead in offering sacrificial victims on behalf of his children. Indeed, from the entrance of sin into the world God established for man what might be called a provisional means of pardon. Adam and Eve were covered in His presence by skin, necessitating the death of an animal; and righteous Abel was instructed (presumably by his parents) to approach God by way of blood sacrifice. None of these sacrifices in reality dealt with the matter of sin, but all pointed forward to what God Himself would make available in the person of His Son, the ultimate offering. Although Hebrews refers to the Levitical system introduced after Job's time, the principle is the same:

> And every priest standeth daily ministering and offering oftentimes the same sacrifices, which can never take away sins: But this man, after he had offered one sacrifice for sins for ever, sat down on the right hand of God (Heb 10.11-12).

As is often remarked, what God's justice demanded, His love provided.

But Job lived before the cross. As far as he can see, the God he has served has turned against him without cause, smiting him with such severity that the only possible outcome is death. Death, he is convinced, is very close: "for now shall I sleep in the dust; and thou shalt seek me in the morning, but I shall not be" (7.21). From dust he was formed originally, and in the dust he will lie down when he dies. Should God come looking for him next day, it will be too late, for he will have passed away in the night. He imagines God as a very human visitor who turns up to check on Job's health, only to discover he has already succumbed to his diseases. The chapter closes soberly with death.

But pause a moment to note the ways in which Job speaks about God in this, his first formal response to his friends. He has seen through the outward politeness of Eliphaz's oriental courtesy to detect an undercurrent of distrust, disapproval and suspicion. Eliphaz may sugar his speech, but he basically believes Job to be a man who has been found out for his wickedness, is being punished, and must repent in order to be restored to God's favour. But Job does not spend all his time remonstrating with Eliphaz and his colleagues. Rather, he talks to and about God.

How does Job speak about God? Three descriptions stand out. He is the Almighty (6.4,14), He is the Holy One (6.10), He is the Watcher of men (7.20). As **the Almighty**, He maintains total control over His universe. This is emphasised by Job's repeated insistence that all his circumstances, whether good or ill, are ultimately traceable to God. We do not live in a capricious, anarchic world, but in one superintended by divine power and wisdom. In reply to the jeering pagans round about, the psalmist has a simple and sufficient answer:

> Wherefore should the heathen say, Where is now their God? But our God is in the heavens: he hath done whatsoever he hath pleased (Ps 115.2-3).

It is still true: whatever men may say, our God is in the heavens and does whatever He pleases, for He "worketh all things after the counsel of his own will" (Eph 1.11).

God is also **the Holy One**. This draws attention to His moral perfections and majestic awesomeness. The name underlines the vast gulf between the creature and the Creator in all His glory. Isaiah spoke of Him as the "Holy one of Israel" (Is 1.4; 5.19,24) before being personally – and devastatingly – confronted with the reality of what the title implies (6.3-5). Witnessing the impact of divine holiness on the grandest of created beings – for the seraphim covered their faces and their feet, continually testifying to the all-consuming purity of Jehovah – caused the prophet to become conscious of his own condition. Like a leper (and the same year King Uzziah died a literal leper) he was unclean before God. It takes a glimpse of what God is to bring us to a realisation of our own sin. As Torrey says, "the man who thinks well of himself has never met God". At this stage, Job still sees himself as the injured innocent (and to some extent he is correct), but he will change his tune when, at the climax of the book, he meets the Lord. In the light of His terrible greatness the patriarch will find it is time for a serious self-reassessment.

Finally, God is **the "watcher"**, or as Darby translates it, the "Observer of men". The word (5341) has the idea of watching over or guarding, and is used of men keeping God's word, and of God keeping men. God "kept [5341] him [Israel] as the apple of his eye" (Deut 32.10), and will "keep [5341] him in perfect peace, whose mind is stayed on thee: because he trusteth in thee" (Is 26.3). Occasionally the word refers to a literal caretaker, one who guards vulnerable property such as a vineyard, and this is how it is used in the only other occurrence in Job: "He buildeth his house as a moth, and as a booth that the keeper [5341] maketh" (27.18). God, then, is the great warden or preserver of the world, ever watching over the creatures of His hand. From the surrounding verses it seems clear that Job uses the term in a negative way: God is a critical onlooker, a detached viewer who operates a persistently intrusive surveillance of His handiwork. Job is subject to "the constant espionage exercised by God over men, that He may detect their sin and bring them to a reckoning".[102] As he said earlier, "thine eyes are upon me, and I am not" (7.8).

But Job, we must remember, is speaking out of the festering confusion of his soul; his words do not constitute a complete doctrinal statement. The Scriptures as a whole reveal that God does watch over His world, but with a tender concern for the needy as well as a judicial investigation of the wicked. The Christian believer rests happy in the knowledge that His Father's eye is always upon him. Around the same period in which Job lived, Hagar learned that truth, and announced a new name of God, the "God of seeing" (ESV):

> And she called the name of the Lord that spake unto her, Thou God seest me: for she said, Have I also here looked after him that seeth me? (Gen 16.13).

The rest of Scripture elaborates on the reality of God's all-seeing eye:

> The Lord is in his holy temple, the Lord's throne is in heaven: his eyes behold, his eyelids try, the children of men (Ps 11.4).

> For the ways of man are before the eyes of the Lord, and he pondereth all his goings (Prov 5.21).

> The eyes of the Lord are in every place, beholding the evil and the good (Prov 15.3).

> Can any hide himself in secret places that I shall not see him? saith the Lord. Do not I fill heaven and earth? saith the Lord (Jer 23.24).

> Neither is there any creature that is not manifest in his sight: but all things are naked and opened unto the eyes of him with whom we have to do (Heb 4.13).

But if God, in His omniscience, perceives, He also graciously preserves. Job is obsessed with the former, but God's benevolent care for His people is taught with equal authority. It is especially the theme of the psalmist:

> Thou shalt keep them [the poor and needy mentioned in v.5], O Lord, thou shalt preserve them from this generation for ever (Ps 12.7).

> O love the Lord, all ye his saints: for the Lord preserveth the faithful, and plentifully rewardeth the proud doer (Ps 31.23).

> Thou art my hiding place; thou shalt preserve me from trouble; thou shalt compass me about with songs of deliverance. Selah (Ps 32.7).

> Casting all your care upon him; for he careth for you (1 Pet 5.7).

That is our position today. Looking back to a finished work of redemption and forward to a soon-coming Saviour to gather His people into His immediate presence, we can rest the meantime in His caring hands. This does not guarantee earthly prosperity but it does guarantee ultimate preservation.

Deep down, Job knows that some of his words, especially those of the initial griping complaint in chapter 3, are ill-judged. He freely admits they are "rash" (6.3, RV) or "vehement" (6.3, JND); they spring from "the anguish of my spirit … the bitterness of my soul" (7.11). Job is no ivory tower theologian pontificating on man's condition, or an academic attempting a technical exposition of Scripture; rather, he is a genuine sufferer (indeed, as far as Scripture is concerned, the greatest of human sufferers, bar one) who can see no light at the end of the tunnel. Nevertheless, he sticks with his God. Ellison puts it well:

> This is one of the greatest lessons we can learn from Jeremiah and Job. They never hesitated to open their hearts to God, even though men might call their words blasphemy.[103]

Whatever happens, this is the best recourse for believers buffeted by life.

SECTION 6
Dialogue: Job 4 – 42.6
Contest: Round 1: Job 4-14
Bildad's 1st Speech: Job 8

One imagines that after Job's long, testy, and closely engaged response to Eliphaz there may have been something of a pause in the debate. Perhaps the three friends looked at one another in puzzlement. Clearly, Job was not going to be the docile patient who swallows his physician's bitter pill without protest. Tougher treatment was called for – so, step forward, Bildad! If Eliphaz, the leader and elder statesman of the delegation, was eloquent and easy-going in his approach (although Job has rightly detected a critical spirit under the benign surface of his words), Bildad is nothing if not blunt. He doesn't say much (his speech is under half the length of Eliphaz's), but what he does say is cutting.

His whole approach is more direct and heartless. Obviously he believed in calling a spade a spade. Job's children must have sinned to deserve their deaths (8.4); if Job really were what he claims to be, God would immediately restore his fortunes (8.6); those who suffer earthly calamity are nothing but hypocrites (8.13). It is all summed up in a condensed statement of his underlying doctrinal principle: "Behold, God will not cast away a perfect man, neither will he help the evil doers" (8.20). The parallelism emphasizes the point: on the one hand God will not abandon the righteous, but neither will He extend help to the wicked. Job evidently has been abandoned, and equally visibly is not in receipt of divine help – therefore he is in danger of being classified among the wicked.

After a brief introduction, the speech falls into three paragraphs:

     1. The Experience of Job: 8.3-7
     2. The Evidence of History: 8.8-10
     3. The Examples of Judgment: 8.11-22.

The introduction gets to the point without beating about the bush: "Then answered Bildad the Shuhite, and said, How long wilt thou speak these things? and how long shall the words of thy mouth be like a strong wind?" (8.1-2).

Bildad's initial move is to condemn Job's language, likening it to a gust of wind, "blowing wildly, noisily, rashly, and purposelessly, with damaging results".[104] Whether he is looking back to Job's shocking outburst in chapter 3, or responding to his protest against Eliphaz's advice, it matters little. So often Job's friends seem oddly insensitive to his terrible trauma, never stopping to think how they might have spoken in similar circumstances. As Robinson remarks, "faultiness in another's speech [is] no excuse for unfeelingness in our own".[105]

The Experience of Job: 8.3-7

Bildad immediately homes in on Job's recent family catastrophes. This section is dominated by second person singular pronouns (I count ten of them in the first seven verses), emphasising the object of his attack: "If thy children have sinned … If thou wouldest seek … If thou wert pure and upright" (8.4-6). The particular focus is the tragic death of Job's children, but Bildad leads into this with a zealous affirmation of God's inflexible justice: "Doth God pervert judgment? or doth the Almighty pervert justice?" (8.3)

The implied answer is "No", and of course he is correct. The God who throughout the Old Testament is constantly associated with righteousness will never misrepresent the right, or perpetrate injustice. The testimony of Scripture is uniform and conclusive:

> Whereupon the princes of Israel and the king humbled themselves; and they said, The Lord is righteous (2 Chr 12.6).

> O Lord God of Israel, thou art righteous: for we remain yet escaped, as it is this day: behold, we are before thee in our trespasses: for we cannot stand before thee because of this (Ezra 9.15).

> Righteous art thou, O Lord, and upright are thy judgments (Ps 119.137).

> Therefore hath the Lord watched upon the evil, and brought it upon us: for the Lord our God is righteous in all his works which he doeth: for we obeyed not his voice (Dan 9.14).

> And I heard another out of the altar say, Even so, Lord God Almighty, true and righteous are thy judgments (Rev 16.7).

Later in the book Elihu will make the same affirmation: "Yea, surely God will not do wickedly, neither will the Almighty pervert judgment" (34.12). God's righteousness is as free as His immutable holiness from the possibility of taint. Indeed, His perfect justice and righteousness are, according to Strong, "simply holiness exercised toward creatures. The same holiness which exists in God in eternity past manifests itself as justice and righteousness, so soon as intelligent creatures come into being".[106]

It is therefore all the more astonishing when we read in the New Testament that this God of absolute righteousness also "justifieth the ungodly" (Rom 4.5). A just God is able to declare wicked people righteous? It flies in the face of Israel's law, in which Jehovah insists that magistrates acquit only the innocent:

> If there be a controversy between men, and they come unto judgment, that the judges may judge them; then they shall justify the righteous, and condemn the wicked (Deut 25.1).

The magistrate's pronouncement does not alter the nature of the contestants in a law suit – it simply declares them publicly to be what they already are: the innocent man is seen to be innocent, the guilty man is seen to be guilty. Further, the Lord says of Himself, "I will not justify the wicked" (Ex 23.7). Yet Paul dares to say that this same God justifies wicked people! The answer to the apparent contradiction is found in Romans chapter 3, where the apostle presents the Lord Jesus Christ as the sufficient sacrifice who meets all God's just claims against His people, allowing Him righteously to pardon believing sinners. Charitie Bancroft's hymn puts it into marvellous words:

> Because the sinless Saviour died
> My sinful soul is counted free;
> For God, the Just, is satisfied
> To look on Him and pardon me.

Bildad knows nothing of this. He knows only the justice that smites the bad and rewards the good. Abraham had daringly approached God on that very basis when pleading for the godly minority in Sodom. He appealed not to God's mercy towards the wicked but to His justice towards the good:

> And Abraham drew near, and said, Wilt thou also destroy the righteous with the wicked? Peradventure there be fifty righteous within the city: wilt thou also destroy and not spare the place for the fifty righteous that are therein? That be far from thee to do after this manner, to slay the righteous with the wicked: and that the righteous should be as the wicked, that be far from thee: Shall not the Judge of all the earth do right? (Gen 18.23-25).

In reality it was a very small minority indeed, smaller even than Abraham had imagined. Nevertheless, God graciously responded to his request, albeit in a manner different from his expectations. But Abraham's prayer was no vain hope, for it was grounded on God's self-revelation. Earlier in the chapter the Lord had spoken of the patriarch's family life:

> I know him, that he will command his children and his household after him, and they shall keep the way of the Lord, to do justice and judgment; that the Lord may bring upon Abraham that which he hath spoken of him (Gen 18.19).

The "way of the Lord", we learn, is "justice and judgment", a moral quality to be reflected in the lives of His people. From that statement, Abraham deduced that God's dealings with men will never contradict His essential character. His response to God's word is a pattern for us all: he listened, he learned, and what he heard he made the burden of his prayer, venturing to rest his case on God's self-declared justice. He reasoned forwards from the divine nature to the way God must therefore treat His creatures. A just God could not possibly condemn righteous people. This, we must notice, begs the question of how any fallen creatures may be considered righteous in God's sight. Not until we reach Romans do we find a cogent exposition of the way God can pardon the guilty, announcing them to be judicially right, without compromising His justice. As has often been pointed out, Paul's letter to the Romans is first of all about the justification or vindication of God Himself.

But let us return to Bildad. He is reasoning backwards, from external circumstances to the divine attribute which (in his opinion) must have caused them. For him, the argument goes like this: if God is inflexibly righteous, it follows that the fate of Job's children must have been the judicial consequence of personal wickedness, for only sinners meet with judgment. This is the connection between the doctrinal statement of verse 3 and the following verses. Bildad offers us a sequence of hypotheses: "If ... If ... If ..." (8. 4-6). The first "If" really has the force of "Since" because of the words that follow: "If thy children have sinned against him, he hath also given them over into the hand of their transgression" (8.4, JND). There could be no doubt about the former statement (the sin of Job's children) in the light of the historical evidence of the latter (their sudden deaths). The second "If" moves into the realm of advice: if only Job would seek the Lord early and diligently make supplication to Him. It is a repetition of Eliphaz's counsel: "I would seek unto God, and unto God would I commit my cause" (5.8). The final "If" touches on the nub of the whole matter: if Job actually were "pure and upright", then unquestionably God would intervene to restore his losses.

The argument is logical and inexorable. The sudden death of Job's children demonstrates God's justice in slaying the guilty (8.4). The only cure is to cast himself unreservedly upon God in prayer (8.5). But the essential condition for answered prayer is that he who prays be practically upright in heart and life (8.6) for, as James teaches us, "The effectual fervent prayer of a righteous man availeth much" (James 5.16). It is that requirement of personal righteousness which is the problem. Once again we meet the frustrating mixture of accuracy and error which makes it so hard to pick the meat off the bones of the friends' advice. Bildad's tracing of Job's trials to the hand of God, his advocacy of the power of prayer, his insistence that God only heeds the upright in heart – all this is doctrinally true. Yet in context he is wrong. Take his critical comment about Job's character: "If thou wert pure and upright; surely now he would awake for thee, and make the habitation of thy righteousness prosperous" (8.6). The underlying implication is that Job is not what he appears to be, a just and pious man. He cannot be "pure and upright" because evil has befallen his family; and since he is already short of the standard, it is therefore impossible for God to hear his prayers. His disasters disqualify him from redress. But the reader knows that Job is "perfect and upright, and one that feared God, and eschewed evil" (1.1). The inspired narrator describes him as "upright"; later Job will insist – and there is no reason to doubt him – that "my prayer is pure" (16.17). Bildad's censorious assumption is off course.

If he is incorrect in his assessment of Job's character, he is oddly very exact in his generous offer of the benefits that follow repentance:

> ... surely now he would awake for thee, and make the habitation of thy righteousness prosperous. Though thy beginning was small, yet thy latter end should greatly increase (8.6-7).

This describes Job's end with unexpected accuracy: the renewal and increase of his material prosperity (42.10-12). However, the man whom Bildad now instructs to pray for God's pardon is the man who will plead with God on behalf of his three, shamefaced friends, counsellors proven completely wrong in their assessment. The book starts with Job interceding for his family; it will end with him interceding for his friends. It can hardly be accidental that James links him with Elijah in adjacent sections of his letter about the importance of patience and prayer (James 5.7-18), for the whole book paints Job as a man who, in joy and sorrow, had constant intercourse with God.

The Evidence of History: 8.8-10

Having addressed Job's circumstances, Bildad now explains the foundations for his belief. Eliphaz had sought to overawe Job with a creepy midnight vision; Bildad rests his case on the weighty authority of history. Since any individual is too short-lived to evaluate God's ways comprehensively, all he can do is resort to the testimony of the fathers. In the words of Delitzsch, "Our ephemeral and shadowy life is not sufficient for passing judgment on the dealings of God; we must call history and tradition to our aid".[107]

There is some truth here. Bildad is treading ground similar to Job's frequent references to the brevity of human life: "we are but of yesterday, and know nothing, because our days upon earth are a shadow" (8.9). We may apply it to Christians. One lifetime is too short to absorb everything in God's Word; therefore only the ignorant and the complacent will deprive themselves of the written ministry of earlier generations of believers. Indeed, we learn much from the discoveries of the past, and the wisdom of our ancestors (whether believers or not) constitutes a treasure house of insights into fallen human nature. Even the apostle Paul was not averse to quoting from pagan poets when their testimony was reliable and apposite (Acts 17.28; 1 Cor 15.33; Titus 1.12). But history requires authoritative interpretation to make sense of it, for human tradition alone is by no means infallible.

Let me illustrate. Hezekiah's Assyrian besiegers assumed that, because he had overthrown the ancient high places in Judah, he had sinned against his God. In reality, of course, all he had done was to return to the ways of Jehovah which his ancestors had abandoned in favour of more fashionable worship practices. Sennacherib obviously had his spies in Jerusalem, but they had not done their homework:

> And if thou say to me, We rely upon Jehovah our God: is it not he, whose high places and whose altars Hezekiah has removed, saying to Judah and Jerusalem, Ye shall worship before this altar? (Is 36.7, JND).

Because of its ignorance of God's Word, the world sometimes mistakes for treasonous departure what is in reality a zealous return to Scripture. More, it generally rejects principle in favour of pragmatism.

Later in the history of Judah, survivors of the destruction of Jerusalem who foolishly fled to Egypt refused Jeremiah's call to repentance, instead looking back longingly to an affluence they credited to the idolatry practised for generations:

> As for the word that thou hast spoken unto us in the name of the Lord, we will not hearken unto thee. But we will certainly do whatsoever thing goeth forth out of our own mouth, to burn incense unto the queen of heaven, and to pour out drink offerings unto her, as we have done, we, and our fathers, our kings, and our princes, in the cities of Judah, and in the streets of Jerusalem: for then had we plenty of victuals, and were well, and saw no evil (Jer 44.16-17).

Their theology was naïve: our forefathers' practices brought us good so they must have been correct. Wise believers will avoid reading apparent outward success as a proof of divine approbation. That procedure would have endorsed Moses's disobedience to the Lord's command to "speak ye unto the rock" (Num 20.8), simply because the water flowed in abundance and the people were blessed. But as a result of their personal rebellion Moses and Aaron were excluded from entering the land.

Again, the Lord Jesus exposed the error of Pharisaic tradition which marginalized the clear teachings of God's word:

> Thus have ye made the commandment of God of none effect by your tradition. Ye hypocrites, well did Esaias prophesy of you, saying, This people draweth nigh unto me with their mouth, and honoureth me with their lips; but their heart is far from me. But in vain they do worship me, teaching for doctrines the commandments of men (Mt 15.6-9).

All this should cause us to be very careful in our use of snappy phrases like, "If it's new it's not true, and if it's true it's not new". Such a mantra is only correct if we establish our baseline as the unambiguous teaching of God's Word, rather than what people have long assumed it to be. It is so easy to omit a bit here or add a bit there. Many deviations are of long standing, for truth is very quickly undermined. It did not take long for Satan to challenge God's command to Adam and Eve, and it did not take them long to sin. If mere antiquity were the touchstone of what is right, Luther would have remained loyal to the ceremonies of Rome, and Darby would have stayed in the Church of Ireland. Not tradition (whether Roman Catholic, protestant, or assembly) but Scripture accurately expounded must be the believer's foundation. That is why local churches of Christians must be engaged in the regular business of teaching directly and systematically from the Word. As long as we are in this world we are prone to error, because the inbuilt tendency of the heart (and therefore of every assembly) is to drift away from, not towards, what is right. If the price of freedom is constant vigilance, then the cost of godliness in personal and assembly life is perpetual exposure to the Word of God in its unedited entirety. Its cutting edge is never blunted. Whatever the catchword of the day, the believer's response must be "To the law and to the testimony: if they speak not according to this word, it is because there is no light in them" (Is 8.20).

The Examples of Judgment: 8.11-22

Bildad now parades a series of images of human vulnerability, all testifying to the hand of God in the affairs of wicked men. His aim is to scare Job into confession and penitence, by demonstrating that hypocrites faced a fearful future. They were like fragile water plants, such as the papyrus (8.11-13). Hartley comments that "papyrus was a very valuable plant, being used for swift skiffs (Is 18.2), baskets (Ex 2.3), mats, and parchments. It grows rapidly to a height of eight to ten feet. A tall, straight plant, it appears stately as it waves gently in the breeze".[108] Just as the papyrus depends on the presence of water, so the wicked thrive only in external prosperity; possessing no inward stability, no deep-grounded roots, their success is like the rapid growth of reeds. Such vegetation withers even before it is cut down.

From the papyrus Bildad switches to the spider's web to illustrate the fragility of godless confidence (8.14-15). It is an apt picture. To place one's hope in anything other than the living God is utter folly, whereas, says the psalmist, "Blessed is that man that maketh the Lord his trust, and respecteth not the proud, nor such as turn aside to lies" (Ps 40.4). To rest on a flimsy support is fatal. The wicked man "shall lean [8172] upon his house, but it shall not stand: he shall hold it fast, but it shall not endure" (8.15). Just as Saul leaned (8172) upon his reliable spear (2 Sam 1.6) and Naaman's master leaned on his loyal servant's hand (2 Kings 5.18), so the child of God can safely rest only on Jehovah (2 Chr 14.11). He alone can bear His people up in every emergency.

Finally Bildad describes a creeping garden plant, possibly a vine or intrusive weed, which shoots up luxuriantly in the sunshine only to be torn out of its place (8.16-19). Although it entwines its roots about the rocks in an endeavour to secure its position, once it is ripped away from the soil it leaves no trace behind. In Bildad's illustration the "he" who tears it out sounds like a gardener, but of course he expects his listeners to realise that this efficient gardener represents God. Once God intervenes in judgment there is neither recourse nor return, and others speedily grow up in the place of the uprooted plant. The irony is sharp: all the hypocrite's "joy" comes to is this – swift removal and irretrievable ruin.

Three metaphors therefore drive home the inevitable destiny of the hypocrite: like the papyrus he withers, like the web he collapses, like the uprooted plant he is speedily replaced and forgotten. It is not a cheerful picture, nor is it meant to be. Bildad is out to shake Job's confidence and rip away the veneer of his reputation for righteousness.

Bildad changes his manner for his conclusion, however, painting a more comforting portrait of restored affluence (8.20-22). As we noted earlier, it is here that he establishes his basic principle: "God will not cast off a perfect man, neither will he take evil-doers by the hand" (8.20, JND). The language suggests a hand stretched out to seize and uphold one about to fall. The imagery is pervasive in the Old Testament:

Nevertheless I am continually with thee: thou hast holden me by my right hand (Ps 73.23).

For I the Lord thy God will hold thy right hand, saying unto thee, Fear not; I will help thee (Is 41.13).

I the Lord have called thee in righteousness, and will hold thine hand, and will keep thee, and give thee for a covenant of the people, for a light of the Gentiles (Is 42.6).

Every believer is at times deeply conscious of the gracious yet firm grasp of Jehovah holding him up in moments of danger, communicating the tender love of His presence. Though spoken to Israel (as witnessed by the second half of the verse, which is rarely quoted) the well-known Deuteronomic promise can be extended to include Gentiles who today trust in Christ:

The eternal God is thy refuge, and underneath are the everlasting arms: and he shall thrust out the enemy from before thee; and shall say, Destroy them (Deut 33.27).

When read carefully in the light of New Testament distinctives, a pledge which includes God's mandate to Israel to exterminate the godless Canaanites provides sweet encouragement for the Christian. Our great enemies today are not Amorites but those insidious fleshly desires which war against the soul (1 Pet 2.11). They too need to be put to death.

But Bildad's words have a barbed edge. The "perfect man" is the basically good man who repents of his wickedness and returns to the Lord. The nudge in Job's direction is hardly subtle. "Evil doers", on the other hand, are those who abuse God's kindness by their recalcitrance. Job must align himself with the former if he wants future blessing; otherwise he will inevitably slide into the camp of the latter. But at least Bildad ends on a positive note: God will not terminate His dealings with Job "Till he fill thy mouth with laughing, and thy lips with rejoicing" (8.21). This conventional summary of earthly blessing is nearer the mark than he might imagine, for God truly will not finish with Job until He has attained the great end He had in view from the start – Job's vindication and super-abundant restoration. And the coda, consigning Job's enemies to shame, will be realised in part in the humiliation experienced by the three friends as the object of Jehovah's rebuke and Job's intercession.

What can we say about Bildad? He is not the most winsome of speakers, but he has a grasp of some basic truths. Sometimes we need to be reminded that, just as the mere presence of teaching gift does not automatically guarantee doctrinal accuracy, so its absence does not prevent a man from occasionally saying what is valuable. Bildad lacks the smooth platform manner of Eliphaz and might be considered too dour for most tastes, but nonetheless he draws attention to much that is right. Let us list some of the solid truths in his speech:

- God is just (8.3)
- God can and does intervene in discipline and judgment (8.4)
- God hears the prayers of His people (8.5)
- Effective prayer requires godliness of life (8.6)
- We can learn useful lessons from the past (8.8)
- One identifying mark of the wicked is that they forget God (8.13)
- Hypocrisy will eventually be exposed (8.13)
- Human life on this planet is precarious (8.14-15)
- Righteousness is blessed and wickedness is punished (8.20).

His limitations become most evident if we look more closely at the first and last statements in that list. Take his doctrine of God. The oral traditions handed down by Adam and his immediate descendants would have taught that God was powerful (as evidenced by the created universe), good (in His abundant provision for mankind), just (in His execution of the promised death penalty on sinful Adam and Eve), and gracious (in His gift of coats of skin to cover our naked parents). Bildad's theology, therefore, is too narrow, with little apparent room for mercy or grace. Take his view of the outworkings of divine justice. Although he is correct to insist that righteousness is rewarded and wickedness punished, he seems unaware of the possibility that there might be a long-term strategy in God's dealings with His creatures. Yes, divine justice requires the punishment of sin – but not necessarily at once. Those who are righteous through confidence in a God who provides a temporary sacrifice to meet their needs will indeed be blessed – but not necessarily immediately. Bildad does not see that "calamity is no proof of guilt in those on whom it falls, and that evil may serve in the hand of God wider uses than the chastisement of individuals".[109]

Reading further into the Word we get a clearer sense of the divine strategy. For example, after testifying to the righteous standing of all who place their faith in Christ, Paul reveals that God is also engaged in putting such people through a long-term training programme, for

> we glory in tribulations also: knowing that tribulation worketh patience; And patience, experience; and experience, hope: And hope maketh not ashamed (Rom 5.3-5).

For tribulation to produce patience requires the passing of time. That is to say, the tribulation needs to be more than some momentary experience for the endurance to mature into a lasting quality. God not only saves souls from hell but uses adverse circumstances in this world to mould lives in godliness. The final difference between the saved and the unsaved awaits eternity for its full unveiling.

SECTION 7
Dialogue: Job 4 – 42.6
Contest: Round 1: Job 4-14
Job's 2nd Speech: Job 9-10

For all the aggressiveness of his manner, Bildad is no more successful than Eliphaz in silencing or subduing the protests of Job against what he sees as God's hostility. In fact he provokes Job's most searing speech yet. Lengthy and convoluted, it does not easily break down into neat components. Commentators have noted the absence of any obvious logical development for, like a dog worrying a bone, Job keeps returning to the same nagging issues. Davidson confesses that the two chapters are difficult to paragraph,

> not being calm and logical, but passionate and hurried, and passing on by rapid steps from one point to another, all more or less connected, and fusing all together in the glow of a fire, the colours of which are awe before an omnipotent Power, and moral terror and indignation mixed with piteous despair at the indiscriminate severity with which it crushes men.[110]

The very language used in the speech illustrates its character. For example, early on Job talks of God's power to uproot mountains (is he thinking of volcanic eruptions?) and cause earthquakes (9.5-6), after which he himself explodes in pent-up frustration: "I will give free course to my complaint; I will speak in the bitterness of my soul" (10.1, JND). What God does in the natural world reflects on a grand scale Job's angry expostulations. His final words, on the other hand, revert to a sorrowful contemplation of the afterlife, so often the burden of his thought during his depression. But *sheol*, the place of departed spirits, is now presented as a destination to be dreaded, a scene in which all light is dimmed and all coherence removed. It is a "land of darkness, as darkness itself; and of the shadow of death, without any order, and where the light is as darkness" (10.22). A pervasive sense of obscurity is suggested by the use of four different Hebrew words denoting the absence of light (10.21-22). "Without any order" (a Hebrew term used only here in the Bible) accurately describes the entire speech, which concludes gloomily with the word "darkness". There is an opacity and disjointedness about the discourse which mirrors Job's mood.

The reason for the confusion in Job's words is that they burst out of the patriarch's mouth as an unconsidered expression of frustration and bewilderment of soul. As a result he darts swiftly from one idea to another, thinking aloud without editing or modifying his remarks. Hartley explains it as follows:

> In this speech Job tends to state a position boldly, then abandon it when he sees its difficulty and jump to another idea, which is also quickly abandoned.[111]

The reason is not hard to grasp: a man who has lived in the consciousness of

God's smile suddenly finds he has become the object of divine disfavour and seeks desperately to understand why.

There are other parts of Scripture possessed of a similar heady energy, streaming like raw lava fresh from a subterranean discharge. The middle chapter of Peter's second letter, for example, has a comparable tempestuous flow of ideas, lacking the normal arrangement we expect in a doctrinal epistle, but the cause is entirely different. The apostle is so enflamed by the poisonous errors against which he is writing that his message has something of the unpredictable fervour of a spontaneous platform harangue rather than a coolly organized thesis.

Job's inability to comprehend God's ways with him, or discover a path through the wilderness of his misery, is thus reflected in his feverish manner of speaking. But of course we must always keep in mind the structural pattern of the entire book. What appears to be disorganization in one passage by no means endangers the careful arrangement of the whole. One of the grave drawbacks of sluggish assembly Bible readings is that a laborious (and sometimes, alas, tedious) concentration upon tiny textual minutiae too often obscures the overarching design. As a result, the saints fail to see the wood for the trees. That is to say, the inspired details of God's Word need to be read in their own equally inspired context, lest we go radically off course in our interpretation. Every book of Scripture has its own distinctive architecture, which we disregard at our peril. The overall shape of the book of Job is outlined in the introduction and visualized in the chart. This structure must constantly be borne in mind as we progress through the book's development. The patriarch's present mental disturbance cannot unsettle the firm pattern of the book any more than an individual believer's moments of doubt and disillusionment can compromise the sovereign purposes of God. Our current experience in this world, chaotic and erratic as it often seems, is firmly bookended by the greatest events in human history, the cross and the second coming of Christ. These divine interventions introduce meaning and stability to what otherwise might appear to be random and aimless. We therefore rejoice that, although we may not always clearly see our way in the present (for we walk by faith, not by sight), it is as securely in the hands of God as are the past and the future.

That said, Job's long answer to Bildad cries out for at least some attempt at structural arrangement so that the reader can get his head around the many ideas jostling within it. Primarily for ease of analysis I therefore suggest that, after its brief introduction (9.1-3), Job's second speech falls into six major sections:

> 1. God's Invincibility: 9.4-10
> 2. Job's Impotence: 9.11-16
> 3. God's Injustice: 9.17-24
> 4. Job's Impermanence: 9.25-31
> 5. God's Inaccessibility: 9.32-35
> 6. Job's Interrogation: 10.1-22.

The introduction (9.1-3) is important as it raises two matters of interpretation and sets the general tone of Job's argument:

Then Job answered and said, I know it is so of a truth: but how should man
be just with God? If he will contend with him, he cannot answer him one
of a thousand (9.1-3).

The first question of interpretation concerns the antecedent to Job's initial
response to Bildad: "I know it is so of a truth: but how should man be just with
God?" (9.2) To what does "it" refer? Zuck relates it specifically to the last words
of Bildad at the close of chapter 8:

They that hate thee shall be clothed with shame; and the dwelling place
of the wicked shall come to nought (8.22).

By way of encouragement (and warning) to Job, Bildad affirms that the wicked
face certain ruin. Other commentators, like Hartley, refer Job's words back to
Bildad's entire argument, which rests on the fundamental assertion that a just
God always rewards the good and punishes the bad (8.20).

Whichever is the correct understanding, the point in the second half of verse 2
is clear. "You tell me that God punishes the wicked and favours the upright? Well,
of course I know that", replies Job. There may be an element of irony in his words,
for his speech will later accuse God of injustice in His ways with men. But be that
as it may, Job's problem is this: even though he is confident that he is personally
blameless, how is it possible for any mere man, subjected to a divine onslaught,
ever to be in the right with God? Whatever he may do or say he is bound to be
proved wrong. You just cannot do battle with One who is omnipotent.

The second interpretative crux involves elucidating the ambiguous third
person pronouns in verse 3: "If he will contend with him, he cannot answer him
one of a thousand". The implication of most of the earlier translations is that
the first "he" refers to God, and the second, to man. If God elects to enter into
conflict with or conduct a lawsuit against any of His creatures, not one of them
has the capacity to outdo Him. How can man effectively argue against God?
Thus the Revised Version puts it like this: "If he be pleased to contend with him,
he cannot answer him one of a thousand" (9.3, RV). By contrast, the English
Standard Version, along with Delitzsch's commentary, takes the view that the
first "he" is a man who daringly chooses to enter into debate with God only to
find himself overawed by God"s majesty: "If one wished to contend with him,
one could not answer him once in a thousand times" (9.3, ESV). The hyperbole
serves to emphasise the sheer impossibility of replying to God. And this is Job's
problem. In the book's great climax Jehovah will in fact bombard the patriarch
with question upon question about creation and providence, all of which he will
find totally beyond his ability to handle.

In one sense it matters little which reading of verse 3 is correct because
the basic meaning is transparent: it is impossible for any man successfully to
challenge or confute the living God of the universe. Since Job is going to reiterate
his conviction that he is the innocent victim of divine hostility, the second
interpretation is perhaps the more attractive. Job longs to approach God and

get Him to explain precisely why He has inflicted such apparently unjustified sufferings on His servant. But he knows deep down that he cannot debate with his Creator on equal terms:

> How much less shall I answer him, and choose out my words to reason with him? (9.14).

> If I justify myself, mine own mouth shall condemn me: if I say, I am perfect, it shall also prove me perverse (9.20).

> For he is not a man, as I am, that I should answer him, and we should come together in judgment (9.32).

It is this deep-rooted persuasion which leads him eventually to cry out for a go-between, a mediator who can "lay his hand upon us both" (9.33), a burning desire which constitutes one of the great high-spots of the speech.

The introductory verses also betray something of the irreverent tone of Job's reply – ironic, bitter, resentful. Simply because of His power God cannot be taken to task or out-argued.

God's Invincibility: 9.4-10

The key idea of this section is posed as a question at the close of verse 4 – "who hath hardened himself against him, and hath prospered?" – with the evidence for God's supremacy adduced in verses 5 to 10. Job is thinking back to his rueful admission that no one can take up a case against God and win. No one can harden himself against God and succeed; Pharaoh certainly did not, even though Scripture reveals that the hardening was instigated by God (Ex 7.3).

Job starts off with a summary of God's unique greatness: He is "wise in heart, and mighty in strength" (9.4). Eliphaz and Bildad both affirmed His power, but Job introduces a new attribute, wisdom. Eliphaz to some extent implied it in his speech (5.13), but Job now brings it to the fore. The word (2450) is used to describe Bezaleel and Aholiab in their tabernacle work (Ex 36.1), the expert artificers involved in the construction of Solomon's temple (2 Chr 2.7), and that vital moral understanding celebrated in the Old Testament wisdom books such as Proverbs and Ecclesiastes (Prov 10.1).

The God of the Bible is impeccable in all His excellencies. His power is unassailable and His wisdom unsurpassable, colouring all His actions, for everything He elects to do is done in wisdom (Prov 8.23-31). At this stage in his spiritual education Job cannot comprehend that God's wisdom may have purposes in affliction which are beyond his understanding. But we who live on this side of the cross have a more privileged and informed perspective. Because all God's ways are wise, believers can afford to lean on His arms knowing that His plan for them must be right. He makes no mistakes. With the coming of the incarnate Son, God has been manifest as never before, because the Lord Jesus is the embodiment of divine wisdom. In His earthly life not only did He work astounding miracles of power, He answered all the tricky questions of men with unflappable serenity and consummate astuteness. As Paul puts it, "unto them which are called, both Jews and Greeks, Christ [is] the power of God, and the wisdom of God" (1 Cor 1.24). Job speaks about divine wisdom and might, but in Christ they are seen perfectly to unite.

Job's demonstration of God's power and wisdom consists of a brief survey of His creative majesty. He overturns mountains in volcanic eruptions, He causes earthquakes, He blots out the sun and stars, either through the clouds of ash accompanying such phenomena or through celestial eclipses (9.5-7). Job, as we have noted before, has that healthy Old Testament mind-set which, by-passing secondary causes, credits all "natural" events to the God of nature. As Delitzsch rightly comments, "Scripture nowhere attempts an analysis of the workings of nature, but only traces them back to their final cause".[112] I call this viewpoint "healthy" because, for the Christian believer, it is of the greatest comfort to know that all the forces of this universe are controlled by the God who gave His Son to death for the sake of His people. What befalls the saints, and what befalls the world, is not merely of God's passive allowance (as though He were standing back from His creation and letting calamities occur willy-nilly) but of His action. In his robust *Letter from a Christian Citizen*, Wilson takes the same line. This is how he responds to atheist Sam Harris's query as to where God was when in 2005 hurricane Katrina wrecked the city of New Orleans:

> You ask, "What was God doing while Katrina laid waste to their city?" Well, to give the biblical answer, during Katrina, *God* was laying waste to the city. This is something even insurance companies know; it was an act of God. He is not an absentee deity; scriptural Christians do not feel in the least bit apologetic about how God governs the world. What He did to New Orleans was holy, righteous, just and good.

He goes on to note that some believers appear to be so embarrassed by such an all-powerful deity that they try, in his phrase, to un-god God:

> and they call their explanation "the openness of God". God troubleshoots as we go, but He actually does not do it very well. In this view, God reacts to disasters as they happen, but His reflexes are pretty poor. He runs after disasters, wringing His hands.[113]

Nothing could be more unlike the God of the Bible. God intervenes in judgment as it pleases Him yet, in all these matters and more, for His saints it can be said that "all things [good things and bad things] work together for good" (Rom 8.28). Job did not, as we do, have access to the full disclosure of God's heart in the Lord Jesus Christ, but he will not surrender what he does know: God is always God.

The next few verses appear to cock an eye back to God's original creative activity in Genesis (9.8-10) rather than His current providential government of the universe. The parallel passages certainly suggest this (Is 40.22; 44.24). But the two doctrines are indissolubly related: He who created also conserves. This is also the teaching of the New Testament, which clearly reveals the Lord Jesus as both Creator and upholder of all things:

> For by him were all things created, that are in heaven, and that are in earth, visible and invisible, whether they be thrones, or dominions, or principalities, or powers: all things were created by him, and for him: And he is before all things, and by him all things consist [hold together]" (Col 1.16-17).

> [God] hath in these last days spoken unto us by his Son, whom he hath appointed heir of all things, by whom also he made the worlds; Who being the brightness of his glory, and the express image of his person, and upholding all things by the word of his power ... (Heb 1.2-3).

It is God who spread out the heavens "as a curtain" (Is 40.22), and trampled triumphantly upon the watery ridges of the sea, restricting it to its place and saying, "Hitherto shalt thou come, but no further: and here shall thy proud waves be stayed" (Job 38.11). The *Jamieson, Fausset and Brown Commentary* interestingly informs us that the Egyptian hieroglyphic for impossibility is a man walking on waves. But on Lake Galilee the incarnate Son did just that, for when the Lord Jesus Christ saw His disciples in difficulties, "about the fourth watch of the night he cometh unto them, walking upon the sea" (Mk 6.48). His miracle proved His deity.

Job then lifts his gaze from the oceans into the heights of heaven to consider the multitudes of stars. God made them all, too, in their innumerably varied and beautiful constellations: the Great Bear, Orion, Pleiades (possibly a group of seven stars), and the "chambers of the south", which are "probably the great spaces and deep recesses of the southern hemisphere of the heavens, with the constellations which they contain".[114] The effortless economy of Genesis 1.16 ("he made the stars also") is here expanded to suggest something of the grand immensity of space.

Job's summary is a testimony to the awesomeness of a God who "doeth great things past finding out; yea, and wonders without number" (9.10). "Past finding out" is the expression used in David's special psalm of praise: "Great is the Lord, and greatly to be praised; and his greatness is unsearchable" (Ps 145.3). It occurs again when Isaiah admits the inability of man to probe the mind of God:

> Hast thou not known? hast thou not heard, that the everlasting God, the Lord, the Creator of the ends of the earth, fainteth not, neither is weary? there is no searching of his understanding (Is 40.28).

"Wonders [6381] without number" captures both the mind-numbing power of One who can do the impossible (the word for "wonder" appears first in Genesis

18.14, translated "too hard", and last in Zechariah 8.6, rendered "marvellous"), and His capacity to do it time and time again. It is not surprising that, years later, David has to confess that "the heavens declare the glory of God; and the firmament sheweth his handywork" (Ps 19.1). Just to observe the heavens is to glimpse the skirts of Omnipotence.

Job, however, is not composing a psalm of praise – indeed, his argument is fast moving towards an indictment of what he considers God's unfairness towards him – yet his words must prompt the Christian reader to worship. Our God is infinitely great, powerful, wise and glorious. The psalmist so often appeals to His creatorial and providential majesty as a reason for adoration:

> For I know that the Lord is great, and that our Lord is above all gods. Whatsoever the Lord pleased, that did he in heaven, and in earth, in the seas, and all deep places. He causeth the vapours to ascend from the ends of the earth; he maketh lightnings for the rain; he bringeth the wind out of his treasuries (Ps 135.5-7).

There is always good cause to praise the Lord.

Job's Impotence: 9.11-16

God is invincible. But this truth fills Job not with thanksgiving but with bitter frustration because he simply cannot comprehend what God is currently doing with him. Nor can he find any answers. The negative language of human inability packs this section:

> I see him not ... I perceive him not ... who can hinder him? who will say unto him, What doest thou? ... How much less shall I answer him, and choose out my words to reason with him? ... yet would I not believe that he had hearkened unto my voice (9.11-16).

God, by contrast, is active, invisible and unstoppable. As Job complains, He "goeth by me", He "passeth on", and He "taketh away" (9.11-12). Everything of Job's He has removed, yet no one can challenge His actions. Daniel later uses similar language in his statement of divine authority, whether in the realm of heavenly power or human politics:

> all the inhabitants of the earth are reputed as nothing: and he doeth according to his will in the army of heaven, and among the inhabitants of the earth: and none can stay his hand, or say unto him, What doest thou? (Dan 4.35).

However, what for the exiled prophet was a profound solace was for the bereaved patriarch a festering sore. God, it seemed, was implacably set against him, and Job could neither see Him nor get in touch with Him for any kind of redress.

Verse 13 involves the strange use of what sounds like mythological language. Job has already referred to pagan magicians who stir up leviathan (3.8), that supposed monster of the deep who represents the enemies of Jehovah. Here he alludes to *Rahab*. Because God "will not withdraw his anger; the helpers of Rahab do stoop under him" (9.13, RV). Delitzsch offers an extended explanation:

> from Ps 89.10 and Is 51.9, it is evident that *Rahab* properly denotes a sea-monster, which has become the symbol of Egypt, like *tannin* and *leviathan* elsewhere. This signification of the word is also supported by Job 26.12 … It is not clear whether these "sea-monsters" denote rebels cast down into the sea beneath the sky, or chained upon the sky; but at any rate the consciousness of a distinct mythological meaning … is expressed by this translation … Job compares himself, the feeble one, to these mythical titanic powers in Job 9.14…. how much less can I, the feeble one, dispute with Him![115]

Rahab appears in several Old Testament texts outside of Job: Psalm 87.4; 89.10; Isaiah 30.7 and 51.9-10. In Psalm 87.4 and Isaiah 30.7 (translated "strength" in the KJV) the word seems to describe the pride of Egypt. The other references, however, picture a cosmic monster whom we may identity with Satan, the archetypal source of all creaturely pride and resentment of Jehovah's majesty. This should not surprise us. Other passages similarly shadow the satanic malice lurking behind individual men. In Isaiah 14.12-15 the king of Babylon is pictured in language which looks beyond him to a greater underlying source of arrogance and hatred of God. In Ezekiel 28.12-17 the prince of Tyre again reflects something of the devilish instigator of his crimes. In Job, then, we may see *Rahab* as a monstrous being who represents every kind of anti-God rebellion. Hartley summarises it well:

> Rahab is one of the monsters along with Leviathan (see 3.8; 41.1-34) and Tannin (see 7.12; 30.29) … who were thought to inhabit the depths of the sea. By reason of their role in the myths of Israel's neighbours, in the OT these creatures symbolize the forces of chaos in opposition to God.[116]

Job's meaning is therefore this: if the strongest opposition (Satan himself) has ultimately to bow before God, overwhelmed by His all-glorious greatness, what little can a frail mortal hope to do even in choosing suitable words with which to make a case before Him (9.13-14)?

Job is forced to admit his utter helplessness. Deep down he is conscious of no specific sin in his life, but even that conviction of innocence (and it is one which he will retain until he meets the Lord at the close of the book) avails nothing. In the presence of such a God what can he do but retreat, covered with confusion? Let us imagine Job somehow managed to summon the great God of the universe to a judicial hearing about his grievance, and God actually answered that summons. Job would still find it impossible to believe God was treating him seriously, or taking the slightest notice of him (9.15-16). Even genuine innocence would wither into an admission of guilt before such a judge. Now, all this is Job's way of reaffirming his personal blamelessness while simultaneously insisting that it is impossible for any man to frame a case before so awesome and unapproachable a God. The reader will note that, when later in the book God answers his repeated requests for an audience, this language will be proved true. The upright man against whom no charge could be brought will voluntarily prostrate himself in the dust, fully conscious for the first time that he has spoken ill-advisedly.

God's Injustice: 9.17-24

We now reach the heart of the matter. Job has been uneasily dodging round it for a while, dropping hints here and there about the consequences of God's irresistible strength, His unaccountability, His awesomeness, but not quite daring to accuse Him of wrongdoing. Now he comes out and says it. God has afflicted him "without cause", filled him "with bitterness", and (as a conclusive rebuttal of Bildad's doctrine of divine justice) is a God who "destroyeth the perfect and the wicked" (9.22). That is to say, God makes no distinction between good and bad, but ruins each alike.

It is a staggering accusation. Few of us would dare directly charge God with injustice, but perhaps we might at times, in the secrecy of our own souls, be tempted to use the lesser word, unfairness. It is a fallen human characteristic to compare our circumstances unfavourably with those of others and grow resentful. The impoverished believer thinks it unfair he wasn't born with a silver spoon in his mouth. The believer who is (to use the jargon of political correctness) vertically challenged thinks it unfair he isn't taller. The man with one ear wishes he had two. The bachelor wishes God had given him a wife. The married man perhaps wishes He hadn't. It's all so deeply unfair. Not one of us has ever faced Job's unique trials, and none of us ever will, but we all know the temptation to complain. In a moment of personal bereavement Jacob cried out, "all these things are against me" (Gen 42.36). Naomi went even further in directly acknowledging God's role in her circumstances, saying that "the hand of the Lord is gone out against me" (Ruth 1.13). Nevertheless it is Job who most eloquently charges God with unrighteousness.

Job first touches on the way God's resources have been marshalled against him. "If I speak of strength, lo, he is strong" (9.19). How strong He is may be seen in the imagery Job employs:

> He, who crusheth me with a tempest, and multiplieth my wounds without cause. He suffereth me not to take my breath, for he filleth me with bitternesses (9.17-18, JND).

"Crush" (7779) translates a rare word which first appears in Genesis 3.16, where it is rendered "bruise". What God was currently doing to Job was what would be done to the seed of the woman when He brought about the final overthrow of the serpent. It is one of those moments in the book suggesting that

Job, in his innocent sufferings, becomes a faint type of the Lord Jesus, the spotless victim upon whom God laid the iniquity of us all (Is 53.6). Job has been battered by a storm. God's control of natural phenomena has already been mentioned (9.5-7), for He uses tempest (8183) and hurricane to accomplish His ends. He has, in fact, quite literally unleashed the forces of nature against Job, as chapter 1 disclosed. Nahum employs the same sort of language to illustrate divine power:

> The Lord is slow to anger, and great in power, and will not at all acquit the wicked: the Lord hath his way in the whirlwind and in the storm [8183], and the clouds are the dust of his feet (Nah 1.3).

Job's wounds (and again the word can be taken perfectly literally) have been multiplied "without cause", as the Lord Himself acknowledged to Satan right at the start (2.3). In contrast to the constant insinuations of his friends, the book repeatedly reminds us of Job's blamelessness despite all that has befallen him. The same language is used of the Messiah, who could say, in the words of David:

> They that hate me without a cause are more than the hairs of mine head: they that would destroy me, being mine enemies wrongfully, are mighty: then I restored that which I took not away (Ps 69.4).

Although he did not know it, in the sovereign design of God Job was entering into something of the experiences of the One who would become the very mediator for whom he so greatly longed.

Yet Job is eaten up with bitterness. The root word is that used by Naomi to describe her penurious condition on returning, with her loyal daughter-in-law, to the land of her nativity (Ruth 1.20). It is also the word employed prophetically to paint repentant Israel's state of mind when they at last recognise their Messiah, "and shall be in bitterness for him, as one that is in bitterness for his firstborn" (Zech 12.10). That final occurrence reminds us that God is wonderfully able, through bitterness, to lead His people into blessing, so that those who pass "through the valley of Baca [weeping] make it a well" (Ps 84.6).

But God is not only supreme over the natural world; He also controls all human systems of justice. After all, is He not the judge of all the earth? "If I speak ... of judgment, who shall set me a time to plead?" (9.19). To whom can Job turn to have his case heard, to be vindicated in front of those friends so unwilling to believe him guiltless? In verses 20-22 Job uses the adjective "perfect" three times as he builds up to an emphatic statement of his own innocence and God's injustice. It is the same word used by the narrator and the Lord to describe Job at the beginning, for the reader is never allowed to forget that Job is, in the relative sense of the word, truly "perfect" or blameless (1.1; 1.8; 2.3). Job is thinking in terms of a legal inquiry in which his case against God (or God's case against him, whatever it may be) can be investigated – but he knows full well, even granted the opportunity to speak and clear himself, that very act would demonstrate his guilt. The language is difficult, but the basic meaning is evident: whatever may happen, the creature will inevitably always be in the wrong. The minute he so much as opens his mouth, he condemns himself. Indeed, "were I perfect, he [God] would prove me perverse" (9.20, JND). "Even though I were in reality completely innocent", confesses Job, "in the event of speaking in the presence of God I would instinctively shrivel up, disown myself and abhor my past life as though I were in fact a guilty man". Job claims that the majesty of Jehovah causes him to "despise [3988]" his life. We shall discover at the end of the book, confronted with the real and not the imagined presence of God, he uses the same word to describe his reaction, but this time without the slightest tinge of irony: "wherefore I abhor [3988] myself, and repent in dust and ashes" (42.6). One of the memorable lessons of the book of Job is that God is irreducibly awesome.

Finally Job comes out with a blanket accusation of God's indifference towards the innocent (9.22-24):

> It is all one; therefore I said, he destroyeth the perfect and the wicked. If the scourge kill suddenly, he mocketh at the trial of the innocent. The earth is given over into the hand of the wicked man; he covereth the faces of its judges. If not, who then is it? (9.22-24, JND).

His point is this. Whether men are upright or wicked, God appears to treat them all the same. He must be completely apathetic towards innocent victims of calamity, for He permits the world to groan under the heel of injustice and oppression. The *Jamieson, Fausset and Brown Commentary* offers this translation and explanation:

> "While [God's] scourge slays suddenly [the wicked, 9.22], He laughs at [disregards; not derides] the pining away of the innocent." The only difference, says Job, between the innocent and guilty is, the latter are slain by a sudden stroke, the former pine away gradually. And since there is no one else who can take the blame for the state of affairs on earth, it must be God Himself who has corrupted judgment.

This translation has the advantage of fitting Job's own situation well – he has not been slain by a stroke, but rather is suffering the long drawn-out misery of chronic pain and loss. In other words, the fate of the innocent man is in fact worse than that of evil men. And as God is supreme over the happenings of this world, so He must be held accountable for the failure of human justice. As Hartley puts it, "Given the fact that injustices exist throughout the land and that there is only one God, one can only conclude that God Himself is the cause of these injustices".[117] John Gill is equally clear:

> this is to be understood of God, who delivers the earth into the hands of the wicked, suffers them to have the rule over it, and permits such things to be done, as already observed; and besides, gives up the judges of the

earth to judicial blindness, so that they cannot discern what is right and just, and do it.

As if in acknowledgment that his hearers might immediately challenge this irreverent thought, he rounds on them with a direct question. "If not, then who is it?" – if God is not ultimately responsible for what goes on down here, then who is?

This is a breath-taking attack on God. We must, of course remember its context. It does not spring from the ordinary conditions of life but from unique depths of dejection. Smick reminds us that

> These are the words of a sick and desperate man. They are a forceful reminder to anyone who has to counsel the sick, that people who face deep trials often say irresponsible things in their struggle to understand their suffering in the light of God's compassion.[118]

Davidson notes that

> In this passage Job's spirit reaches the lowest abyss of its alienation from God. From this time onwards his mind is calmer and the moral idea of God begins to reassert its place in his thoughts.[119]

I am not convinced that Job's mind is demonstrably more serene from this moment onwards, as his thoughts and feelings still fluctuate wildly. Nonetheless, there is a general lowering of the emotional temperature. However, Job's essential point (in response to the contention of his friends) must not be overlooked. Without agreeing with his denunciation of divine injustice – for even Job in his calmer moments will recognise that everything God does is right – we can at least see how it interrogates the neat theology of his comforters. If what he says is correct, no one can judge a man's state of soul merely by his outward circumstances. And in this he is correct.

It is only proper to pause a moment to reassert the biblical doctrine of God's unimpeachable righteousness. Isaiah records one of the clearest statements:

> Tell ye, and bring them near; yea, let them take counsel together: who hath declared this from ancient time? who hath told it from that time? have not I the Lord? and there is no God else beside me; a just God and a Saviour; there is none beside me (Is 45.21).

The prophet teaches God's unparalleled omniscience in His revelation of the future, His uniqueness, His righteousness, and His ability to save. There is no one like Him. Yes, God is in control of this fallen world, superintending the affairs of men in ways we cannot presently comprehend. What seem so often like capricious and even cruel actions will finally be unveiled as the wholly righteous, good and glorious dealings of an unerring God. Perhaps not surprisingly, it is the book of Revelation which especially highlights the rightness of His ways in judgment:

> And I heard the angel of the waters say, Thou art righteous, O Lord, which art, and wast, and shalt be, because thou hast judged thus (Rev 16.5).

> And I heard another out of the altar say, Even so, Lord God Almighty, true and righteous are thy judgments (Rev 16.7).

> For true and righteous are his judgments: for he hath judged the great whore, which did corrupt the earth with her fornication, and hath avenged the blood of his servants at her hand (Rev 19.2).

Job, then, is right in tracing everything to His hand, but wrong in ascribing injustice to Him, for God is always upright. Robinson remarks that

> the nature of the flesh is to put a wrong construction upon God's dealings. The object of Satan is to misrepresent God, as arbitrary, cruel and tyrannical. Hard thoughts of God [are] a special temptation in time of trouble.[120]

Job, let's face it, was going through a greater time of trouble than any of us can imagine. As a result, he cannot yet see the wonderful harmony between God's justice and His saving grace. That will be the argument of Paul's letter to the Romans – that God can remain wholly just and at the same time justify guilty, helpless sinners. Nevertheless, before his story concludes, the protagonist will come to confess that God is without flaw in His ways with men, and with Job in particular.

Job's Impermanence: 9.25-31

Anger gives way to grief. From the blatant injustice which surrounds him Job returns to a pained consciousness of his own mortality. His life on earth is flashing past. This is no mere generalization about human transience, but the confession of a man convinced by sickness and sorrow that he is about to die:

> And my days are swifter than a runner: they flee away, they see no good. They pass by like skiffs of reed; as an eagle that swoops upon the prey (9.25-26, JND).

Like the swift couriers who (in later history) ran bearing official messages throughout the Persian Empire (Esth 3.15), his days flit past empty of profit or joy, bringing him no glad tidings of blessing. Like the light Egyptian skiffs or canoes made out of papyrus which sailed the Nile (Is 18.2), his life speeds by. The suddenly down-swooping eagle which descends on its hapless victim reminds him that his life is liable at any moment to be snatched away. Job chooses the fastest movers on earth, sea and sky to suggest the terrible brevity of his blighted existence as it hurtles pell-mell to its close.

Perhaps at that instant he reads in the expression of his friends the unbelievably insensitive hint that he really ought to pull himself together and put a brave face on things:

> If I say, I will forget my complaint, I will leave off my sad countenance, and brighten up, I am afraid of all my sorrows [6094]; I know that thou wilt not hold me innocent (9.27-28, JND).

The wounded and the broken-hearted cannot cheer up at the flick of a switch. God alone can meet their needs by His grace. At this point in the text Delitzsch draws our attention to the significant fact that Job is now addressing God: "Job does not speak of God without at the same time looking up to Him as in prayer. Although he feels rejected of God, he still remains true to God".[121] This is one of the greatest testimonies to a durable work of divine grace in Job's soul: throughout all his protracted, inexplicable miseries he keeps speaking to God. Never does he throw in the towel or abandon his faith.

The full testimony of the Old Testament looks ahead to the arrival of a divine Messiah who, in the administration of His perfect Kingdom of righteous and peace, would be able to heal broken-hearted people. What is said of Jehovah in Psalm 147 is fulfilled by the Messiah in Isaiah 61:

> He healeth the broken in heart, and bindeth up their wounds [6094] (Ps 147.3).

> The Spirit of the Lord God is upon me; because the Lord hath anointed me to preach good tidings unto the meek; he hath sent me to bind up the brokenhearted, to proclaim liberty to the captives, and the opening of the prison to them that are bound; To proclaim the acceptable year of the Lord, and the day of vengeance of our God; to comfort all that mourn; To appoint unto them that mourn in Zion, to give unto them beauty for ashes, the oil of joy for mourning, the garment of praise for the spirit of heaviness; that they might be called trees of righteousness, the planting of the Lord, that he might be glorified (Is 61.1-3).

Job's great distress is that he is on the brink of death, yet remains unvindicated by God. All his efforts are a waste of time because God, being infinitely powerful, can simply overrule all protests (9.29-31). He offers a hyperbolical illustration to make his point. Though he were to bathe himself in melted snow, often considered the purest of waters, though he were to wash himself "never so clean", or, more likely, "with lye" (ESV), God would still cast him out as morally foul. The *International Standard Bible Encyclopaedia* tells us that "soda or lye has been used as a cleansing agent from earliest times. It effervesces energetically, when treated with an acid". Jeremiah refers to it as a powerful purifying tool; nevertheless it cannot expunge sin:

> For though thou wash thee with lye, and take thee much soap, yet thine iniquity is marked before me, saith the Lord God (Jer 2.22, RV).

Job is right to imply that human notions of purity cannot satisfy God. What men consider good is utterly polluted in His sight, for "we are all as an unclean thing, and all our righteousnesses are as filthy rags; and we all do fade as a leaf; and our iniquities, like the wind, have taken us away" (Is 64.6). Man at his best is still under condemnation because, as Paul argues in Romans,

> There is none righteous, no, not one: There is none that understandeth, there is none that seeketh after God. They are all gone out of the way, they are together become unprofitable; there is none that doeth good, no, not one (Rom 3.10-12).

But Job is not thinking, like the apostle, in rigorous doctrinal terms. Rather, he is immersed in his own immediate situation. It is as if he is saying, "No matter what I do, God will not go public to admit that I am not being punished for any specific wrongdoing". The accusation of divine injustice still rankles in his mind. The imagery is painfully graphic: though he took bath after bath so as to present himself in sparkling cleanliness, God would simply hurl him into a filthy ditch. God wilfully bespatters him with muck so that his very clothes are disgusted with him. Later he will use the same word "abhor" to describe the revulsion of erstwhile friends and enemies:

> All my inward friends abhorred me: and they whom I loved are turned against me (19.19).

> They abhor me, they flee far from me, and spare not to spit in my face (30.10).

The language describes a man ostracized by the very people from whom he might have expected loyalty and support.

God's Inaccessibility: 9.32-35

But what, for Job, is far more painful than this social opprobrium is that the God he has adored and served seems to have repudiated him. Worse, unlike men, God cannot easily be contacted or appealed to. This provokes an expression of longing which momentarily lifts Job's thoughts beyond his immediate ills:

> For he is not a man, as I am, that I should answer him; that we should come together in judgment. There is not an umpire between us, who should lay his hand upon us both (9.32-33, JND).

Job articulates the unbridgeable gulf between deity and humanity so as to sum up his frustrations. God is God, immense, transcendent, holy, and free from all taint; but Job is a mere man, created, limited, weak, damaged by Adam's sin. How can such radically different beings meet together? As Eli said to his rebellious sons,

> If one man sin against another, the judge shall judge him: but if a man sin against the Lord, who shall intreat for him? (1 Sam 2.25).

Who indeed? What is needed is a go-between, an umpire or arbiter, who can relate to both parties and bring them into restored fellowship. According to Zuck, the Hebrew word (3198) Darby translates "umpire" in Job 9.33 "comes from a verb meaning to argue, reason or convict".[122] It is rendered by a range of words in the KJV, such as "reprove" (Gen 20.16), "judge" (Gen 31.37), "chasten" (2 Sam 7.14), and "reason" (Job 13.3). Writes Hartley:

> An earthly arbiter may resolve an issue between two parties ... he listens to both sides of the controversy and works out a solution that is binding on both of them. Job wishes for such a heavenly umpire, one who could lay his hands on both God and himself and effect a reconciliation.[123]

But Job knows of no such mediator. His spirit cries out instinctively for a provision as yet undisclosed in Scripture.

The poet George Herbert expressed something of this in one of his devotional sonnets, called "Redemption". Like all good poetry, it demands careful reading:

> Having been tenant long to a rich lord,
>   Not thriving, I resolvèd to be bold,
>   And make a suit unto him, to afford
> A new small-rented lease, and cancel th' old.
> In heaven at his manor I him sought;
>   They told me there that he was lately gone
>   About some land, which he had dearly bought
> Long since on earth, to take possessiòn.
> I straight returned, and knowing his great birth,
>   Sought him accordingly in great resorts;
>   In cities, theatres, gardens, parks, and courts;
> At length I heard a ragged noise and mirth
>   Of thieves and murderers; there I him espied,
>   Who straight, *Your suit is granted,* said, and died.[124]

The poem acts as a kind of parable. Wishing, because of a deep consciousness of his own bankruptcy, to get in touch with God and solicit His mercy, the speaker makes his way to heaven where he discovers, to his chagrin, that his Lord has already descended to earth. After fruitless searching he eventually finds

Him in the unlikeliest of locations – a shameful place of execution. Herbert employs the day to day language of seventeenth-century commerce and travel as a striking metaphor for a profound spiritual quest. The poem's narrator is, from the start, ignorant that his Lord has long known his need and provided the remedy.

So too Job cannot know that his cravings will find their satisfaction in Christ; only the New Testament answers his heartfelt cry. First, it tells us that, though man cannot climb into heaven, a divine person has come down to earth to reveal all that God is:

> And no man hath ascended up to heaven, but he that came down from heaven, even the Son of man which is in heaven (Jn 3.13).

Second, that same One has taken on Himself genuine yet sinless manhood without in the least compromising the fullness of His deity:

> And the Word was made flesh, and dwelt among us, (and we beheld his glory, the glory as of the only begotten of the Father,) full of grace and truth (Jn 1.14).

Third, because He unites in His person unabridged deity and perfect humanity, He can, on the basis of His atoning sacrifice, uniquely relate to both parties as the ideal mediator:

> For there is one God, and one mediator between God and men, the man Christ Jesus; Who gave himself a ransom for all, to be testified in due time (1 Tim 2.5-6).

The Christian reader can supply all this information from his superior vantage point, but Job of course has no knowledge of this ideal mediator, and therefore ends the chapter by retreating into his earlier depression.

> Let him take his rod away from me, and let not his fear terrify me: Then would I speak, and not fear him; but it is not so with me (9.34-35).

The "rod" here speaks of divine power and judgment. The same word (7626), first translated "sceptre" in Genesis 49.10, is used most frequently of the tribes of Israel, but returns in the sense of an instrument of discipline and authority in the Psalms (2.9; 23.4; 89.32). Job asks that the heavy hand of divine oppression might be removed from him and the terror of God's majesty withdrawn, so that he might do what he wants to do, and make a case against God's treatment of him. He makes his plea – but there is no miraculous change in his circumstances: the weight of misery still hangs over him as he languishes under God's anger. The contest between an all-powerful God and a puny mortal is so unequal that he finds himself incapable of voicing his objections.

Job's Interrogation: 10.1-22

The subdued, dejected mood with which chapter 9 ended is only passing, because chapter 10 starts with Job bracing himself afresh for desperate action. The first verse needs to be read in a translation more recent than the KJV in order to grasp the idea:

> My soul is weary of my life: I will give free course to my complaint; I will speak in the bitterness of my soul (10.1, JND).

It is as if Job suddenly decides that he is so tired of his miserable life that he may as well blurt out all his frustrations to God regardless of the consequences. "Complaint" (7879) is a common word on his lips (7.13; 9.27; 21.4; 23.2), and sums up his simmering discontent.

The rest of the chapter therefore constitutes a kind of prayer, but what a prayer! It is packed full of queries, seething with irritation, and shaped as a series of direct challenges to God. As is customary in Job's speeches at this stage in the book, it veers erratically between the reverently accurate (10.10-12) and the outspokenly defiant (10.4-5, 16-17). That is why I have entitled the whole section "Job's interrogation", for he audaciously takes it upon himself to question God's character and God's conduct. It is initiated by the phrase, "I will say unto God", so that everything that follows up to verse 22 forms the draft of a proposed address to the Almighty.

It may help to approach the chapter as a series of interrelated questions:

1. Why does God afflict me? 10.2-3
2. Are His actions governed by human limitations? 10.4-7
3. Is He simply going to return me to the dust? 10.8-9
4. Did He create me with the aim of destroying me? 10.10-17
5. Why did He cause me to be born? 10.18-22.

If we contrast this sequence of tortuous demands with the ceremonial parade of avowals of innocence which makes up chapter 31, we can get a sense of the range of moods through which Job passes. Feeling at the end of his tether, he assembles in his mind everything he has ever wished to ask God about his life and his sorrows. Because he is so exasperated, he lets loose with savagely irreverent language, the whole point of which is to get God's attention.

The first question, **Why does God afflict me?** (10.2-3), is one constantly on Job's mind, although his friends have no doubt about the answer. As far as they are concerned Job is suffering because he deserves it. But Job knows this is not the case; therefore for him to raise the matter is a vital necessity. It is noteworthy that he makes no attempt to shuffle off responsibility from God to something or someone else. He does not blame the weather, or hostile tribes, or supernatural enemies. It is God who brings suffering on His servant. However, he pleads that God would not condemn him without explanation. "Condemn" (7561) is a key word in the book, appearing eleven times (9.20,29; 10.2,7,15; 15.6; 32.3; 34.12,17,29; 40.8), and – most importantly – is used finally by God Himself when He asks Job, "Wilt thou also disannul my judgment? wilt thou condemn me, that thou mayest be righteous?" (40.8). Although he does not yet realise it, in his obsession with the supposed injustices done to him, Job is implicitly reproving God.

Feeling so unfairly treated, Job, in his resentment, casts doubt on God's goodness:

> Doth it please thee to oppress, that thou shouldest despise the work of thy hands, and shine upon the counsel of the wicked? (10.3, JND).

To accuse God of vindictiveness is deliberately shocking. The God of the Bible does not oppress (6231), deceive, defraud, or do wrongful violence (the Hebrew word is translated by the KJV in all these ways). Indeed, the teaching of Israel's law is "thou shalt not defraud [6231]" (Lev 19.13), and "thou shalt not oppress [6231]" (Deut 24.14). The Lord takes up the cause of the underdog and "executeth judgment for the oppressed" (Ps 146.7), pledging through the coming messianic King to "break in pieces the oppressor" (Ps 72.4). When Christ reigns in glory all human tyranny will be terminated.

Can it bring God pleasure to turn His back on His own handiwork (specifically, Job), and instead look with favour on wicked men and their evil practices? Does God really find satisfaction in inflicting pain on the good while allowing the bad to prosper? The question "why?" raised in verse 2 is now elaborated in the hypothetical and deliberately hyperbolical suggestion of verse 3, to which the implied answer is "surely not!"

Thinking aloud and scarcely bothering to organise his ideas, Job moves rapidly on to a related question: **Can it be that God's actions, like men's, are affected by ignorance and transience** (10.4-7)?

> Hast thou eyes of flesh? or seest thou as man seeth? Are thy days as the days of man? are thy years as man's days, That thou enquirest after mine iniquity, and searchest after my sin? Thou knowest that I am not wicked; and there is none that can deliver out of thine hand (10.4-7).

With a kind of self-conscious absurdity he engages in theological conjecture. Is it conceivable that the living God sees in the same way men see, judging only on the basis of outward appearance? Job's friends have looked on his terrible condition and from that presumed to read his heart. But God is different. In His infallible knowingness, He is infinitely removed from human limitations of understanding and lack of generous sympathy.

How right he is! This outrageous manner of speech is designed in part to bring his human hearers up with a jerk, for although he is speaking to God he does so audibly in the presence of his critical friends. His speeches therefore have a double audience. The wild speculations of Job can be answered by the clear revelation of Scripture as a whole, which offers an unambiguous response to his question. However ignorant man may be, God is intuitively and infallibly all-knowing. "The ways of man are before the eyes of the Lord, and he pondereth all his goings" (Prov 5.21), for "the eyes of the Lord are in every place, beholding the evil and the good" (Prov 15.3). As Hannah says, "the Lord is a God of knowledge, and by him actions are weighed" (1 Sam 2.3). There are no blinkers on His eyes and no errors in His understanding, because "all things are naked and opened unto the eyes of him with whom we have to do" (Heb 4.13). The believer takes delight in the doctrine of divine omniscience and, like the psalmist, gladly invites God to probe the inmost recesses of the heart so that sin might be detected and purged:

> Search me, O God, and know my heart: try me, and know my thoughts: And see if there be any wicked way in me, and lead me in the way everlasting (Ps 139.23-24).

Just as there are no restrictions to God's knowledge about His creatures, so He is not, like man, under the pressure of fleeting time to accomplish His purposes:

> Are thy days as the days of a mortal? are thy years as a man's days, That thou searchest after mine iniquity, and inquirest into my sin? (10.5-6, JND).

Verse 5 uses two distinct words for "man". The first (translated "mortal" by Darby), suggestive of man in his impermanence and frailty, is used eighteen times in Job; the second, used fifteen times, refers to man in his strength. Either way, pitiful or powerful, men are shackled by time and forced to prosecute their plans with haste lest they act too late. But God, infinite, eternal, all-knowing, gloriously wise, indefatigable, cannot, like His feeble creatures, be at the mercy of such hindrances. Job could understand it if a man had inflicted these sufferings on him to probe his heart, because man is constrained by time and ignorance. But although men may have been used as God's instruments, Job is under no illusions: his distresses sprang ultimately from the Lord. Why then did God's blows fall on him in such rapid succession? God, because He is God, must know, without resorting to such methods of inquisition, that Job was not a wicked man deserving of punishment; and God, because He is God, had no need to batter him with terrible waves of misery as though pushed for time (10.7). Since He is omnipotent, no one could impede Him, for "there is none that can deliver out of thine hand" (10.7).

The language lingers in the mind. Job, understandably, is thinking in terms of deliverance from God's anger (and he is right), but the Christian delights to meditate on another impossibility. The Lord Jesus promised His sheep absolute preservation:

> I give unto them eternal life; and they shall never perish, neither shall any man pluck them out of my hand. My Father, which gave them me, is greater than all; and no man is able to pluck them out of my Father's hand (Jn 10.28-29).

Job felt himself brutally gripped in the hand of God's wrath; believers know themselves safe and secure in the tender hand of Christ"s protective care.

Longfellow wrote of the processes of divine judgment that

> Though the mills of God grind slowly,
> Yet they grind exceeding small;
> Though with patience he stands waiting,
> With exactness grinds he all.[125]

In the course of human history this seems often to be true. Over long stretches of time, evil empires climb to a pinnacle of influence and then slowly collapse into a God-ordained decay; wicked men flourish a while and then succumb to death. One of the functions of the book of Daniel is to record the rise and fall of world powers. But such leisurely progression does not square with Job's experience. In his case, disasters descended on one another's heels, like sudden thunderbolts from a tranquil sky.

Job's point, then, is a simple one: since God is not in any sense hamstrung by the limitations of His creatures, why has He attacked Job with all the urgency we might expect from one who has an eye on the clock?

Allowing no pause either to answer or qualify this question, he rushes on to another. **Is God simply planning to consign me to the dust from which man was originally created** (10.8-9)?

> Thy hands have bound me together [6087] and made me as one [6213], round about; yet dost thou swallow me up! Remember, I beseech thee, that thou hast made me as clay, and wilt bring me into dust again (10.8-9, JND).

The rough hands of divine wrath which clutch Job are the same hands that originally created him. Can it be that the God who fashioned him in the first place now plans to destroy him or, literally, to devour him? The word (1104) is used of the sea swallowing up the Egyptian army (Ex 15.12), and the earth engulfing the rebellious Korah (Num 16.32). Was this God's plan for Job? In calling on God to look on him with favour, his language echoes the Genesis creation account while in context describing the formation of each subsequent generation. Here is Delitzsch's useful comment:

> According to the view of Scripture, a creative act similar to the creation of Adam is repeated at the origin of each individual; and the continuation of development according to natural laws is not less the working of God than the creative planting of the very beginning.[126]

Job, we notice, bypasses the instrumentality of his parents to credit God with his making. This perspective should govern every believer's thinking, for it rightly foregrounds the divine. Job uses an infrequent word which the KJV translates "made" (6087), rendered "framed" in the RV and "bound" by Darby. It appears to derive from a root meaning to carve, fabricate, or stretch into shape. Probably drawing on the fact that the same term is sometimes translated "grieve" (as in Genesis 6.6 and 34.7) the *Jamieson, Fausset and Brown Commentary* glosses the word succinctly as meaning "with pains; implying a work of difficulty and art; applying to God language applicable only to man". The construction of mankind was a divine work of the utmost delicacy and skill.

He couples this with a more common word (6213) which first appears in Genesis 1.7 ("And God made the firmament"). Together with the adverbial clause "together round about", which hints at the remarkable unity of the human body, these terms suggest the marvellous complexity of man, a complexity famously celebrated by the psalmist:

> For thou hast possessed my reins; thou didst cover me in my mother's womb. I will praise thee, for I am fearfully, wonderfully made. Marvellous are thy works; and that my soul knoweth right well. My bones were not hidden from thee when I was made in secret, curiously wrought in the lower parts of the earth. Thine eyes did see my unformed substance, and in thy book all my members were written; during many days were they fashioned, when as yet there was none of them (Ps 139.13-16, JND).

Man was fashioned from the clay and, because of sin, eventually returns to the dust (10.9). "Clay" (2563) first appears in the context of building operations (Genesis 11.3 and Exodus 1.4), where it is rendered "mortar". "Dust" (6080) is found first in Genesis 2.7 and in 3.19 in relation to man's construction and the passing of his death sentence. The psalm which most poignantly testifies to human transience in contrast to the glorious eternality of God reaffirms this truth: "Thou makest mortal man to return to dust, and sayest, Return, children of men" (Ps 90.3, JND). But Job employs this diction in conjunction with a heart-felt appeal that God would "remember" him. That is, he longs for God to act kindly towards him, as He did to Noah (Gen 8.1), and as Joseph asked for practical thoughtfulness from the chief butler (Gen 40.14). It is often the habit of godly men to pray that God would do what in His deity He cannot fail to do – that is, look with grace and mercy upon His needy people. It is no surprise, then, to discover that "remember" is constantly on the lips of the psalmist as he sues for aid. In confessing that he is God's workmanship, Job is appealing to his Creator's tender compassion on the works of His hands.

The next question is really a poetic expansion of its predecessor, putting into words the stark implication that God lavished all that attention on Job with the deliberate intention of destroying him. Here is the sadistic deity beloved of atheistic caricature. Yet the speaker is no godless infidel but a man of tested piety and reverence. That he can be brought to such an utterance shows just how corrosively Job's sorrows have gnawed away at his heart. The question is a searing one: **Did God create me only with the aim of bringing me to ruin** (10.10-17)?

> Hast thou not poured me out as milk, and curdled me like cheese? Thou hast clothed me with skin and flesh, and knit me together with bones and

sinews; Thou hast granted me life and favour, and thy care hath preserved my spirit; And these things didst thou hide in thy heart; I know that this was with thee. If I sinned, thou wouldest mark me, and thou wouldest not acquit me of mine iniquity. If I were wicked, woe unto me! and righteous, I will not lift up my head, being so full of shame, and beholding mine affliction; - And it increaseth: thou huntest me as a fierce lion; and ever again thou shewest thy marvellous power upon me. Thou renewest thy witnesses before me and increasest thy displeasure against me; successions of evil and a time of toil are with me (10.10-17, JND).

Part of the unsettling impact of this disturbing passage is the sudden shift from cosy tenderness to the nightmare vision of a Creator who delights in destruction. The superb precision of Job's initial language, its descriptive power, the awe-struck reverence with which he traces every aspect of the human body to God's fingers, makes the first few verses both memorable and moving. Job's account of the way a baby is made is astonishing. Each tiny detail of his formation in the womb was a divine action: it was God who poured, curdled, clothed, knit together, favoured and preserved the patriarch. Exquisite craftsmanship combined with personal attention to detail constitutes the keynote of the poetic vocabulary. The moulding of the human body, the breathing of life into that body, the gracious divine provision for every daily need ("thy care hath preserved my spirit") all remind the reader of the Genesis creation narrative. Job presents himself as one both framed and favoured by God. He even uses that word which in the Old Testament is so often associated with Jehovah's special covenant goodness towards Israel. "Favour" (2617) translates the term elsewhere rendered "mercy" (Gen 19.19), "kindness" (Gen 20.13) and "lovingkindness" (Ps 17.7; 25.6; 36.7). Every believer can appropriate this language, knowing that he is physically formed, providentially sustained, and spiritually blessed by God. All the good things we enjoy come from His hand.

But so, says Job, do the bad. Three wonderful verses witness to God's benign involvement in Job's life (10.10-12). Thereafter, one verse fires an explosive salvo into all the heartening implications of love, gentleness, and skilled craftsmanship, by hinting that, even as He shaped Job, God secretly had in mind the savage afflictions He planned to unleash on him (10.13). The meaning of verse 13 is not too obvious in the KJV, but the ESV makes it clearer: "Yet these things you hid in your heart; I know that this was your purpose" (10.13, ESV). Hartley expounds the point:

> Job imagines that God must have been his foe from the start. During the days of Job's prosperity, when he thought that God was showing him love in giving him an abundant life, God had hid in His heart the trials that He was going to bring against Job.[127]

All God's ways with Job – in creation, preservation, and present affliction – were bound up in His eternal counsels. For Job, the whole idea is stupefying.

The way he expresses it is designed to make God seem some kind of monster who wilfully smashes what He has made. But Job only blurts out such bitter accusations because grief has beclouded his vision and distorted his judgment. These are the things he claims he would say to God, given the opportunity. But when in chapter 42 the opportunity is granted, his actual words are entirely different. Bodily and mental pain can savagely undermine our peace of soul; but a glimpse of God adjusts our perspective. It is of the greatest encouragement to sorely tried saints to know that, "Like as a father pitieth his children, so the Lord pitieth them that fear him. For he knoweth our frame; he remembereth that we are dust" (Ps 103.13-14). If no one else understands the sorrows believers endure, we can be certain that our God does.

Now, in terms of total biblical revelation, Job cannot be faulted in what he says – save that he has seriously misjudged the divine motivation. Jeremiah went through a similar torment of mind as he watched the sufferings and endured the hatred of his fellow citizens in besieged Jerusalem. However, he eventually reached a faith-based conclusion. God, he knew, was the author of Judah's well-deserved calamities. Nevertheless, "though he cause grief, yet will he have compassion according to the multitude of his mercies. For he doth not afflict willingly nor grieve the children of men" (Lam 3.32-33). Jehovah chastised rebellious Judah with the aim in view of their restoration to Himself. Jehovah brought sorrow upon sorrow on His faithful servant Job with a view to an equally glorious end – that Job would be blessed even more wonderfully than in the past, not only with restored well-being but with a new appreciation of Himself. All this – and more – was hidden in God's heart.

Christian believers rejoice that they were individually chosen in Christ

> ... before the foundation of the world, that we should be holy and without blame before him in love: Having predestinated us unto the adoption of children by Jesus Christ to himself, according to the good pleasure of his will, To the praise of the glory of his grace, wherein he hath made us accepted in the beloved (Eph 1.4-6).

Part of God's gracious plan for His people involves a spiritual toughening up in what people have come to call the school of suffering (which might also be termed the college of calamity or the academy of affliction). However we describe it, the fact remains: God's training programme necessitates that we pass through adversity. The precise details for each individual believer (and they will vary according to the divine wisdom) are hidden in His heart; the basic principle, however, is spelt out in Scripture, which informs us that "through many tribulations we must enter into the kingdom of God" (Acts 14.22, RV).

Job goes on:

> If I sin, then thou markest me, and thou wilt not acquit me from mine iniquity. If I be wicked, woe unto me; and if I be righteous, yet shall I not lift up my head; being filled with ignominy and looking upon mine

affliction. And if my head exalt itself, thou huntest me as a lion: and again thou shewest thyself marvelous upon me. Thou renewest thy witnesses against me, and increasest thine indignation upon me; changes and warfare are with me (10.14-17, RV).

Whichever way he turns and however he behaves, He is trapped. If he sins, there can be no escape because God is constantly (and, Job assumes, disapprovingly) scrutinizing him. "Markest" (8104) translates a word elsewhere in Job rendered "lookest narrowly" (13.27) and "watch" (14.16). It means (according to Brown, Driver and Briggs) "to keep, guard, observe, give heed". His sins (and he uses three distinct words: sin, iniquity, and wickedness) will inevitably be detected and punished. If, on the other hand, he were deemed comparatively righteous, he still would not dare hold up his head like an innocent man. The instinctive honesty of Job's soul is revealed in the way he presents the two moral possibilities: in terms of descriptive detail the balance is tipped in favour of wickedness. That is to say, Job, like all genuine believers, has an intuitive awareness of his own indwelling sin. He says more about that than about his innocence. Even a man who, throughout the debate, has insisted that he is not guilty of any behaviour to account for his current sufferings, knows deep down that he is a sinner.

Something of the dreadful wretchedness he feels spills out in his next words. The KJV translates "I am full of confusion"; but the word (7036) is normally rendered "shame" (Ps 83.16), "dishonour" (Prov 6.33), "ignominy" (Prov 18.3), or "reproach" (Prov 22.10). For all his conviction of innocence, Job is covered with humiliation, conscious that his affliction seems to bear incontrovertible witness to his guilt. No wonder he is downcast. If, contrary to what he has said in verse 15, he were to lift up his head boldly (which is what the first phrase in verse 16 appears to mean), then God would hunt him down like a lion that catches then toys with its prey, inventing new ways of tormenting its victim.

Readers of English poetry will recognise the source of the imagery in one of the Roman Catholic Gerard Manley Hopkins's unconventional sonnets. The searing language of "Carrion Comfort" draws on Job's terrifying emblem of the ferocious lion to express the poet's sense that God, infinite and inescapable, has turned against him:

But ah, but O thou terrible, why wouldst thou rude on me
Thy wring-world right foot rock? lay a lionlimb against me? scan
With darksome devouring eyes my bruisèd bones? and fan,
O in turns of tempest, me heaped there; me frantic to avoid thee and flee?[128]

The simile expands upon the stomach-churning thought of verse 13 – that God has always had his destruction in view. But the unexpected animal imagery takes the concept even further: God actively and cruelly sports with the objects of His wrath. The idea is horrifying.

We have to ask ourselves, is God *really* like a lion? At times He is. The same word (7826) is used in Hosea to describe Jehovah's solemn judgmental dealings with His disobedient people:

> For I will be unto Ephraim as a lion, and as a young lion to the house of Judah: I, even I, will tear and go away; I will take away, and none shall rescue him (Hosea 5.14).

> Therefore I will be unto them as a lion: as a leopard by the way will I observe them (Hosea 13.7).

There can be no doubting the genuineness of God's anger against sin and His disciplinary actions towards His people in both Testaments. Job's imagery may bring us up with a start, but it is a healthy reminder that the God of the Bible is terrible, and rightly to be feared.

The speaker's final outcry in this paragraph (10.17) is a baffled protest against the way his perpetual miseries batter him, like damning proofs of guilt. The KJV ("Thou renewest thy witnesses against me, and increasest thine indignation upon me; changes and war are against me") is best supplemented by other translations. Each new affliction is like yet another witness that God brings into the courtroom to testify to all and sundry that Job – despite all his denials – is a wicked man. They come unceasingly, these evidences of divine anger, like the relentless advance of hostile warriors. Delitzsch's translation, though unidiomatic, makes the point:

> Thou wouldst ever bring fresh witnesses against me,
> And increase Thy wrath against me,
> I should be compelled to withstand continuously advancing troops and a host.[129]

Beset on all sides – by God, by multiple afflictions, by men, through the unsympathetic reproaches of his friends – Job feels himself the abject victim of oppression.

His final query spells out the frightening depression of his current mood: **Why did God cause me to be born?**

> And wherefore didst thou bring me forth out of the womb? I had expired, and no eye had seen me. I should be as though I had not been; I should have been carried from the womb to the grave. Are not my days few? cease then and let me alone, that I may revive a little, Before I go, and never to return, - to the land of darkness and the shadow of death; A land of gloom, as darkness itself; of the shadow of death, without any order, where the light is as thick darkness (10.18-22, JND).

His emotions have reverted to the black misery of chapter 3, with its plaintive desire that he had never seen daylight. So low is Job's mood that he considers it would have been better had he died at the moment of birth, transported instantly from womb to tomb. In any case, his life, he is convinced, must be drawing rapidly to its close. He therefore appeals to God to allow him one last breathing space in which to "take comfort a little". Apart from the present example, the word for "take comfort" (1082) is found only three times in the Bible (Job 9.27; Ps 39.13; Amos 5.9). In the Psalm, the KJV translates it "recover strength", which suits the context of Job: he longs for a brief revival of energy before passing away. He is in no doubt about his destination – the place of the dead, the dread region of darkness.

The use of four distinct words for darkness in verses 21-22 has a double function: it emphasises the inescapable gloom of *sheol*, the place of the departed, as well as expressing the present condition of Job's soul. *Sheol* is "the land of darkness [2822] and the shadow of death [6757]; A land of darkness [5890], as darkness [652] itself; and of the shadow of death [6757], without any order, and where the light is as darkness [652]" (10.21-22). The first word is a common one, used in Genesis 1.2; the second, "the shadow of death", is found ten times in Job, but most memorably in Psalm 23.4; the third is used elsewhere only in Amos 4.13; the fourth (another favourite of this book, appearing six times) suggests dusk and obscurity. Alongside these synonyms we find, as noted earlier, a unique term for arrangement and orderliness which is prefixed by a negative: *sheol* is a frightening world of disorder.

This accumulation of synonyms tells us far more about Job's dejected mood than about the Old Testament place of departed spirits. In any case, he is not promulgating doctrine but unburdening his soul. At this stage in the book his mind is so wrenched by his multiple sorrows that his mental processes have become almost deranged. Can we blame him? According to Delitzsch, the sixteenth century scholar Jerome Weller, who wrote on the first twelve chapters of Job, maintained that "An expositor of Job … must have lain on the same bed of sickness as Job, and have tasted in some measure the bitter experience of Job".[130] Since none of us can be said to have done this, we must treat his unique sighs and tears with due humility. Only God knows what any of us might have said and done in similar circumstances.

Let us sum up what we may learn from this section of Job, which is as difficult as it is disturbing.

First, we are confronted by the essential **frailty of man**. It is a sobering lesson. Even the best of men, under extreme pressure, can give way to wrong and resentful thoughts about his Creator. The flesh, by its very nature, is at constant war against God. That is why every believer at times finds himself engaged in bitter internal struggles, digging in his heels, straining at the leash, wilfully resisting God's Word and God's ways with him. It was even the experience of Paul:

> For I know that in me (that is, in my flesh,) dwelleth no good thing: for to will is present with me; but how to perform that which is good I find not. For the good that I would I do not: but the evil which I would not, that I do (Rom 7.18-19).

Under the almost unendurable strain of physical, emotional and spiritual trauma, Job gives voice to thoughts that flash through every believer's mind in times of deep trial, but which he normally supresses, knowing that they are the rebellious murmurings of the flesh.

Our pains may be less than Job's, and we possess by grace a resource denied to him. Purely because of our historical circumstances, we look back to Calvary's finished work and say of God, with Horatius Bonar:

> He spared not His Son!
> 'Tis this that silences each rising fear,
> 'Tis this that bids the hard thought disappear;
> He spared not His Son!

What is the abiding proof of God's love for His own? Calvary. What is the saint's sure recourse when his feelings are so over-clouded by present difficulties that he can scarcely join up words to stammer out a prayer? Calvary. Paul condenses it into one verse: "God commendeth his love toward us, in that, while we were yet sinners, Christ died for us" (Rom 5.8). The flesh is weak; but in Christ we have an infinitely powerful Saviour.

Second, we note the astonishingly uncensored **honesty of Scripture**, which faithfully registers the failings of its heroes. A human writer would have been tempted, for the sake of reverence, to edit out, or at least tone down, some of the more outrageous of Job's complaints. But the inspired Word, which faithfully chronicles Moses's fit of temper, David's adultery, Elijah's suicidal depression, and Peter's repeated denials, records them for our learning. These were men of passions like our own. From their struggles we can take heart, because Scripture deals not with ciphers or automata but with real people in the thick of real problems.

Third, we trace the marvellous **strategy of God** in permitting Job, amidst his grumbles and gripes, to voice a desire for the mediator it was God's eternal purpose to provide. In the well-chosen expression of Parsons, "Although Job did not realise it, he was sighing for Christ".[131] If we forget all else, we should make sure Job's words burn into our minds: "There is not an umpire between us, who should lay his hand upon us both" (9.33, JND). While the expression is grammatically negative ("There is not"), testifying to Job"s despondency, the aspiration is positive in its careful definition of what Job knew he needed: an umpire, a mediator, a go-between who could lay his hand on both parties, God and man, in order to draw them into reconciliation. This, in the person of Christ, has been achieved so that all sinners may have access by faith to the living God.

SECTION 8
Dialogue: Job 4 – 42.6
Contest: Round 1: Job 4-14
Zophar's 1st Speech: Job 11

The third and final of Job's three visitors now adds his pennyworth to the debate. Zophar the Naamathite is, if anything, even terser and tetchier than Bildad. Perhaps he is the youngest of the group because he speaks last. He gives the impression that he has been impatiently straining at the leash while silently listening to Job's complaints and protestations. Unlike Eliphaz, he does not ground his statements on a mysterious (and dubious) revelation, nor does he, like Bildad, rely on hoary tradition. Instead, he applies what might be called a crude reasoning process: Job has been battered, therefore Job has been bad. It is in essence the same theory espoused by all the debaters, but Zophar does not even attempt to verify its correctness. He simply assumes it must be right. No other possibility seems to occur to his small mind. As a character remarks in Dorothy L Sayers's detective novel *Whose Body?*, "there's nothing you can't prove if your outlook is only sufficiently limited". He is the most impetuous and curt of the three, sallying forth into verbal battle with a man whom he considers to be suffering far less than his sins deserve (11.6). Zophar does not mince matters in the least: there is not the slightest trace of restraint, courtesy, or sympathy in his voice. Far from applying soothing oil to Job's wounded spirit, he liberally pours in vinegar. His brief argument divides into three sections:

> 1. Job's Speech: 11.1-6
> 2. God's Supremacy: 11.7-12
> 3. Zophar's Solution: 11.13-20.

Job's Speech: 11.1-6

Like his colleague Bildad, Zophar's first line of attack is not Job's subject matter but his manner of speaking. A man who could give vent to such a "multitude of words", and be so "full of talk" must not be allowed to go answered (11.2). It is true that Job has much to say (his last speech consisted of fifty-seven verses), but then he has had much to suffer. The Lord Jesus taught that what is in our hearts will inevitably shape our speech:

> A good man out of the good treasure of his heart bringeth forth that which is good; and an evil man out of the evil treasure of his heart bringeth forth that which is evil: for of the abundance of the heart his mouth speaketh (Lk 6.45).

Job, we know, is a good man whose heart has been bruised beyond comprehension and whose words are therefore full of anguish. None of his friends seem sensitive to the extreme tenderness of his mind and body. These callous comforters stand in Scripture as a permanent reminder of the need for genuine sympathy when dealing with the distressed. According to Zophar, Job is guilty of speaking "lies" and indulging in mockery (picking up the same word Job daringly uses when in 9.23 he charges God with cynical indifference to the afflictions of the innocent), and therefore must be quickly put to shame lest he encourage others in irreverence (11.3). But not only is his form of speech worthy of censure because it goes on so long, so too is his content, for he has claimed to be without fault: "For thou hast said, My doctrine is pure, and I am clean in thine eyes" (11.4).

It is undeniable that no man is of himself "pure" (2134) in God's eyes. The word reappears in Proverbs where we learn that "All the ways of a man are clean [2134] in his own eyes; but the Lord weigheth the spirits" (Prov 16.2). However well we may think of ourselves – and it is in the nature of fallen man to overlook his own faults – it is God who assesses reality. On the other hand, it is possible in measure to be "clean" (1249) in the sense of being, by grace, right with God. The one qualified to ascend to the hill of the Lord is such a man, possessed of "clean hands, and a pure [1249] heart; who hath not lifted up his soul unto vanity, nor sworn deceitfully" (Ps 24.4).

Zophar's hackles rise at what he judges to be Job's wholly inadmissible assertion of sinlessness. But is that really what Job has been saying? Let's listen again to his own words rather than their reported (and distorted) version:

> If I justify myself, mine own mouth shall condemn me: if I say, I am perfect, it shall also prove me perverse. Though I were perfect, yet would I not know my soul: I would despise my life. This is one thing, therefore I said it, He destroyeth the perfect and the wicked (9.20-22).

> Thou knowest that I am not wicked; and there is none that can deliver out of thine hand (10.7).

Job describes himself both positively and negatively: positively he is prepared to employ the term "perfect", though aware that in the overawing presence of God such a word would freeze on his lips, while negatively he is "not wicked". It is important to recall what has been said before – that the concept of perfection in Scripture can be used in a relative as well as an absolute way. When used of men it is always a relative quality; the consistent testimony of the Bible is that God alone is without spot or flaw in all His attributes. Yet so often, in the Old Testament especially, good men make claims which at first blush sound outrageous. Here, for example, is David:

> Thou hast proved my heart, thou hast visited me by night; thou hast tried me, thou hast found nothing: my thought goeth not beyond my word. Concerning the works of men, by the word of thy lips I have kept from the paths of the violent man. When thou holdest my goings in thy paths, my footsteps slip not (Ps 17.3-5, JND).

This kind of statement is common in David's poetry and, in the words of Davis, it gives "some readers a case of the jitters". Is he not treading on the brink of smug self-satisfaction and pride? Who, save the person of Christ, can possibly claim a spotless track record? The same expositor provides a lucid and logical answer:

> Psalm writers are aware that there is a sense in which no one can stand up to the full blaze of God's scrutiny … But David is playing in a more minor key here. He is not claiming sinlessness but steadfastness; he is not boasting of his perfection but arguing for his consistency; he is saying he has been loyal, not impeccable.[132]

The same applies to Job. He is well aware of indwelling sin (7.21), but also conscious that he has been steadfast in his desire to honour God. Throughout his life he has endeavoured to be upright in the personal, familial and social realms. If we are in any doubt about his conduct or his claim we have only to refer back to the inspired narrative description of a man who "was perfect and upright, and one that feared God, and eschewed evil" (1.1). Zophar's affronted repudiation is therefore mistaken. He is crediting Job with a claim to sinlessness he never makes. What Job has maintained, and will maintain to the end of the debate, is that he has, to the best of his knowledge, done nothing to merit the treatment he has received. As Hartley comments,

> Job holds tenaciously to his innocence … but he prefers the word *tam*, "blameless" [the word translated "perfect" in 1.1 and 9.20-22], a word that means personal integrity more than spotless purity.[133]

Zophar's error should remind us of the need for care when quoting from others, making sure we get our citations correct and understand what they mean before we embark on criticism. The New Testament records examples of people who slipped into the mistake of putting words into others' mouths. The Jewish opponents of the Lord Jesus falsely accused Him of claiming that He would destroy and rebuild their temple (Jn 2.19-21; Mt 26.60-61), while even the disciples misquoted His words to Peter about John's life-span (Jn 21.21-23). The first acted with wilful malice, distorting a prediction of the resurrection, the second with carelessness, but both were wrong.

Zophar goes further. Appalled by what appears to him to be Job's irreverent self-confidence and refusal to confess the sin which must lie at the back of his current situation, he desires God to step in and put Job in his place:

> But oh that God would speak, and open his lips against thee; And that he would shew thee the secrets of wisdom, how that they are the double of what is realised; and know that God passeth by much of thine iniquity! (11.5-6, JND).

The preposition translated "against" does not appear to have a necessarily adversarial meaning. Young's Literal Translation offers a more neutral rendering

("And yet, O that God had spoken! And doth open His lips with thee"), as does the ESV ("But oh, that God would speak and open his lips to you"), although the context indicates that Zophar expects Job to receive divine rebuke rather than support. When God does indeed speak, contrary to all the expectation of the friends, it will be to reprove Eliphaz, Bildad and Zophar.

Job, we know, has increasingly been expressing a similar longing that God would make Himself known, if only to explain His purpose in this extended period of misery. His fevered prayers have raised questions only God can answer. But Zophar is confident he knows what God ought to say to Job – that His wisdom is double that of man, and that Job's sufferings are less than his desert. Once again, as so often with this book, we have to sift the wheat from the chaff. When speaking of divine wisdom Zophar's words are perfectly accurate. Man cannot attain to it. "Secret" (8587) only appears twice elsewhere, once in Job 28.11 (translated "hid") and once in the Psalms: "Shall not God search this out? for he knoweth the secrets [8587] of the heart" (Ps 44.21). God knows the hidden things of the human heart and, in a coming day, will bring them to light (1 Cor 4.5), but man can never plumb the depths of God. Immeasurable, unsearchable, incomprehensible He is in all His actions. This truth is beautifully illustrated in Psalm 147, where it is placed in the context of God's gracious dealings with His people:

> He telleth the number of the stars; he calleth them all by their names. Great is our Lord, and of great power: his understanding is infinite. The Lord lifteth up the meek: he casteth the wicked down to the ground (Ps 147.4-6).

Divine wisdom and omniscience are never mere intellectual attributes. God's understanding is so all-embracing that, without effort, He numbers and knows all the stars, but more importantly, fully comprehends His human creatures so as to distinguish infallibly between the "meek" and the "wicked". Zophar has seriously misjudged Job, but God makes no mistakes. When, at the close of the book, Jehovah intervenes to challenge Job directly, the wisdom of His activities in creation and providence will be one of the means by which He restores Job to a proper state of mind. At the same time, He will raise up this meek and misunderstood man so that his final blessings marvellously exceed what he lost.

In this sense Zophar is correct. God's wisdom so greatly exceeds man's (and Job's) that no one has the competence to take Him to task for His actions. Before His wisdom we simply have to bow in submission and faith. But when he presumes to affirm that Job is receiving less chastisement than he deserves, Zophar steps beyond the bounds of that fallible human knowledge he has already pronounced inadequate. Having placed God's wisdom out of man's reach, he contradicts his own doctrine by daring to diagnose Job's situation. It is a dangerous thing to claim to interpret God's purposes in His dealings with specific men. Unbelieving Israel fell into this trap when it assumed that the sufferings of the Lord Jesus at Calvary were an evidence of divine displeasure:

Surely he hath borne our griefs, and carried our sorrows: yet we did esteem him stricken, smitten of God, and afflicted (Is 53.4).

They had the same outlook as Zophar: a man's outward circumstances are proof of his spiritual state. But Isaiah's language gazes ahead to Israel's future conversion. Speaking from the vantage point of spiritual restoration, repentant Israel will look back aghast to its national misjudgment of Messiah. The first half of the verse documents the reality (Messiah was actually bearing the penalty for His people's sins) while the second half records the nation's blindness (they considered Him to be suffering at the hands of God the consequences of His own wickedness). It is a solemn lesson in the fallibility of human assessment.

God's Supremacy: 11.7-12

Having castigated Job for verbosity, prevarication and presumption, Zophar now expands upon the theme of God's immeasurable wisdom with a view to bringing Job down to earth. God is supreme over all; what then can Job hope to know about Him and the reasons behind His actions? His three-fold challenge ("canst thou?", 11.7-8) anticipates in miniature Jehovah's later series of queries (38.31-35) while of course remaining ignorant of the real reason for God's dealings with His servant. The transcendence of God means that He is, in every excellence, wholly beyond human comprehension. Verse 7 is well-known in the KJV, but more recent translations amplify its implications:

Can you find out the deep things of God? Can you find out the limit of the Almighty? (11.7, ESV).

The idea is one of probing the very nature of what God is. Delitzsch's own rendering is useful:

Canst thou find out the nature of Eloah, and penetrate to the foundation of the existence of the Almighty?

He goes on with this comment:

The nature of God may be sought after, but cannot be found out; and the end of God is unattainable, for He is both the Perfect One ... and the Endless One.[134]

Zophar is not incorrect in saying that God can neither be discovered nor discerned by man. Were that the whole truth, however, we should be in the most miserable of conditions, shut up to perpetual ignorance. But the testimony of Scripture is that God can and does make Himself known to His creatures. Divine self-revelation is an act of grace without which no man could ever know God. First, the physical creation is a standing evidence of His reality, for that which may be known of God is manifest in them; for God hath shewed it unto them. For the invisible things of him from the creation of the world are clearly seen, being understood by the things that are made, even his eternal power and Godhead; so that they are without excuse (Rom 1.19-20).

Second, man's conscience, though damaged by sin, bears witness to a standard of conduct beyond himself against which his actions can be measured:

For when the Gentiles, which have not the law, do by nature the things contained in the law, these, having not the law, are a law unto themselves: Which shew the work of the law written in their hearts, their conscience also bearing witness, and their thoughts the mean while accusing or else excusing one another (Rom 2.14-15).

Third, God has entered historically into unique covenant relationship with one particular nation, Israel, entrusting them with a clearly defined code of conduct which reveals something of His own nature. In a world given over to pagan idolatry, their national life was intended to bear witness to Jehovah's character:

Ye are my witnesses, saith the Lord, and my servant whom I have chosen: that ye may know and believe me, and understand that I am he: before me there was no God formed, neither shall there be after me. I, even I, am the Lord; and beside me there is no saviour (Is 43.10-11).

Fourth, and conclusively, He has unveiled Himself fully and finally in the person of the incarnate Son, in whom "dwelleth all the fulness of the Godhead bodily" (Col 2.9). All that God is, Christ is, for although "No man hath seen God at any time; the only begotten Son … hath declared him " (Jn 1.18).

Zophar's attempt to illustrate God's incomprehensibility is almost bound to make believers think, by contrast, of the New Testament testimony to the boundlessness of God's love in Christ. Here is Zophar:

It is as high as heaven; what canst thou do? deeper than hell [*sheol*]; what canst thou know? The measure thereof is longer than the earth, and broader than the sea (11.8-9).

By contrast, Paul's desire for the saints at Ephesus is

That Christ may dwell in your hearts by faith; that ye, being rooted and grounded in love, May be able to comprehend with all saints what is the breadth, and length, and depth, and height; And to know the love of Christ, which passeth knowledge, that ye might be filled with all the fulness of God (Eph 3.17-19).

Whereas Zophar is trying to convince Job of pitiful ignorance of divine matters, Paul is praying that, as believers come to appreciate the indwelling power of Christ, they might be able to enter the more fully into the infinite riches of His love. Beyond the scope of human knowledge they may be; nonetheless the secrets of God's heart have been laid bare to believers in the person of Christ. It is in the nature of progressive revelation that what is withheld or obscured in the Old Testament is made beautifully plain in Christ Jesus, even though in its magnificence it remains unfathomable.

Zophar is determined to be emphatic. God cannot be understood, nor can anyone hinder Him in the accomplishment of His ends, or escape the all-seeing eye of His omniscience:

> If he pass by, and shut up, and call to judgment, who can hinder him? For he knoweth vain men, and seeth wickedness when man doth not consider it (11.10-11, JND).

The verb the KJV translates "cut off" ("pass by", JND) is a word (2498) it elsewhere renders, for example, "passed" (4.15), "passeth on" (9.11), and "passed away" (9.26). The idea seems to be that as God moves to inspect His creatures, He shuts up the wicked for future judgment, bringing them forth later to the assizes. No one can stay His hand. After all, He knows vain (or lying) men through and through, being fully aware of their wickedness even when they, because of sin-hardened hearts, are scarcely conscious of wrong-doing. Man is not the best judge of his own folly. All this is designed to silence and humiliate Job. If God has, in his present afflictions, imprisoned him with a view to trial, there is nothing he can do about it.

He concludes this part of his argument with a snappy proverbial expression which has exercised the commentators (11.12). Here are a few selective attempts at translation and elucidation:

> For vain man would be wise, though man be born like a wild ass's colt (KJV).

> Yet a senseless man will make bold, though man be born like the foal of a wild ass (JND).

> But a stupid man will get understanding when a wild donkey's colt is born a man! (ESV).

> As it is impossible for a donkey to be sired by a wild ass, so it is impossible for a stubborn person to become truly wise by his own efforts.[135]

For all its awkwardness of expression, the basic idea seems reasonably clear. Man is so empty-headed (the word "vain" here means "hollow", and is so translated in its three other occurrences: Exodus 27.8; 38.7; Jeremiah 52.21) that it is as likely that he will attain wisdom as that a wild ass will give birth to a man. In short, it is impossible. By nature man is incurably foolish. But even so early a book as Job offers a glimmer of light when it tells us later that "the fear of the Lord, that is wisdom; and to depart from evil is understanding" (28.28). Further, to the believer in the Lord Jesus Christ the New Testament offers this encouraging invitation: "If any of you lack wisdom, let him ask of God, that giveth to all men liberally, and upbraideth not; and it shall be given him" (James 1.5). For those willing to admit their ignorance and cast themselves on the Lord there is an offer of enlightenment from the God who delights to instruct His creatures.

Zophar's middle-eastern proverb does not stand in a vacuum; it is the climax of a deliberate and unsubtle attempt to give Job a stiff rap over the knuckles. We need to read it in direct application to its target audience, accompanied by finger-jabbing and (perhaps) sage nods of agreement or even audible "amens" from the others. If Job had been wearing a jacket, Zophar would doubtless have grabbed him by the lapels. As Smick says, Job is being informed that he is "a witless, empty-headed man with as much chance to become wise as a wild donkey has to be born tame".[136] It is not the most comforting of comparisons. As they say, with friends like this, who needs enemies? It is sadly true that oftentimes a believer's greatest sorrows come from the insensitivity of his own brethren. And yet the New Testament local assembly is intended to be a place of mutual support and sustenance, where the saints are to

> consider one another for provoking to love and good works; not forsaking the assembling of ourselves together, as the custom is with some; but encouraging one another, and by so much the more as ye see the day drawing near (Heb 10.24-25, JND).

In such a spiritual environment it is possible to "warn them that are unruly, comfort the feebleminded, support the weak, be patient toward all men" (1 Thess 5.14). Job's friends lack the tender touch. To offer counsel, however correct, without love, and exhortation without grace, will only ratchet up a man's sufferings.

Zophar's Solution: 11.13-20

Zophar moves now into his concluding advice. Job has been foolish in his speech but Zophar has the solution. The course of action he recommends, along with its attendant results, is clearly charted out in the "if ... then" structure of his exhortation. Let us first consider the **conditions** he lays down (11.13-14):

> If thou prepare thy heart and stretch out thy hands toward him, If thou put far away the iniquity which is in thy hand, and let not wrong dwell in thy tents (11.13-14, JND).

Job must repent ("prepare thy heart"), make supplication to God ("stretch out thy hands toward him"), and renounce his sinful ways ("put far away the iniquity which is in thy hand, and let not wrong dwell in thy tents"). He needs to cultivate a prepared heart (11.13a), because Zophar is convinced that he is insincere in his repeated claims to blamelessness. He requires pure hands for his prayers to be heeded (11.13-14), because Zophar believes him guilty of serious iniquity. And he should endeavour to ensure the domestic piety of his household (11.14), for the wholesale slaughter of his children proves, to Zophar's satisfaction, that they must all have been godless.

Allowing for its inevitable lack of New Testament clarity, Zophar and his contemporaries knowing nothing of faith in the finished work of Christ, it would be hard to find fault with this appeal as part of an evangelistic address. It accurately lists the requirements of the sinner: he must change his mind and agree with God's verdict on his helpless condition, turn to the Lord in humble quest of mercy, and be ready for a radical alteration in lifestyle. It parallels Paul's summary of his early preaching when he

shewed first unto them of Damascus, and at Jerusalem, and throughout all the coasts of Judaea, and then to the Gentiles, that they should repent and turn to God, and do works meet for repentance (Acts 26.20).

Repent, turn to God, do suitable works: the sequence is the same. The trouble is that Zophar directs his advice to the wrong audience. He is treating one of God's choicest Old Testament saints as though he were a deep-dyed sinner requiring a preliminary course in the way of salvation. Of course, from the platform it is impossible for a preacher to know everything about the people he addresses. It is therefore as appropriate to include in an evangelistic message some teaching for believers as it is to insert a gospel appeal in a meeting designed primarily for Christians. In its wonderful variety the Word of God is sufficient for any heart in any condition. But Zophar is not speaking to a mixed crowd; he is offering personal counsel to one distressed friend. His willingness to believe the worst about Job suggests a crass lack of understanding, and demonstrates gross presumption in being so dogmatic about the cause of his friend's sufferings.

But what about the beneficial **consequences** which will follow Job's compliance (11.15-19)? Zophar offers an attractive concatenation of blessings. The first is renewed fellowship with God:

For then shalt thou lift up thy face without spot; yea, thou shalt be stedfast, and shalt not fear (11.15).

A downcast face suggests sorrow and estrangement (22.29), but a repentant Job would be able to lift up his countenance in the assured enjoyment of being right with God, secure in contentment of soul. The second blessing is that blissful forgetfulness of past sorrows which is so rarely the lot of man (11.16). The imagery of "waters that pass away" may be intended to make us think of a stream that dries in the hot sun and is forgotten (6.15), or a torrent that once threatened destruction but is now gone. The idea is simple: the danger and distress are past.

In this life pain may cease, but its bitter memory may linger for a long time. One of the brightest blessings of the new heaven and earth is the guarantee that

> God shall wipe away all tears from their eyes; and there shall be no more death, neither sorrow, nor crying, neither shall there be any more pain: for the former things are passed away (Rev 21.4).

Pain will be banished, but so too all sorrow will be obliterated. The third blessing in Zophar's list is emergence from obscurity into the brilliance of divine favour (11.17) so that the contrast will be as dawn to darkness. Zophar's picture language is compelling:

> And life shall arise brighter than noonday; though thou be enshrouded in darkness, thou shalt be as the morning (11.17, JND).

After the spiritual gloom and mental depression which has been his lot, Job will be ushered into a sphere of illumination so dazzling it will outshine the sun at its zenith. His will be the dawn of a new day. Zophar's language anticipates the glowing description of the pathway of the righteous in Proverbs: "But the path of the just is as the shining light, that shineth more and more unto the perfect day" (Prov 4.18).

More, Job will enjoy a new security, free from fear, with no possible threat of another sudden removal of his possessions (11.18-19a). Zophar's phrase, "thou shalt lie down" (11.19), uses the same word (7257) which David employs to describe God's goodness in making him "lie down in green pastures" (Ps 23.2). It is a lovely tableau of serenity, security and satisfaction. Finally, he will be restored to his honourable position of social eminence so that, as in the past, "many shall seek thy favour" (11.19b, JND).

The poignant irony of Zophar's description of blessings awaiting a repentant Job is that it foreshadows the book's conclusion, where Job's prosperity is restored double. But Zophar could never have imagined that he and two other crest-fallen friends would be instructed by God to make suit to Job for his intercession:

> So Eliphaz the Temanite and Bildad the Shuhite and Zophar the Naamathite went, and did according as the Lord commanded them: the Lord also accepted Job. And the Lord turned the captivity of Job, when he prayed for his friends (42.9-10).

They would become in reality the first of the "many [who] shall seek thy favour". The man they so derided would be the means of their reconciliation with a displeased God.

But let us revisit that list of the results of repentance: fellowship with God, forgetfulness of past sorrows, illumination, security, and positive influence among men. Those who today repent and place their faith in Christ Jesus do indeed come right now into such spiritual blessings. By faith we enter a sphere of divine fellowship, for "being justified by faith, we have peace with God through our Lord Jesus Christ: By whom also we have access by faith into this grace wherein we stand" (Rom 5.1-2). We thereby enjoy "fellowship … with the Father, and with his Son Jesus Christ" (1 Jn 1.3). No longer do we live embittered by the failures of the past but, like the apostle, "forgetting those things which are behind, and reaching forth unto those things which are before … press toward the mark for the prize of the high calling of God in Christ Jesus" (Phil 3.13-14). In Christ we have a new understanding of the grand purpose of God, having passed out of ignorance into the light of His revelation. Paul, accosted by the risen Christ accompanied by "a light from heaven, above the brightness of the sun" (Acts 26.13), could pray for believers

> That the God of our Lord Jesus Christ, the Father of glory, may give unto you the spirit of wisdom and revelation in the knowledge of him: The eyes of your understanding being enlightened; that ye may know what is the hope of his calling, and what the riches of the glory of his inheritance in the saints, and what is the exceeding greatness of his power to us-ward who believe, according to the working of his mighty power, Which he wrought in Christ, when he raised him from the dead, and set him at his own right hand in the heavenly places (Eph 1.17-20).

The simplest believer potentially knows more about the gracious purposes of God than the cleverest of academics. Further, all in Christ have an eternal security which can never be compromised, for the Lord Jesus says about His sheep

> I give unto them eternal life; and they shall never perish, neither shall any man pluck them out of my hand. My Father, which gave them me, is greater than all; and no man is able to pluck them out of my Father's hand (Jn 10.28-29).

Finally, being in the good of God's salvation truth, all believers have the privilege of informing an unknowing world about its wonders. This is why Peter encourages saints to

> sanctify the Lord God in your hearts: and be ready always to give an answer to every man that asketh you a reason of the hope that is in you with meekness and fear (1 Pet 3.15).

As a summary of the benefits of New Testament salvation, Zophar's words warm the soul.

Thus far he has announced the conditions and consequences of Job's repentance. But now, as a parting shot, he adds a final **caution** (11.20):

> But the eyes of the wicked shall fail, and all refuge shall vanish from them, and their hope shall be the breathing out of life (11.20, JND).

Zophar holds out to Job two distinct destinies – that of the humbly repentant man, and that of the stubbornly wicked man. In contrast to the blessings which grace the penitent, the wicked will find that the good they seek will fail them, they will have no escape from coming disaster, and their only hope will be death. The writer of Proverbs makes a similar contrast: "The fear of the wicked, it shall come upon him: but the desire of the righteous shall be granted" (Prov 10.24). By ending his advice on this solemn note, Zophar, like Bildad before him (8.22b), leaves us with the impression that he has serious doubts about Job's spiritual condition.

Like the earlier speakers, Zophar, for all his irrelevance and dogmatism, says much that is theologically correct. Let us list some of his positive teachings:

- In the depths of His eternal excellence God is ultimately unknowable (11.7-9)
- He is irresistible in His power and inescapable in His omniscience (11.10-11)
- Sinful men are foolish by nature (11.12)
- Sinful man must repent and turn to God for mercy (11.13)
- Genuine repentance will be accompanied by a right lifestyle (11.14)
- The blessings of a right relationship with God include the banishment of fear, sorrow, darkness, and anxiety (11.15-19)
- God's people are possessed of a sure hope (11.18)
- The terrible destiny of the wicked is certain (11.20).

Nevertheless, taken as a response to the trials of a believer, Zophar's view of life is remarkably simplistic. As far as he is concerned, physical suffering proves personal sin, whereas repentance guarantees material reward. Both theories are incorrect. In the wisdom of God, the good may be afflicted in this world, and a genuine turning to the Lord does not of itself assure instant material prosperity. Many a new believer has discovered that it is a costly business to trust in God. Because he believed God's word, Abram uprooted himself and his family and travelled to a land he had never seen, only to discover once he got there that it was already occupied and ravaged by famine (Gen 12.4-6,10). In his case faith did not lead to immediate felicity. Having received his sight by the Saviour's gracious miracle, the man born blind found himself the instant target of religious hostility and persecution, culminating in expulsion from the synagogue (Jn 9.34). In the light of Scripture and human experience Zophar's cosy philosophy will not stand up to scrutiny.

SECTION 9
Dialogue: Job 4 – 42.6
Contest: Round 1: Job 4-14
Job's 3rd Speech: Job 12-14

Zophar's crabby contribution to the verbal contest taking place around the out-of-town ash-heap may have been the briefest so far, but Job's response is the longest speech yet, consisting of seventy-five verses. This protracted rejoinder, bringing to a close the first round in the debate, can be examined in several possible ways. As we might expect, it constitutes an **answer** to some of the points raised in Zophar's preceding remarks, but at the same time it is structured as a controlled if complex **argument** in itself, leading towards a melancholy expectation of death. It also divides into two sections, aimed at two distinct **audiences**.

As a direct **answer** to Zophar, Job's riposte picks up and analyses three of his ideas. Zophar accused Job of a defective understanding, hinting obliquely that Job has no more intelligence than "a wild ass's colt" (11.12). Job retorts with an extended hymn of praise, acknowledging total divine authority over the affairs of men, in which he implicitly demonstrates that it is an oversimplification to insist that the good are always rewarded and the bad judged (12.9-25). Zophar asserted that, though Job is undoubtedly guilty of dreadful sin, he is in fact being treated leniently, "less than thine iniquity deserveth" (11.6), to which Job responds with a plaintive avowal of personal innocence (13.15-28). Zophar offered him the neat prospect of restoration once he owned up to his sin and repented: "thou shalt be secure, because there is hope" (11.18). Job's answer is to point out the sharp contrast between a tree, which though cut down may indeed sprout again, and a man like himself on the edge of death, for whom there is no ultimate restoration, because "thou [God] destroyest the hope of man" (14.19).

As an **argument** in its own right, the speech, taken chapter by chapter, permits us to see Job's gaze moving in different directions. Looking outward to the world around, he affirms God's irresistible sovereignty over all created things (chapter 12). Looking inwards to his own soul, he defends his personal integrity in the face of the secret sins his friends claim must have caused his sufferings (chapter 13). Looking onwards, he unveils deep misery as he anticipates the desolation of the grave (chapter 14). The general tone is bleak, but there are isolated pockets of renewed faith which reveal in the patriarch's heart a briefly kindled but swiftly suffocated hope.

As a speech directed to a double **audience**, it first of all addresses the three friends (12.1 – 13.19), using the plural pronouns "ye" and "your". Job may be answering some of Zophar's specific contentions, but his words are aimed at all the friends. This is hardly surprising as the three, despite differences of manner, are singing from the same hymn sheet. Then he turns his attention to God personally (13.20 – 14.22), now using the singular pronouns "thou" and "thy". This shift reflects a feature already noted in the debate: that Job, disappointed by his comforters, increasingly resorts to God as the only reliable source of relief.

In this sense, Job's reply may be seen to divide either into three sections, corresponding broadly to the chapters, or two sections (of about a chapter and a half each) addressed respectively to the three friends and God.

Much of what has been said earlier comes back in these three chapters. The book of Job is not a logical, forward-moving argument like Paul's letter to the Ephesians, or a chronological sequence of events, like those recorded in the Old Testament historical books. Rather, it circles around the same problems with increasing acerbity as Job and his friends stubbornly dig in their heels. Like the stagnant trench warfare on the Western Front, there is little movement save for a constant strengthening of defences. This is one of the factors which make the book so hard to read and understand. Jerome is said to have commented that the story of Job was like an eel: the more tightly one tried to hold on to it, the faster it wriggled away. On the other hand, Delitzsch offers practical help in suggesting that we view Job as a greatly expanded version of what is found in the book of Lamentations and some of the Psalms. He is dealing specifically with the great dirge of chapter 3, but his comment has a much wider application because it sheds light on the structure of the whole book. This is what he writes:

> … what in Jeremiah and several of the psalms is compressed into a small compass, - the darkness of temptation and its clearing up, - is here the substance of a long entanglement dramatically presented, which first of all becomes progressively more and more involved, and to which this outburst of feeling gives the impulse.[137]

We have only to read, say, Psalms 38, 69 or 74, to see what he is getting at. In the comparatively short space of a lyrical poem, an initial expression of distress and doubt finally gives way to the sunshine of renewed faith in God. Because we can read the whole in a few minutes we are conscious of the pattern. A man's spiritual experience is condensed into a snapshot. But Job is such a huge book that we can easily lose the thread as we wander through the tortuous labyrinth. The depression of the early and middle chapters threatens to overwhelm the whole. Nevertheless, the overarching design is essentially the same: the misery and despair so eloquently articulated in the body of the book eventually disperse with the intervention of Jehovah's voice and the rebirth of Job's submissive confidence. But the route to this glad conclusion involves long, convoluted pathways which meander apparently aimlessly around the same insistent assertions and counter-assertions. In fact, the book of Job is remarkably like the experience of the believer's life in this world: for all our underlying faith, doubts and difficulties will occasionally overwhelm our minds, until the moment when everything is resolved by the intervention of the Lord Jesus to take His people home.

For the purposes of analysis and commentary, I shall treat the speech as an argument consisting of three main sections with subsections. The chapters, which constitute the major sections, may be headed as follows:

1. The Outward Look – God's Sovereignty: Chapter 12
2. The Inward Look – Job's Integrity: Chapter 13
3. The Onward Look – Job's Misery: Chapter 14.

The Outward Look – God's Sovereignty: Chapter 12

In this chapter, Job offers a rebuttal of the kind of wisdom his friends have displayed. Despite a reputation for knowledge and an unyielding dogmatism, they possess no greater understanding than he does. Indeed, their statements are tired and stale, for "who knoweth not such things as these?" (12.1-3). Both Job's personal experience and the witness of observable facts contradict any neat notion that in this life the good prosper and the bad suffer (12.4-6). Even animals and rocks could teach them something about God's overwhelming and destructive sovereignty (12.7-10). All teaching has to be tested to validate its accuracy, and Job proceeds to put their blinkered philosophy to the proof by embarking on an extensive investigation of God's works (12.11-25).

The subsections, which attempt to locate the paragraphs, may be headed as follows:

1. Job undercuts his friends' understanding: 12.1-3
2. Job denies their doctrine: 12.4-6
3. Job implies their ignorance: 12.7-10
4. Job trumps their theology: 12.11-25.

Job undercuts his friends' understanding: 12.1-3

It is with heavy sarcasm that Job rounds on his friends. Of course, they are the ultimate depositories of wisdom and no one else can get a look in! But Job also has a grasp of reality. For all his physical and mental pain he has not lost the spiritual acumen for which he was once so highly regarded.

It is a sad thing when spiritual counsellors or assembly shepherds give an impression of superiority, or pompously talk down to the saints in their care. Unlike the failing leaders of Israel in Ezekiel's day, a true shepherd moves humbly among the flock, with tender consideration binding up the sick and ministering to the diseased; he does not stand aloof and pronounce judgment. Behind Ezekiel's stern indictment we can glimpse what true pastors ought to be:

> The diseased have ye not strengthened, neither have ye healed that which was sick, neither have ye bound up that which was broken, neither have ye brought again that which was driven away, neither have ye sought that which was lost; but with force and with cruelty have ye ruled them (Ezek 34.4).

Job's self-satisfied critics have in fact only been propounding ideas about God's greatness and power well known to all. There is, it needs to be said, nothing wrong with teaching long-established truth (as long, of course, as it is truth and not merely man-made tradition); after all, in one sense, all truth is old, sourced in the infallible Word which, in its completeness, has been available to the people of God for nearly two thousand years. What is reprehensible is if we present the plain teaching of the Word as if it was something we alone have uncovered. There is always a temptation to sensationalise, if only to grab the attention of an audience and massage our own egos. How vital it is that what we say, whether on the platform or in personal counsel, is biblical, sensitive, and suitably unassuming.

Job denies their doctrine: 12.4-6

Despite their pretensions, Job's friends have no monopoly on wisdom or knowledge. Their basic contention, that suffering proves sinfulness, and that prosperity is the invariable accompaniment of piety, just does not work out in practice. Job challenges their idea by offering two counter examples: the personal one of his own current experience (12.4-5), and the more general one of the common lot of wicked men in this world (12.6). First, he sums up his own case:

> I am as one that is a laughing–stock to his neighbour, a man that called upon God, and he answered him: the just, the perfect man is a laughing–stock (12.4, RV).

Since his disasters fell on him he has become an object of mockery; and the prime culprits are his so-called friends. Another faithful man who used similar language was Jeremiah, complaining to God that "I am in derision daily, every one mocketh me" (Jer 20.7), and "I was a derision to all my people; and their song all the day" (Lam 3.14). Rejection and scorn have often been the lot of good men.

In no uncertain terms Job asserts his personal integrity and uprightness. He is a man whose habitual exercise was to pray and, what is more, have his prayers answered. The language affirms a genuine, longstanding relationship with God. The reader will think back to the piety noted in the prologue (1.1), where his godliness was specifically demonstrated in regular intercession on behalf of his sons:

> Job sent and sanctified them, and rose up early in the morning, and offered burnt offerings according to the number of them all: for Job said, It may be that my sons have sinned, and cursed God in their hearts. Thus did Job continually (1.5).

Here was a man, then, who prayed and whose prayers were heard for, until the intervention of Satan, Job's family had obviously been a pattern of earthly prosperity. Further, he describes himself as "the just [6662] upright [8549] man". Both adjectives are used first of Noah, who stood out from a world heading for judgment as "a just [6662] man and perfect [8549] in his generations" (Gen 6.9). It is no wonder Job's name is coupled with Noah's in Ezekiel 14.14 and 20 as outstanding examples of righteousness.

Job's point is that although he was a man of prayer, although he was both just and upright in his life, his present misery has made him an object of derision. People's memories can be so short. Old friends had once rejoiced in his wisdom and public esteem, but now they implicitly lined up with the population of Job's city to ridicule him. Those who knew all about the gracious miracles of the Lord

Jesus, and had perhaps even benefited from His bounty, were eager to jeer at His
sufferings on Calvary:

> And they that passed by reviled him, wagging their heads, And saying,
> Thou that destroyest the temple, and buildest it in three days, save thyself.
> If thou be the Son of God, come down from the cross. Likewise also the
> chief priests mocking him, with the scribes and elders, said, He saved
> others; himself he cannot save. If he be the King of Israel, let him now
> come down from the cross, and we will believe him. He trusted in God;
> let him deliver him now, if he will have him: for he said, I am the Son of
> God. The thieves also, which were crucified with him, cast the same in his
> teeth (Mt 27.39-44).

The language of their ridicule testifies to a lively remembrance of His words,
His works and the God-honouring conduct of His life. Yet far from inducing
pity, such knowledge only stimulated the sharper scorn. When good men fall into
adversity we should not forget what once they were.

But that is exactly what Job's friends did. From the comfortable vantage point
of the moral high ground, they look down on him as one who has justly fallen into
disaster: "In the thought of him that is at ease there is contempt for misfortune;
it is ready for them whose foot slippeth" (12.5, RV).

The language of the RV in verse 5 is different from the translation of the KJV
or Darby, but Delitzsch's rendering takes a similar line: "Contempt belongs to
misfortune, according to the ideas of the prosperous; It awaits those who are ready
to slip". When great men fall from their elevated pedestal, those still enjoying
worldly prosperity look on them with suspicion. The Hebrew word translated
"at ease" (7600) is often negative in tone, suggesting arrogant complacency. For
example:

> Our soul is exceedingly filled with the scorning of those that are at ease,
> and with the contempt of the proud (Ps 123.4).

> Rise up, ye women that are at ease; hear my voice, ye careless daughters;
> give ear unto my speech (Is 32.9).

> And I am very sore displeased with the heathen that are at ease: for I was
> but a little displeased, and they helped forward the affliction (Zech 1.15).

In these passages the word is paralleled with terms indicating haughty
contempt and self-confidence ("proud", "careless"), or accusations of deliberate
malice ("they helped forward the affliction"). The psalmist deplores the scornful
attitude of Israel's enemies; Isaiah warns the affluent women of Jerusalem that
judgment is impending; and Zechariah pronounces Jehovah's anger on nations
who, though used as His tools in disciplining delinquent Israel, relished their
role too much by intensifying their victim's anguish. Job's language is studiedly

indirect and aphoristic in style, but he is clearly having a tilt at his companions, whose present security encourages them to sneer at their downcast friend.

May God grant that we never gloat over the fall of either friend or foe. That was one of the sins for which Edom was condemned: "thou shouldest not have … rejoiced over the children of Judah in the day of their destruction; neither shouldest thou have spoken proudly in the day of distress" (Obad v.12). David behaved very differently to his enemies:

> They rewarded me evil for good to the spoiling of my soul. But as for me, when they were sick, my clothing was sackcloth: I humbled my soul with fasting; and my prayer returned into mine own bosom. I behaved myself as though he had been my friend or brother: I bowed down heavily, as one that mourneth for his mother (Ps 35.12-14).

Since we are incapable of knowing what lies ahead for us in this present age, it is advisable to be circumspect in our comments on those who, for one reason or another, have suffered a reversal. Life in this world is at best a slippery pathway. David reminds us that it was only of God's mercy that he kept his balance: "Thou hast enlarged my steps under me; so that my feet did not slip" (2 Sam 22.37). Again: "The mouth of the righteous speaketh wisdom, and his tongue talketh of judgment. The law of his God is in his heart; none of his steps shall slide" (Ps 37.30-31). Job presents his own case as an example of innocence enduring inexplicable affliction.

On the other hand, "The tabernacles of robbers prosper, and they that provoke God are secure; into whose hand God bringeth abundantly" (12.6). Do the just always prosper? No – he is the living proof. Do the unjust always suffer prompt judgment? No – it is a truism that the wicked can do very well in this world. Job overstates his argument; it is not always the case that the wicked are invariably at ease, but then, in view of his appalling circumstances, he is almost bound to exaggerate. The psalmist had a similar misapprehension about the condition of evil men, until he "went into the sanctuary of God" and had his outlook adjusted in line with the divine perspective:

> I was envious at the foolish, when I saw the prosperity of the wicked. For there are no bands in their death: but their strength is firm. They are not in trouble as other men; neither are they plagued like other men. Therefore pride compasseth them about as a chain; violence covereth them as a garment (Ps 73.3-6).

The prosperity of the wicked is temporal, their security ultimately an illusion. The KJV translation of Job 12.6 implies that it is God who showers blessings on them in abundance. True, everything ultimately derives from Him, for "he maketh his sun to rise on the evil and on the good, and sendeth rain on the just and on the unjust" (Mt 5.45). However, more recent versions offer a different view. Here is the ESV:

The tents of robbers are at peace, and those who provoke God are secure, who bring their god in their hand (12.6, ESV).

The idea is that such people make a god out of their own thieving skills, idolizing their strength and cunning in robbery. Such people view themselves as masters of their fate and captains of their soul. And they do well, so it seems. Job's point is that, for all the sage philosophizing of his friends, the simple facts of life contradict them.

Again we note that, in his frustration and annoyance, Job makes exaggerated claims. A calmer analysis of the situation would avoid such naïve black and white contrasts. But then we have always to bear in mind his position as the beleaguered victim of equally black and white dogmatism. Job, unlike the psalmist, cannot retreat into the sanctuary to have his outlook clarified and his sores soothed. Nevertheless, the last few chapters of the book will see him, if we may use this language, privileged to have the sanctuary brought down to him, so that, in his stupendous encounter with Jehovah, his eyes will be opened to the infinite wisdom of God.

Job implies their ignorance: 12.7-10

Reverting to his initial sardonic comment about the second-hand nature of their advice (12.3), Job now urges his friends to take a tour around the marvels of God's world. Beasts, birds, earth and fish can all testify, by their very existence, that God is in control of His handiwork. As Delitzsch puts it,

> The working of God, which infinitely transcends human power and knowledge, is the sermon which is continuously preached by all created things; they all proclaim the omnipotence and wisdom of the Creator.[138]

Verse 7 brings together land animals and those of the air; verse 8 joins the earth (meaning presumably the soil and the rock formations) and the sea with its own population. Wherever one looks there is a forthright witness to the greatness of God. In Delitzsch's words, "Creation is the school of knowledge, and man is the learner".[139] The psalmist agrees, but his language is that of jubilant praise, lacking the complex and understandably jaundiced tone of a man deprived of every earthly comfort:

> O Lord, how manifold are thy works! in wisdom hast thou made them all: the earth is full of thy riches. So is this great and wide sea, wherein are things creeping innumerable, both small and great beasts (Ps 104.24-25).

Look around you, says Job – don't you know that God is the doer of all? Just as His hand wrought creation in the beginning, so His hand maintains everything He has made, including man (12.9-10). The New Testament presents this in the clearest doctrinal terms as God's creative and conserving ministry. It is specifically said of the Lord Jesus that not only did He make all things but that He also sustains what He made. We read that "by him all things consist" (Col 1.17), in the sense that He is constantly "upholding all things by the word of his power" (Heb 1.3). Job's words anticipate the language of Daniel to Belshazzar: "the God in whose hand thy breath is, and whose are all thy ways, hast thou not glorified" (Dan 5.23). The difference is that Job is no Belshazzar in his insolence but rather a humble if bewildered worshipper.

Grief has not erased his grasp of sound doctrine. Although he has no written scriptures, Job knows that God is the unique Creator and keeper of all things, comprising both the animal kingdom and man (whom he places last in testimony to man's position as the apex of God's work, given dominion over the lower creation). Like a man adrift in a savage sea, the current taking him he knows not where, Job clings desperately onto the lifebelt of his knowledge of God.

Job trumps their theology: 12.11-25

Job now responds more directly to the theological tirades with which he has been assaulted, proving beyond doubt that he is as capable as anyone of giving God the glory for His supremacy. He starts with the important principle that everything has to be tested, be it the meals we eat or the messages we hear: "Doth not the ear try words, as the palate tasteth food?" (12.11, JND).

Just as the proof of the pudding is in the eating, so arguments must be carefully assessed rather than swallowed without question. We eat what suits our taste, and we take note of words which stand up to the test of reality. Of course, we are in a far better position than Job because we have the completed Word of God against which every idea, every doctrinal suggestion, every platform pronouncement must be measured. Paul encouraged the saints in Thessalonica to "Prove all things; hold fast that which is good" (1 Thess 5.21), and experienced the testing process himself when the people of Berea checked his preaching against the only infallible source of truth open to them, the Old Testament. Far from acting presumptuously in their meticulous investigation of apostolic teaching, they were commended as "noble" (Acts 17.11). If they were applauded for testing an apostle's words, how much more must we test all we hear today, when there are no inspired preachers but only imperfect men who seek to open up the riches of the inerrant Scriptures.

There follows a verse which must be read as heavy sarcasm: "With the ancient is wisdom; and in length of days understanding" (12.12). Bearing in mind everything Job has said so far about his friends' counsel, this can hardly be taken as a ringing endorsement of their sagacity; rather, it stands in contrast to the affirmation in the following verse that true wisdom, knowledge and understanding belong uniquely to God. If we were to insert a question mark at the end of the sentence it might make the point. "Are you really telling me that the mere passing of years automatically endows a man with wisdom and understanding? Come off it!" The friends have implied that they alone know all about God and His ways, but Job is not impressed. He too knows that God possesses both wisdom and power (12.13-25). Nonetheless, His actions with men and nations do not bear out the simple theory that He instantly awards blessing to the good or retribution to the bad. What Job sees around him – and it dizzies him to contemplate it – is "the uncontrolled movement of God in the affairs of the world".[140]

There is here an apparent imbalance between Job's testimony to God's wisdom and His testimony to God's might. One verse acts as a summary, including both "wisdom and strength" (12.13), but emphasising the former with its two synonyms ("counsel and understanding"), while the following twelve verses appear to concentrate on varied demonstrations of divine power. Nevertheless, as the local outworking of God's power is always guided by His wisdom, in the final analysis the two are inseparable.

God's wisdom has already been touched upon in the debate, but never before has so much space been devoted to the evidence of His power. The key thing to notice about this extended description of omnipotence is the simple fact that God is the prime actor. Job uses twenty-three verbs to give some idea of the extensiveness and irresistibility of His actions. What does God do? He "breaketh down … shutteth up … withholdeth … sendeth … leadeth … maketh … looseth … girdeth … leadeth … overthroweth … removeth … taketh away … poureth … weakeneth … discovereth … bringeth out … increaseth … destroyeth … enlargeth … straiteneth … taketh away … causeth to wander … maketh". Notice that God is the subject of all these different verbs. Most of them are what we might call negative or destructive actions, suggesting the jaw-dropping unstoppability of God's overwhelming authority as He interferes in the lives of men. They all testify to absolute supremacy over the affairs of creation. Obviously Job does not believe in some kind of absentee landlord who, having created the universe, stands back to let it take its course. On the contrary, God is ceaselessly at work in His world.

God is both active and unthwartable in everything He elects to do. One verse is devoted to His power over the natural world (12.15), but the rest concern His involvement in the lives of men and nations. However, if, as Henry Morris argues, verse 15 includes a description of the Noahic flood which so devastated the earth that the apostle Peter refers to the pre-flood world as "the world that then was" (2 Pet 3.6), then even this verse is primarily about God's dealings with men. Here is Morris's comment:

> God had "withheld the waters" in the primeval "waters which were above the firmament" (Gen 1.7), so that there was no "rain upon the earth" (Gen 2.5) in the antediluvian period. But then, when their iniquity was full, He "sent them out" and they "overturned the earth".[141]

The word "overturn" (2015) indicates monumental force and upheaval. It is used three times in Genesis 19 (translated "overthrow" in the KJV) to describe the obliteration of Sodom and Gomorrah. Whether Job is specifically alluding to the great flood or not, his words teach God's unhampered control over the processes of the natural world.

Further, what He does cannot be undone (12.14) for, as Solomon was well aware, whatsoever God doeth, it shall be for ever: nothing can be put to it, nor any thing taken from it: and God doeth it, that men should fear before him (Eccl 3.14).

Is Job thinking particularly of his own situation when he says "If he tears down, none can rebuild; if he shuts a man in, none can open" (12.14, ESV)? There is certainly an echo of Zophar's earlier comment that "If he cut off, and shut up, or gather together, then who can hinder him?"(11.10). Job's response is an expansion of Zophar's remark. The word "tear down" (2040) is used elsewhere of the destruction of Moabite cities by the Israelite army (2 Kings 3.25), the overthrow of Jerusalem (Lam 2.2), and the future wasting of Babylon (Jer 50.15). The strongest barricades cannot withstand the slightest assault by the Almighty. This language describes Job's experience with painful accuracy. His comfortable life has been suddenly shattered like a flimsy city wall, with the loss of family and possessions; he has been hedged in to inescapable suffering and distress.

Job considers all this with bitterness of heart. He cannot undo what God has done. But Christian believers view God's irreversible activities in a very different way, because we come to this truth in the light of Calvary. That work, done once and once only, is unrepeatable. It stands untouchable for ever as the magnificent groundwork of salvation, for the Lord Jesus Christ, "after he had offered one sacrifice for sins for ever, sat down on the right hand of God" (Heb 10.12). Neither angels nor men can overturn what God in grace has accomplished for the eternal blessing of His people.

For Job, God's power is seen primarily in His unchallengeable authority over the great men of the world. Job lists only the prominent and powerful. He is not concerned here with social nonentities like the riffraff mentioned in chapter 30, but with counsellors and judges (12.17), kings and priests (12.18-19), princes and "chiefs of the people" (12.21,24). We must remember that Job himself was one of the elite of the land, famous for his wisdom, revered for his charity, respected for his wealth. If God has absolute power over such notables, He obviously has everyone else well in hand. In these twelve verses Job's argument is that small and great alike are subject to the same unpredictable ups and downs of experience, the same anomalies or apparent inequalities of circumstance. But, contrary to pagan thinking, life is not governed by some capricious or fractious fate, but by the living God of the universe. And how extraordinary is His complete hands-on involvement in the lives of men! "With him is strength and wisdom: the deceived and the deceiver are his" (12.16). In what sense may it be said that "the deceived and the deceiver are his"? Of course they both belong to Him, in that they are His creatures. But Job is saying more than that. Whether a man is misled by another is, in the final analysis, a result of God's action in withholding from his mind the sharp-wittedness and insight which might allow him to penetrate the fraud. Furthermore, the deceiver himself is only able to weave a web of trickery around his victim because God has granted him the faculty of seductive speech and persuasive argument. John Gill's comment is worth quoting because it so clearly explains how God works everything for the glory of His name:

all the deceptions that are suffered to be among men, they are all wisely ordered and overruled to good purposes, so as to issue well. The deception of our first parents was suffered and willed, that the grace of God might be displayed in the salvation of men. Errors and heresies are and must be for the trial and discovery of sound believers, that they which are approved might be manifest … Now all this shows the infinite and consummate wisdom of God; it is brought to prove, not only that He "knows" deceivers, and all their arts and tricks, through which men are deceived by them … but He is the fountain of all that wisdom and knowledge in them, superior to others, which they abuse, nor can they use it without His leave; and He can and does counterwork them, and restrains them as He pleases, and makes all to work for and issue in His own glory.

In case anyone should suggest that Job's comment is merely the cynical outburst of a traumatized man (and of course the speakers in the debate, Job included, are by no means infallible), we have only to turn to a confirmatory scripture:

And if the prophet be deceived when he hath spoken a thing, I the Lord have deceived that prophet, and I will stretch out my hand upon him, and will destroy him from the midst of my people Israel (Ezek 14.9).

Prophets who claimed to speak from God but propounded lies were in fact, albeit unconsciously, fulfilling His purpose in offering a wilfully disobedient audience the kind of easy, "feel-good" message they longed to hear. The wicked King Ahab and his apostate people wanted a neat prediction of military success, and therefore, as Micaiah informed them, "the Lord hath put a lying spirit in the mouth of all these thy prophets, and the Lord hath spoken evil concerning thee" (1 Kings 22.23). The preacher and teacher of God's Word must not edit out the difficult and the unfashionable but faithfully proclaim what people need to hear rather than what they want to hear. Evil and lies do not originate in God, but He overrules in them for the fulfilment of His purposes, just as the book of Job as a whole shows how Satan's malice only served to highlight God's gracious educational programme for His servant.

It is hard to discern any immediately obvious pattern in verses 13-25, but the broad drift is evident. Whatever men may think, God is constantly at the helm in His universe, steering it to accomplish His own purposes as He pleases. Job already knows – and still knows, despite his personal sufferings – what it took seven years to teach Nebuchadnezzar; that "the most High ruleth in the kingdom of men, and giveth it to whomsoever he will", and that "all the inhabitants of the earth are reputed as nothing: and he doeth according to his will in the army of heaven, and among the inhabitants of the earth: and none can stay his hand, or say unto him, What doest thou?" (Dan 4.25,35). How this brings human pride crashing to the ground! Do men boast in their smart wisdom and intelligence?

Listen:

> He leadeth counsellors away spoiled, and maketh the judges fools … He
> removeth away the speech of the trusty, and taketh away the understanding
> of the aged (12.17,20).

Do men parade their military might, leaning on international prestige and
pretended invincibility? Listen:

> He weakeneth the government of kings, and bindeth their loins with
> a fetter; He leadeth priests away spoiled, and overthroweth the mighty
> … He poureth contempt upon nobles, and slackeneth the girdle of the
> mighty (12.18-19,21, JND).

Do powerful nations ride roughshod over their weaker neighbours, swelling
with pride at their global reputation? Listen:

> He increaseth the nations, and destroyeth them: he enlargeth the nations,
> and straiteneth them again (12.23).

Whether nations rise or fall, God is in control.

Later in the Old Testament Isaiah puts the world powers of his day firmly in
their place with his delicious imagery of an insignificant drip falling unnoticed
from a bucket full of water, or the invisible dust which no one bothers to blow off
the scales as it is of no account in the weighing process:

> Behold, the nations are like a drop from a bucket, and are accounted as
> the dust on the scales; behold, he takes up the coastlands like fine dust (Is
> 40.15, ESV).

Every great world leader or tyrant has eventually succumbed to the death
penalty which hangs over all sinners, and has sometimes suffered severe reversals
even before that final hour. God holds the reins of power. When, at the close
of the Great Tribulation, the Lord Jesus returns in glory and His magnificent
procession across the skies is seen by the entire population of the earth, men will
hastily mobilise in a vain attempt to oppose His arrival (Rev 19.19). Yet all this is
ultimately moved by God Himself for, as He announced earlier, "I will gather all
nations against Jerusalem to battle" (Zech 14.2). For all their boasts, no nation,
no individual is autonomous.

The history of Israel's Old Testament kingdom, as well as the experience
of Gentile monarchs, is a standing testimony to the vulnerability of human
leadership. God delights in subverting the expectations of sinful men. We have
only to think of the second psalm, which sums up the impotent fury of rebel man
against his Creator:

Why do the heathen rage, and the people imagine a vain thing? The kings of the earth set themselves, and the rulers take counsel together, against the Lord, and against his anointed, saying, Let us break their bands asunder, and cast away their cords from us. He that sitteth in the heavens shall laugh: the Lord shall have them in derision. Then shall he speak unto them in his wrath, and vex them in his sore displeasure (Ps 2.1-5).

When God laughs in judgment, men have to tremble. Job has a similar insight into the frailty of human power, but he is unable to go as far as the psalmist, who sees past the upheavals among nations to the grand end, the exaltation of the Son in His kingdom glory: "Yet have I set my king upon my holy hill of Zion" (Ps 2.6). It is the teaching repeated in Ezekiel when the Lord declares "I will overturn, overturn, overturn, it: and it shall be no more, until he come whose right it is; and I will give it him" (Ezek 21.27). Whatever men may say or do, and however much replacement theologians may strain to erase Israel from Scripture, God's purpose is sure: Christ will reign from Zion.

Job's paean of praise for divine power comes to a close with one verse which interestingly speaks of God's ability to uncover things hidden in darkness (12.22), and two verses which graphically describe the fate of those subject to His judgment:

He taketh away the understanding of the chiefs of the people of the earth, and causeth them to wander in a pathless waste. They grope in the dark without light, and he maketh them to stagger like a drunkard (12.24-25, JND).

Men under God's hand grope in darkness, lost, confused, and disorientated. When the Sodomites demanded that Lot deliver up his angelic visitors, the latter "smote the men that were at the door of the house with blindness, both small and great: so that they wearied themselves to find the door" (Gen 19.11). The picture of men desperately feeling their way for what they cannot get sums up the dissatisfaction of man's quest for lasting pleasure in this world. But darkness hides nothing from the all-seeing eye of Jehovah for, as the psalmist says, "the night shineth as the day: the darkness and the light are both alike to thee" (Ps 139.12). As well as affirming His wisdom and power, Job bears testimony to God's omniscience. At the back of his mind does he perhaps wonder whether such a God can shed light on his own personal nightmare of hurt and ignorance? If God has the ability to uncover "deep things out of darkness", and bring "out to light the shadow of death" (12.22), then can He not make sense of Job's sufferings? In the middle of a night of pain it is sometimes almost impossible to imagine a glad outcome with the break of dawn, but Job's darkness will eventually be dissipated at the close of his story. Not that he will be informed of the reasons behind his afflictions, but rather he will be brought as never before into the satisfying light of Jehovah's greatness.

What is the overall effect of Job's survey of God's work in the world? It suggests that in His power and wisdom He is mysterious and unpredictable. There is no neat correlation between wickedness and misery, or between uprightness and prosperity. Men and nations are victims of divinely instigated calamities regardless of their social, spiritual or moral character. Smick expresses it like this: "Job saw God so wise and powerful that He cannot be put into a box. He has sovereign freedom".[142] Of course, what Job saw, he saw with eyes blinded by his own tears. At this point in his story it appears to him that God is powerful yet unpityingly capricious in His activities. But we have to remember that this is only a stage in his spiritual education.

Before we move on to chapter 13, one other feature of the passage may be worth comment. In verse 9 Job refers, for the first and last time in the dialogue, to God as "LORD". The proper name "Jehovah" appears in the narrative framework of the book but never elsewhere in the debate. Because of this, critical and technical commentators like Hartley dismiss it as "a scribal error of one who had in mind a familiar phrase".[143] But this overlooks the possibility that divine inspiration might move in ways that transcend the expectations of human scholarship. Indeed, this exceptional use of the personal name of the God of the Bible may give us an unconscious anticipation of the revelation which awaits Job in chapter 38 when "the LORD answered Job out of the whirlwind" (38.1). What does Job say about Jehovah here? "Who knoweth not in all these, that the hand of Jehovah hath wrought this?" (12.9, JND). His great list of divine activities strangely avoids naming God, replacing the noun with the repeated pronoun "he". But ultimately – and Job is correct – the hand of the LORD *has* done it all. He will learn more of God's marvellous ways in the final chapters of the book. All Job's circumstances, the joys of the past, the pains of the present, and the blessings of the future, are of His doing. To know that everything, good and ill, that befalls us comes from the hand of the One who is self-existent, self-sufficient, and changeless in His eternal excellence (for these are the implications built into the great name of Jehovah) is of the greatest comfort to suffering saints of all times. Christians know even more, for they can identify that hand as belonging to the Saviour of Calvary.

The Inward Look – Job's Integrity: Chapter 13

The previous chapter concluded with the image of proud men reduced to the plight of the blind and the drunk, ever wandering around to no purpose. There is perhaps some intentional parallel between this vivid picture of human ineptness and Job's view of his friends' useless efforts at comfort. Their arguments simply go round in circles without making progress.

But now Job takes up Zophar's charge (and it is the view of all three comforters) that he is guilty of some unnamed but serious sin. In response he reasserts his integrity but, more important, turns away from his friends to address God directly. Repeating from the previous chapter his rather peppery dismissal of their arguments as facile, second-hand, and untrustworthy, he now longs for a personal audience with God (13.1-5). He denounces their defence of divine judgment on him as a tissue of false ideas and flimsy propositions which would not stand up to scrutiny were God Himself to test them (13.6-12), Finally, he reaffirms a conviction of his innocence before the God in whose presence he must stand. In his impassioned protestations from verse 20 onwards it is as though Zophar and company are no longer present, for Job ignores them and speaks directly to God.

The subsections may be headed as follows:

> 1. The friends' wisdom: 13.1-5
> 2. The friends' wickedness: 13.6-12
> 3. Job's witness: 13.13-28.

The friends' wisdom: 13.1-5
Reaffirming his intellectual and spiritual credibility, Job refuses to be browbeaten by the opposition. Though outnumbered he is by no means outgunned. Their whole approach to him has brought nothing but disappointment and annoyance. It is plain from verse 3 that he wishes to engage directly with God rather than with men whose opinions are warped by a traditional theology which cannot face up to reality. When we hear his charge that they are guilty of constructing artful lies, and that their words have no healing properties (13.4), we can understand why Job would want to turn to the Almighty. God alone is true both in His essential being and in His words. It was this that drew the Thessalonians to Him, when they "turned to God from idols to serve the living and true God" (1 Thess 1.9). Though earthly doctors fail, God is the great physician who announced to Israel, "I kill, and I make alive; I wound, and I heal: neither is there any that can deliver out of my hand" (Deut 32.39). The sequence of actions, from the negative to the positive ("kill ... make alive; wound ... heal"), is exactly the order of the book of Job; before he can be lifted up into blessing hitherto unimagined Job has to be knocked down. Before the doctor can heal he must first hurt. It is no wonder that Job requests his tormentors to be quiet. The wisest thing for them is to stop talking, as their silence would at least offer respite to a man battered by incessant nagging (13.5).

The friends' wickedness: 13.6-12
Job goes on to ask them not only to be quiet but also to listen carefully to what he has to say. He accuses them of wicked words – of speaking unrighteously and deceitfully on behalf of God (13.7). This is a startling allegation. We must remember that these were religious sages, men of seasoned wisdom, piety and orthodoxy. But Job says they were, in effect, lying in support of God. Their motive – to defend the ways of God – was doubtless laudable, but their method – to insist that Job must have sinned to merit his sufferings – was radically flawed, because it was built on a complete misunderstanding. In essence, they were using wrong means to support what they thought was a right cause. Zuck pushes the point further: "Thinking they were defending God, they were really defending only their view about God".[144]

This continues to be a problem. It is very easy to wax warm in support of what is merely human tradition (however venerable) rather than revealed truth. The

Pharisees were marked by a chronic inability to distinguish between what God actually said and what they thought He ought to have said:

> But he answered and said unto them, Why do ye also transgress the commandment of God by your tradition? For God commanded, saying, Honour thy father and mother: and, He that curseth father or mother, let him die the death. But ye say, Whosoever shall say to his father or his mother, It is a gift, by whatsoever thou mightest be profited by me; And honour not his father or his mother, he shall be free. Thus have ye made the commandment of God of none effect by your tradition (Mt 15.3-6).

Human tradition which, either by adding, subtracting or altering, displaces God's Word has become serious error.

It is possible to become very impassioned in our stand for what we think is truth when in fact we may be misrepresenting it. Some of the doctrinal battles in the history of Christendom seem, in part at least, to have been brought about by a failure to comprehend the breadth of divine revelation. As Cromwell famously wrote to the Church of Scotland in 1650:

> I am persuaded that divers of you, who lead the people, have laboured to build yourselves in these things; wherein you have censured others, and established yourselves "upon the Word of God." Is it therefore infallibly agreeable to the Word of God, all that *you* say? I beseech you, in the bowels of Christ, think it possible you may be mistaken.[145]

To ask ourselves whether, perhaps, we might be mistaken in our inherited interpretations of the Word is never a bad thing, if it sends us hastening back to the Scriptures of truth.

Certainly, to use unrighteous means to vindicate or serve a righteous God is a contradiction. The cause of the living God is never served by falsification of truth, underhand practices, or corrupt behaviour. Paul, for example, was quick to insist on the absolute transparency of his gospel work:

> For our exhortation was not of deceit, nor of uncleanness, nor in guile: But as we were allowed of God to be put in trust with the gospel, even so we speak; not as pleasing men, but God, which trieth our hearts. For neither at any time used we flattering words, as ye know, nor a cloke of covetousness; God is witness: Nor of men sought we glory, neither of you, nor yet of others, when we might have been burdensome, as the apostles of Christ (1 Thess 2.3-6).

Not only did he preach a truthful message, he did it in a way which was worthy of such a great God. The content of the message and the mode of its delivery are inseparable. That is why the evangelist cannot indulge in the sharp practices of the salesman or the politician, soft-pedalling unpleasant realities, or appealing to baser human instincts. Nor will he sensationalise in order to attract attention. If people are (by the grace of God) genuinely saved under frothy and diluted preaching, they are almost bound to imagine that regular Bible instruction will be equally slick and easy. If they are saved in a context of loud music, gimmickry, prizes and entertainment, they will expect this to continue. To proclaim the gospel of God involves a serious and accurate presentation of a divine message, a presentation which must not be compromised because it sets up expectations of the way the Christian life is to be conducted.

Deceit is a particularly noxious sin. The psalmist prayed that he might be delivered from "lying lips, and from a deceitful tongue" (Ps 120.2), for such weapons inflict the most corrosive of wounds. The body's physical hurts may be healed, but a scarred memory and a bruised soul can last until memory itself fails. The psalmist's is a prayer we all need to offer, asking not only to be preserved from the malicious tongues of our enemies, but also (and this is even more important) from contracting such diseased speech patterns ourselves. It is so easy to imitate the ways of a godless world. The apostle Peter reminds us of the impeccable character of the Lord Jesus Christ, whose speech and life were free from any kind of pretence or falsity:

> For even hereunto were ye called: because Christ also suffered for us, leaving us an example, that ye should follow his steps: Who did no sin, neither was guile found in his mouth: Who, when he was reviled, reviled not again; when he suffered, he threatened not; but committed himself to him that judgeth righteously (1 Pet 2.21-23).

Despite all His suffering He never resorted to untruthfulness, and stands as the everlasting model for His people.

Job goes on with his scathing indictment of his religious friends. They purported to take up arms in God's cause against what they considered to be the blasphemous tone of Job's complaints, in order to defend His ways with Job. But could they and their rhetoric really stand up to divine scrutiny? Not only were they speaking deceitfully, but in unjustly favouring God in the argument they were guilty of the very partiality which the rest of the Bible shows He abhorred (13.8). The divine rejection of preferential treatment is evident in both the Old and the New Testaments. Here is the Mosaic instruction to magistrates:

> Ye shall do no unrighteousness in judgment: thou shalt not respect the person of the poor, nor honour the person of the mighty: but in righteousness shalt thou judge thy neighbour (Lev 19.15).

Righteous dealings were to be maintained in the administration of justice in Israel, whoever the plaintiff might be. The poor were not to be favoured because of their poverty, nor the rich because of their influence. Timothy was exhorted to observe the same scrupulous even-handedness when censuring errors among believers in the church at Ephesus. It might have been to his advantage to keep quiet about the faults of prominent and wealthy men in the assembly, but Paul's words make no allowance for prejudice:

> I charge thee before God, and the Lord Jesus Christ, and the elect angels, that thou observe these things without preferring one before another, doing nothing by partiality (1 Tim 5.21).

Family loyalties can be very powerful; blood and bankrolls can stifle the voice of justice. But a God who has no favourites will have no favouritism among His people.

With unconscious irony Job anticipates a time when they, their words and their motives would all be laid bare before the majesty of the all-knowing God. In that day they would be terrified by His rebuke (13.9-11). As we know, the story of Job goes on to record that very moment when the three friends are put to shame (42.7). Those who take it on themselves, for good or ill, to pontificate to their brethren should always remember that one day they will, with those very brethren, stand before a righteous Judge whose eyes penetrate all defences and uncover all subterfuges.

Job's terse summation of the combined wisdom of his friends is that their "memorable sayings are proverbs of ashes, [their] bulwarks are bulwarks of mire" (13.12, JND). The metaphors are hard-hitting. Their wise saws were about as fresh and lively as the scattered ashes of burned books, their strong arguments as frail and tottering as walls made of mud or crumbling clay. If they took refuge behind these fragments of old clichés, they would soon find that none could stand against the might of God. But the same imagery recurs in Job's final words when, in a very different mood from the caustic criticism with which he now treats his comforters, he confesses the utter ruin to which God has reduced him: "He hath cast me into the mire, and I am become like dust and ashes" (30.19). As Abraham knew, man at best is but "dust and ashes" (Gen 18.27), and it is wise for each of us to remember our frailty. Nevertheless, even if we forget, God in grace treats us with tender consideration: "he knoweth our frame; he remembereth that we are dust" (Ps 103.14).

Job's witness: 13.13-28

Again requesting silence that he might formulate his thoughts, Job now embarks on a self-defence which he knows is audacious in the extreme. The phrase "let come on me what will" (13.13) is a key statement, because it indicates that, although he does not move into the second person singular until verse 20, he is already contemplating a direct appeal to God. It is a risky business to demand an audience with God, far riskier than Paul's appeal to Caesar. Verses 14 and 15 spell out the danger:

> Wherefore should I take my flesh in my teeth, and put my life in mine hand? Though he slay me, yet will I wait for him: nevertheless I will maintain my ways before him (13.14-15, RV).

The proverbial expression of verse 14 seems to mean that, unlike an animal jealously clutching in its jaws the meat it plans to eat, or a man tenaciously clinging to what means most to him, Job has lost interest in life. He has already admitted he looks only for death. Perhaps his desire to speak to God will immediately lead to his dissolution – no matter: "Though he slay me, yet will I wait for him".

Verse 15 is one of those memorable moments in the book of Job which most believers can recognise and quote, even if they are ignorant of the context. And there is no doubt that the traditional rendering of the verse, long made familiar by the KJV, has been a source of deep encouragement to the people of God over the centuries: "Though he slay me, yet will I trust in him: but I will maintain mine own ways before him". Spurgeon calls it "one of the supreme sayings of scripture", adding that "in these words Job answered both the accusations of Satan and the charges of his friends". He continues:

> Our text exhibits a child of God under the severest pressure, and shows us the difference between him and a man of the world. A man of the world under the same conditions as Job would have been driven to despair, and in that desperation would have become morosely sullen, or defiantly rebellious. Here you see what in a child of God takes the place of despair. When others despair he trusts in God.[146]

Interestingly, however, Spurgeon's moving sermon on the verse deals only with the first half. He does not tackle the second part, which is less easily slotted into a confession of humble faith.

Despite having passed into common speech, this famous verse in fact raises two serious problems: how exactly should it be translated, and what is the relationship between the two halves? What, first is all, is Job saying? Zuck argues that, while the KJV translation is a lovely and practical truth sanctified by long use, it is probably not what Job meant. His alternative is "behold, he will slay me; I do not have hope. I will present my case to His face".[147] Readers who wish to explore the technical matters involved in this translation crux will consult Delitzsch and the more recent academic commentators but, put simply, it is the difference between the reading of the traditional Hebrew text and its margin. The text reads, "he will slay me; I have no hope". The margin reads, "though he slay me, I will hope in him". The word rendered "trust" or "hope" (3176) means primarily to wait, hope for, expect. It is used, for example, in Lamentations 3.21 and 24, where the prophet expresses hope in the Lord despite all the turmoil around him. Job is therefore either saying that, even though the Lord should slay him for his temerity in insisting upon an audience, he will continue to hope in God's goodness; or that he looks only for death and can entertain no hope because the One who has brought him into misery will shortly end his life. After all, he is putting himself in jeopardy merely by asking to plead his case before God's presence.

How can we choose between the Hebrew text (with its negative "no hope") and the more positive margin? The translation which best fits the context of Job's words would seem to be the one to adopt. Job's anticipation of fast-approaching death and his frequent expressions of dejection (6.11; 7.21; 10.20; 14.19) appear to support the negative rendering. The words of the KJV perhaps better express the attitude of the quiet, restrained Job of the first two chapters rather than the voluble Job of the dialogue who, in his desperation, is keen to take his case to the highest court whatever the outcome.

On the other hand, it has to be admitted that Job, in the distress of his soul, tends to swing swiftly within a short space between contradictory moods. His thought is so mercurial it is never easy to pin down. The strains placed on him by his terrible circumstances, the disappointment experienced listening to unsupportive friends, the tension between confidence that God is righteous and a feeling that God is dealing unjustly with him – all these factors lead to an instability of soul reflected in his ever-shifting outlook. A reader of his story may feel inclined to accept the traditional rendering as one equally in tune with this unpredictable turn of mind. It has to be added that a good number of recent Bible versions (including the ESV, the CEV, and the ISV) favour the familiar translation. Smick goes so far as to say that "whatever the reading, the context appears to require a translation that expresses Job's faith, not his doubt".[148] But Job's faith ebbs and flows with his feelings. Although it is impossible to be dogmatic, Zuck's position seems justified by the immediate setting of Job's argument, that he will press ahead with his call for a divine hearing, even though he fears it will be the end of him.

But we still have to discover how the two halves of the verse relate. The verse is structured as an antithetical parallelism:

(a) Behold, he will slay me, I have no hope:
(b) nevertheless I will maintain my ways before him (ASV).

Section (a) testifies to an open-eyed awareness of divine power, while section (b) is a statement of what we might call a bold resolution. They balance dejection (I have no hope) and determination (nevertheless I will argue my case). Job has no prospect of restored life down here but, despite all the objections of his friends, despite the terrors associated with appearing at the divine assizes, he is equally certain of the innocence he plans to assert in the very presence of God. As Constable puts it, "Job evidently expected God to kill him for what he was about to say, but he wanted answers more than life".[149]

He speaks as a man resigned to his fate but nonetheless one who has ordered his case, certain he has a just cause (13.16-19). To assert innocence before God as he plans to do ("I will maintain my ways before him") will not be an act of presumption, as his friends think, but one of simple integrity: "This also shall be my salvation; for a godless man shall not come before him" (13.16, RV). He has a deep-seated faith that, though he cannot comprehend God's current dealings, God is just and will uphold what is right. A hypocrite cannot swagger into His presence and get away with it, but Job is no hypocrite. His friends should pay heed to what he is saying (13.17), because he has prepared his case for the judicial inquiry, sure that he will be upheld as an innocent man (13.18). He may die as a result of his boldness, but at least he will finally be vindicated.

The language of verse 18 refers to Job's unique situation, the daring expectation that he will be declared innocent of all culpability for his sufferings: "I know that

I shall be justified". But the Christian believer rejoices in a grander blessing. We have already been justified, that is, declared eternally right with God, on the basis of faith in the finished work of Christ. We are not awaiting some great heavenly assessment at which it will be determined whether we are right with God or not, but rest now in a settled salvation. Paul's summary is definitive:

> Therefore being justified by faith, we have peace with God through our Lord Jesus Christ: By whom also we have access by faith into this grace wherein we stand, and rejoice in hope of the glory of God. And not only so, but we glory in tribulations also: knowing that tribulation worketh patience (Rom 5.1-3).

Justification is appropriated by faith, and results in a present peace with God, access into a gracious standing before Him, and a future hope of glory. But it also includes the resources to endure tribulation in the present scene. These resources consist primarily in an intelligent awareness of the value of hardship in cultivating those Christian graces which testify to a genuine work of God in our souls. This is one reason why reading Job can be such an encouragement. Lacking our accumulated knowledge of God he nevertheless endured, confident in God's justice though perplexed by his afflictions.

Job's final word, before embarking upon direct address to God, is to confess that if anyone were to refute his protestations of innocence, he would abandon speaking altogether and die: "Who is he that will contend with me? for now shall I hold my peace and give up the ghost" (13.19, RV). Here is a man utterly – and, we know, rightly – persuaded that he is not guilty of any crime to account for the distresses which have befallen him.

At this point, he turns from his human audience to God, making a double request (13.20-22). If he is to stand before God and state his case without intimidation, two hindrances must be overcome. The "two things" he wants removed are, first, God's hand of affliction, which impedes his self-expression; and, second, that manifestation of divine majesty which will terrify him so greatly as to prevent him opening his mouth at all. The "dread" (367) which makes him "afraid" is described by the psalmist:

> I am afflicted and ready to die from my youth up: while I suffer thy terrors [367] I am distracted. Thy fierce wrath goeth over me; thy terrors have cut me off (Ps 88.15-16).

God's terribleness is a forgotten truth. It is worth remembering that before ever he tells us, to our comfort, that "God is love", the apostle John insists that "God is light" (1 Jn 1.5; 4.8). The order is not without significance. We should not emphasise the former at the expense of the latter.

Once God removes any obstructions to Job's freedom of speech, he will take his stand. Verse 22 seems to use the technical language of a formal trial. Job boldly offers God the choice: either He can speak first and then let Job respond in his own defence; or Job is willing to present his case, to which God may then reply.

It is a daring plea. Perhaps at this stage there is a breathless pause, as Job and his human audience wait to see if God will respond audibly to a creature's rash challenge. But the heavens are silent. Since there is no evident answer, Job plunges ahead by demanding that God explain what he has done to provoke the sufferings he has had to endure: "How many are mine iniquities and sins? make me to know my transgression and my sin" (13.23). Three distinct words illustrate the breadth of human sin against God. "Iniquity" (5771) suggests perversity or depravity; "sin" (2403) comes from a verb meaning to miss (used literally in Judges 20.16 of the sharp-shooting Benjamites); and "transgression" (6588) implies revolt. The combination of the three sums up every possible way of offending God and His law. Job wants to know precisely what he has done to deserve punishment.

But the following verse hints at the greater distress in his heart: "Wherefore hidest thou thy face, and holdest me for thine enemy?" (13.24). More painful to Job than the material losses he has suffered is the loss of glad fellowship with the God he loves. He has boldly demanded a divine answer to his challenge, and yet the heavens remain ominously hushed. All Job's bravado collapses in the face of this seeming indifference; he cannot understand why the God he has known so long should remain concealed and unresponsive. It is a key moment because, for the reader at least, it sweeps away any suspicions the friends may have provoked and confirms everything we learned about Job in the prologue. "My servant Job", God called him, with evident approval. It is the consciousness of divine favour, the enjoyment of God's company, the sweetness of fellowship with his Creator, that Job misses most of all.

It is here that Job resembles the psalmist, whose spiritual ardour is expressed in terms of a hunted animal panting for refreshment:

> As the hart panteth after the water brooks, so panteth my soul after thee, O God. My soul thirsteth for God, for the living God: when shall I come and appear before God? My tears have been my meat day and night, while they continually say unto me, Where is thy God? (Ps 42.1-3).

The situations are not dissimilar. David felt estranged from God because of his adverse circumstances, and longed for a renewed enjoyment of the divine nearness, the absence of which provoked the mockery of his enemies. Spurgeon writes in his *Autobiography* about the painful reality of such moments of desolation in a believer's life:

> I believe it is a shallow experience that makes people always confident of what they are, and where they are, for there are times of terrible trouble, that make even the most confident child of God hardly know whether he is on his head or his heels.[150]

Of all the godly men in Old Testament times, those into whose naked heart we get the closest glimpses are those who encounter serious affliction: Job, David, Jeremiah. Is it accidental that each of these men is, in measure, a foretaste of the Messiah in His innocent sufferings?

Why, asks Job, is God so insistent on persecuting him? After all, what is he? His picture language is heart-breaking. In his mortal insignificance and frailty he likens himself to "a leaf driven to and fro", "dry stubble" (13.25), and "a rotten thing … a garment that is moth-eaten" (13.28). Stubble or chaff often represents the wicked blasted by God's judgments. Here is Moses, exulting in the destruction of Egypt's army:

> And in the greatness of thine excellency thou hast overthrown them that rose up against thee: thou sentest forth thy wrath, which consumed them as stubble (Ex 15.7).

Here, similarly, is the psalmist calling on the Lord to overwhelm his enemies:

> O my God, make them like a wheel; as the stubble before the wind (Ps 83.13).

In like manner, Isaiah predicts Babylon's overthrow:

> Behold, they shall be as stubble; the fire shall burn them; they shall not deliver themselves from the power of the flame: there shall not be a coal to warm at, nor fire to sit before it (Is 47.14).

Trouble is, Job is no brazen opponent of God, but a humble servant. Why then is he being treated like a dangerous antagonist? That God should expend such effort in harassing a fragile leaf driven by the wind, or in pursuing the dry straw as though it were of value, seems absurd. What can a rotting garment do against God? In between passages describing his frailty come verses lamenting God's persecution:

> For thou writest bitter things against me, and makest me to possess the iniquities of my youth; And thou puttest my feet in the stocks, and markest all my paths; thou settest a bound about the soles of my feet (13.26-27, JND).

It is as if God has penned a serious criminal charge against him, intent on bringing down on him all the consequences of his thoughtless youthful follies, follies which Job can hardly remember. Once again we notice that Job never claims absolute sinlessness: rather, there are no errors of his mature years to account for his misery. He is like a prisoner condemned to sit in the stocks, immobilised and humiliated: God has limited his movements so that he is shut up to misery. The idea that God has deliberately boxed him in to suffering is a recurring one:

> Why is light given to a man whose way is hid, and whom God hath hedged in? (3.23).

> Behold … he shutteth up a man, and there can be no opening (12.14).

> He hath fenced up my way that I cannot pass, and he hath set darkness in my paths (19.8).

From God's designs there can be no escape. But Job's words may have a more precise meaning. Hartley, among others, notes that "the prisoner's feet were marked or branded in order that he might be easily tracked".[151] Even were he to make a dash for freedom he would be relentlessly pursued. For Job the thought of constant divine surveillance is oppressive. For the psalmist, the same thought offers comfort:

> Thou knowest my downsitting and mine uprising, thou understandest my thought afar off. Thou compassest my path and my lying down, and art acquainted with all my ways ... Thou hast beset me behind and before, and laid thine hand upon me. Such knowledge is too wonderful for me; it is high, I cannot attain unto it. Whither shall I go from thy spirit? or whither shall I flee from thy presence? If I ascend up into heaven, thou art there: if I make my bed in hell, behold, thou art there. If I take the wings of the morning, and dwell in the uttermost parts of the sea; Even there shall thy hand lead me, and thy right hand shall hold me (Ps 139.2-3, 5-10).

The difference, of course, is that the psalmist is not, like Job, undergoing intense and unrelieved suffering, convinced that God has turned against him.

In chapter 13 Job's witness on his own behalf is that, examining his soul, he is innocent of any known crime yet impotent to resist God's remorseless persecution. In the light of God's greatness, he is but "a rotten thing ... a garment that is moth eaten" (13.28). With this searing picture of personal corruption, the chapter ends. But the imagery of human weakness will continue in chapter 14.

The Onward Look – Job's Misery: Chapter 14
The subsections in this rather difficult chapter seem to run as follows:

> 1. Man's innate defilement: 14.1-6
> 2. Man's irreversible death: 14.7-15
> 3. Man's inevitable destruction: 14.16-22.

Despite baring his soul in chapter 13, Job looks gloomily ahead to a bleak future. Zophar glibly promised hope of recovery if only he repented, but Job sees no hope at all. God has not responded to his urgent plea for a formal hearing. His language therefore switches from the deeply personal register, which concluded the previous chapter, to the more universal, as he meditates on the human condition in this world. Man is defiled by inherited sin (14.1-6). His life is brief and, unlike a tree, has no expectation of revival after death (14.7-15), for God watches over him with a view to his destruction (14.16-22). All this is a detached observation of mankind in general. Nevertheless, in verses 13-17 the intensely individual language returns with twelve first person pronouns which focus attention on Job's yearning for a restoration to fellowship with God.

Man's innate defilement: 14.1-6

Like the psalmist, Job raises a basic question about human nature (7.17; Ps 8.4;144.3). His diction, coloured by the bitter personal experience of sorrow, emphasises the brevity, misery, fragility, and depravity of human life (14.1-2,4). Since all men are damaged by Adam's sin, why is God so set on hounding Job in particular (14.3,5-6)?

The **brevity** of life is plain to all: "Man that is born of a woman is of few days" (14.1). Job is speaking during the patriarchal era, when human lifespan was considerably longer and the body stronger than today. Nevertheless, compared with God's eternity, it is but passing. As Moses wrote:

> Before the mountains were brought forth, or ever thou hadst formed the earth and the world, even from everlasting to everlasting, thou art God. Thou turnest man to destruction; and sayest, Return, ye children of men. For a thousand years in thy sight are but as yesterday when it is past, and as a watch in the night. Thou carriest them away as with a flood; they are as a sleep: in the morning they are like grass which groweth up. In the morning it flourisheth, and groweth up; in the evening it is cut down, and withereth. For we are consumed by thine anger, and by thy wrath are we troubled (Ps 90.2-7).

Job is talking specifically about "Man ... born of a woman". That is to say, he is thnking of everyone since Adam the first man, who entered the world uniquely and innocently as a result of God's creative handiwork. All born subsequently are damaged by sin; hence their life is curtailed, for they commence living already under the death penalty.

Equally obvious is life's **misery**, "full of trouble" (14.1). This noun (7267) appears seven times in the Old Testament, of which five are in Job (3.17,26; 14.1; 37.2; 39.24), and conveys the idea of "agitation, excitement, raging, trouble, turmoil, trembling" (Brown, Driver and Briggs). Instead of long life and little distress, fallen man faces exactly the opposite. This jaundiced account of existence on planet earth has to be understood as a reflection of Job's condition. Had he spoken during the days of his prosperity he would doubtless have used very different language, for present experience tends to govern our moods and our words.

Jacob provides a fascinating case history of the mesmerising power of the present. Conscious only of the fact that he had been deprived of two sons, he became blind to all God's past goodness to him:

> And Jacob their father said unto them, Me have ye bereaved of my children: Joseph is not, and Simeon is not, and ye will take Benjamin away: all these things are against me (Gen 42.36).

Speaking later to Pharaoh, he is still wearily negative in mood:

> And Jacob said unto Pharaoh, The days of the years of my pilgrimage are an hundred and thirty years: few and evil have the days of the years of my

life been, and have not attained unto the days of the years of the life of my fathers in the days of their pilgrimage (Gen 47.9).

But when the time comes for him to bless Joseph and his two boys, the whole atmosphere has changed:

And he blessed Joseph, and said, God, before whom my fathers Abraham and Isaac did walk, the God which fed me all my life long unto this day, The Angel which redeemed me from all evil, bless the lads; and let my name be named on them, and the name of my fathers Abraham and Isaac; and let them grow into a multitude in the midst of the earth (Gen 48.15-16).

What made the difference? God had not altered, nor had His covenant promises to Abraham and his descendants. It was Jacob's immediate circumstances which had improved; he was now settled comfortably in Egypt, restored to the sons he thought lost, and blessed with the proof of an expanding family. How often our feelings are chained to current experience instead of being anchored to the unchangeable promises of Scripture! Paul provides the positive example in Romans 8.31: "If God be for us, who can be against us?"

> "All these things are against me,"
> Cried Jacob in despair;
> "All these things are against me;
> To turn I know not where.
> My sons are taken from me,
> My heart is full of grief;
> With everything against me
> Where can I find relief?"
>
> "If God the Lord be for us,"
> Wrote Paul to Roman saints;
> "If God the Lord be for us,
> Who then can be against?
> Though all seek to despatch us,
> Below, around, above,
> I know that nought can snatch us
> From Jesus and His love."

Job had no such promises, either spoken or written, and yet, as we shall see, for all his despondency he never finally abandons a rooted confidence that God is righteous even when His ways are incomprehensible and apparently contradictory.

Job has no illusions about life's **fragility**: man "cometh forth like a flower, and is cut down: he fleeth also as a shadow, and continueth not" (14.2). Flowers may be beautiful but they are a traditional emblem of human frailty. Hartley gives us a glimpse of the scene Job might have had in mind: "In Palestine after the spring rains, flowers bloom in abundance and the fields glow from their splendour. But they last only for a moment. They soon fade from the hot desert winds".[152] It may remind us of the attractive picture painted by the wooer in Song of Solomon 2.11-13 to mark the passing of winter, although that love song interestingly is silent about the transience of earthly beauty. "Cut down" (5243) is another word used mainly in Job (14.2; 18.16; 24.24) and once by the psalmist, describing the fate of wicked men who "shall soon be cut down like the grass, and wither as the green herb" (Ps 37.2). Just as the mower scythes the grass, so God takes away in death. Shadows are equally evanescent, intangible and insubstantial. To try and pick up a shadow is to be baffled. David had a similar understanding of the flimsiness of life:

> For we are strangers before thee, and sojourners, as were all our fathers: our days on the earth are as a shadow, and there is none abiding (1 Chr 29.15).

Behind it all lies the inescapable root cause, human **depravity,** which shortens man's life and spoils his pleasures. Job's words sum up the frustration he feels as he asks, "Who can bring a clean thing out of an unclean? not one" (14.4). Delitzsch's expanded paraphrase is helpful:

> Would that perfect sinlessness were possible to man; but since (to use a New Testament expression) that which is born of the flesh is flesh, there is not a single one pure.[153]

It may well be that this is a legal plea of mitigation, for Job still hankers after a direct judicial audience with God. Since man is congenitally ruined, how can God expect anything of him other than failure? Job was fully aware of Adam's sin and its consequences in the race. However, although he is correct in his theology as far as it goes, he is not fully informed of God's gracious purpose in redemption. He must have known about the promise of a deliverer who, while being the seed of the woman, would nonetheless bruise the serpent's head, but he was unaware of exactly what this would entail. When the eternal Son, equal in every way with the Father, took on Himself sinless humanity, the impossibility Job articulates came amazingly true in time and space. The only One able to bring out of an unclean womb a clean offspring is God Himself, and at the incarnation He did just that. As the angel said to Mary,

> The Holy Ghost shall come upon thee, and the power of the Highest shall overshadow thee: therefore also that holy thing which shall be born of thee shall be called the Son of God (Lk 1.35).

The Lord Jesus was genuinely "born of a woman, born under the law" (Gal 4.4, RV), and yet continued to be what He eternally was, the spotless Son of God. Even in his confession of the utter failure of Adamic humanity, Job's language makes the Christian believer think of the perfection of the Second Man.

But this is beyond Job's immediate concern or comprehension. His mind is wrapped up with man's innate failings, the brevity of his earthly life, and the dread sense of divine scrutiny resting on him throughout this fleeting existence. That God's eyes are upon him (14.3) is no cause for thanksgiving but a source of terror, for he is subject to the surveillance of a sovereign judge. It is another example of Job's rapidly and unpredictably changing mood. He has been demanding a formal audience with God (13.18,22), yet now the very thought of it fills him with fear. Because the duration and conditions of man's life on earth are fixed by God, Job wishes God would turn away His searching gaze, allowing him to reach his appointed end, just as a hired servant does his duty until sundown (14.5-6). Job has used the same imagery before (7.1-4) to express the weariness he feels while waiting the closure of a life of toil.

Job may long for "rest", but the attraction is primarily the relief of release from backbreaking labour. Death will remove present pains and distresses. As far as the believer is concerned, "rest" is a much more positive blessing which accompanies the return of the Lord Jesus Christ in His glory. Paul promised the persecuted Thessalonian saints "rest with us, when the Lord Jesus shall be revealed from heaven with his mighty angel" (2 Thess 1.7). But there is more. In Christ we enjoy rest of soul right now, having turned from futile human efforts to trust wholly in Him for salvation: "he that is entered into [God's] rest, he also hath ceased from his own works, as God did from his" (Heb 4.10). Those gladly reposing in the work of Christ can look forward to the fullness of joy in His presence.

Man's irreversible death: 14.7-15

Job now elaborates further on his gloomy mood. He embarks on a brief **meditation**, highlighting the contrast between a tree, which can at least shoot again after being felled, and man, who has no future beyond this life (14.7-12). Then, unexpectedly, he breaks into an impassioned **aspiration**, pleading for the very resurrection which he has just declared impossible (14.13-15).

Here is Darby's translation of the tree image:

> For there is hope for a tree: if it be cut down, it will sprout again, and its tender branch will not cease; Though its root grow old in the earth, and its stock die in the ground, Yet through the scent of water it will bud, and put forth boughs like a young plant (14.7-9, JND).

The idea is not unique to Job. Similar imagery appears in the prophets. Isaiah, for example, uses it to picture the blessed future awaiting Israel despite its sin and chastisement:

> And if there be yet a tenth in it, it shall again be eaten up: as a terebinth, and as an oak, whose stock remaineth, when they are felled; so the holy seed is the stock thereof (Is 6.13, RV).

God would remove His people into captivity; but in due time a tiny remnant ("a tenth") would return, though facing severe persecution in the land ("it shall again be eaten up"). Perhaps the ESV most clearly gives the sense of the verse: "though a tenth remain in it, it will be burned again, like a terebinth or an oak, whose stump remains when it is felled". Israel would return to its land only to be razed down to the roots. Yet, as Nebuchadnezzar learned in Daniel 4.26, a tree stump can sprout once more. A great world ruler was quite literally brought down to the ground that he might be lifted up to blessing. So will it be in a coming day when, its eyes miraculously opened to its Messiah, "all Israel shall be saved" (Rom 11.26; Zech 12.10). How much His ancient people mean to God, and what free grace blessings He has in store for them!

In Isaiah and Daniel the felled but sprouting tree speaks respectively of national and personal restoration. But Job knows nothing of the glory God has planned for Israel, nor has he any notion of God's disciplinary ways with a Gentile emperor who lived centuries after his own time. His outlook is that of the wise man who intelligently observes God's works in the natural world. Even mere trees have a hope of restoration after disaster. He sets up the negative ("Though") in order to contrast it with the natural miracle of revival ("Yet"). Out of the ashes of catastrophe comes unlooked for renewal.

However, the grammatical construction leads inexorably to a bitter recognition that man has no such hope: "For there is hope of a tree ... Though ... Yet ... But man dieth, and wasteth away: yea, man giveth up the ghost, and where is he?" (14.7-10). Job brings together two of the Hebrew words for man, the first meaning a strong or valiant man, the second referring to Adam, made out of red earth. Despite his vigour, and in part because of his construction from dust, man inevitably dies and is reduced to nothing. "Wasteth away" (2522) translates a word appearing only three times in the Old Testament, describing how Amalek was "discomfited" (Ex 17.13), and Lucifer's ability to "weaken [2522] the nations" (Is 14.12). Whoever he may be, man is finally brought low in death – "and where is he?" The question expresses the speaker's overwhelming sense of despair.

To underline his current feeling of pessimism Job offers another natural analogy:

> [As] the waters recede from the lake, and the river wasteth and drieth up:
> So man lieth down, and riseth not again; till the heavens be no more, they
> do not awake, nor are raised out of their sleep (14.11-12, JND).

Delitzsch explains it well: "this vanishing away without hope and beyond recovery is contemplated under the figure of running water, or of water that is dried up and never returns again to its channel".[154] It is not meant to be a cheerful image. The same simile is used by the wise woman of Tekoa: "For we must needs die, and are as water spilt on the ground, which cannot be gathered up again" (2 Sam 14.14). Just as water soaks into the ground and evaporates, so man's life ends with no hint of return.

But let us look more closely at Job's words. Bearing in mind the erratically fluctuating state of his thoughts, it is not to be wondered at that his outlook is so negative. Though a tree may recover, man cannot. Is Job saying there is no hope of an individual resuscitation in the present state of things, as is the experience of the tree; or is he denying the possibility of a future life in a raised body? Remembering that his great desire is for a public exoneration, a vindication in the presence of his sceptical friends, the first option seems more likely. Only in the present order of things can such an acquittal make sense. On the other hand, his language suggests a future bodily resurrection ("riseth not again … they do not awake, nor are raised"), if only to repudiate it. The word "awake" (6974) translates a term which, in at least two places, speaks directly of resurrection. It is used in Psalm 17.15 of David's glad hope of satisfaction "when I awake, with thy likeness", and in Daniel 12.2 of the post-tribulational resurrection of godly Israelites to enter Messiah's kingdom on earth. It seems reasonable therefore to infer that it may well carry the same kind of significance here. Yet Job negates any resurrection hope. His negation is qualified by a temporal clause: "till the heavens be no more". This could possibly allow for a resurrection at the very close of the present created order (only when the heaven and earth which now exist are removed can there be a resurrection). However, his deep despondency makes it more likely that the language is simply a poeticism for "never" (under no circumstances whatever is there any possibility of resurrection). The prospect is unutterably dreary.

Job's negativity is partly the result of his accumulated griefs, and partly the inevitable consequence of living at an early stage in the progress of revelation. Hartley points out that the vocabulary to express a hope in resurrection did not even exist when Job was alive:

> Since there was no technical word for resurrection when the book of Job was written, the concept was expressed by the piling up of words associated with "awakening from sleep": "arise", "awake, "stir up, rouse".[155]

Everything changes once we reach the New Testament. There the Greek word for resurrection literally means "a standing up again" (Strong's Concordance), thus dramatically picturing the action of a body rising to its feet.

The Christian, possessed of God's completed Word, can turn from Job's pardonable agnosticism to Paul's assurance. First, we are informed that at death the believer enters into the conscious delight of the Lord's presence. Although the word "sleep" may accurately describe the condition of the body in the grave, it cannot do justice to the spirit's blessedness of being "at home with the Lord" (2 Cor 5.8, RV). The body sleeps but the soul rejoices. Second, Paul elaborates on the Saviour's seed teaching recorded in John 11 and 14 to affirm the certainty of a glorious resurrection:

> Behold, I shew you a mystery; We shall not all sleep, but we shall all be changed, In a moment, in the twinkling of an eye, at the last trump: for the trumpet shall sound, and the dead shall be raised incorruptible, and we shall be changed (1 Cor 15.51-52).

The mystery, or secret, which Paul discloses is not, of course, the truth of resurrection itself, which had been partially unveiled in later Old Testament times (Ps 16.10; Dan 12.1-2), but the doctrine of the living believer's transformation at the moment of the Lord's coming. The Lord had taught the disciples that He would come for them, but did not make plain that at that moment they would instantaneously receive a glorified body without passing through the article of death. Whether living or dead when Christ comes, the believer will be eternally fitted for His presence.

To a man living in an era of partial revelation and burdened down by his own pains, death appeared irreversible. Without the shining light of New Testament teaching, Job can only conclude that death is final. For the Christian, however, death has already been overturned in the historical resurrection of Christ, and will be completely destroyed in the future completion of that "first resurrection". Even that is not the end, for the ungodly dead will also be raised, not in glorified bodies suited to eternal bliss, but in sinful bodies which will everlastingly continue in the torments of the lake of fire.

Immediately after this grim meditation on life's transience comes another of those astonishing swivels in Job's thinking. It takes the form of a passionate **aspiration** (14.13-15), in which he prays directly for the very thing he seems just to have denied:

> Oh that thou wouldest hide me in Sheol, that thou wouldest keep me secret until thine anger be past, that thou wouldest appoint me a set time, and remember me, - (If a man die, shall he live again?) all the days of my time of toil would I wait, till my change should come: Thou wouldest call, and I would answer thee; thou wouldest have a desire after the work of thy hands (14.13-15, JND).

Although vague in its notions of resurrection, the Old Testament is clear that death does not terminate a man's existence. As Davidson summarises it, "the dead person subsisted, but he did not live. He descended into *sheol*, the abode of deceased persons. His existence was a dreamy shadow of his past life".[156] Job wants *sheol* to be a kind of ark of safety in which he would be kept secure until God's anger was abated. We note that all the doing is God's. The sequence of verbs describes a divine work: hide, keep, appoint, call, desire. Job may be without strength and without assured hope, yet he is still confident that God has all the power necessary to resolve the situation.

However we look at it, verses 13 to 15 constitute a marvellous passage. Job's plea is that, after his death, God would nestle him safely in the place of departed spirits until His wrath was past, so that he might finally be called forth for vindication and restoration to the fellowship with God he so earnestly craved. He wants to be secretly hidden, much in the way that the psalmist was confident that "in the time of trouble he shall hide me in his pavilion" (Ps 27.5), and "Thou shalt hide them in the secret of thy presence from the pride of man" (Ps 31.20). Whatever their circumstances, God alone has the power to preserve His people. Job's prayer to be remembered picks up a word that first appears in Genesis, describing God's gracious activity on Noah's behalf: "And God remembered Noah, and every living thing, and all the cattle that was with him in the ark: and God made a wind to pass over the earth, and the waters assuaged" (Gen 8.1). The man hidden in the ark was not forgotten but brought forth into a bright new world after the outpouring of divine anger had ceased. The parallel with Job's request can hardly be accidental. Job will wait (3176) until his change (2487) comes. The word "wait" was used in the previous chapter (13.15, as "trust", KJV). It appears eight times in Job and means to trust, wait, or hope. The word for "change" appears only twelve times in the Old Testament, usually associated with a change of clothing (Gen 45.22; Judg 14.12ff; 2 Kings 5.5). Read in New Testament light, it hints at the dramatic change which comes with resurrection, when the saints are raised in glorified bodies. Job is sure that God will call him (we might think of the Lord Jesus summoning Lazarus out of the tomb) and he in turn will answer. The language echoes his earlier demand for an immediate judicial audience: "call thou, and I will answer" (13.22).

But it is worth looking more closely at Job's explanation of exactly why he believes God will call him, for we cannot forget that at this moment he is deeply conscious of being abandoned and assaulted by the God he has served. What will bring about the alteration? It is because "thou wilt have a desire to the work of thine hands" (14.15). The Hebrew word for "desire" (3700) is used only on five occasions in the Old Testament, each time in a context of intense and urgent yearning:

> And now, though thou wouldest needs be gone, because thou sore longedst [3700] after thy father's house (Gen 31.30).

> Like as a lion that is greedy [3700] of his prey, and as it were a young lion lurking in secret places (Ps 17.12).

> My soul longeth [3700], yea, even fainteth for the courts of the Lord: my heart and my flesh crieth out for the living God (Ps 84.2).

> Gather yourselves together, yea, gather together, O nation not desired [3700] (Zeph 2.1).

Strong's Concordance informs us that the word basically means to be pale with longing. How daringly and how memorably this godly man puts into words an intuitive awareness that the living God has such a tender affection for His people that He can never finally give them up!

Putting all the information together, what Job is saying is this. Once His anger is over, God will so greatly long for His personally hand-made creature that He will call him forth in resurrection. As a result, the fellowship so inexplicably broken (as far as Job understands it) will be wonderfully restored. Darby's translation of verse 14 puts the key question, "If a man die, shall he live again?", in parenthesis, which offers some assistance in grasping the fidgety, tentative movement of Job's unsettled thinking process. Pleading for a temporary hiding place until he can stand before God, his innocence attested and his fellowship restored, he revisits in his mind the whole question of resurrection. In verses 10 to 12 he categorically denied any future hope. But now, in spite of everything he has said earlier, we sense the dawning of an almost unbelievable insight. Might it be that there *will be* a resurrection after all? Surely there will have to be, if God is to maintain His essential character as righteous and good. Just as his near contemporary Abraham posited a special resurrection as the only way for the God who had commanded Isaac's death to be true to His promises about Isaac's seed, so Job emerges from the darkness of ignorance into the light of future hope. Such a flash of understanding fits well with his concluding – and intensely emotional – image of God having a rekindled fondness for His handiwork. Job is His creation, His loyal worshipper. Amidst the ruins of his earthly blessings he is touchingly sure that God will eventually turn back to him in renewed affection. Though his intelligence cannot comprehend the concept of bodily resurrection, his heart yearns for it; in so doing, Job anticipates a truth that comes to its full flowering in the New Testament.

Man's inevitable destruction: 14.16-22

Alas, the speech does not end on this wonderful high note. Some expositors and translations view verses 16-17 in a positive light, as though they continue to describe the blessedness of the restoration envisaged in the previous three verses. Here, for example, is the rendering offered by the ESV:

> For then [that is, at the time when God again longs for the work of His hands] you would number my steps; you would not keep watch over my sin; my transgression would be sealed up in a bag, and you would cover over my iniquity (14.16-17, ESV).

This takes the passage as describing a renewal of God's gracious care for Job, which involves the covering over of any sins he may have committed. The Christian believer can certainly bask in the enjoyment of what has been done for him through the finished work of Christ, guaranteeing both pardon and protection. In Him "we have redemption through his blood, the forgiveness of sins" (Eph 1.7), and are "kept by the power of God through faith unto salvation" (1 Pet 1.5).

However, all expositors have to acknowledge that by the close of the chapter Job's outlook has reverted to one of deep despondency. That being the case, it seems reasonable to locate the change of mood at this point. The language of verse 16, then, brings Job, and the reader, down to earth with a bump: "but now". His dream of future vindication and restored fellowship is burst like a bubble as he awakes to his continuing misery. God's attitude is, alas, not one of deep desire for his company, but rather one of unfeeling hostility. Like a stern magistrate He counts Job's steps, keeps implacable watch over his sin, sealing it up in a bag with a view to exposure and punishment.

The destruction of man is illustrated by the imagery of natural erosion:

> And indeed a mountain falling cometh to nought, and the rock is removed
> out of its place; The waters wear the stones, the floods thereof wash away
> the dust of the earth; and thou destroyest the hope of man (14.18-19,
> JND).

If the world around is susceptible to inevitable decay, what hope is there for
puny man? Job's eye moves from the monumentally great right down to the
infinitesimally tiny. The mountain, the rocks, the individual stones, even the
powdery dust of the ground – they are all brought to nothing. Frail man therefore
has nothing to look forward to save death, with no glimmer of light at the end.
The picture is bleak in the extreme. But Job has not finished. He presents a chilling
glimpse of a deathbed scene: "Thou prevailest for ever against him, and he passeth:
thou changest [8138] his countenance, and sendest him away" (14.20). The God
who destroys the mountains overcomes every individual man, dismissing him
from life. The shocking close-up of a human face undergoing physical change at
the moment of death, as the spirit is sent away to *sheol*, is harrowing. Sinful man
is headed for decomposition. Men change and decay. But when we reach the
end of the Old Testament – and here is the great comfort – God says, "I am the
Lord, I change [8138] not" (Mal 3.6). Job would have assented to the words of
the hymn writer:

> Change and decay in all around I see,
> O Thou who changest not, abide with me!

Once snatched away in death, man becomes oblivious to everything that
happens afterwards. Perhaps his children rise to a high position in society,
perhaps they fall into degradation and poverty, but he knows nothing about it.
As Solomon puts it, "Whatsoever thy hand findeth to do, do it with thy might;
for there is no work, nor device, nor knowledge, nor wisdom, in the grave [*sheol*],
whither thou goest" (Eccl 9.10).

The man in *sheol* has no awareness of what is taking place on earth, for Job tells
us that "his flesh hath pain for himself alone, and his soul mourneth for himself"
(14.22, JND). Delitzsch offers this commentary:

> He has no knowledge and interest that extends beyond himself; only he
> himself is the object of that which takes place with his flesh in the grave,
> and of that on which his soul reflects below in the depths of [*sheol*] … [so
> that] the process of the decomposition of the body is a source of pain and
> sorrow to the departed spirit.[157]

Although this is a possible understanding of the verse, it seems more likely
that Job is describing the physical ("flesh") and mental ("soul") sufferings of an
individual approaching death. Even before he leaves the world for the place of

departed spirits, he is so self-preoccupied that he can think of nothing else. As Hartley explains it, "before death the entire person is caught in the throes of pain and is reduced to mourning solely for himself".[158] The chapter which rose to the anticipation of a glorious resurrection and restored communion ends with pain and mourning.

It is a grim outlook. Job concludes the first round of the verbal debate with a return to the kind of melancholy which expressed itself so disturbingly in his great complaint of chapter 3. Nevertheless, we must not forget those oases of confidence which hint at the development of faith in his soul. There are three great moments:

> With him is wisdom and strength, he hath counsel and understanding (12.13).

> Behold, he will slay me; I have no hope: Nevertheless I will maintain my ways before him (13.15, ASV).

> O that thou wouldest hide me in the grave, that thou wouldest keep me secret, until thy wrath be past, that thou wouldest appoint me a set time, and remember me! If a man die, shall he live again? all the days of my appointed time will I wait, till my change come. Thou shalt call, and I will answer thee: thou wilt have a desire to the work of thine hands (14.13-15).

The first is an acknowledgement of God's supreme wisdom and power, faintly anticipating the trembling reverence with which Job will respond to Jehovah's awesome self-disclosure in chapters 38 to 41. Whatever our circumstances, God eternally combines wisdom and might, a truth which should generate in His people both assurance and adoration. The second balances a resigned awareness that nothing but death lies ahead ("I have no hope") against a confidence that God hears His children's cries ("I will maintain my ways before him"). When everything seems dark as night, it is always possible to pray. Friends may fail but God is faithful. As David put it later, "I am in a great strait: let us fall now into the hand of the Lord; for his mercies are great: and let me not fall into the hand of man" (2 Sam 24.14). The third rises to an amazing prayer for a resurrection of the just which had not yet been revealed to men. Momentarily Job enters into the heart of God in the same way that Moses, interceding for guilty Israel, delighted the Lord by expressing before Him His own feelings for His erring people. With the atoning death of the incarnate Son it becomes evident as never before that God has "a desire to the work of [His] hands", seeing that He was willing to pay such a price to redeem them.

But these are just glimmerings in the gloom. We are as yet only one third of the way through Job's education.

SECTION 10
Dialogue: Job 4 – 42.6
Contest: Round 2: Job 15-21
Eliphaz's 2nd Speech: Job 15

By this stage in the book, one entire round of debate has taken place, with Job ceaselessly bombarded on all sides by his friends. But though verbally and emotionally battered he remains unbowed, resolute in his refusal to agree with their unanimous verdict on his sudden calamities. The reader, privy to the information in the prologue, is of course fully aware of his innocence, though perhaps a trifle perplexed by his increasingly self-righteous attitude. It is undeniably true that Job has done nothing to deserve the miseries which have been inflicted on him; indeed, it was ironically his very uprightness which qualified him to bear the full brunt of satanic malice. Nevertheless, under the constant criticism of his friends, he has given way to remarks about God's justice and goodness which he will later regret.

As the senior member of the opposition, Eliphaz initiates Round Two, responding to Job's unyielding defiance with a blistering attack on his character. There is a notable difference between this speech and his first in chapters 4 and 5. Gone is the sweet talk about Job's past virtues, gone is the gentle suggestion that God may be chastening him with a view to blessing, gone is the kindly exhortation to repentance. He now views Job as "a hardened sinner in arrogant rebellion against God".[159] Under the velvet glove is the mailed fist, for Eliphaz proceeds to treat Job with the disparagement displayed in the earlier comments of Bildad and Zophar. If the reader was fooled into thinking Eliphaz a sympathetic old man, now is the time to think again!

His verbal attack is three-pronged. First, he reprimands the patriarch for his irreverent speeches (15.1-13), signalled by the frequent allusions to conversation: "utter … talk … speeches … mouth … tongue … lips". Then he puts on record an uncompromising diagnosis of what he considers to be Job's basic problem – his innate wickedness (15.14-16). Finally, he pulls back the curtain from the future in a lengthy and no-holds-barred description of the inevitable destiny of the wicked (15.17-35). He begins and ends with a reference to the belly. The Hebrew word (990) is translated in the KJV in a variety of ways, such as belly, womb, or body; here it refers to the innermost parts of man. According to Eliphaz, Job's words reveal him as no more than a motor mouth, giving vent to meaningless blasts of hot air (15.2). More damning still is his concluding verdict on evil men (of whom, naturally, Job is the prime example), men who "conceive mischief, and bring forth vanity, and their belly prepareth deceit" (15.35). The imagery of childbirth suggests how natural, how instinctive are the godless man's lies. A rotten tree will yield only rotten fruit.

The speech therefore breaks up into the following sections:

   1. Eliphaz Rebukes Job's Disrespect: 15.1-13
   2. Eliphaz Records his Diagnosis: 15.14-16
   3. Eliphaz Reveals Job's Destiny: 15.17-35.

Eliphaz Rebukes Job's Disrespect: 15.1-13

This section is peppered with thirteen questions, as Eliphaz interrogates the hapless Job much like an energetic prosecution counsel laying into his victim. The twenty-three second person singular pronouns leave no doubt about the target. The jabbing finger points constantly at the beleaguered invalid. Eliphaz first deplores the emptiness of Job's answers (15.2-6) and then concentrates his attack on the expression of his arrogance (15.7-13).

This has been called "a reprimand speech". The **emptiness of Job's answers** (15.2-6) is evident because everything he has said is simply hot air. Clearly Eliphaz thinks Job talks far too much. His allusion to the east wind refers to "the strong, hot wind that blows off the desert. It is dreaded in the Near East because its dry burning heat brings days of irritability and listlessness".[160] To Eliphaz, it is astonishing that Job has the effrontery to claim to be "a wise man" (v.2), on a par with his distinguished visitors. The word (7307) translated "vain" (which in its context is a disparaging criticism of Job's verbal windiness) appears thirty-one times in this book, bearing a range of meanings. It describes, for example, the hurricane that destroyed Job's son's house (1.19), God's anger (4.9), the mysterious spirit that communicated with Eliphaz (4.15), the transience of human life (7.7), the natural process of respiration (9.18), the human spirit (15.13), and the Spirit of God (26.13; 33.4). Interestingly, Job himself first employs this imagery. Fully admitting that his words are blustery, he excuses his intemperate speeches as the utterances of "one that is desperate, which are as wind" (6.26). Eliphaz is therefore hardly saying anything new. Job has already confessed that distress provoked his outbursts of passion, which his friends should treat with allowance, bearing in mind his sufferings. We may agree with Eliphaz that such language has no beneficial value: "Should he reason with unprofitable talk? or with speeches wherewith he can do no good?" (15.3). But can people in appalling pain be judged by the normal standards of polite, rational discourse?

Eliphaz, however, is unwilling to make any concessions. On the contrary, he diagnoses Job's words as proof of headstrong irreverence: "thou makest piety of none effect, and restrainest meditation before God" (15.4, JND). Worse even than Job's recalcitrance, is his influence on others. In Davidson's words, "The tendency of his conduct and principles must be to diminish and do away with devoutness and religion among men".[161]

Every believer must bear in mind the wider effect of his words and actions. Abraham's disastrous flight into Egypt gave his nephew Lot a taste for luxurious ease which ruined his pilgrim life, luring him in the direction of Sodom. David's polygamy must have had some impact on Solomon, who saw no reason not to outdo his father. Manasseh's flagrant idolatry so infected the nation of Judah that not even his unexpected repentance could cancel the ill he had caused. A good question to ask is this: would it be glorifying to God if every believer in my local assembly behaved like me? That said, when we look back at Job's earlier speeches, noting how often he takes refuge in prayer, we can only feel that Eliphaz is guilty of exaggeration and misrepresentation. Without adducing any shred of evidence, he accuses Job of wickedness and guile, asserting that "thine iniquity teacheth thy mouth, and thou choosest the tongue of the crafty" (15.5, RV). This is the unvarying position of the three friends. Though Job's reputation for godliness was without parallel, and his outward conduct towards to his neighbours a model of charity, the sudden reversal of his circumstances is the only data with which his friends are prepared to work. All past behaviour and blessings are conveniently forgotten. Whatever he may say, he stands condemned, and any attempt at self-defence only exacerbates his guilt. According to Eliphaz, no upright man would ever stoop to put into words what Job has been uttering: "Thine own mouth condemneth thee, and not I: yea, thine own lips testify against thee" (15.6).

Though admittedly unorthodox, Job's words have been spoken to a select company of friends who travelled to visit him in his sickness. He has not been promoting doctrinal error from the platform, or publishing his doubts and anxieties to all and sundry. Just as there is a difference between those personal psalms of David which unveil the apprehensions of his soul, and his formal public prayers and poems as the nation's leader, so too there is a difference between the public teaching of the Word and the innermost confessions of a saint undergoing acute trial. Those who honestly but discreetly unburden themselves to intimate friends and responsible brethren cannot be charged with perverting the people of God.

Eliphaz now turns his attention to what he considers the shocking **expression of Job's arrogance** (15.7-13). The questions come thick and fast, all designed, in their snide sarcasm, to humiliate the patriarch. Was Job as old as Cain ("the first man to be born"), or does he antedate the hills which, in their relative immovability, seemed to a man like Jacob to be everlasting (Gen 49.26)? "Hast thou listened in the secret council of God? And hast thou absorbed wisdom for thyself?" (15.8, JND). The contempt is laid on with a trowel. Has Job a special pass admitting him to the secret counsels of the Godhead, or has he assimilated all the wisdom of heaven? Eliphaz is attempting to return the aces Job served in his earlier speeches when challenging his friends' smug self-confidence and trite sayings (12.2-3; 13.2).

Some of this language anticipates the Proverbs, with its testimony to the eternity of divine wisdom:

I was set up from everlasting, from the beginning, or ever the earth was. When there were no depths, I was brought forth; when there were no fountains abounding with water. Before the mountains were settled, before the hills was I brought forth: While as yet he had not made the earth, nor the fields, nor the highest part of the dust of the world. When he prepared the heavens, I was there: when he set a compass upon the face of the depth: When he established the clouds above: when he strengthened the fountains of the deep: When he gave to the sea his decree, that the waters should not pass his commandment: when he appointed the foundations of the earth: Then I was by him, as one brought up with him: and I was daily his delight, rejoicing always before him; Rejoicing in the habitable part of his earth; and my delights were with the sons of men (Prov 8.23-31).

But there is a huge difference. What in the book of Job is caustic irony is in Proverbs a moving hymn in celebration of a glorious divine attribute which, like God Himself, has neither beginning nor end. This famous personification of God's wisdom has, not surprisingly, reminded many believers of the eternal Son in His uncreated excellence (Micah 5.2). The Son's active involvement in creation (Col 1.16), His face to face fellowship with God (Jn 1.1-2), the pleasure He constantly brought to God (Mt 3.16-17), and the delight He finds in man (1 Jn 4.19) seem to be sketched out here. Only the Son has unhindered access to the Father's heart and unlimited ability to make Him known:

> Then answered Jesus and said unto them, Verily, verily, I say unto you, The Son can do nothing of himself, but what he seeth the Father do: for what things soever he doeth, these also doeth the Son likewise. For the Father loveth the Son, and sheweth him all things that himself doeth: and he will shew him greater works than these, that ye may marvel (Jn 5.19-20).

> I speak that which I have seen with my Father (Jn 8.38).

The Son of God remains gloriously unique in all His excellences, especially His function of revealing deity, for "in him dwelleth all the fulness of the Godhead bodily" (Col 2.9).

Nevertheless, it is the marvel of God's grace that He loves to disclose some of His inscrutable secrets to His people. Thus it was Abraham (rather than Lot) who learned first about the divine plan for Sodom for, as God said, "shall I hide from Abraham that thing which I do?" (Gen 18.17). But the New Testament is far more expansive in unveiling God's heart: the coming of the Son has made the Father known. The key verse is John 1.18: "No man hath seen God at any time; the only begotten Son, which is in the bosom of the Father, he hath declared him". As to His divine essence, God is invisible to all creaturely eyes, yet the incarnation of the Son has revealed God as Father in a way never known in Old Testament times. Thayer's *Lexicon* informs us that the word for "declare" was "used in Greek writing of the interpretation of things sacred and divine, oracles, dreams". We may therefore appropriately say that the Son has uniquely interpreted or exegeted the Father to men. The same Son says to His disciples, "Henceforth I call you not servants; for the servant knoweth not what his lord doeth: but I have called you friends; for all things that I have heard of my Father I have made known unto you" (Jn 15.15). Astonishing though it may sound, the simplest believer in the Lord Jesus Christ today possesses an insight into the heart of God and His plans for this universe surpassing that of the world's universities.

Eliphaz's intention is to prick what he considers the dangerous bubble of Job's self-conceit. His diction, however, betrays the fact that his own ego has been severely bruised. After all, Job has failed to assent to his mature advice. This is why he angrily closes ranks with his colleagues to defend their joint reputation for pious wisdom:

What knowest thou, that we know not? what understandest thou, which
is not in us? With us are both the grayheaded and very aged men, much
elder than thy father (15.9-10).

Trading insults or building truth on mere antiquity is scarcely persuasive. It is
rather like defending a doctrine on the grounds that "this is what assemblies have
always taught", a line of argument which smacks of special pleading instead of
biblical reasoning, When men cannot find scripture to support their views they
sometimes, alas, resort to bullying tactics or retreat behind weight of numbers.
Eliphaz, we may note, is condemning Job for arrogance while his own approach
is no better.

His reference to the "consolations of God" has to be understood in its context:
"Are the consolations of God too small for thee? and the word gently spoken to
thee?" (15.11, JND). It seems clear from the immediately preceding verses and the
second part of verse 11 that he is alluding, not to divine comfort in general, but
to the specific advice he and the other sages have been offering. We, he is saying,
are venerable purveyors of gracious encouragement from God Himself which you
refuse at your own peril, Job. It is clear that Job's friends have a disturbingly high
view of themselves and their ministry.

Nevertheless, we may be profoundly thankful that it is indeed possible to
receive genuine consolation from the Lord. The Hebrew word (8575) occurs only
five times in the Old Testament, and its appearances suggest something of its
range of meaning. Here are the other occasions:

Hear diligently my speech, and let this be your consolations [8575] (21.2).

When I said, My foot slippeth; thy mercy, O Lord, held me up. In the
multitude of my thoughts within me thy comforts [8575] delight my soul
(Ps 94.18-19).

Rejoice ye with Jerusalem, and be glad with her, all ye that love her: rejoice
for joy with her, all ye that mourn for her: That ye may suck, and be
satisfied with the breasts of her consolations [8575]; that ye may milk out,
and be delighted with the abundance of her glory (Is 66.10-11).

Neither shall men tear themselves for them in mourning, to comfort them
for the dead; neither shall men give them the cup of consolation [8575] to
drink for their father or for their mother (Jer 16.7).

The first of these examples is Job returning Eliphaz's word in 15.11 back to
the three friends. One has to admit that their debate does at times resemble a
fast-moving game of verbal tennis in which terms and topics are batted to and
fro as each seeks to score a winning point. The second, however, is a very positive
example. The psalmist finds an oasis of sustaining joy amidst his current distresses
by meditating on God's goodness. Even though his wayward thoughts were many

and various, he gains genuine solace in reflecting upon divine mercy. John Gill helpfully explains the context:

> The word for thoughts [Ps 94.19] is used of branches of trees, thick and entwined, and so denotes perplexed and distressing thoughts, such as good men sometimes have concerning God; his awful and tremendous majesty; the perfections of his nature, particularly his power, purity, and holiness; concerning their relation to him, his presence with them, and good will towards them, which, because of their sins, they are ready to doubt of; thoughts concerning sin; that there are no sins like theirs, attended with such aggravated circumstances; that they are such as will not be forgiven; or they fear their corruptions will be too many for them, and they shall perish by them; or that they shall so fall as to bring dishonour on the ways of God.

In the midst of so many unsettling meditations, the psalmist is stabilized by concentrating his mind on God's grace. This is still the believer's experience as he turns from self-contemplation, always a recipe for misery, to immerse himself in the blessings God lavishes on His redeemed. The third example looks ahead to Israel's glorious future, when all who recognise God's grand purpose for His ancient people will rejoice in Jerusalem's revived prosperity under her reigning Messiah. The final instance is the Lord's instruction to Jeremiah in the light of Jerusalem's imminent fall to the Babylonian army in 586 BC. Death and destruction would be so commonplace that there would be no time for the normal cultural ceremonies of mourning, such as passing the "cup of consolation". If nothing else, these examples testify that genuine solace is found only in the Lord.

Human comfort is at best a let-down – which was certainly Job's bitter experience with his friends – but the real "consolations of God", those grounded upon His infallible revelation, never fail. Further, they so often deal with us gently, tenderly reminding our souls of the abundance of God's mercies. What the KJV translates as "secret" is a word (328) occurring only five times elsewhere and rendered "softly" (Gen 33.14; 1 Kings 21.27; Is 8.6), "gently" (2 Sam 18.5), and once "the charmers" (Is 19.3), alluding to occult practitioners who in their mystic trances make faint murmurings. The idea is best illustrated in the 2 Samuel reference which reports David's earnest desire that his soldiers, pursuing the rebel army, "Deal gently [328] for my sake with the young man, even with Absalom". Where the hard-hearted Joab failed to "deal gently", the Scriptures perfectly apply divine comfort to the aching heart.

Our privilege outstrips that of Job's era because we possess the completed word in which is found everything needed for life and godliness. Neither he nor his visitors could turn to the Bible. Little wonder they were so obviously short of authority for their ideas! We have only to contrast the situation in the New Testament. What followed when the letter from the Jerusalem elders, about not imposing Jewish ways on Gentile believers, was read out at Antioch? The result was what God's Word should always produce in our hearts: "Which when they had read, they rejoiced for the consolation" (Acts 15.31). If Scripture fails to engender joy, it is likely that we are reading it inattentively.

Eliphaz concludes this part of his attack by accusing Job of an undisciplined heart, angry eyes, and a spirit in revolt against God:

> Why doth thy heart carry thee away? and why do thine eyes wink? That thou turnest thy spirit against God, and lettest words go out of thy mouth? (15.12-13, JND).

Winking eyes (the ESV suggests that they "flash") indicate indignation or pride (Young's Literal Translation offers this: "And what – are thine eyes high?"). Whatever the case, the outcome is clear: in speaking the way he does, Job is guilty of setting himself against God.

As we make our way through the book of Job, we must never forget that Eliphaz and his companions see themselves as the official spokesmen for orthodox godliness. As far as Eliphaz is concerned, his words are a divinely inspired ministry of advice, which Job has the impudence to resist. To reject the friends' counsel is therefore to reject God. That Eliphaz has an absurdly inflated and erroneous view of himself will become evident at the close, when the God on whose behalf he claims to speak announces, "My wrath is kindled against thee, and against thy two friends: for ye have not spoken of me the thing that is right" (42.7). On the other hand, in reading the words of the apostle Paul in the New Testament we encounter the mind of God, for he taught with genuine divine authority. His claim is unabashed and straightforward:

> What? came the word of God out from you? or came it unto you only? If any man think himself to be a prophet, or spiritual, let him acknowledge that the things that I write unto you are the commandments of the Lord. But if any man be ignorant, let him be ignorant (1 Cor 14.36-38).

> For this we say unto you by the word of the Lord, that we which are alive and remain unto the coming of the Lord shall not prevent them which are asleep (1 Thess 4.15).

> By revelation he made known unto me the mystery; (as I wrote afore in few words, Whereby, when ye read, ye may understand my knowledge in the mystery of Christ) Which in other ages was not made known unto the sons of men, as it is now revealed unto his holy apostles and prophets by the Spirit; That the Gentiles should be fellowheirs, and of the same body, and partakers of his promise in Christ by the gospel: Whereof I was made a minister, according to the gift of the grace of God given unto me by the effectual working of his power (Eph 3.3-7).

This was no delusion of grandeur but simple truth. To Paul was entrusted a unique unveiling of God's mind concerning the present age. Like salvation itself, it had nothing to do with his merits but sprang entirely from God's sovereign grace and purpose. That being the case, we can legitimately affirm that "what Paul says, God says". Some are eager to demean what they disparage as "Paul's ideas", not because they are in any sense ambiguous but because they run counter to modern fashions. To be palatable to a modern world, Pauline teaching must be adjusted in the light of the latest fads. But God's Word, mediated through Paul or anyone else, has never been and never will be acceptable to a world system governed by Satan. Opposition to Paul is nothing new; a reading of the Corinthian letters indicates early hostility to his authority and his message. Notwithstanding, the testimony of Scripture is clear: Paul, unlike Eliphaz, wrote under full inspiration. To resist his teaching is to reject the Lord's Word.

Eliphaz Records his Diagnosis: 15.14-16

Repeating a question Job has raised in earlier chapters, Eliphaz now pronounces verdict upon "abominable and filthy man", speaking obliquely yet evidently with one particular man in view – Job. His language combines echoes of his original teaching in 4.17 and Job's question in 7.17, along with Job's recent comment about "man that is born of a woman" (14.1). This last verse alone demonstrates the redundancy of Eliphaz's argument, because Job has never denied the fact of human sinfulness. Nevertheless Eliphaz presses on:

> What is man, that he should be pure? and he that is born of a woman, that he should be righteous? Behold, he putteth no trust in his holy ones, and the heavens are not pure in his sight: How much less the abominable and corrupt, - man, that drinketh unrighteousness like water! (15.14-16, JND).

How can man, with his inherited depravity, be clean in God's sight? Even the angels and the created heavens are impure compared with the ineffable holiness of God, so what hope is there for sin-stained humanity? The adjectives assault human self-satisfaction. What is man? He is abominable, or morally detestable. He is unspeakably filthy, sour or morally corrupt. The KJV's word "filthy" (444) only appears here and in the psalmist's repeatedly negative assessment of mankind: "They are all gone aside, they are all together become filthy: there is none that doeth good, no, not one" (Ps 14.3; 53.3). And what is man's characteristic activity? He gulps down iniquity and unrighteousness as though it were the elixir of life.

In context, Eliphaz's indignant assessment of man is aimed primarily at Job. It is a rhetorical strategy designed to discomfit the target of his eloquence. As a strategy it is flawed, for, as mentioned above, Job is well aware of man's fallen nature. Nevertheless there is important truth in Eliphaz's words. We are all – to use the language of the theologians – totally depraved. The terminology is frequently misunderstood. It does not mean that every man is as bad as he possibly can be, but rather that he is bad in every area of life. Like a stick of seaside rock, his ingrained sin nature goes all through him from the first bite to the very last, influencing and polluting every thought, word, and deed. Even what he might pride himself on as his best moments are only filthy rags in God's sight (Is 64.6).

We are, in other words, as badly off as we can possibly be, "alienated from the life of God" (Eph 4.18) and heading inexorably towards eternal judgment. There is nothing we can do to please God, nor can we lift a finger to save ourselves. If there is in any man the slightest distaste for his own wickedness, the slightest yearning for deliverance, it is a testimony to the sovereign movement of the Holy Spirit. Those who have by grace been rescued from the terrible everlasting consequences of their sinfulness on the basis of the saving work of Christ will be the very last to forget the wretchedness of their condition by nature. To minimize the awful sinfulness of man is to demean the work of Calvary.

Eliphaz Reveals Job's Destiny: 15.17-35

Although, apart from verse 17, this section, like the previous three verses, avoids addressing Job directly, there can be no doubt that "the wicked man" (15.20) refers to him. After an introduction (15.17-19) which does no more than reiterate Eliphaz's assertion that his words rest upon personal experience ("that which I have seen I will declare") and the wisdom of the ages ("Which wise men have told from their fathers"), we are offered an inside view of the wicked man's fear (15.20-24), folly (15.25-27) and future (15.28-35). All this is designed to contradict Job's insistence that bad men often prosper down here.

The wicked man's fear (15.20-24) is discovered in the torments and terrors which dominate his lifetime, however long it may last. Regardless of outward prosperity, his doom is sealed. Smick puts it like this: "the wicked never escape the torment they deserve; and even if they do, for a moment, trouble is just around the corner".[162]

The language of the KJV suggests that this underlying fear derives from a man's ignorance of how long he will live: "The wicked man travaileth with pain all his days, and the number of years is hidden to the oppressor" (15.20). But the word "hidden" (6845) is elsewhere translated "laid up" (as, for example, in Job 21.19; Ps 31.19; Prov 2.7), which at least raises the possibility that it is not so much the wicked man's ignorance of his life-span which is the issue here, but the fact that his days are fixed by God. This is certainly the way other translations render the verse:

> The wicked man travaileth with pain all his days, even the number of years that are laid up for the oppressor (15.20, RV).

> All his days the wicked man is tormented, and numbered years are allotted to the violent (15.20, JND).

> The wicked man writhes in pain all his days, through all the years that are laid up for the ruthless (15.20, ESV).

From the start his days are numbered, because God alone determines whether a man's life is long or brief, just as He "removeth kings, and setteth up kings" (Dan 2.21). For the believer this is a salutary reminder that our pilgrimage in this world is comparatively short, its duration preordained of God. That is why we are exhorted to a wise employment of our time. Moses's prayer is that the Lord would "teach us to number our days, that we may apply our hearts unto wisdom" (Ps 90.12), while Paul urges us to "walk circumspectly, not as fools, but as wise, Redeeming the time, because the days are evil" (Eph 5.15-16), walking "in wisdom toward them that are without, redeeming the time" (Col 4.5). The wicked man resents life's transience; the child of God rejoices that it is all in His hands, and therefore seeks to live it out to His glory.

What Eliphaz describes in some detail seems to be the corrosive effect of an evil conscience. Even amidst success, the sinner dreads what lies over the horizon, terrified of possible disasters, for "The wicked flee when no man pursueth" (Prov 28.1). The feverish apprehensions of his guilt-ridden thinking processes are graphically laid bare:

> The sound of terrors is in his ears: in prosperity the destroyer cometh upon him. He believeth not that he shall return out of darkness, and he is singled out for the sword. He wandereth abroad for bread, - where may it be? He knoweth that the day of darkness is ready at his hand. Distress and anguish make him afraid; they prevail against him, as a king ready for the battle (15.21-24, JND).

The impact of a guilty conscience has long been the opportunity for a literary *tour de force*. Shakespeare dramatised it in *Macbeth*, Sir Henry Irving created a sensation in Victorian London with his performance in Leopold Lewis's melodrama *The Bells*, and Dickens sketched its effects in the character of Jonas Chuzzlewit. But Eliphaz produces his own tableau of a sin-burdened mind, constantly on the edge of uncertainty, alert for calamity, living in anticipation of violent death, fearful of famine in the midst of plenty. It is exactly the opposite of the picture he painted earlier of the godly man:

> there shall no evil touch thee. In famine he shall redeem thee from death: and in war from the power of the sword. Thou shalt be hid from the scourge of the tongue: neither shalt thou be afraid of destruction when it cometh. At destruction and famine thou shalt laugh: neither shalt thou be afraid of the beasts of the earth. For thou shalt be in league with the stones of the field: and the beasts of the field shall be at peace with thee (5.19-23).

But that was when he felt able to offer Job the blessings of recovery, were he only to repent and return to the Lord. By this stage Eliphaz has changed his mind about Job, and is persuaded of his irretrievable guilt. Despite his reputation for godliness, he must all the time have been deceiving his friends with a crafty veneer of hypocrisy. There is a clear tilt at Job in the description of one who "believeth not that he shall return out of darkness", for Job has constantly confessed a dread that his death is imminent. It is as if Eliphaz is saying, "Look Job, this is the real face of the guilty man – do you not recognise yourself in the mirror of my description?"

He moves on to explain the reason for such misery by unfolding **the wicked man's folly** (15.25-27): "he stretcheth out his hand against God, and strengtheneth himself against the Almighty" (15.25). To oppose God is to be guilty of overweening stupidity. Eliphaz describes the wicked man's rash actions. Verse 25 speaks of wilful arrogance, for he "behaveth himself proudly against the Almighty" (15.25, RV), while verse 26 pictures him like a warrior who defiantly "runneth against him [God], with outstretched neck, with the thick bosses of his bucklers [4043]" (15.26, JND). Bosses are the hard outward projections of a shield. Ironically this military word is first used in Scripture of God's great promise to Abram that "I am thy shield [4043], and thy exceeding great reward" (Gen 15.1). Seeking to rescue his nephew Lot, Abram had attacked and defeated an army many times larger than his own household militia. More, he had refused the spoil offered him by the grateful king of Sodom. Now, however, he might have had second thoughts. Would he be the object of a devastating reprisal attack? Had he lost valuable possessions? Jehovah's assurance met both his anxieties: God Himself was his defence and his wealth. Those who place their faith in God find Him to be their protection, while those who use their utmost force against Him are doomed to defeat. Their inevitable failure is emphasised in Eliphaz's choice of the word "Almighty" for God (15.25).

But why does the wicked man behave so foolishly? The answer is given in verse 27: "he hath covered his face with his fatness, and gathered fat upon his flanks" (15.27, JND). The God-hater is one whose material prosperity has given him a fleshly solidity which encourages conceit: his face and waistline broadcast his self-indulgence. We might remember Eglon the king of Moab, "a very fat man" (Judg 3.17), whose cruel dominion over Israel was brought to an abrupt end by the remarkable one-man enterprise of Ehud. Scripture often uses fatness as a symbol of material abundance, whether human self-sufficiency and pride ("Their eyes stand out with fatness: they have more than heart could wish", Ps 73.7) or the result of divine blessing ("I will satiate the soul of the priests with fatness, and my people shall be satisfied with my goodness, saith the Lord", Jer 31.14). Since every material blessing ultimately comes from above, no man can boast in his riches, for "The rich and poor meet together: the Lord is the maker of them all" (Prov 22.2). Nevertheless, the current affluence of the western world seems to spawn atheism rather than grateful dependence on God.

Has Eliphaz's military imagery in these verses been influenced by Job's own picture language? He spoke earlier of "the arrows of the Almighty" and "the terrors of God [which] do set themselves in array against me" (6.4). He saw himself as a target for divine archery, one against whom God's hosts were formed up in battle order. If Eliphaz is thinking of this, then he has turned the image back against Job. Far from being the innocent victim of heavenly aggression, Job is a deliberate rebel whose insolence has stirred up retribution.

This retribution is spelled out in greater detail as Eliphaz looks ahead to **the wicked man's future** (15.28-35). He lives in desolation, deprivation and darkness:

> And he dwelleth in desolate cities, in houses that no man inhabiteth, which are destined to become heaps. He shall not become rich, neither shall his

substance continue, and their possessions shall not extend upon the earth.
He shall not depart out of darkness; the flame shall dry up his branches;
and by the breath of his mouth shall he go away (15.28-30, JND).

It is probable that in verse 28 Eliphaz is describing the haunt of robbers and
brigands, so as to contradict Job's rash assertion about their invariable prosperity.
Job had said that "The tabernacles of robbers prosper, and they that provoke God
are secure; into whose hand God bringeth abundantly" (12.6), but Eliphaz's picture
is entirely different. The language of ruined dwellings looks back the catastrophic
destruction of Job's eldest son's house (1.18-19), while the prophecy that the wicked
man will never again be rich recollects the sudden removal of Job's wealth. The
darkness of verse 30 not only reflects such a man's innate fear of the future (15.22)
but also, in its reference to withered branches, hints at the slaughter of Job's children
(1.18-19). With gratuitous cruelty, Eliphaz reminds Job of his losses in order to
drive home the conclusion (a false one) that Job is a great sinner.

In the middle of this account of the evil man's inescapable ruin, Eliphaz offers
a word of advice: "Let him not trust in vanity, deceiving himself: for vanity shall
be his recompence" (15.31, RV). To shelter behind the emptiness of false ideas
about man and God is only to delude oneself and discover too late the failure of
one's boasted security. Sinful man constructs "wishful thinking" defences against
the judgment of God. Perhaps there is no God at all or, if there is, perhaps He
will be tolerant of evil, or perhaps my good deeds will outweigh my bad. In
his excellent book, *Ten Lies about God*, Lutzer analyses the way people redefine
their idea of God to suit their own desires. He becomes a cosy non-judgmental
god (unworthy of an upper case letter) who conveniently affirms our personal
preferences, glosses over our sins, and functions to make us feel good. But as
Lutzer says, "the biblical God … stands in sharp contrast to all options on today's
spiritual smorgasbord".[163] From Him there is no escape. Eliphaz is correct as far
as he goes. Those who trust in themselves will find no shelter from the wrath of a
God who is holy, all-knowing, and omnipotent. But Christians know that there
is a shelter in the person of Christ, who bore in His own body on the tree the
terrible penalty His people deserve. To be found in Him is to be eternally secure.

Eliphaz does not linger over his advice. Back in chapter 5 he devoted eleven
verses to an exposition of the blessings awaiting a repentant Job. But there is no call
here to a spiritual change of mind, only a catalogue of the calamities overhanging
the wicked. The recompense of the wicked man "will be paid in full before his
time, and his branch will not be green" (15.32, ESV). God will intervene to
"shake off his unripe grapes as a vine, and shall cast his flower as an olive" (15.33,
JND), so that the man is removed before his prime, cut down before he reaches
fruition. The imagery of unripe grapes and cast off olive blossom again looks back
to the annihilation of Job's family. According to Hartley, "every other year the
olive tree produces a vast number of blossoms that never set. In these years the
early promise of fruit never materialises".[164] The "fire" that "shall consume the
tabernacles of bribery" is the same word for the lightning which incinerated Job's
sheep and servants (1.16). Eliphaz will not let Job forget his pains.

It is worth observing that his underlying imagery gives the lie to Job's insistence that "there is hope of a tree, if it be cut down, that it will sprout again, and that the tender branch thereof will not cease" (14.7). Allusions to dried and withered up branches (15.30,32) not only remind Job of the tragedy of his children, but also implicitly contest any notion of hope for man beyond the grave. Hartley sums it up like this:

> In the Old Testament the tree serves as a symbol of an upright dignified person. But Eliphaz observes that a stately tree may wither and die ... Renewal is not possible for this tree, because an austere environment squeezes out its energy, its life. With this illustration from nature Eliphaz is discouraging Job's speculation that there might be hope beyond death.[165]

The tree can indeed speak of the godly man. We need only think of Psalm 1.3, Psalm 52.8, and perhaps especially Jeremiah 17:

> Blessed is the man that trusteth in the Lord, and whose hope the Lord is. For he shall be as a tree planted by the waters, and that spreadeth out her roots by the river, and shall not see when heat cometh, but her leaf shall be green; and shall not be careful in the year of drought, neither shall cease from yielding fruit (Jer 17.7-8).

Such scriptures do not support Eliphaz's pessimism. God promises the ability to endure hardships because a tree planted beside waters possesses an unfailing source of nourishment. Here we should pause to notice that the parallel with Job is remarkable. He is a man who has long trusted in the Lord, and even though he is currently enduring a season of drought – creating waves of anxiety in his mind – he still remains convinced deep down that his God is in control, and will in due time vindicate him. Though we may never face the onslaughts which battered Job, we enjoy an unfailing supply of spiritual refreshment far exceeding anything available to Old Testament believers: the written Word in its infallible sufficiency, the indwelling Holy Spirit, the interceding High Priestly ministry of the exalted Christ, the fellowship of saints in the local assembly. Such advantages are invisible to the world, but nonetheless blessedly real.

Eliphaz not only reminds Job of his tragedy, he also presumes to explain it: Job belongs to the "company of the godless", and is ominously associated with "the tents of bribery" (15.34, RV). He is, says Eliphaz, a radically impious man guilty of corruption in his financial dealings. Both Godward and manward, Job falls short. The final verse brings together three words expressive of Job's condition: "mischief", "iniquity", "deceit" (15.35, JND and RV). The lexis is interesting. "Mischief" (5999) is translated various ways in the KJV: labour, mischief, misery, travail, trouble, sorrow, grievance, pain, perverseness. "Iniquity" (205) is a word Brown Driver and Briggs define as "trouble, wickedness, sorrow". The word rendered "deceit" (4820) signifies, according to the same authority, "deceit, treachery". It is first used by Isaac to describe Jacob's "subtilty" (Gen 27.35) in robbing Esau of his blessing. The first two of Eliphaz's three words come together when Balaam confesses, against his will, that despite Israel's failures, God in grace refused to acknowledge their sins: "He hath not beheld iniquity [205] in Jacob, neither hath he seen perverseness [5999] in Israel: the Lord his God is with him, and the shout of a king is among them" (Num 23.21). The language looks beyond the fickle Israel of the wilderness wanderings to a nation spiritually regenerated, nationally restored, and blessed with its Messiah in the midst. A greedy pagan prophet was granted a foreview of Israel's future glory.

Under the superintending hand of divine inspiration, Balaam had to speak truly about Israel, though it went against the grain of his covetous nature. Eliphaz, on the other hand, is not speaking accurately about Job. His words apply to a hardened rebel, not to a saint undergoing terrible trial. This is one of the great failings of the comforters. They say what is right, but to the wrong person at the wrong time for the wrong reason.

Delivering a sermon on verse 11 of this chapter, Spurgeon said the following:

> However wrong Eliphaz may have been in reference to Job – and in reference to him his remarks were grossly unjust – yet many of them are correct in themselves, and may usefully be applied to our own hearts.[166]

It is therefore appropriate to pause and list some of the things Eliphaz says which, although improper in their application, are still true and profitable as doctrinal statements:

- True wisdom teaches humility of speech (15.2,7-8)
- God's consolations are sweet to the soul (15.11)
- Man should not turn against God (15.13)
- Man is innately sinful from birth (15.14,16)
- God is incomparably holy (15.15)
- Outward prosperity may conceal inner insecurity (15.20-24)
- It is folly to oppose God (15.25-27)
- God is the only safe object of trust (15.31)
- Retribution awaits the wicked (15.31-34)
- Sinful action is the natural product of a sinful heart (15.35).

Eliphaz, however, makes a serious mistake in treating a suffering saint as though he were a stubborn sinner. His theology lacks room for the grace and love of God toward His people. One of the Puritans observed that the preacher of the Word should make it his aim to disturb the comfortable (pricking the sinner's bubble of complacency), and comfort the disturbed (soothing the genuine believer's anxieties). Eliphaz's harsh approach can only distress further one who has already been troubled both by adverse circumstances and by the failure of God to respond to his pleadings. It is sad when friends only add to our grief.

SECTION 11
Dialogue: Job 4 – 42.6
Contest: Round 2: Job 15-21
Job's 4th Speech: Job 16-17

The relentless opposition of his three so-called comforters, demonstrating a conspicuous failure to live up to their name, now provokes Job's infamously stinging comment, "miserable comforters are ye all" (16.2). One might have thought that his unyielding resistance to their combined assault might have caused them to give up their attempts at advice as a bad job, and make tracks for home. Why continue when they are making no headway? But nothing seems able to shake them out of their fixed mind-set, nor their determination to impose their opinion upon a sceptic. But as the old adage has it, "convince a man against his will – he's of the same opinion still". It is a truism which should be borne in mind, whether we are speaking about the claims of the gospel or the teachings of the Word. Mere intellectual disputation or, worse, psychological bullying will never genuinely change anyone's mind. Paul knew that well enough. As he wrote to the believers at Corinth,

> I was with you in weakness, and in fear, and in much trembling. And my speech and my preaching was not with enticing words of man's wisdom, but in demonstration of the Spirit and of power: That your faith should not stand in the wisdom of men, but in the power of God (1 Cor 2.3-5).

Those won over by clever arguments will always be at the mercy of anyone who comes along with even cleverer ones.

But the friends are adamant. Not even the reasonable answers of Job, or the possibility that they may be doing their old friend a serious injustice, will halt their steamroller assault in its tracks. It is possible to be so enamoured of our theory that we fail to notice that it does not square with the facts.

After Eliphaz's savage attack upon his integrity, Job pauses briefly to contrast the kind of consolation he is being offered with what he would say were circumstances reversed (16.1-5). But he then straightway lays into Eliphaz's charge that he is guilty of warring against God; on the contrary, it is God who has declared war on him (16.6-17). Nevertheless, although picturing God as a bitter enemy, he still clings to his paradoxical conviction that the same God will eventually speak up for him (16.18 – 17.5). That said, the time is short: his days are numbered and death looms on the horizon (17.6-16).

The speech can be divided into four paragraphs:

1. Job's Answer: 16.1-5
2. God's Antagonism: 16.6-17
3. Heaven's Advocate: 16.18 – 17.5
4. Death's Approach: 17.6-16.

As always, it is worth noting precisely to whom Job addresses himself. He starts with a word to all three visitors ("ye all", 16.2), momentarily focussing on the previous speaker Eliphaz ("what provoketh thee", 16.3, JND), before returning to the trio as a whole ("I also could speak as ye do", 16.4-5). In verses 7 and 8 he starts addressing God ("thou hast made desolate all my company"), although most of the time he alludes to Him obliquely in the third person ("he hath made me weary"). Verse 18 is an apostrophe (an exclamatory address to a third party, often a personified abstraction or inanimate object) to the earth, in expectation of his approaching death ("O earth, cover not thou my blood"). Chapter 17 verses 3 and 4 again address God ("be surety for me with thyself", RV), but verse 10 reverts to the friends ("return ye, all of you", RV), while the chapter concludes with a double apostrophe, this time to "corruption" ("Thou art my father", 17.14a) and the worm, another emblem of death ("Thou art my mother, and my sister", 17.14b).

Although in this speech Job does not spend as much time as before in speaking directly to the Lord, the undergirding of his defence is still the same: his only hope is in a God who must eventually vindicate him.

Job's Answer: 16.1-5

Job begins by complaining about the staleness of his friends' words. He has heard it all before. Their comfort is worthless, doing nothing but add to his pain. Eliphaz accused him of not appreciating the "consolations of God" (15.11), but then Eliphaz, like all the friends, made the unjustifiable assumption that his verdict coincided with the viewpoint of heaven. If we seek to console the weary or comfort the distressed we shall find a frustratingly negative pattern in Job's visitors. As Robinson says, "the tongue of the wise [is] nowhere more needed than in the house of sorrow".[167] Is it wise, let alone gracious, to chide or insult those undergoing unbearable misery? By contrast, the New Testament records a positive example in the life of Paul:

> When we were come into Macedonia, our flesh had no rest, but we were troubled on every side; without were fightings, within were fears. Nevertheless God, that comforteth those that are cast down, comforted us by the coming of Titus; And not by his coming only, but by the consolation wherewith he was comforted in you, when he told us your earnest desire, your mourning, your fervent mind toward me; so that I rejoiced the more (2 Cor 7.5-7).

Paul's honest account of his sufferings for Christ in Macedonia informs us of external and internal trials, yet highlights the sovereign grace of God in arranging for Titus to return at just the right moment to encourage the apostle both by his presence and by the good news he brought from Corinth. Only in despondency do we learn that God "raiseth up all those that be bowed down." (Ps 145.14); only in loneliness do we fully appreciate the value of fellowship (2 Tim 1.4). Although Paul took no personal pleasure in exposing the Corinthians' sin, he rejoices that their sorrow "after a godly manner", unlike fruitless worldly grief, had led to repentance (2 Cor 7.8-9). Lonely and anxious in mind about the Corinthians' spiritual well-being, he was lifted by the opportune arrival of Titus with the welcome news that they were distressed about their failure to deal with the sins that so grieved the apostle. But the most remarkable thing about Paul's words is that he credits all this to God.

God does the comforting when we are cast down, but He often does it through the saints. On the Damascus Road Paul learned that to touch one of Christ's people is to touch the Lord Himself. The Saviour's words must have engraved themselves on his heart: "Saul, Saul, why persecutest thou me?" (Acts 9.4). The indissoluble union between Christ and His people means that those who attack them, whether they know it or not, attack Him. But it also means that He will often minister to His saints, not by direct miraculous provision from the heavens, but by means of other saints. The truth of the body of Christ involves the vital interconnection of all believers, united "in the bundle of life" (1 Sam 25.29). God's message of special comfort for Paul came *via* Titus.

This should teach us to be grateful to God for the encouragement we receive from one another, and to seek in turn to lift up those who are disheartened rather than tread them further into the dust. If, like Job, we have ever been on the receiving end of hostility from those who should be offering support, then a comment by Wiersbe provides help: "Sometimes we have to experience misunderstanding from unsympathetic friends in order to learn how to minister to others".[168] Even negative role models, properly viewed, may be beneficial.

Job may be severely stressed but he is not silent, nor will he suffer fools gladly. He is not averse to returning the swingeing criticisms he receives. Eliphaz had accused him of filling his belly "with the east wind" (15.2), to which Job retorts that if anyone is a windbag, it is Eliphaz himself: "Shall words of wind have an end? or what provoketh thee that thou answerest?" (16.3, JND). The second half of the verse inquires why Eliphaz feels so personally irritated that he has to bombard Job in this way: "What", asks Job, "have I done to provoke you?"

More significant, however, is Job's brief but telling comment about the ministry of consolation. He first describes the kind of treatment he is currently receiving: "I also could speak as ye: if your soul were in my soul's stead, I could join together words against you, and shake my head at you" (16.4, JND). Says Job, were roles reversed I could do just as you have been doing: I could marshal all my linguistic forces against you. The verb "heap up" in the KJV (2266) is pictorially impressive but linguistically imprecise, for the Hebrew term is first used in Genesis 14.3 of the five kings from the Sodom area who formed a military coalition against their regional overlords. It is the first war recorded in the Bible. The idea of battle suits the context here. Job is under rhetorical attack by men who can draw on an armoury of arguments, words, figures of speech, and anything which might pummel him into submission. As so often in the Middle East, their words are accompanied by histrionic body language, such as the emphatic shaking of the head. The *Jamieson, Fausset and Brown Commentary* notes that this action was done "in mockery; it means *nodding*, rather than *shaking*; nodding is not with us, as in the East, a gesture of scorn". A glance at other occurrences of the word confirms the implication of derision. It is used similarly in 2 Kings 19.21, Psalm 22.7, Psalm 109.25, Lamentations 2.15 and Zephaniah 2.15. Perhaps most noteworthy is its appearance in two messianic psalms:

> All they that see me laugh me to scorn: they shoot out the lip, they shake the head, saying, He trusted on the Lord that he would deliver him: let him deliver him, seeing he delighted in him (Ps 22.7-8).

> My knees are weak through fasting; and my flesh faileth of fatness. I became also a reproach unto them: when they looked upon me they shaked their heads (Ps 109.24-25).

Man's sneering contempt for the afflicted Messiah, expressed historically at Calvary, is faintly foreshadowed in the treatment Job received from his fellows. His current speech will several times make the reader think ahead to the sufferings of Christ. Job never knew that he was privileged to pave the way for the truly innocent victim, but believers in the Lord Jesus, informed by the completed Word, can take heart from the fact that their unjust sufferings in this world, however trivial, unite them in a special fellowship with their Master:

> Beloved, think it not strange concerning the fiery trial which is to try you, as though some strange thing happened unto you: But rejoice, inasmuch as ye are partakers of Christ's sufferings; that, when his glory shall be revealed, ye may be glad also with exceeding joy (1 Pet 4.12-13).

We have an insight into our circumstances and an incentive unknown to Job.

It is easy to blame and condemn, says Job. But were I in your shoes, I would behave differently. In fact, "I would strengthen you with my mouth, and the moving of my lips should assuage your grief" (16.5). Commentators differ as to whether he is speaking ironically or not. Some detect a satirical contrast. On the one hand there are words which come merely from the mouth and lips; on the other, genuine counsel emanates from the depths of the heart, as described in Proverbs, where we learn that as "Ointment and perfume rejoice the heart: so doth the sweetness of a man's friend by hearty counsel" or, as Young"s Literal Translation has it, "counsel of the soul" (Prov 27.9). Certainly the Bible sometimes discloses the gulf between fair words and a foul heart. This was the condition of the Pharisees during the earthly ministry of the Lord Jesus, who drew on Isaiah to rip the veneer off their hypocrisy: "this people draw near me with their mouth, and with their lips do honour me, but have removed their heart far from me, and their fear toward me is taught by the precept of men" (Is 29.13; Mt 15.8). If the language is ironic, then Job is jibing at the wordy, superficial consolation he is receiving and claiming, with heavy sarcasm, that he could easily return such useless talk with interest. But it is not necessary to take this view. We know from Eliphaz's first speech (4.3-4) and from Job's own final avowal of innocence

(29.11-16, 25) that he had a reputation for succouring the needy with genuine tenderness and sympathy. It is therefore entirely likely that he is deploring their failure as comforters in contrast to his own compassionate ministrations.

The power of the written or spoken word should never be undervalued. It is possible by means of words to strengthen those undergoing trial, and to relieve pain with the lips. This is done, not with aimless talk, but through the careful application of appropriate scriptures to the needs of the patient. Just as the doctor selects his medicines with expert skill, so does the spiritual physician, knowing that "A word fitly spoken is like apples of gold in pictures of silver" (Prov 25.11). Anticipating the nearness of the messianic Kingdom, Isaiah demonstrates the way "counsel of the soul" can spiritually reinvigorate the downcast:

> Strengthen ye the weak hands, and confirm the feeble knees. Say to them that are of a fearful heart, Be strong, fear not: behold, your God will come with vengeance, even God with a recompence; he will come and save you (Is 35.3-4).

What is it that revitalizes the flagging saint? Weak hands, feeble knees, and fearful hearts – picturing failure in the believer's work and walk, springing from unbelief at the core of his being – are remedied by a potent dose of the undiluted Word. The passage demonstrates the cure being administered: "Say to them ... Be strong, fear not: behold, your God will come". Just as the remnant of Israel in the tribulation period will be cheered by the news of Messiah's imminent advent for their deliverance, so too the Christian is encouraged in daily continuance by the sure hope of the Lord's return for His church. We are spiritually edified by being taught about God's gracious provision in Christ, about His purpose for our lives, about His infallible programme for the universe. To see such verbal tonic at work in the New Testament we have only to turn to the letters, especially those written to saints going through times of sore trial, such as 1 Peter or 1 and 2 Thessalonians. In each case the writer reminds his readers of the joys awaiting the saints at the Lord's return, and the way in which current distresses give us the opportunity to follow the perfect example of Christ (1 Pet 1.6-7; 2 Thess 1.4-10). The better we know the Scriptures, the better we are equipped to apply their healing balm to those in need.

God's Antagonism: 16.6-17

Alas, talking theoretically about the possibility of comfort affords Job no relief. The good he might be able to do for others has no present benefit in his own soul. The repetition of the word "assuaged" from verse 5 makes his point: his aching heart and body are not soothed by anything he can say. Nonetheless, though speaking brings him no consolation, neither does remaining silent. He will therefore speak on (16.6).

As he has done before, Job boldly traces all his miseries to God. It is, writes Robinson, "the part of a sanctified nature to see God in every event of our lot, whether prosperous or adverse".[169] The same attitude was displayed by Naomi, whose understanding of the God of Israel (the ultimate source of both blessing and bitterness) informed her Moabite daughter-in-law's confession of whole-hearted allegiance to Jehovah (Ruth 1.8-9,13,16-17). The way we speak about God influences those around us for good or ill. More, it brings solace to the soul to trace everything to an infallible Father. Here is the Puritan Thomas Watson:

> It is one heart-quieting consideration in all the afflictions that befall us, that God has a special hand in them: "the Almighty hath afflicted me". Instruments can no more stir till God gives them a commission, than the axe can cut of itself without a hand. Job eyed God in his affliction: therefore, as Augustine observes, he does not say, "The Lord gave, and the devil took away," but "The Lord hath taken away".[170]

But what precisely has God taken from Job? Systematically he catalogues his complaints. God has robbed him of **family** (16.7), bodily **health** (16.8-9), social **status** (16.10-11), **peace** (16.12-14), and **joy** (16.15-17).

Because of God's actions in chapter 1 he has lost his **family**: "But now he hath made me weary; thou hast made desolate all my family" (16.7, JND). The word "weary" (3811) carries the idea of exhaustion, grief and impatience. It is used, for example, of the Sodomites who wore themselves out trying to locate the door of Lot's house (Gen 19.11), of the privation facing the Israelites *en route* to Canaan, which God graciously remedied with water and manna (Ps 68.9), of God's displeasure at Israel's hypocritical worship (Is 1.14), and of Jeremiah's fatigue in trying to keep up with the infantry (Jer 12.5). Job was utterly worn down by his sorrows. Chief among them was the removal of "all my company" (KJV). The word is normally rendered "congregation" or "assembly", but the context indicates that it refers to Job's household – his wife, his children, his many servants. Those who would normally gather around to offer support and solace were the very ones of whom he had been robbed. Human suffering is intensified by solitariness.

He has likewise lost his bodily **health** (16.8-9): "And thou hast filled me with wrinkles, which is a witness against me: and my leanness rising up in me beareth witness to my face" (16.8). The language of the KJV is vivid in its description of the physical effects of disease and distress. But the word for wrinkles appears only here and in 22.16, where it is translated "cut down". Darby and the ESV both translate the phrase about wrinkles as "shrivelled me up", suggesting a rather more comprehensive idea, including not only crumpled and rumpled skin but also a general emaciation of the frame. Job is cadaverous and shrunken, his once healthy body reduced to skin and bones, a dreadful reality which testifies loudly against him. That is to say, his sickness and its impact stand as an apparently unimpeachable witness to his guilt – who but one under the immediate judgment of God would suffer such a devastating plague? This is what grieves him so much. In the words of Delitzsch,

> God has shrivelled him up; and this suffering form to which God has reduced him, is become an evidence, i.e., for himself and for others, as

the three friends, an accusation *de facto*, which puts him down as a sinner, although his self-consciousness testifies the opposite to him.[171]

The word "leanness" (3585) is elsewhere translated "lies" (as, for example, Hosea 7.3; 10.13; 11.12), which may hint that the state of Job's health is in fact an unreliable witness to his guilt before God. Nevertheless, everything is against him – the ravages of disease upon his body, the pains he constantly bears, the disbelieving attitude of his friends. He is, notwithstanding, innocent, as he will firmly attest in verse 17. The outward appearance is no infallible guide to what is inside. A marred countenance and a wasted frame may betoken grief rather than guilt (Is 52.14).

Yet all this adversity comes from God: "His anger teareth and pursueth me; he gnasheth with his teeth against me; as mine adversary he sharpeneth his eyes at me" (16.9, JND). Job does not hold back from ascribing animosity to the Almighty. Like a wild beast, God has pursued him and torn him (the same word is used by Jacob in Genesis 37.33 when he believes Joseph has been mauled to death by a savage animal). Job earlier spoke of God hunting him "as a fierce lion" (10.16), and the imagery lingers in his mind. Lion-like claws, powerful teeth and gleaming eyes are all directed against him. "[He] sharpeneth his eyes upon me" is an odd phrase, but presumably means that God has darted hostile glances at him, with eyes as sharp and penetrating as swords. The picture is of an implacable foe. Just as in days past his outward circumstances unanimously testified to divine approval, so now they signal his rejection.

But there is more. God has also deprived him of his social **status** and the moral support to which he might be entitled (16.10-11):

> They gape upon me with their mouth; they smite my cheeks reproachfully; they range themselves together against me. God hath delivered me over to the iniquitous man, and hurled me into the hands of the wicked (16.10-11, JND).

Job's calamities have lost him the high esteem he once enjoyed among his peers. It seems that all his associates have now abandoned him or, worse, collaborated in abusing him. They open their mouths wide to heap insults on him, they treat him with contempt ("to smite the cheek" is picture language for insolent disrespect), they conspire together to degrade him further. But – and once again Job looks past second causes to see God's behind-the-scenes direction – the men that line up against him are there only because God has given him over into their hands. The final cause is God, who has wilfully cast him over to the tender mercies of wicked men. When he speaks of "the wicked" Job may be thinking of his three so-called friends, but he is more likely to have in mind the outcast rabble who take special delight in harassing him, gloating over the fall of a righteous man. These people, malicious and malevolent, are described specifically in 30.1-10.

Two of the words in this passage ("smite" and "cheeks") recur in Isaiah's prophetic account of Messiah's sufferings at the hands of men: "I gave my back to the smiters, and my cheeks to them that plucked off the hair: I hid not my face from shame and spitting" (Is 50.6). If Job unconsciously previews something of the afflictions of the Lord Jesus Christ, he does so with the significant difference that the Saviour voluntarily gave Himself over to His enemies. Everything He went through He suffered freely, fully knowing what lay ahead, including the glorious eternal consequences of His work. Job's pains were intense, and were ultimately inflicted on him by God, but they had no atoning value. How could they, since Job – like the rest of us – was only a man, and a sinful man at that? What the Lord Jesus endured from His creatures, He endured willingly and knowingly; yet at the same time it was God who handed Him over to men that they might do their worst. Behind human malice lies divine permission. Paul uses the identical word to describe Calvary from the point of view of the Father's purpose and the Son's devoted act of surrender:

> He that spared not his own Son, but delivered [3860] him up for us all, how shall he not with him also freely give us all things? (Rom 8.32).

> I am crucified with Christ: nevertheless I live; yet not I, but Christ liveth in me: and the life which I now live in the flesh I live by the faith of the Son of God, who loved me, and gave [3860] himself for me (Gal 2.20).

The Father gave, and the Son gave. Amazing as it may seem, the context of both statements is blessing for the saints: "how shall he not with him also freely give us all things?" (Rom 8.32). Out of infinite distress and unjust suffering, God brought eternal, immeasurable good for His people.

God has also deprived Job of **peace** and rest (16.12-14) by precipitously declaring war on him:

> I was at rest, but he hath shattered me; he hath taken me by the neck and shaken me to pieces, and set me up for his mark. His arrows encompass me round about, he cleaveth my reins asunder and doth not spare; he poureth out my gall upon the ground. He breaketh me with breach upon breach; he runneth upon me like a mighty man (16.12-14, JND).

December 7th 1941 saw the unexpected and unannounced attack by Japan on the USA Pacific Fleet at the naval base of Pearl Harbour in Hawaii. It was, according to President F D Roosevelt, "a date which will live in infamy", largely because no formal declaration of war had been made. Yet Japan and the United States had been on a collision course for years, so in one sense the attack hardly came out of the blue. By contrast, the sudden calamities which beset Job were entirely unforeseen, unpredictable and unprecedented. There were no warnings given, there had been no failure in Job's devotedness to his God, there were no prior examples of God turning against a faithful servant. And still the multiple blows had fallen. Like the peacetime vessels resting in Battleship Row, Job had been enjoying inner and outer serenity, only to have it all shattered by a surprise attack.

The Hebrew word "at ease" (7961) implies quietness, wealth, prosperity and security. It is used of the area invaded by the descendants of Simeon who, seeking extra living space, came upon "fat pasture and good, [where] the land was wide, and quiet, and peaceable [7961]" (1 Chr 4.40). It appears also, for example, in Job 20.20 ("quietness") and 21.23 ("quiet"). Job dwelt with his family and his possessions in apparently justifiable security, but God launched a pre-emptive attack. The language describes a blitzkrieg. Job has been broken into fragments, seized by the scruff of the neck and shaken (some of us may think instinctively of a terrier worrying a rat), and set up as the target for God's arrows. The word "mark" (4307), usually translated "prison", first occurs in the context of Jonathan engaging in simulated archery practice as a signal to David (1 Sam 20.20). Jeremiah, speaking as a representative inhabitant of Jerusalem during the terrible Babylonian siege, uses similar language: "He hath bent his bow, and set me as a mark for the arrow. He hath caused the arrows of his quiver to enter into my reins" (Lam 3.12-13). Whatever the parallel, and the language is remarkably close, we must never forget that the city of Jerusalem (though not the faithful prophet Jeremiah) was suffering God's judgment because of her sins, whereas Job has done nothing to deserve his pains.

Job develops his archery imagery – picture language introduced as early as chapter 6 when speaking about the "arrows of the Almighty" (6.4) – by imagining himself surrounded by a host of bowmen: "his archers [7228] compass me round about" (16.13). Jeremiah uses the same word in connection with Babylon's destruction:

> Call together the archers [7228] against Babylon: all ye that bend the bow, camp against it round about; let none thereof escape: recompense her according to her work; according to all that she hath done, do unto her: for she hath been proud against the Lord, against the Holy One of Israel (Jer 50.29).

Babylon fell historically (and a future Babylon will one day fall again) because of her wickedness. God conscripted the Medes and Persians to bring about her collapse. But Job is being wounded by three friends, whose stinging words have invaded his soul like poisoned darts. With gruesome detail, he pictures a man so transfixed by showers of arrows that his body has been broken open, spilling his vital organs ("reins [kidneys] … gall") upon the earth. Though primitive arrows could not do what heavy artillery managed to do in mangling human bodies during the First World War, they could nevertheless cause real carnage.

More, God "doth not spare". The word (2550) is often translated using the vocabulary of compassion. It is first used of Pharaoh's daughter taking pity on the baby Moses: "she saw the child: and, behold, the babe wept. And she had compassion [2550] on him, and said, This is one of the Hebrews' children" (Ex 2.6). It last appears in the lovely assurance of God's tender concern for His faithful remnant: "they shall be mine, saith the Lord of hosts, in that day when I make up my jewels; and I will spare [2550] them, as a man spareth [2550] his own son that serveth him" (Mal 3.17). An Egyptian princess had pity on a vulnerable infant; Jehovah will take pity on the elect minority of Israel during the Great Tribulation – but, says Job, God has no compassion on me. The language makes us think again of Romans 8. It may be customary for a man to spare a son who faithfully serves him but, as the hymn writer paraphrases it,

> Thou didst not spare Thine only Son
> But gav'st Him for a world undone,
> And freely with that Blessed One
> Thou givest all.

Not only has God ordered His archers to fire at Job, He has personally assaulted him with the bloodthirsty ferocity of a mighty warrior (16.14). The language pictures a besieged city, its defensive wall breached by numerous gaps because of the severity of the onslaught. Eliphaz had sketched Job as a brazen and foolhardy rebel who "stretcheth out his hand against God, and strengtheneth himself against the Almighty. He runneth upon him, even on his neck, upon the thick bosses of his bucklers" (15.25-26), but Job's answer is that Eliphaz has everything back to front. Job, not God, is the victim of devastating attack. As Zuck comments, Job has amassed "a forceful colocation of word-pictures to portray the intensity of his emotional writhing and the helplessness of his pitiable condition".[172]

Finally, God has stolen all his **joy**: "I have sewed sackcloth upon my skin, and rolled my horn in the dust. My face is red with weeping, and on my eyelids is the shadow of death" (16.15-16, JND). Sackcloth was the conventional garb of the Middle Eastern mourner (Gen 37.34; 2 Sam 3.31; Lam 2.10), but Job is so identified with grief that it is as if he has actually stitched the coarse fabric to his body. Because of its association with animals, the horn was emblematic of physical power and dignity (Deut 33.17; Ps 18.2). Davidson explains the imagery:

> To lift up the horn is to increase in power or eminence, or to show a proud sense of greatness … to thrust it into the dust … is to feel the sense of deepest humiliation. Job's once honoured head which he held erect was brought down low in shame.[173]

Job's horn has been rolled humiliatingly in the dirt as a testimony to his terrible abasement. His face is flushed and distorted with tears, while the discoloration of his eyelids seems the harbinger of imminent death. All this contrasts with the prosperous Job of the past. Here are his own words, looking back on happier days:

> Oh that I were as in months past, as in the days when God preserved me; When his candle shined upon my head, and when by his light I walked through darkness; As I was in the days of my youth, when the secret of God was upon my tabernacle; When the Almighty was yet with me, when my children were about me (29.2-5).

Job has presented a formidable list of grievances. Robinson sums it up like this:

> Children gone; property lost; wife alienated; body covered from head
> to foot with the most grievous and loathsome disease that ever afflicted
> fallen humanity; mind harassed, depressed, distracted; sleep taken away
> … horrifying dreams; his sincerity and piety more than suspected by his
> friends in consequence of his sufferings.[174]

Has anyone ever suffered such wholesale reversal for no discernible cause? Job's final word is to maintain his innocence. All these dreadful calamities have befallen him despite the fact that "there is no violence in my hands, and my prayer is pure" (16.17, JND). The conciseness of this avowal should not be allowed to undermine its clarity. He was guiltless of injustice to men or insincerity toward God. The word Darby translates as "violence" (2555) first appears in Genesis 6.11 to describe the condition of the ante-diluvian world in its rampant brutality and godlessness. But Job was just in his dealings with men, and genuine in his devotion to God. Eliphaz had accused him of restraining prayer and piety (15.4) but Job, as we learn from the first chapter of the book, was a man of earnest intercession. To assert that his prayer was pure was not, of course, to claim perfection but rather a blameless and honest commitment to the things of God. Paul expected no less of believers when he wrote, "I desire therefore that the men pray in every place, lifting up holy hands, without wrath and disputing" (1 Tim 2.8, RV). That said, Job's words are true in the absolute sense when applied to the person of Christ, for "men appointed his grave with the wicked, but he was with the rich in his death, because he had done no violence, neither was there guile in his mouth" (Is 53.9, JND). The Saviour was guilty of no violence against men, despite all their assaults against Him, and no hypocrisy towards God, whose honour He constantly maintained and whose will He uncomplainingly fulfilled.

Heaven's Advocate: 16.18 – 17.5

The charge-sheet against God is long and detailed, but still Job clings to his deep-rooted conviction that God Himself will finally rise to his defence. First, he appeals to the earth not to cover him up in death. The Revised Version makes the sense clear: "O earth, cover not thou my blood, and let my cry have no resting place" (16.18, RV). Like a murder victim whose blood shouts aloud to the heavens against his slayer, Job appeals to the ground not to stifle his appeal for justice. He does not want to be forgotten when he dies. Was he thinking back to the history of the first man to be killed? The story of Cain and Abel must have been passed down orally by Adam and Eve to many generations of their descendants. As far as the Genesis record is concerned, Abel was a righteous, God-fearing man whose worship was endorsed by heaven but resented by his brother:

> And Cain talked with Abel his brother: and it came to pass, when they
> were in the field, that Cain rose up against Abel his brother, and slew him.

And the Lord said unto Cain, Where is Abel thy brother? And he said, I know not: Am I my brother's keeper? And he said, What hast thou done? the voice of thy brother's blood crieth unto me from the ground (Gen 4.8-10).

The irony in Job's case is that it was no fellow man but God Himself who conspired against him with a view to causing his death. God was both, unaccountably, his greatest enemy and yet simultaneously the source of all his hopes.

This is one of the astonishing things about the book of Job. In Delitzsch's words, "in the very God who appears to him to be a blood-thirsty enemy in pursuit of him, Job nevertheless hopes to find a witness of his innocence".[175] The patriarch knew that all his ills came from God (he had no illusions about the extent of divine sovereignty), therefore God was against him; at the same time he clung to an awareness that God was inflexibly righteous and tender towards His creatures, therefore He must – in due time – speak up for him.

Would it have made things easier to bear had he revised his theology and robbed God of His absolute power, reducing Him to a combatant engaged in doubtful warfare with a malevolent enemy who thirsted for Job's blood? In that case it was not God who was responsible for his sufferings but another supernatural power against whom God had no final answer. But such a viewpoint would only raise other and greater problems. If God is not sovereign, then the universe is in a state of anarchy, pain has no purpose, and man is merely the shuttlecock batted to and fro in an unpitying game between cosmic forces. Then again, would it have brought him relief to renounce his God, abandoning his faith altogether? By no means. It is our response to suffering (for whatever reason) which shows what we really are at root. One of the mysterious effects of a work of divine grace in the soul is that the same distresses which drive the unbeliever further away from God serve only to draw the believer closer to Him. And there is no doubt that Job, in all his pains and perplexities, clings ever closer to the Lord.

Job never permits his personal trials, however puzzling, to alter his deep-rooted worldview. Possessed of the completed Word, the Christian has far less excuse to adjust his understanding of God's revealed truth because of local circumstances. We are not to read Scripture in the light of our experiences any more than we should interpret it through the distorting lens of human scientific opinion, philosophy or history. These constantly change; Scripture does not. Rather, it is the pure and unvarying beam of God's Word which must be brought to bear on the shifting opinions and conditions of men.

But now comes a grand moment. Rising to a towering pinnacle of faith, Job expresses his confidence that, whatever may be the case on earth, there is at least in heaven someone able to stand up for him: "Even now, behold, my Witness is in the heavens, and he that voucheth [or testifies] for me is in the heights" (16.19, JND). This verse in fact speaks of a double witness. Despite his dejection and disappointment, in the midst of misery Job bears testimony to the certainty of divine omniscience and righteousness. To call God "my Witness" assumes that God knows all the facts, and is concerned about what is right. More, Job is certain that God Himself will eventually intervene to endorse his innocence. He has no confidence in the so-called friends around him, but there is One above on whom he can rely.

Living as we do in a world which attempts to censor all references to the divine, it is easy to forget that the living God is always in perfect control. But Job never forgets. Indeed, the following verses set up a contrast between the failure of his friends and (implicitly) the faithfulness of God, the connection between them being brought out best by the RV:

> My friends scorn me: but mine eye poureth out tears unto God; That he would maintain the right of a man with God, and of a son of man with his neighbour! (16.20-21, RV).

His colleagues only mocked (3887) him (the word is used of the scornful in Psalm 1.1, and appears extensively in the book of Proverbs), but in his deep desire for an intercessor he found tearful recourse to God.

In a fallen world it is a common experience that men let down those who appeal to them for aid. The ironic blessing built into this failure is that it propels the believer all the more into the arms of the Lord. Scripture is littered with examples of this abiding principle – when man fails, God in grace steps in to succour His servants:

> And David was greatly distressed; for the people spake of stoning him, because the soul of all the people was grieved, every man for his sons and for his daughters: but David encouraged himself in the Lord his God (1 Sam 30.6).

> When my father and my mother forsake me, then the Lord will take me up (Ps 27.10).

> I heard the defaming of many, fear on every side. Report, say they, and we will report it. All my familiars watched for my halting, saying, Peradventure he will be enticed, and we shall prevail against him, and we shall take our revenge on him. But the Lord is with me as a mighty terrible one: therefore my persecutors shall stumble, and they shall not prevail (Jer 20.10-11).

> Jesus heard that they had cast him [the cured blind man] out; and when he had found him, he said unto him, Dost thou believe on the Son of God? (Jn 9.35).

> At my first answer no man stood with me, but all men forsook me: I pray God that it may not be laid to their charge. Notwithstanding the Lord stood with me, and strengthened me (2 Tim 4.16-17).

Every child of God can be thankful that, although there is failure all around (and especially within), there is never any failure in the Lord.

Finding no support among his friends, Job looks to God to supply him with a spokesman who can argue his case against God's injustice towards him. The paradox is self-evident. It is God who is against him, of this he has no doubt (16.12-14); and yet it is only God who can defend him from such attacks. He therefore seeks shelter *from* God *in* God. We should pause to savour the wonder of this realisation. Job's dilemma, from which the oral revelation of his era can supply him with no clear escape, has driven him to anticipate, albeit unconsciously, the essentials of God's way of salvation in Christ. Sinful man stands under the wrath of God's infinite holiness, and the only hope lies in God Himself to provide a rescue from His own just judgment. The atoning death of Christ did exactly this, for the Lord Jesus rendered to God what was due to His name while receiving from God the full penalty that our sins deserve. To be "in Christ" is therefore to be in a sphere of eternal safety from God's wrath against the ungodly. This explains Paul's delighted doxology: "Blessed be the God and Father of our Lord Jesus Christ, who hath blessed us with all spiritual blessings in heavenly places in Christ" (Eph 1.3). Every good for the believer is "in Christ". It is as though Job's thought unconsciously rushes ahead to the future revelation that "there is one God, and one mediator between God and men, the man Christ Jesus; Who gave himself a ransom for all, to be testified in due time" (1 Tim 2.5-6).

But even as Job makes a marvellous declaration of confidence in the divine ability to meet his need, he confesses that his life is fast approaching the deadline: "When a few years are come, then I shall go the way whence I shall not return. My breath is corrupt, my days are extinct, the graves are ready for me" (16.22 – 17.1). In reading this book we need to keep in mind the progressively deteriorating condition of Job's body. He is conscious of the unlikelihood of any recovery. The sombre announcement of no return is not in itself necessarily a denial of a future resurrection, but rather an assertion that his life in this world is swiftly terminating. His breath is offensive because of his multiple diseases (although the ESV suggests the idea is that his "spirit is broken"), his lifespan is coming to its end – and, with the extinction of his children, so too is his lineage – with the result that the graveyard yawns hungrily for him. The word "grave" (6913), first used in Genesis 23.4 to describe the last resting place of Sarah, is found here in the plural, perhaps to visualize a burial ground: nothing but death looms ahead.

And still, in the face of his impending demise, his friends persist in promising him a rosy-tinted future of restored life and prosperity if only he would knuckle down and repent! Job's contempt is cutting: "Surely there are mockers with me, and mine eye abideth in their provocation" (17.2, RV). We can imagine him looking balefully around at the three friends and saying, in effect, "I have to sit here and endure your derision, my eyes fixed on nothing but men who provoke me with clumsy words". "Provocations" (4784) is normally rendered by "rebellion" or some similar term; the advice offered him, because of its utter inappropriateness, could only irritate his spirit. Moses used the word of the grousers in Israel whose unbelief put God to the test with their constant murmuring (Num 20.10),

although of course (alas) he too spoke ill-advisedly, being himself accused of
rebellion by Jehovah (Num 20.24).

Having put the friends in their place, Job turns back to God: "Lay down now
a pledge, be thou surety for me with thyself: who is he that striketh hands with
me? For thou hast hidden their heart from understanding; therefore thou wilt not
exalt them" (17.3-4, JND). The vocabulary of pledges, surety and striking hands
places us squarely in a law court scene. While admitting to ignorance of ancient
legal conventions, Barnes helps us grasp the judicial implications of the language:

> The whole passage here is obscure, because we are in a great measure
> ignorant of the ancient practices in courts of law, and of the ancient
> forms of trial. The general sense seems to be, that Job desires the Deity to
> enter into a judicial investigation, and to give him a "pledge" – or, as we
> should say, a "bond," or "security" – that he would not avail himself of his
> almighty power, but would place him on an equality in the trial, and allow
> him to plead his cause on equal terms.

"Surety" (6148) is first used by Judah when promising his anxious father to
engage himself for his young brother Benjamin's safety: "I will be surety for him; of
my hand shalt thou require him: if I bring him not unto thee, and set him before
thee, then let me bear the blame for ever" (Gen 43.9). The word also appears in
conjunction with the practice of striking hands, obviously the accepted cultural
signal of a binding agreement: "My son, if thou be surety for thy friend, if thou hast
stricken thy hand with a stranger" (Prov 6.1; and compare Proverbs 17.18; 22.6).
The writer of Proverbs strongly urges his readers to avoid hastily taking on a legal
obligation on behalf of a stranger. Poor Job cannot even get friends to believe him,
let alone undertake his cause. Since none of them will take the risk, who else has he,
apart from God? Hartley sums it up: "There is none to whom Job can turn as his
guarantor, one who will seal the agreement to defend him with a handshake, save
God Himself".[176] God, we should note, is both judge and counsel for the defence.
Like Asaph, Job might have said, "Whom have I in heaven but thee? and there is
none upon earth that I desire beside thee. My flesh and my heart faileth: but God is
the strength of my heart, and my portion for ever" (Ps 73.25-26). Another psalmist
appealed similarly to God, using the language of legal protection: "I have done
judgment and justice: leave me not to mine oppressors. Be surety for thy servant for
good: let not the proud oppress me" (Ps 119.121-122).

Having demonstrated that he looks to God alone for support, Job pauses
for a moment, seeking to account for his friends' abject failure: "thou hast hid
their heart from understanding: therefore shalt thou not exalt them. He that
denounceth his friends for a prey, even the eyes of his children shall fail" (17.4-
5, RV). This is a very tough passage. As usual, however, Delitzsch offers help in
making sense of the difficulties:

> God has closed the heart of the friends against understanding … i.e.,
> He has fixed a curtain, a wall of partition, between their hearts and the

right understanding of the matter; He has smitten them with blindness, therefore He will not (since they are suffering from a want of perception which He has ordained, and which is consequently known to Him) allow them to be exalted, i.e., to conquer and triumph.[177]

It is God who stands behind his afflictions, and it is God who has blinded the would-be comforters so that they are unable to comprehend the problem or offer aid. It is yet another evidence of the startling clarity of Job's understanding of God, even without access to written revelation. Is he in distress? God brought it about. Is he disowned and misunderstood by those to whom he looked for encouragement? God has hidden the truth from their minds, just as Jochabed concealed the baby Moses, and Rahab the spies. Since, because of this divine action, his friends are unable to sympathise with him, it is therefore up to God to vindicate him before them all as an innocent and misunderstood man. They must not be permitted to triumph in their faulty judgment of him; God Himself will have to intervene on Job's behalf.

On the other hand, he is equally clear that his friends' gross insensitivity to his grief is itself culpable and deserves recompense, for

> he who offers his friends as spoil for distribution will be punished most severely for the same upon his children: he shall not escape the divine retribution which visits him … for the wrong done to his friends … i.e., he who so faithlessly disowns the claims of affection is punished for it on that which he holds most dear.[178]

Obviously Job does not consider that divine sovereignty contradicts or neutralises human responsibility. God has closed their minds, yet they are still accountable for their failure to speak truthfully about him. The same paradox persists into the New Testament. Calvary was the fulfilment of "the determinate counsel and foreknowledge of God", while simultaneously being the work of man's "wicked hands" (Acts 2.23). In verse 5 Job utters what appears to be a "cryptic proverb"[179] about the dangers of false testimony, a warning to his friends that they will face serious consequences for their heartless abandonment of him in his hour of need. They looked unfeelingly on his family tragedies, seeing them as proof of wickedness; they too were in danger of suffering the loss of their children.

Death's Approach: 17.6-16

To Job death seems always near at hand. He cannot forget that God has brought about the degradation which is rapidly leading to his demise: "And he hath made me a proverb of the peoples; and I am become one to be spit on in the face" (17.6, JND). Job, a man once synonymous with righteous prosperity, has become a by-word (4914) for disgrace. The word appears only here, but similar terms suggest the range of its meaning. On the borders of the land Moses tells Israel that future disobedience leading to captivity would cause it to become "an astonishment, a proverb, and a byword, among all nations whither the Lord shall lead thee" (Deut 28.37). What people have called "the wandering Jew", brought low into servitude, desolation and shame, would become the world's whipping boy. The same kind of language is used by David: "I made sackcloth also my garment; and I became a proverb to them. They that sit in the gate speak against me; and I was the song of the drunkards" (Ps 69.11-12). There may also be, in part, a glimpse ahead to the rejected Christ, although this is one of those Psalms in which not every verse is unambiguously messianic.

However, the pre-echo of the Saviour's humiliation in the second part of Job 17.6 is inescapable: "I am become one to be spit on in the face" (JND). The KJV's "tabret" refers to a tambourine, an instrument used in festal music and dance, but modern translations take the Hebrew word, found only here, to mean that Job had become an object of the utmost contempt, one whom passers-by spat upon. Relevant prophetic, historical and doctrinal passages spring to mind:

> I gave my back to the smiters, and my cheeks to them that plucked off the hair: I hid not my face from shame and spitting (Is 50.6).

> Then did they spit in his face, and buffeted him; and others smote him with the palms of their hands (Mt 26.67).

> Looking unto Jesus the author and finisher of our faith; who for the joy that was set before him endured the cross, despising the shame, and is set down at the right hand of the throne of God (Heb 12.2).

Although in life Job never learned the reasons for his trials, come the full unveiling of God's purposes in the future it will without doubt be a cause of wonderment for him to discover that in his afflictions, though he did not realise it, he was truly "looking unto Jesus". His guiltless sufferings made him an honoured forerunner of God's Son. When we reach the vantage point of eternal glory, much we cannot comprehend in this world will fall into place as part of the divine design.

> When at the last I reach the heav'nly haven
> Where hidden purposes are brought to light,
> Then shall I praise Thee for my pilgrim journey,
> Knowing that all Thy ways with me were right.

In words like "sorrow" and "shadow", we detect something of his weariness: "Mine eye also is dim by reason of sorrow, and all my members are as a shadow" (17.7). As a consequence of physical and emotional humiliation, his eye has lost its healthy sparkle, while his body, with all its individual members, is robbed of substance, becoming a mere shade. The following two verses raise problems of interpretation:

Upright men shall be astonished at this, and the innocent shall be stirred up against the ungodly; But the righteous shall hold on his way, and he that hath clean hands shall increase in strength (17.8-9, JND).

What does Job mean? His words are, in part, an answer to Eliphaz's accusation that "thou castest off fear, and restrainest prayer before God" (15.4). "Your kind of argumentation, Job, your refusal to acknowledge your terrible sins, will only encourage ungodliness and irreverence in others". No, answers Job, my experience – though I cannot understand it at the moment – will actually fortify the saints of God. He imagines godly people – is he thinking ahead to the way his story will affect future generations? – viewing his afflictions (they are obviously to be distinguished from his three unfeeling friends), and becoming so indignant at the way the wicked prosper while Job (the upright man) has to suffer, that they resolutely refuse to abandon their own godly lifestyle. On the contrary, they grow "stronger and stronger" (the language of the KJV) in their spiritual convictions. Just as tribulation draws the genuine believer closer to the Lord while hardening the unbeliever against Him, so news about suffering saints in other countries does not stumble God's people. Instead, it stimulates them to redoubled efforts in holy living. Paul, we may recollect, gloried in the faithful continuance of Thessalonian believers despite terrible persecution:

We are bound to thank God always for you, brethren, as it is meet, because that your faith groweth exceedingly, and the charity of every one of you all toward each other aboundeth; So that we ourselves glory in you in the churches of God for your patience and faith in all your persecutions and tribulations that ye endure (2 Thess 1.3-4).

Comments Delitzsch, "These words of Job (if we may be allowed the figure) are like a rocket which shoots above the tragic darkness of the book, lighting it up suddenly, although only for a short time".[180] Beyond all expectation, Job has risen above his immediate circumstances to look ahead to a day when his story would be retold to the blessing of genuine believers. The nearest parallel is in the New Testament, when the Lord Jesus speaks up to defend Mary's silent act of devotion in anointing His body for burial before his death: "Verily I say unto you, Wheresoever this gospel shall be preached in the whole world, there shall also this, that this woman hath done, be told for a memorial of her" (Mt 26.13). Misunderstood at the time, Mary would be venerated thereafter. In a similar way, the patriarch, though despised and rejected by his contemporaries, would be a source of spiritual encouragement to saints in times to come. As we read about Job's endurance (so human in its ups and downs) under unimaginable pains, we are given strength to persevere in our lesser trials.

From this sublime glance ahead Job returns to the bemused trio sitting beside him. Their faces indicate a total inability to follow his argument. All right, says Job, come on at me again with your criticism and contempt, for I have given up expecting to find one intelligent man among you (17.10). Trouble is, he knows his time on earth is limited. He sums up his condition in a three-part statement: "My days are past [5674], my purposes are broken off, the cherished judgments of my heart" (17.11, JND). His life is virtually gone. The first and last occurrences of this common word illuminate its meaning. It describes the wind that God caused to "pass over" the earth so that the flood waters abated (Gen 8.1), and the removal of false prophecy and occultism from Israel in its days of millennial revival: "I will cause the prophets and the unclean spirit to pass [5674] out of the land" (Zech 13.2). Just as swiftly Job's life sweeps to its close. The last two parts of the verse are synonymous. His "purposes" (the word normally refers to wicked or mischievous plans, so one wonders whether Job is bitterly employing the kind of language which might be expected to come from his suspicious friends) are broken, just as easily as Samson snapped the fresh cords that bound him (Judg 16.9), and all his "cherished thoughts" (the dearest ambitions of his heart) have come to nothing. Despite this, his friends glibly assure him that there are blue skies just around the corner if only he will swallow their medicine. "They change the night into a day: the light, say they, is near unto the darkness" (17.12, RV). "They" must refer to the friends who, in the midst of his darkness of mind and sorrow of spirit, cheerfully promise him the dawning of a bright new day.

Job's friends had no grounds for making such rash promises. The whole foundation of their belief-system was askew. Believers should never offer consolations they have no right to advance. The Christian approaching death is not helped by those who come with slick charismatic pledges of miraculous restoration, or who persuade him to jettison his medication in the hope of instantaneous healing. Lazarus's sisters provide a reliable model of how to pray for the terminally ill: "Lord, behold, he whom thou lovest is sick" (Jn 11.3). Although looking for the Saviour's speedy response, they did not presume to tell Him what to do, but simply informed Him of the situation. Sometimes we can do no better. On the other hand, the Christian believer has biblical revelation which tells him that, for all saints of this dispensation, "The night is far spent, the day is at hand" (Rom 13.12). We may rejoice, because "we have the word of prophecy made more sure; whereunto ye do well that ye take heed, as unto a lamp shining in a dark place, until the day dawn, and the day-star arise in your hearts" (2 Pet 1.19, RV). That is the kind of genuine encouragement which may be safely proffered to every child of God. The arrival of "the bright and morning star" (Rev 22.16) draws nearer every hour.

Job's final words, reverting to the language of humiliation and physical disintegration used earlier (17.6-7), are bleak in the extreme. Here is Darby's rendering of the closing section:

> If I wait, Sheol is my house; I spread my bed in the darkness: I cry to the grave, Thou art my father! to the worm, My mother, and my sister! And where is then my hope? yea, my hope, who shall see it? It shall go down to the bars of Sheol, when our rest shall be together in the dust (17.13-16, JND).

What, asks Job, really lies ahead for me? *Sheol*, the place of departed of spirits, will be my home, darkness will be my environment (in contrast to the daylight promised by his friends), the grave (or corruption) and the worm will become my intimate family. Job has no qualms about particularising the horrors of bodily disintegration. Anyone who considers that the Bible shies away from the painful realities of human life would do well to ponder Job's shockingly frank language. Three other times he mentions the worm (7415), and always in connection with putrefaction:

> My flesh is clothed with worms and clods of dust; my skin is broken, and become loathsome (7.5).

> They shall lie down alike in the dust, and the worms shall cover them (21.26).

> The womb shall forget him; the worm shall feed sweetly on him; he shall be no more remembered; and wickedness shall be broken as a tree (24.20).

But if, as he firmly believes, he is heading inexorably towards death, darkness and dissolution, where is his expectation? By "hope", he may refer either to the prospects of renewed life held out by the friends in their exhortations to repentance (11.18), or to his own ingrained sense that God must ultimately arise for his defence. In either case, if death is imminent, what hope has he? It looks as though his hope will descend with him into the dust of the grave. When and how can he be exonerated? God has not deigned to answer his calls for an audience, his friends are as hostile as ever, his physical condition has not improved. Those earlier flashes of illumination and assurance seem to have been wiped from his mind so that he now sees nothing but the shadow of the tomb. Eight times *sheol* appears in the book, and that grim word (translated "the grave", "hell" and "the pit" in the KJV) bookends this short passage (17.13,16).

As we have observed before, Job's moods during his trials are alarmingly volatile, rising at times to an outstanding confession of assurance in God, then sinking into gloomy presentiments of death and oblivion. A realistic portrayal of a traumatised man of faith is one of the unforgettable aspects of this often intractable book. But even amidst Job's most negative thoughts we find glimpses of hope, as long as we read his statements in the light of the rest of Scripture. Take the word "dust" (17.16), the final word of the chapter. For Job, it sums up the grim reality of death. It is a common word in the book, appearing twenty-six times, reminding us of man's humble origins (Gen 2.7) and his earthly destiny as a result of sin (Gen 3.19), facts Job knew well. But at the centre of Scripture stands a truth which lifts the heart, a reminder of God's tender understanding of and fatherly concern for man's natural frailty:

> Like as a father pitieth his children, so the Lord pitieth them that fear him.
> For he knoweth our frame; he remembereth that we are dust (Ps 103.13-14).

According to the *Oxford Online Dictionary*, dust is "fine, dry powder consisting of tiny particles of earth or waste matter lying on the ground or on surfaces or carried in the air".[181] To most of us it is the irritating cause of unending housework. A creature made out of dust is the flimsiest of beings; his body, ruined by sin, tends ever to the grave. Yet the God who made him knows all about his weaknesses, his aches and pains, his inbuilt infirmities. More, He cares for him just as a father pities his children.

We may go further. Daniel the prophet looks forward to a day when the death penalty announced in Eden will be reversed:

> And many of them that sleep in the dust of the earth shall awake, some to everlasting life, and some to shame and everlasting contempt (Dan 12.2).

He refers specifically to the elect of Israel, raised up at the close of the Great Tribulation to share in the millennial Kingdom, when "they that be wise shall shine as the brightness of the firmament; and they that turn many to righteousness as the stars for ever and ever" (Dan 12.3). The doctrine of bodily resurrection is of the utmost importance for every believer of the current church age, for it assures us that we shall enter eternal blessing complete with glorified bodies to equip us for the unimpeded enjoyment of our everlasting home.

Job did not have the benefit of the book of Psalms, or the prophecy of Daniel, but he had a grasp of God which still takes the breath away. If pain does nothing else, it makes a man think. And Job certainly thought deeply about what he knew. He knew that God was absolutely sovereign in all the affairs of His universe; therefore God brought about his problems as He also blinded his would-be comforters. He knew that God had such a concern for righteousness that He would, in due time, stand up for Job's defence. He knew that God was ever approachable in prayer as the sure recourse for His people in distress. In the middle of the insoluble riddle of pain, these are real supports. But the Christian believer has so much more. Kelly says of Job, that "he saw God's hand without in the least entering into His mind about the trial, still less His love".[182] From our privileged vantage point, we recognise the heart behind the hand, and in Calvary we marvel at the great unveiling of divine love. Our benefits as far outstrip Job's as our testings fall short of his.

SECTION 12
Dialogue: Job 4 – 42.6
Contest: Round 2: Job 15-21
Bildad's 2nd Speech: Job 18

If Bildad was peppery in his previous contribution to the debate, he certainly has not improved in listening to the heated exchanges of the last few chapters. The passing of time is supposed to mellow men, but not Bildad. At least his first speech, recorded in chapter 8, offered a dutifully contrite Job the possibility of light at the end of the tunnel, whereas he now speaks as one convinced that there can be no hope for a man so hardened in sin. Since he cannot seduce or shame Job into repentance, perhaps he can scare him? From blandishments, he therefore resorts to threats pure and simple, proving himself to be, in Robinson's words, "the bitterest and most hostile of the three friends".[183]

His simple strategy is to dismiss all Job's arguments with a sweep of the hand before moving into a detailed and deliberately blood-curdling catalogue of the miseries which inevitably accompany wickedness in this world, a catalogue which constitutes "a passionate oration on the terrors that await the evildoer". It is indeed "a bleak picture without a single bright stroke".[184] Its purpose is evident: to prove that if such things are currently happening to Job, then he must be, beyond doubt, one of the wicked.

His second speech falls into two unequal paragraphs:

> 1. Bildad's Repudiation of Job's Wordiness: 18.1-4
> 2. Bildad's Denunciation of Job's Wickedness: 18.5-21.

Bildad's Repudiation of Job's Wordiness: 18.1-4

One of the things we discover as we wend our way through the book of Job is the sheer tedium involved in listening to stale repetition. If the reader finds the experience wearying how much more did Job! Bildad has nothing new to offer; indeed, he begins with words almost identical to those of his first speech. Compare his two opening gambits:

> How long will it be ere ye make an end of words? mark, and afterwards we will speak (18.2).

> How long wilt thou speak these things? and how long shall the words of thy mouth be like a strong wind? (8.2).

There is nothing wrong with repeating when necessary what is reliable and good. The immutable truth of God has to be taught systematically over and over again, especially as every new generation of believers urgently needs to hear it plainly communicated. That is why Paul urges Timothy to "Hold the pattern of sound words which thou hast heard from me, in faith and love which is in Christ Jesus" (2 Tim 1.13, RV), and "the things that thou hast heard of me among many witnesses, the same commit thou to faithful men, who shall be able to teach others also" (2 Tim 2.2). The apostle's choice of the words "the same" indicates that divine truth is to be passed on without addition, without subtraction, and without alteration. The book of Deuteronomy (which means, significantly, "the second law") consists of a lengthy address by Moses to the younger Israelites on the borders of the Promised Land, recounting the privileges and experiences of their parents: God's instruction to His people had not changed with the passing of time. During His earthly life the Lord Jesus frequently delivered identical teaching (just as He worked similar miracles in different locations); and Peter specifically dedicated himself to a ministry of recapitulation and revision:

> I will not be negligent to put you always in remembrance of these things, though ye know them, and be established in the present truth. Yea, I think it meet, as long as I am in this tabernacle, to stir you up by putting you in remembrance (2 Pet 1.12-13).

Concerning the preacher who boasted that he had never delivered the same message more than once, someone drily commented that it was only because he had never said anything worth repeating. And yet there is in the Word of God an infinite variety of spiritually nourishing information which is marvellously susceptible to different kinds of exposition. No two Bible teachers will ever open up a chapter of Scripture in exactly the same way, because God has so packed His Word with unfathomable riches that each believer can come to it afresh, drawing on the unique personal capacities with which God has endowed him. This is not to say that Scripture defies rational explanation, or that it resists any settled contextual meaning. The normative historical-grammatical method of exegesis is grounded on the confidence that God's Word has but one interpretation, though many applications. To approach the Bible with any other presupposition is to be at the mercy of the latest interpretative fashion. The modish literary philosophy of post-modernism may thrive on what it calls "indeterminacy of meaning" (except of course in books written by its proponents, who seem to expect their words, if no one else's, to be understood as they intended them), but in Scripture, as in common sense, grammar and context safely regulate meaning. Ramm summarises the principle well: "the interpreter must give attention to *grammar*; to the *times, circumstances, and conditions* of the writer of the biblical book; and to the *context* of the passage".[185]

But Job is not sitting comfortably in a Gospel Hall listening to edifying ministry. On the outskirts of his town, perched uncomfortably on an ash pile, suffering the continuing pains of multiple diseases, he has to endure the persistently recycled theories of unsympathetic men who have dug themselves into a hole with no way out.

The testy Bildad first charges him with wilfully tracking down meaningless verbiage in order to prolong the contest:

> How long will ye hunt for words? Be intelligent, and then we will speak.
> Wherefore are we counted as beasts, and reputed stupid in your sight?

> Thou that tearest thyself in thine anger, shall the earth be forsaken for thee?
> and shall the rock be removed out of its place? (18.2-4, JND)

There is an immediate oddity in the momentary use of the second person plural ("ye … your") as Bildad initiates his address. To whom is he speaking? Not the two other friends, for sure, because there is no evidence of any crack in their coalition. They may have different personalities but they hold the same basic presuppositions. Smick suggests that he has chosen "to categorise Job as one of those problem people … who make life difficult by being unreasonable".[186] More likely, Bildad views Job as the representative of a larger company; he has, in effect, become the spokesman for the whole congregation of the godless. Not only is he a sinner, he has taken the lead among those who rebel against God, deliberately searching out clever arguments with which to repel the attacks of pious orthodoxy. If he would use his head and control himself, then his friends would better be able to express themselves. His pig-headed resistance to their combined wisdom, and his sarcastic insults, mean that he is treating them as less than human, almost as though they were brute beasts, devoid of reason.

Bildad has obviously been stung by some of Job's comments. His reference to "beasts" (literally, "cattle", as in Genesis 1.24) is a conscious echo of Job's earlier challenge to "ask now the beasts, and they shall teach thee; and the fowls of the air, and they shall tell thee" (12.7). Job has argued that even the dumb animals realise, in contrast to the cosy theology of the friends, that there is no neat correlation between goodness and success: violence and brute strength hold sway in a fallen world. Bildad goes on, in his turn, to accuse Job of throwing a temper tantrum to no purpose. Listening, with increasing disgust, to the patriarch's case against God, he picks up a key word. "He [God] teareth [2963] me in his wrath, who hateth me" (16.9), complained Job. "No", answers, Bildad; "in your insane frenzy you are guilty of tearing yourself" (2963). We should note that as he describes Job's senseless raging he changes to the second person singular (18.4). Yet all Job's fury is pointless: as a mere individual he cannot hope to shake the fixed conditions of the physical world ("the earth … the rock") any more than he can change the moral principles of God's universe. In his pathetic madness Shakespeare's King Lear tries in vain to out-storm the tempest in which he finds himself, but to no avail, because weather conditions are beyond the control of even the most powerful of mortals. Huff and puff all you wish, says Bildad, but you can change neither God's world nor God's ways. We would not disagree. Puny man cannot overturn creation, or overcome the basic principles of cause and effect which God in wisdom has built into His world. The divine promise given after the flood assures us that, whatever the prognostications of climate change scientists, "While the earth remaineth, seedtime and harvest, and cold and heat, and summer and winter, and day and night shall not cease" (Gen 8.22). However much inflationary circumstances may disturb human financial systems, under all conditions it remains true that "the wages of sin is death" (Rom 6.23). Divine judgment takes its course with the inevitable outcome, as Bildad goes on to argue, that the lights in the tent of the wicked man will be put out. Retribution is inescapable.

Where Bildad is wrong – and it is a serious error – is in assuming among his fixed moral principles that earthly distress is an invariable symptom of heavenly disapproval. This blunder lies at the root of the rest of his speech. He accuses Job of ranting, but to the unprejudiced observer he seems little better himself. Robinson shrewdly comments, "a great part of wisdom is to govern one's temper … loss of temper generally proves weakness in argument".[187] As the three friends re-tread their limited spot of argumentative and rhetorical ground, we may well get the impression that, though there is a distinct increase in heat, little true light is being generated.

Bildad's Denunciation of Job's Wickedness: 18.5-21

This extensive account of the fate of bad men subdivides into four main paragraphs. Bildad paints a lurid sketch of the terrible judgment awaiting the ungodly even while they are alive. It is no accident that he describes the object of his condemnation in the singular, for it is of course Job who is in his mind. There is nothing abstract or theoretical about his language. The wicked man finds himself surrounded by darkness (18.5-6), ensnared by disaster (18.7-10), weakened by disease (18.11-14), and robbed of descendants (18.15-19). The topics move from the broadly general (18.5-10) to the uncomfortably and unkindly specific (18.11-19), the last two answering Job's complaint that God had burdened him with sickness and taken away his family. If He has, says Bildad, it is only a proof that you are one of the ungodly.

To be **surrounded by darkness** (18.5-6) suggests a picture of gloom not unlike Job's own assessment of his situation. His previous speeches have drawn on the imagery of darkness to express both his mood and his expectation of imminent departure into the obscurity of *sheol* (3.4-6; 10.21-22; 17.13). Bildad uses four different nouns relating to light (in the KJV, "light", "spark", "fire" and "candle") in order to snuff them all out: it is a dramatic representation of the sudden extinguishing of prosperity in the home of the wicked man. Light speaks of warmth, domesticity, health, and happiness. While Egypt shivered in a divinely imposed thick darkness, "all the children of Israel had light in their dwellings" (Ex 10.23). But for the wilful sinner, all enjoyment of earthly blessing will be removed. Jamieson, Fausset and Brown comment that "Arabian hospitality … prided itself on welcoming the stranger to the fire in the tent, and even lit fires to direct him to it. The ungodly shall be deprived of the means to show hospitality. His dwelling shall be dark and desolate".

The wicked man is also **ensnared by disaster** (18.7-10). Bildad pictures him making his perilous way along a track littered with obstacles and traps:

The steps of his strength shall be straitened, and his own counsel shall cast him down. For he is sent into the net by his own feet, and he walketh on the meshes; The gin taketh him by the heel, the snare layeth hold on him; A cord is hidden for him in the ground, and his trap in the way (18.7-10, JND).

In biblical metaphor the walk illustrates the pathway of life. The poetry of the Psalms is full of this imagery:

> Blessed is the man that walketh not in the counsel of the ungodly, nor standeth in the way of sinners, nor sitteth in the seat of the scornful (Ps 1.1).

> The wicked walk on every side, when the vilest men are exalted (Ps 12.8).

> Judge me, O Lord; for I have walked in mine integrity: I have trusted also in the Lord; therefore I shall not slide (Ps 26.1).

> For the Lord God is a sun and shield: the Lord will give grace and glory: no good thing will he withhold from them that walk uprightly (Ps 84.11).

The highway of life is often a minefield of concealed snares and pitfalls, laid on purpose to stumble the believer. The psalmist is well aware of the grim fact that, in David's words, "there is but a step between me and death" (1 Sam 20.3):

> When my spirit was overwhelmed within me, then thou knewest my path. In the way wherein I walked have they privily laid a snare for me (Ps 142.3).

> They have prepared a net for my steps; my soul is bowed down: they have digged a pit before me (Ps 57.6).

Nevertheless, those who belong to the Lord and seek to follow His ways may pray with confidence, "Hold up my goings in thy paths, that my footsteps slip not" (Ps 17.5). In a hazardous world we find spiritual safety only in Him.

Bildad, however, is not thinking of the malicious snares laid by the wicked to bring down the child of God; rather, he is describing the judicial calamities God has planned for the evil man. His firm, strong strides, the outward evidence of health and vitality, will be "straitened". Writes Davidson, "the widening of the steps is a usual oriental figure for the bold and free movements of one in prosperity, as straitening of them is for the timid and constrained action of one in adversity".[188] The word "straitened" (3334) only appears nine times in Scripture and carries the idea of cramped, uncomfortably narrowed circumstances. It is first used of Jacob as he fearfully approached a meeting with his estranged brother Esau: "Then Jacob was greatly afraid and distressed [3334]" (Gen 32.7). It is promised of the son who heeds his father's wise counsel that "When thou goest, thy steps shall not be straitened [3334]; and when thou runnest, thou shalt not stumble" (Prov 4.12). The lot of the ungodly is very different. Instead of marching forth with the bold, self-confident stride of a man in the peak of condition, he will be reduced to infirm tottering. And what is it that casts him down? "His own counsel". That is to say, his wicked schemes and plans will be his undoing, just as Haman's plot against Mordecai rebounded fatally on his own head.

To hammer home his point that the godless man is hemmed in by potential risks on every side, Bildad uses six synonyms. The sinner's feet carry him into a "net"; he walks upon "meshes"; a "gin" seizes him by the heel; a "snare" holds him; a "cord" or noose is laid in the ground to catch him; a "trap" is spread in his pathway. The language is designed to make us think of the fowler seeking to catch a wild bird, or the hunter laying snares for an animal. However carefully he treads, the victim is bound to fall through the network of woven branches and leaves which cover the pit, or be caught by his heel in a snare, or find his feet lashed helplessly in a noose.

Bildad's lesson about the vulnerability of the wicked is in principle accurate, and accords with other scriptures. There is often a terrible irony in their fate, for "The heathen are sunk down in the pit that they made: in the net which they hid is their own foot taken" (Ps 9.15). David's language about his enemy is striking in its imprecation: "Let destruction come upon him at unawares; and let his net that he hath hid catch himself: into that very destruction let him fall" (Ps 35.8). The judgment that befell the bad king Zedekiah at the overthrow of Jerusalem by the Babylonian army is described in similar terms: "My net also will I spread upon him, and he shall be taken in my snare: and I will bring him to Babylon to the land of the Chaldeans; yet shall he not see it, though he shall die there" (Ezek 12.13). Even in this life sin may sometimes receive severe punishment, but it will be dealt with completely when men stand at the Great White Throne judgment where, in John's vision, "the dead were judged out of those things which were written in the books, according to their works" (Rev 20.12). But Bildad is addressing his solemn warning to the wrong man: Job, we know from the prologue, is one of the godliest men of his day.

Remorselessly, however, Bildad ploughs on. The sinner is also **weakened by disease** (18.11-14), reduced to a shadow of his former self, and brought down to bodily dissolution. The paragraph moves from "terrors" to "terrors", starting with a general reference to the symptoms of a guilty conscience (18.11), and climaxing in an encounter with "the king of terrors" himself (18.14), a personification of death. Here is the passage in the Revised Version:

> Terrors shall make him afraid on every side, and shall chase him at his heels. His strength shall be hunger–bitten [literally, "hungry"] and calamity shall be ready for his halting ["misfortune is ready for his fall", Delitzsch]. It shall devour the members of his body, yea, the firstborn of death shall devour his members. He shall be rooted out of his tent wherein he trusteth; and he shall be brought to the king of terrors (18.11-14, RV).

This deliberately creepy scenario includes psychological paranoia, the collapse of bodily health, the gradual withering of the limbs, violent uprooting from the sphere of security and confidence, with the result that the wicked man finally stands quaking in the presence of death itself. "The firstborn of death" paints a grisly picture, because in Semitic culture the firstborn held pride of place as the chief, the ultimate. When God says of David, "I will make him my firstborn, higher than the kings of the earth" (Ps 89.27), He is announcing in the strongest terms the primacy of David's lineage. This promise will find its fulfilment in the millennial rule of Christ when, for the first time in human history, "a king shall reign in righteousness, and princes shall rule in judgment" (Is 32.1). If "the firstborn of the poor" (Is 14.30) means the very poorest, then "the firstborn of death" means the most extreme manifestation of death one could imagine. This obscene thing will proceed to "devour" (the common Hebrew word for "eat") the sinner's limbs and body parts.

In order to underline the gratuitously unfeeling character of Bildad's diatribe, we must pause to remind ourselves of Job's appalling physical state. He is suffering from, among other things, hideous boils which produce an irritating skin condition (2.7-8), a disfiguration which makes him almost unrecognisable (2.12), suppurating sores infested with worms (7.5), red and swollen eyes (16.16), stinking breath (19.17), drastic weight loss (19.20), unsightly withering of the skin (30.30), and chronic bowel trouble (30.27). Certainly he appears to be a living illustration of Bildad's words. Later he will say of himself that "Terrors are turned upon me: they pursue my soul as the wind: and my welfare passeth away as a cloud" (30.15). He has repeatedly assured his audience that nothing but death lies ahead of him (7.21; 10.20-22; 14.19-22; 17.1,13-16). The heartless image that Bildad paints is aimed to offer a shocking verbal mirror to the patriarch's gaze. Here, says Bildad, look; that's you, Job, isn't it?

But he has not finished. He leaves his most crushing blow to the end. The wicked man will be **robbed of descendants** (18.15-19), because

> They who are none of his shall dwell in his tent; brimstone shall be showered upon his habitation: His roots shall be dried up beneath, and above shall his branch be cut off; His remembrance shall perish from the earth, and he shall have no name on the pasture-grounds. He is driven from light into darkness, and chased out of the world. He hath neither son nor grandson among his people, nor any remaining in the places of his sojourn (18.15-19, JND).

This snapshot of a family home occupied by strangers introduces an account of total oblivion. The loss of one's posterity and therefore one's name was a catastrophic disaster to a man of Job's day. Writes Delitzsch: "the desolation of his house is the most terrible calamity for the Semite, i.e., when all belonging to his family die, or are reduced to poverty, their habitation is desolated, and their ruins are become the byword of future generations".[189] The unexpected military defeat at Ai caused Joshua to fear the utter extinction of Israel, because "the Canaanites and all the inhabitants of the land shall hear of it, and shall environ us round, and cut off our name from the earth" (Josh 7.9). Saul, in one of his saner moments, pressed David to swear "that thou wilt not cut off my seed after me, and that thou wilt not destroy my name out of my father's house" (1 Sam 24.21). David himself prays, concerning the evil man, "Let his posterity be cut off; and in the generation following let their name be blotted out" (Ps 109.13). Jehovah's judgment of Babylon meant that He would completely annihilate its ruling dynasty and "cut off from Babylon the name, and remnant, and son, and nephew" (Is 14.22). In stunning contrast, the amazing promise of blessing held out to believing eunuchs, men who could produce no natural issue, is that "unto them will I give in mine house and within my walls a place and a name better than of sons and of daughters: I will give them an everlasting name, that shall not be cut off" (Is 56.5).

These examples all testify to the importance of the family name in Old Testament times. But the drying up of his roots and the cutting off of his branch announced the complete extermination of Job's lineage. The allusion to brimstone may be designed to remind him – as if he needed it – of the "fire of God" which fell from heaven to consume his flocks, and the supernaturally "great wind" which demolished his son's house, killing his children. It may even echo the appalling divine judgment on Sodom and Gomorrah, implicitly placing Job's offspring in a similar category. The sinful man's name would be completely forgotten and he would be driven out into permanent exclusion, leaving no memorial, no record, no remembrance.

As he concludes his list of the disasters which form the earthly lot of the wicked man, Bildad imagines the reactions of a spell-bound audience:

> They of the west are appalled at his day, and horror seizes them of the east.
> Surely such are the dwellings of the unrighteous, such is the place of him
> who knows not God (18.20-21, ESV).

The ESV makes best sense of verse 20. The word rendered "come after" in the KJV is used in the expressions "uttermost sea" and "hinder sea" (the Mediterranean, or western sea) in Deuteronomy 11.24 and Zechariah 14.8, while "went before" appears as "east sea" (the Dead Sea or eastern sea) in Ezekiel 47.18. Delitzsch comments that "it is much more suited both to the order of the words and the usage of the language to understand … the former of those dwelling in the west, and the latter of those dwelling in the east".[190] In other words, the dramatic destruction of the hardened sinner ("his day" of ruin and disaster) causes worldwide shock as the news is flashed around the globe.

Bildad ends censoriously: "Surely such are the dwellings of the wicked, and this is the place of him that knoweth not God" (18.21). His target is unmistakable. As Davidson puts it, "every sentence of Bildad's speech carries with it the charge, Thou art the man".[191]

Throughout this chapter Bildad makes two assumptions, without offering any supporting evidence. First, he assumes that the ungodly meet their fate primarily *in this world;* second, that everyone who is afflicted with outward misery must therefore be numbered amongst the ungodly. He appears to have little sense of judgment to come, and no awareness of the diverse educational dealings of God with His people. A fuller biblical picture of the former is spelt out by the apostle Paul in his letter to the Romans. There he teaches that there is indeed a present penalty for sin, meted out in various ways in this life; Romans chapter 1 teaches, among other things, that God often punishes sin with yet more sin. That is to say, He judicially abandons man to the gross built-in earthly consequences of his rebellion. Hence we read that "the wrath of God is revealed [not, will be revealed] from heaven against all ungodliness and unrighteousness of men, who hold the truth in unrighteousness" (Rom 1.18), a wrath expressed in the terrible fact that "God also gave them up ... gave them up ... gave them over to a reprobate mind" (Rom 1.24,26,28). There is therefore a present tense manifestation of divine anger against sin. Paul's examples focus on particularly nasty sins of deliberate vileness. But this does not contradict or replace the future display of wrath about which Paul writes in chapter 2. There he warns the hardened, unbelieving sinner that "after thy hardness and impenitent heart [thou] treasurest up unto thyself wrath against the day of wrath and revelation of the righteous judgment of God; Who will render to every man according to his deeds" (Rom 2.5-6).

The coming eschatological day of wrath is both unavoidable and just, involving a full and final assessment of each individual in the presence of the all-knowing God. The result is clearly narrated in the book of Revelation:

> And the sea gave up the dead which were in it; and death and hell delivered up the dead which were in them: and they were judged every man according to their works. And death and hell were cast into the lake of fire. This is the second death. And whosoever was not found written in the book of life was cast into the lake of fire (Rev 20.13-15).

Present manifestations of divine wrath, on the other hand, vary considerably according to God's sovereign purposes. Asaph looked at some of the evidently wicked people around him, and saw little sign of conscience-stricken misery either in their life or in their death:

> For there are no bands in their death: but their strength is firm. They are not in trouble as other men; neither are they plagued like other men. Therefore pride compasseth them about as a chain; violence covereth them as a garment. Their eyes stand out with fatness: they have more than heart could wish (Ps 73.4-7).

John Bunyan's *Life and Death of Mr Badman*, a kind of inverted *Pilgrim's Progress*, is equally realistic in its account of the deathbed of the anti-hero, a brazenly rebellious man whose life has been lived in open defiance of God. In keeping with the literary strategy of the book, the matter is handled in question and answer form:

> Pray, how was he in his death? Was death strong upon him? Or did he die with ease, quietly? As quietly as a lamb. There seemed not to be in it, to standers by, so much as a strong struggle of nature. And, as for his mind, it seemed to be wholly at quiet.[192]

The epitome of the bad man dies, ironically, in peace and tranquillity. But, as Bunyan is at pains to point out, "there is no judgment to be made by a quiet death, of the eternal state of him that so dieth".[193] A prosperous life and a speedy, painless death no more prove that a man is saved than a life full of suffering witnesses that a man is lost.

By this stage in the book, Bildad and his friends are beginning to treat Job not as a good man who has stumbled but as an irredeemably bad man who is receiving the due reward of his deeds. As far as they are concerned he is, in his outrageous arguments, the mouthpiece of the wicked. In reality, the reader knows that he is "the representative of the suffering and misjudged righteous, in other words, of the congregation whose blessedness is hidden beneath an outward form of suffering".[194] Indeed, in contrast to Bildad's harsh verdict upon Job, "his patience and piety have diffused a fragrance throughout the world. His name [is] one of the brightest constellations in the firmament of Holy Scripture".[195] Far from being the hypocrite his friends imagine, Job is in many ways a type of the Lord Jesus Christ, the ultimate Just One who suffered at the hands of God and man. Bildad has been preaching to the wrong person (for Job is one of the righteous) with the wrong motives (completely lacking any tenderness of heart).

Nevertheless, even poor preachers can say something valuable. Paul rejoiced when Christ was accurately proclaimed, even though some of the evangelists currently filling the platform were motivated by envy of the imprisoned apostle, betraying a malicious glee in his sufferings. He is frank in his exposure:

> Some indeed preach Christ even of envy and strife; and some also of good will: The one preach Christ of contention, not sincerely, supposing to add affliction to my bonds: But the other of love, knowing that I am set for the defence of the gospel. What then? notwithstanding, every way, whether in pretence, or in truth, Christ is preached; and I therein do rejoice, yea, and will rejoice (Phil 1.15-18).

If Paul could find something positive in such adverse circumstances, we can pick some tasty meat off the bones of Bildad's second contribution to the debate. Here are some of the valid points he makes:

- Wickedness will eventually receive its just reward (18.5)
- A man's own trickery often proves his undoing (18.7)
- Our pathway through this world is fraught with perils (18.8-10)
- Sin may have a direct impact on a man's health (18.12-13)
- Death is inescapable (18.14)
- An individual's sin often brings dire consequences to his family (18.16)
- God's visible judgment strikes men with terror (18.20)
- The root of unrighteousness is ignorance of God (18.21).

Bildad's analysis of the fate of the evil man (18.5-19) may stimulate us to trace, by contrast, the biblical promises held out to those who trust the living God. The impenitent sinner may indeed be surrounded by darkness (18.5-6), for as Solomon puts it, "The way of the wicked is as darkness: they know not at what they stumble" (Prov 4.19), and his destiny will be "outer darkness" (Mt 8.12). On the other hand, "the path of the just is as the shining light, that shineth more and more unto the perfect day" (Prov 4.18). Though the sinner may be ensnared by disaster (18.7-10), his way pockmarked with potholes and pitfalls, the believer can "say of the Lord, He is my refuge and my fortress: my God; in him will I trust. Surely he shall deliver thee from the snare of the fowler, and from the noisome pestilence" (Ps 91.2-3). While the wicked man may be enfeebled by disease (18.11-14), the believer rejoices that, though he has no guaranteed immunity to sickness in this life, "The Lord will strengthen him upon the bed of languishing" and "make all his bed in his sickness" (Ps 41.3). Paul goes further, announcing the principle that the Christian's physical weakness may constitute a positive blessing, "for when I am weak, then am I strong" (2 Cor 12.10). The ungodly may lose their descendants (18.15-19), but the believer in Christ has a remarkable compensation:

> Verily I say unto you, There is no man that hath left house, or brethren, or sisters, or father, or mother, or wife, or children, or lands, for my sake, and the gospel's, But he shall receive an hundredfold now in this time, houses, and brethren, and sisters, and mothers, and children, and lands, with persecutions; and in the world to come eternal life (Mk 10.29-30).

The blessing offered by the Lord Jesus to His disciples is threefold: a recompense "now in this time", which takes the form of a vast spiritual family (found today in the practical fellowship of saints in the local assembly where God has placed us), a reminder by means of "persecutions" of the Saviour's rejection by this present age, and a final reward in the millennial Kingdom ("the world [age] to come").

Perhaps the last verse of Job 18 contains in miniature the greatest impact for the believer. As we might expect, its application is wholly wrong but at least the principle is right. The poetic parallelism establishes a connection between unrighteousness and not knowing God: "Surely, such are the dwellings of the unrighteous man, and such the place of him that knoweth not God" (18.21, JND). If unrighteousness and ignorance of God go hand in hand, the same is true of their opposites, justification and the knowledge of God. It is only by faith in Christ Jesus that we are counted judicially right in God's sight and thereby enter into the blessing of a personal knowledge of and relationship with the living God: "being justified by faith [there's the righteousness], we have peace with God [there's the relationship] through our Lord Jesus Christ" (Rom 5.1). Though Job lived so long ago, the consistent teaching of the book is that he, by grace, enjoyed both a righteous standing and a genuine relationship with his God. Neither the trials he endured, nor the friends who intensified them, could rob him of these blessings.

SECTION 13
Dialogue: Job 4 – 42.6
Contest: Round 2: Job 15-21
Job's 5th Speech: Job 19

I suppose all Bible readers are familiar with at least two passages in the book of Job: the prologue, with its sturdy testimony to faith under fire, and the midpoint, chapter 19, with its astonishing expression of confidence in a doctrine as yet not clearly disclosed in God's Word. Since Job seems unable to find vindication in the present world, and certainly receives no support from his friends, he peers ahead to a coming day when a divine Redeemer will stand up in his defence. When Charles Jennens, Handel's librettist, compiled his selection of verses for the 1742 oratorio *Messiah*, he significantly combined Job 19 with 1 Corinthians 15, placing Job's anticipation of a future exoneration in the full light of the historical resurrection of the Lord Jesus Christ. Thus the soprano soloist beautifully runs together slightly modified extracts from one of the oldest and one of the most recent books of the Bible:

> I know that my redeemer liveth, and that he shall stand at the latter day upon the earth: And though ... worms destroy this body, yet in my flesh shall I see God: [for] now is Christ risen from the dead ... the firstfruits of them that sleep (Job 19.25-26; 1 Cor 15.20).

Jennens's theology cannot be faulted. The triumphant resurrection of Christ in the past guarantees the resurrection of His people in the future.

Commentators agree that this is one of the grandest moments in the entire book of Job. It is, writes Zuck, "a skyscraper among the 42 chapters of Job",[196] a book which itself constitutes, in the opinion of Bullard, "the literary Everest of the Bible".[197] As far as Robinson is concerned, it is the "crowning part of the controversy", being both "in form and in fact the centre of the whole book".[198]

But Job's memorable statement of faith is found in the context of continuing emotional turbulence and mental distress. Before he reaches his mountaintop of serene trust Job plunges into a valley of bitter accusation in which he berates his friends for their hard words, charges God with wilfully subverting his cause, and cries out for sympathy. He starts with a disgusted rejection of his friends' brutal criticisms, claiming that their words have broken him in pieces (19.2); he ends with a deep longing for his own words of impassioned self-defence to be recorded permanently, written in a book or carved on the rock (19.23-24). We should not miss the irony that his desire was granted, for we are reading, in the imperishable record of Scripture, the very words he wanted preserved.

The chapter can be broken down into four unequal paragraphs as follows:

1. Job's Introduction: 19.1-4
2. Job's Explanation of his Reproach: 19.5-22
3. Job's Anticipation of his Redeemer: 19.23-27
4. Job's Intimation of coming Retribution: 19.28-29.

Job's Introduction: 19.1-4

Job's bitter grief is evident from the beginning in his linguistic choices:

> How long will ye vex my soul and break me in pieces with words? These
> ten times have ye reproached me: ye are not ashamed that ye deal hardly
> with me (19.2-3, RV).

His friends have afflicted or tormented him (the word "vex", not common, is
used most frequently in Lamentations), broken him in pieces (a word used six
times in Job and translated, for example, "crushed" or "destroyed"), reproached
him, and injured him (the word is found only here). Further, this has been their
constant theme, ever harping on his theological and moral failures, failures
which they have been unable to prove. "These ten times" is a Hebraism meaning
frequently or often. Jacob claimed that Laban had similarly defrauded him: "your
father hath deceived me, and changed my wages ten times" (Gen 31.7). In the
same way the Lord charged Israel with provocation, for "all those men which have
seen my glory, and my miracles, which I did in Egypt and in the wilderness …
have tempted me now these ten times, and have not hearkened to my voice" (Num
14.22). Job has been suffering the irritation of constant carping. As Delitzsch puts
it, "This controversy is torture to Job's spirit; enduring in himself unutterable
agony, both bodily and spiritually, and in addition stretched upon the rack by the
three friends with their united strength".[199]

Persistence in prayer to God is a good thing (Col 4.2), but persistence in
negative criticism is abrasive. It is counter-productive to nag incessantly even in
what may appear to be a good cause. When Paul had to write a corrective letter
to an erring assembly he finds something positive to commend, and never resorts
to unjustifiable or unfeeling abuse. The Corinthians, for example, who would
probably win the prize for the worst local church in the New Testament, are
praised for the evidence of God's grace among them (1 Cor 1.4,6), their possession
of spiritual gifts (1 Cor 1.5,7), their anticipation of the Lord's return (1 Cor 1.7-
8), and their enjoyment of divine fellowship (1 Cor 1.9). And Paul assured them
that his serious disciplinary ministry was in no way a denial of his love for them
(2 Cor 2.4), for his correction was accompanied by tears.

Words can be potentially destructive. We are taught in childhood that, though
sticks and stones may break our bones, words will never hurt us, but Job's
testimony is that not only do they hurt, they leave lingering sores. Many a believer
can recall the unkind remarks of fellow saints, words uttered thoughtlessly on the
spur of the moment and never intended to inflict permanent injury. None of us
should have the reputation for a cruel tongue.

Job's response to his friends (19.4) is to say something like this: "Even if I have
made some kind of mistake" – and his word choice is important because he uses a
term which first appears in Leviticus 4.13 to describe a sin of ignorance – "I am the
one responsible for it, and must myself stand before God to answer for it. It's not
your place to pass judgment". He is not, we should note, admitting the possibility
of serious sin, but rather of "an inadvertent mistake, the kind of wrongful act that

everyone commits by reason of being human. Remaining confident that he has never sinned as gravely as his misfortune suggests, Job refuses to concede that he has done anything more serious than some unintentional blunder".[200]

Job's Explanation of his Reproach: 19.5-22

But of course his friends are still working on the tired and faulty assumption that his intense sufferings are irrefutable proofs of guilt. This lies behind Job's argument in verses 5 and 6:

> If indeed ye will magnify yourselves against me, and plead against me my reproach: Know now that God hath subverted me in my cause, and hath compassed me with his net (19.5-6, RV).

His friends, comfortably settled on a pinnacle of piety, take it for granted that his calamities confirmed his wickedness; Job, on the contrary, asserts that far from demonstrating his sinfulness they were the evidence that God had wronged him. It was not his iniquity but God's injustice which explained his dreadful circumstances. Job has been here before, making the kind of shockingly heretical accusations which outraged the devoutness of his friends and would undoubtedly alienate the reader were it not that we know he is partly correct. I say partly, because while he is unquestionably right to claim that he has done nothing to deserve his sufferings, he is wrong to charge God with unrighteousness. What we blurt out in pain and perplexity sometimes borders on the seriously irreverent. That is why James reminds us that control of the tongue is the most demanding of human accomplishments (James 3.1-2).

Job is not the only biblical example of outspokenness under pressure. Even Jeremiah, that most loyal of prophets, when faced with the opposition of powerful enemies, was driven to charge God with misleading him: "O Lord, thou hast deceived me, and I was deceived: thou art stronger than I, and hast prevailed: I am in derision daily, every one mocketh me" (Jer 20.7). Thinking back to the Lord's words to him in chapter 1, the prophet complains that he was promised immunity from persecution in his unpopular ministry and yet he has become the target of national hostility. His misunderstanding of what was in reality a pledge of preservation, rather than exemption from distress, leads him to accuse God of prevarication. Nevertheless, despite their very similar accusations, neither Jeremiah nor Job are guilty of blasphemy, if by blasphemy we mean a fixed attitude of wilful antagonism towards God expressed in a defamation of the divine character. Neither Job nor Jeremiah stoops to such folly. According to Zuck, "Job's opinion did not amount to blasphemy; instead it revealed an honest assessment of the facts as he saw them".[201]

Whether his words are rash or simply honest, from the start of his speech his immediate focus is God (19.6), drawing attention to the One who is the real theme of the chapter. Whatever his friends might think, he is convinced that God is his opponent and, however inconsistent the idea might appear, he believes also that God is his only reliable recourse.

He has no doubt that God has deliberately enclosed him in His net (19.6b). The Hebrew word for "net" is different, but Job is possibly responding to Bildad's charge that the wicked man is "cast into a net [of his own making] by his own feet, and he walketh upon a snare" (18.8). His point is that, in contrast to Bildad's moralising, he is not suffering the painful consequences of his own evil devices; rather, God has arbitrarily entangled him. He is trapped and cannot escape. That is why he clamoured aloud for justice, although no one takes any notice (19.7). The unfairness of his situation and God's inexplicable silence in the face of all his appeals fills him with the utmost dejection of spirit.

He now embarks on a detailed analysis of his condition as he sees it, a condition brought about by God's hostility. Although the grammatical subject governing the next six verses remains unnamed, identified only by the pronoun "he", the referent is clear from verse 6. Job feels that he has been trapped (19.8), robbed (19.9), broken (19.10), attacked (19.11-12), and thoroughly isolated (19.13) by God Himself. His picture language is powerful and very painful.

For a start, he has been subjected to **oppression from above** (19.6-13). God is the source of all his troubles. "He hath hedged up [1443] my way that I cannot pass, and he hath set darkness in my paths" (19.8, JND). Like a benighted traveller hastening homewards he has found the pathway blocked on every side. Jeremiah uses the same language in Lamentations:

> He hath hedged [1443] me about, that I cannot get out: he hath made my chain heavy. Also when I cry and shout, he shutteth out my prayer. He hath inclosed [1443] my ways with hewn stone, he hath made my paths crooked (Lam 3.7-9).

Try as he might, Job cannot break out from the pathway of pain that God has mapped out for him. He feels like a man spoiled of all his possessions, for "he hath stripped me of my glory, and taken the crown from my head" (19.9). The removal of his crown is meant to make us think of deposed royalty. Though Job was never literally a king, he did enjoy a position of almost regal dignity and prominence in his society. But his power, his riches, his esteem, his honour have all been savagely torn away. The verb "stripped" (6584) is graphic in its intensity, being used first to describe Joseph robbed of his special robe (Gen 37.23), and next of the flaying of the burnt offering (Lev 1.6). Job has been devastated: "He hath broken me down [5422] on every side, and I am gone: and mine hope hath he plucked up like a tree" (19.10, RV). "Break down" (5422) was what Israel was instructed to do to the altars of their idolatrous neighbours (Ex 34.13), or to kitchen equipment contaminated by an unclean creature (Lev 11.35), or to a house infected with leprosy (Lev 14.45). More ominously, it was exactly what the Babylonians did historically to the walls of Jerusalem (2 Kings 25.10). Even his hopes of some future restoration in this life, as held out to him by Zophar (11.18), have been uprooted like a tree ripped from its soil.

As a result of all this violent harassment, Job looks for nothing but death. "The words, *and I am gone*, refer to his inevitable death from his disease, which he regards as already virtually come".[202]

He now moves into military metaphor. Of verses 6 to 12 as a whole Smick writes, "Reverse this order and you have a step-by-step description of what happens in siege warfare",[203] but in fact the battle imagery does not become apparent until verses 11 and 12. Job feels as if he has been battered by divine storm troopers: God "hath kindled his anger against me, and hath counted me unto him as one of his enemies. His troops have come together and cast up their way against me, and have encamped round about my tent" (19.11-12, JND). The language borrows from ancient warfare, tracing the encounter from the initial animosity in the enemy commander's heart to the arrival of the besieging army with all the heavy equipment needed to blockade a town. The ESV helpfully renders the second part of verse 12: "they have cast up their siege ramp against me and encamp around my tent". All the sorrows and trials which have beset him are like a horde of fierce warriors out for his destruction.

Finally, God has cut him off from both relatives ("brethren") and friends ("acquaintance"): "He hath put my brethren far from me, and mine acquaintance are wholly estranged from me" (19.13, RV).

Trapped, robbed, broken, attacked, and isolated as a result of God's dealings with him, in his unrelieved misery Job faintly prefigures aspects of the Lord Jesus in His sufferings. Just as the psalmist seems to look ahead to Messiah's desertion when he writes, "My lovers and my friends stand aloof from my sore; and my kinsmen stand afar off" (Ps 38.11), so Job anticipates the Calvary narratives in the Gospels: "And all his acquaintance, and the women that followed him from Galilee, stood afar off, beholding these things" (Lk 23.49). Forsaken by the fickle crowd, deserted by the disciples, the Saviour was finally exposed to all God's judicial anger against man's sin, causing Him to ask – employing prophetic words we shall never fathom – "My God, my God, why hast thou forsaken me? why art thou so far from helping me, and from the words of my roaring?" (Ps 22.1) The only innocent man was treated like the worst of criminals.

But it is that last point, the experience of terrible isolation, which Job now particularly develops as he charts something of the **oppression from around** which has been his lot (19.14-19). Aloneness and loneliness should be carefully distinguished; it is possible to endure the one without the other. Job was not physically alone, for he had three – and later four – friends close at hand to sit with him in his affliction. But he was nevertheless acutely lonely, for there was no one who really understood or sympathised with his situation.

Delitzsch comments:

> One result of this condition of siege in which God's wrath has placed him is that he is avoided and despised as one smitten of God: neither love and fidelity, nor obedience and dependence, meet him from any quarter. What he has said in Job 17.6, that he is become a byword and an abomination (an object to spit upon), he here describes in detail.[204]

This is a new manifestation of sorrow, for hitherto it has been primarily the loss of divine fellowship and the ruin of earthly security which has plagued him. Here we become conscious of the acute social stigma Job suffers because of his calamities. While verses 6-13 traced everything to God, Job now views his kinsfolk and household servants as fully accountable for their hostile actions. It is the balance which Peter carefully maintained when speaking of the source of Messiah's sufferings:

> Ye men of Israel, hear these words; Jesus of Nazareth, a man approved of God among you by miracles and wonders and signs, which God did by him in the midst of you, as ye yourselves also know: Him, being delivered by the determinate counsel and foreknowledge of God, ye have taken, and by wicked hands have crucified and slain (Acts 2.22-23).

Divine sovereignty ("delivered by the determinate counsel and foreknowledge of God") never justifies sinful human activity ("ye have taken, and by wicked hands have crucified and slain").

Job's catalogue of human failure seems to move deliberately from the outside inwards. He starts with friends (he is presumably thinking primarily of the three sages by his side) and ends with his wife:

> My kinsfolk have failed, and my known friends have forgotten me. The sojourners in my house and my maids count me as a stranger; I am an alien in their sight. I called my servant, and he answered not; I entreated him with my mouth. My breath is strange to my wife, and my entreaties to the children of my mother's womb (19.14-17, JND).

"Kinsfolk" literally means those who are near at hand, and first occurs when Lot describes Zoar as a "city near to flee unto" (Gen 19.20); Young's Literal Translation renders it "neighbours". "Known friends" are those most familiar to him. But both have let him down. The neighbours have "failed" (2308), like the builders of Babel who "left off [2308] to build the city" (Gen 11.8), while close friends have forgotten him just as the chief butler forgot Joseph (Gen 40.23). Even his household is guilty of neglect, treating their master as though he were a stranger in his own home. Those whom he had graciously received as temporary visitors into his house ("sojourners") contemptuously treated their host as an outsider, while his female slaves ignored him. His own personal servant failed to respond to his calls for attention. Worse, even his wife would have nothing to do with him. Her lack of sympathy with her husband's distress was the culminating blow he suffered in chapter 2, and she appears again here as the final straw in Job's misery as a social outcast. The language suggests both emotional and mental estrangement, as well as the terrible effects of the multiple diseases which make his breath so odiously foetid.

As it stands in the KJV, the second part of verse 17 sounds odd: "though I intreated for the children's sake of mine own body" (19.17). For a start, Job is well aware that all his children have been killed (1.19-21). Second, the word "body" (990) is normally translated "womb" or "belly" (as, for example, in Genesis 25.23 and Numbers 5.21). In the light of this, more recent translators reasonably opt for a rendering which refers the phrase to his brothers, that is, the children of his mother's womb. He is therefore saying that, owing to his sicknesses, his breath has become insufferable to his wife, and an unbearable stench to his own brothers. All those closest to him have been alienated.

The passage frankly spells out Job's shameful ostracism. In the west, where families are commonly fractured, we find it hard to grasp how humiliating it must have been for Job, a distinguished eastern sheik with a large household of domestic retainers, to be shunned by his nearest relatives. How much more for the Creator of all things to be so despised by His creatures that He could confess, in the prophetic words of David, "I am become a stranger unto my brethren, and an alien unto my mother's children" (Ps 69.8)? The prediction was fulfilled in part in John's terse narrative comment, "neither did his brethren believe in him" (Jn 7.5).

But Job descends deeper still into shame, so that "even young children [5759] despise me; I rise up, and they speak against me" (19.18, JND). The word, a rare one, means "babe" or "little one". Job uses it later to describe the undeserved domestic bliss of the wicked: "They send forth their little ones [5759] like a flock, and their children dance" (21.11). So profound are his sorrows, and so repulsive his sores, that even small children, accustomed in oriental culture to show nothing but the utmost respect for the elderly, mock him in public.

Verse 19 effectively sums up his grief: "All my intimate friends abhor me, and they whom I loved are turned against me" (19.19, JND). Davidson asserts that "the reference is to such as his three friends, men whose high converse and fellowship seemed to Job, as a thoughtful godly man, something almost better than relationship",[205] but the language may equally describe the host of acquaintances and loved ones from whom he has found nothing but indifference or positive loathing.

Few of the Lord's people can enter into anything like Job's experience. Nevertheless, there are times when we may briefly know what it is to be misunderstood and abandoned by those dearest to us. There are scriptural examples. Hagar and her child were driven out from their home by Sarah's anger (Gen 21.14); Joseph was sold into slavery by his envious brothers (Gen 37.19-30); Moses sent his wife back to her parents (Ex 18.2); Miriam and Aaron slandered their brother (Num 12.1); young David faced the envious resentment of an older sibling (1 Sam 17.28). The Lord Jesus warned His disciples that they would inevitably be exposed to the hostility of a world that spurned Him, a hostility which would be felt especially in the home:

> Think not that I am come to send peace on earth: I came not to send peace, but a sword. For I am come to set a man at variance against his father, and the daughter against her mother, and the daughter in law against her mother in law. And a man's foes shall be they of his own household (Mt 10.34-36).

Darkness, however, only emphasises the light of God's promises. The picture may seem bleak, yet the great pledge of the Old Testament still holds true: "When my father and my mother forsake me, then the Lord will take me up" (Ps 27.10). Indeed, it is often only when we are faced with the utter failure of earthly kindred that we discover the sufficiency of God's love. As someone has said, it is precisely when we find the living God is all we have that we realise He is all we need. Hence it is that Job, throughout his trials, even when he is convinced that heaven itself has turned against him, speaks constantly to and about God. Affliction never drives him into atheism.

His final complaint is about physical **oppression from within**: "My bone cleaveth to my skin and to my flesh, and I am escaped with the skin of my teeth" (19.20). Persecuted by God, deserted by friends, he is also a chronic victim of the many internal pangs springing from his multiple diseases. Sickness has taken its toll. As Delitzsch puts it, "the bones may be felt and seen through the skin, and the little flesh that remains is wasted away almost to a skeleton".[206] The phrase "escaped with the skin of my teeth" has become proverbial, and some commentators have expended much ingenuity in explaining it as a clinical description of Job's dental health. Smick, for example, argues that "only Job's gums were left unaffected by his ailment".[207] Nevertheless, in the words of Davidson, "it seems more natural to suppose Job to mean that there has been but the 'skin of the teeth', i.e., next to nothing, between him and death".[208] It is best read as an idiomatic expression paralleling verse 10 and summing up the extremity of his situation.

Having so vividly catalogued his sorrows, Job ends this section of his speech by turning back to the three friends with a moving plea for understanding: "Have pity upon me, have pity upon me, O ye my friends; for the hand of God hath touched me. Why do ye persecute me as God, and are not satisfied with my flesh?" (19.21-22).

He implores them for mercy, that they would spare him the tactless, inconsiderate speeches which only increased his misery. Even if God had stretched out His hand against him, was it necessary that they should follow suit? Were they imitating God in a relentless pursuit of his life? The imagery implicitly likens the friends to wild animals ravenously devouring their prey. But Job calls out for humane pity. According to Strong, the word "have pity" (2603) means "to *bend* or *stoop* in kindness to an inferior", and is used of the psalmist imploring mercy of God (Ps 4.1; 6.2; 9.13; 25.16; 26.11), and by the writer of Proverbs to distinguish the behaviour of the godly man:

> He that despiseth his neighbour sinneth: but he that hath mercy [2603] on the poor, happy is he (Prov 14.21).

> He that oppresseth the poor reproacheth his Maker: but he that honoureth him hath mercy [2603] on the poor (Prov 14.31).

> He that hath pity [2603] upon the poor lendeth unto the Lord; and that which he hath given will he pay him again (Prov 19.17).

Because "the Lord is very pitiful, and of tender mercy" (James 5.11), those who have benefitted from His mercy should be prompt to show it to others. The Lord Jesus told a parable about a man who had been forgiven a huge debt yet could not find it in his heart to be merciful to one who owed him a paltry sum (Mt 18.23-35). The solemn lesson is put into the mouth of the king in the story: "Shouldest not thou also have had compassion on thy fellowservant, even as I had pity on thee?" (Mt 18.33). All believers should take note of the challenge.

Although Job is wholly in the dark about the heavenly events related in the first two chapters of the book, his diagnosis of his situation is accurate. Behind all the satanic assaults he has endured lies God, without whose permission Satan would have no ability to touch him at all. Naomi, often unjustifiably maligned by commentators, had a similarly exact sense of her circumstances, honestly acknowledging to her pagan daughters-in-law that "the hand of the Lord is gone out against me" (Ruth 1.13). This frank testimony to the disciplinary power of Jehovah, the God of Israel, far from doing harm, served to bring out the genuine faith of Ruth. She at least was under no illusions of an easy life when she accompanied her mother-in-law.

There is an important lesson in Job's heart-rending appeal for pity. Though affliction, whatever form it may take, is always ultimately traceable to God, there is no call for men to add to it. Indeed, those who try to exceed God's purpose find themselves facing severe reprisal. One of the striking verses of the Old Testament is Zechariah's indictment of those nations God used in His chastisement of erring Israel. Says the Lord, "I am very sore displeased with the heathen that are at ease: for I was but a little displeased [with the nation of Israel], and they helped forward the affliction" (Zech 1.15). So gleeful were Israel's enemies at the opportunity to wreak their hatred on the chosen people that they tried to go beyond the limits of God's disciplinary programme. Now, in one sense this is clearly impossible. No creature can step outside the bounds of God's purpose. To countenance the idea is to rob God of His sovereign control and surrender the universe to anarchy. But the prophet's language – which in some ways is similar to the common biblical procedure of crediting God with human characteristics (such as the capacity to repent) – is making an emphatic point. The Gentiles so relished their power that, to satisfy their own malicious vengeance, they wanted to exterminate the nation completely. History is not lacking in examples of this, nor of the retribution which has befallen those peoples who have particularly victimised the Jews.

If pagan nations, used as instruments of divine judgment, were wrong to try and punish the objects of God's afflicting hand beyond His intention, how much more should believers today refrain from adding to human pain. The Christian's basic obligation towards those who suffer is one of sympathy and support. Here is Robinson's incisive comment: "God's apparent severity towards any of His creatures [is] no reason for man's severity to his suffering fellow-creature. In all circumstances God makes humanity man's duty".[209] The Judean famine of Acts 11.28-30 may well have come as a divine judgment upon the area, but the responsibility of the saints was to seek to alleviate suffering. A tsunami may be an expression of God's anger against human wickedness, but believers will where possible try to display practical love and care. Paul's instruction prioritises the saints, but expands to embrace humanity in general:

> And let us not be weary in well doing: for in due season we shall reap, if we faint not. As we have therefore opportunity, let us do good unto all men, especially unto them who are of the household of faith (Gal 6.9-10).

The Saviour provides the great example. In a world where men and women were suffering under the divinely-imposed judicial consequences of human sinfulness, the Lord Jesus "went about doing good, and healing all that were oppressed of the devil; for God was with him" (Acts 10.38).

Job's Anticipation of his Redeemer: 19.23-27

Turning finally from his disillusionment with his friends, Job now pours out his heart, not directly *to* God in prayer (as he has done in previous chapters) but *about* the God in whom he rests for his vindication. Men dismissed him as a hypocrite; he alone maintained his innocence; only God could settle the matter once and for all by speaking up in his defence. Lacerated by the wounding words of his peers, Job longs for the indelible preservation of his personal testimony:

> Oh would that my words were written! oh that they were inscribed in a book! That with an iron style and lead they were graven in the rock for ever! (19.23-24, JND).

The Hebrew noun for "word" (4405) used here pervades Job: thirty-four of its thirty-eight Old Testament appearances are found in this book. "Written" (3789) first occurs in Exodus 17.14, where Moses is told to write in a book for the benefit of Joshua. But Job's literary aspiration predates Moses. Ordinary writing on flimsy surfaces is perishable, so Job desires his words to be hewn or carved out in rock using an iron stylus, with molten lead run into the traces in the stone so that the engraving would last for ever. Hartley tells us that "inscribed stone monuments called stelae were erected as witnesses of various matters, including laws, events, boundary marks, and personal accomplishments".[210] Years later, the prophet Jeremiah declared that "the sin of Judah is written with a pen of iron, and with the point of a diamond: it is graven upon the table of their heart, and upon the horns of your altars" (Jer 17.1). Judah's wickedness was carved deep in the hearts of the people and displayed outwardly on the pagan altars which bore witness to their idolatry. Job's testimony, on the other hand, which he wanted faithfully preserved against the ravages of time, was one of innocence. Despite everything against him, he still perseveres in the hope that eventually God Himself would intervene for him.

The boldness and yet the contradictory nature of Job's confidence should not be overlooked. He is bold in affirming so unshakeably God's knowledge of his personal uprightness. In this he parallels Paul solemnly insisting on his honesty and integrity: "I say the truth in Christ, I lie not, my conscience also bearing me witness in the Holy Ghost" (Rom 9.1); "The God and Father of our Lord Jesus Christ, which is blessed for evermore, knoweth that I lie not" (2 Cor 11.31); "For neither at any time used we flattering words, as ye know, nor a cloke of covetousness; God is witness" (1 Thess 2.5). Yet Job's argument seems oddly inconsistent because he has been asserting at the same time that God is his enemy, One who has unaccountably turned against him. Nevertheless, that very God whom he blames for his deplorable condition is the God in whom he places all his hopes.

Job's policy is a model for believers going through inexplicable circumstances of trial and distress. When, in memorable words of comfort, the psalmist urges the suffering saint to "cast thy burden upon the Lord, and he shall sustain thee" (Ps 55.22), he uses a word for "burden" which appears only here. According to the lexicons the word basically means "that which is given". Young's Literal Translation renders it thus: "Cast on Jehovah that which He hath given thee". In other words, every burden (be it sickness, sorrow, persecution, impoverishment, desertion, misunderstanding) is allocated by the Lord Himself so that we might return it to Him, who alone is truly able to bear it. In simple faith and confidence we are to give back to God what He has placed upon us. He is both the origin of the load and the occasion of its lifting.

And so we arrive at Job's grand expression of hope, best captured in the well-known language of the KJV:

> For I know that my redeemer liveth, and that he shall stand at the latter day upon the earth: And though after my skin worms destroy this body, yet in my flesh shall I see God: Whom I shall see for myself, and mine eyes shall behold, and not another; though my reins be consumed within me (19.25-27).

The passage, however familiar, is not straight-forward. One of the first things to notice is how many of the words are in italics, especially key nouns like "day", "worms", and "body". The KJV translators used italics to signal their own editorial insertions, which were designed to make sense of the original Hebrew text. The heavy italicisation here suggests that the text is particularly difficult. Not surprisingly, then, the 1881 Revised Version offers a rather different rendering:

> But I know that my redeemer liveth, and that he shall stand up at the last upon the earth: And after my skin hath been thus destroyed, yet from my flesh shall I see God: Whom I shall see for myself, and mine eyes shall behold, and not another. My reins are consumed within me (19.25-27, RV).

The body and the worms, we observe, are missing, and the phrase "in my flesh" has become the more ambiguous "from my flesh". In order to help us unpack and understand Job's words we shall ask five questions: what, who, when, where, and why.

What is the passage all about? The crucial verb at the start is "I know", which asserts the speaker's unshakeable confidence. In the preceding eighteen chapters Job has come through a hailstorm of divinely instigated affliction and unrelenting human criticism with his basic trust in God amazingly intact. His family and friends may spurn him, but he knows that there is One on whom he can rely. In New Testament times another suffering servant of God could use similar language. Persecuted and imprisoned for his faith, Paul recognised the connection between his responsibility as preacher, teacher and apostle, and his current trials:

> For the which cause I also suffer these things: nevertheless I am not ashamed: for I know whom I have believed, and am persuaded that he is able to keep that which I have committed unto him against that day (2 Tim 1.12).

The words are simple but substantial: "I am not ashamed: for I know whom I have believed". New Testament Christianity is all about knowing God. This is far more than a mere intellectual awareness, although it certainly includes an intelligent surrender to a body of doctrine; rather, it is a deep personal relationship with the living God grounded upon gratitude for His gracious provision in Christ. That is why the Lord Jesus sums up real life in these words: "this is life eternal, that they might know thee the only true God, and Jesus Christ, whom thou hast sent" (Jn 17.3). Paul knew whom he believed and so, despite his position at the dawn of revelation, did Job. What Job's words prove is his undimmed faith in God.

But **who** exactly was it that Job claimed to know? The One he calls "God" in verse 26 he calls "my redeemer" in verse 25. To Job, God was more than just the supreme Creator of the universe and the Master over all his circumstances. He was Job's personal Redeemer. The word (1350) refers to "a person who provided protection or legal preservation for a close relative who could not do so for himself".[211] This important term appears 104 times in the Old Testament, translated sometimes as a noun ("redeemer"), sometimes as a verb ("redeem"). According to the law God gave Israel, a redeemer had to be physically related to those he desired to help, wealthy enough to meet their need, and genuinely willing to undertake their cause. The whole concept of redemption was built into the family, social and national fabric of Old Testament Israel so that God's people would be fully accustomed to its meaning. The nation was educated to recognise the role of the family defender, the *goel* (1350), one who avenged unlawful killing and bought back family property which had been sold because of poverty. The law summarises it like this: "If thy brother be waxen poor, and hath sold away some of his possession, and if any of his kin come to redeem [1350] it, then shall he redeem that which his brother sold" (Lev 25.25). Most significant of all, God Himself was the Redeemer of the entire nation, having rescued them historically from their dreadful Egyptian bondage:

> Thou in thy mercy hast led forth the people which thou hast redeemed: thou hast guided them in thy strength unto thy holy habitation (Ex 15.13).

Fear not, thou worm Jacob, and ye men of Israel; I will help thee, saith the Lord, and thy redeemer, the Holy One of Israel (Is 41.14).

But it may come as a surprise to discover that the word first occurs before the Mosaic law was given. Listen to Jacob's prayer: "The Angel which redeemed [1350] me from all evil, bless the lads; and let my name be named on them, and the name of my fathers Abraham and Isaac; and let them grow into a multitude in the midst of the earth" (Gen 48.16). This angel, the supernatural source of redemption and blessing, can be none other than a divine person and, if we take John 1.18 seriously, must therefore be a pre-incarnate manifestation of the Son of God, always the great expositor of the Father. Long before the laws of kinsman redemption were laid down through Moses, God was seen by Jacob as the Redeemer. If Job lived before Jacob's Egyptian sojourn, which the book certainly implies, then Job is the first man on record ever to use this remarkable language of God.

For Job, then, God is his Redeemer, able to stand up in his defence against all his enemies. Luther claimed that the essence of the gospel was found in the pronouns, and Job's use of the possessive pronoun here is a powerful testimony to his faith. Spurgeon puts it beautifully in one of his sermons on this verse:

> Job had lost everything – every stick and stone that he possessed, he had lost his children, he had lost his wife, too, for all practical purposes, for she had not acted like a wife to him in his time of trial. Poor Job, he had lost everything else, but he had not lost his Redeemer.[212]

Reading Job's words in the light of later revelation we can see a powerful anticipation of the Lord Jesus Christ, the complete fulfilment of the kinsman redeemer. He alone meets the requirements. He entered by incarnation into a genuine relationship with those He would redeem (Heb 2.14-16); in His eternal deity He possessed all the resources needed to render in full the payment of His people's obligation (Gal 4.4-5); and He was in His love willing to undertake our cause (Gal 2.20). How much Job may have understood we do not know, but his use of the word "redeemer" is an amazing foreview of the person and work of Christ.

But Job says yet more. His Redeemer, he tells us, in contrast to his own deplorable condition teetering on the brink of death, was blessedly alive. God is essentially both the living One and, if we consult Young's Literal Translation of the verse, the last One: "I have known my Redeemer, The Living and the Last" (19.25, YLT). The same word translated "last" (314) appears in Isaiah as a testimony to the uniquely eternal existence of Jehovah:

> Who hath wrought and done it, calling the generations from the beginning? I the Lord, the first, and with the last [314]; I am he (Is 41.4).

> Thus saith the Lord the King of Israel, and his redeemer the Lord of hosts; I am the first, and I am the last [314]; and beside me there is no God (Is 44.6).

Hearken unto me, O Jacob and Israel, my called; I am he; I am the first, I also am the last [314] (Is 48.12).

Eternal in His being, and unanswerable in His every utterance, Job's Redeemer is therefore unsurpassable: none can come before Him and none can come after Him. Job's "living Vindicator, who will be the last One and thus will have the final word, will stand on the earth as a witness stands in a trial and will testify to Job's innocence for all to hear".[213] Again, the New Testament believer is bound to think of the Saviour's self-description in the concluding book of Scripture: "Fear not; I am the first and the last" (Rev 1.17); "these things saith the first and the last, which was dead, and is alive" (Rev 2.8); "I am Alpha and Omega, the beginning and the end, the first and the last" (Rev 22.13). As the *Jamieson, Fausset and Brown Commentary* so fittingly puts it, "at the winding up of the whole scheme of revelation [the Lord Jesus] announces Himself as the One *before whom and after whom there is no God*". He who possesses such an everlasting Redeemer can rise above the mists and storms of temporal human experience. Job's faith, writes Robinson, is "neither to be shaken by his terrible losses, nor his wife's reproaches, nor his friends' suspicions and accusations. [It is] like the lifeboat which, buried for a few moments in the surging billows, comes again to the surface".[214] **Who** Job's words bear witness to is the God who acts as kinsman Redeemer on behalf of His needy people.

But the next question is trickier. **When** would this Redeemer intervene? Job clearly points to a moment in the future, a time "after my skin hath been thus destroyed". Heaven's failure to respond to his earlier cries for justice has convinced him that death is his inevitable lot, yet his hope does not terminate with death. After bodily dissolution has taken place he still anticipates seeing God. But how could this be? It is here the biggest problem arises in understanding Job's meaning. The KJV says that Job will see God "in my flesh", while the RV says "from my flesh". The noun is perfectly clear-cut. It means literal flesh, whether in normal earthly conditions (Gen 2.21,23) or in a resurrection state (Ezek 37.6,8), although it has to be admitted that the Ezekiel references describe a visionary revivification scene which in reality pictures not resurrection but a future national regathering and restoration of Israel. The problem lies in the preposition. According to Davidson, "the Hebrew preposition *from* has the same ambiguity as *from* in English".[215] For example, when we speak of answering a letter "from home", the phrase could equally mean "while staying at home", or "while away from home". And this is the crux of the matter here. Archer, who takes the traditional view embodied in the KJV translation, summarises it like this:

The interpretation hinges upon the meaning of the preposition *min*, which sometimes does signify "without"; yet it is fair to say that in connection with the verb "to see", *min*, in its usage elsewhere almost always indicates the vantage point from which the observer looks. It is fair to conclude that a Hebrew listener would have understood this statement to mean, "And from the vantage point of my flesh, I shall see God".[216]

But we are running ahead of the argument. Job is absolutely certain that he faces death. His words therefore cannot be read as suggesting that he anticipates a divine intervention while he is still in his present mortal body. That leaves us with two viable possibilities. Either Job means that while he is *in* his flesh he will see God (which presupposes a future bodily resurrection), or that he will see God while he is *away* from his flesh (language alluding to the place of departed spirits, or *sheol*, to which he has made reference in earlier speeches). Doctrinally speaking, both readings of the text are biblically unexceptionable. Job has already spoken of his awareness that man's existence continues even after this mortal life has ended (3.13; 10.21-22). We know from the complete revelation of the New Testament that at death the Christian believer goes to be with the Lord in a condition of existence which is vastly superior to that of life on earth. Paul informs us that he has "a desire to depart, and to be with Christ; which is far better" (Phil 1.23), because "to be absent from the body" means "to be at home with the Lord" (2 Cor 5.8, RV). We also know that the Christian's great hope is not death as such, however attractive it might at times seem to be, but the coming of the Lord Jesus to grant His people their imperishable resurrection bodies of glory. The essential character of New Testament saints is that they daily await God's "Son from the heavens, whom he raised from among the dead, Jesus, our deliverer from the coming wrath" (1 Thess 1.10, JND).

But although, as far as we are aware, Job possessed no clear revelation of a future resurrection of the body, and certainly could not know about the blessed state of those who die in Christ, he nonetheless looks ahead to a hope inextricably connected with a divine person. Not surprisingly, his words, read in a New Testament context, have traditionally been taken as a direct anticipation of resurrection. The seventeenth century commentator Matthew Henry writes as follows:

> though the revelation of the promised Seed, and the promised inheritance, was then discerned only like the dawning of the day, yet Job was taught of God to believe in a living Redeemer, and to *look for the resurrection of the dead and the life of the world to come*, for of these, doubtless, he must be understood to speak.[217]

However, by the nineteenth century, Delitzsch, one of the most thoughtful and scholarly of commentators, is taking a more cautious line:

> by far the majority of modern expositors have decided that Job does not indeed here avow the hope of the resurrection, but the hope of a future spiritual beholding of God, and therefore of a future life; and thus the popular idea of Hades, which elsewhere has sway over him, breaks out.[218]

As a result, some commentators view Job's affirmation as a testimony not to future resurrection but to the reality of a conscious afterlife. In the words of Ellison, "it is continued conscious communion with God after death rather than the resurrection of the body that Job is proclaiming".[219] Constable puts it like this:

Evidently Job expected to see God after death, but there is no indication in the text that Job knew God would resurrect his body after he died. He believed in life after death, but he evidently did not know about the certain resurrection of the body. This revelation came from God after Job's lifetime.[220]

That said, a check on some of the more recent translations of Job 19.26 suggests evidence of a return to the older understanding of the text. The three main translation possibilities work out like this:

(i)   Preserving the ambiguity of the Hebrew: "from my flesh [or, body]": RV (1881), JND (1889), YLT (1898), CEV (1995)

(ii)   Implying a reference to *sheol*, the place of departed spirits: "without my flesh": ASV (1895), JPS (1917), BBE (1965)

(iii)   Implying a hope of future bodily resurrection: "in my flesh": MKJV (1962-1998), ESV (2001), ISV (1996-2010).

The immediate context does not appear to be determinative, as the antithetical poetic parallelism which most translations indicate ("though … yet") could support either a contrast between mortal life and the after-life, or a contrast between the mortal body and a resurrection body. No matter whether Job is thinking of a disembodied state or looking ahead to a resurrection, he has no doubt that his Redeemer will stand up for him so that he will be granted the privilege of seeing his God. Before a decision is made between these alternatives, however, it would be wise to consider the final two questions.

Where would the Redeemer's wondrous activity take place? Job's language posits an earthly situation: "he shall stand up at the last upon the earth [6083]" (19.25, RV). The word translated "earth" is rendered "dust" in the vast majority of its appearances, from Genesis 2.7 to Zechariah 9.3, which suggests that Job is emphasizing the inescapable physicality of the location. Death would reduce his shrunken body to dust, but on that same dusty earth his Redeemer would undoubtedly stand. Further, Job describes his anticipated glimpse of God in these words: "I shall see for myself, and mine eyes shall behold, and not another". This is the summit of his longing. Writes Davidson, "the whole of his misery might be expressed in saying that God hid Himself from him, and the whole of his redemption and joy will consist in seeing God".[221] But we must take careful note of the diction: the specific allusion to "dust" and "eyes" strongly supports the idea of a bodily resurrection.

Finally, **why** would his Redeemer take His stand on the dust of the earth? Hartley points out that the word for "stand" is, in this context, "a technical legal term meaning to 'stand up' as a witness in court. Job is thus saying that his kinsman will fulfil his responsibility as redeemer by giving decisive testimony in Job's defence".[222]

On balance, it seems that all these considerations, culminating with the inescapable allusions to "earth" and "eyes", endorse the notion that in some way Job anticipates a future bodily resurrection in which he will actually behold the God who will stand up in his support. But we should be wary of reading too much into this. It does not necessarily indicate that Job had, as part of his creed, confidence in a future resurrection of men in general. That concept seems not be established clearly in Scripture until the prophetic portion of the Old Testament. Isaiah glances forward to a time when

> Thy dead men shall live, together with my dead body shall they arise. Awake and sing, ye that dwell in dust: for thy dew is as the dew of herbs, and the earth shall cast out the dead (Is 26.19).

Furthermore, Daniel has a revelation of a raising up of godly Israelites after a future period of intense and unique national distress:

> And at that time shall Michael stand up, the great prince who standeth for the children of thy people; and there shall be a time of distress, such as never was since there was a nation until that time. And at that time thy people shall be delivered, every one that is found written in the book. And many of them that sleep in the dust of the earth shall awake, some to everlasting life, and some to shame, to everlasting contempt (Dan 12.1-2, JND).

Daniel learns about the physical preservation of a godly remnant of Israel through the predicted tribulation ("thy people shall be delivered, every one that is found written in the book"), followed by a selective resurrection of "some to everlasting life", which we may assume to include the enjoyment of millennial blessing, while others will be raised later "to shame, to everlasting contempt".

Job, however, is more likely to be thinking of a special individual resurrection God would arrange so that His servant might be finally freed from the false charges men had levelled against him. In a similar way, Abraham, with no spoken or written information on which to base his confidence, trusted that God would raise his son Isaac from the ashes of the altar on Moriah in order to fulfil His infallible promises (Heb 11.17-19). But Abraham was not expecting either a universal resurrection of the dead, or a resurrection which resulted in a glorified body. Those doctrines came later in the progress of revelation. What both patriarchs believed was that, in order to be true to Himself, God would have to return certain individuals back to human life; Isaac, so that the promises of global blessing through him could be fulfilled, and Job, so that his innocence could be attested before men. In the words of Delitzsch:

> Upon the dust in which he is now soon to be laid, into which he is now soon to be changed, will He, the Rescuer of his honour, arise … and set His divine seal to Job's own testimony thus made permanent in the monumental inscription.[223]

Here is the marvel. As Job's mortal body weakens under the weight of multiple ailments, and as his mind aches because of the suspicions of his friends, his faith rises. Indeed, he seems to be consciously overwhelmed by the words he finds himself uttering. Who is this God whom he expects to see? He is the Redeemer "Whom I, even I, shall see, on my side, and mine eyes shall behold, and not as a stranger" (19.27, ASV). The ASV brings out more clearly than other versions the note of sublime confidence. The divine One whom Job will see will at last be "on my side", and will be glimpsed, "not as a stranger" or a hostile enemy, as He has hitherto seemed to be, but as a trustworthy friend. Darby hit a similar note of joyful assurance in his hymn "Rise, my soul, thy God directs thee", a hymn which fast-forwards to the believer's glad entrance into heaven:

> There no stranger - God shall meet thee;
> Stranger thou in courts above!
> He who to His rest shall greet thee
> Greets thee with a well-known love.

Job falls back momentarily exhausted, at a loss for words at the contemplation of such a feast of spiritual satisfaction. The KJV translates with accuracy, but perhaps misses the point of the final phrase of verse 27. When Job says "*though* my reins be consumed within me", we should omit the italicized word and understand him to be concluding his remarkable statement of faith with a confession of unspeakable delight. The ESV appropriately renders it as an overjoyed exclamation: "my heart faints within me!"

This can be seen as the third of Job's great mountain-tops of faith. Out of the morass of his bitter grief he rises, first, to anticipate a time when God would renew His affections towards him:

> O that thou wouldest hide me in the grave, that thou wouldest keep me secret, until thy wrath be past, that thou wouldest appoint me a set time, and remember me! If a man die, shall he live again? all the days of my appointed time will I wait, till my change come. Thou shalt call, and I will answer thee: thou wilt have a desire to the work of thine hands (14.13-15).

Second, he affirms that, despite the failure of his fellows, he still has a faithful witness in heaven:

> Also now, behold, my witness is in heaven, and my record is on high. My friends scorn me: but mine eye poureth out tears unto God. O that one might plead for a man with God, as a man pleadeth for his neighbour! (16.19-21).

Third, as death looms on the horizon, he looks ahead to a miraculous raising up after death in which God will finally take up his cause as his reliable kinsman Redeemer.

New Testament believers come to Job's words with all the extra information found in the completed Scriptures. We rightly lay hold of his assurance in the knowledge that the living Redeemer of whom he speaks is none other than the Lord Jesus Christ, who has "abolished death, and hath brought life and immortality to light through the gospel" (2 Tim 1.10).

Job's Intimation of Coming Retribution: 19.28-29

Mountain peaks of spiritual serenity are rarely sustained down here. In case anyone thinks Job was alone in a sudden return to earth, there are plenty of examples in the Psalms (89.1-2, 49-51), Jeremiah (15.15-18; 20.7-18) and the Gospels (Mt 16.16-23). After a breath-taking confession of future hope, for which his own mind can offer no rational foundation save that it springs from confidence in a God who cannot fail, Job slips back into the reproachful tone with which he earlier castigated his friends. His words are a solemn warning to them. How could they continue to harass him so remorselessly seeing that "the root of the matter", that is, a genuinely righteous integrity, was evident in him? To persist in such injustice would expose them, in due time, to the judgment of God: "Be ye afraid of the sword: for wrath bringeth the punishments of the sword, that ye may know there is a judgment" (19.29). The implication is that the God who would rise in defence of His vilified servant Job would also move in judgment on those who had so unfairly persecuted him.

Unknowingly, Job anticipates the future. The God who is going to intervene before the book's close and (to Job's surprise) while the patriarch is still alive, will speak aloud on Job's behalf in the hearing of his shamed friends. Their punishment would not be a literal sword, but piercing words of rebuke addressed publicly to Eliphaz as their spokesman: "My wrath is kindled against thee, and against thy two friends: for ye have not spoken of me the thing that is right, as my servant Job hath" (42.7).

Yet what lingers most in our minds as we read this chapter is not Job's closing warning to his friends, deserving as they are of humiliation. Instead, it is his assured commitment to a divine vindicator who will at last act for his deliverance. But the unsympathetic friends nevertheless play an unlooked for and wholly unintentional role in the growth of Job's soul. It is their unyielding opposition to his protestations of innocence which has driven Job into God's arms. Delitzsch has a fine summary:

> The speech of Job, now explained, most clearly shows us how Job's affliction, interpreted by the friends as a divine retribution, becomes for Job's nature a wholesome refining crucible.[224]

The suffering through which he has passed has caused him to rise to a height of spiritual insight: although he may not fully comprehend his own words, he has in seed form anticipated the great truth of resurrection when all God's redeemed people will behold their Redeemer.

SECTION 14
Dialogue: Job 4 – 42.6
Contest: Round 2: Job 15-21
Zophar's 2nd Speech: Job 20

One of the sad things the reader discovers on wading through the book of Job is how little Job's friends seem to attend to what he says. He has just put into memorable words a remarkable confidence in God's coming to his defence as his kinsman Redeemer, a concept as yet unheralded in the Old Testament and not truly explained until the incarnation and its consequences. But no one seems to have been listening.

One of my friends has, as his regular email signature, the pithy but pointed sentence, "A big part of loving is listening". Job's comforters have not learned that true friendship and true pastoral care involve the self-discipline of sympathetic attentiveness, without which there can be no genuine dialogue. Zophar simply continues with his version of the old, old story of the terrible judgments awaiting the wicked man in this world, almost as though Job had not spoken at all. Granted, he has heard "the reproof which putteth me to shame" (20.3, RV), and seethes with indignation that Job dares to rebuke his friends. But this matter really dominates only the first few verses of the previous chapter (19.2-5). Everything else Job mentions he ignores. Like a grumpy visitor invited to look at an album of wedding photographs, Zophar can see nothing but himself among the many guests and smarts at the unflattering way the camera has captured him. As a result, his words are precipitate, irritable and intemperate. In the words of Robinson, "with less haste in Zophar's spirit, there had been more humanity in his speech".[225] But then, as Delitzsch justly remarks, "a man is never more eloquent than when he has to defend his injured honour".[226]

This is Zophar's second and final contribution to the discussion, and its distance from his earlier words signals how far his attitude to Job has hardened. His first speech in chapter 11 set up a dramatic contrast between the godly man and the wicked man, which at least allowed for the possibility that Job might be a good man who had slipped and who, with repentance, might be restored to the pathway of righteousness. But his second speech allows no such hope. His blistering description of the fate awaiting the godless announces in no uncertain terms his opinion that Job falls squarely into that category. His carefully chosen terminology insinuates that Job is no hapless victim of temptation but a heartless oppressor, guilty of extorting wealth from the poor (20.10,15), savouring his lusts like a favourite delicacy (20.12-13), abandoning his social responsibility of care for the needy (20.19), and insatiable in his greed for gain (20.21).

This extended diatribe on the fate of the evil man may be broken down into the following paragraphs:

> 1. Introduction: 20.1-3
> 2. The Wicked Man's Death will be Swift: 20.4-11

3. The Wicked Man's Delights will be Surrendered: 20.12-21
4. The Wicked Man's Destruction will be Spectacular: 20.22-28
5. Conclusion: 20.29.

Introduction: 20.1-3

Job's rejection of his friends' unanimous advice stimulates in the indignant Zophar a feisty response. The RV brings out the sense:

> Therefore do my thoughts give answer to me, even by reason of my haste that is in me. I have heard the reproof which putteth me to shame, and the spirit of my understanding answereth me (20.2-3, RV).

"Haste" (2363) is used in narrative passages to describe a military vanguard moving into battle or an ambush being sprung (Num 32.17; Judg 20.37), and the speed with which God's vengeance pursues the ungodly (Deut 32.35). Most commonly, however, it figures in the psalmist's calls for divine assistance in the midst of distress (Ps 22.19; 38.22; 40.13; 70.1,5). Zophar's haste is purely for the preservation of his own self-esteem. It is interesting to note how those who are lavish in their criticism of others often become acutely sensitive when criticised themselves. When we rush to our own defence we are liable to make mistakes. That stinging email, that inflammatory letter, that tetchy text, or that peppery phone-call we plan to make would probably be all the better for a decent night's rest, after which calmer thoughts are likely to mollify our passions. It is with good reason that the wisdom writers of the Old Testament counsel caution in speech:

> He that is slow to wrath is of great understanding: but he that is hasty of spirit exalteth folly (Prov 14.29).

> Seest thou a man that is hasty in his words? there is more hope of a fool than of him (Prov 29.20).

> Be not hasty in thy spirit to be angry: for anger resteth in the bosom of fools (Eccl 7.9).

Alacrity is only a recommended course of action when it involves practical, intelligent submission to God's revealed word. When the psalmist says, "I made haste, and delayed not to keep thy commandments" (Ps 119.60), he speaks as one responding to God's known will. Saul of Tarsus clearly took that injunction to heart when, his sight miraculously restored, he was baptised even before breaking his self-inflicted three-day fast: "And immediately there fell from his eyes as it had been scales: and he received sight forthwith, and arose, and was baptized" (Acts 9.18). Here was a man who started as he would go on, prioritizing prompt obedience to scriptural truth.

But Zophar is too much in love with his own dignity to think judiciously about his counsel to Job. His words, therefore, although true as far as they go, fail to embrace the whole truth or offer the comfort an afflicted soul craves. Zeal and eloquence he has aplenty, but completely lacks that compassionate understanding which wisely urges a spiritual counsellor to consider himself lest he also be tempted (Gal 6.1). Drawing on his not inconsiderable poetic resources, he launches into an angry response with all guns blazing.

The Wicked Man's Death will be Swift: 20.4-11

The first point provides a snappy summary of his entire argument. The doctrine is an old one, traceable to man's earliest days: "the triumphing of the wicked is short, and the joy of the hypocrite but for a moment" (20.5). The early history of humanity had been passed down orally, so Zophar may well be thinking of God's speedy judgment on Adam and Eve. They were the first human transgressors, who had been warned of the death penalty should they eat of the forbidden tree: "thou shalt not eat of it: for in the day that thou eatest thereof thou shalt surely die" (Gen 2.17). The phrase, "in the day", may well be an idiomatic equivalent to "when", but there seems little doubt that both their sin and its sentence took place within a brief space of time. It is equally true that Cain's murder of his brother was promptly avenged by God, leading not in this case to instant spiritual death but to lifelong punitive expulsion from the benefits of human society (Gen 4.14-15). From the Bible as a whole the Christian believer knows that sinful joy at best is pitifully short-lived compared with the endlessness of eternity. Recognising that the living God offered blessing that outlasted this world, Moses made the informed choice "to suffer affliction with the people of God, [rather] than to enjoy the pleasures of sin for a season" (Heb 11.25). We should always look to the long-term.

Zophar's aphorism therefore has a solid basis. But his use of it is ill-judged and unsympathetic. The impression he gives, and means to give, is that divine judgment falls on men precipitately in this life. Job's case is the example burning in his mind. But Scripture gives the lie to such oversimplification. Jeremiah, for example, knew that evil men could do well down here, living out a long and leisurely lifespan:

> Righteous art thou, O Lord, when I plead with thee: yet let me talk with thee of thy judgments: Wherefore doth the way of the wicked prosper? wherefore are all they happy that deal very treacherously? Thou hast planted them, yea, they have taken root: they grow, yea, they bring forth fruit: thou art near in their mouth, and far from their reins (Jer 12.1-2).

Like Job, he knew that God was righteous in all His ways, and therefore he found it hard to reconcile a just God with a world where, to all intents and purposes, the wicked appeared to be more than comfortable. It was not simply that they prospered awhile, for that might have been dismissed as a momentary aberration, but that they did so over a considerable stretch of time, taking deep root and bearing abundant fruit, disturbingly like the righteous man of Psalm One. Moreover, his firm hold on divine sovereignty led him to acknowledge that all this was God's work, for "Thou hast planted them". Men's circumstances are governed by God's hand. Yet the men of whom Jeremiah wrote were rank hypocrites, guilty of pious words coupled with sinful behaviour.

Scripture provides plenty of examples to support Jeremiah's viewpoint. Jeroboam II of the apostate northern kingdom of Israel was a bad man, but enjoyed a long and materially affluent reign of forty-one years. Even though "he did that which was evil in the sight of the Lord", continuing in "all the sins of Jeroboam the son of Nebat, who made Israel to sin" (2 Kings 14.24), he was used of God to restore the nation's boundaries and revive its military prestige. In the providence of God bad men may be instrumental in doing good things. Nor were such anomalies restricted to the breakaway north. In the southern kingdom of Judah, Manasseh was the worst monarch ever to occupy David's throne, his blatantly immoral and idolatrous excesses being the final straw that brought about the Babylonian captivity, because he "made Judah and the inhabitants of Jerusalem to err, and to do worse than the heathen, whom the Lord had destroyed before the children of Israel" (2 Chr 33.9). Yet this man was permitted to reign for fifty-five years.

We can supplement this evidence by turning from individuals to nations. The inhabitants of Canaan, whose egregious wickedness caused their extermination at the hands of Israel, were suffered to continue for some four hundred years before judgment fell because, as the Lord told Abraham, "the iniquity of the Amorites is not yet full" (Gen 15.16). The notes in the 1599 Geneva Bible make the point: "Though God tolerates the wicked for a time, yet His vengeance falls on them when the measure of their wickedness is full". But how gracious and longsuffering to hold back retribution for so long! The almost limitless riches of divine forbearance are one of the great marvels of human history. In the era before the Flood human wickedness rose to heaven like a foul stench, yet God delayed for one hundred and twenty years before sending the global deluge. Of this long deferral Peter writes that "the longsuffering of God waited in the days of Noah" (1 Pet 3.20). In the same way the city of Nineveh, capital of the barbaric Assyrian empire, was granted forty days in which to repent and avoid destruction. The extensions of God's forbearance may vary from forty days to four hundred years; but the principle remains true that God is "merciful and gracious, slow to anger, and plenteous in mercy" (Ps 103.8). Every believer must be unceasingly grateful for the Lord's longsuffering towards him.

These biblical examples serve to demonstrate that, in the sovereign grace of God, men sometimes profit from divine forbearance. One of the most astonishing testimonies to the Lord's mercy is that Manasseh, that monster of wickedness, repented when God brought him into affliction, spending the remainder of his reign in an earnest but vain attempt to make amends for earlier misdeeds (2 Chr 33.12-19). But some things cannot be undone. Not even a reformed Manasseh could erase the disastrous impact of his former behaviour on his own son.

To underline his stern message, Zophar analyses under three headings what might be called the typical career of the godless man. He foregrounds his insolence (20.5-7), his impermanence (20.8-9), and his eventual impoverishment (20.10). His summary statement in verse 5 brings together two words for evil ("wicked" and "godless", RV), two words for exultation ("triumphing" and "joy"), and two words for brevity ("short", and "for a moment"), with the result that we are struck by the rapid end to the bad man's success. His triumph and joy, suggestive of vaunting pride, are dispelled in an instant.

To illustrate the sinner's **insolence** (20.5-7), Zophar focusses on the unholy delights of the wicked man, using a word, "triumphing" (7445), which appears only four times in the Old Testament, and normally in the context of legitimate pleasures. Job uses it of the joy associated with childbirth (3.7), while the psalmist employs it of songs of praise which accompany the worship of God (Ps 63.5; 100.2). Here, however, it describes the happiness of the sinner. Though he has turned his back on the God of all true blessing, he nevertheless appears free to revel in his jubilation. But it is all short-lived. The construction of verses 6 and 7 sets up a sharp contrast: "Though ... Yet". Though in his pride he seems to mount to the very heavens, lifting his head among the clouds, he will eventually perish like his own dung so completely that those who recollect his haughty demeanour will wonder where he has gone. The language may make us think of the archetypical example of sinful pride, Lucifer, who strove to imitate God but was instead cast down to the depths:

> How art thou fallen from heaven, O Lucifer, son of the morning! how art thou cut down to the ground, which didst weaken the nations! For thou hast said in thine heart, I will ascend into heaven, I will exalt my throne above the stars of God: I will sit also upon the mount of the congregation, in the sides of the north: I will ascend above the heights of the clouds; I will be like the most High. Yet thou shalt be brought down to hell, to the sides of the pit (Is 14.12-15).

This description relates historically to the king of Babylon, while anticipating the character of the coming man of sin – yet behind both stands the original enemy of God (Lk 10.18). Lucifer's self-deluded soliloquy is x-rayed: "I will ascend ... I will exalt ... I will sit ... I will ascend ... I will be like". Against all those impressively assertive "I wills" stands the simple divine pronouncement: "Yet thou shalt be brought down". We might think back to Pharaoh's fruitless effort to round up the escaping Israelites at the time of the exodus. Moses's song of praise superbly exposes the boastful mind-set of the pursuing Egyptian host:

> The enemy said, I will pursue, I will overtake, I will divide the spoil; my lust shall be satisfied upon them; I will draw my sword, my hand shall destroy them. Thou didst blow with thy wind, the sea covered them: they sank as lead in the mighty waters (Ex 15.9-10).

But, as with Lucifer, all those human "I wills" collapse like a pack of cards as God simply blows on them with His breath. No one can set himself against the God of heaven and prosper.

No mean poet himself, Zophar makes his point in verses 6 and 7 by contrasting the vocabulary of sublime exaltation ("excellency … heavens … clouds") with that of bathetic humiliation ("perish … dung"). He uses the same word for dung (1561) which so distressed the prophet Ezekiel who, to illustrate in dramatic parable form the degradation facing Judah, was told to "eat … barley cakes, and thou shalt bake it with dung [1561] that cometh out of man, in their sight" (Ezek 4.12). Because of his natural abhorrence of this appalling public shame, the Lord permitted him to use as his fuel dried cow's dung (a different Hebrew word) rather than human excrement (Ezek 4.15). Zophar's word occurs for the final time in Zephaniah, describing the horrors of the future day of the Lord when God will "bring distress upon men, that they shall walk like blind men, because they have sinned against the Lord: and their blood shall be poured out as dust, and their flesh as the dung" (Zeph 1.17). When God's wrath is unleashed on an unsuspecting world, human blood and flesh will literally be reduced to dust and dung.

The sudden descent from the "heavens" to the "dung" could not be more shattering of human arrogance. The Bible affirms that, in the final analysis, the way up is down, and the way down is up. That is to say, if we really wish to be exalted, the road is the deliberate downhill one to self-denial, self-humbling, and lowly service for others. The Lord Jesus is the perfect example. He who was eternally "in the form of God, thought it not robbery to be equal with God: But made himself of no reputation, and … humbled himself, and became obedient unto death, even the death of the cross" (Phil 2.6-8). Those, on the other hand, who propel themselves into prominence, aspiring to worldly greatness, will find the end of their road is ruin.

The divine reply to the wicked man's pride is a revelation of his **impermanence** (20.8-9). Though he may seem securely settled in the delights of this world, "He shall fly away as a dream, and shall not be found: yea, he shall be chased away as a vision of the night. The eye also which saw him shall see him no more; neither shall his place any more behold him" (20.8-9). Zophar has chosen his verbs to good effect. The godless man will "fly away", just as a dream evaporates at the approach of day, and "be chased away", like a defeated army scuttling off in full retreat from the field of battle. Those who saw him will find no trace of him left; all memory of his life and achievements will be erased. Scripture insistently teaches the evanescence of human life. That is why men are so often likened to grass in its frailty, insignificance, and transience:

Thou carriest them away as with a flood; they are as a sleep: in the morning they are like grass which groweth up. In the morning it flourisheth, and groweth up; in the evening it is cut down, and withereth (Ps 90.5-6).

As for man, his days are as grass: as a flower of the field, so he flourisheth. For the wind passeth over it, and it is gone; and the place thereof shall know it no more (Ps 103.15-16).

The voice said, Cry. And he said, What shall I cry? All flesh is grass, and all the goodliness thereof is as the flower of the field: The grass withereth, the flower fadeth: because the spirit of the Lord bloweth upon it: surely the people is grass (Is 40.6-7).

The lesson, all the more needed in days of affluence and material prosperity, is not to set our hopes on a passing world. Moses encourages us "to number our days, that we may apply our hearts unto wisdom" (Ps 90.12), for those who belong to the God of eternity must live with eternity in view.

But there is more in Zophar's argument. The wicked man, snatched from the scene of his short-lived triumph, leaves nothing behind for his descendants but shameful **impoverishment** (20.10). The penalty for his social crimes will fall on his children, who will "seek to please the poor, and his hands shall restore their goods" (20.10). The implication is that the wicked man has enriched himself at the expense of others so that his heirs, instead of inheriting his wealth, find themselves forced to repay his ill-gotten gains. Zophar's allusion to children must have grated on Job's ears: in one fell swoop he lost all his offspring. He was in that sense far worse off than the imaginary villain of Zophar's sermon; he at least left a family behind him, even though they would be reduced to begging favours of the poor.

Zophar concludes this section of his speech by emphasising the contrast between the wicked man's apparent strength and his inescapable destiny: "His bones were full of his youthful strength; but it shall lie down with him in the dust" (20.11, JND). The KJV's reference in this verse to "sins" is italicised, as it does not appear in the Hebrew text. Darby's rendering makes better sense: for all his youthful vigour, the godless man will end up in the dirt. The sharp antithesis between "heavens" and "dung", highlighted in verses 6 and 7, is here repeated in the words "youth" and "dust". As the Israelite preacher reminds his reader, "Rejoice, O young man, in thy youth; and let thy heart cheer thee in the days of thy youth, and walk in the ways of thine heart, and in the sight of thine eyes: but know thou, that for all these things God will bring thee into judgment" (Eccl 11.9). In Shakespeare's comedy *Twelfth Night* the jester Feste urges his frivolous audience to pursue the pleasures of love while they may because "Youth's a stuff will not endure". "Eat, drink and be merry" has always been the slogan of men on the run from God; Scripture, however, pulls back the curtain to reveal the dread inevitability of judgment after death. Since, apart from that generation of Christian believers to be caught up alive at the rapture of the church, all the Lord's people of this dispensation will eventually "lie down ... in the dust", how imperative it is to invest our time and energies in what will last.

The Wicked Man's Delights will be Surrendered: 20.12-21

Zophar moves into a close-up of the impending punitive sufferings awaiting the wicked man. His sharp eye for detail suggests a gloating pleasure in announcing the terrible fate of the godless. But no man should expatiate gleefully on the solemn truth of retribution. When we speak to men about coming judgment, an essential component of the gospel message, it should not be done with lip-smacking relish.

The example of the Saviour, wailing aloud over the fate of rebellious Jerusalem (Lk 19.41-44), exemplifies the right way to warn about impending doom.

Zophar, however, savours the fate of the evil man. Not only will his death be swift, all the things that mean most to him in life will have to be rendered up. Zophar's diction draws on the common human pleasure of eating in order to describe the sinner's lingering enjoyment of his sins; they are like syrupy delicacies he wants to retain under his tongue as long as possible, almost loathe to swallow them down and lose their delicious taste. God's Word is starkly honest: sin does have its own sweetness, for "Stolen waters are sweet, and bread eaten in secret is pleasant" (Prov 9.17). Ever since Adam's disobedience, men have been fascinated by the forbidden, supposing that true pleasure resides in what God withholds. The opposite is true. "Bread of deceit is sweet to a man; but afterwards his mouth shall be filled with gravel" (Prov 20.17). Zophar is keen that his audience be aware of the solemn "afterwards" of sinful behaviour. He therefore organises his words so that for two whole verses the luscious morsel is kept in the mouth before it descends to the intestines. The result is unexpected: "Yet his meat in his bowels is turned, it is the gall of asps within him" (20.14). What seemed so pleasurable turns out to be poisonous, and the appetizing meal ends up as nauseous vomit.

Who can deny that he is right? What is sweet to the taste buds may sometimes be sour to the stomach. Twice the writer of the Proverbs reminds us that "There is a way which seemeth right unto a man, but the end thereof are the ways of death" (Prov 14.12; 16.25). The apostle John was instructed to eat a little book which he found to be "in my mouth sweet as honey: and as soon as I had eaten it, my belly was bitter" (Rev 10.10). There was nothing intrinsically evil about the book, but John's experience illustrates the paradox that the Word of God, a delight to the believer's soul, may bring discomfort as we digest its stern announcements of coming judgment on a rebel planet. Even the gospel message which heralds God's mercy in Christ simultaneously affirms the fearful destiny of unbelievers. But there is all the difference in the world between the poison which the wicked man fatally absorbs into his system with his sin, and the bitterness which the genuine believer may have to experience as he becomes aware of the solemn ramifications of God's revealed truth. Unlike the disgusting aftermath of sinful self-indulgence, the ultimate effects of God's Word are always beneficial, even when it speaks of judgment. The psalmist is a good witness: "How sweet are thy words unto my taste! yea, sweeter than honey to my mouth!" (Ps 119.103). So too is Jeremiah: "Thy words were found, and I did eat them; and thy word was unto me the joy and rejoicing of mine heart: for I am called by thy name, O Lord God of hosts" (Jer 15.16). This testimony is all the more powerful because it comes in the middle of a complaint about the faithful but beleaguered prophet's ill-treatment by an audience unwilling to receive his unpalatable message.

But Zophar is still keen to bring home his suspicion that Job's calamities prove Job's culpability. At the beginning, Job was one of the wealthiest men of his day. But how did he obtain all his riches? Listen to Zophar: "He hath swallowed down riches, and he shall vomit them up again: God shall cast them out of his belly" (20.15). What Job acquired unjustly (in the speaker's view) he has already had to surrender

– hence the depredations recently suffered at the hands of marauding tribesmen. At this stage Zophar avoids directly charging Job (who represents the wicked man) with extortion and injustice (this will come later), but the implication is clear enough. Along with the removal of his affluence comes anguish of heart. On the positive side he "shall suck the poison of asps: the viper's tongue shall slay him" (20.16), that is to say, what he fondly imagined as assets will turn out to be the griping pains of deadly venom; on the negative side, "he shall not see the rivers, the floods, the brooks of honey and butter" (20.17), traditional middle eastern emblems of prosperity. He gains what he does not want and forfeits the good he desires.

At the end of this section the underlying accusation, which has been in Zophar's mind all the time, is brought to the fore:

> That which he laboured for shall he restore, and not swallow down; its restitution shall be according to the value, and he shall not rejoice therein. For he hath oppressed, hath forsaken the poor; he hath violently taken away a house that he did not build. Because he knew no rest in his craving, he shall save nought of what he most desired. Nothing escaped his greediness; therefore his prosperity shall not endure (20.18-21, JND).

We should be in no doubt as to what Zophar is saying. The wicked man will have to surrender all he has worked for and make restitution for his unjust gains. The restoration of things stolen by force or guile was later built into God's law for Israel:

> Then it shall be, because he hath sinned, and is guilty, that he shall restore that which he took violently away, or the thing which he hath deceitfully gotten, or that which was delivered him to keep, or the lost thing which he found (Lev 6.4).

So eager is the speaker to ram home his point, that the godless man's wealth will be given back, that his earlier prediction – placing this responsibility on his heirs (20.10) – now changes to an assertion that it will be extracted directly from the guilty party while he lives (20.15,18,21). The imagery of eating continues ("swallow down … greediness"), but more important is the explanation of why these penalties fall on him: "For he hath oppressed, hath forsaken the poor; he hath violently taken away a house that he did not build" (20.19). In Zophar's eyes, Job is no common or garden sinner but a wilful tyrant, a robber, an oppressive bully who victimisd the very people he should have protected. Further, he is a man of avaricious passion, constantly wanting more. His life is a parade of sinful acts of commission ("he hath violently taken away a house") and omission ("he … hath forsaken the poor"), all sourced by a selfish attitude of heart ("he knew no rest in his … greediness").

The Wicked Man's Destruction will be Spectacular: 20.22-28

Drawing to the climax of his denunciation, Zophar points out that even at the height of his prosperity the wicked man is deeply uneasy in his heart. "In the fulness of his sufficiency he shall be in straits: the hand of every one that is in misery shall come upon him" (20.22, RV). "Straits" (3334) simply means distress. It first appears in the story of Jacob, when the patriarch, enriched with flocks and herds, suddenly heard that his estranged brother Esau was coming to meet him: "Then Jacob was greatly afraid and was distressed [3334]" (Gen 32.7). It is possible to be inwardly fearful even in the midst of material plenty. This, says Zophar, is the fate of the ungodly man. The specific reason for his internal terror is that he knows all those he has wronged have joined forces against him. Jacob's story is apt, for he faced the ire of a brother whom he had tricked out of his birthright and blessing. Affluence is no substitute for a clear conscience. Although some may foolishly suppose that material "gain is godliness", the reality is that "godliness with contentment is great gain" (1 Tim 6.5-6).

But this inner pain is as nothing compared to the appalling calamities to come, when God intervenes in wrath. "It shall be that, to fill his belly, he will cast his fierce anger upon him, and will rain it upon him into his flesh" (20.23, JND). Although the grammatical subject of this verse remains unnamed it clearly refers to God. Zophar mentions God directly only three times in this speech (20.15,29), but His involvement is assumed in verses 23 (where the KJV supplies "God" in italics) and 28. Reverting to his favourite imagery of the feast which turns sour, Zophar tells us that God will fill the bad man's belly, not with satisfying food, but with His devastating anger. If verse 14 described the inbuilt misery of sin, this verse looks ahead to an overt demonstration of divine fury. It is the difference between Romans chapter 1 (describing the present results of sin in the life) and chapter 2 (which fast forwards to the future day of God's public anger). As we might expect from Zophar, the language is energetic and graphic. The ungodly man is suddenly engulfed in God's "fierce anger", which will "rain" down into his very flesh. Imagery of severe weather conditions (one wonders if Zophar is glancing back to the events of the first chapter) swiftly changes into a scene of bloodthirsty warfare. It leaves little to the imagination:

> If he have fled from the iron weapon, the bow of brass shall strike him through. He draweth it forth; it cometh out of his body, and the glittering point out of his gall: terrors are upon him. All darkness is laid up for his treasures: a fire not blown shall devour him; it shall feed upon what is left in his tent (20.24-26, JND).

When God strikes, the sinner has nowhere to turn. Fleeing in terror from an iron weapon he runs full tilt into an even more horrific one of bronze or copper, becoming gruesomely transfixed by a shaft which penetrates his body so that its point comes out of his gallbladder. The Bible tells of men who fled one peril only to meet a worse. The scattered Syrian army which retreated from Ahab's victorious troops into the apparent safety of the city of Aphek faced something more catastrophic than capture, for "a wall fell upon twenty and seven thousand of the men that were left" (1 Kings 20.30). The irony is cutting. Jeremiah states the principle, this time in relation to the fate of Moab, with customary clarity: "He that fleeth from the fear shall fall into the pit; and he that getteth up out of the pit shall be taken in the snare" (Jer 48.44).

The judgment of God is a serious business, and Scripture does not sugar the pill. Violent death can be very messy. With the kind of detail which appeals to small boys weaned on lurid stories of blood and gore, the book of Judges records the ghastly end of King Eglon of Moab, a vicious enemy of God's people. He was struck down in his palace by the left-handed judge, Ehud:

> And Ehud put forth his left hand, and took the dagger from his right thigh, and thrust it into his belly: And the haft also went in after the blade; and the fat closed upon the blade, so that he could not draw the dagger out of his belly; and the dirt came out (Judg 3.21-22).

No mincing of words here. Zophar would doubtless gladly shake hands with the writer of Judges, for both have a healthy respect for the severity of God's anger. "Terrors are upon him" (20.25) is his punchy summary statement. Truly, terrors in abundance will fall on the entire world during the tribulation. When the sixth seal of Revelation is broken, unleashing yet more horrifying global disasters, the reaction of ungodly men is recorded:

> And the kings of the earth, and the great men, and the rich men, and the chief captains, and the mighty men, and every bondman, and every free man, hid themselves in the dens and in the rocks of the mountains; And said to the mountains and rocks, Fall on us, and hide us from the face of him that sitteth on the throne, and from the wrath of the Lamb: For the great day of his wrath is come; and who shall be able to stand? (Rev 6.15-17).

No earth dweller will be able to stand before the wrath of the Lamb. All credit to Zophar, therefore, for uncompromising honesty in preaching the inescapability of God's vengeance on the wicked. It all comes to a grand climax in the final few verses:

> All darkness is laid up for his treasures: a fire not blown shall devour him; it shall feed upon what is left in his tent. The heavens shall reveal his iniquity, and the earth shall rise up against him. The increase of his house shall depart, flowing away in the day of his [God's] anger (20.26-28, JND).

There is no hope for the wilful sinner. The weather is against him, his enemies pursue him, darkness embraces him, a supernatural fire devours him. When the day of God's anger comes, all his valued possessions will be removed, and his cherished goods "flow away" (5064) just like "waters that are poured down [5064] a steep place" (Micah 1.4). Again, Zophar is implicitly glancing back at Job's recent losses, thinking of that "fire of God [which fell] from heaven, and ... burned up the sheep, and the servants, and consumed them" (1.16). Jamieson,

Fausset and Brown suggest, rather unconvincingly, that "tact is shown by the friends in not expressly mentioning, but alluding under colour of general cases, to Job's calamities", but one can hardly argue that diplomacy is Zophar's strong suit. Throughout his speech he has been rubbing it in with a will. It is as if he is saying to Job, "You simply cannot escape God's wrath, as you should know if you analyse your recent experiences. The entire created universe has joined hands against you (20.27), testifying to God's righteous anger at your sins". Job had earlier appealed to the sympathy of the earth (16.18), and claimed he had a Witness and Redeemer in heaven (16.19; 19.25), but Zophar brutally denies the possibility of either.

Conclusion: 20.29

Zophar's conclusion is unambiguous and uncompromising: "This [that is to say, everything listed in such detail in the previous verses] is the portion of a wicked man from God, and the heritage appointed unto him by God" (20.29). According to this so-called friend, Job has only got what he deserves.

Chapter 20 is not an attractive portion of Scripture to read, for it neither warms the heart nor usefully informs the mind. One has to agree with Zuck's comment that Zophar's words are "as venomous as the cobras and vipers he mentioned (20.14,16)".[227] His viewpoint is so narrowly focussed on retribution that it lacks the balance of Scripture. For a start, he is completely silent about God's longsuffering and grace. Nevertheless, one has to admit that much of Zophar's impassioned sermon is built on accurate principles. He correctly reminds us that sin is punished. He warns us that selfish indulgences are short-lived. His perspective, however, is distorted: he assumes that recompense always falls speedily in this life, but says nothing about judgment after death. Scripture teaches that sin faces divine judgment, sometimes in this life, and certainly after death. The final book in the canon sums it up with devastating clarity. Revelation chapters 6 to 19 visualize the terrible experience of a future generation of earth dwellers who will endure God's wrath in the tribulation era (sins punished in this life), before they experience the eternal penalty of the lake of fire (endless retribution after death). Though Zophar's lesson contains much that is correct, his greatest error – and it is one shared with the other friends – is that he is preaching to the wrong person. This is the persistent blunder of Job's associates. Though their doctrine is generally sound, their application is wholly mistaken.

However, to give Zophar his due, let us list some of the positive truths he mentions:

- Man is a created being, placed upon the earth by God (20.4)
- Wickedness will eventually be repaid (20.5,27)
- In the light of eternity, the prosperity of the wicked is brief (20.5)
- A man's sins affect his children (20.10)
- For all its irrepressible vigour, youth ends in the dust (20.11)
- Sweet tastes can produce a sore tummy (20.13-14)
- Violence will get its just deserts (20.19)
- God's wrath falls unexpectedly (20.23).

These are serious lessons which a God-hating world needs to hear before it is shocked into a belated recognition of His power, when the long-silent heavens begin to thunder disaster. But Job is no anti-theist. He is a saint of God undergoing incomprehensible sufferings, and requiring a ministry of tenderness, not savage criticism. Still, even the unforgiveable words of Zophar have their positive value, viewed from the perspective of the book's ultimate purpose. The same God, who at the beginning permitted Satan's malice to erupt so violently upon Job, also allowed the three friends to castigate him with their ungracious and ill-informed speeches. Divine sovereignty comprehends the small as well as the great. Delitzsch is right to see past a failing friend to the unfolding of God's programme:

> The uncharitableness of the friends must be to [Job] the thread by which he finds his way through the labyrinth of his sufferings to the God who loves him, although He seems to be angry with him.[228]

Astonishing as it may seem, God uses the unjustified verbal abuse of people like Zophar in drawing Job closer to Himself. After all, when a man like Zophar offers such counsel, where can you turn but to God?

SECTION 15
Dialogue: Job 4 – 42.6
Contest: Round 2: Job 15-21
Job's 6th Speech: Job 21

As we come to the close of Round Two of this prolonged and increasingly irritable verbal battle between Job and his three friends, it is worth pausing to sum up the state of play. Nothing has changed. The two sides have not altered or compromised their positions; all they have done is dig down deeper. The parallel with the trench warfare on the Western Front is patent, for there has been no break-through. The words found in a letter written by a First World War soldier could sum up the book of Job so far:

> On 28th October, 1914 Wilfred Abel-Smith wrote: "I can't see how these battles are to end. It becomes a question of stalemate. With a line of this length you can't get ahead anywhere (or else you get in a dangerous position) and you can't get on because there are no flanks, and you cannot therefore get round them. As soon as you outflank, an aeroplane gives away the show, the enemy meets it, and vice versa with us, so it is a never-ending business".[229]

So continues the never-ending business of attempting to account for Job's personal tragedies. His great affirmation of faith in a divine Redeemer who would stand up in his defence was the grand climax of chapter 19. Not even Zophar's tediously repetitive diatribe on the fate of the wicked can obliterate from the reader's memory those wonderful words. Though Job descends from that high water mark, he never again completely relapses into the searing bitterness which coloured so many of his earlier speeches.

Nevertheless, in chapter 21 Job resorts to doing again what he did at the close of the first round of the debate (chapters 12-14): he ceases to foreground either his own personal misery or his deep theological convictions, and instead engages rigorously and critically with the notion underlying the arguments of his friends. They have insistently bombarded him with the simple formula that because the wicked are summarily punished in this life, whereas the righteous enjoy prosperity, it must automatically follow that a man suffering misfortune is a bad man. Both their premise and their conclusion are faulty. Job energetically applies his mind – and he is obviously not only a godly man but one of remarkable intelligence – to analyse this inflexible presupposition.

One of the interesting features of this chapter is the way Job shows he has been listening attentively to what has been said. His speech is full of quotations and half-quotations as he puts the thesis of the friends to the test. The following chart catalogues some of the ways in which Job responds to earlier comments:

Job's Friends' Remark	Job's Response
20.5, 11: the wicked perish	21.7: the wicked prosper
18.19; 20.10: their children suffer	21.8: their children are established
20.16: they suffer painful illness	21.23: they live and die at ease
18.5: their lamp is extinguished	21.17: how often is their lamp extinguished?
5.4; 20.10: their children are vulnerable	21.11, 19: their children do well
20.4: Zophar appeals to history	21.29: Job appeals to experience

Zophar, for example, had asserted that though the evil man may boast of youthful vigour, in the final count all that vitality will join him in the dust of death (20.11), but Job asks by way of counterblast, "Wherefore do the wicked live, become old, yea, are mighty in power?" (21.7). Bildad had insisted that the sinner "shall neither have son nor nephew among his people, nor any remaining in his dwellings" (18.19), to which Job responds that, on the contrary, "Their seed is established in their sight with them, and their offspring before their eyes" (21.8). Again, Bildad had said that "the light of the wicked shall be put out, and the spark of his fire shall not shine" (18.5), to which Job answers by questioning his accuracy: "How oft is it that the lamp of the wicked is put out? that their calamity cometh upon them? that God distributeth sorrows in his anger?" (21.17, RV). Near the start of the debate Eliphaz had spoken of the disaster awaiting the wicked man's descendants: "His children are far from safety, and they are crushed in the gate, neither is there any to deliver them" (5.4). But Job doubts it: "Ye say, God layeth up his iniquity for his children. Let him recompense it unto himself, that he may know it" (21.19, RV). It is all very well to claim that God's retribution is delayed in order to fall on the children, but is that borne out by the facts, and even if it were, would it constitute a just punishment of a bad man? Zophar had grounded his argument on antiquity (20.4), but Job appeals to unprejudiced travellers' observation of the way things really are in the world (21.29). The speech demonstrates a close interconnection between Job's words and the earlier comments of his companions. At least he has been listening carefully. The same cannot always be said of his friends.

During the debate he has contested their neat theory that a man's earthly circumstances infallibly testify to his state of soul. Such a system, he argues, does not stand up to the light of day. Suffering no more proves that the sufferer is guilty of specific acts of sin, than outward affluence demonstrates the presence of genuine piety. The friends have assumed that bad men have a miserable time down here, but their assumption is open to serious challenge. In unpicking their premise, Job concentrates his fire on the case of the bad man who prospers rather than the good man who suffers, since it is not hard to show that open godlessness, evidenced in speech and conduct, can coexist with material success. If that is the case, then the naïve philosophy of the friends is immediately found wanting. The victim of affliction, on the other hand, cannot so easily prove his innocence because, though like Job he may to all outward appearances have a clean slate, he might be guilty of secret sins in the heart. Job therefore focuses his attention on the case of the evil man. Hartley offers a useful précis of his thesis:

> many who are rich in material things reject God openly and blatantly. If this is true so is the opposite, i.e., those suffering beneath heavy burdens are not necessarily sinners. If in God's providence the wicked can prosper, surely the devout may suffer.[230]

Job's argument falls into three parts. He starts with a **complaint** to his friends, soliciting their attention in such a way that his bitingly ironic undertone cannot be missed (21.1-6). He then issues his **challenge** to their theory by focussing on the indisputable earthly blessings of the ungodly (21.7-26). This is in direct response to the recent words of Zophar, who depicted the wicked man as living in constant fear and facing instant destruction. Job by contrast paints a completely different picture highlighting the success (21.7-15) and the security (21.16-26) of wickedness in this world. His **conclusion** (21.27-34), in which he reverts to addressing his audience directly, invites them to examine the real facts about the wicked man's fate. Far from facing devastating judgment, such a man goes comfortably to his grave in peace and honour.

> 1. Job's Complaint: 21.1-6
> 2. Job's Challenge: 21.7-26
> 3. Job's Conclusion: 21.27-34.

Job's Complaint: 21.1-6

The direct address with which Job opens his speech fairly drips with cumulative irony. Darby's translation effectively brings out the tone:

> Hear attentively my speech, and let this replace your consolations. Suffer me and I will speak; and after I have spoken, mock on! As for me, is my complaint to a man? or wherefore should not my spirit be impatient? Mark me, and be astonished, and lay the hand upon the mouth (21.2-5, JND).

His plea is that they should "hear", "suffer" and "mark" him. The so-called solace they have offered has been of no value whatsoever. Eliphaz, rather patronisingly, had described their combined efforts at spiritual counselling as "the consolations of God" (15.11), but they had brought Job no relief. Indeed, what they considered comfort he pronounced sheer mockery. The word (3932) first appears in 2 Kings 19.21 when Jerusalem was besieged by an Assyrian army, yet Jehovah announced that the daughter of Zion "despised … and laughed … to scorn [3932]" all the vain boastings of Sennacherib's generals. It last appears when Jeremiah protests "I am in derision daily, every one mocketh [3932] me" (Jer 20.7). Job therefore urges them to be silent and listen to what he has to say. Once he has expressed his point of view they can then revert to their predictable jeering, for by this stage in the contest he has no doubt that nothing would alter their attitude to him. They are beyond the possibility of a change of heart.

It is sad when we are so wedded to our opinions as to be wilfully deaf to any information which might cause a rethink. It is even possible to come to God's Word with inherited and preconceived interpretations rather than a heart open to the teaching of the text. Solomon prayed that God would "Give therefore thy servant an understanding heart to judge thy people" (1 Kings 3.9). "Understanding" translates a word (8085) elsewhere rendered by various forms of the verb to hear – in fact it is translated "understanding" only on this one occasion. What Solomon wisely requested was a "hearing heart", one that paid careful attention to evidence so that he could properly assess and pronounce judgment in the many cases of injustice which would be brought before his throne. That is the attitude all believers need when coming to the Word of God. It is not a prejudiced mind-set which blithely approaches the text along the well-worn grooves of human tradition, but one open to truth however uncomfortable which will lead us into paths of spiritual wisdom and growth.

But the minds of Job's friends were set in concrete. In any case, it mattered little what they said, as his major complaint was against God, not against men. God had brought him into appalling misery and yet would not intervene audibly to explain His apparent disapproval of Job. "Wherefore should not my spirit be impatient?" (21.4b, JND), asks Job. We might paraphrase his words like this: "Why shouldn't I be irritable and peppery, bearing in mind all I have to endure? Look closely at my sufferings, be awe-struck at everything I have had to bear, and put your hand on your mouths to suppress any more ill-judged words. After all, simply to think about my personal circumstances causes me to be terrified and tremble".

It was not primarily the awful corporeal and mental suffering that he had to endure that so overwhelmed Job. As the debate has continued it has been noteworthy that he has said much less than we might expect about the dreadful agonies of body and mind which must have wrenched his soul. More painful for him by far was a sense of spiritual desolation. The God to whom he had been so close, and whose favour had been his constant delight, had withdrawn into silence and obscurity.

Job's Challenge: 21.7-26

But now he enters the fray to attack the presuppositions upon which the debate seemed to rest. What he provides is a series of snapshots of the wicked at the height of their unassailable prosperity. Zophar had limited himself to the singular, speaking always of the individual wicked man (20.5-29), obviously with an eye clearly fixed on Job, but Job responds by outlining the earthly success of a whole tribe of godless people. For him, the general **well-being of the wicked** (21.7-15) collapses the assumption of his friends. They maintained that sin received its recompense down here; Job asserts the contrary. First of all, then, he points to the earthly success of such people (21.7-15). Systematically he takes apart the fabric of his friends' thesis, noting the power (21.7), prolonged life (21.8), preservation (21.9), possessions (21.10), progeny (21.11), pleasures (21.12), prosperity

(21.13) and philosophy of the godless (21.14-15), those whose entire lifestyle is built upon wilful ignorance and independence of God.

His first remark is framed as a question about the **power** of godless men, a question which acts as a summary of the challenge to follow: "Wherefore do the wicked live, become old, yea, are mighty in power?" (21.7) Why is it that men whose conduct and outlook are utterly opposed to the living God are permitted to live at all? Why do they enjoy long lives on earth? Why do they become influential in the world? The three questions anticipate the anxieties of the psalmist:

> I was envious at the foolish, when I saw the prosperity of the wicked. For there are no bands in their death: but their strength is firm. They are not in trouble as other men; neither are they plagued like other men. Therefore pride compasseth them about as a chain; violence covereth them as a garment. Their eyes stand out with fatness: they have more than heart could wish. They are corrupt, and speak wickedly concerning oppression: they speak loftily. They set their mouth against the heavens, and their tongue walketh through the earth (Ps 73.3-9).

It is helpful to see Psalm 73 as an inspired commentary on Job 21. "The foolish" are men whose entire demeanour flaunts their contempt for God and His saints, but still they are permitted to succeed and even glory in their arrogance, affluence and violence. Like the psalmist, Job's bewilderment is not simply that such people exist, but that they rise to positions of authority and influence in the world. He echoes his own words in chapter 9, that "the earth is given into the hand of the wicked" (9.24). Bildad had said that their doom came speedily:

> Whilst it is yet in his greenness, and not cut down, it withereth before any other herb. So are the paths of all that forget God; and the hypocrite's hope shall perish: Whose hope shall be cut off, and whose trust shall be a spider's web (8.12-14).

Not so, answers Job. On the contrary, their lives are greatly **prolonged** (21.8) so that they are able to rejoice in an abundant and vigorous posterity. It is a terrible ordeal for a parent to bury any of his children (we have only to consider the extreme grief of David as he mourned for Absalom), but Job has had to do that with all ten of his. Yet, on looking around, he saw wicked men with extended years and flourishing families. They benefitted from physical **preservation** (21.9). Their houses – referring both to the material structure and the domestic community sheltered inside – seemed immune to the kind of disasters which had befallen him, for God's rod of correction was, unaccountably, withheld. Bildad had confidently stated of the hypocrite that "He shall lean upon his house, but it shall not stand: he shall hold it fast, but it shall not endure" (8.15). Again, Job denies this cosy theory. In doing so and in crediting such events to God, he must be thinking back on his own circumstances; he knew full well that the calamities that descended on him in chapter 1 came from above. What of the wicked? "Their houses are safe from fear, neither is the rod of God upon them" (21.9). "Safe" translates the word (7965) most often rendered "peace". According to Isaiah "There is no peace [7965], saith the Lord, unto the wicked" (Is 48.22); but Job, whose eye is fixed, understandably, on immediate events in the present world, finds that the wicked are favoured with unruffled contentment. God had afflicted him but left untouched those most deserving of judgment.

His attention turns to their **possessions**. He notes that their livestock proliferate in abundance: their cattle conceive successfully and give birth without mishap (21.10). His own vast herds of cattle, once the talk of the neighbourhood, had been snatched away by raiding parties, leaving him destitute.

But if their livestock were astonishingly fertile, so too was their family life. They could boast a plentiful and happy **progeny**, here likened to a flock of sheep in their numerical strength, and pictured dancing in evident contentment (21.11). They had no fears for their children's safety ("They send forth their little ones") for danger seems entirely foreign to them. The language may remind us of the millennial descriptions of Zechariah:

> Thus saith the Lord of hosts; There shall yet old men and old women dwell in the streets of Jerusalem, and every man with his staff in his hand for very age. And the streets of the city shall be full of boys and girls playing in the streets thereof (Zech 8.4-5).

But such idyllic scenes, where old and young can coexist in mutual joy and safety, await the time when the nation of Israel, repentantly trusting its Messiah, will bask in the holy security of His righteous reign over the earth. Peace and security in the fullest sense can only come about when the Prince of peace establishes His throne in the same world where He was rejected. The pastoral utopia briefly sketched by Job, on the other hand, is a testimony to his own bitterness as he imagines the undimmed delight of those whose families remained untouched by tragedy. In referring to their offspring as "little ones" he employs the same word he used in 19.18 to complain that "young children despised me". In his mind the unmerited domestic bliss of the wicked is conflated with the personal abuse he has received at the mouths of local youngsters: their idle joys are associated with his own deep griefs.

He goes further. Not only are wicked people blessed with children; they enjoy all the **pleasure** the material world can offer (21.12). Whether this verse describes the youthful activities of infants or the amusements of their parents it matters little. Clearly the ungodly are musically proficient, gifted with artistic and cultural talents which afford them relaxation. It is certainly true historically that there is no simple correlation between artistic taste and morality. The blood-stained hands of Hitler's henchmen greedily plundered the art treasures of war-torn Europe for their own private collections. It is possible to be culturally sophisticated yet spiritually dead. It was, we may recall, the descendants of Cain, the first human murderer, who were noted as pioneers in musical accomplishment (Gen 4.21).

They are therefore blessed with unalloyed **prosperity** lasting their lifetime:

"They spend their days in prosperity, and in a moment go down to Sheol" (21.13, JND). This verse is not designed to make us think of their removal into the place of departed spirits as a fearful penalty suddenly inflicted on them; rather, the idea is that they live out a satisfying life on earth and then are taken away without fuss or undue distress. The adverbial phrase "in a moment" (7281) comes from a word alluding to the wink of an eye (7280), which is sometimes translated so as to suggest ease:

> And among these nations shalt thou find no ease [7280], neither shall the sole of thy foot have rest: but the Lord shall give thee there a trembling heart, and failing of eyes, and sorrow of mind (Deut 28.65).

> The wild beasts of the desert shall also meet with the wild beasts of the island, and the satyr shall cry to his fellow; the screech owl also shall rest [7280] there, and find for herself a place of rest (Is 34.14).

> Hearken unto me, my people; and give ear unto me, O my nation: for a law shall proceed from me, and I will make my judgment to rest [7280] for a light of the people (Is 51.4).

> O thou sword of the Lord, how long will it be ere thou be quiet? put up thyself into thy scabbard, rest [7280], and be still (Jer 47.6).

It is therefore understandable that the Jewish Publication Society Bible renders Job 21.13 like this: "They spend their days in prosperity, and peacefully they go down to the grave". In other words, even the king of terrors holds no fears for them – they serenely slip out of this world, wracked neither with physical pains nor with mental apprehensions. As the psalmist puts it, "they have no pangs in their death, and their body is well nourished" (Ps 73.4, JND).

How completely different is Job's portrait of the wicked to the grim sketch offered unanimously by his companions. As Davidson says,

> This idyllic picture of a joyous, untroubled life, rich in possessions and filled with all that gives a charm to existence, and having a peaceful close, forms the counterpart to the picture drawn by the friends.[231]

Before we consider the way Job sums up the philosophy of people who have no time for God, it may be worth noting that, verses 14-15 apart, his description of the earthly felicity of the wicked sounds disturbingly like the blessings promised to obedient Israel. God gave His elect people a land and all the material wealth associated with earthly possessions, but the condition for the enjoyment of such benefits was national obedience to His law. The terms are laid down clearly in the Pentateuch and reiterated elsewhere in the Old Testament. Here is one of the earliest passages spelling out the link between behaviour and blessing:

And all these blessings shall come on thee, and overtake thee, if thou shalt hearken unto the voice of the Lord thy God. Blessed shalt thou be in the city, and blessed shalt thou be in the field. Blessed shall be the fruit of thy body, and the fruit of thy ground, and the fruit of thy cattle, the increase of thy kine, and the flocks of thy sheep. Blessed shall be thy basket and thy store. Blessed shalt thou be when thou comest in, and blessed shalt thou be when thou goest out. The Lord shall cause thine enemies that rise up against thee to be smitten before thy face: they shall come out against thee one way, and flee before thee seven ways (Deut 28.2-7).

Just as in Job's account of the well-being of the wicked, faithful Israel are promised an abundance of specific material benefits if they heed the Lord, healthy children, crops and cattle among them. Such promises are repeated in Leviticus 26.3-12, Psalm 144.13-15, and Malachi 3.10-12. Although Job lived before the law was given through Moses, and belonged to a people outside of God's gracious mainstream dealings with the chosen nation, the similarity between Israel's rewards for obedience and the success of the godless is indisputable. By the time a systematic reader of the Old Testament reaches the book of Job he has already encountered God's call of Israel and observed her sad failure to live up to the terms of the agreement by which she was to enjoy her territory. The parallels are therefore all the more obvious. In placing the story of Job where He does in the canon of Scripture, the Spirit of God expects us to feel as shocked as Job himself at the picture of flagrantly sinful people revelling in the sweets of peace and prosperity.

But now Job comes to his devastating point. The very people who bask in luxury and ease are those who contemptuously and openly dismiss God from their thinking. He sums up their **philosophy**:

Yet they said unto God, Depart from us; for we desire not the knowledge of thy ways. What is the Almighty, that we should serve him? and what profit should we have, if we pray unto him? (21.14-15, RV)

Though the words may sound similar, their cheap dismissal of God is completely different from Peter's New Testament request that the Lord Jesus leave him. The context highlights the contrast: "When Simon Peter saw it, he fell down at Jesus' knees, saying, Depart from me; for I am a sinful man, O Lord" (Lk 5.8). Simon had witnessed a stunning miracle, fell prostrate in worship, instinctively acknowledging his own unworthiness in the presence of such a glorious Person. To approach the Almighty is to become aware of our own sinfulness. But the people about whom Job is speaking are completely removed from the reverential awe of Peter, even though they deign to give God His name of *El Shaddai*, the great name by which He revealed Himself to Abraham, saying, "I am the Almighty God; walk before me, and be thou perfect" (Gen 17.1).

Coverdale's 16th century translation beautifully captures their deliberately insulting irreverence: "What manner of fellow is the Almighty that we should serve him?"[232] They are characterised by outrageous insolence ("Depart from us"), wilful ignorance ("we desire not the knowledge of thy ways"), and foolish independence ("What is the Almighty, that we should serve him?"). Such is the mindset of men today, because the human heart has not altered in the slightest since sin entered the world. For all their vaunted achievements in the fields of science, technology and art – themselves only the gifts of God's grace – men still have "the understanding darkened, being alienated from the life of God through the ignorance that is in them, because of the blindness of their heart" (Eph 4.18).

There are echoes here of Pharaoh's disdain for Jehovah as one unworthy of his notice: "Who is the Lord, that I should obey his voice to let Israel go? I know not the Lord, neither will I let Israel go" (Ex 5.2). Perhaps that Egyptian monarch judged Jehovah by the degraded condition of His enslaved people, perhaps in his sheltered polytheistic culture he had never heard the personal name of God, perhaps he simply wanted to be as offensive as possible. Whatever the reason, he soon learned, to the bitter cost of his family and his nation, that Jehovah was not a deity to be treated with scorn. Whatever men may say, God is still the Almighty, the supreme ruler of heaven and earth, who accomplishes His purposes as He pleases. In response to the taunts of the heathen, the psalmist wisely retreats behind God's sovereignty:

> Wherefore should the heathen say, Where is now their God? But our God
> is in the heavens: he hath done whatsoever he hath pleased (Ps 115.2-3).

In all circumstances of bewilderment and distress this is still the safest place for the believer.

The proper outlook of the Christian is exactly the opposite of the wicked men of Job's day. They had no desire to know God's ways, they resented His service, and they mocked the value of prayer. By contrast, the child of God finds the greatest delight in all these things.

Let us take them one at a time. To learn about God's ways brings the believer a joy that thrills his heart and satisfies his mind. It was Israel's duty to "fear the Lord thy God, to walk in all his ways, and to love him, and to serve the Lord thy God with all thy heart and with all thy soul" (Deut 10.12). It is therefore unsurprising that the godly psalmist prayed, "Shew me thy ways, O Lord; teach me thy paths" (Ps 25.4). The natural man has no love for God's ways, because he "receiveth not the things of the Spirit of God: for they are foolishness unto him: neither can he know them, because they are spiritually discerned" (1 Cor 2.14). It takes an initiative of divine grace for anyone to thirst after the spiritual. Since "Thy way, O God, is in the sanctuary" (Ps 77.13), it follows that an understanding of His counsels and movements requires extensive and reverent meditation. In the final analysis, the things of God are not learned through the textbook, the academic lecture, or the internet, but through time spent poring over the written Word. There we discover that all God's actions, whether directly or indirectly, are an expression of His glorious character, for "The Lord is righteous in all his ways, and holy in all his works" (Ps 145.17).

And what of His service? The unbeliever misrepresents Christian duty as oppressive servitude, but in reality to serve the Most High is the most honourable and fulfilling of activities. Whether they realise it or not, all men serve somebody; if not God, they simply slave for Satan and themselves. Paul puts the point in memorable language. Warning the saints to beware of all who oppose the truth of God, he writes,

> Now I beseech you, brethren, mark them which cause divisions and offences contrary to the doctrine which ye have learned; and avoid them. For they that are such serve not our Lord Jesus Christ, but their own belly; and by good words and fair speeches deceive the hearts of the simple (Rom 16.17-18).

The contrast could scarcely be plainer: we serve either the Lord or our own lusts. Paul is not blind to the paradox that perfect freedom is found only in submission: "he that is called in the Lord, being a servant, is the Lord's freeman: likewise also he that is called, being free, is Christ"s servant" (1 Cor 7.22). The most powerful of men, once saved, become the glad bondservants of Christ; and the most menial of slaves, once saved, enjoy a spiritual liberty in Christ which far outweighs their earthly condition of life.

The unbeliever laughs at prayer. People often jeer at what they cannot comprehend – it offers them short-term compensation for the nagging fear that they may be missing out on something wonderful. But the child of God values prayer as one of his great invisible resources. Whether confined to a prison cell or a hospital bed, he can nonetheless "come boldly unto the throne of grace [to] … obtain mercy, and find grace to help in time of need" (Heb 4.16). It may be significant that, according to Job, the unbelievers' objection to prayer is not that it is wrong but that it does not profit. Men of the world prefer a quick gain, whereas the believer habitually looks to the long-term. Even so, there is still an immediate value in communion with God. It soothes the soul, enlightens the understanding, and brings the mind into line with the purposes of heaven.

Job's speech has so far offered a revisionary sketch of the career of the wicked. They detest God, yet they do well. Now he turns to an **analysis of the argument** of his friends by looking more closely at the earthly security of those who have no place for God in their lives (21.16-26). This section needs careful reading because, at first glance, it seems at times as though Job agrees that sinners receive their due deserts in this world (21.17-20). But the best way to understand his words is to take them as referring back to the specific arguments of his friends. He quotes or paraphrases their propositions, then refutes them.

Before he gets down to business, however, he wants it clearly understood that he has no truck with the tribe of the godless, even though, unlike himself, they seem on top of the world: "Lo, their good is not in their hand: the counsel of the wicked is far from me" (21.16). He makes two points. First, the material success of bad people is not completely under their control – that is, it is ultimately not of their own making, for all human circumstances and conditions of life are traceable to God. As always, Job bypasses secondary causes (such as human endeavour or external accidents) and goes straight to the source. Just as he has no doubt that his own distresses have come from God's hand, so too he is convinced that it is the same God who has blessed the wicked. He cannot understand it, but nor can he deny it. His second point, however, is a marvellous testimony to a faith which survives the furnace. Even though pragmatism might encourage him to abandon godliness in order to reap the harvest of blessing enjoyed by bad people, he steadfastly refuses to pursue that pathway. The wicked may prosper, but they are still wrong. Doing what is right purely because it is right, and not for external reward, bespeaks a rare dedication. Daniel's three colleagues demonstrated it when they refused to bow to Nebuchadnezzar's image, even though they were fully aware that it might not be the Lord's will to snatch them from a gruesome death:

> If it be so, our God whom we serve is able to deliver us from the burning fiery furnace, and he will deliver us out of thine hand, O king. But if not, be it known unto thee, O king, that we will not serve thy gods, nor worship the golden image which thou hast set up (Dan 3.17-18).

They knew God had the power to rescue them from danger ("our God whom we serve is able to deliver us"), but they had no assurance that it was necessarily His will. That seems to be the meaning of the qualifying phrase, "But if not". Whether they were going to be supernaturally saved from peril or whether they had to face the flames, they would still not compromise their loyalty to Jehovah. Their polite but firm statement of allegiance is a model to us all.

Something similar seems to be Job's idea here. The godless might prosper (and, conversely, he, Job, might continue to suffer), but he will not align himself with wicked men and their ways. As Delitzsch puts it, "verse 16a is therefore to be taken as Job's judgment, and 16b as the moral effect which it produces upon him".[233] Job fully acknowledges their prosperity but equally abhors the principle governing their lives. In so doing he is, unbeknown to himself, once again refuting the charge Satan laid against him at the start of the book. That challenge was very direct:

> Doth Job fear God for nought? Hast not thou made an hedge about him, and about his house, and about all that he hath on every side? thou hast blessed the work of his hands, and his substance is increased in the land. But put forth thine hand now, and touch all that he hath, and he will curse thee to thy face (1.9-11).

Why do men serve the living God? Simply for what they can get out of it? Or might there be a deep-seated recognition that God is worthy of His people's service and worship regardless of whatever earthly benefits they might receive? Job is a living testimony to the sturdiness of a faith that honours God not because of blessings but in spite of calamities.

In the next few verses Job repeats and refutes some specific assertions of his friends as to the fate of the wicked. He deals first with two examples of what we might call their theological **fantasy** (21.17-21). The words are best read in a translation which supplies interrogation marks instead of the exclamation points of the KJV. This emphasises the fact that, far from endorsing, Job is questioning their viewpoint:

> How often is the lamp of the wicked put out, and cometh their calamity upon them? Doth he distribute sorrows to them in his anger? Do they become as stubble before the wind, and as chaff that the storm carrieth away? (21.17-18, JND).

As Hartley says, "Each of Job's questions expects the answer, "very few times, if any".[234] The original words were Bildad's in 18.5-6. He spoke of the lights going out in the tents of the godless. But Job demurs. It is as if he is asking, let's be honest now, is it really the case that God invariably and immediately snuffs out their lives and showers them with misery? The picture language of stubble is a common Old Testament image of worthlessness and fragility. The psalmist memorably contrasts the rooted living stability of the righteous with the "The ungodly [who] are … like the chaff which the wind driveth away" (Ps 1.4), and later prays that his enemies will be "as chaff before the wind: and let the angel of the Lord chase them" (Ps 35.5). Isaiah foresees the destruction of godless Gentile nations in similar terms:

> The nations shall rush like the rushing of many waters: but God shall rebuke them, and they shall flee far off, and shall be chased as the chaff of the mountains before the wind, and like a rolling thing before the whirlwind (Is 17.13).

Old Testament history loudly testifies that God can indeed drive wicked men like chaff. But He does not always do so at once, or even during their lifetime. We have to bear in mind that Job is responding to men who have constructed a rigid theory which admits of no exceptions. According to them, the wicked are always punished here and now. Job collapses the theory by asking whether this is demonstrably the case every time.

In the next two verses he takes up Zophar's conviction that bad men are punished in their children, who suffer the evil consequences of their parents' sins (20.10). Again, the passage is best read in a translation which inserts the assumed words, "you claim" or "you say", to indicate that Job is citing another's argument. Here is the Revised Version:

> Ye say, God layeth up his iniquity for his children. Let him recompense it unto himself, that he may know it. Let his own eyes see his destruction, and let him drink of the wrath of the Almighty. For what pleasure hath he in his house after him, when the number of his months is cut off in the midst? (21.19-21, RV).

Job's answer to their proposal is simply to question its justice, for it hardly deals directly with the transgressor. It would be much better, says Job, for God to pour out His retribution on the head of the guilty party, rather than wait until he is dead and cannot care less what happens to his house or his heirs. Punishment deferred until the next generation is no punishment at all.

Having punched some holes in their fantasy view of the world, Job now proceeds to draw his friends' attention to the **facts** (21.22-26). He starts by making the point that it is impossible for men to predict God's ways with His creatures: "Shall any teach God knowledge? seeing he judgeth those that are high" (21.22). His friends have been expecting God to conform to their neat ideas of how He should deal with men on earth, instead of looking carefully at the historical evidences of His activities. Different destinies are not automatically determined by differences of moral character, for God distributes circumstances as He pleases. His ways are inscrutable precisely because He is the supreme ruler of the universe, able to judge the highest of created beings. Since God judges the heavens, have mere men any right to tell Him how to handle things on earth?

All Job and his contemporaries had to go on was their knowledge of human history. They had no access to the inspired written Word, in which we learn not only the facts of history but also the way God's hand directs it according to His good pleasure. Scripture insistently teaches that God is answerable to no man. Isaiah had to remind Israel that it had no right to complain about God's disciplinary ways. He could use a Gentile like Nebuchadnezzar to chastise them, or another Gentile like Cyrus to restore them, for He can do what He will:

> Woe unto him that striveth with his Maker! Let the potsherd strive with the potsherds of the earth. Shall the clay say to him that fashioneth it, What makest thou? or thy work, He hath no hands? (Is 45.9)

God consults with no one in His administration of the world, for "Who hath directed the Spirit of the Lord, or being his counsellor hath taught him?" (Is 40.13), or "who hath known the mind of the Lord, that he may instruct him?" (1 Cor 2.16). But whereas the Old Testament prophet simply leaves the believer humbled by God's unsearchable greatness, the New Testament apostle adds a footnote: "But we have the mind of Christ" (1 Cor 2.16). The climactic disclosure of God's heart in the incarnate person of Christ has brought saints today into a vastly more privileged position than that of Israel. Indeed, we are informed that, though it is of course uniquely God who judges "those that are high" (21.22), believers of the present church age will be His servants in this exercise (1 Cor 6.3).

Having put his companions in their place by reminding them that God does not bend His ways to match any man's theories, Job confronts them with two imaginary but representative men whose pathway through life is quite distinct:

> One dieth in his full strength, being wholly at ease and quiet; His sides are full of fat, and the marrow of his bones is moistened; And another dieth in

bitterness of soul, and hath not tasted good: Together they lie down in the dust, and the worms cover them (21.23-26, JND).

The structure of the passage is simple. We are introduced to "one", who is contrasted with "another", and yet in the final analysis they lie down in the dust of death "together", just as though there were no perceptible difference between them. The first man enjoys a life of abundance and luxury, "his breasts ... full of milk, and his bones ... moistened with marrow" (21.24), and dies painlessly. The word translated "breasts" appears only here, and probably refers to containers or pails, suggesting the rich yield of his dairy cattle. Zophar had claimed that the wicked man "shall not see the rivers, the floods, the brooks of honey and butter" (20.17), but Job imagines a man blessed both in his substance and in his physical vigour. The second man, on the other hand, misses out on all this prosperity, dying in bitterness of soul having never drunk deeply of the world's pleasures. Job describes him by using the same word ("bitterness") he has earlier used of himself:

Wherefore is light given to him that is in misery, and life unto the bitter in soul (3.20).

Therefore I will not refrain my mouth; I will speak in the anguish of my spirit; I will complain in the bitterness of my soul (7.11).

My soul is weary of my life; I will leave my complaint upon myself; I will speak in the bitterness of my soul (10.1).

But it would be wrong to draw the conclusion that the second man represents Job, for, after all, Job had enjoyed many years of material blessing. Only recently has he been stripped of all his goods, whereas the man in the illustration has had no earthly success at all. The first man in Job's illustration does well in this world, the second does badly, yet there is nothing to indicate any moral or spiritual difference between them. The reason for his little parable is to highlight the fact that "it is impossible to derive a just law of retribution from what we observe in the present world".[235] What distinguishes the two men is not that one is good and the other bad, but that one is what the world would call fortunate, and the other unfortunate. Regardless, both end up in exactly the same place – the grave. Death, says Job, is the great leveller; it fails to differentiate between the righteous and the unrighteous. As the preacher says,

All things come alike to all: there is one event to the righteous, and to the wicked; to the good and to the clean, and to the unclean; to him that sacrificeth, and to him that sacrificeth not: as is the good, so is the sinner; and he that sweareth, as he that feareth an oath (Eccl 9.2).

Neither Job nor Solomon is looking beyond the immediate reality of physical death. They make no mention of an afterlife or a judicial assessment. Their aim is only to show that all men die. Other scriptures make it plain that there are two separate eternal destinies for men, depending entirely upon a man's relationship with God.

Job's Conclusion: 21.27-34

Bringing his speech to a close, Job turns to his companions and tells them that he is well aware of their thinking processes, the theological system which requires them to assess him by outward circumstances. They conjecture that great sufferers are great sinners, but Job wants them to realise that such a naïve mind-set fails to do justice to the facts of life.

Sarcastically putting words into their mouths, he captures their worldview: "For ye say, Where is the house of the prince? and where are the dwelling places of the wicked?" (21.28). Maybe he is looking back to Zophar's recent comment on the complete obliteration of the hypocrite so that his contemporaries find no trace of him: "he shall perish for ever like his own dung: they which have seen him shall say, Where is he?" (20.7). Assuming that Job's words constitute an example of synonymous parallelism, "the prince" and the "wicked" must therefore be identical in meaning. The "dwelling places" are, according to Young's Literal Translation, "the tent – The tabernacles of the wicked", hinting at the spacious pavilions of an eastern sheik. The verse does not contrast a noble prince with wicked men, but rather asserts that the unjust, however exalted, are heading for devastating judgment. In using such language as he credits to them, Job's friends doubtless have in mind the destruction of Job's son's house with all its inhabitants.

That is the claim. But Job counters by asking whether his friends have ever bothered to check the accuracy of their opinions. Since they refuse to believe his words, considering him a prejudiced witness, can they not bother to take the testimony of unbiased onlookers who have travelled the world and seen what truly goes on? "Have ye not asked the wayfarers? and do ye not regard their tokens" (Job 21.29, JND). The friends rely on tradition and handed-down orthodoxy (8.8; 20.4), but truth does not fly in the face of reality. And what is the reality experienced travellers have seen?

> That the wicked is reserved to the day of destruction? they shall be brought forth to the day of wrath. Who shall declare his way to his face? and who shall repay him what he hath done? Yet shall he be brought to the grave, and shall remain in the tomb. The clods of the valley shall be sweet unto him, and every man shall draw after him, as there are innumerable before him (21.30-33).

In the KJV Job's language implies that the wicked man is destined for future punishment. It is indeed possible that Job is looking ahead to a final judgment after death in which the apparent inequities of this life will be dealt with. The Saviour's narrative of the rich man and Lazarus demonstrates the accuracy of such a belief. The man who had basked in earthly wealth finds things are reversed after death:

But Abraham said, Son, remember that thou in thy lifetime receivedst thy good things, and likewise Lazarus evil things: but now he is comforted, and thou art tormented (Lk 16.25).

The apostle Paul later explains it in terms designed to encourage believers enduring the hardships of life: "For our light affliction, which is but for a moment, worketh for us a far more exceeding and eternal weight of glory" (2 Cor 4.17).

But is that the case in the book of Job? We must resist the temptation to read this early Old Testament story as though it were part of the New Testament. "Reserved" translates a word (2820) whose meaning is illustrated by its earlier appearances in the Scriptures. For example, it is used when God tells Abimelech that "I also withheld [2820] thee from sinning against me" (Gen 20.6), when the angel of the Lord praises Abraham because "thou hast not withheld [2820] thy son, thine only son from me" (Gen 22.12), and when Joseph says to Mrs Potiphar (about her husband's trust in him) "neither hath he kept back [2820] anything from me but thee, because thou art his wife" (Gen 39.9). These examples suggest that the word used by Job could refer to the wicked man's escape from disaster rather than his being fingered to face it. Thus the ESV renders the verse: "the evil man is spared in the day of calamity … rescued in the day of wrath" (21.30, ESV). This fits well with Job's argument. Far from agreeing with his friends' idea that sin is promptly punished, he insists that eyewitness testimony affirms the opposite. In this world (and that is the focus of his outlook here) wicked men are safe from calamity and delivered from wrath.

He goes further: "Who shall declare his way to his face? and who shall repay him what he hath done?" (21.31). Who in this world, he asks, has either the power or the authority to expose the sinner's wickedness, or reward him with his due deserts? He paints a scene where evil gets away with it right to the very end of life. With some cynicism, he imagines the tranquil setting of the wicked man's grave:

> Yet is he carried to the graves, and watch is kept over the tomb. The clods
> of the valley are sweet unto him; and every man followeth suit after him,
> as there were innumerable before him (21.32-33, JND).

Bildad had asserted of the wicked that "His remembrance shall perish from the earth, and he shall have no name in the street" (18.17), but Job gives us a glimpse of something like a state funeral with all its public pomp and splendour. The sinner is carried in dignity to the cemetery, his tomb adorned with costly memorials to ensure a continued remembrance. Hartley informs us that "in many ancient near eastern countries the rich made endowments to ensure the proper care of their tombs … to guarantee the continuation of the honour of the deceased".[236] Even in death the bad man's blessings continue, for the earth in which his body rests is "sweet unto him". In life he was prosperous; in death he is peaceful. What more could he want? And this is no aberration, but the general state of affairs, for "every man followeth suit after him, as there were innumerable before him". This particular wicked man is but one of a vast host stretching out to the horizon; they live regardless of God and go to their graves in quiet.

Job's frank description of the way of the world explodes the stale theory of his companions. "How then comfort ye me in vain, seeing in your answers there remaineth falsehood?" (21.34). They came, supposedly, to console their friend, but their boasted comfort was futile being built on a false perception of reality. They might be in the majority (three against one), they were pious men, they were sincere, they were fluent of speech, they were impressively dogmatic – but they were wrong.

There are two matters of interest in this chapter. First, because his friends have been arguing in black and white terms, allowing no possibility of variation in the experience of the godly or the ungodly, Job is almost forced into following suit. The result is that his response to their oversimplification is, at times, equally oversimplified. They tell him that bad men without fail receive their just deserts down here; he replies that, as far as he can see, they never do. His picture of the glowing worldly success of the wicked exaggerates the reality. We know from other scriptures that God can and does step in to punish sin when it pleases Him. Adam and Eve were driven out of Eden; Cain was exiled; Uzzah (2 Sam 6.3-8), Pelatiah (Ezek 11.13), Ananias and Sapphira (Acts 5.1-11) were smitten on the spot; Korah was swallowed up by the earth (Num 16.32). But Job has been boxed into this corner by the false overgeneralisations with which he has been assaulted. A man suffering from extreme physical and emotional distress is not in the best position to assess things with the calm balance and clear-sightedness of the detached observer, and Job cannot be blamed for the hyperbole with which he answers back. Extremism begets extremism. The 16th century Reformers learned their own intolerance towards dissent at least in part from the brutal violence they received at the hands of the Roman Catholic system. Their persecution of godly Anabaptists[237] is a terrible blot on their record. When they attained political power they treated Roman Catholics with similar cruelty. Nevertheless, it is a lesson to us to avoid arguing or acting unjustly lest we simply browbeat others into doing the same.

It is not hard to score an ungracious hit. I recall hearing someone describe a brother who believed that the saints of the church age would go through the rigours of Daniel's 70th week as a man who "looks as though he's going to go through the tribulation". This cheap jest was designed to cast scorn on his doctrine. But to use a man's customary facial expression as a reason for rejecting his teaching is both morally unfair and intellectually unconvincing. When people resort to the *ad hominem* argument it suggests they have nothing better to offer. The error of a post-tribulation rapture should be answered by a reasoned and systematic exposition of Scripture. Even there we must avoid hyperbole. The exaggeration or falsification of biblical data is to be avoided because it involves playing fast and loose with the evidence. It is easy to claim, for example, that "the Bible never says so and so", but, as Darby remarks somewhere, one can only justifiably make such a sweeping statement if one knows everything in the Bible. It is tough to prove a negative. It is better to argue on the basis of what the Bible *does* say, because that is demonstrable by simple quotation.

The other matter is the conformity of doctrinal truth to historical reality. Job charges his friends with maintaining a theory unsupported by the hard evidence of daily life. Now, the Christian believes Scripture because it is the word of a God who cannot lie. Though none of us were present when God created the universe, we trust the divine record: "Through faith we understand that the worlds were framed by the word of God, so that things which are seen were not made of things which do appear" (Heb 11.3). But when the Bible testifies to matters which pertain to the realms of recorded history, experimental science, and common experience, we expect it to harmonise with the facts. In that case there is a place for outside verification. Even the Son of God made sure that His first miracle was publically validated by a significant and unprejudiced observer so that the astonishing quality of the wine He had created was affirmed to all (Jn 2.8-10). In the same way, He sent cured lepers to the priest for careful inspection so that the ceremony for the leper's cleansing might be carried out in fulfilment of the Law of Moses. Biblical miracles are testable within the normal rules of evidence, just as the results of a genuine conversion will be visible to an onlooker. Those who are saved by the power of God should certainly show it. But when a claim does not stand up to investigation, something must be wrong. People who profess the doctrine that godliness is rewarded with instant health and wealth in this world come unstuck when they examine history and Scripture. History records the lives of countless godly men and women who endured suffering and poverty; Scripture confronts us with Job in the Old Testament and Paul in the New. Of both it may be said that, in their different ways, they "suffered the loss of all things" (Phil 3.8). Paul suffered loss in the knowledge that in Christ he had blessings which outweighed the world; Job suffered so that, in the good providence of God, he might eventually understand that his God had the right to do as He pleased with His servant. Once he submitted to that truth, Job was finally restored to even greater earthly blessing than before.

The book of Job is, among many other things, a stunning rebuttal of prosperity theology, an appeal to fair and logical argument, and a challenge to all believers to offer sympathetic understanding to those in distress.

SECTION 16
Dialogue: Job 4 – 42.6
Contest: Round 3: Job 22-31
Eliphaz's 3rd Speech: Job 22

Job's previous speech, implying that the prosperity of the wicked denies any simple correlation between sin and suffering in human life, has made it clear that he is still in no mood to surrender to the combined assault of his friends. Eliphaz is therefore compelled to bring out his big guns to demolish Job's defences. The sustained artillery barrage which preceded the Battle of the Somme in 1916 was designed to pulverise German dugouts and obliterate their barbed wire emplacements. History testifies that it did nothing of the sort, so that the advancing British infantry found themselves facing a hail of machine gun fire for which they were ill prepared. By the end of Round Three, Eliphaz's moral and theological bombardment (Job 22), poorly supported by the pitiful contribution of Bildad (Job 25) and the complete silence of Zophar, will be found to have been equally unsuccessful in achieving its object. Job's replies, which terminate the formal contest between him and his friends, are deafening in their robust defiance (Job 23-24, 26-31).

Unaware of his impending failure, however, urged on by a conviction that Job's calamities must be the result of personal sins, and genuinely concerned that the patriarch be recovered, Eliphaz now resorts to fabricating a catalogue of crimes of which Job has been guilty. We must take careful note that he has no supporting evidence for any of these, but is simply pursuing the logic of his erroneous presuppositions. It is tragic when a theological assumption forces us into downright lying to sustain our beliefs.

Eliphaz's attack first of all aims to expose Job's fundamental mistake in maintaining his own righteousness (22.1-5), after which he describes two kinds of sin which have tainted the patriarch's life. Guilty of both exploiting and neglecting the weak and vulnerable in society (22.6-9), he is now suffering the consequences (22.10-11). But he has also been infected by serious theological error, implicitly harbouring the notion that a transcendent God is so removed from human life that He is unconcerned about man's misdemeanours (22.12-14). A glance at the evidence of history should put him right: God can and does step in to punish wicked men because, in His omniscience, He knows all about them (22.15-20). Finally, Eliphaz reverts to the more benign demeanour which was so apparent in his first speech back in chapters 4 and 5, holding out the benefits awaiting the repentant backslider if only he heeded such good advice (22.21-30). This, then, is the development of his final contribution to the debate:

> 1. An Exposé of Job's Hypocrisy: 22.1-5
> 2. An Exposition of Job's Sin: (i) Inhumanity: 22.6-9
> 3. An Explanation of Job's Calamities: 22.10-11
> 4. An Exposition of Job's Sin: (ii) Impiety: 22.12-14
> 5. The Evidence of History: 22.15-20
> 6. An Exhortation to Repentance: 22.21-30.

An Exposé of Job's Hypocrisy: 22.1-5

No space is wasted on a prolonged introduction – Eliphaz gets straight into his subject. The logic of the first five verses is not immediately easy to grasp, but the RV helps make sense of it. It stands as an **accusation** of hypocrisy:

> Can a man be profitable unto God? surely he that is wise is profitable unto himself. Is it any pleasure to the Almighty, that thou art righteous? or is it gain to him, that thou makest thy ways perfect? Is it for thy fear of him that he reproveth thee, that he entereth with thee into judgment? Is not thy wickedness great? neither is there any end to thine iniquities (22.2-5, RV).

The passage begins with morally positive words ("wise … righteous … perfect") and ends with negative ones ("wickedness … iniquities"). It is as though Eliphaz lists the commendable characteristics of Job (features all his friends hitherto believed were genuinely true of him) only to assert that they must have been a façade concealing a cesspool of filth. Why? Because of the evident punishments he is now suffering. He was reputed to be a wise man ("he that is wise"), an upright man ("thou art righteous"), and a blameless man ("thou makest thy ways perfect"). Everyone thought well of Job. But wait, says Eliphaz. Is it conceivable that God is afflicting you because of your reverence for Him? Surely not. Can He be entering into judgment with you (as witnessed by your calamities) because of your piety? It just does not make sense. No, it must be because all the time you have been a religious fraud, guilty of gross wickedness and innumerable iniquities. You may have fooled your friends and acquaintances, but you have not hoodwinked God. Only a monumental sinner could suffer such mega-disasters.

That is the broad accusation. Job has flaunted his virtue, but underneath he has been a great offender. Behind the accusation lies a theological **assumption**. Job might have the public reputation for being a righteous, blameless sage but, even supposing that were true (and, as we have seen, Eliphaz dismisses it as a sham), would it oblige God to be grateful? Eliphaz maintains that a man's virtue does not enhance, nor does a man's viciousness reduce, the happiness of God. If a man is especially wise, his wisdom benefits himself, not God. That being the case, it cannot be that God awards prosperity to some and calamity to others for His own personal advantage; the cause of good and ill in human experience must lie in man himself. Therefore – and this is his key point – Job must be suffering because of personal failures.

In one sense Eliphaz is perfectly correct in what he says about God. Delitzsch's comment is helpful:

> God is in Himself the all-sufficient One; … no advantage accrues to Him from human uprightness, since His nature, existing before and transcending all created things, can suffer neither diminution nor increase from the creature.[238]

This is the great blessedness of the God of the Bible. His unshakeable sovereignty and unassailable glory place Him far above the storms of this world, so that man's sin harms not God but himself, and man's goodness in no way increases the eternal divine pleasure. The Lord Jesus gave His disciples a salutary lesson designed to puncture human self-esteem: "So likewise ye, when ye shall have done all those things which are commanded you, say, We are unprofitable servants: we have done that which was our duty to do" (Lk 17.10). If the believer does, to his limited ability, everything required of him in Scripture (if that were possible), he would still have nothing in which to boast. More, his faithfulness will have added nothing to God's infinite majesty, for God is not to be served or worshipped "as though he needed any thing, seeing he giveth to all life, and breath, and all things" (Acts 17.25).

In his marvellous study of the Old Testament Christophanies, *The Companion of the Way*, Hewlett puts into words the essential autonomy of God:

> In His kindness [God] gives to His creation all that it needs, but He Himself is in need of nothing from it … All His works and ways in the universe have their fount in His own nature. Nothing external can impose any necessity upon Him, or add to Him, or take away from Him. Dependence is a basic law of all created existence. The Creator alone possesses the freedom of an absolute independence.[239]

The name of Jehovah, revealed to Moses, means "I AM THAT I AM" (Ex 3.14), an outstanding demonstration that God is in Himself eternally self-existent and self-sufficient. He needs nothing and no one. But creatures are by definition dependent beings. That is why the divine name, "I AM", on the lips of the Lord Jesus becomes a glorious testimony to His infallible ability to meet all *our* needs, and we have many. If I need spiritual sustenance, He is "the bread of life"; if I need illumination, He is "the light of the world"; if I need guidance, He is "the way". God did not create man to satisfy some deficiency in Himself, but for His own wise purposes of grace. Within the eternal fellowship of the triune Godhead there has always been infinitely perfect love and mutual satisfaction (Jn 17.5,24).

It is important for the believer to grasp this fact, lest he develop an inflated ego. We all have a tendency to think ourselves indispensable in our little sphere of service, but God is too great to be assisted by our obedience or thwarted by our failure. Paul's counsel is direct:

> For I say, through the grace given unto me, to every man that is among you, not to think of himself more highly than he ought to think; but to think soberly, according as God hath dealt to every man the measure of faith (Rom 12.3).

Man can never put God under obligation.

On the other hand, it is equally true that Scripture does not present the living God as coldly remote or untouched by human behaviour. He is not the armchair First Cause of the deists who sits aloof from the world He has created. Rather, it is His deep desire to bless His people. The words spoken to Israel on the borders of the Land make this plain: "O that there were such an heart in them, that they would fear me, and keep all my commandments always, that it might be well with them, and with their children for ever!" (Deut 5.29). The longing of Jehovah to see His people come into the practical benefits of obedience to His Word is expressed with undisguised feeling. This is all the more remarkable when we realise that it is God alone who can grant innately wicked people such a submissive heart (1 Chr 29.18-19).

Just as God delights in our obedience, so He is genuinely grieved by our sin. This is the teaching of both Testaments:

> And it repented the Lord that he had made man on the earth, and it grieved him at his heart (Gen 6.6).

> Forty years long was I grieved with this generation, and said, It is a people that do err in their heart, and they have not known my ways (Ps 95.10).

> And when he had looked round about on them with anger, being grieved for the hardness of their hearts, he saith unto the man, Stretch forth thine hand. And he stretched it out: and his hand was restored whole as the other (Mk 3.5).

> And grieve not the holy Spirit of God, whereby ye are sealed unto the day of redemption (Eph 4.30).

The biblical position is this: God's immutable blessedness is neither increased by man's obedience, nor diminished by his sin, and yet it is still true that He rejoices in our faithfulness (Mt 25.21,23) and grieves at our failures (Lk 22.61-62). But none of this really touches on the specific case of Job, for the Almighty had specially chosen him to be an instrument through whom He would glorify Himself and humiliate the accuser.

Being completely in the dark as to the divine purposes, Eliphaz's words to Job are totally off the point. But blindly he blunders on.

An Exposition of Job's Sin: (i) Inhumanity: 22.6-9

In his zeal to take Job to task for some specific misdeeds, Eliphaz draws, not on known facts (for he has none), but on his fertile imagination. He has extravagantly accused Job of great wickedness and iniquities without number (22.5). Somehow he must pierce his friend's complete armour and cause him to blush for shame. Lack of evidence might be an impediment to some, but it is no hindrance to Eliphaz's eloquence, for where he has no facts he simply makes them up. Surely Job must have been guilty of some serious sins of deliberate commission (22.6) and inexcusable omission (22.7):

> thou hast taken pledges of thy brother for nought, and stripped the naked

of their clothing. Thou hast not given water to the weary to drink, and thou hast withholden bread from the hungry (22.6-7, RV).

Determined to accuse Job of what Hartley calls "violating the highest standards of patriarchal piety",[240] Eliphaz speculates about the kind of iniquities to which a well-to-do sheik might be prone. Material affluence easily spawns indifference to the needs of others, and social eminence fosters smug pride. Though by no means a Christian novel, Dickens's *Christmas Carol* does at least express in memorable language the perils of human selfishness. As the Ghost of Christmas Present says to Scrooge:

> Will you decide what men shall live, what men shall die? It may be, that in the sight of Heaven, you are more worthless and less fit to live than millions like this poor man's child. Oh God! to hear the Insect on the leaf pronouncing on the too much life among his hungry brothers in the dust![241]

Solomon reminds us that "The rich man's wealth is his strong city", while "the destruction of the poor is their poverty" (Prov 10.15). It is easy to become self-satisfied and self-absorbed with one's blessings, to the disadvantage of others less favoured. Encouraging saints to supply the needs of their brethren, Paul argues for "an equality, that now at this time your abundance may be a supply for their want … that there may be equality" (2 Cor 8.13-14). True godliness will be expressed in generosity.

Perhaps smug affluent isolationism was a temptation from which Eliphaz himself was not entirely free, which explains why it forms the substance of his charge against Job. We are quick to see our own failings reflected in others. The sins he lists are the kind which involve the abuse of social power, failing to provide support for the weak and vulnerable. The accusation relates to the importance of consideration and charity in Middle Eastern culture. The law God gave Moses was notable for its humanity, and the way it preserved the personal dignity of even the poorest members of society. For example, "If thou at all take thy neighbour's raiment to pledge, thou shalt deliver it unto him by that the sun goeth down" (Ex 22.26). This brief instruction, uttered at the same time as the Decalogue, is elaborated in Deuteronomy:

> When thou dost lend thy brother anything, thou shalt not go into his house to fetch his pledge. Thou shalt stand abroad, and the man to whom thou dost lend shall bring out the pledge abroad unto thee. And if the man be poor, thou shalt not sleep with his pledge: In any case thou shalt deliver him the pledge again when the sun goeth down, that he may sleep in his own raiment, and bless thee: and it shall be righteousness unto thee before the Lord thy God (Deut 24.10-13).

As the *Jamieson, Fausset and Brown Commentary* informs us,

No Orientals undress, but, merely throwing off their turbans and some of their heavy outer garments, they sleep in the clothes which they wear during the day. The bed of the poor is usually nothing else than a mat; and, in winter, they cover themselves with a cloak – a practice which forms the ground or reason of the humane and merciful law respecting the pawned coat.

The law ordained that no one was to be deprived of his bedclothes, even as security for a loan. But, according to Eliphaz, Job – a man originally possessed of fabulous wealth – had for no good reason demanded pledges from his own relatives, and ruthlessly stripped the helpless of their essential protection.

More, he had failed to offer that practical kindness to the weary and hungry traveller which was expected behaviour in his society. Upon seeing three strangers approach his tents in the heat of the day and without yet knowing who they were, the elderly Abraham busied himself in arranging for suitably lavish hospitality (Gen 18.1-8). Job, however, had failed to offer even a cup of cold water to the thirsty, and cruelly withheld bread from the hungry. Genuine hospitality (the New Testament Greek word means "love shown to strangers") is one of the outward marks of God's work in the soul. It is to be manifest not merely by local church leaders (1 Tim 3.2; Titus 1.8), but by all believers, who should be "given to hospitality" (Rom 12.13), eager to "Use hospitality one to another without grudging" (1 Pet 4.9). This is not to be confused with the kind of socialising in which long-established friends are constantly visiting one another's homes. Though unobjectionable, it is not to be identified with hospitality. The biblical emphasis, with an eye on Abraham's example, is on meeting the needs of visiting strangers, "for thereby some have entertained angels unawares" (Heb 13.2).

Behind all Eliphaz's allegations, however baseless, lies an important truth. Sin is far more than simply the wilful practice of what is wrong; it includes the omission of what is right. The Decalogue, part of God's code of behaviour uniquely entrusted to the nation of Israel while at the same time designed to lay bare the failure of all humanity, lists eight negative injunctions but only two positive ones (keeping the Sabbath, and honouring parents). The preponderance of negative commands ("Thou shalt not") comments on the innate wickedness of the human heart, which requires constant restraint from evil-doing, so prone is it to err. Nonetheless, positive commands are included in Israel's rule of life. Indeed, when we think about it, even negative directives imply a positive attitude: instead of harming our fellow-man (by murder, adultery, theft and deception) we should seek his good. As the ideal Israelite and the perfect man, the Lord Jesus not only "did no sin, neither was guile found in his mouth" (1 Pet 2.22), but positively "went about doing good, and healing all that were oppressed of the devil; for God was with him" (Acts 10.38). He is the model of freedom from all wickedness and fulfilment of all righteousness. It is not surprising, then, that the rest of the New Testament urges believers to "Awake to righteousness, and sin not" (1 Cor 15.34), to "do good unto all men, especially unto them who are of the household of faith" (Gal 6.10).

According to Eliphaz, Job, by contrast, had devoted himself to wickedness while unpardonably abstaining from generous kindness. He had no excuse, being a man of high estate and powerful influence: "But the powerful man, he had the land; and the man of high rank dwelt in it" (22.8, JND). Young's Literal Translation brings out the picture language of the Hebrew text: "As to the man of arm - he hath the earth, And the accepted of face - he dwelleth in it". "Powerful" (2220) translates a word relating to the arm. It is first used when Jacob, blessing his son Joseph, tells us that "his bow abode in strength, and the arms [2220] of his hands were made strong by the hands of the mighty God of Jacob" (Gen 49.24). It is used to describe God's mighty power delivering Israel out of Egypt (Ex 6.6; 15.16; Deut 4.34; 5.15; 7.19; 9.29), and the "shoulder" of the sacrificial victim (Num 6.19; Deut 18.3). Job, then, is a powerful man who is "accepted of face", respected and welcome in every reputable gathering, one to whom others looked up in admiration. The language signals social and material renown, in contrast to the marginalised people he has despised – the naked, the weary, the hungry. What could such a man, already wealthy beyond measure and esteemed by all, hope to gain in withholding benevolence from the impoverished?

Paul's New Testament teaching about material resources is beautifully sane. There is nothing intrinsically wrong with wealth, but believers who have been so blessed are to use their assets responsibly:

> Charge them that are rich in this world, that they be not highminded, nor trust in uncertain riches, but in the living God, who giveth us richly all things to enjoy; That they do good, that they be rich in good works, ready to distribute, willing to communicate (1 Tim 6.17-18).

As CHM writes somewhere, "the very best thing we can do with our money is to spend it for the Lord; and then instead of being rust on our souls it will be treasure in heaven".

Back in his denunciation of Job, Eliphaz, warming to his task, proceeds in his wholly fictional portrait of a penny-pinching tyrant. Not only has he abused the poor and refused to aid the needy, Job has actually "sent widows away empty, and the arms of the fatherless have been broken" (22.9). Those who were the special objects of God's gracious care in the commonwealth of Israel have become the innocent targets of Job's malice. The Lord instructed Israel, "Ye shall not afflict any widow, or fatherless child" (Ex 22.22), and the prophets exhorted the failing nation to put into practice that humane but neglected command: "Learn to do well; seek judgment, relieve the oppressed, judge the fatherless, plead for the widow" (Is 1.17). Persistently, however, Israel rebelled, and its continued disobedience met with catastrophic national discipline. When, under divine inspiration, Zechariah looks back to Judah's captivity he sees it as Jehovah's response to that generation's failure to uphold the humane commands of the law:

> Thus speaketh the Lord of hosts, saying, Execute true judgment, and shew mercy and compassions every man to his brother: And oppress not the widow,

nor the fatherless, the stranger, nor the poor; and let none of you imagine evil against his brother in your heart. But they refused to hearken, and pulled away the shoulder, and stopped their ears, that they should not hear. Yea, they made their hearts as an adamant stone, lest they should hear the law, and the words which the Lord of hosts hath sent in his spirit by the former prophets: therefore came a great wrath from the Lord of hosts (Zech 7.9-12).

The historical case against Israel is incontestable.

But Job's situation is entirely different. Eliphaz, unlike Zechariah, is not uttering an inspired prophetic word. He is simply expressing a personal opinion that Job must have done something dreadful to merit his distresses. Exactly how dreadful Eliphaz indicates by the use of the adjectives "empty" and "broken". "Empty" (7387) translates a word first used by Jacob in addressing his mean father-in-law:

> Except the God of my father, the God of Abraham, and the fear of Isaac, had been with me, surely thou hadst sent me away now empty [7387]. God hath seen mine affliction and the labour of my hands, and rebuked thee yesternight (Gen 31.42).

God's disapproval of the greedy, hypocritical Laban is evident in Jacob's implied rebuke. But both Jacob and Laban were shrewd, capable farmers, well able to defend themselves. In meeting Laban, Jacob only encountered another trickster like himself. Naomi, on the other hand, was a vulnerable widow, bereft of husband, sons and resources:

> I went out full, and the Lord hath brought me home again empty [7387]: why then call ye me Naomi, seeing the Lord hath testified against me, and the Almighty hath afflicted me? (Ruth 1.21).

It was such people that the local emir, possessed of property and wealth, was expected to assist. The fatherless, too, should have been the objects of his charity, but Job (according to Eliphaz) had treated them with gratuitous violence, leaving their arms "broken". This word (1792) is cutting in its suggestions of brute force and spite. Six of its eighteen occurrences are found in the book of Job, where it is translated in the KJV variously as "crushed" (4.19; 5.4), "destroyed" (6.9; 34.25), and "break in pieces" (19.2). Movingly, the same word appears in Isaiah's description of Messiah's atoning sufferings: "he was wounded for our transgressions, he was bruised [1792] for our iniquities: the chastisement of our peace was upon him; and with his stripes we are healed" (Is 53.5). The Son of God was Himself subjected to violence so that guilty sinners might be pardoned.

What, according to Eliphaz's fiction, Job failed to do as an Old Testament saint, remains the Christian believer's responsibility in a world suffering the consequences of human sin. James's definition of what he calls "pure religion" is challengingly direct: "Pure religion and undefiled before God and the Father is this, To visit the fatherless and widows in their affliction, and to keep himself unspotted from the world" (James 1.27). The combination of visitation for the purposes of practical relief, and separation from the defiling nature of a sinful world, prompts the believer towards a standard of conduct which finds its highest expression in the incarnate Son of God. He was tenderly kind to the widows and the fatherless, as exemplified in the remarkable miracle just outside the town of Nain (Lk 7.11-16) and, as our high priest, was ever "holy, harmless, undefiled, separate from sinners" (Heb 7.26) in the perfection of His earthly pathway.

Eliphaz's uncharitable suppositions about Job's guilt are entirely wide of the mark. We have as our evidence the unqualified commendation of the prologue (1.1) and, in Job's later riposte to these make-believe accusations, will encounter a convincingly detailed blow-by-blow repudiation of the charge-sheet (29.11-16). Eliphaz's moral sermon may well have been needed by many, but categorically not by Job. As is so often the case in this book, we are hearing right things said to the wrong person.

An Explanation of Job's Calamities: 22.10-11

Eliphaz proceeds to draw his deductions. Job is currently suffering under the disciplinary hand of God because of his social failures:

> Therefore snares are round about thee, and sudden fear troubleth thee; Or darkness, that thou canst not see, and floods of waters cover thee (22.10-11, JND).

The "Therefore" is the logical connective that handcuffs Job's calamities to Job's conduct. He is justly plagued by snares, fear, darkness, and floods of waters. The psalmist speaks in similar terms of the terrible judgments of God upon the wicked, those on whom "he shall rain snares, fire and brimstone, and an horrible tempest: this shall be the portion of their cup" (Ps 11.6). The "snare" is literally the animal trap (Ps 91.3; 124.7; Eccl 9.12), but is also used metaphorically of the malicious designs of evil men who delight in causing God's people to stumble (Ps 119.110; 140.5; 141.9; 142.3). Although obviously speaking about the divinely-ordained calamities which have befallen Job since chapter 1, Eliphaz is himself guilty of seeking to ensnare the patriarch. He aims to browbeat him into conforming to a false understanding of God's strategy. But Job will not surrender to the insistent clamourings of his friends.

If the "snare" is the trap itself, then "fear" describes Job's terrified reaction to his predicament. This word (6343) may be used positively of an intelligent reverence for the living God (Gen 31.42; 2 Chr 19.7), but here it relates to the horror experienced by a man suddenly and unexpectedly receiving the just reward of his misdeeds. Job used it of himself when he confessed that "the thing which I greatly feared [6343] is come upon me, and that which I was afraid of is come unto me" (3.25). As recently as the previous chapter he claimed that the houses of evil men were "safe from fear [6343], neither is the rod of God upon them" (21.9), but Eliphaz inverts this by cruelly pointing to Job's situation. It is the characteristic of wicked man that "there is no fear of God before his eyes" (Ps 36.1), but Job is introduced to the reader, using a different Hebrew verb, as a man who consistently "feared God" (1.1). He feared God, and yet he was not spared from catastrophe. Job was uniquely tested. Nevertheless, the gracious promise of God to the one who "dwelleth in the secret place of the most High" (Ps 91.1) remains true:

> Thou shalt not be afraid for the terror [6343] by night; nor for the arrow that flieth by day; Nor for the pestilence that walketh in darkness [2822]; nor for the destruction that wasteth at noonday (Ps 91.5-6).

It is worth noting that the psalm promises, not absolute immunity from trouble, but serenity within times of trouble. The terror, the arrow, the pestilence and the destruction are all very real. If the saint were snug within a cocoon of safety he would not even be aware of them. But it is Job who demonstrates the psalm's truth for, despite all the disasters that befall him (the terror, arrow, pestilence and destruction), he never abandons his confidence in God.

"Darkness" (2822), a word found twenty-three times in Job, can be used to describe absence of physical light (Gen 1.2; Job 38.19) or the spiritual and emotional depression of soul brought about by grief and affliction (12.25; 17.12; 19.8). Job will have to wait until the Lord intervenes in chapter 38 for his personal darkness to be dispelled, but the believer today may appropriate the guarantee that "thou wilt light my candle: the Lord my God will enlighten my darkness" (Ps 18.28). As we read the Scriptures – the written revelation of God denied to Job – our mind is illuminated so that we may walk in a manner worthy of Him, for

> Through thy precepts I get understanding: therefore I hate every false way. Thy word is a lamp unto my feet, and a light unto my path … The entrance of thy words giveth light; it giveth understanding unto the simple (Ps 119.104-5,130).

Only as we surrender daily to the teaching of God's Word can we be guided safely through the hidden minefield of this world.

Job's fourth punishment, according to Eliphaz, is floods of waters, a metaphor for the multiple disasters which have overwhelmed him. Jehovah uses the same phrase later in the book to point out Job's inability to summon the rain: "Canst thou lift up thy voice to the clouds, that abundance of waters may cover thee?" (38.34). This is the prerogative of deity for, as Jeremiah asks, "Are there any among the vanities of the Gentiles that can cause rain? or can the heavens give showers? art not thou he, O Lord our God? therefore we will wait upon thee: for thou hast made all these things" (Jer 14.22). Eliphaz will shortly refer to the historical inundation of Noah's cataclysm which devastated the entire world and etched itself into the collective memory of mankind, as witnessed in the flood mythologies with which ancient civilizations abound. But here he speaks primarily of the recent personal calamities which have shattered his friend.

There are times when the child of God finds himself engulfed with sorrows, when it seems as though snares, fear, darkness and floods have blotted out the light of the sun and extinguished any sense of the Lord's presence. That was Job's situation. We may be thankful that none of us will ever meet such a combined onslaught as that unleashed against him. For all his rash outspokenness, his response remains a model of faith in the dark. Faced with human misunderstanding and divine silence, he continued to rest in the God who, he was sure, could not fail to be true to Himself. Believers of this age have so many advantages. As Paul writes to the Ephesians, the Christian's course in the evil day is to dig in his heels and hold his ground:

> Wherefore take unto you the whole armour of God, that ye may be able to withstand in the evil day, and having done all, to stand. Stand therefore, having your loins girt about with truth, and having on the breastplate of righteousness (Eph 6.13-14).

When disaster strikes, we are to remember that because our God is sovereign He permits nothing contrary to His programme, and because He is loving all is organized by His wisdom for our spiritual benefit. Possessing the written assurance Job lacked, "we know that all things work together for good to them that love God, to them who are the called according to his purpose" (Rom 8.28).

An Exposition of Job's Sin: (ii) Impiety: 22.12-14

Eliphaz now supplements his catalogue of Job's supposed social failures with a spiritual one. Not only has Job been guilty of inhumane behaviour towards his fellow men, he has harboured irreverent thoughts of God. Eliphaz mentions the infinite distance between God and man in order to claim, without warrant, that Job's refusal to concede that the wicked are summarily punished implicitly denies God's thorough knowledge of His creatures:

> Is not God in the height of heaven? and behold the height of the stars, how high they are! And thou sayest, What doth God know? can he judge through the thick darkness? Thick clouds are a covering to him, that he seeth not; and he walketh in the circuit of heaven (22.12-14, RV).

According to Eliphaz, the fact of God's transcendence had blinded Job to God's omniscience.

Scripture teaches that God is infinitely elevated above His creatures. Instructed to build Jehovah a house in Jerusalem, Solomon was acutely aware that Israel's God was not like the petty deities of the neighbouring heathen, restricted to their locations and powerless beyond their confines. His prayer is a remarkable statement of theological precision: "But will God indeed dwell on the earth? behold, the heaven and heaven of heavens cannot contain thee; how much less this house that I have builded?" (1 Kings 8.27). Years later, the Syrians who invaded the northern kingdom foolishly assumed that Israel's "gods are gods of the hills; therefore they were stronger than we; but let us fight against them in the plain, and surely we shall be stronger than they" (1 Kings 20.23). They only displayed their ignorance in crediting Israel with a plurality of gods who were hamstrung outside their comfort zone. That was the hallmark of paganism. But the God of the Bible is of immeasurable, illimitable grandeur. That is why His ways with His people are beyond the capacity of our cramped minds to grasp. The unattainable heights of the heavens become the yardstick for His wisdom:

> For my thoughts are not your thoughts, neither are your ways my ways, saith the Lord. For as the heavens are higher than the earth, so are my ways higher than your ways, and my thoughts than your thoughts (Is 55.8-9).

Such a passage would have been a real solace to Job, for it would have offered him a thread through the labyrinth of his inexplicable misery. But Isaiah had not been written. All Job could do was cling on to what he knew of God.

Sinful men have commonly used the absence of obvious divine surveillance as an excuse for selfish indulgence. Because God is not visibly present overseeing them, they assume, like the ostrich with its head buried in the sand, that they cannot be detected in their wickedness:

> And they say, How doth God know? and is there knowledge in the most High? (Ps 73.11).

> Yet they say, The Lord shall not see, neither shall the God of Jacob regard it (Ps 94.7).

> Woe unto them that seek deep to hide their counsel from the Lord, and their works are in the dark, and they say, Who seeth us? and who knoweth us? (Is 29.15).

There is something sadly amusing about the damaged thinking processes of men who, denying the Creator, have only succeeded in sliding into foolishness, for "even as they did not like to retain God in their knowledge, God gave them over to a reprobate mind" (Rom 1.28). Those who boast most in their intellect often only display their spiritual witlessness.

God is indeed in the heights of heaven. He is the Creator of the stars (which, as Abraham learned in Genesis 22.17, are as numerous as the grains of sand on the sea shore), and yet is willing to enter into the most intimate personal relationship with those who humbly bow to His Word:

> For thus saith the high and lofty One that inhabiteth eternity, whose name is Holy; I dwell in the high and holy place, with him also that is of a contrite and humble spirit, to revive the spirit of the humble, and to revive the heart of the contrite ones ... to this man will I look, even to him that is poor and of a contrite spirit, and trembleth at my word (Is 57.15; 66.2).

In verses 13 and 14 Eliphaz puts words into Job's mouth. God is so high up that He cannot, or does not, concern Himself with the petty affairs of men. But this is to create a God in man's image. It is true that the higher man rises, the more diminutive and indistinguishable people on earth appear to be; one need only take an aeroplane trip to discover that height reduces sight. Not so for the God who is privy to the secrets of every human heart. As Jeremiah solemnly tells us:

> The heart is deceitful above all things, and desperately wicked: who can know it? I the Lord search the heart, I try the reins, even to give every man according to his ways, and according to the fruit of his doings (Jer 17.9-10).

The God who made men infallibly knows men. Distance and darkness are no hindrance to His perfect understanding for, confesses the psalmist,

> If I say, Surely the darkness shall cover me; even the night shall be light about me. Yea, the darkness hideth not from thee; but the night shineth as the day: the darkness and the light are both alike to thee (Ps 139.11-12).

Robinson reminds us that "God [is] higher than the highest star, yet nearer to both reader and writer than his nearest friend".[242] This assurance should bring comfort to the believer's soul.

But Job has never demonstrated such a gross misunderstanding of the living God as Eliphaz charges to his account. On the contrary, he has already testified to God's knowledge of every detail of his life (7.8,12,20; 10.7,14), and his constant resort to prayer affirms a settled conviction that God both hears and knows. Eliphaz is preaching to the converted.

The Evidence of History: 22.15-20

Having, to his own satisfaction, arraigned Job for the serious sins of inhumane behaviour and irreverence, Eliphaz now looks back to history for evidence of God's interventions in judgment. He is making the point that sinners do not get away with it.

He therefore asks Job, "Dost thou mark the ancient path which wicked men have trodden?" (22.15, JND). "Mark" (8104) is rendered "keep" in the RV, because the word, a very common one, has a range of meanings, including that of treading or following a pathway. David claims that "I have kept [8104] the ways of the Lord, and have not wickedly departed from my God" (2 Sam 22.22), which obviously signifies a loyal adherence to divine instructions. But Eliphaz implicitly accuses Job of following the trail blazed by evil-doers. Stick to that well-worn highway, says Eliphaz, and you'll end up facing the same terrible destiny.

Continuing a theme he introduced back in his first speech, that "they that plow iniquity, and sow wickedness, reap the same" (4.8), Eliphaz now offers a specific historical example to support his general assertion. He refers to the gross wickedness which corrupted the world before the flood. What happened to that generation?

[They] were carried off before the time, whose foundation was overflowed with a flood; Who said unto God, Depart from us! and what could the Almighty do to them? Yet he filled their houses with good. But the counsel of the wicked is far from me (22.16-18, JND).

Although the word Darby translates "flood" (5104) means basically a river or stream (as in Genesis 2.10 and 15.18), Eliphaz's historical context strongly suggests that he is thinking of the Noahic flood, that global inundation which extinguished all land life outside of the ark, sweeping away the foundations upon which men had built their security. Delitzsch writes of the people living then, that

> the ground on which they and their habitations stood was placed under water and floated away: without doubt the flood is intended; reference to this perfectly accords with the patriarchal pre-and extra-Israelitish standpoint of the book of Job; and the generation of the time of the flood … is accounted in the holy scriptures of the Old and New Testament as a paragon of godlessness.[243]

An entire generation was "snatched away before their time" (22.16, RV), cut off in the midst of their sins by devastating judgment. Like Eliphaz, the Lord Jesus also used the Genesis flood as an historical pattern of divine intervention which typified His own future return in glory, for

> as were the days of Noah, so shall be the coming of the Son of man. For as in those days which were before the flood they were eating and drinking, marrying and giving in marriage, until the day that Noah entered into the ark, and they knew not until the flood came, and took them all away; so shall be the coming of the Son of man (Mt 24.37-39, RV).

We should be in no doubt that the God who has in the past intervened so dramatically in human history to punish wickedness (and, we might add, left an earth whose surface is indelibly scarred with traces of that judgment) will do so again when the Lord Jesus Christ unleashes divine wrath against an intractably rebellious planet. But Eliphaz, wrongly, has Job in his sights. Without saying so directly, he is linking his old friend with the egregiously sinful men of Genesis chapter 6, of whom it is said that "every imagination of the thoughts of [their] heart was only evil continually" (Gen 6.5).

In verses 17 and 18 he deliberately quotes from Job's words in the previous chapter. Job had recounted the blasphemous disregard for God that characterises prosperous wicked men:

> they say unto God, Depart from us; for we desire not the knowledge of thy ways. What is the Almighty, that we should serve him? and what profit should we have, if we pray unto him? Lo, their good is not in their hand: the counsel of the wicked is far from me (21.14-16).

Back comes the language in Eliphaz's ironic citation: "[they] said unto God,

Depart from us! and what could the Almighty do to them? Yet he filled their houses with good. But the counsel of the wicked is far from me" (22.17-18, JND). While emphatically repudiating their philosophy of life, Job had claimed that such people did well in the world, even though they denied God. Eliphaz asserts the opposite: those who mocked God, whatever prosperity they may have once enjoyed, were suddenly destroyed by the flood He sent on a godless world. He also sarcastically parrots Job's earlier disclaimer of any personal adherence to godlessness – "but the counsel of the wicked is far from me" – as if to say, "you, Job have been found to be one of the wicked because of the evils you suffer, and yet you attempt hypocritically to distance yourself from their philosophy".

To remove any doubt that he is alluding to Job's terrible disasters at the start of the book, Eliphaz significantly alters the mode of divine judgment. In the time of Noah God had intervened with a deluge so that, in Peter's words, "the world that then was, being overflowed with water, perished" (2 Pet 3.6). But no water had been involved in the many blows which fell on Job. There had, however, been fire from above, for the sole surviving servant had reported that "The fire of God is fallen from heaven, and hath burned up the sheep, and the servants, and consumed them" (1.16). Accordingly, Eliphaz relates the reaction of the godly as they behold God's judgments in operation:

> The righteous see it, and are glad; and the innocent laugh them to scorn:
> Saying, Surely they that did rise up against us are cut off, and the remnant
> of them the fire hath consumed (22.19-20, RV).

The flood, we notice, is silently transmuted into fire, a fire which reminds us of Job's experience. The words put into the mouth of righteous people seem to identify them with two groups: the three friends who unanimously pronounce Job's sufferings a consequence of his sin, and the victims of Job's inhumanity and indifference, who speak of the wicked as "they that did rise against us". Job, we recall, has been pilloried as a man guilty of serious social ills.

There is no doubt that Eliphaz here employs language the Old Testament sometimes uses of the godly as they behold Jehovah's righteous response to human sin. The following quotations are representative:

> The righteous shall rejoice when he seeth the vengeance: he shall wash his
> feet in the blood of the wicked (Ps 58.10).

> As smoke is driven away, so drive them away: as wax melteth before the
> fire, so let the wicked perish at the presence of God. But let the righteous
> be glad; let them rejoice before God: yea, let them exceedingly rejoice (Ps
> 68.2-3).

> In the transgression of an evil man there is a snare: but the righteous doth
> sing and rejoice (Prov 29.6).

Nor is this response confined to the Old Testament. The book of Revelation unfolds in unambiguous clarity the future outpouring of divine wrath on a rebel planet, but always frames its accounts of judgment with outbursts of heavenly praise and worship. Here are the twenty-four elders rejoicing in God's works of retribution:

> We give thee thanks, O Lord God Almighty, which art, and wast, and art to come; because thou hast taken to thee thy great power, and hast reigned. And the nations were angry, and thy wrath is come, and the time of the dead, that they should be judged … and [thou] shouldest destroy them which destroy the earth (Rev 11.16-18).

Just before the final bowls of wrath are emptied out these are the words uttered by those who had resisted the temptation to take the mark of the beast:

> Great and marvellous are thy works, Lord God Almighty; just and true are thy ways, thou King of saints. Who shall not fear thee, O Lord, and glorify thy name? for thou only art holy: for all nations shall come and worship before thee; for thy judgments are made manifest (Rev 15.3-4).

Those who belong to a God who is both light and love gladly assent to His ways, whether in grace or in government, for what He does is always right. Judgment, especially meted out upon His own people, may be what Isaiah calls "his work, his strange work" (Is 28.21), but it is always righteous. In fact, one of the evidences of spiritual life in our souls is that we agree with God's verdict on man.

This does not mean, however, that we have the right to lick our lips in pleasure at the fate of the unsaved. Like Zophar before him, Eliphaz gives the impression that he looks at Job's trials with superior, self-righteous complacency. As always, the ideal example of faithfulness combined with compassion is the Lord Jesus. If anyone had the right to gloat over the impending destruction of Jerusalem, guilty of rejecting its promised Messiah, it was He. Instead, He wept aloud in the deepest grief:

> And when he was come near, he beheld the city, and wept over it, Saying, If thou hadst known, even thou, at least in this thy day, the things which belong unto thy peace! but now they are hid from thine eyes. For the days shall come upon thee, that thine enemies shall cast a trench about thee, and compass thee round, and keep thee in on every side, And shall lay thee even with the ground, and thy children within thee; and they shall not leave in thee one stone upon another; because thou knewest not the time of thy visitation (Lk 19.41-44).

Jonah, the most successful preacher in history, bitterly resented the salvation of repentant Gentiles in Nineveh; the Saviour, spurned by His own people, sorrowed over the hard-heartedness of Israel. Though it brings glory to God when His righteous judgment is displayed, it is never to be a cause for callous jubilation.

Ezekiel 24 announces in pictorial form the coming fall of Jerusalem and its temple because of the nation's sins, but the following chapter promises equally terrible judgments upon the surrounding countries (Ammon, Moab, Edom and Philistia) which thoughtlessly rejoiced in Judah's sufferings.

An Exhortation to Repentance: 22.21-30

There now begins one of the most moving and spiritually rich exhortations to repentance found anywhere in the Word of God. It is made all the more appealing by a poetically compelling presentation of the practical benefits to be enjoyed by the restored backslider. Eliphaz, who earlier compiled a catalogue of what he falsely imagined were Job's sins, is on much firmer ground in listing the steps to restoration and the advantages of returning to the Lord. He counsels reconciliation with God (22.21), receptiveness to His word (22.22), and the removal of anything which might have replaced God in his affections (22.23-25). This, he tells Job, will result in joy (22.26), fellowship (22.27-28), and the ability to intercede on behalf of others (22.29-30). The vital connection between Job's humble turning back to God and his future blessings is spelled out by the simple "if … then" construction:

> **If** thou return to the Almighty, thou shalt be built up, thou shalt put away iniquity far from thy tabernacles. **Then** shalt thou lay up gold as dust, and the gold of Ophir as the stones of the brooks (22.23-24).

Bible readers will not be unfamiliar with this formula. It highlights the condition of obedience upon which Israel was to enjoy material blessing in the land, and the necessity for diligence if we would truly grow in the knowledge of God:

> **If** ye walk in my statutes, and keep my commandments, and do them; **Then** I will give you rain in due season, and the land shall yield her increase, and the trees of the field shall yield their fruit (Lev 26.3-4).

> And it shall come to pass, **if** ye diligently hearken unto me, saith the Lord, to bring in no burden through the gates of this city on the sabbath day, but hallow the sabbath day, to do no work therein; **Then** shall there enter into the gates of this city kings and princes sitting upon the throne of David, riding in chariots and on horses, they, and their princes, the men of Judah, and the inhabitants of Jerusalem: and this city shall remain for ever (Jer 17.24-25).

> My son, **if** thou wilt receive my words, and hide my commandments with thee … **Then** shalt thou understand the fear of the Lord, and find the knowledge of God (Prov 2.1-5).

The first step in restoration is **reconciliation**. "Acquaint now thyself with him", urges Eliphaz (22.21). The word "Acquaint" (5532), not a common term, means "to *be familiar* with; by implication to *minister* to, *be serviceable* to" (Strong's

Concordance). It is used, for example, of Abishag who "cherished [5532] the king" in order to increase his warmth (1 Kings 1.4), and of the God who is "acquainted [5532] with all my ways" (Ps 139.3). Eliphaz has used it already when he asked, at the start of his speech, "Can a man be profitable [5532] unto God?" (22.2). But here the idea is of a close relationship. Delitzsch's rendering is happily modest in its vocabulary: "Make friends now with Him, so hast thou peace; Thereby good will come unto thee".[244] Equally direct is Darby's translation: "Reconcile thyself now with him, and be at peace: thereby good shall come unto thee" (22.21).

Wonderful benefits follow from being restored to living fellowship with God, summed up here as "peace" and "good". The Hebrew word for "be at peace" (7999) can sometimes carry the idea of making amends. In the KJV it is rendered, for example, "rewarded" (Gen 44.4), "make it good" (Ex 21.34), "restore" (Ex 22.1), "make restitution" (Ex 22.12). Paul teaches us that justification brings the believer into the enjoyment of peace with God, that is to say, a settled relationship where all hostilities have ceased, for "being justified by faith, we have peace with God through our Lord Jesus Christ" (Rom 5.1). But this is possible only because the finished work of Christ on the cross has made complete restitution to God, all the believing sinner's debts having been paid in full so that the guilty one now stands judicially acquitted. Peace with God, of course, is not to be understood as an armistice with a godless world; on the contrary, salvation places the believer instantly out of step with a system of values controlled by Satan. Hostilities with the world, the flesh and the devil only commence with salvation. But even the hatred of sinful men cannot disturb the fact that we have entered into a relationship of unchanging serenity with the Ruler of the universe.

Moreover, we bask in the sunshine of God's favour, for He organises the lives of His people so that "all things work together for good to them that love God" (Rom 8.28). Again, we must take note that the "good" towards which all things work is not to be confused with material success, for many saints are deprived of riches, health, and earthly comforts. Nevertheless they are, according to this promise, heading for a far greater good, which is "to be conformed to the image of his Son, that he might be the firstborn among many brethren" (Rom 8.29). God's great goal for the creation is the public exaltation of Christ, "that in all things he might have the preeminence" (Col 1.18).

The second step is **receptiveness** to God's Word (22.22). Without willing submission to the Word we cannot hope to enjoy any consciousness of divine blessing. Therefore Eliphaz counsels wisely: "Receive, I pray thee, instruction from his mouth, and lay up his words in thy heart. If thou return to the Almighty, thou shalt be built up" (22.22-23a, JND). Where the KJV translates "the law", which may mislead the reader into thinking of the Law of Moses, Darby renders "instruction", making allowance for the fact that the story of Job predates the calling of Israel. Nevertheless, men had information from and about God, oral revelation passed down from Adam to subsequent generations. Eliphaz knew what a man should do with that heritage of spiritual teaching: he should receive it as though it had come straight from God's mouth, and store it up in his heart, the command and control centre of his life. Similar language is used when God addresses Israel:

> And thou shalt love the Lord thy God with all thine heart, and with all thy soul, and with all thy might. And these words, which I command thee this day, shall be in thine heart: And thou shalt teach them diligently unto thy children (Deut 6.5-7).

What a man receives from God he is responsible to treasure up and pass on to others. The Lord Jesus quoted from Deuteronomy the solemn command that "Man shall not live by bread alone, but by every word that proceedeth out of the mouth of God" (Mt 4.4). All divine revelation, however mediated, is as authoritative as if God had audibly spoken from heaven. Much to his astonishment, Job will literally hear such a voice in the latter part of his book; but that is no longer the case today, nor is it necessary. The canon of Scripture being complete, the believer is shut up to God's written self-disclosure. Nonetheless, it remains true that the word needs to be assimilated and retained in our hearts. One of the marks of a real work of God in the soul is a child-like willingness to be taught from the Scriptures. He who has no appetite for the Word is probably not saved at all.

In his fascinating *Worthies of England*, first published in 1662, Fuller tells a fascinating story about Lawrence Chaderton, one of the translators of the King James Bible:

> He had a plain but effectual way of preaching. It happened that he visiting his friends, preached in this his native country, where the word of God (as in the days of Samuel) was very precious. And concluded his sermon, which was of two hours continuance at least, with words to this effect, "That he would no longer trespass upon their patience." Whereupon all the auditory cried out, (wonder not if hungry people craved more meat) "For God's sake, sir, go on." Hereat Mr Chaderton was surprised into a longer discourse.[245]

That certainly suggests a healthy appetite for the Word! We might recall the hunger displayed on the Day of Pentecost, when "they that gladly received his word were baptized: and the same day there were added unto them about three thousand souls" (Acts 2.41). Since "received" is used in Luke 8.40 of the crowds eagerly welcoming the Lord Jesus to the other side of the lake, we may assume that it implies genuine enthusiasm. We should not receive the Word of God with the same indifference or regret with which we receive a council tax demand or a gas bill. Jeremiah's experience is one to be emulated: "Thy words were found, and I did eat them; and thy word was unto me the joy and rejoicing of mine heart: for I am called by thy name, O Lord God of hosts" (Jer 15.16). God's word was found, eaten, and enjoyed – the enduring recipe for spiritual growth.

The third step is a determined **removal** from the life of what is wrong (22.23-25), with its consequent spiritual compensations. We should again take careful note of the encouraging "if ... then" construction:

> **If** thou return to the Almighty, thou shalt be built up. **If** thou remove unrighteousness far from thy tents, And put the precious ore with the dust, and the gold of Ophir among the stones of the torrents, **Then** the Almighty will be thy precious ore, and silver heaped up unto thee (22.23-25, JND).

A true return to the Lord involves a restoration of purloined goods. Eliphaz's language insinuates that Job has been guilty of theft or, at the very least, has placed his trust in riches: the abstract "unrighteousness" is equated with the concrete "precious ore" with which Job has crammed his house. He must get rid of it; in so doing he will find he has not lost, but gained.

When Paul preached in Ephesus, that notorious haunt of occult practices, the reality of salvation was demonstrated by a public abandonment of witchcraft:

> And many that believed came, and confessed, and shewed their deeds. Many of them also which used curious arts brought their books together, and burned them before all men: and they counted the price of them, and found it fifty thousand pieces of silver. So mightily grew the word of God and prevailed (Acts 19.18-20).

In the same way, the returning backslider will repudiate the sins which lured him from the Lord. In Job's case (so Eliphaz assumes) the insidious appeal of wealth led him astray. Get rid of that gold, that "precious ore" which has seduced your affections, he urges. Put it back in the ground from which it came, treat the precious metal as though it were in reality nothing but worthless dust, and you will discover that God Himself will become your real treasure. The word Darby translates as "precious ore" only appears in these two verses; the parallel constitutes a beautiful illustration of the way in which godliness brings its own reward. God Himself is His people's recompense. Abraham discovered this when, having refused the gifts offered him by a grateful King of Sodom, he heard the heartening words, "Fear not, Abram: I am thy shield, and thy exceeding great reward" (Gen 15.1). No man loses out by giving God His place, for "them that honour me I will honour, and they that despise me shall be lightly esteemed" (1 Sam 2.30).

The lesson is as pertinent as ever. In both Testaments the believer is exhorted to trust exclusively in the Lord.

> They that trust in their wealth, and boast themselves in the multitude of their riches; None of them can by any means redeem his brother, nor give to God a ransom for him (Ps 49.6-7).

> Thus saith the Lord, Let not the wise man glory in his wisdom, neither let the mighty man glory in his might, let not the rich man glory in his riches: But let him that glorieth glory in this, that he understandeth and knoweth

me, that I am the Lord (Jer 9.23-24).

Paul tells us to place our confidence not "in uncertain riches, but in the living God, who giveth us richly all things to enjoy" (1 Tim 6.17). Just as Jehovah graciously declared Himself to be the inheritance of the Levites, given no tribal allocation in Canaan (Deut 10.9), so God is the ultimate inheritance of His people today.

The results of genuine restoration are breath-taking. The first is unalloyed **gladness of soul**: "For then shalt thou have thy delight in the Almighty, and shalt lift up thy face unto God" (22.26). To return to the Lord in humility of heart is to find joy in the things of God. Instead of dejection of spirit, the weight of a guilty conscience, and the consciousness of unease in the presence of God (such as caused Adam and Eve to hide themselves among the trees of the garden), the repentant backslider enters into a spiritual satisfaction the world can never comprehend. True godliness is not sour-faced and grim; rather, it is that deep sensitivity to divine goodness which lightens the heart and irradiates the face. The message by which we are saved is called "the glorious gospel of the blessed God" (1 Tim 1.11). The *Jamieson, Fausset and Brown Commentary* makes the point that "the term, 'blessed,' indicates at once *immortality* and *supreme happiness*. The supremely blessed One is He from whom all blessedness flows". If God is supremely happy in providing salvation for helpless sinners, then certainly the beneficiaries of His love should rejoice "with joy unspeakable and full of glory" (1 Pet 1.8).

The second blessing is renewed **fellowship with God,** issuing in the experience of divine favour in daily life:

> Thou shalt make thy prayer unto him, and he shall hear thee, and thou shalt pay thy vows. Thou shalt also decree a thing, and it shall be established unto thee: and the light shall shine upon thy ways (22.27-28).

No longer at a distance, the restored backslider may be assured his prayers are heard, and therefore he will be able to pay the vows he promised as a response to answered petitions. Further, success will crown his plans, for "You will decide on a matter, and it will be established for you, and light will shine on your ways" (22.28, ESV). Like the blessed man of Psalm One, "his leaf also shall not wither; and whatsoever he doeth shall prosper" (Ps 1.3). It echoes the route to earthly prosperity offered by another psalm: "Delight thyself also in the Lord; and he shall give thee the desires of thine heart" (Ps 37.4). The language harmonises with the particularly but not exclusively earthly character of Israel's blessings. It remains true, however, that those whose hearts align with God's mind are bound to desire the things He longs to grant them. This is the secret of prayer: to bring our deceitful and rebellious hearts into harmony with the will of heaven.

The third blessing is **an ability to intercede** successfully on behalf of others (22.29-30). These verses have been interpreted in a variety of ways, as witnessed in the differences between the major translations.

The RV, ASV and JPS join to offer this rendering of verse 29: "When they cast thee down, thou shalt say, There is lifting up; and the humble person he shall save" (22.29, RV). Although ambiguous, this seems to focus the attention on Job himself as the man under affliction who, now humbly acknowledging his folly, sees a way out of misery into restored divine favour.

Other Bible versions (for example, the ESV and the ISV) recognise that the word for "lifting up" (1466) only appears three times in the Old Testament and, apart from this verse in Job, is translated "pride" (Job 33.17; Jer 13.17). Instead of describing the raising up of the humble man to prosperity, the verse may therefore be explaining why he fell into wretchedness in the first place. Here is the ESV: "For when they are humbled you say, 'It is because of pride'; but he saves the lowly" (22.29, ESV). Having trodden the same pathway, Job will be able to diagnose the failings of other men who succumb to pride.

Darby represents a viewpoint taken also by the KJV and the CEV:

> When they are made low, then thou shalt say, Rise up! and he shall save
> him that is of downcast eyes. Even him that is not innocent shall he deliver;
> yea, he shall be delivered by the pureness of thy hands (22.29-30, JND).

Delitzsch offers a similar rendering:

> If they are cast down, thou sayest, "Arise!"
> And him that hath low eyes He saveth.
> He shall rescue him who is not guiltless,
> And he is rescued by the purity of thy hands.[246]

The idea is this. When other men are cast down in mind by affliction or distress, the restored backslider (Job) will be able to minister to them by advocating an appropriate humility. It may be that James is thinking of this verse when he tells us that "God resisteth the proud, but giveth grace unto the humble" (James 4.6). Those who accept their humbling as from the Lord's hand, responding with contrite repentance, may as a consequence be raised up to blessing. But there is more. Because of his renewed fellowship with God, and with hands now cleansed from defilement, Job will be in an ideal position to intercede on behalf of the guilty ("him that is not innocent"), causing him to escape divine judgment.

This last view seems consistent with the idea that Job's spiritual renewal will be a gateway to blessing so tremendous that it will spread out to embrace others. It forms a fitting climax to Eliphaz's exhortation. The backslider who is the beneficiary of God's grace is best placed to encourage others into similar good. The experiences through which God leads us are aspects of His training programme to equip us to serve others in need. Paul's words to the Corinthian assembly are designed to give an insight into the purpose of the believer's trials. Speaking about his own intense sufferings in the cause of Christ, he writes:

Blessed be God, even the Father of our Lord Jesus Christ, the Father of mercies, and the God of all comfort; Who comforteth us in all our tribulation, that we may be able to comfort them which are in any trouble, by the comfort wherewith we ourselves are comforted of God (2 Cor 1.3-4).

Why do God's people suffer? We may divide trials into at least three kinds: the common sufferings of man in a fallen world (Gen 3.16-19; Job 5.6-7), such as illness, death, disappointment, reversal; corrective sufferings from God's hand for the discipline of His children (Heb 12.5-11; 1 Pet 2.20; 4.15); and distinctively Christian sufferings which befall believers because of their testimony for Christ in the scene of His rejection (Jn 15.18-21; 16.2-3,33; 1 Pet 4.16; 5.9). Dealing in 2 Corinthians 1 primarily with the last, Paul reveals the glorious aim ("that", v.4), which is to equip us to encourage others in like circumstances. Troubles are alleviated by the enjoyment of divine comfort which we in turn pass on. For the Christian, affliction can become the royal road to blessing (2 Cor 12.9).

Eliphaz's words form a grand culmination to his appeal for Job to admit his sins and cast himself on God's mercy. Look at the benefits, says Eliphaz – you'll be able to help those who fall into the same misery because of personal failure. Perhaps, despite everything he has said against the patriarch, he intuitively recognises that Job was the kind of man who loved helping those in need. Trouble is, at root it is all wrong: Job is *not* being punished for his sins. As Delitzsch writes,

Thus do even the holiest and truest words lose their value when they are not uttered at the right time, and the most brilliant sermon that exhorts to penitence remains without effect when it is prompted by pharisaic uncharitableness.[247]

Looked at in isolation from its context, Eliphaz's final message is packed with valuable spiritual instruction. Spurgeon, for example, delivered an encouraging sermon based on verse 26, reprinted in *The Suffering of Man and the Sovereignty of God*. Read as part of a coherent investigation of Job's sufferings, however, most of what Eliphaz says has little bearing on the case. Mere knowledge, however impressive and accurate, should not be mistaken for wisdom. The two are distinct: knowledge constitutes a storehouse of information; wisdom is the rare ability to use that information appropriately.

And yet, as we have already noticed, the unexpected by-product of the ignorance, dogmatism, and misunderstanding of Eliphaz and his colleagues is to drive Job all the more into the arms of a God whose ways he cannot comprehend but whose righteousness he cannot doubt. Friends fail but God remains eternally faithful.

Despite all that has been said about his basic misapprehension, Eliphaz touches on much that is profitable. What positive truths can we learn from his final words?

- Human virtue in no way increases God's felicity (22.3)
- Sin involves both the omission of the good as well as the practice of the

bad (22.6-7)
- Men are responsible to share the blessings God has given (22.6-7)
- The godly will protect the vulnerable (22.9)
- Divine transcendence does not neutralise divine omniscience (22.12-14)
- History shows that God can intervene in judgment as He pleases (22.15-16)
- The godly rejoice in God's judgments (22.19-20)
- True peace flows from being reconciled to God (22.21)
- Men are responsible to receive and heed God's word (22.22)
- Repentance involves the practical repudiation of evil (22.23)
- God Himself is His people's greatest treasure (22.25)
- Prayer is a precious blessing (22.27)
- Godliness promotes guidance in life (22.28)
- The restored backslider is able to help others (22.29).

Great lessons, indeed, but we should not miss the greatest irony in the speech. In his desire to coax his friend into repentance, Eliphaz rises to the generous promise that a restored Job would even be able to intercede on behalf of the guilty. Though he does not know it, he has, for once, hit the nail on the head. In chapter 42, under divine direction, Job will do just that for Eliphaz, Bildad and Zophar: "my servant Job shall pray for you: for him will I accept" (42.8). It will be a jaw-dropping fulfilment of Eliphaz's prediction, but not the one he anticipated.

SECTION 17
Dialogue: Job 4 – 42.6
Contest: Round 3: Job 22-31
Job's 7th Speech: Job 23-24

Job's response to Eliphaz's final appeal in chapter 22 is strangely oblique in the sense that he never once addresses either him or any of the friends directly as we might expect, but rather focuses his attention entirely on God. In many ways the speech is a kind of soliloquy in which Job articulates his deepest thoughts and feelings without reference to a specific audience.

The two chapters which make up this speech constitute two distinct sections of the monologue. In chapter 23 he considers with some bitterness the adversity unjustly endured by the guiltless (clearly a portrait of Job himself, as seen by the thirty-five or so first person pronouns). His language at the chapter's beginning and end leaves us in no doubt as to his distress. He speaks of "my complaint … my stroke" (23.2), and confesses that he is "troubled at his presence … [and] afraid of him. For God maketh my heart soft, and the Almighty troubleth me" (23.16). But his primary grievance is that he cannot get in touch with the God who is the source of his suffering. Yet whereas an innocent man, though wronged, can find no redress, it seems that the wicked thrive. Therefore in chapter 24 he moves on to examine the unaccountable prosperity enjoyed by the guilty, whether they are marauding brigands in the countryside or criminals in the city. This involves a longshot which takes in both rural and urban communities, alternating between glimpses of the villains and their victims. The chapters may be captioned thus:

   1. The Adversity Endured by the Guiltless: 23.1-17
   2. The Prosperity Enjoyed by the Guilty: 24.1-25.

Job will come to the same conclusion he has reached before – that there is no supporting evidence for his friends' theory that in this world the godless are promptly punished and the righteous vindicated. He goes further: it seems that, whether men are good or bad, they are all treated alike because, eventually, they all die (24.21-24). No special vengeance is reserved for the egregiously wicked.

Although the presence of the Lord pervades the entire speech – as can be seen by the thirty personal pronouns referring to Him in chapter 23 alone – God is mentioned by name only four times: 23.16 ("God … the Almighty"), 24.1 ("the Almighty") and 24.12 ("God"). As usual, Robinson concisely draws out the implications: "God [is] so familiar to Job's thoughts as to be spoken of without being named".[248] God is always the presiding object of Job's meditations, his instinctive recourse in times of trouble, the assumed audience of all his complaints. Even when grumbling, Job is God-centred. It would be well for every believer to bear in mind that, whether we address Him directly or not, God is the silent listener to every conversation and the infallible reader of all our unspoken thoughts.

The Adversity Endured by the Guiltless: 23.1-17

After a brief introduction (23.1-2), the first section of the speech breaks down into four paragraphs as Job graphically expresses his frustrations:

> 1. Job's Desire: 23.3-7
> 2. Job's Disappointment: 23.8-9
> 3. Job's Defence: 23.10-12
> 4. Job's Distress: 23.13-17.

The introduction is a candid admission of misery:

> Then Job answered and said, Even to day is my complaint bitter: my stroke is heavier than my groaning (23.1-2).

Although this prologue indicates that what follows is ostensibly an answer to Eliphaz, it is unusual because Job does not engage directly with his friend. Instead, he embarks on a monologue recounting his fruitless quest for God. He cannot contact the One who is responsible for his misery. The mood is signalled at the start: "Even to day is my complaint bitter: my stroke is heavier than my groaning" (23.2). The RV alters "bitter" to "rebellious", because the Hebrew word (4805) is thus translated in the vast majority of its occurrences in the Old Testament. For example,

> Rebellion [4805] is as the sin of witchcraft, and stubbornness is as iniquity and idolatry. Because thou hast rejected the word of the Lord, he hath also rejected thee from being king (1 Sam 15.23).

The ideas are linked: bitterness of spirit so often leads to active rebellion. Job is saying that his complaints against God are viewed by his friends as tantamount to an act of revolt, even though in reality the terrible load of suffering he has to bear ("my stroke" means effectively "the hand of God which has been laid upon me") far exceeds the cries of distress which have escaped his mouth.

By contrast, the ESV rendering ("Today also my complaint is bitter; my hand is heavy on account of my groaning") understands the second part of the verse to mean that he has to bite his tongue because of his excruciating pain. He is tempted to blurt out even more than he does. In Hartley's words, "His groanings, evoked by his agony, are so severe that he has to control himself with a heavy hand. His pain is pushing hard against the threshold of self-control".[249]

Whatever way the statement is read, it reveals the nagging anguish Job has endured perhaps for many days. On its own the verse is a testament to the patriarch's longstanding grief of body and mind, and we might expect it to herald a fresh lament. But it does not.

Job's Desire: 23.3-7

What Job laments is his alienation from God. His deep yearning, indeed the priority of his life, is to find God. He may have confessed the extremity of his physical torments in verse 2, but thereafter it is a spiritual bereavement which weighs heavily on his thoughts. This has been evidenced earlier in the debate: the greatest loss he feels is not the removal of property and family and health, but his estrangement from God. It is in chapter 9 that he first puts into words his frustration with God's inaccessibility:

> For he is not a man, as I am, that I should answer him, and we should come together in judgment. Neither is there any daysman betwixt us, that might lay his hand upon us both. Let him take his rod away from me, and let not his fear terrify me: Then would I speak, and not fear him; but it is not so with me (9.32-35).

It is a constant source of despondency that, despite all his longings, the way to God seems barred: "Surely I would speak to the Almighty, and I desire to reason with God" (13.3). The insistent silence of God in the face of his trials is Job's greatest affliction: "Oh that I knew where I might find him! that I might come even to his seat!" (23.3). He longs for converse, for communion, for comfort. Job would certainly have been able to identify with the confession of Asaph: "Whom have I in heaven but thee? and there is none upon earth that I desire beside thee. My flesh and my heart faileth: but God is the strength of my heart, and my portion for ever" (Ps 73.25-26). As we read the book we come to understand more and more why the Lord referred approvingly to Job as "my servant" (1.8).

Spurgeon agrees, making the point that Job's desire for God is the great proof of his genuineness:

> He wanted his God; he did not long to see Bildad, or Eliphaz, or Zophar, or any earthly friend; but his cry was "Oh, that I knew where I might find HIM!" ... This is one of the marks of a true child of God – that even when God smites him, he still longs for His presence . An ungodly man, if he has made any pretence of fellowship with God in his days of prosperity, forsakes Him as soon as adversity comes; but the true child of God clings to his Father however roughly He may deal with him ... This is the mark of our regeneration and adoption, - that, whatever happens, we still cling to our God.[250]

Job's earnest yearning is met with what, to him, appears to be persistent divine indifference. Hence his frustration: "Oh that I knew where I might find him!" Although the Christian believer may for a while be deprived of a sense of God's gracious nearness (and in His sovereign purposes God deals with His people in many and different ways) we would not use Job's precise language. Why not? Because we are informed in His Word of the exact location of our God, fully revealed as He has been in the incarnate Son. The faithful Israelite in Old Testament times had no doubts either, even when taunted by his heathen neighbours: "Wherefore should the heathen say, Where is now their God? But our God is in the heavens: he hath done whatsoever he hath pleased" (Ps 115.2-3). Jehovah might condescend to locate His earthly rule in Zion, but His eternal residence was in the heavens. Today our Saviour, the ascended Christ, is enthroned there at God's right hand, accessible to all His people at all times on the grounds of His completed atoning work, so that we have perpetual "boldness to enter into the holiest by the blood of Jesus" (Heb 10.19), and are freely able to approach "the throne of grace, that we may obtain mercy, and find grace to help in time of need" (Heb 4.16).

Still, God's tantalising unapproachability in Job's great hour of need in no way dampens his ardour. On the contrary, his spiritual desire is the more enflamed. It is in moments of personal crisis that what means most to us rises to the surface. In his final moments, the elderly priest Eli unexpectedly displayed a similar priority. As a judge he had lacked spiritual discernment, mistaking a godly, grief-stricken woman for a drunkard (1 Sam 1.13-14); as a father he had been a dismal failure, over many years indulging his sons' waywardness (1 Sam 2.29); as a priest he had been pointedly bypassed in favour of a small child when God wished to communicate His word (1 Sam 3.11-18). When, in due time, Israel was defeated in battle and his sons were slain according to God's solemn judgment message, the old man's heart broke. The biblical narrative is moving in its simplicity:

> And there ran a man of Benjamin out of the army, and came to Shiloh the same day with his clothes rent, and with earth upon his head. And when he came, lo, Eli sat upon a seat by the wayside watching: for his heart trembled for the ark of God. And when the man came into the city, and told it, all the city cried out. And when Eli heard the noise of the crying, he said, What meaneth the noise of this tumult? And the man came in hastily, and told Eli. Now Eli was ninety and eight years old; and his eyes were dim, that he could not see. And the man said unto Eli, I am he that came out of the army, and I fled to day out of the army. And he said, What is there done, my son? And the messenger answered and said, Israel is fled before the Philistines, and there hath been also a great slaughter among the people, and thy two sons also, Hophni and Phinehas, are dead, and the ark of God is taken. And it came to pass, when he made mention of the ark of God, that he fell from off the seat backward by the side of the gate, and his neck brake, and he died: for he was an old man, and heavy. And he had judged Israel forty years (1 Sam 4.12-18).

Baffled, blind and fearful, Eli waited for news from the front line. When it came, it could not have been worse. But we must not miss the main point: Eli's fatal sorrow sprang not so much from his personal bereavement as from the news that the ark had been captured. In the end his real affections were centred on the things of God. The man accused of honouring his sons above Jehovah died because, in the final analysis, he had a genuine heart for God's honour.

What became true of Eli only toward the close of his life, however, was constantly true in the case of Job for, as we know, he was God's showcase model of reverential fear (1.8). Nevertheless, his hunger for communion with his God went unanswered. In verses 4 to 7 he therefore envisages how wonderful it would be were God to respond to his entreaties and unveil His presence. We might note the irony that, in this wild flight of fancy to heaven's court where he would express his grievances before the King of the universe, Job credits himself with a freedom of speech which, in the event, completely deserts him. When Jehovah really speaks, Job is silenced (40.3-5; 42.1-6). His boldness right now is the result of sheer desperation: "I would order my cause before him, and fill my mouth with arguments. I would know the words which he would answer me, and understand what he would say unto me" (23.4-5).

To order one's cause is to arrange one's material methodically and appropriately. The verb "order" (6186) appears several times in the book, and is used earlier when Job says that "the terrors of God do set themselves in array [6186] against me" (6.4), and, anticipating his day in God's court-room, "I have ordered [6186] my cause; I know that I shall be justified" (13.18). Just as God has marshalled His forces against Job, so Job, like an astute lawyer, will organise his verbal opposition against God. Job claims that, when he stood before God to plead his cause, his briefcase would bulge with irrefutable arguments. The noun "arguments" (8433) is usually translated by words indicating disapproval or censure, words such as "reproof" or "rebuke"; only in its two appearances in Job is it treated differently, and translated "reasoning" (13.6) or "arguments" (23.4). This should not blind us to its generally critical character: Job plans to defend himself robustly with an array of rebuttals against what he sees as God's unjust treatment of him. Furthermore, he claims that on the trial day he would be enabled – the implication is that *God* would enable him – to comprehend anything the Almighty said. This is not an example of astounding arrogance but a deep-seated certainty that, come his day in court, he would at last be placed in a position to get his head round God's verdict. It signified little what men might say – his unsympathetic friends in particular – if only God were to speak. God's judgment was all that mattered. And, however much he might be perplexed *now*, it would all make sense to him *then*.

Job is confident that, standing before God, he would neither be overwhelmed nor shattered in the presence of the divine majesty: "Will he plead against me with his great power? No; but he would put strength in me" (23.6). Far from crushing Job with the invincibility of His omnipotence (the word translated "plead" in the KJV first appears in Genesis 26.20 to describe the local herdsmen of Gerar striving with Isaac's retainers), God would be favourable to His servant. The KJV phrase, "put strength in me", makes us think of God's contest with Jacob narrated in Genesis 32.24-31, an episode which reappears in Hosea 12.4, where we learn, amazingly, that the patriarch "had power over the angel". That is to say, God would empower Job to stand and speak where no mere mortal could possibly stand. We might recollect Daniel's bodily collapse in the presence of a heavenly visitor:

And, behold, one like the similitude of the sons of men touched my lips: then I opened my mouth, and spake, and said unto him that stood before

me, O my lord, by the vision my sorrows are turned upon me, and I have
retained no strength. For how can the servant of this my lord talk with
this my lord? for as for me, straightway there remained no strength in
me, neither is there breath left in me. Then there came again and touched
me one like the appearance of a man, and he strengthened me, And said,
O man greatly beloved, fear not: peace be unto thee, be strong, yea, be
strong. And when he had spoken unto me, I was strengthened, and said,
Let my lord speak; for thou hast strengthened me (Dan 10.16-19).

The greatly beloved man chosen by God to be the special recipient of prophetic
revelation could only endure that awe-inspiring experience with heavenly aid. In
His grace God continues to fortify His people despite their human weakness.
Paul tells us that, because "we know not what we should pray for as we ought ...
the Spirit [Himself] maketh intercession for us with groanings which cannot be
uttered" (Rom 8.26). The simplest spiritual exercise is totally beyond us because
it requires divine enablement; both reading the Scriptures and engaging in prayer
call for help from above.

But the RV renders the verse a little differently: "Would he contend with
me in the greatness of his power? Nay; but he would give heed unto me" (23.6,
RV). Here the idea is not the special impartation of strength but the willingness
of God to pay attention to Job's pleadings. His friends had taken little notice
of what he had been saying, obsessed as they were with defending their own
theology. But God at least would give him a courteous audience. Indeed, as Job
discovers when God eventually does speak, none of his utterances has escaped
the ear of the Almighty, for the Lord addresses him as one that "darkeneth
counsel by words without knowledge" (38.2). From beginning to end all Job's
words, as well as those of the friends (42.7), have been carefully registered in
heaven, "for the Lord heareth the poor, and despiseth not his prisoners" (Ps
69.33).

Were he able to approach God's throne, Job is confident he would feel at
liberty to state his case: "There would an upright [3477] man reason with him;
and I should be delivered for ever from my judge" (23.7, JND). Job looks forward
to his appearance before the Supreme Court, sure that the outcome would be
complete acquittal. Rather than accuse him, God would publicly acknowledge
his righteousness. Again, this is no example of brazen effrontery or shameless
immodesty but a simple statement of fact: Job, we know, is indeed an upright,
righteous (3477) man. The first three of the eight appearances of this word in the
book describe the protagonist without the slightest ambivalence (1.1,8; 2.3). He
is not, as we have noted before, claiming sinless perfection, but freedom from
any crime to account for the dreadful penalties meted out on him. The very fact
of his constant longing to draw near to God proves his blamelessness. In this he
anticipates the language of John's Gospel:

For every one that doeth evil hateth the light, neither cometh to the light,
lest his deeds should be reproved. But he that doeth truth cometh to the

light, that his deeds may be made manifest, that they are wrought in God (Jn 3.20-21).

The evildoer naturally shrinks from the light of exposure, but the genuine believer, whose good works are only brought about by the prior operation of God's grace, gladly draws near to the God he worships. Even though, in the event, the final revelation of Jehovah in chapters 38 to 42 will produce in righteous Job a stunned confession of utter worthlessness, there is never any thought in his heart of flight. Job always longs for fellowship with the God he loves. Like every genuine believer he knows instinctively that "it is good for me to draw near to God" (Ps 73.28).

Job's Disappointment: 23.8-9

The problem is, Job's eager anticipation of an opportunity to plead his case has not been granted. The heavens remain obdurately silent. His fond dream of a personal audience with the Creator tumbles to the ground in a reluctant admission that, wherever he has searched for God, he has been confronted with a blank wall. Of the language "forward … backward … on the left hand … on the right hand" (23.8-9), Zuck informs us that "these words suggested east, west, north and south, for directions in the ancient Near East were determined from the perspective of a person facing east".[251] It is as though Job has unsuccessfully scoured the world for the One he desperately desires to confront. But God's absence from all points of the compass is, of course, only illusory. Though Job cannot locate Him, He is there throughout His universe, as David well knew:

Whither shall I go from thy spirit? or whither shall I flee from thy presence? If I ascend up into heaven, thou art there: if I make my bed in hell, behold, thou art there. If I take the wings of the morning, and dwell in the uttermost parts of the sea; Even there shall thy hand lead me, and thy right hand shall hold me (Ps 139.7-10).

David thinks vertically (heaven and *sheol*) and horizontally ("the wings of the morning" speaks of the east, and "the uttermost parts of the sea" refers westwards to the Mediterranean); no matter which way he flees, God is there before him. Job too is not ignorant of unceasing divine activity; he confesses that God is at work in the north, and hides Himself in the south. The language of verse 9, "On the left hand, where he doth work, but I cannot behold him: he hideth himself on the right hand, that I cannot see him" (23.9), implicitly testifies to One ever moving in His universe. "Work" (6213) translates a very common verb which first appears in the creation account to describe the formation of the expanse of the heavens: "And God made [6213] the firmament, and divided the waters which were under the firmament from the waters which were above the firmament: and it was so" (Gen 1.7). Though, in the excellence of His ineffable glory, God is personally invisible, "for there shall no man see me, and live" (Ex 33.20), His marvellous handiwork is around for all to contemplate.

Back in chapter 9 Job had acknowledged God's omnipotence with a similar confession of His invisibility: "Lo, he goeth by me, and I see him not: he passeth on also, but I perceive him not" (9.11). But whereas the emphasis there was on the irresistibility of God's infinite power, the focus here is on His inaccessibility. Though he so urgently pushes for an audience with the Creator of the universe, it seems to Job that God is deliberately keeping Himself in the background.

The natural man is by nature blind to God's presence in history, but the spiritual man, in reading Scripture, has the privilege of a peep behind the scenes. Though, for example, the book of Esther never mentions His name, the hand of Jehovah is everywhere evident superintending the destiny of His imperilled people. What the unbeliever may dismiss as coincidence – the deposition of Vashti, the choice of Esther, the role of Mordecai in thwarting a palace coup, the king's unaccountable insomnia – the believer recognises as providence. We may go further. Not only does God arrange human events for His glory, He is in His essential splendour simultaneously present in every part of His universe, even though He may choose to make Himself specially known in particular ways and in specific places. Writes Robinson, "God's absolute presence [is] everywhere; His gracious manifested presence only as He is pleased to afford it".[252] Jacob's awe-struck confession that "the Lord is in this place; and I knew it not" (Gen 28.16) means that, while in His infinite immensity "the heaven and heaven of heavens cannot contain him" (2 Chr 2.6), in His grace He condescended to make Himself known at Bethel. More wondrously still, that same God tabernacled among men in the person of the incarnate Son (Jn 1.14), and will yet in the new universe make His residence permanently among His people. John the apostle had an advance glimpse of that long-expected day: "Behold, the tabernacle of God is with men, and he will dwell with them, and they shall be his people, and God himself shall be with them, and be their God" (Rev 21.3).

Job's Defence: 23.10-12

Despite his failure to find God or fathom His purpose, Job takes comfort in the thought that God is not ignorant of him. His assurance is marvellous in its simplicity: "But he knoweth the way that I take: when he hath tried me, I shall come forth as gold" (23.10).

The first part of the sentence is ambiguous. Young's Literal Translation gives an idea of the original: "For He hath known the way with me, He hath tried me – as gold I go forth". "The way with me" could refer either to "the way that I take", that is to say, Job's personal direction in life, or it could allude to God's current dealings with him. If the first, it means that the God who seems now to be evading Job nevertheless knows his integrity and will, in due course, vindicate him. If the second, it might be explained like this:

"He [God] knows [His] way with me." Because God knows what He is doing with Job, Job is coming to a point where he will be satisfied even if God never explains the reason for His strange conduct. Earlier Job had demanded to know why God was dealing with him thus, and he found his trial insufferable (7.18). Now he accepts the testing, because he knows: *I shall come forth as gold.*[253]

Either understanding of the verse would be doctrinally true. It is the profoundest of consolations for the believer to know that, when he cannot make out his own way, the Lord can. Robinson comments, "If in our trouble we cannot see God, it should be our comfort that God sees us, and knows all about us".[254] If, as is often the case in Scripture, the verb "know" extends beyond mere intellectual acquaintance to embrace the meaning of "approval", then Job's affirmation agrees with the psalmist: "the Lord knoweth the way of the righteous" (Ps 1.6). Whatever men might say, God fully knows each of His own. We can be sure that He will without fail accomplish His gracious purposes in His people.

The language of coming forth like gold draws on the imagery of the refining process. Poor Job was going through the fire of affliction, and he knew it. But, as Wiersbe puts it,

> When God puts His own people into the furnace, He keeps His eye on the clock and His hand on the thermostat. He knows how long and how much.[255]

The New Testament equivalent is found in Peter's first epistle, where the apostle encourages saints under persecution with the assurance that

> the trial of your faith, being much more precious than of gold that perisheth, though it be tried with fire, might be found unto praise and honour and glory at the appearing of Jesus Christ: Whom having not seen, ye love; in whom, though now ye see him not, yet believing, ye rejoice with joy unspeakable and full of glory (1 Pet 1.7-8).

At the same time the differences are as great as the similarities. Peter could look back to the first coming of Christ and forward to His second coming as the historical events which bookend the believer's pathway in this world, giving stability amidst the turbulence of earthly difficulties. What the Christian believer suffers is designed, in God's providence, to test and toughen his faith, faith which is far more valuable than the most precious of earthly commodities. Indeed, the hotter the furnace, the brighter the gold. Job knew nothing of Peter's privileged perspective, but nevertheless he rested on his limited grasp of God in the hope that the divine purpose, whatever it was, would be finally accomplished. Then the gold would shine bright. Hartley views this as a moment of tremendous significance in the book:

> Here Job's assurance that God is concerned with his well-being rises to its highest point. Job's use of the analogy of purifying gold for his own testing is another indication that the basic motivation behind the lament is the restoration of his own honour, not the restoration of his wealth … rather than owning the precious metal, Job longs for a golden character.[256]

Not surprisingly, Spurgeon waxes lyrical as he elaborates on the paradox that the fire, however hot, can never damage genuine gold:

> No gold is ever injured in the fire. Stoke the furnace as much as you may, let the blast be as strong as you will, thrust the ingot into the very centre of the white heat, let it lie in the very heart of the flame; pile on more fuel, let another blast torment the coals till they become most vehement with heat, yet the gold is losing nothing, it may even be gaining. If it had any alloy mingled with it, the alloy is separated from it by the fire, and to gain in purity is the greatest of gains. But the pure gold is not one drachma less; there is not a single particle of it that can be burnt. It is there still, all the better for the fiery trial to which it has been subjected.[257]

Rightly, he applies this lesson to the believer. Though it may bring short-term hurt, nothing that God puts His people through can ultimately harm them – rather, it enhances their brightness.

> "He knoweth the way that I take",
> Though His purpose we cannot unfold;
> Yet the furnace exposes the fake,
> While refining the godly as gold.
> When the pathway seems weary and worn
> May our confidence never grow dim,
> For our God, knowing all we have borne,
> Will reward us in glory with Him.

But as we shall see, Job's moods are still subject to considerable fluctuation. The confidence of verse 10 will soon give way to the dejection of verse 15. At this stage in his pilgrimage he cannot speak with a calm, unwavering assurance about the infallibility of the divine mind superintending his sufferings. After all, he was only half-way through the refining process.

Only when we reach the end of the journey will we have the opportunity to look back and see the reason for the route. The act of climbing a steep and treacherous hill makes it impossible to look around with safety as body and mind are concentrated on attaining the high ground, but once firmly settled on the pinnacle we can gaze back at the pathway which led to the peak. Securely exalted in Egypt and reunited with his perfidious but now repentant brothers, Joseph was able to marvel in retrospect at the divine purpose which had brought him to that position: "ye thought evil against me; but God meant it unto good, to bring to pass, as it is this day, to save much people alive" (Gen 50.20). But midway in his story even Joseph was perplexed. The psalmist offers an illuminating insight into his very real misery while languishing for years in an Egyptian prison: "They have afflicted with fetters his feet, Iron hath entered his soul" (Ps 105.18, YLT). If iron "entered the soul" of one already informed of coming glory, how much more did it fret the mind of a godly man who had none of Joseph's golden dreams.

Job now explains the reason for his confidence with a frank confession of piety:

> My foot hath held fast to his steps; his way have I kept, and turned not aside.
> I have not gone back from the commandment of his lips; I have treasured
> up the words of his mouth more than my necessary food (23.11-12, RV).

This personal testimony is constructed in the form of a chiastic sentence, which can best be seen by breaking it up into component parts:

(a) My foot hath held fast to his steps; his way have I kept,
    (b) And turned not aside.
    (b) I have not gone back from the commandment of his lips;
(a) I have treasured up the words of his mouth more than my necessary food.

The (a) sections consist of positive statements, while the (b) sections are negative. Job is affirming his loyalty to God in a two-fold way: he has done what is right, and he has avoided what is wrong. He also moves from his feet, which have kept to God's pathway, to his heart, where he has treasured up the divine words. We shall only walk in paths of righteousness if God's Word, which alone instructs in godly behaviour, has taken root in the centre of our being (Prov 4.23).

When Job says that his foot has "held fast" to His steps, he is using a word (270) which suggests a firm grasp. It is used of the ram "caught [270] in a thicket by his horns" (Gen 22.13) which Abraham offered instead of Isaac, and of Jacob's action at birth when "his hand took hold [270] on Esau's heel" (Gen 25.26). Although there might at times have been every temptation to deviate from the pathway of godliness, against all odds Job held firm. Like the psalmist who wrote, "Our heart is not turned back, neither have our steps declined [5186] from thy way" (Ps 44.18), Job has not "turned aside" (5186) or wandered from the right road. In chapter 31 he returns to this word in his final avowal of personal innocence:

> If my step hath turned [5186] out of the way, and mine heart walked after
> mine eyes, and if any blot hath cleaved to mine hands; Then let me sow,
> and let another eat; yea, let my offspring be rooted out (31.7-8).

Nor has he departed from God's commandments (4687). This noun is first used to describe the exemplary obedience of Abraham who "obeyed my voice, and kept my charge, my commandments [4687], my statutes, and my laws" (Gen 26.5). Even before the written law was entrusted to Moses as Israel's rule of life, God pronounced commandments for His people to obey. This helps us understand Job's situation. Like Abraham, he had no written code of conduct from heaven but was nonetheless aware of basic divine standards of behaviour. At the same time, while we have biblical evidence that God spoke personally to Abraham, directing his steps out of Ur towards the land of Canaan and establishing His unconditional covenant with the patriarch and his seed, we have no such data about Job. All we can do, therefore, is presume that the instructions God gave

Adam and Eve and the history of His dealings with them were handed down to subsequent generations, so that people like Job had a fundamental idea of the character and requirements of the Creator. This inherited knowledge of God, along with the testimony of conscience, is what Job describes as "the words of his mouth".

Obedience to the Creator has been paramount in Job's life, for His words have meant more to Job than "my necessary food". "Food" is italicised in the KJV because the phrase literally means "my allotted portion", whether referring to physical sustenance or personal inclinations. Darby renders it, "the purpose of my own heart". With impressive self-discipline, Job has placed God's commands above his bodily needs or his deepest desires. Likening God's word to nourishment is a common biblical testimony to its vital importance for the health of the soul:

> man doth not live by bread only, but by every word that proceedeth out of the mouth of the Lord doth man live (Deut 8.3).

> How sweet are thy words unto my taste! yea, sweeter than honey to my mouth! (Ps 119.103).

> Thy words were found, and I did eat them; and thy word was unto me the joy and rejoicing of mine heart: for I am called by thy name, O Lord God of hosts (Jer 15.16).

> As newborn babes, desire the sincere milk of the word, that ye may grow thereby (1 Pet 2.2).

In a time period before God's revelation was written down, Job simply had recourse to memorised oral history and instructions on which to feed his soul and by which to guide his life. Today we are privileged to have the completed canon of Scripture as our sure instruction manual, yet how few can claim (like Job) to be living in the good of what we know? Gaius is a positive New Testament example. The apostle John "rejoiced greatly, when the brethren came and testified of the truth that is in thee, even as thou walkest in the truth" (3 Jn v 3). The truth of God was in Gaius (residing in his heart and mind), but he also walked in truth, because it formed the yardstick for his lifestyle. That, in measure, is what Job is claiming for himself, and there is nothing in the divine record of his history to contradict his self-assessment.

Job's Distress: 23.13-17

From a plateau of serene confidence in God's knowledge of him Job suddenly plummets into a vale of grief. Despite a conviction of personal uprightness and integrity, Job is unable to read his current circumstances as anything other than evidence that God is against him. Nothing he can do or say will alter One who is all-powerful. He is innocent of any gross sin, yet he is being treated as though he were a criminal of the deepest dye. Eclipsed is his glad hope of coming forth like gold tried in the furnace. Although verse 13 stands as a condensed testimony to the unfailing power of God to accomplish His will, in context it is Job's bitter confession that, as far as he can understand, God is determined to prove him guilty:

> But he is in one mind, and who can turn him? And what his soul desireth, that will he do. For he will perform what is appointed for me; and many such things are with him (23.13-14, JND).

The sovereignty of God over every aspect of His universe is essential to any understanding of the divine programme, and its truth is affirmed throughout Scripture. Here are just a few samples from the Old Testament:

> But our God is in the heavens: he hath done whatsoever he hath pleased (Ps 115.3).

> Whatsoever the Lord pleased, that did he in heaven, and in earth, in the seas, and all deep places (Ps 135.6).

> I have spoken it, I will also bring it to pass; I have purposed it, I will also do it (Is 46.11).

> The Lord hath done that which he had devised; he hath fulfilled his word that he had commanded in the days of old (Lam 2.17).

> And the captain of the guard took Jeremiah, and said unto him, The Lord thy God hath pronounced this evil upon this place. Now the Lord hath brought it, and done according as he hath said (Jer 40.2-3).

> And all the inhabitants of the earth are reputed as nothing: and he doeth according to his will in the army of heaven, and among the inhabitants of the earth: and none can stay his hand, or say unto him, What doest thou? (Dan 4.35).

The last two passages are particularly impressive since they are the unexpected evidence of Gentiles who had seen something of Jehovah's irresistible power. The Babylonian captain had witnessed God's dealings with His backsliding people Israel, and Nebuchadnezzar had personally experienced God's chastening hand. What such a God elected to do, He did. Even Job used similar language earlier in his book: "Behold, he taketh away, who can hinder him? who will say unto him, What doest thou?" (9.12). The God of the Bible has never abdicated from supreme control of His universe and therefore effects His will without any possibility of failure.

But at this point in his pathway, the thought brings Job no sweetness. Even though his abstract statement of divine sovereignty (23.13) is coupled with an application relating the doctrine to his own circumstances (23.14), it affords no relief. Knowing that God will perform His plan for Job only fills him with the nightmarish dread that yet more calamities loom on the horizon. Because "many such things are with him", Job is bracing himself for the next display of divine malevolence. Delitzsch speaks of Job anticipating "the wondrously inventive hostility of God [which] can heap up ever new troubles for him".[258] For Job, the outlook seems bleak.

Let us turn, for contrast, to the language of David in one of his times of distress:

> Though the Lord be high, yet hath he respect unto the lowly: but the proud he knoweth afar off. Though I walk in the midst of trouble, thou wilt revive me: thou shalt stretch forth thine hand against the wrath of mine enemies, and thy right hand shall save me. The Lord will perfect that which concerneth me: thy mercy, O Lord, endureth for ever: forsake not the works of thine own hands (Ps 138.6-8).

David knew God was for him (Ps 56.9) and would "perfect that which concerneth me"; such a heart-warming assurance was hidden from Job. What made the difference? It was not that David was a better man but simply that he lived in a different era. David was able to rest in the revealed promises of God enshrined in the great covenant Jehovah had made with him concerning his house, his kingdom, and his throne (2 Sam 7.12-16). Job faced circumstances far grimmer than anything David suffered, and he had no heavenly pledges on which to rely. He had neither prophetic word nor written law. It is therefore all the more breath-taking that he could on occasion rise to a confidence – fluctuating and erratic as it was – in a God of infinite uprightness.

But at the present moment his thoughts are far from tranquil. Because God seems to be so set against him, he lives in a state of constant trepidation:

> Therefore am I troubled at his presence: when I consider, I am afraid of him. For God maketh my heart soft, and the Almighty troubleth me: Because I was not cut off before the darkness, neither hath he covered the darkness from my face (23.15-17).

Job is "troubled" (926) and "afraid" in God's presence – the former word (926) can also be rendered "afraid", as in Job 21.6 and Psalm 83.15 – just as Joseph's older brothers were uneasy as they stood before one they had so greatly wronged (Gen 45.3). The cause of his terror, however, is not the same. Joseph's brothers had a long-standing guilty conscience. Job, by contrast, has been persistently denying any consciousness of sin great enough to explain his afflictions. He is troubled because "the Almighty troubleth [926] me". The reason, in other words, lies not in himself but in God. Our reading of the prologue has shown his instinct to be correct. Satan may have been the tool God used in unleashing a battery of unexpected calamities on the patriarch, but God remained the initiator. Job has not retreated one inch from the great statements he made at the start: "the Lord gave, and the Lord hath taken away … shall we receive good at the hand of God, and shall we not receive evil?" (1.21; 2.10).

God has softened his heart, making it faint and feeble so that his courage melts away, unable to bear up under his insupportable load of grief. His particular regret is that he was not "cut off", that is to say, removed out of the world in death before the present darkness of sorrow engulfed him. Far from shielding him from the raging storm, God has, as it were, wilfully thrust him out into it. The language may reflect his memory of a recent unsympathetic comment from Eliphaz, that "darkness, that thou canst not see; and abundance of waters cover thee" (22.10-11). Job is, for the moment, back in something like the despondent mood of the early chapters where he wished he had never been born (3.11).

The Prosperity Enjoyed by the Guilty: 24.1-25
The darkness alluded to at the close of the previous chapter is not so much a metaphor for Job's intense sufferings as an emblem of his consciousness that God is no longer his benefactor and friend. This sense of loss is exacerbated by the realisation that, in the world around, those who live in defiance of God seem to escape judgment. Delitzsch presents the case well. It is, he writes,

> the thought that God stands forth in hostility against him, which makes his affliction so terrific, and doubly so in connection with the inalienable consciousness of his innocence. From the incomprehensible punishment which, without reason, is passing over him, he now again comes to speak of the incomprehensible connivance of God, which permits the godlessness of the world to go on unpunished.[259]

This forms the kick-start to chapter 24. Where is God when wickedness is rampant (24.1)? His friends have blithely assured him that divine retribution is everywhere visible, falling inexorably on evil men. In response, Job takes a tour of the country and the city, observing violent criminals and their hapless victims (24.2-17), and finally coming to an unsatisfactory conclusion: although God rarely intervenes immediately, He does eventually deal with sinners in the simple sense that wicked men, like the rest, die (24.18-25). This observation, as we shall see, is insufficient to offer the solution Job seeks. The paragraphs may be seen to run as follows:

> 1. The Silence of God: 24.1
> 2. The Suffering of Man: 24.2-17
> 3. The Solution to the Problem: 24.18-25.

The Silence of God: 24.1
Job has raised this question before. Back in chapter 9 he complained that "The earth is given into the hand of the wicked: he covereth the faces of the judges thereof; if not, where, and who is he?" (9.24). If the sovereign God is not responsible for the gross anomalies evident in the world – the innocent trampled

underfoot and the wicked triumphant – then who is? Here his challenge is even more direct: "Why are times not laid up by the Almighty? and why do not they which know him see his days?" (24.1, RV). The "times" (6256) to which he refers are those formal occasions of divine judgment when the Creator steps into history to punish the bad. The word is used in a similar way when Ezekiel the prophet announces the coming of God's vengeance on Gentile nations: "For the day is near, even the day of the Lord is near, a cloudy day; it shall be the time [6256] of the heathen" (Ezek 30.3). Job cannot understand why God does not instantly hold tribunal and deal with blatant injustice so that those who love Him might witness, with praise and thanksgiving, His "days" of righteous retribution. After all, He is the "Almighty", and there is no power in the universe that can stay His hand. Job's grievance is summarised by Davidson: "This is Job's complaint, that God the judge and ruler of the world fails to judge and rule it in righteousness. Men do not behold Him appointing times and holding days for doing judgment on wrong, and righting the oppressed".[260]

The problem is the more aggravated by Job's knowledge that God had so intervened in the past. The oral history of mankind recorded the deadly and pervasive consequences of Adam's sin (Gen 3.17), the judgment of the flood (Gen 6-8) – indeed the many legends of a global cataclysm bear witness in distorted form to the historicity of the event – and the confusion of tongues at the building of Babel (Gen 11.1-9). These spectacular irruptions of divine anger had left unambiguous traces upon the earth. The first imposed the death penalty on all mankind, while the second so radically altered the planet's surface that the world before the Noahic flood is described in the New Testament as "the world that then was", as opposed to "the heavens and the earth, which are now" (2 Pet 3.6-7). The reality of God's displeasure at the tower of Babel is still evidenced in the variety of languages which divide humanity.

Does written revelation offer an answer to Job's challenge? One response to his bewilderment at God's apparent indifference to the state of the world is the doctrine of divine longsuffering. Jehovah's gracious dealings with Israel form a record of astonishing patience under the provocation of human sinfulness. After the initial disclosure of this attribute to Moses in Exodus 34.6, where longsuffering appears as an essential ingredient of Jehovah's name, the lesson is reiterated in the law, the psalms and the prophets:

The Lord is longsuffering, and of great mercy, forgiving iniquity and transgression, and by no means clearing the guilty, visiting the iniquity of the fathers upon the children unto the third and fourth generation (Num 14.18).

But thou, O Lord, art a God full of compassion, and gracious, longsuffering, and plenteous in mercy and truth (Ps 86.15).

O Lord, thou knowest: remember me, and visit me, and revenge me of my persecutors; take me not away in thy longsuffering (Jer 15.15).

Presumably it was known in Job's time period that "the longsuffering of God waited in the days of Noah, while the ark was a preparing, wherein few, that is, eight souls were saved by water" (1 Pet 3.20), but this marvellous unfolding of the divine character was not indelibly inscribed until the law was written. The history of Israel, favoured but faithless, is one of the most convincing demonstrations of the longsuffering of God – but it was not available to Job.

With the coming of the New Testament, however, Paul relates God's longsuffering not simply to the chosen people but to mankind as a whole. There we learn of human culpability in the light of "the riches of his goodness and forbearance and longsuffering" (Rom 2.4), and discover that the work of Calvary is gloriously retroactive in declaring God's "righteousness for the remission of sins that are past, through the forbearance of God" (Rom 3.25). In reply to scoffers who mocked at the chronic inactivity of the heavens, the apostle Peter offers a sobering explanation: "The Lord is not slack concerning his promise, as some men count slackness; but is longsuffering to us-ward, not willing that any should perish, but that all should come to repentance" (2 Pet 3.9). Job, as we have seen, had no access to Israel's written law, nor could he anticipate the full disclosure of God's heart which came with the person of Christ. We should not be too surprised at his inability to understand God's patience with men.

Another answer to Job's problem is what might be called the doctrine of the divine strategy. That is to say, God has a predetermined programme which will be fulfilled only in His own good time. Divine judgment may appear to be deferred, but that does not mean it has been cancelled. As Peter writes immediately after his lesson in God's forbearance,

> the day of the Lord will come as a thief in the night; in the which the heavens shall pass away with a great noise, and the elements shall melt with fervent heat, the earth also and the works that are therein shall be burned up (2 Pet 3.10).

"The day of the Lord", the very moment for which Job longed, "will come". Then the living God of the universe will intervene, with devastating effect, in human history. Though the Old Testament has many glimpses of this period, especially in the writings of the prophets who predicted the coming and character of the "day of the Lord", the sequence of events is not clearly unfolded until chapters 6 to 20 of the book of Revelation. But when Job lived, such details had not been disclosed.

Truths unknown to Job are precious to us. If the knowledge of divine forbearance is of immense consolation to believers well acquainted with their daily failings, a grasp of God's strategy safeguards us against false expectations. Christians who look for instant bodily health in this age fail to understand that divine healing awaits the coming of the Lord Jesus, "who shall transform our body of humiliation into conformity to his body of glory, according to the working of the power which he has even to subdue all things to himself" (Phil 3.21, JND). Until that grand event, every generation of believers, just like the unsaved, will succumb to disease and death.

The Suffering of Man: 24.2-17

Job now assembles a body of data to prove that wickedness prevails both in the countryside (24.2-11) and in the city (24.12-17). In contrast to his friends, with their idyllic vision of a world where the righteous prospered and the unrighteous were summarily punished, Job paints a picture of wide-spread oppression and misery. To him, "God's administration of justice seems sporadic, partial, and inconsistent".[261] No matter where one looks, sin leaves its terrible mark.

Job starts by surveying the situation in the **countryside** (24.2-11). In considering the rural community, Job's attention alternates between the villains (24.2-4a, 9) and their innocent victims (24.4b-8, 10-11). The latter are described as "the fatherless", "the needy", "the poor" (24.3-4,9). But first he considers the bold perpetrators of injustice.

> Some remove the landmarks; they violently take away flocks, and feed thereof. They drive away the ass of the fatherless, they take the widow's ox for a pledge. They turn the needy out of the way (24.2-4a).

Job's words may well remind us of Eliphaz's recent unfounded accusation that "thou hast taken a pledge from thy brother for nought, and stripped the naked of their clothing … Thou hast sent widows away empty, and the arms of the fatherless have been broken" (22.6,9). Job agrees that such dreadful things are indeed being done, but not by him. Israel, on entering the Promised Land, was instructed not to remove "thy neighbour's landmark, which they of old time have set in thine inheritance" (Deut 19.14), because it was crucial for social harmony that property markers be accurately preserved. The *Jamieson, Fausset and Brown Commentary* points out that in the Middle East

> boundaries of arable fields are marked by nothing but by a little trench, a small cairn, or a single erect stone, placed at certain intervals. It is manifest that a dishonest person could easily fill the gutter with earth, or remove these stones a few feet without much risk of detection and so enlarge his own field by a stealthy encroachment on his neighbour's.

But avarice knows no bounds. Job lists three particular crimes: dishonest extension of estates, theft of livestock, and inhumane abuse of the poor. Greedy men sneakily enlarged their holdings, and appropriated by force other people's possessions. "Violently take away" (1497) translates a word which first appears when Abraham had to reprove Abimelech "because of a well of water, which Abimelech's servants had violently taken away [1497]" (Gen 21.25). It describes one of the lawless periods recorded in the book of Judges when "the men of Shechem … robbed [1497] all that came along that way by them" (Judg 9.25). It is also used of David's mighty man Benaiah who "slew an Egyptian, a goodly man: and the Egyptian had a spear in his hand; but he went down to him with a staff, and plucked [1497] the spear out of the Egyptian's hand, and slew him with his own spear" (2 Sam 23.21). The idea is one of forceful, irresistible seizure.

Not only do these people brazenly rob, they flaunt their spoil by openly pasturing their stolen flocks on stolen fields, so secure they are in their wrongdoing. Not surprisingly, such men lack any pity for the weakest members of society and have no compunction about plundering widows and orphans, deliberately depriving them of their means of livelihood. Their cruelty is summed up in verse 4a, which the ISV renders by the phrase, "They push the needy off the road". This snapshot of loutish discourtesy, with swaggering thugs elbowing the frail and elderly off the pathway, pictures a much greater and more extensive evil – that of wilfully taking advantage of the most vulnerable.

But then Job's attention shifts to the hapless victims of such violence. How do these people, bullied by their powerful neighbours, manage to survive in such a lawless environment?

> The poor of the earth hide themselves together. Behold, as wild asses in the desert they go forth to their work, seeking diligently for meat; the wilderness yieldeth them food for their children. They cut their provender in the field; and they glean the vintage of the wicked. They lie all night naked without clothing, and have no covering in the cold. They are wet with the showers of the mountains, and embrace the rock for want of a shelter (24.4b-8, RV).

Because the pronoun "they" is used in this passage without any specific identification, some translations, such as the KJV and Darby, assume that it continues to describe the brigands of verses 2-4a who prey on the poor. But it is much more likely that the phrase "the poor of the earth" (24.4b) governs the verses that follow, so that the camera shifts its attention away from the guilty to their innocent victims. Having spotlighted the evildoers, Job now concentrates on their prey. This is the viewpoint taken by the RV and the ESV. The contrast between persecutors and persecuted is very pointed for, as Hartley says, "while the poor must move about stealthily in fear for their own safety, the rich revel in luxury at the expense of those they oppress".[262] The needy, robbed of their possessions, have to "hide themselves" from their oppressors (the same word is used in the very different context of Adam and Eve concealing themselves from the Lord), desperately seeking employment and food to support their families. Reduced to the level of wild animals, they roam the inhospitable wilderness with no fixed abiding place, gratefully taking advantage of any shelter from the inclement elements they can find, and accepting whatever paid labour comes their way. It probably makes best sense to understand the phrase "they glean the vintage of the wicked" (24.6) as meaning that they find themselves obliged to slave for harsh and unsympathetic employers. Job paints a canvas of degradation, misery, helplessness and want. The "needy" (34) and the "poor" (6041) have little going for them.

The placing of Job just before Psalms in our Bible occasionally throws up some fascinating juxtapositions. The psalmist takes up the same words Job has used in order to look ahead to the blessings of the kingdom age, when the rightful

Davidic king will "deliver the needy [34] when he crieth; the poor [6041] also, and him that hath no helper" (Ps 72.12). Only when Christ reigns will there be an end to poverty, injustice, and inhumanity. But Job, we may assume, knew nothing of this grand expectation.

In the middle of his pathetic account of human suffering, he briefly returns to the oppressors as he speaks of those who callously "pluck the fatherless from the breast, and take a pledge of the poor" (24.9). Although the language may simply be a broad-brush if graphic metaphor for cold-hearted cruelty, Delitzsch suggests that it literally describes "inhuman creditors [who] take the fatherless and still tender orphan away from its mother, in order to bring it up as a slave, and so to obtain payment".[263] If this is the case, it makes sense of the passage to assume that those described in verses 10 and 11 are the slave-labour victims of the merciless creditors mentioned in verse 9: "These go naked without clothing, and, hungry, they bear the sheaf; They press out oil within their walls, they tread their winepresses, and suffer thirst" (24.10-11, JND). Lacking adequate food and clothing, they are forced to toil for taskmasters who even refuse to provide them with liquid refreshment. "Though labouring amidst the abundant harvest of their master they are faint with hunger themselves".[264] Hartley is correct to argue that "sapping a worker's strength without giving him any nourishment or allowing him a share in the joy of his toil is the height of inhumane labour practices".[265] The contrast between the benevolent labour relations enshrined in Israel's law and practised by Boaz in Bethlehem (Ruth 2.4-16), and the working conditions imposed by these people traffickers, could not be more marked.

We might pause to notice a poignant fact. Job's own sufferings have obviously made him acutely sensitive to the injuries of others. In contrast to his wholly unsympathetic friends, he has a heart deeply touched and troubled by human pain. For a moment he seems almost unmindful of his own sorrows as he responds to the distresses of the disadvantaged. When Shakespeare wants to dramatise ignorant pomp and splendour suddenly confronted with the reality of human misery in a fallen world, he drives King Lear out from the cosy shelter of his fastness onto a storm-swept heath. There the proud king learns how little he has done to remedy the ills of his people:

> Poor naked wretches, wheresoe'er you are,
> That bide the pelting of this pitiless storm,
> How shall your houseless heads and unfed sides,
> Your loop'd and window'd raggedness, defend you
> From seasons such as these? O, I have ta'en
> Too little care of this![266]

But Job is no Lear. He is a man "perfect and upright" (1.1), whose life has been devoted to providing for the poor and needy, as we shall see when we reach his final protestation of innocence in chapter 31. Nevertheless, it may be that one of the reasons God conducts His people through times of deep distress is that they might be the better equipped to sympathise with others in like condition.

Now, however, Job turns his attention to the crimes of the **city** (24.12-17). As before, he distinguishes between villains, specified here in the singular as "the murderer", "a thief", and "the adulterer" (24.14-15), and their victims, identified as "the poor and needy" (24.14).

Since the first city mentioned in Scripture was constructed by the murderer Cain (Gen 4.17), it is perhaps not surprising that the city should become a haunt of those who shed blood. The last Old Testament reference to the word is in Zechariah, where it describes Jerusalem pillaged by Gentiles just before the return of Christ in glory, an event which terminates a barbaric period of slaughter and sexual depravity when "the city shall be taken, and the houses rifled, and the women ravished" (Zech 14.2). It is therefore with relief that we turn to the Bible's final allusion to a city. Genesis starts with man in a garden, but Revelation concludes with a city of such beauty and moral perfection that it stretches the imagination to breaking point. Specifically excluded from this "holy city" are the very people who cause such havoc and misery in the city of Job's indictment: "But ... murderers, and whoremongers ... shall have their part in the lake which burneth with fire and brimstone: which is the second death" (Rev 21.8). Towards that holy, happy city the believer is heading.

In the present world, the outcry of those abused by human agency is loud but apparently unavailing:

> From out of the populous city men groan [5008], and the soul of the wounded [2491] crieth out: yet God imputeth it not for folly (24.12, RV).

The only other occurrence of the verb "groan" (5008) is found in Ezekiel, where it refers to Pharaoh's death rattle as he and his troops are massacred by the Babylonians. The verse is interesting because it also includes Job's word "wounded": "I will strengthen the arms of the king of Babylon, and put my sword in his hand: but I will break Pharaoh's arms, and he shall groan [5008] before him with the groanings of a deadly wounded [2491] man" (Ezek 30.24). The Hebrew adjective translated "wounded" first appears in the unsavoury story of Dinah and her vengeful brothers, where we read that "the sons of Jacob came upon the slain [2491], and spoiled the city, because they had defiled their sister" (Gen 34.27). Clearly the idea is not a minor scratch but a mortal wound. The city, Job asserts, is a place where men in their death throes groan in pain and scream for aid, but God does not interpose to deal with their oppressors. By His non-intervention He effectively charges no one with wrong-doing.

Who exactly are the people who engage in criminal activities in the city streets?

> They are of those that rebel against the light; they know not the ways thereof, nor abide in the paths thereof (24.13).

Job's description is both moral and literal: crime springs essentially from godlessness, from a rejection of the pathway of light and goodness, and tends often to take place under cover of night. It is the same whatever the culture. When, in *Oliver Twist*, a novel which leads us through the twisted and murky streets of vice-ridden London, Bill Sykes brutally murders the kind-hearted Nancy, Dickens pulls out all the stops to foreground the melodrama:

> Of all the bad deeds that, under cover of the darkness, had been committed within wide London's bounds since night hung over it, that was the worst. Of all the horrors that rose with an ill scent upon the morning air, that was the foulest and most cruel.[267]

What Dickens omits is the spiritual dimension of human wickedness. Job, however, offers a summary statement tracing sinful deeds to that spiritual and moral darkness which blinds men's minds to the requirements of a holy God. As Paul teaches the Roman believers, light and darkness are opposite principles of the spiritual world:

> The night is far spent, the day is at hand: let us therefore cast off the works of darkness, and let us put on the armour of light. Let us walk honestly, as in the day; not in rioting and drunkenness, not in chambering and wantonness, not in strife and envying (Rom 13.12-13).

Because sin is deep-rooted in man's heart, neither political programmes of moral education nor social improvements in living conditions can ever eradicate the desire to rob or kill. On the other hand, the believer in the Lord Jesus, having surrendered to Him who is "the light of the world", will gladly endeavour to walk in a manner worthy of his Saviour. Paul's exhortation to the Ephesian saints contrasts what they were by nature with what they are by grace:

> ye were once darkness, but now light in the Lord; walk as children of light, (for the fruit of the light is in all goodness and righteousness and truth,) proving what is agreeable to the Lord; and do not have fellowship with the unfruitful works of darkness, but rather also reprove them (Eph 5.8-11, JND).

It is an unmistakable signal of the genuine child of God that he seeks to steer away from a lifestyle which dishonours God.

Having traced urban criminality to its origin, Job cites three specific examples:

> The murderer riseth with the light, killeth the afflicted and needy, and in the night is as a thief. And the eye of the adulterer waiteth for the twilight, saying, No eye shall see me; and he putteth a covering on his face. In the dark they dig through houses; by day they shut themselves in (24.14-16a, JND).

The murderer, the adulterer, and the thief stand as the most serious representatives of the many sins of city life. The murderer (7523) follows in the blood-stained footsteps of Cain. Significantly, the word first occurs in the Ten Commandments: "Thou shalt not kill [7523]" (Ex 20.13). Such a man rises with the dawn so that he can lie in wait for solitary travellers, or those whose poverty requires them to leave early for their labour and make their way through still darkened streets. His activities in the obscurity link him with thieves who also ply their trade when men are most weary and least watchful.

The adulterer equally keeps a wary eye on the coming of dusk so that he can stealthily make his way to the place of his illicit assignation, his face veiled so as to prevent recognition. Again, the Hebrew word makes its first appearance in the law: "Thou shalt not commit adultery [5003]" (Ex 20.14). As the Proverb writer says, "whoso committeth adultery [5003] with a woman lacketh understanding: he that doeth it destroyeth his own soul" (Prov 6.32). Those who resist the light of divine instruction about the sanctity and perpetuity of the marriage relationship pursue short-term pleasure at the cost of terrible long-term loss. The blame is not always one-sided. Job casts his spotlight upon the predatory male, but the female may be equally guilty, as seen in the more expansive illustration recorded by the book of Proverbs, which again sets the episode in the shelter of dusk:

> And beheld among the simple ones, I discerned among the youths, a young man void of understanding, Passing through the street near her corner; and he went the way to her house, In the twilight, in the evening, in the black and dark night: And, behold, there met him a woman with the attire of an harlot, and subtil of heart. (She is loud and stubborn; her feet abide not in her house: Now is she without, now in the streets, and lieth in wait at every corner.) So she caught him, and kissed him, and with an impudent face said unto him, I have peace offerings with me; this day have I payed my vows. Therefore came I forth to meet thee, diligently to seek thy face, and I have found thee. I have decked my bed with coverings of tapestry, with carved works, with fine linen of Egypt. I have perfumed my bed with myrrh, aloes, and cinnamon. Come, let us take our fill of love until the morning: let us solace ourselves with loves. For the goodman is not at home, he is gone a long journey: He hath taken a bag of money with him, and will come home at the day appointed (Prov 7.7-20).

Whoever may be the instigator and whatever the provocation, adultery is wrong. The naïve optimism of the sinner is momentarily disclosed in Job's brief glimpse into his thinking processes: "No eye shall see me" (24.15). The Christian reader, of course, knows that the God who sets standards for human behaviour is privy to all that takes place in His universe, for "The eyes of the Lord are in every place, beholding the evil and the good" (Prov 15.3). Nevertheless, in the context of Job's argument – that God does not step in to uphold justice – it appears that He neither sees nor cares.

The third example is not named directly but appears to be the house breaker who, like his partners in crime, uses the dark to prosecute his burglarious enterprises.

The verb to "dig through" (2864) occurs in the account of Ezekiel's acted out parable of King Zedekiah's vain efforts to escape from besieged Jerusalem (Ezek 12.5). Though he tried to dig his way out of the city wall under cover of night he was still captured by the Babylonians. The word means to force one's way, and aptly describes the practices of the Middle Eastern criminal who craftily breaks through the sun-dried mud bricks with which most houses were constructed. The language of the Lord Jesus, advising His disciples not to store up their wealth in this world, assumes a similar environment where "thieves break through and steal" (Mt 6.19). If the home owner had known "in what watch the thief would come, he would have watched, and would not have suffered his house to be broken up" (Mt 24.43). The KJV translation of Job 24.16 suggests that the thief has been surveying his prospective target during daylight hours ("houses, which they had marked for themselves in the daytime"), but since the word "marked" (2856) means primarily to seal or close up it is more likely Job describes him cunningly lying low until dark for his own safety.

Job's three examples of city crime are, we may note, infringements of the fifth, sixth and seventh commandments recorded in Exodus 20. Though men like Job lived before the law was given we may assume that the creation principle of fidelity in marriage (Gen 2.24), the punishment inflicted on Cain (Gen 4.11-12), and the story of the fate – at the hands of Abram's private security force – which befell an invading coalition of kings who plundered Sodom (Gen 14), would have been handed down as a lesson in the folly of crime against one's fellow man.

Job's final word on such people is, like verse 13, another summary statement:

> they know not the light: For the morning is to them all as the shadow of death; for they are familiar with the terrors of the shadow of death (24.16b-17, JND).

These people shun any fellowship with light, which to them represents the dread possibility of detection and punishment. They are estranged from the God who is light, and furtively conduct their wicked occupations away from the blaze of publicity. The light of day, welcome to the majority of men, is to them a source of anxiety lest it lead to their betrayal. They are at home only in the darkness.

But we must not forget the introduction to this section. Verse 12 asserted that, despite all city crime, God appears indifferent. No one is charged. Delitzsch sums up Job's argument:

> Thus by their skill and contrivance they escape danger, and divine justice allows them to remain undiscovered and unpunished – a fact which is most incomprehensible.[268]

As might be expected in the conduct of an emotional debate, Job is wilfully exaggerating his case. Cities are not normally wholly given over to crime and injustice. Sodom was exceptional, lacking even ten righteous inhabitants, yet even there the environment must have been sufficiently attractive and secure for Lot's family to remain in their adopted home. But it is understandable that Job feels compelled to bolster his case with hyperbole in response to the equally over-inflated claims of his opponents.

Another observation might be made. Literary convention from classical times has, generally speaking, portrayed the countryside as an idyllic retreat of simple innocence, free from the contaminating evils of the corrupt city. The poet Shelley represents one side of that tradition, writing in 1819 about the ills of the English capital:

> Hell is a city much like London –
> A populous and a smoky city;
> There all sorts of people are undone,
> And there is little or no fun done;
> Small justice shown, and still less pity.[269]

Job, however, weighs both locations in the balance, country and city, and finds them wanting. His point is a devastating indictment of mankind as a whole: there is no place on earth free from the deleterious effects of human sinfulness for, to use the language of the apostle John, "the whole world lieth in the evil one" (1 Jn 5.19, RV).

The Solution to the Problem: 24.18-25

Now follows one of those troublesome sections of Job, a passage which at first sight appears to contradict everything the patriarch has been saying. His basic contention, in contrast to his friends, is that God does not seem to intervene directly in judgment on the wickedness of man (24.1,12). How then are we to understand verses 18 to 20?

> He is swift upon the face of the waters; their portion is cursed in the earth: he turneth not by the way of the vineyards. Drought and heat consume the snow waters: so doth Sheol those which have sinned. The womb shall forget him; the worm shall feed sweetly on him; he shall be no more remembered: and unrighteousness shall be broken as a tree (24.18-20, RV).

This sounds remarkably like the kind of argument adduced by the friends, that the wicked man is speedily dispatched. Perhaps a paraphrase of the language will make clear what Job is saying. He (the wicked man) is quickly swept away like flimsy debris on the surface of the waters, the property he leaves behind is treated as worthless, and he is no longer able to visit his estates and land holdings. Just as heat evaporates snow waters, so *sheol*, the place of departed spirits, gobbles up sinners, for in death they all descend into its depths. The evil man's mother will forget him, the worms in the grave will feast on him, and he will be lost to human memory. Like a tree uprooted by savage winds, the wicked man will be cut down. The lexical collocation of "tree" (6086) and "broken" (7665) is not common, but a parallel in the Psalms is interesting: "He smote their vines also and their fig trees; and brake [7665] the trees [6086] of their coasts" (Ps 105.33). What God's destructive hail did to Egypt's plantations, God does to the sinner.

Now, that sounds like a description of severe judgment. But Job's invariable contention is that wicked men seem to get away with it. Is this then an example of his inconsistency?

It is important to remember that the greater part of this book is dialogue; that is to say, we are given an inspired account of the words of the disputants, without any disclosure of important non-verbal signals of meaning (tone of voice, bodily gestures, pace and pause) which add so much to the accuracy and subtlety of communication. Electronic mailing, which purports to bring people closer together, simultaneously prizes them apart because of its easy susceptibility to misunderstanding. Texts, emails and other screen-restricted messaging systems lack the amazing versatility of the human voice. Doubtless Job and his friends have accompanied their speeches with the dramatic gestures which we know, from other parts of Scripture, were the cultural conventions of the east. We have already observed how they regularly refer to one another's words, making to and fro connections in a determination to expose the folly of the other's argument. It is therefore perfectly possible that Job is here offering a précis of the friends' viewpoint – presenting it, of course, with an audible coating of mockery – before he counters it with his own opinion.

This is the perspective of the ESV, which introduces verses 18 to 20 with the editorial insertion, "You say". This announces that Job is sarcastically using his friends' arguments against them. In other words, Job is turning on his audience and saying, Now, you insist that criminals are swiftly executed by God's intervention, leaving no trace. But is that really the case? Although there is no basis in the Hebrew text for the additional words, it has to be admitted that, for example, back in chapter 21.17-18 Job quoted the opinion of Bildad with a thick layer of irony. The *Jamieson, Fausset and Brown Commentary* supports this understanding of the passage, as does Davidson's commentary. It is a derisive summary of the popular creed with its dogma of instant retribution, after which Job presents the hard reality (24.21-24).

Another, and perhaps more plausible, way of understanding the paragraph is to take the language at its face value and acknowledge that, while Job, goaded by his discomfort, often launches into hyperbole, he is in fact a wise man fully aware that God remains the judge of all the earth. Here is Zuck's caution: "Job never said the wicked do not suffer. Instead, Job said that both the righteous and the wicked suffer, and both prosper".[270] Hartley argues that it is "not correct to assume that because Job questions God's method of governing, he puts aside all belief in retributive punishment".[271] Delitzsch takes a similar tack. That is to say, Job acknowledges that even though divine judgment is rarely immediate, in the long run it is inevitable for the simple reason that all wicked men finally perish.

This involves the consequence that, in the meantime, there appears to be little practical difference between the earthly lot of the godly and the ungodly. The wicked do indeed eventually die, depart into *sheol*, leaving little trace behind them. But then so too do the godly. The evil man carries out his career of crime, and then he dies. Yet how unsatisfying is this fate, with gross violators of the Creator's standards slipping smoothly into eternity after a lifetime of open and unpunished sin! Job's gaze reverts to the base villainy of the kind of men he has been describing. Again, it is their wilful cruelty towards the destitute that particularly kindles his anger:

> He devoureth the barren that beareth not; and doeth not good to the widow.
> He draweth away the mighty also by his power: he riseth up, and no man
> is sure of life. God giveth them to be in security, and they rest thereon; and
> his eyes are upon their ways. They are exalted; yet a little while, and they are
> gone; yea, they are brought low, they are taken out of the way as all other,
> and are cut off as the tops of the ears of corn (24.21-24, RV).

The evil man abuses the helpless ("the barren ... the widow"), and even manages to manipulate the more powerful members of society to his advantage. He "draweth away" (4900) the mighty with far greater success than Job would enjoy in a fishing expedition against Leviathan: "Canst thou draw out [4900] leviathan with an hook?" (41.1). Once he rises up (the word is first used of Cain rising up against his brother), no one can be assured of safety. From top to bottom of the social ladder he holds sway in his violence. The frightening thing is that God, who knows all about the wicked because they are constantly under His surveillance, permits such people to live out their life in earthly security. They have their time of glory in this world, which in the final analysis is fleeting ("yet a little while"), and then they are gone, just like everybody else.

Job's verbs in verse 24 offer an insight into the reality of death. He brings home the brevity of life by balancing the single word "exalted" (describing the sinner's earthly experience) against four synonyms for death: "gone [369] ... brought low [4355] ... taken out of the way [7092] ... cut off [5243]". The first term, very common in the Old Testament, is used of the world before Adam was placed upon it, when "there was not [369] a man to till the ground" (Gen 2.5), and of the removal of Enoch who "was not [369]; for God took him" (Gen 5.24). It is traceable to "a primitive root meaning to be nothing or not exist" (Brown, Driver and Briggs). The second only appears twice elsewhere:

> Many times did he deliver them; but they provoked him with their counsel,
> and were brought low [4355] for their iniquity (Ps 106.43).

> By much slothfulness the building decayeth [4355]; and through idleness
> of the hands the house droppeth through (Eccl 10.18).

Like impudent Israel receiving the reward of its folly, and like a building that crumbles because of lack of maintenance, so the wicked man is brought into death. The third word is also rare (Brown, Driver and Briggs define the meaning as "to draw together, close, shut, shut up, stop up") but some translations link it to the final image of the cornfield, rendering it "gathered up" (JND and ESV). The last verb turns up in three other places, and always in the context of death:

> He cometh forth like a flower, and is cut down [5243]: he fleeth also as a shadow, and continueth not (14.2).

> His roots shall be dried up beneath, and above shall his branch be cut off [5243] (18.16).

> For they shall soon be cut down [5243] like the grass, and wither as the green herb (Ps 37.2).

In the first example, Job is describing the common lot of mankind, while in the second Bildad pronounces the fate of the specifically wicked man. The psalmist likewise deals with the destiny of evildoers.

This takes us to the kernel of the issue. The fact that the same harvest imagery is used both of men in general (Job 14.2) and of wicked men in particular (Job 18.16; Ps 37.2) only underlines Job's niggling anxiety about God's government of the world. It would appear that "the wicked are exalted, rise high in life, and suddenly, with no pain, they die … It is a natural death that overtakes them, like that of all others. … they are cut off like the tops of the ears of corn, not prematurely, but having attained to full ripeness".[272] To Job this seems grossly unfair. Here is a man guilty of all kinds of infamy, and yet he dies "as all other", just like everybody else. He is not seen to receive the "due reward" of his deeds. Good men prosper; bad men prosper; good men fall ill and die; bad men fall ill and die. So where is God's justice? His position, writes Robinson, is "the same as Asaph, that the ungodly often live long and prosper in this world, and are without any 'bands in their death', though [they are] ultimately brought to judgment".[273]

Job's final word is to ask if anyone dare deny what he affirms: "And if it be not so now, who will prove me a liar, and make my speech nothing worth?" (24.25, RV). His challenge is not addressed to the friends; rather, it is a cry to the heavens, which have remained stubbornly silent throughout a speech insistently and unrepentantly questioning the ways of God.

Job has a real point. In a world under the curse there is, generally speaking, no unambiguous evidence of the solemn judgment of God against specific acts of human sinfulness, apart from the Adamic death penalty which falls indiscriminately on all alike. One could argue that some men suffer an outstandingly "bad death"; clearly the robber alongside the Lord Jesus believed he and his fellow criminal were receiving, in the horrific agonies of crucifixion, what they deserved (Lk 23.41). But then, good men have been crucified too.

Because of his time period, Job had no ability to look beyond physical death to the eternal dimension of human existence, which is "now made manifest by the appearing of our Saviour Jesus Christ, who hath abolished death, and hath brought life and immortality to light through the gospel" (2 Tim 1.10). The coming of Christ has, for the believer, swept aside the veil of obscurity so that every child of God rejoices in the hope of resurrection. Then, and not before, he will be kitted out everlastingly with a glorious body suited to the New Jerusalem, his final home. But the Lord Jesus also frankly revealed, for the first time, the full condition of the wicked for eternity in a place where "their worm dieth not, and the fire is not quenched" (Mk 9.44). The last verse of Isaiah's prophecy chillingly previews the place, but the Lord Jesus brings home the deadly peril of going there. It is John's vision of a Great White Throne, where men are raised and judged specifically according to the infallible record of their works, which finally answers Job's anger that the godless escape their due reward:

> And I saw a great white throne, and him that sat on it, from whose face the earth and the heaven fled away; and there was found no place for them. And I saw the dead, small and great, stand before God; and the books were opened: and another book was opened, which is the book of life: and the dead were judged out of those things which were written in the books, according to their works. And the sea gave up the dead which were in it; and death and hell delivered up the dead which were in them: and they were judged every man according to their works. And death and hell were cast into the lake of fire. This is the second death (Rev 20.11-14).

SECTION 18
Dialogue: Job 4 – 42.6
Contest: Round 3: Job 22-31
Bildad's 3rd Speech: Job 25

Bildad the Shuhite's final contribution to the Job debate, a mere six verses, is
the most attenuated speech in the entire book. As a result some commentators,
apparently embarrassed by its brevity, have sought to pad it out with additions.
This they do by arbitrarily picking out sections from Job's concluding defence in
chapters 26 to 31, sections they deem inconsistent with Job's general stance in the
discussion, and reallocating them to Bildad. Hartley, for example, pronounces
chapter 25 "far too short",[274] and suggests that verses 13 to 23 of chapter 27
originally formed part of Bildad's final word, while Davidson opts for verses 5 to
13 of chapter 26.

It is, however, safest to take the text as it stands. In any case, on what grounds
can a reader decide that some part of God's Word is of insufficient length?
Measuring it according to our theological standards or literary tastes is pure
subjectivism. No man can sit in judgment on Scripture: rather, God's Word
assesses *us*. As the Lord Jesus said to those in the nation of Israel who had no
time for Him, "He that rejecteth me, and receiveth not my words, hath one that
judgeth him: the word that I have spoken, the same shall judge him in the last
day" (Jn 12.48). Instead of rearranging the text to suit his fancies, the reader
with a due respect for the face-value of Scripture will seek a contextual reason
for the conspicuous abridgement of this chapter. And there is an appropriate
explanation. As the debate has progressed, it has become increasingly obvious
that, while Job has steadily grown in verbal strength and moral confidence, his
opponents have gradually run out of steam. Their speeches have become shorter,
and his longer. Taken in the context of the controversy as a whole, then, Bildad's
impoverished words fittingly dramatise the failure of any of Job's friends to
answer his questions or relieve his afflictions. In the same way the complete
non-participation of Zophar in Round Three is satisfactorily accounted for:
if Bildad runs dry, Zophar (already shown to be the least fluent of the three
speakers) is rendered wholly dumb. They lapse into a humiliated silence,
whereas in chapters 26 to 31 Job rises to his most extensive, rhetorically poised,
and spiritually assured self-defence. The contrast between Bildad's pitiful six
verses and Job's one hundred and sixty-one speaks for itself.

At the same time, although the shortness of the speech testifies to Bildad's
inability to pull anything new out of the bag – and we shall see that his entire
approach is derivative – we must not suppose that his intelligence has been
neutralised. We might not wish to go so far as Robinson, who generously sums
up the chapter as "true in its statements, just in its sentiments, sublime in its
poetry",[275] but we may nonetheless admit that Bildad retains all the rhetorical
powers of an eastern sage, able to organise his words with oratorical polish. The
speech is a carefully crafted chiastic stanza:

Then answered Bildad the Shuhite, and said,

(a)   Dominion and fear are with him, he maketh peace in his high places.

    (b)   Is there any number of his armies? and upon whom doth not his
          light arise?

        (c)   How then can man be justified with God? or how can he
             be clean that is born of a woman?

    (b)   Behold even to the moon, and it shineth not; yea, the stars are
          not pure in his sight.

(a)   How much less man, that is a worm? and the son of man, which is a
     worm? (25.1-6)

The central idea (c) which holds the stanza together is the sheer impossibility
of man being right with God. God is far too great and man far too grimy. The (a)
sections set up the dizzying contrast between God's supreme exaltation "in his high
places" and man's degradation on earth as "a worm". The (b) sections parallel aspects
of the divine majesty: the heavenly host is as innumerable as the all-searching light
of God is unavoidable (v.3), and yet the same celestial bodies which to us appear
so brilliant against their backcloth possess no intrinsic purity but are merely the
products of almighty power (v.5). Compared with His ineffable excellence they, for
all their apparent brightness, are polluted. How much more is man!

All this is designed to counter Job's persistent championing of his innocence, and
his longing to stand before God to be cleared of all the charges his friends have filed
against him. Bildad is outraged that Job presumes to maintain that "there [in God's
courtroom] would an upright man reason with him; and I should be delivered for
ever from my judge" (23.7, JND). This appears to be the only point from Job's
protest in the previous two chapters that Bildad bothers to address. The rest of Job's
argument, especially his analysis of the way good and bad alike suffer distressingly
similar experiences in this world, he entirely overlooks. Convinced that Job, with
his claim to be "an upright man", needs to be brought low by a theological lesson in
the overwhelming splendour of the divine majesty, Bildad reasserts God's greatness
and man's guiltiness. Delitzsch tellingly reduces the argument to two standard ideas:

> Bildad only repeats the two commonplaces, that man cannot possibly
> maintain his supposedly perverted right before God, the all-just and all-
> controlling One, to whom, even in heaven above, all things cheerfully
> submit, and that man cannot possibly be accounted spotlessly pure, and
> consequently exalted above all punishment before Him, the most holy
> One, before whom even the brightest stars do not appear absolutely pure.[276]

Because God is so pure, man cannot but deserve judgment; because God is so powerful, man cannot possibly evade judgment. We have been here before. The old line of argument has in fact been completely exhausted, because Bildad is simply rehashing the original position of Eliphaz. Right at the start he insisted that God is both powerful (4.9-11) and pure (4.18-21), while frail man can be crushed like a moth (4.19). In common with his colleagues, Bildad is guilty of arguing dogmatically on the basis of insufficient data. What he says is true, but it is not the whole truth, either about God, who is merciful as well as powerful (James 5.11), or man, who is dignified by his creatorial position in the universe even though damaged by sin (Heb 2.6-9). Furthermore, like Eliphaz and Zophar in their turn, Bildad is compromised by a callously insensitive attitude towards a man bruised by crippling blows.

The chapter may be broken up into its three main ideas:

> 1. God is Powerful: 25.2-3
> 2. God is Pure: 25.5
> 3. Man is Puny: 25.4,6.

God is Powerful: 25.2-3

God is possessed of absolute dominion (4910) over the entire universe, provoking the utmost dread in those conscious of His authority. Having the strength to quell any opposition in the heights of the heavens, God can certainly put down the feeble resistance of men. This doctrine pervades the Old Testament, providing stability for God's people Israel and offering a constant theme for national praise:

> Thine, O Lord, is the greatness, and the power, and the glory, and the victory, and the majesty: for all that is in the heaven and in the earth is thine; thine is the kingdom, O Lord, and thou art exalted as head above all. Both riches and honour come of thee, and thou reignest [4910] over all; and in thine hand is power and might; and in thine hand it is to make great, and to give strength unto all (1 Chr 29.11-12).

Bildad's word "fear" is certainly the right response to God's excellence. Jacob goes so far as to use the word as a title for the God of his ancestors when he says to Laban, "Except the God of my father, the God of Abraham, and the fear of Isaac, had been with me, surely thou hadst sent me away now empty" (Gen 31.42). God was the "fear" of Isaac in the sense that He uniquely was the One Isaac reverenced and worshipped. This God is so infinite in His power that He is the great peace-maker of the heavens, whether we think of Him calming atmospheric storms or presiding with indisputable sovereignty over the celestial beings who surround His throne. Bildad's rhetorical questions implicitly maintain that God's hosts are as incalculable in their numbers as His global influence is inescapable.

Jehovah instructed Israel to look above to gain some sense of His incomparable majesty:

To whom then will ye liken me, or shall I be equal? saith the Holy One. Lift up your eyes on high, and behold who hath created these things, that bringeth out their host by number: he calleth them all by names by the greatness of his might, for that he is strong in power; not one faileth (Is 40.25-26).

It is still fitting that believers gaze upwards to marvel at God's wondrous handiwork, for "the invisible things of him from the creation of the world are clearly seen" (Rom 1.20). The universe, with its hosts (whether of stars or angels), is a dazzling testimony to divine power. The angels, we know, men are not normally permitted to see, but Daniel's privileged vision of God as the Ancient of days gave him a glimpse of the myriads that make up His heavenly courtiers:

A fiery stream issued and came forth from before him: thousand thousands ministered unto him, and ten thousand times ten thousand stood before him (Dan 7.10).

God's entourage stretches into infinity, and His light illuminates every part of His dominion. When Bildad asserts that this light shines on all, he is referring not so much to the light of His essential being as to His indisputable sway over all His creatures.

As far as he goes, Bildad is correct. The God of the Bible is gloriously omnipotent and all-embracing in His power. The day to come, when demonic hordes and human armies mobilize in desperate coalition against the return of Christ in messianic splendour, will be the predetermined day of their eternal defeat. John's viewpoint in the book of Revelation allows him to see satanic energy working at full blast, while he is simultaneously aware that behind it all the hand of God is accomplishing His purposes of judgment:

the spirits of devils, working miracles ... go forth unto the kings of the earth and of the whole world, to gather them to the battle of that great day of God Almighty ... And he [God] gathered them together into a place called in the Hebrew tongue Armageddon (Rev 16.14-16).

The armies of the world are called together by demonic influence (v.14), but they are also assembled by the power of God (v.16). Those who incline to accept a textual reading in verse 16 which once again traces the gathering force to demons ("they gathered them", RV; "they assembled them", ESV) need only turn to Zechariah 14.2 to have the matter clarified. There the voice of Jehovah unambiguously announces His climactic interference in the affairs of men: "I will gather all nations against Jerusalem to battle". The book of Job starts by giving us the inside information that Satan cannot move a muscle without a divine say-so; and this remains true until the passing of the present heavens and earth.

However, although no reader can object to Bildad's testimony to God's mightiness, it has to be admitted that he is simply parroting what Eliphaz said earlier about One who "doeth great things and unsearchable; marvellous things without number" (5.9). Further, as Wiersbe justly comments, "knowing a few facts about the creation of God is not the same as knowing truths about the God of creation".[277] Job has nowhere challenged this doctrinal commonplace. Bildad's pennyworth adds nothing to the progress of the discussion. Indeed, Job already knows far more than Bildad about His works; where he has sought help, to no avail, is in comprehending God's mysterious ways.

God is Pure: 25.5

Omnipotence is not the sum total of the divine attributes. He who is all-powerful is also all-holy in His being. Bildad considers the moon and the stars as glittering representatives of the vast created universe, so awe-inspiring from the vantage point of earth, yet tainted in comparison with the moral magnificence of divine holiness. The parade of the galaxies seems fascinatingly endless in its breath-taking splendour, but it is as nothing compared with the infinite majesty of God Himself. That "The heavens declare the glory of God; and the firmament sheweth his handywork" (Ps 19.1) indicates that their function is to honour God; nonetheless, they all fall short of His excellence. The point behind Bildad's words is patent: he aims to reduce man in general – and Job in particular – to insignificance. Hartley summarises it like this:

> Even though the moon and the stars, members of God's heavenly army, appear so bright to mankind, they have no innate purity that gives them any position with God. They too must serve Him out of contrition and unworthiness. If this is true of these marvellous heavenly bodies, how much more true is it of mankind?[278]

We can agree with this assessment of God's ineffable purity. According to Isaiah, the refrain "Holy, holy, holy, is the Lord of hosts: the whole earth is full of his glory" (Is 6.3), is the perpetual testimony of the seraphim standing before the throne. But again Bildad is simply aping Eliphaz. He started off the debate by asking the question, "Shall mortal man be more just than God? shall a man be more pure than his maker? Behold, he put no trust in his servants; and his angels he charged with folly" (4.17-18). His second speech trod similar ground, throwing up some of the very terms Bildad borrows in order to expose human fragility and failure:

> What is man, that he should be clean? and he which is born of a woman, that he should be righteous? Behold, he putteth no trust in his saints; yea, the heavens are not clean in his sight. How much more abominable and filthy is man, which drinketh iniquity like water? (15.14-16).

Bildad is saying nothing that has not been said before, and the paucity of his words betrays his discomfiture at being unable to develop the case against Job.

Man is Puny: 25.4,6

In these verses Bildad turns his whole attention to humanity. His two descriptions of man in verses 4 and 6, designed to put Job in his place, draw on contrasting viewpoints. He is first of all "man" (582), frail, mortal and weak (25.4). It is the word used by the psalmist to suggest human transience:

> For he knoweth our frame; he remembereth that we are dust. As for man [582], his days are as grass: as a flower of the field, so he flourisheth (Ps 103.14-15).

But he is also "born of a woman" and therefore heir to inherited sin and guilt, for we read that "Adam lived an hundred and thirty years, and begat a son in his own likeness, after his image" (Gen 5.3). The death penalty Adam acquired through rebellion against God he passed on to his children. Though the first word ("man") may legitimately define Adam after his act of disobedience, the second descriptive phrase has to be limited to his descendants, for the simple fact that Adam was not "born of a woman". Nevertheless, he is responsible for the sinful condition of those who are, for "by one man sin entered into the world, and death by sin; and so death passed upon all men, for that all have sinned" (Rom 5.12). In verse 6 "man" (582) is paralleled with "son of man [120]", where the second word is basically the name Adam, reminding the reader of his physical constituents, made out of the common red dust of the earth. Bildad is referring back to the first man Adam ("man" in verses 4a and 6a) and all his children ("he … that is born of a woman", and "the son of man", in verses 4b and 6b).

But Bildad also introduces a disparaging metaphor, teaming up two words for worm (25.6). If the heavenly bodies, the moon and stars, are impure in God's sight, "How much less man, that is a worm [7415]? and the son of man, which is a worm [8438]?" (25.6) Bildad's first noun (7415) appears seven times in the Old Testament, of which five are in Job. It is first used literally of the worms which bred in manna kept past its use-by date (Ex 16.24); but thereafter it is a metaphorical term suggestive of human feebleness and mortality (Job 7.5; 17.14; 21.26; 24.20; 25.6; Is 14.11). The second word (8438) appears forty-three times, of which by far the majority of occasions are rendered "scarlet", as in Exodus 25.3-4, or (once) "crimson" (Is 1.18). Cansdale informs us that

> colours were seldom named accurately in ancient languages. Scholars have suggested that the need for a full and precise vocabulary had not yet arisen and that such colours as were recognised took their names from the materials providing them … the insect from which this dye was prepared belongs to the Coccidae, the Scale Insects and Mealy Bugs. This family includes several other dye-producers, e.g., the cochineal insect and lac insect of India (from which came the name crimson lake) … All these insects are small, about the size of Aphids, or plant-lice, to which they are related, and this may suggest that the basic meaning of *tole'ah* [8438] is a very small grub.[279]

This word is used of the tiny bug which ate up Jonah's gourd (Jonah 4.7), and figuratively describes Israel's national insignificance in the eyes of hostile Gentiles:

> Fear not, thou worm Jacob, and ye men of Israel; I will help thee, saith the Lord, and thy redeemer, the Holy One of Israel (Is 41.14).

Perhaps most interestingly, it is the word used by David in a moment of utter dereliction. At that time, unbeknown to himself, he prefigured the Messiah in His future humiliation, despised and rejected of men, oppressed by Satan, and forsaken by His God: "But I am a worm [8438], and no man; a reproach of men, and despised of the people" (Ps 22.6). In diminishing man to the level of a humble worm, Bildad unintentionally reminds the Christian reader of the riches of God's grace which caused the eternal Son to take on Himself spotless humanity that He might redeem sinners. As Robinson says, "the Son of God became a worm with man, to make worms sons of God with Himself".[280] Bildad's intention of course, is far narrower. His message is this: if God is so infinitely great in power, and so dazzlingly spotless in His holiness, how can any mortal man possibly call His ways into question, as Job presumes to do?

As we have seen before, Job's friends, though often misguided in their aim and imperfect in their knowledge, can certainly articulate solid truths which have real value for Christian believers. For example, Bildad draws attention to four great doctrinal facts:

- The unopposable power of God (25.2)
- The unsullied light of divine holiness (25.3,5)
- The creaturely frailty of man (25.6)
- The congenital sinfulness of Adam's descendants (25.4).

Yes, the living God is almighty and ineffably holy, whereas man is both frail and corrupted by sin. But the speaker is too coolly clinical in his analysis. His bleak language, entirely lacking in warmth or sympathy, resembles the academically logical propositions of a textbook systematic theology. And yet Bildad, with his two associates, has travelled a distance with the purpose of offering comfort to the beleaguered Job! Cold comfort, this. Bringing the comprehensive light of completed revelation to bear on these concepts adds a cordial tenderness entirely absent from Bildad's austere summary. For example, we now know that the ability of God to make "peace in his high places" (25.2) goes far beyond Bildad's limited understanding. The New Testament unveils a grand strategy whereby He has made peace for guilty sinners "through the blood of his [Christ's] cross, by him to reconcile all things unto himself; by him, I say, whether they be things in earth, or things in heaven" (Col 1.20). A sin-damaged universe will be gloriously restored by Christ on the basis of His atoning death, for He is the great peacemaker.

But even reading Bildad's words in the context of his own understandably restricted knowledge-base highlights a failure to do justice to the breadth of what

God had revealed to early generations of mankind. For example, in his efforts to reduce Job to a sense of his nothingness, he conspicuously omits any mention of the original dominion mandate with which God entrusted man. Man may be dust as far as his physical constitution is concerned, but he was made uniquely in God's image and given special dignity:

> And God said, Let us make man in our image, after our likeness: and let them have dominion over the fish of the sea, and over the fowl of the air, and over the cattle, and over all the earth, and over every creeping thing that creepeth upon the earth. So God created man in his own image, in the image of God created he him; male and female created he them. And God blessed them, and God said unto them, Be fruitful, and multiply, and replenish the earth, and subdue it: and have dominion over the fish of the sea, and over the fowl of the air, and over every living thing that moveth upon the earth (Gen 1.26-28).

Further, man's inexcusable sinfulness has been graciously provided for. Immediately after Adam's disobedience, God first of all promised the coming of a deliverer who would Himself be man, and then illustrated the results of His deliverance in the coats of skin with which He covered human nakedness (Gen 3.15,21). All these facts would have been handed down as part of the original information Adam and Eve bequeathed their descendants – and yet Bildad, obsessed with mankind's degradation, is completely silent about them. It is pardonable to be ignorant of what has not yet been revealed; but it is inexcusable to proffer a deliberately skewed account of God's dealings with creatures He made to relate uniquely to Himself. All too often, in order to address a particular problem, the Bible teacher may succumb to the temptation to misrepresent the broad witness of Scripture. But when we handle the Word of God we must endeavour at all costs to be scrupulously accurate. It does no honour to Him and no good to men if we twist Scripture to suit our predilections.

We may contrast Bildad's bilious view of man with that of the psalmist. In answer to a query about the nature of humanity in the context of a vast cosmos, the latter refers back to the authoritative Genesis creation account:

> What is man, that thou art mindful of him? and the son of man, that thou visitest him? For thou hast made him a little lower than the angels, and hast crowned him with glory and honour. Thou madest him to have dominion over the works of thy hands; thou hast put all things under his feet (Ps 8.4-6).

The Genesis narrative gives the indispensable inspired background. For all Bildad's fulminations, men are far more than worms.

Despite his genuine reverence, Bildad, anxious to humiliate Job, ironically treads close to the errors of modern secular humanism. Thinking, wrongly, that the more he degrades Job the more he magnifies God, Bildad offers a warped vision of humanity which is ultimately self-defeating. Evolutionary mythology, with its not-so-hidden agenda of banishing the Creator God of the Bible from His universe, wilfully demeans man by reducing him to the accidental outcome of random events over billions of years. But that only undermines the very person who propounds the argument, for who can take seriously the speculations of those who, on their own admission, are descended from jumped-up pond scum? Bildad, of course, is no supporter of the folly of atheism, but his virulent attack on human dignity equally rebounds on his own head, for in reviling Job he reduces himself and diminishes the entire debate to a quarrel between maggots.

Only a rigorously scriptural worldview offers a correct, comprehensive view of humanity. Created directly, deliberately and uniquely in the image of God to rule the earth, man, though damaged body and soul by his inherited and personal sinfulness, may be restored to a relationship with God through the perfect man, the Lord Jesus Christ, whose sacrificial death has satisfied all God's righteous demands. We may go still further. In the Lord Jesus, "the second man ... the Lord from heaven" (1 Cor 15.47), the whole of God's grand purpose for the creation will ultimately and unfailingly be fulfilled.

Although C S Lewis is best known for his children's stories, he also penned some effective poems. One of these is a cheekily satirical hymn in mock praise of evolutionary theory. Christians will recognise a distorted version of "Lead us, heavenly Father, lead us" in the following tongue-in-cheek parody, which beautifully sums up the futility of a materialistic world-view:

> Lead us, Evolution, lead us
> Up the future's endless stair:
> Chop us, change us, prod us, weed us,
> For stagnation is despair:
> Groping, guessing, yet progressing,
> Lead us nobody knows where.
>
> Wrong or justice in the present,
> Joy or sorrow, what are they
> While there's always jam tomorrow,
> While we tread the onward way?
> Never knowing where we're going,
> We can never go astray.
>
> To whatever variation
> Our posterity may turn
> Hairy, squashy, or crustacean,
> Bulbous-eyed or square of stern,
> Tusked or toothless, mild or ruthless,
> Towards that unknown god we yearn.

Ask not if it's god or devil,
Brethren, lest your words imply
Static norms of good and evil
(As in Plato) throned on high;
Such scholastic, inelastic,
Abstract yardsticks we deny.

Far too long have sages vainly
Glossed great Nature's simple text;
He who runs can read it plainly,
"Goodness = what comes next."
By evolving, Life is solving
All the questions we perplexed.

On then! Value means survival-
Value. If our progeny
Spreads and spawns and licks each rival,
That will prove its deity
(Far from pleasant, by our present
Standards, though it may well be).[280]

In contrast to the ghastly pointlessness of the secular evolutionary mind-set, biblical Christianity offers a blessed hope inextricably tied up with the person of Christ the Creator. He who permanently added to His eternal deity sinless humanity will return to the very planet where He was rejected in order to seize the reins of world government. And – wondrous to relate! – those who belong to Him will reign with Him. Far from being abject worms, believers in the Lord Jesus are vested with the utmost dignity as the undeserving objects of God's eternal electing purposes of grace in Christ. As Paul says,

> whom he did foreknow, he also did predestinate to be conformed to the image of his Son, that he might be the firstborn among many brethren. Moreover whom he did predestinate, them he also called: and whom he called, them he also justified: and whom he justified, them he also glorified (Rom 8.29-30).

Unlike the pitiful agnosticism of Lewis's parody hymn, and unlike the dangerous lop-sidedness displayed in Bildad's negative assessment of humanity, Scripture is beautifully clear. It is the privilege of the Bible-believer to know where he has come from, why he is here, and where he is going.

SECTION 19
Dialogue: Job 4 – 42.6
Contest: Round 3: Job 22-31
Job's 8th and Final Speech: Job 26-31
Part One: Job 26

One of the dangers associated with reading the book of Job is the temptation to expect at least one of the human disputants to offer an infallible analysis of the situation. We would love to find someone with whom we can whole-heartedly identify. However, as Ellison reminds us, "We know that Job's friends were wrong; we must not jump to the conclusion that Job was right".[281] Much as we long to hear an authoritative voice, the book remains an inspired record of men's uninspired attempts to understand God's ways with Job, attempts coloured by incomplete information, prejudice, theological obsession, and the tendency of men always to view themselves and their opinions in the best possible light. No one in the story of Job has access to the whole truth.

This needs to be specially borne in mind as we approach Job's final contribution to the verbal contest, a long speech in which he very movingly sums up his sense of injured innocence. Job, we know from the prologue, is guiltless of any sin for which he is being punished. Further, he is an outstandingly godly man. Nevertheless, this does not mean that everything he says is either wholly accurate or wholly wise. The reader has to recognise that this is no academic disputation in which Job is a detached promulgator of ideas. Rather, he is a man brought to his knees, suffering unimaginable bodily and mental anguish, yet constrained to defend himself in the face of what he can only view as unjustified human and divine opposition. A balanced and objective statement of his situation is therefore not to be expected. Rather, his language is highly impassioned in its poetic energy, at times absurdly hyperbolical in its avowals, and often logically inconsistent in its unpredictable shifts in direction. Job is trapped on an emotional rollercoaster.

In this sense it could be argued that Job is one of the most realistic books in the Bible. It offers an honest record of the attempts of ordinary people to explain the inexplicable – why a good man is suffering a bad time. Christians conversing today, though illuminated by access to the completed canon of Scripture, may nonetheless be equally in the dark as to the precise reasons for the circumstances of any individual child of God. When disaster strikes, when sorrow comes, when the unthinkable descends on us and we try to work out why, we are in many ways in the position of the Job debaters. Even Christians are susceptible to uninspired, unsympathetic, and unwise speculations when they consider the adversities which befall fellow saints.

But Job's last words demand careful attention. They are so extensive and wide-ranging that, to follow the complex logic of this lengthy argument, we need to summarise the gist of each chapter. This commentary takes the biblical text at face value, and therefore accepts chapter 27 as Job's words, even though parts of it seem, *prima facie*, to fly in the face of some of his earlier assertions. Chapter 28 is also to be viewed as an essential component of his speech, not some hymnic insertion in praise of wisdom by the anonymous writer of the book. The series of chapters is significantly broken up by two brief narrative links ("Job continued his parable", 27.1; 29.1), allowing a pause for the silent Zophar to contribute his anticipated third speech if willing and able.

Chapter 26, the introduction, consists of a sarcastic retort to the summary account of God's greatness in the previous chapter. Job expands Bildad's rather skimpy ideas well beyond his own feeble outline, showing that he can, as it were, out-Bildad Bildad when he wants to. Along with his three friends, he is perfectly aware of the majesty and power of God. It is therefore perhaps all the more surprising to find that, when Jehovah does eventually intervene vocally, it is precisely this point on which He expatiates.

Chapter 27 goes on, daringly, to charge this great God, whose created works are but the whisper of His ways, with depriving Job of his rights and subjecting him to utter misery. Job will neither agree with his friends' crude account of his situation (that he is being punished for his sins), nor will he abandon his claims to innocence. But he is as well instructed in the righteous judgments of God as anyone, knowing that, in the final analysis, the wicked are dealt with. This knowledge, however, does not explain or soothe his present condition.

Chapter 28 sounds at first reading like a free-standing poem in praise of wisdom, with little bearing on the immediate controversy. But in fact it fits well into the broad development of the argument. Men – that is to say, Job and his three friends – have been attempting to comprehend God's ways with Job, only to discover that this requires a wisdom beyond their reach. How can man acquire the understanding to solve the riddle of Job? Although miners dig into the bowels of the earth to search industriously for precious metals, no one has managed to uncover the most valuable commodity of all, real wisdom, for it belongs uniquely to God. Because creaturely insight will never stretch to a comprehension of God's actions, man's safest course in the face of the mysterious is to maintain a steadfast reverence of attitude and righteousness of behaviour.

Chapter 29 is a nostalgic flashback, looking regretfully over Job's past life of prosperous ease when he basked in the conscious enjoyment of divine blessing. He was everywhere noted for personal uprightness, social conscience, and inestimable wisdom. It is a rosy-tinted picture of an eastern sage at the height of his reputation.

Chapter 30 violently bursts the cosy bubble of memory by setting up the deplorable contrast with his present condition as a social outcast, despised, diseased, and heading for death. Job is offering us a view of the "then" and "now" of his life.

Chapter 31 forms the grand climax to all his utterances, at the close of which we read "The words of Job are ended" (31.40). The whole point of this chapter is to list frankly the misdeeds of which he might have been guilty (sins particularly open to a wealthy eastern sheik), only to affirm, in the most emphatic language, his total innocence. He will neither surrender his integrity nor compromise his self-knowledge. A formal avowal of blamelessness (cataloguing a variety of personal and public sins) is accompanied by solemn maledictions upon himself were he to be found guilty of any. This terminates Job's confession and defence.

Since the narrative insets divide the speech into three distinct sections, it makes sense to handle it as a three-part discourse, with each part of increasing length. The three sections, then, consist of the following chapters:

> (i) 26.1-14
> (ii) 27.1 – 28.28
> (iii) 29.1 – 31.40.

Chapter 26 forms a general introduction. Job, with biting sarcasm, lambasts Bildad for his failure to offer seasonable advice (26.1-4), before proceeding to show how pitiable is Bildad's grasp of God's greatness (26.5-13), which is in fact immeasurable (26.14). The three paragraphs of this introduction may be set out thus:

> 1. Job's Response: 26.1-4
> 2. Job's Revision: 26.5-13
> 3. Job's Revelation: 26.14

Job's Response: 26.1-4

The first four verses constitute a blistering **response** to Bildad (26.1-4), and are best read in a translation (such as the RV or Darby) which replaces the question marks of the KJV with exclamation marks. This draws attention to the caustic irony of the language, by means of which Job "pours out the full vials of his sarcasm on Bildad's irrelevant statements":[282]

> And Job answered and said, How hast thou helped the powerless; how saved the arm that is without strength! How hast thou counselled him that hath no wisdom, and abundantly declared the thing as it is! For whom hast thou uttered words? and whose spirit came from thee? (26.1-4, JND).

Job's words are carefully chosen to highlight the gulf between him and Bildad. He, the object of divine hostility, is, in the eyes of his unsympathetic friends, "powerless", "without strength", and possessed of "no wisdom" to understand the reason for his tragedy. But if he is indeed as helpless as they say, why then do his friends not offer effective support? As a purveyor of practical assistance Bildad is a complete failure. In a tone of heavy-handed mockery, the positive verbs ("helped … saved … counselled … declared") are inverted in meaning to show how far short he has fallen. Job is saying that Bildad has conspicuously *not* helped, *not* saved, *not* counselled, and *not* informed him. The phrase "abundantly declared" drips with irony: the friends have made such pretentious claims for their intellectual powers, but what have they achieved? Their combined efforts have been fruitless; indeed, they have succeeded only in intensifying Job's misery. Two key ideas controlling these words are strength ("helped … saved") and sagacity ("counselled … declared"): Bildad can neither rescue him from his plight nor satisfactorily explain the reason for it. This gives Job two crucial concepts with which to shape the whole chapter. As we shall see, he argues that God alone knows what man cannot know (26.5-6), and does what man cannot do (26.7-14). He possesses true wisdom and true power.

But Job is not yet finished with Bildad. He insinuates, correctly, that the previous speaker has been trafficking with other people's thoughts (26.4). It is as if he challenges his opponent by inquiring, with sardonic politeness, who his scriptwriter was, and whose mind he pillaged for his arguments. We have already seen that chapter 26 is lifted from the earlier speeches of Eliphaz. Bildad the philosopher is in fact Bildad the plagiarist.

Job's bitter experience of let-down is not unique in human history. When it comes to offering soothing encouragement to souls in time of trouble, men at best, even "mine own familiar friend, in whom I trusted" (Ps 41.9), may prove broken reeds. But we need not end with this depressing observation. What neither Bildad nor any other of the friends can do for Job, God is able to do for His people. As the hymn writer puts it:

> When other helpers fail and comforts flee,
> Help of the helpless, oh, abide with me.

We have only to research into Job's vocabulary to tease out the truth. The first time the verb "help" (5826) occurs is when Jacob promises Joseph that "the God of thy father … shall help [5826] thee" (Gen 49.25). The last time the verb "save" (3467) appears is in the eschatological setting of Israel's future deliverance from her foes, when "The Lord also shall save [3467] the tents of Judah first" (Zech 12.7). In the poetical and prophetic books, "counsel" (3289) describes the blessing of divine direction and guidance, reaching a grand climax in Isaiah's great revelation of Messiah's name:

> I will bless the Lord, who hath given me counsel [3289]: my reins also instruct me in the night seasons (Ps 16.7).

> I will instruct thee and teach thee in the way which thou shalt go: I will guide [3289] thee with mine eye (Ps 32.8).

> For the Lord of hosts hath purposed [3289], and who shall disannul it? And his hand is stretched out, and who shall turn it back? (Is 14.27)

> For unto us a child is born, unto us a son is given: and the government shall be upon his shoulder: and his name shall be called Wonderful, Counsellor [3289], The mighty God, The everlasting Father, The Prince of Peace (Is 9.6).

The rather odd phrase in the KJV and Darby, "the thing as it is [8454]" (26.3), is by others translated "sound knowledge" (RV, ASV, ESV). It means "sound wisdom", and the KJV renders it this way in Proverbs 2.7, 3.21 and 8.14, where it describes God's guidance of those who rely on Him. God alone is the reliable source of help, salvation, guidance and wisdom for His people. When others prove a disappointment – and ultimately they always will – we can be sure of finding our resources in the unfailing Lord.

Job's Revision: 26.5-13

Job now proceeds to offer an extensive **revision** of Bildad's theology, demonstrating that he knows as much as his friend about the power of God over the created universe. His language in fact reveals that he knows far more. Zuck writes that "it is typical of Job to outdo his friends-turned-rivals in his understanding of God's transcendence".[283] This magnificent survey of creation, ranging vertically from things in the depths (26.5-6) to things in the heights (26.7-13), is a symphonic tone-poem compared with Bildad's feeble five-finger exercise.

Job's first point is that God's power extends beyond the land of the living, because He also exercises supervision over the invisible region of the dead:

> The shades [7496] tremble beneath the waters and the inhabitants thereof; Sheol [7585] is naked before him, and destruction hath no covering (26.5-6, JND).

Job's is the first of eight Old Testament appearances of a word which Darby translates "shades" (7496), indicating that it refers to the spirits of the dead. It sometimes turns up, as here, in parallel with the word for the place where these spirits are currently confined, *sheol* (7585):

> But he knoweth not that the dead [7496] are there; and that her guests are in the depths of hell [7585] (Prov 9.18).

> Hell [7585] from beneath is moved for thee to meet thee at thy coming: it stirreth up the dead [S7496] for thee, even all the chief ones of the earth; it hath raised up from their thrones all the kings of the nations (Is 14.9).

If, as some lexicons suggest, the Hebrew word for "dead" (7496) is related to *rephaim* (7497), a term describing the fearsome giants who inhabited Canaan (Gen 14.5; Deut 2.11), the shades to which he refers might be paraphrased as "the elite among the dead".[284] Job's point is that God is infinitely greater than Bildad's perfunctory summary might suggest. His all-seeing eye lays bare the location of departed souls, so that even the most potent among them "tremble" (2342) beneath His gaze. There are no loud-mouthed atheists among the ranks of the dead, just as there are none among the hosts of evil spirits (atheism is a peculiarly human foolishness), for "The demons even believe, and tremble" (James 2.19, JND). Brown, Driver and Briggs define this verb "tremble" in Job 26.5 as meaning "to twist, whirl, dance, writhe, fear, tremble, travail, be in anguish, be pained". It is used of the abject terror God brought on the indigenous Canaanites (despite their boasted giants) as they became aware of Israel's approach to the land:

This day will I begin to put the dread of thee and the fear of thee upon the nations that are under the whole heaven, who shall hear report of thee, and shall tremble, and be in anguish [2342] because of thee (Deut 2.25).

The same word describes the daughters of Shiloh who "danced" before being ambushed by the Benjamites (Judg 21.21,23), Saul sore "wounded" by archers (1 Sam 31.3), the "fear" which all men owe God (1 Chr 16.30), the wicked man's "pain" (Job 15.20), and the voice of the Lord that "shaketh" the wilderness (Ps 29.8). God's power causes the inhabitants of *sheol* to shake.

The other key term is "destruction" (11), a Hebrew word transliterated *abaddon*, a noun frequently found in connection with death and *sheol*. It resurfaces in the book of Revelation to describe "the angel of the bottomless pit, whose name in the Hebrew tongue is Abaddon, but in the Greek tongue hath his name Apollyon" (Rev 9.11). The book of Proverbs argues pointedly that, since "Hell and destruction [11] are before the Lord: how much more then the hearts of the children of men?" (Prov 15.11). If the invisible world of the dead cannot hide from God, how much more are living men's hearts utterly exposed to Him, for "all things are naked and opened unto the eyes of him with whom we have to do" (Heb 4.13).

Not only, then, does God hold sovereign sway in "his high places", as Bildad correctly states (25.2), He rules the underworld too. Delitzsch sums it up:

> The operation of the majesty of the heavenly Ruler extends even to the realm of shades; the sea with the multitude of its inhabitants forms no barrier between God and the realm of shades; the marrowless, bloodless phantoms or shades below writhe like a woman in travail as often as this majesty is felt by them, as, perhaps, by the raging of the sea or the quaking of the earth.[285]

It is worth emphasising that, whatever the pretensions of spiritists and occultists, the dead are beyond men's reach. They rest secure in the keeping of the living God for, when life terminates, "Then shall the dust return to the earth as it was: and the spirit shall return unto God who gave it" (Eccl 12.7). The departed spirits of unsaved people are not at the beck and call of necromancers, but are confined until the day when, in John's vision, "the sea gave up the dead which were in it; and death and hell [*hades*, the New Testament equivalent of the Old Testament *sheol*] delivered up the dead which were in them: and they were judged every man according to their works. And death and hell [*hades*] were cast into the lake of fire. This is the second death" (Rev 20.13-14).

God controls the depths and the heights. Job now shifts his attention from the unseen world below to the visible evidences of God's creative excellence in His universe. Just as Bildad arranged his material into a chiastic structure, so does Job:

(a) He stretcheth out the north over empty space, he hangeth the earth upon nothing;

  (b) He bindeth up the waters in his thick clouds, and the cloud is not rent under them.

    (c) He covereth the face of his throne, he spreadeth his cloud upon it.

      (d) He hath traced a fixed circle over the waters, unto the confines of light and darkness.

    (c) The pillars of the heavens tremble and are astonished at his rebuke.

  (b) He stirreth up the sea by his power, and by his understanding he smiteth through Rahab.

(a) By his Spirit the heavens are adorned; his hand hath formed the fleeing serpent (26.7-13, JND).

The (a) sections, which frame the stanza, consider the stellar heavens and the vastness of outer space; the (b) sections parallel the waters above, held in cloud formations, with the waters of the sea; the (c) sections describe the skies and the mountains that seem to uphold them by using the language of palatial architecture ("throne", "pillars"); and the central line (d) focusses on light and darkness.

In a few verses, Job gives us a good deal to think about. Like the writer of Psalm 104 he is constructing a poetic celebration of creation which complements without contradicting the prose narrative of Genesis 1 and 2. Despite his terrible physical and mental sufferings, he has not lost his sense of wonderment at the handiwork of God. All around him and above him is refreshing proof of divine power. The passage is packed with verbs of majestic divine action: "stretcheth out … hangeth … bindeth … covereth … spreadeth … stirreth up …. smiteth".

God "stretcheth out [5186] the north". The word is used to describe men pitching their tents (Gen 12.8; 26.25; 33.19; 35.21), or Aaron holding forth his rod (Ex 7.19; 8.5,17). What men do in daily life without effort God has done with equal ease in spreading out the immense expanse of the sky. Most relevant to the present context is this word's appearance in the great creation passages in the psalms and prophets:

[Thou] coverest thyself with light as with a garment: who stretchest out [5186] the heavens like a curtain (Ps 104.2).

It is he that sitteth upon the circle of the earth, and the inhabitants thereof are as grasshoppers; that stretcheth out [5186] the heavens as a curtain, and spreadeth them out as a tent to dwell in (Is 40.22).

Thus saith the Lord, thy redeemer, and he that formed thee from the womb, I am the Lord that maketh all things; that stretcheth forth [5186] the heavens alone; that spreadeth abroad the earth by myself (Is 44.24).

I have made the earth, and created man upon it: I, even my hands, have stretched out [5186] the heavens, and all their host have I commanded (Is 45.12).

I, even I, am he that comforteth you: who art thou, that thou shouldest be afraid of a man that shall die, and of the son of man which shall be made as grass; And forgettest the Lord thy maker, that hath stretched forth [5186] the heavens, and laid the foundations of the earth; and hast feared continually every day because of the fury of the oppressor, as if he were ready to destroy? and where is the fury of the oppressor? (Is 51.12-13).

He hath made the earth by his power, he hath established the world by his wisdom, and hath stretched out [5186] the heavens by his discretion (Jer 10.12; 51.15).

The repetition testifies to the importance of the visible heavens as a silent but sufficient universal witness to the "eternal power and Godhead" of the Creator (Rom 1.20). Only the wilfully blind fail to see God in His handiwork. In the poetical parts of Scripture the north appears to refer to the most exalted and unattainable aspect of the heavens (a comparison of Psalm 48.2 and Isaiah 14.13 suggests this). In contrast to the lowest depths (*sheol* and *abaddon*) over which He exercises effortless control, God also reigns supreme in the highest height (the north). Further, in His amazing creatorial wisdom He suspends the entire earth upon nothing. Our modern familiarity with this scientific fact should not lessen its wonder.

Kenny Barfield's fascinating book, *Why the Bible is Number 1*, which documents the difference between the breath-taking scientific precision of the Bible and the gross fallacies taught in the "sacred" writings of the Babylonians, Chinese, Greeks, Romans, Hindus and Moslems, makes the following observation:

Ancient authors conceived of the earth as resting on a strange foundation. Some pictured it as riding upon the back of four giant elephants, which perched atop a giant turtle that spent its days meandering about in a sea of milk. Others surmised that the earth was astride a large catfish that swam in some sort of primal ocean. Those who were repulsed by such ideas placed the world on the shoulders of Atlas. On the other hand, the writer of Job correctly observed that "the earth hangs upon nothing" (Job 26.7). Literally, the phrase implies that the earth is suspended in space without observable means of support. Scholars of Job's day certainly had no such conception.[286]

Even allowing, as we must, that not all the words of Job or his friends are necessarily inspired, it is astonishing that such an early book has such an accurate view of the world.

Job goes further in his exploration of God's miraculous power by looking at an aspect of the world's weather systems, specifically "the wonders of the clouds, floating reservoirs of water, which do not burst under the weight of the waters which they contain".[287] The meteorological laws governing rain are of God's appointment. Again, Barfield is worth quoting:

> Prior to the seventeenth century, theorizing about the origin of rainfall was drenched either in magic, ridiculous speculation, or false science. It was said that rain originated in response to good-luck charms, amulets, and incantations. It was also said that rain fell when sluice gates were opened in the solid vault of heaven, allowing water to fall from a celestial ocean that encompassed the globe. Another idea argued that plain, simple air (*not* water vapour) was transformed into rainwater … Historians document that no correct scientific understanding of rainfall and the water cycle existed prior to the days of French scientists Pierre Perrault [1608-1680] and Edme Mariotte [1620-84].[288]

Yet Job knows that God "bindeth up" (6887) rainwater in the clouds "as one stores wine in a wineskin".[289] And for all the huge load of water they enclose, the clouds are not "rent" asunder (1234). The account of the wily Gibeonites who gulled Joshua with their artificially frayed and repaired wineskins, designed to simulate a long and wearisome journey, uses both words employed metaphorically by Job, but in a literal context (Josh 9.4).

All this emphasises God's miraculous power. Bildad had sketched broad generalities but Job impresses us with sharp detail. "The heavens are visible; yet they do not fall to earth".[290] "The sky which vaults the earth from the arctic pole, and the earth itself, hang free without support in space".[291] The clouds retain their reservoirs of water until the time comes for rain to fall. John Buchan is credited with wittily defining an atheist as a person "with no invisible means of support", but every believer gladly rejoices that he is sustained daily by the God of miracles whose power upholds the universe.

Verse 9 continues with a tantalising glimpse of God's inaccessible majesty. The *Jamieson, Fausset and Brown Commentary* notes that "God makes the clouds a veil to screen the glory not only of His person, but even of the exterior of His throne from profane eyes. His agency is everywhere, yet He Himself is invisible". Oddly, the ESV translates the standard Hebrew word for "throne" as "moon", which seems a weak and needless obfuscation. Taken at its face value, the picture language of verses 9 and 11 sketches the outline of a glorious celestial palace complete with royal throne and structural or ornamental columns (the word is used for the pillars of the Old Testament tabernacle and temple). God's sanctuary is beyond the reach of the most powerful telescope, concealed by clouds and inviolable in its splendour. Yet it is real. Something of that heavenly temple is revealed more fully in the book of Revelation. In his lead-up to the spectacular disclosure of the New

Jerusalem, the eternal abode of the saints, John is granted privileged glimpses into an actuality of which earthly sanctuaries are but a shadow.

The central line of Job's chiastic stanza is verse 10, which focuses attention on the borderline between day and night, echoing the Genesis creation narrative where "God divided the light from the darkness" (Gen 1.4). Davidson's account of the verse offers a clear explanation:

> Around the surface of the earth flows the ocean … upon this like a circle all around the earth the arch of heaven comes down; all within this band is light, for the sun rises on one side of it and goes down at the other.[292]

The language implies the spherical shape of the earth, itself remarkable in an era when many thought the world was flat. Nothing is accidental in the planet which God so beautifully made as man's habitation; all is planned according to His wise will for His glory and our benefit.

Verses 11, 12 and 13 introduce a new element into this hymn of praise to God the Creator by referring to His ability to put down all potential opposition. Heaven's pillars (that is to say, the mountains which, viewed poetically, constitute the sky's supporting columns) quiver with fear at His rebuke (26.11), Rahab the proud denizen of the deep is shattered by His power (26.12), and He pierces the fleeing serpent (26.13). God's greatness holds the very heavens in awe, destroying all who rise against Him, whether they be in the depths (as in 9.13 Rahab may describe a mythological sea-monster, or simply personify the pride of the ocean) or in the heights (the "fleeing serpent" refers both to a particular constellation in the stellar heavens and to the ultimate enemy of God, identified with the serpent of Eden).

The language testifies to the startling efficacy of divine energy. "Rebuke" (1606) is often used of Jehovah's spoken word intervening in the regular processes of nature to accomplish His will:

> And the channels of the sea appeared, the foundations of the world were discovered, at the rebuking [1606] of the Lord, at the blast of the breath of his nostrils (2 Sam 22.16).

> At thy rebuke [1606], O God of Jacob, both the chariot and horse are cast into a dead sleep (Ps 76.6).

> [The vineyard representing Israel] is burned with fire, it is cut down: they [the people] perish at the rebuke [1606] of thy countenance (Ps 80.16).

> Thou coveredst it with the deep as with a garment: the waters stood above the mountains. At thy rebuke [1606] they fled; at the voice of thy thunder they hasted away (Ps 104.6-7).

The last example may refer to creation or, perhaps, to the Noahic flood which brought about a radical transformation in the face of the earth. God's rebuke, which accomplishes His purposes without fail, is of such colossal impact as to shake the heavens.

But He also controls the waters, arousing, dividing or stilling (7280) the oceans as it pleases Him: "He stirreth up [7280] the sea by his power, and by his understanding he smiteth through Rahab" (26.12, JND). The verb "stir up" is capable of a range of translations. If we take the rendering of the RV and Darby, the verse teaches that God initiates storms in order to demonstrate His authority over the ocean. Job's language recurs in the prophets, where Jehovah tells Israel that "I am the Lord thy God, that divided [7280] the sea, whose waves roared" (Is 51.15; Jer 31.35). Though some readers might consider it disturbing, the Bible is unashamed in its affirmation that the same God who calms the sea (a truth we are quick to appreciate) also stirs it up into tempests:

> For he commandeth, and raiseth the stormy wind, which lifteth up the waves thereof. They mount up to the heaven, they go down again to the depths: their soul is melted because of trouble. They reel to and fro, and stagger like a drunken man, and are at their wits' end. Then they cry unto the Lord in their trouble, and he bringeth them out of their distresses. He maketh the storm a calm, so that the waves thereof are still (Ps 107.25-29).

The psalmist, we notice, is not theologically uneasy at the fact that God both "raiseth the stormy wind" and "maketh the storm a calm". This is the story of Job in a nutshell. God brought disasters on him that he might be the more cast on his God. Every believer ought to store this principle away in his mind as a source of comfort and stability when trouble comes.

But the verb may also have a more pacific meaning, teaching that God stills the storms, bringing "rest" (as the Hebrew word is translated in Jeremiah 31.2; 47.6; 50.34). In this case, Job may be thinking back to the end of the global flood when "God remembered Noah, and every living thing, and all the cattle that was with him in the ark: and God made a wind to pass over the earth, and the waters assuaged" (Gen 8.1).

Perhaps we do not need to choose between alternatives, as both ideas are doctrinally true: God creates and calms storms for the furtherance of His own good purposes. The Galilean tempest recorded in Matthew 8.24, a sudden squall miraculously quelled by the Lord Jesus, could never have arisen in the first place without His will. After the upheavals (both political and geographical) of the great tribulation period – catastrophic disruptions brought about by direct divine intervention in world history – will come the glorious rest of the kingdom age on earth when the messianic King "shall come down like rain upon the mown grass" (Ps 72.6), wonderfully reviving a ruined planet.

Further, God both beautifies and exercises total authority over heavenly bodies, because "By his Spirit the heavens are adorned; his hand hath formed the fleeing serpent" (26.13, JND). This is one of those Old Testament verses (like Genesis 1.2, Job 33.4 and Psalm 104.30) which credit the Spirit of God with the work of creation. Delitzsch rather reduces its significance by translating the passage "By His breath the heavens become cheerful; His hand hath formed the fugitive dragon",[293] but this seems an unnecessary dilution. Though the New Testament specially discloses the creative activity of the Son, this by no means cancels the testimony of the Hebrew Bible. The word "adorned" (or "garnished", as the KJV felicitously retains from the earlier Bishops' Bible, of which it was the official revision) is found only here. The Brown, Driver and Briggs lexicon relates it to another word appearing in Psalm 16.6 and rendered "goodly". It means, according to Strong's Concordance, "to glisten". The Spirit of God lavishly bespangled the sky with innumerable stars to give it its outstanding brilliance and beauty.

But what about "the fleeing serpent"? This phrase likely refers specifically to the constellation called Serpens (the serpent), and thus by extrapolation demonstrates God's power over everything in the heavenly realms. But it may also hint at the great enemy we met in the prologue and who returns towards the end of the book (suggestively at least) in the guise of the monstrous leviathan, whom God alone can curb. Some commentators, rightly sensing this connection, argue (on the basis of the linguistic equivalent in Isaiah 27.1) that "the fleeing serpent" is identical with leviathan, and that the second half of verse 13 therefore describes not the skies but the sea. Though plausible, this is not entirely persuasive because it destroys the synonymous parallelism in the verse by which the "heavens" garnished by God's Spirit balance the fleeing serpent made by His hands. It makes better sense to see both parts of the verse as dealing with things above.

Another problem relates to the verb. Darby (along with the KJV) tells us that God's hand "formed" this serpent, whereas other versions (RV, ASV, ESV) inform us that He "pierced" it. The word seems capable of bearing both positive (begin, form) and negative meanings (wound, defile, pierce). Whatever the case, this much is clear: God exercises supreme power. He makes and unmakes as it pleases Him.

In summary, verses 5 to 13 constitute a paean of praise to a God whose authority is limitless and whose activity is exhaustless. Whether we peer below (to the unseen landscape of *sheol* or the hidden depths of the oceans) or gaze above (to the impenetrable heavens) we see a testimony to His infinite majesty.

Job's Revelation: 26.14

Perhaps the most astounding aspect of Job's grasp of God's greatness is his shrewd awareness of how little he really knows. He concludes with a candid **revelation** of his ignorance (26.14). The final verse of the chapter ascribes to God's works an incomprehensibility which defeats the greatest of human intelligence:

> Lo, these are the borders of his ways; but what a whisper of a word do we hear of him! And the thunder of his power, who can understand? (26.14, JND)

The spectacular wonders Job has described in the previous verses ("these") are merely the outskirts of God's creatorial works – they are but the edges of His excellence, the outer suburbs of his splendour, the merest sigh of His speech. But were He to intervene in the awe-inspiring fullness of His power, who could possibly stand before Him? Men would be instantaneously bowled over.

Moses, daringly requesting to see God's glory, was told "Thou canst not see my face: for there shall no man see me, and live" (Ex 33.20); nevertheless, he was graciously permitted a passing glimpse, for "I will put thee in a clift of the rock, and will cover thee with my hand while I pass by: And I will take away mine hand, and thou shalt see my back parts: but my face shall not be seen" (Ex 33.22-23). Moses therefore had a peep at what someone has aptly called the divine after-glow. The full dazzle of glory he knew he could not see. Like Moses, hidden snugly in the shelter of God's protecting hand, Job knows that the visible heavens are but a faint glimmer of God's essential and inaccessible splendour. So much of His creatorial wisdom remains beyond men's reach. Unlike his rather smug friends, Job is under no illusions about the limitations of his understanding. However, the reader who is privy to the book's structure might detect an added irony: Job speaks here of God's whisper, but in chapters 38 to 41 God will thunder out of a whirlwind in challenging him with some of His most inscrutable marvels.

One of the many paradoxes of Christian growth is this: the more we get to know the Scriptures and their mind-blowing testimony to the greatness and wisdom of our God, the more we become increasingly conscious of how little we grasp. John's Gospel uses the simplest of vocabularies and yet contains depths of spiritual truth beyond the capacity of the greatest mind. The horizon of divine magnificence is always receding into the distance. It is to Job's credit that he is acutely aware of his own intellectual weakness.

Perhaps one other point ought to be raised. Job's language in this chapter bears eloquent testimony to the staggering grandeur of God's creative acts which rightly provoke the utmost wonder and worship. But the Christian believer knows of an even greater demonstration of His power: "the gospel of Christ … is the power of God unto salvation to every one that believeth; to the Jew first, and also to the Greek" (Rom 1.16). Samuel Davies' hymn puts this truth into memorable words:

> Great God of wonders! All Thy ways
> Are matchless, Godlike and divine;
> But the fair glories of Thy grace
> More Godlike and unrivaled shine.
> Who is a pardoning God like Thee?
> Or who has grace so rich and free?
>
> Crimes of such horror to forgive,
> Such guilty, daring worms to spare;
> This is Thy grand prerogative,
> And none shall in the honour share.

Angels and men, resign your claim
To pity, mercy, love and grace:
These glories crown Jehovah's Name
With an incomparable glaze.

In wonder lost, with trembling joy,
We take the pardon of our God:
Pardon for crimes of deepest dye,
A pardon bought with Jesus' blood.

O may this strange, this matchless grace,
This Godlike miracle of love,
Fill the whole earth with grateful praise,
And all th'angelic choirs above.[294]

Far surpassing God's power in creation is His ability and willingness, on the righteous basis of the work of Calvary, to pardon helpless sinners.

SECTION 20
Dialogue: Job 4 – 42.6
Contest: Round 3: Job 22-31
Job's 8th and Final Speech: Job 26-31
Part Two: Job 27-28

Chapter 27 is generally considered a particularly difficult section of Job's final speech, largely because verses 7 to 23 seem, at first sight, to contradict everything that Job has hitherto been arguing. His friends have insisted that, because evil men cannot escape divine punishment, the invasion of misery into a man's life testifies to personal wickedness. Job, by contrast, has challenged this notion by arguing that, far from receiving instant justice, the lawless frequently prosper in the world. That being the case, any naïve correlation between physical circumstances and spiritual condition, such as that deduced by his friends, is simply untenable. However, in chapter 27 Job starts using language which reminds us of the earlier speeches of his opponents, insisting that divine judgment inevitably falls on sin: "This is the portion of a wicked man with God, and the heritage of oppressors, which they shall receive of the Almighty" (27.13). Has Job changed his mind?

One common, if arbitrary, way out of the apparent problem is to attribute Job's words to one of his three friends, normally Zophar, who has so far had nothing to say in the third round of the debate. But this procedure involves a radical rearrangement of the biblical text for which there is no real justification. Job's point of view, as we have seen, can chop and change erratically in response to fluctuating emotions and frustrations. There is therefore no reason why he should not, at this advanced stage in the debate, to some extent concede what his opponents have been urging, while rejecting their specific application of the point. In any case, the plural "you" in 27.5,11-12 would sit uncomfortably on the lips of Zophar; were he to speak, he would surely address Job as an individual ("thee"). It is far simpler to take this pronoun as Job alluding to the "three wise men" who have been bombarding him with their collective eloquence. Zophar's complete silence, though unexpected, is, in point of fact, not unaccountable in the light of the gradual fading out of the opposition voices in Round Three: Bildad was reduced to six verses, Zophar to nothing.

Similarly, there are problems with chapter 28, which suddenly embarks without warning upon a strangely impersonal survey of man's quest for spiritual enlightenment. It reads almost like a free-standing poem in praise of that rare and much-sought-after wisdom which can grasp God's mysterious ways with His people. But to ascribe this to the anonymous author of the book, as some have done, is to raise even more difficulties. Why should the narrator who, since the prologue, has been silent apart from brief bridging passages ("But Job answered and said"), make such an unprecedented and substantial intrusion into the book's story-line? Once again, it is better to take the text as it stands and credit this matchless piece of poetry to Job, a man who has already proved himself a master wordsmith. Everything he has said so far testifies to his ability to construct a psalm in honour of wisdom.

These two chapters, then, may be seen broadly to address two distinct but ultimately related matters: the judicial sentence of God on the wicked (Job 27), and man's fruitless search for the wisdom needed to understand God's dealings with him (Job 28). They may be divided up into the following four sections:

> 1. Job's Affirmation – of his Innocence: 27.1-6
> 2. Job's Denunciation – of his Friends' Impertinence: 27.7-12
> 3. Job's Elucidation – of the Wicked Man's Destiny: 27.13-23
> 4. Job's Aspiration – True Wisdom: 28.1-28.

Job's Affirmation – of his Innocence: 27.1-6

Job starts chapter 27 by expressing a resolute **confidence** in God (27.2a,3). At the same time he voices a bitter **complaint** that God has deprived him of justice, treating him with outright hostility (27.2b). Nonetheless he continues to maintain a steadfast **confession** of personal integrity (27.4-6).

Unusually, the narrative introduction employs the word "parable", first found in Balaam's oracular pronouncements over Israel recorded in Numbers 23.7. The psalmist takes up the same term to describe the highly figurative and aphoristic style beloved of oriental poetry: "I will incline mine ear to a parable: I will open my dark saying upon the harp" (Ps 49.4). In Job this word suitably prepares us for the imagery found in the latter part of chapter 27 and (in conjunction with its repetition in 29.1) chapters 29 and 30. Job is speaking with all the self-assured poise and gravitas of an eastern sage, drawing on the rich resources of his lexical and rhetorical skills. His friends may have drained their reservoirs of theological insight, but Job's capacity to argue continues unabated. Indeed, he seems to thrive under pressure.

His initial expression of **confidence** is remarkable. "As God liveth" (27.1) is basically a solemn oath, much in the vein of David's famous statement to Jonathan about his imminent peril:

> And David sware moreover, and said, Thy father certainly knoweth that I have found grace in thine eyes; and he saith, Let not Jonathan know this, lest he be grieved: but truly as the Lord liveth, and as thy soul liveth, there is but a step between me and death (1 Sam 20.3).

The narrative comment, "And David sware", reinforces the point. This is a linguistic register of the utmost seriousness, where the name of God is invoked to endorse and solemnise the speaker's bold claim. The fourth commandment given to Israel is sometimes misunderstood. It did not forbid an individual from taking God's name on his lips, but rather warned him not to "take the name of the Lord thy God in vain" (Ex 20.7), that is to say, to bring God's name into his conversation irreverently and uselessly. It remains wonderfully true that creatures made out of dust are permitted humbly to name the all-glorious God of heaven. Indeed, salvation comes to all who "call on the name of the Lord" (Acts 2.21). David, of course, used the divine name with due respect and care. Presumably this was the kind of language to which poor Peter resorted when desperately (and deviously) seeking to convince his audience in the high priest's palace that he knew nothing of the Lord Jesus (Mt 26.72,74). How sad when a disciple stoops to invoking God's name in order to deny all knowledge of His Son! The apostle Paul, in a very different context, used similar language to highlight the transparency of his gospel ministry:

> For neither at any time used we flattering words, as ye know, nor a cloke of covetousness; God is witness (1 Thess 2.5).

> Ye are witnesses, and God also, how holily and justly and unblameably we behaved ourselves among you that believe (1 Thess 2.10).

> The God and Father of our Lord Jesus Christ, which is blessed for evermore, knoweth that I lie not (2 Cor 11.31).

> Now the things which I write unto you, behold, before God, I lie not (Gal 1.20).

In Job's case – a man of unimpeachable integrity – such language demonstrates how genuine was his deep-seated claim to innocence.

But it does more than that. It testifies to an ineradicable consciousness that, despite all the suffering he has been through, his God remains the true and only living God, the One who created and sustained him (27.3). Job may not be able to reconcile God's eternal existence with his current misery, but nothing will blot the knowledge of God from his mind. The almighty upholder of the universe was Job's sustainer, the foundation of his hopes, and yet simultaneously the source of his grief. The language seems to echo the Genesis account of creation where "the Lord God formed man of the dust of the ground, and breathed into his nostrils the breath of life; and man became a living soul" (Gen 2.7). Job will not retract his protestations of innocence "all the while my breath is in me, and the spirit of God is in my nostrils" (27.3). Come what may, Job remains doggedly entrenched in his belief in God.

For all that, his **complaint** does not mince its words: God hath "taken away my right, and ... embittered my soul" (27.2, JND). Bildad spoke earlier of the impossibility of sinful men being right with God, for "How then can man be justified with God? or how can he be clean that is born of a woman?" (25.4). That, of course, was a calculated tilt against Job's protestations that he was "not guilty". But Job daringly turns the idea on its head by accusing God Himself (the origin and arbiter of justice) of treating him unjustly. His impudence is staggering. It is tantamount to broadcasting an allegation that the highest court of the land is guilty of partiality and corruption. Job has insinuated similar charges throughout the debate (6.4; 7.20; 10.2-3; 13.24; 16.12-13), yet he knows instinctively that there is no higher tribunal to which he can appeal. The God who has vexed his soul is the One by whom he swears, for there is none greater.

At the same time he cannot stifle a conviction that God has treated him unjustly and "embittered" (4843) him. Jacob uses the same word when he says of Joseph that "the archers have sorely grieved [4843] him, and shot at him, and hated him" (Gen 49.23). It is used of the Egyptians who "made [the Israelites'] lives bitter [4843] with hard bondage" (Ex 1.14), of Israel instructed to "obey [the angel's] voice, [and] provoke [4843] him not" (Ex 23.21), and in Naomi's confession that "it grieveth [4843] me much for your sakes that the hand of the Lord is gone out against me" (Ruth 1.13). Usage illustrates meaning: the idea is profound grief, bitterness, and provocation. Job makes no effort to soft-pedal his misery under God's hand.

Spurgeon's comment on this verse (27.2) is worth quoting:

> He is a truly brave man who can say with Job, "Though he slay me, yet will I trust in him". Let God deal with me as he will, yet he is good, and I will praise his name. What if he has vexed my soul? He hath a right to vex me, so I will not kick against the pricks. Let him grieve me, let him put gall and wormwood into my cup if so it shall please him; but still will I magnify his name, for he is good, and only good. Here is the strength of the saints, here is the glory which God getteth out of true believers – that they cannot and will not be soured against their God.[295]

Wonderful words of genuine encouragement to a Christian audience they are, but not entirely true to the text of Scripture. The exigencies of extracting a positive exhortation out of an Old Testament record have caused Spurgeon to confuse what Job actually said with what the preacher obviously thinks he *ought* to have said. Three times we are told (in Spurgeon's loose paraphrase) that Job refers to God as "good". But in reality this attribute of the Almighty is never mentioned directly at all in Job's final speech. Of course Job has benefited from divine goodness in the past (2.10), but that is not the point here. Lacerated to the very heart by his sufferings, and exasperated to breaking point by the unkind insinuations of so-called friends, he frankly expostulates against God's dealings with him. We must not expect him to behave with the saintly submissiveness of an ideal New Testament believer who, with the full revelation of Scripture at his finger-tips, can shelter behind God's gracious self-disclosure in Christ. We only do justice to Job by reading the book honestly in its context.

Nevertheless, for all his accusations of injustice and hurt, Job keeps on clinging to his God. In this he anticipates the attitude of the writer of Psalm 44 who, perplexed that Jehovah has turned against His elect people despite their loyalty to the covenant, still casts himself upon the Lord:

> But thou hast cast off, and put us to shame; and goest not forth with our armies. Thou makest us to turn back from the enemy: and they which hate us spoil for themselves. Thou hast given us like sheep appointed for meat; and hast scattered us among the heathen. Thou sellest thy people for nought, and dost not increase thy wealth by their price. Thou makest us a

reproach to our neighbours, a scorn and a derision to them that are round about us. Thou makest us a byword among the heathen, a shaking of the head among the people. My confusion is continually before me, and the shame of my face hath covered me, For the voice of him that reproacheth and blasphemeth; by reason of the enemy and avenger. All this is come upon us; yet have we not forgotten thee, neither have we dealt falsely in thy covenant. Our heart is not turned back, neither have our steps declined from thy way; Though thou hast sore broken us in the place of dragons, and covered us with the shadow of death (Ps 44.9-19).

This poetic complaint needs to be measured against Psalm 89, where Ethan the Ezrahite contrasts the current weakened condition of Judah's ruling dynasty with the glowing promises contained in the Davidic covenant. He recognises that the nation's recent defeats and disasters are of God:

But thou hast cast off and abhorred, thou hast been wroth with thine anointed. Thou hast made void the covenant of thy servant: thou hast profaned his crown by casting it to the ground. Thou hast broken down all his hedges; thou hast brought his strong holds to ruin (Ps 89.38-40).

But he also knows the reason. Earlier he has carefully recorded the precise terms of the covenant, which include the threat of discipline upon disobedience:

If his children forsake my law, and walk not in my judgments; If they break my statutes, and keep not my commandments; Then will I visit their transgression with the rod, and their iniquity with stripes (Ps 89.30-32).

The present diminished state of Judah is therefore entirely understandable, because sin brings punishment. The principle remains true in New Testament times, "for whatsoever a man soweth, that shall he also reap" (Gal 6.7). In both Psalms 44 and 89 the elect nation is suffering calamity by divine design, but in the one it is *because of* their failure to keep the covenant (89), while in the other it is *in spite of* their faithfulness to the covenant (44).

The parallels between Job and Psalm 44 are therefore especially evident. Both speakers are going through inexplicable adversity. Both feel abandoned, weakened, exposed to hostile forces and, though tracing their distresses to an omnipotent God, remain determined to plead their integrity to the very One they recognise as the source of their ills.

In the face of all the storms that batter him, Job's **confession** of innocence stands unshaken:

My lips shall not speak unrighteousness, nor my tongue utter deceit! Be it far from me that I should justify you; till I die I will not remove my blamelessness from me. My righteousness I hold fast, and will not let it go: my heart reproacheth me not one of my days (27.4-6, JND).

Despite his friends' combined attempts to get him to admit some personal sin, Job will not falsify the truth to justify their lies. It would be "wickedness" to fabricate an error of which he was not guilty simply to agree with them; it would be blatant "deceit" to own up to some secret misdeed he had never committed in order to relieve himself of the pains he was currently suffering. Clearly Job is a man of unshakable integrity. The word translated "wickedness" (5766) first appears in connection with the impartiality of Israel's judicial system, in which there was to be "no unrighteousness [5766] in judgment: thou shalt not respect the person of the poor, nor honour the person of the mighty: but in righteousness shalt thou judge thy neighbour" (Lev 19.15). As an eminent magistrate involved in the local administration of justice (29.12-17), Job abhors the thought of injustice or false testimony. Paralleled in 27.4 with wickedness is deception, a sin especially connected with the faculty of speech. Job earlier accused his friends of talking "deceitfully" (13.7), while the psalmist and the prophet Micah were well aware of the dangers of a guileful tongue (Ps 52.2; 101.7; 120.2-3; Micah 6.12). Job is determined not to sin against his conscience, even to escape misery.

The word in 27.5 which Darby renders "blamelessness" (8538) occurs only five times in Scripture, and all but one are in Job. In the KJV it is translated "integrity" (2.3,9; 27.5; 31.6; Prov 11.3). Most significant is the first appearance, where Jehovah uses the term approvingly of His servant Job to sum up his moral wholeness, saying to Satan, "still he holdeth fast his integrity [8538], although thou movedst me against him, to destroy him without cause" (2.3). It remains true that – regardless of the assaults of Satan and the suspicions of his friends – Job has held firm to his innocence, his blamelessness, his moral completeness. Lest the reader fall into the trap of comparing Job with himself, and thereby doubting the honesty of such a glowing self-assessment, we must not forget that Job was unique in his uprightness and that the positive assessment is God's. However – and this is important – Job was by no means perfect in the sense of being without sin. There was only ever one wholly blameless, sinless man (which Job never claims to be), and that was the incarnate Son of God in whom the Father was "well pleased". Of Him alone it can be said, in Peter's paraphrase of Isaiah, that He "did no sin, neither was guile found in his mouth" (1 Pet 2.22). In Christ no one could discover either wickedness or deception.

Nevertheless Job emphatically claims for himself a general uprightness of conduct and a clear conscience: "My righteousness I hold fast, and will not let it go: my heart shall not reproach me so long as I live" (27.6). Darby's translation gets nearer the meaning of the latter part of the verse: "my heart reproacheth me not one of my days". The idea is that Job, reflecting upon a long life, can find not a single day in which he did anything he regretted. Nothing in the book suggests he was deluding himself. Nonetheless, the Christian reader may begin to feel (and has possibly had niggling doubts for a while) that there is in Job's attitude a degree of fulsome self-righteousness which ill becomes a creature, however virtuous. The final intervention of God into the debate will have the double effect not only of vindicating Job in the eyes of his super-critical friends but also of humbling him before God's infinite majesty.

More to the point at the moment, however, is what might be called a nagging tension within Job's understanding of God. Who is the God he worships and serves? He is, Job knows, the God of incorruptible righteousness, and yet He is also the God who has (apparently) wronged Job. Hartley sums it up: "Two views of God are struggling against each other in Job's thinking; God his accuser and God the source of justice".[296] In essence, Job, in his language of prayer and protestation, is appealing to God against God. Does that mean he believes God makes mistakes? Of course not. Smick's explanation is worth quoting in full:

> We can all agree with Elihu that God does no wrong (34.10) – we can agree till tragedy comes into our lives. Then we may begin to ask ourselves what we have done wrong, or we may even question God's goodness. Deep down we know that neither question is right. So Job too emphatically denied either alternative. He was throwing the mystery into God's lap, as it were, and leaving it there.[297]

As we have seen in relation to resurrection truth, this remarkable man Job is tentatively anticipating something as yet unrevealed in redemptive history. Why should the innocent man suffer? This is the question he faced and could not answer. Though he did not know it, his bitter personal experience, however imperfectly, looked forward to the ministry of the truly perfect man – just as Old Testament types foreshadowed the glorious antitype in Christ. Smick goes on to say that the book of Job

> lays the theological foundation for an answer that Job's faith anticipated but which Job did not fully know. God, the sovereign and therefore responsible Creator, would Himself in the person of His eternal Son solve the human dilemma by bearing the penalty of the sins of mankind, thus showing Himself to be both just and the justifier (vindicator) of all who trust in Him (Rom 3.26).[298]

Deep down in his wounded soul Job is convinced that God is righteous and must eventually speak up on behalf of His innocent servant.

Job's Denunciation – of his Friends' Impertinence: 27.7-12

In the wake of this robust assertion of guiltlessness Job proceeds to cast on his friends some of the opprobrium they have, for the past twenty or so chapters, been heaping on him. Verse 7 expresses the startling wish that those who have afflicted him with insensitive accusations be associated with the wicked in the rebuke awaiting them: "Let mine enemy be as the wicked, and he that riseth up against me as the unrighteous". In some ways Job reminds us of the psalmist who pleads for divine judgment upon those who "persecute him whom thou hast smitten; and … talk to the grief of those whom thou hast wounded" (Ps 69.26). We shall learn in chapter 30 that, since the reversal of his fortunes, he has become a pitiful object of ridicule for the baser members of his society, but the context here relates to those he thought his special friends. Certainly they have only added to the troubles which he traces ultimately to God.

But it is here that the problems begin. Hitherto Job has been at pains to deny any simplistic correlation between wickedness and punishment, but now he seems certain in his own mind that evildoers will receive their due deserts. He offers what might be called a **précis** of their destiny (27.8-12), before embarking on a more detailed **portrayal** of their terrible doom (27.13-23).

In order to sum up the hopelessness of sinful man when God intervenes, Job asks a series of four rhetorical questions:

> For what is the hope of the ungodly, when God cutteth him off, when God taketh away his soul? Will God hear his cry when distress cometh upon him? Doth he delight himself in the Almighty? will he at all times call upon God? (27.8-10, JND).

The first two questions relate to his hopelessness; the second two to his godlessness. This man's **death** is meted out by God (27.8), the ultimate executioner of the wicked. Death, like life, is His prerogative: He alone can cut off and take away the soul. The challenge of the Lord Jesus rings in our ears: "what shall it profit a man, if he shall gain the whole world, and lose his own soul?" (Mk 8.36). The KJV translation of Job 27.8 contrasts the hypocrite's "gain" in this world with his inexorable demise, but it is more likely that the language is designed to establish a linguistic parallel between cutting off and taking away in death. By means of the repetition Job is underlining the certainly of death. In the face of the divine judicial sentence, men have no hope.

Further, despite his cries of **distress** the wicked man will not be heard (27.9). The man who ignores God in prosperity will not be heeded in adversity. He will then discover to his cost that there is no one else to whom he can turn in time of need. At the start and close of Israel's history in the land there are sad allusions to the senseless folly of departure from the living God. On both occasions the nation is warned of the uselessness of reliance on the idols they have served:

> Go and cry unto the gods which ye have chosen; let them deliver you in the time of your tribulation (Judg 10.14).

> Then shall the cities of Judah and inhabitants of Jerusalem go, and cry unto the gods unto whom they offer incense: but they shall not save them at all in the time of their trouble (Jer 11.12).

The book of Revelation offers a chilling glimpse into the mind-set of earth dwellers in the future tribulation era when, conscious that their calamities are traceable to the Creator, men will not repent but rather blaspheme the God of heaven (Rev 16.9,11). Scripture makes it plain that men are to seek the Lord "while he may be found", and call on Him "while he is near" (Is 55.6), for the time will come when it is too late for mercy. As Robinson puts it, "he who will not pray when he might, perhaps cannot pray when he would".[299]

In the face of God's judgment the sinner is hopeless because he has been godless. Caustically, Job sums up the wicked man's **delight** in life (27.10). Alas, whatever else his soul may fancy, he has no relish for the Almighty. Men vainly scour the world for pleasures which cannot last because they are tied to the temporal. Only in the eternal God is there lasting satisfaction; as David says, "Thou wilt shew me the path of life: in thy presence is fulness of joy; at thy right hand there are pleasures for evermore" (Ps 16.11). To be contented with anything less than Jehovah is to court inevitable disappointment. The negative characteristics of the wicked man are that he takes no pleasure in God, nor does he call on Him in prayer. But what the sinner shuns, Job, we recall, diligently practised.

As if to remind us that not all joy need be empty, the word "delight" (6026) is also used in the Old Testament in a positive context. The psalmist's advice is to "Delight [6026] thyself also in the Lord; and he shall give thee the desires of thine heart" (Ps 37.4), while the godly Jew who keeps the Lord's commands is told, "Then shalt thou delight [6026] thyself in the Lord; and I will cause thee to ride upon the high places of the earth, and feed thee with the heritage of Jacob thy father" (Is 58.14). Attaining unalloyed pleasure is not a mere daydream. Scripture speaks of the blessednesses (in the plural) of

> the man that walketh not in the counsel of the ungodly, nor standeth in the way of sinners, nor sitteth in the seat of the scornful, But his delight is in the law of the Lord; and in his law doth he meditate day and night (Ps 1.1-2).

In a world so devoid of moral guidelines that anything goes, it seems odd to learn that lasting happiness is found in repudiating one's personal desire in favour of meditation in God's law. The believer, however, knows that time spent with the Word is never wasted, and brings its own inimitable satisfaction.

Job genuinely hopes in God, constantly calls upon God, delights in God – and is therefore sharply distinguished from the ungodly. As Delitzsch writes, "Job's fellowship with God rests upon the freedom of the most intimate confidence. He is not one of the godless".[300] We might particularly notice the central feature in that brief list: unlike the wicked, he calls upon his God "at all times" (27.10). One of the marks of the real believer is that, whatever his current circumstances, he instinctively turns to the Lord. Sometimes God's people find it easier to pray and praise in moments of settled ease. When Saul of Tarsus, converted by the power of the risen Christ, returned to his home town, there was a brief pause in the hostility which had battered the early saints. The disciples must have breathed a collective sigh of relief:

> Then had the churches rest throughout all Judaea and Galilee and Samaria, and were edified; and walking in the fear of the Lord, and in the comfort of the Holy Ghost, were multiplied (Acts 9.31).

With its intimation of numerical growth, godly reverence and spiritual encouragement among local assemblies, Luke's language is wholly optimistic. The cessation of persecution, we notice, did not cause those believers to slacken in their zeal for God. Tranquillity allowed them to "lead a quiet and peaceable life in all godliness and honesty" (1 Tim 2.2). Nevertheless, it is also true that it often takes times of distress to drive saints into the Lord's loving arms. In trouble, where else can they turn? Earlier, threatened by the religious establishment, the apostles promptly closed ranks in the fervour of spiritual fellowship:

> And being let go, they went to their own company, and reported all that the chief priests and elders had said unto them. And when they heard that, they lifted up their voice to God with one accord (Acts 4.23-24).

Thomas Watson has a homely illustration:

> Afflictions quicken our pace in the way to heaven; it is with us, as with children sent on an errand, if they meet with apples or flowers by the way, they linger and make no great haste home, but if anything fright them, then they run with all the speed they can to their father's house: so, in prosperity, we are gathering the apples and the flowers, and do not much mind heaven, but if troubles begin to arise, and the times grow frightful, then we make haste to heaven, and with David, "run the way of God's commandments".[301]

In storm and sunshine, in sickness and health, in depression and exhilaration, the believer speaks gladly to his God. That is perhaps why the early followers of Christ were described as those "that call on thy name" (Acts 9.14), for this precious relationship was the very lifeblood of their existence. An outstanding feature of the book of Job is the patriarch's constant converse with heaven. Neither calamities nor friends can interrupt his unceasing verbal engagement with God. Even a lack of response fails to dampen his ardour.

True, in his multiple distresses he has felt the heavy hand of God on him, but he is still a man of unimpeachable character against whom his friends have not been able to prove a single charge. It is on account of his experiences that Job is in a unique position to instruct his peers:

> I will teach you concerning the hand of God; what is with the Almighty will I not conceal. Behold, ye yourselves have all seen it; and why are ye thus altogether vain? (27.11-12, JND).

For the past three rounds of argument they have sought to educate him in the proper response to God's punitive dealings with him; now Job announces that he will enlighten *them*.

A man who has been the special object of God's mysterious ways in government – ways which he does not fully understand and, indeed, in one sense never will – is better placed to teach others than those who dabble in theory or speculate in academic theology. That is why in Lamentations chapter 3 the prophet Jeremiah holds up his own example of endurance as a pattern for Israel's behaviour under the rod of divine discipline. The friends' exhortations have been based on traditional dogma; Job's words, like Jeremiah's, spring from a personal encounter with God. They may have "all seen" that wickedness receives its just deserts (although, of course, in God's own time and way), yet they are "altogether vain" in their speeches, arguing back from external suffering to internal sin. The word "vain (1891)", with the implication of being led astray, first appears describing the apostate northern kingdom of Israel which "rejected [God's] statutes, and his covenant that he made with their fathers, and his testimonies which he testified against them; and they followed vanity, and became vain [1891], and went after the heathen that were round about them" (2 Kings 17.15). In the same way, Job's comforters have been misled into serious error in their attempts to interpret what has happened to Job. Though they have "seen" what has come upon him, their insights into the reasons behind it have been worthless.

Job's Elucidation – of the Wicked Man's Destiny: 27.13-23

Job's lengthy investigation of what lies ahead for God's enemies starts with a caption statement for the rest of the chapter: "This is the portion of a wicked man with God, and the heritage of oppressors, which they shall receive of the Almighty" (27.13).

His language slips easily from the singular ("a wicked man") to the plural ("oppressors") for, although the remainder of the paragraph focusses on the individual, Job, like the psalmist, knows full well that in this world "the congregation of evil doers" (Ps 26.5) embraces a vast company. It always seems that the saints are hopelessly outnumbered down here. That is why the wonderful story of Elisha and his timid servant opens our eyes to see that, in the final analysis, "they that be with us are more than they that be with them" (2 Kings 6.16). In the same way, though the first psalm starts with an individual separating himself from a threatening horde of evil people ("the ungodly ... sinners ... the scornful"), it concludes with a vast and blessed company – "the congregation of the righteous". Believers in the present era may appear to be only a "little flock", yet in the ages to come they will populate the new heavens and the new earth.

Job's language parallels "wicked" (7563) and "oppressors" (6184), making the point that one of the common consequences of sin against God is violent injustice towards fellow men. The psalmist uses both words when he sketches the apparently water-tight security of the bad man on the eve of his sudden removal from the world: "I have seen the wicked [7563] in great power [6184], and spreading himself like a green bay tree" (Ps 37.35). For all his boasted immovability he will find that he has to do with a God who is Almighty, sufficient for every situation and possessed of true power. However the godless may delude themselves, lying in wait is a "portion" they will "receive" from God. The Hebrew word for "portion" (2506) first appears in the story of Abram's daring rescue bid to snatch his wayward nephew Lot from the marauding armies who had taken him captive. Refusing the glittering prizes offered by the king of Sodom, Abraham would only take, on behalf of others, "that which the young men have eaten, and the portion of the men which went with me, Aner, Eshcol, and Mamre; let them take their portion [2506]" (Gen 14.24). That portion was material and financial gain; what lies ahead for the wicked man is terrible everlasting judgment, meted out by a God who is never mocked.

Job does not suggest that the wicked man's destiny arrives instantly. It is inevitable but it is not necessarily immediate. The distinction is important. It is here that he significantly differs from his friends, who have worked on the consistent but unproven assumption that a man's current circumstances are an infallible index of his state of soul.

After the caption verse comes a catalogue of the evils to descend upon the sinner. Job considers first what happens to his **possessions** (27.14-18), and then what happens to his **person** (27.19-23).

As to his **possessions**, everything belonging to him, family (27.14-15), wealth (27.16-17), and house (27.18), will be brought to ruin. Those emotional and material blessings which make life in this world so sweet are found to be fragile. In Middle Eastern culture children were rightly considered a particular benefit. The psalmist sums up a point of view sadly overlooked in our secular society:

> Lo, children are an heritage of the Lord: and the fruit of the womb is his reward. As arrows are in the hand of a mighty man; so are children of the youth. Happy is the man that hath his quiver full of them: they shall not be ashamed, but they shall speak with the enemies in the gate (Ps 127.3-5).

Children are a gift from God and a positive asset to their parents if they grow up to be sturdy defenders of the family. But Job speaks here of children tragically multiplied only for violent death or penury: "If his children be multiplied, it is for the sword: and his offspring shall not be satisfied with bread. Those that remain of him shall be buried in death: and his widows shall not weep" (27.14-15).

Those who survived sword and starvation would succumb to the plague. As in Jeremiah 15.2 and 43.11, "death" in this context implies pestilence. So complete will be the obliteration of these sons that their widows, emotionally exhausted, will be incapable of tears. As Delitzsch puts it,

> the women that he leaves behind do not celebrate the usual mourning rites … because the decreed punishment which, stroke after stroke, deprives them of husbands and children, prevents all observance of the customs of mourning, and because the shock stifles the feeling of pity.[302]

If the sinner's family faces extermination, his wealth, whether estimated in money or expensive clothing, will be scattered. Job's words form a chiastic statement with money (a) as the slices of the sandwich, and clothing (b) the filling:

        (a) Though he heap up silver as the dust,
            (b)and prepare raiment as the clay;
            (b) He may prepare it, but the just shall put it on,
        (a) and the innocent shall divide the silver (27.16-17).

The verb "heap up" (6651) is only found seven times in the Old Testament. Joseph uses it when he advises Pharaoh to "lay up" corn for the coming famine (Gen 41.35), and it also describes the Egyptians gathering dead frogs during the second plague (Ex 8.14). More significantly it pictures those who hoard material wealth:

> Surely every man walketh in a vain shew: surely they are disquieted in vain: he heapeth up [6651] riches, and knoweth not who shall gather them (Ps 39.6).

> And Tyrus did build herself a strong hold, and heaped up [6651] silver as the dust, and fine gold as the mire of the streets. Behold, the Lord will cast her out, and he will smite her power in the sea; and she shall be devoured with fire (Zech 9.3-4).

Whether we consider individuals (Psalm 39) or entire cities (Zechariah 9) the outlook is the same: men amass material treasure without the ability to guarantee either its preservation during their lifetime or its safe transference to their heirs. In both Job and Zechariah the similes are telling: men heap up silver "as the dust" and the purest gold "as the mire of the streets". The disturbing collocation of the precious and the worthless reminds us that eventually even the valuable things of this world are reduced to rubble. Men build to the skies but are finally brought down to the "dust" from which they were formed (Gen 2.7; 3.19). "What did he leave?" asked a man of one who had recently died. "He left it all", was the laconic answer. No matter the size of a man's bank balance while he is alive; in death, as far as he is concerned, it is nothing. Dust and dirt, according to Delitzsch, are "the emblem of a great abundance that depreciates even that which is valuable".[303] The godless man accumulates money and stores up fashionable raiment but eventually others enjoy it. "The just" wear his expensive clothes, and "the innocent" divide up his caches of silver.

Even his dwelling place is rickety. It is likened to the delicate sheath in which the clothes moth's larva secretes itself, and to a vineyard caretaker's booth: "He buildeth his house as a moth, and as a booth that the keeper maketh" (27.18). The moth has already been mentioned in Job (4.19; 13.28) and, appropriately enough, appears here immediately after a reference to clothing. According to Cansdale, its "grub-like larvae make a silk-lined case, covered on the outside with debris, out of which only the head protrudes".[304] The shaking or brushing of clothes easily destroys this frail nest. The "booth" suggests a small, temporary shelter, such as might be constructed for cattle (Gen 33.17), for the celebration of the feast of tabernacles (Lev 23.42), or for the short-term accommodation of soldiers in the field (2 Sam 11.11). Job is thinking specifically of "the flimsy hut erected in vineyards or gardens as a post for the watchman, who protects the fruit from theft or destruction by wild beasts".[305] Under Job's scornful gaze, the great man's mansion, built as a monument to his pride and prestige, shrinks to a mere tent. Not even the grandest palaces can last.

From the wicked man's possessions Job turns to his **person** (27.19-23), imagining with grim irony the moment of his death:

> He lieth down rich, but will do so no more; he openeth his eyes, and he is not. Terrors overtake him like waters; a whirlwind stealeth him away in the night. The east wind carrieth him away and he is gone; and as a storm it hurleth him out of his place. And God shall cast upon him and not spare: he would fain flee out of his hand. Men shall clap their hands at him, and shall hiss him out of his place (27.19-23, JND).

Delitzsch's explanation of verse 19, like Darby's, follows the reading of the Septuagint: "he lieth down to sleep rich, and he doeth it no more, since in the night he is removed from life and also from riches by sudden death".[306] The KJV phrase, "but he shall not be gathered", suggests, with its hint of the common Hebrew idiom of being gathered to one's ancestors, a sudden death lacking the dignity of an honourable burial. Either way the picture is of unexpected removal from life and pleasures into the chilling void of death. Job gives us a glimpse into the horror-stricken feelings of the wicked man confronted with his appalling destiny: "Terrors overtake him like waters". Five of the ten appearances of the word "terrors" (1091) are found in Job (18.11,14; 24.17; 27.20; 30.15), but it also turns up in Psalm 73 in a similar context to describe the abject misery of the sinner: "How are they brought into desolation, as in a moment! they are utterly consumed with terrors [1091]" (Ps 73.19). Fear will cascade upon him like the waters of the global cataclysm in Noah's day, waters which engulfed an unsuspecting world of people who "knew not until the flood came, and took them all away" (Mt 24.39).

Job draws freely on the language of natural disaster, alluding to "waters" and "a whirlwind", "the east wind" and "a storm". These dread phenomena metaphorically (and perhaps also literally) describe the devastating judgments of God descending upon the wicked. Delitzsch provides useful information about the "east wind":

> The east wind is dry; it excites the blood, contracts the chest, causes restlessness and anxiety, and sleepless nights or evil dreams. Both man and beast feel weak and sickly while it prevails. Hence that which is unpleasant and revolting in life is compared to the east wind.[307]

Job employs a variety of verbs to describe the impact of these natural disasters: they "overtake" the evil man, and "[steal] him away", they "[carry] him away" and "[hurl] him out of his place". However firmly he may be rooted in the world, when God strikes he is swept off the stage.

The word "steal" (1589) is mainly used in the context of straightforward theft, such as "thou shalt not steal" (Ex 20.15). But it also describes the furtiveness with which Jacob "stole away unawares" (Gen 31.20) from his father-in-law, the way Joseph was snatched "out of the land of the Hebrews" (Gen 40.15), and the craft whereby "Absalom stole the hearts of the men of Israel" (2 Sam 15.6). Retribution falls without warning on those who dwell in apparent security, haling them swiftly into disaster. The storm that "hurleth [8175] him out of his place" uses an expression variously translated in the KJV "feared" (Deut 32.17), "tempestuous" (Ps 50.3), "whirlwind" (Ps 58.9; Dan 11.40), "horribly afraid" (Jer 2.12; Ezek 32.10), and "sore afraid" (Ezek 27.35). It seems to combine the source of peril with the emotion it produces in its victims.

The last two verses of the chapter have been variously understood. The KJV (along with the RV, ASV, and Darby) makes "God" (27.22) and "Men" (27.23) the subjects respectively although, in keeping with its honest policy of alerting the reader to translator's insertions, the KJV places both words in italics. Other translations (such as YLT, ISV, CEV) view these verses as continuing, from what precedes, the imagery of a hostile storm. Here, for example, is the ESV:

> It hurls at him without pity; he flees from its power in headlong flight. It claps its hands at him and hisses at him from its place (27.22-23, ESV).

The tempest is personified as a malicious antagonist that launches itself on the wicked man, expressing its contempt by rejoicing at his fall ("claps its hands") and jeering him off the scene of his earlier triumphs ("hisses at him"). But perhaps the ambivalence of the text is deliberate: behind all the forces of nature which assault men, behind the terrible judgments which engulf the ungodly, is the hand of Jehovah Himself. As the reader has already discovered in the prologue to the book of Job, though He may use instruments as He pleases, ultimately He is the prime mover.

Let us consolidate what we are learning. As we look back over what Job has just said, he appears to be treading the same ground as his would-be comforters. It is this which has driven some expositors to desperate speculations. Some seek to distribute the contentious words among Job's friends. But, as has been noted, there is no textual justification for this expedient. Moreover, if these are meant to be the final words of, say, Zophar, then why does Job not reply to them as he has done hitherto? Chopping up the text of Scripture is simply not a viable option. Others follow the tactic of Miles Coverdale, in his sixteenth century translation of the Old Testament, by implicitly inserting the word "saying" at the close of verse 12. A modern-spelling online edition of Coverdale reads as follows:

> I will teach you in the name of God: and the thing that I have of the Almighty, will I not keep from you. Behold, ye stand in your own conceit, as though ye knew all things. Wherefore then do ye go about with such vain words, saying, This is that portion that the wicked shall have of God, and the heritage that Tyrants shall receive of the Almighty? (27.11-13).[308]

In other words, verses 13 to 23 are treated as Job's recapitulatory paraphrase of what his friends have argued over the history of the debate. There is something to be said for this way of understanding the text. Job has quoted ironically from his friends in past speeches (although never so extensively) and it might be considered apt that in this, his final address, he does so at length.

Those, however, who prefer to take Scripture at its face value, have sought to explain the difficulty with a minimum of manipulation and a reverent acceptance of the text as it stands. Older commentators like Matthew Henry are acutely sensitive to the understandable fluctuations within Job's moods as the debate progresses. Though the following extract is a long one, it is worth citing if only to express a straightforward and intelligent answer to the problem. Matthew Henry writes this about Job's words in chapter 27:

> Now that the heat of the battle was nearly over he was willing to own how far he agreed with them, and where the difference between his opinion and theirs lay. 1. He agreed with them that wicked people are miserable people, that God will surely reckon with cruel oppressors, and one time or other, one way or other, his justice will make reprisals upon them for all the affronts they have put upon God and all the wrongs they have done to their neighbours. This truth is abundantly confirmed by the entire concurrence even of these angry disputants in it. But, 2. In *this* they differed - they held that these deserved judgments are presently and visibly brought upon wicked oppressors, that *they travail with pain all their days,* that in prosperity *the destroyer comes upon them,* that they *shall not be rich,* nor their *branch green,* and that *their destruction shall be accomplished before their time* (so Eliphaz, Job 15.20-21,29,32), that the *steps of their strength shall be straitened,* that *terrors shall make them afraid on every side* (so Bildad, Job 18.7,11), that he himself *shall vomit up his riches,* and that *in the fulness of his sufficiency he shall be in straits,* so Zophar, Job 20.15,22). Now Job held that, in many cases, judgments do not fall upon them quickly, but are deferred for some time. That vengeance strikes slowly he had already shown (Job 21 and 24); now he comes to show that it strikes surely and severely, and that reprieves are no pardons.[309]

In brief, Job fully agrees that the wicked are judged, but he parts company with his friends in their insistence that such judgment is immediate and that the evidence in this life of God's governmental hand is therefore proof of a man's sin. Solomon expressed a similar understanding in Ecclesiastes:

> Though a sinner do evil an hundred times, and his days be prolonged, yet surely I know that it shall be well with them that fear God, which fear before him: But it shall not be well with the wicked, neither shall he prolong his days, which are as a shadow; because he feareth not before God. There is a vanity which is done upon the earth; that there be just men, unto whom it happeneth according to the work of the wicked; again,

there be wicked men, to whom it happeneth according to the work of the righteous: I said that this also is vanity (Eccl 8.12-14).

In other words, although their lives may be greatly extended the wicked cannot escape ultimate judgment. Nonetheless – and here Solomon gives voice to the kind of anxiety which perplexes Job – earthly experience does not invariably testify to a neat correlation between a man's character and his circumstances. The just man suffers while the evil man flourishes.

Job's words may therefore legitimately be viewed as a tempered, judicious assessment of the situation. Others have followed a comparable pathway of exegesis. Delitzsch, always pertinent in his remarks, rejects alternative explanations of the section before concluding, much like Henry, that what we see is a realistic record of a man's viewpoint subtly modulating under the pressure of argument. As he writes,

> had Job's standpoint been absolutely immoveable, the controversy could not possibly have come to a well-adjusted decision, which the poet must have planned, and which he also really brings about, by causing his hero still to retain an imperturbable consciousness of his innocence, but also allowing his irritation to subside, and his extreme harshness to become moderated.[310]

Job is a real man, "subject to like passions as we are" (James 5.17), by turns perturbed, angry, sarcastic, devout, dejected and elated. F B Meyer puts it well in his *Through the Bible Day by Day:*

> Zophar and the rest could hardly have spoken more strongly [than Job did in 27.13-23]. Though Job denied the application to himself, he was willing to admit the general truth of these propositions. Through what marvellous alternations the mind of man passes – now on the crest of the wave and again in the trough; arguing, debating, questioning; now antagonizing a position, and then almost accepting it!

There is therefore no good reason for not accepting the words as Job's own, nor for acknowledging their psychological appropriateness at this stage in the contest. The heat of battle has died down and a mood of calmer reflection has taken over, allowing Job, as it were, to give credit where credit is due. Like his friends, he fully affirms the reality of divine judgment. There is, however, this difference. First, Job does not make the dangerous (and biblically ill-founded) assumption that divine judgment is invariably instantaneous. It comes, but not always at once. His account of the wicked man assumes that he has lived out a long and prosperous life on the earth, although he is eventually swept away in death. The poetic language which so graphically describes his moment of dying hints, perhaps, at the terrible consequences which await him afterwards. Second, in so honestly testifying to the dreadful fate of the wicked, Job effectively distances himself from such people. As Robinson argues, "that Job could maintain the facts as decidedly as [the friends] themselves [constitutes] a proof that he was not the wicked man they had represented him to be".[311]

Job's Aspiration – True Wisdom: Chapter 28

Yes, the wicked will be judged, of that there can be no doubt. But what about the innocent man who has to endure the kind of calamities one would expect to be reserved for the bad? What about, in Solomon's words, those "just men, unto whom it happeneth according to the work of the wicked" (Eccl 8.14)? What about the specific case of Job?

At this point there comes a sharp change of mood, subject, and poetic manner. For the past twenty or so chapters, Job has been addressing either the three friends or God, and engaging closely – and sometimes very irritably – with the terms of the debate about God's dealings with him. Now, by contrast, he addresses no one in particular, and appears to deviate from the topic at hand in order to deplore the apparent inaccessibility of divine wisdom. Indeed, there is little sense of any speaker's identity in what sounds like a detached, impersonal account of the efforts men make chasing temporal wealth in contrast to their failure in the quest for wisdom. The language is also strangely subdued; after the storm of the earlier chapters comes the serenity of meditation. Such a passage will remind readers of the great wisdom literature sections of the Old Testament – the books of Proverbs and Ecclesiastes in particular. Nevertheless, in its context the topic makes good sense. Job, having conceded that God eventually judges the wicked, cannot as yet comprehend why He permits the righteous to be afflicted in this world. For that, he needs an insight which God alone can provide. None of his friends has been able to supply him with a satisfying answer to the problem. As Zuck comments, "this chapter is fittingly Job's, for he had been refuting the three counsellors, who had maintained that they knew God's ways".[312] But, as the hymn to wisdom demonstrates, God's ways are wholly beyond the mind of man.

Chapter 28 is particularly interesting for other reasons as well. Its technical vocabulary (containing some twelve different words for precious metals), its reiterated key question ("where shall wisdom be found? and where is the place of understanding?", 28.12, 20), its contrast between man's craving for riches and his implied indifference towards wisdom, and its concluding intimation of a vital distinction between that inscrutable divine wisdom which governs the world and the wisdom required for daily living (28.28) – all these features demand our attention.

The chapter is held together by the key word "place" (4725), which appears five times (28.1,6,12,20,23), and forms the link with what goes before. The previous chapter ended with the wicked man, despite his material riches (27.16), hurled and hissed out of his "place" (27.21,23). But now we are encouraged to hunt for a very different location. Where can one find wisdom and understanding? Man has the God-given ability to mine deep in the bowels of the earth for precious metals but, paradoxically, he misses out on the more valuable pursuit of wisdom, for that dwells only with God. Of what value are riches without the understanding of how best to use them? Or, to relate the question to Job's personal situation, how can anyone respond properly to sudden impoverishment without the resources of wisdom? Men may eagerly scour the caverns of the earth but they cannot penetrate the counsels of heaven.

The chapter may be divided into two main paragraphs: **the pursuit of wealth** (28.1-11), in which Job investigates man's quest for precious metals, and **the place of wisdom** (28.12-28), which highlights the frustrating inaccessibility of wisdom before finally locating it ultimately in the presence of Jehovah. He alone can instruct man in the right way to live.

The paragraph describing **the pursuit of wealth** (28.1-11) constitutes an astonishingly detailed account of early mining and refining techniques, which includes references to smelting (28.2), tunnelling beneath the earth's surface (28.3-4), blasting the rock (28.9), and damming up intrusive underground streams (28.10-11) in order to reach hidden treasures.

The first two verses of chapter 28 combine the processes of discovering the raw **materials** and preparing them for industrial use:

> Surely there is a vein for the silver, and a place for gold which they refine;
> Iron is taken out of the dust, and copper is molten out of the stone
> (28.1-2, JND).

The metals are categorised: silver, gold, iron, copper. If man is going to benefit from minerals hidden deep in the earth, they have to be found and then worked. Although silver appears in Genesis to describe the patriarchal affluence of "Abram [who] was very rich in cattle, in silver, and in gold" (Gen 13.2), iron and brass (possibly bronze) were first employed by Tubal-Cain, who became "the forger of every kind of tool of brass and iron" (Gen 4.22, JND). The word Darby translates "copper" (28.2) (5154) first appears in God's warning to Israel that if they are faithless to the covenant, "I will break the pride of your power; and I will make your heaven as iron, and your earth as brass" (Lev 26.19). It is characterised by toughness and durability.

In all, Job lists silver, gold (he employs three different words in the chapter), iron, copper, and sapphires. Although there was no gold in the land of Palestine, and Israel originally lacked the technical skills of smelting and smithing (1 Sam 13.19-21), silver was mined in Arabia (2 Chr 9.14) and Tarshish (Jer 10.9), while gold was obtained from Arabia (2 Chr 9.14), Ophir (1 Kings 10.11), and Sheba (1 Kings 10.2).

That gold first appears in Scripture in the Garden of Eden (Gen 2.11; Ezek 28.13) intimates that the precious metals found beneath the earth's surface are neither dangerous nor intrinsically evil, but have been placed there by divine provision for man's benefit. What has been called the "dominion mandate" – the instruction to Adam and Eve to "replenish [fill] the earth, and subdue it: and have dominion over the fish of the sea, and over the fowl of the air, and over every living thing that moveth upon the earth" (Gen 1.28) – gave man license to exploit (but not abuse) the created world. After all, gold and silver were conspicuous in the construction of both the tabernacle and the temple (in accordance with the divine blueprint) to teach Israel and her neighbours important lessons about the surpassing excellence of God their Redeemer. The best of this world was required to illustrate, albeit in a limited way, His ineffable glories. Though sinful human avarice is a root of all kinds of evil (1 Tim 6.10), things precious, beautiful and rare in themselves are not necessarily corrupt. The dazzling description of the New Jerusalem in Revelation 21 and 22 (and there seems no good reason not to take it literally) is sufficient to demonstrate God's appreciation of the aesthetically satisfying and His provision of it for the eternal delight of His people. Even the sin-marred creation around us still acknowledges a Creator who originated the concept of beauty. It is the mismanagement of the material which the Bible condemns.

But metals, once found, have to be purged of impurities before they can be fashioned into practical and attractive artefacts, hence Job's immediate allusion to the work of the refiner. The uncommon word for "refine" (28.1) (2212) is first used of the altar of incense in Solomon's temple, which was constructed of "refined [2212] gold by weight" (1 Chr 28.18). But it is also used metaphorically to describe the inerrancy of Scripture: "the words of the Lord are pure words: as silver tried in a furnace of earth, purified [2212] seven times" (Ps 12.6). The psalmist's language constitutes one of those great rock-solid assurances that there is nothing in God's written word which ought not to be there. No blot or blemish mars the perfection of Scripture: we can trust the Bible through and through. The same word turns up in another metaphorical refining context, this time related to Messiah's coming in glory to revive and restore Israel, specifically the priestly tribe of Levi:

> And he shall sit as a refiner and purifier of silver: and he shall purify the sons of Levi, and purge [2212] them as gold and silver, that they may offer unto the Lord an offering in righteousness (Mal 3.3).

Just as the Scriptures are intrinsically pure, so God's elect people Israel will in the future be purged of sinful dross to become, in a rejuvenated earth, a bright testimony to His holiness. When the Lord Jesus reigns in righteousness from Zion, Israel, repentant and trusting in the value of Calvary's finished work, will for the first time become what it was always meant to be – "a kingdom of priests, and an holy nation" (Ex 19.6). The extended use of the refining concept in other parts of Scripture, embracing the purity of divine words and the cleansing of sinful people, may suggest another thought. Is it possible that, deep down in his soul, Job is groping towards an idea faintly dawning on his consciousness – the idea that his own experiences, painful as they were, perhaps had a purgative function? The furnace of affliction may be God's means of burning away the dross of self-satisfaction, self-confidence and self-righteousness, and drawing His saints closer to Himself. Elihu will press the idea home in chapter 33. But we are running ahead of the text.

Refined raw materials may be worked into objects of profit and pleasure to man. Tragically, in a ruined world, these products often merely reflect human folly and sinful ignorance. Isaiah describes a smith energetically working away at the forge, exhausting himself in the pointless manufacture of an idol to become the object of his worship:

> The smith with the tongs both worketh in the coals, and fashioneth it with hammers, and worketh it with the strength of his arms: yea, he is hungry, and his strength faileth: he drinketh no water, and is faint (Is 44.12).

All that effort to promote useless superstition! Yet much of modern Christendom perpetuates similar absurdities in its veneration of man-made tradition, images, and the external trappings of religious ceremony.

After his catalogue of raw materials comes Job's account of primitive **mining** technology (28.3-4). With its foregrounding of human inventiveness and (in the background, suggested by Job 27.16 and 19, where we met a "rich man" who heaped up "silver as the dust") human greed, it hints at the false sense of values which dominates mankind. Material wealth is preferred to wisdom, and gold pursued rather than godliness (1 Tim 6.5). But at this stage Job is thinking primarily in literal terms. Indeed, his vivid description is unique in Scripture. The *International Standard Bible Encyclopaedia* offers the following information about ancient mining:

> In Job 28.1-11 we have the only biblical reference to mines. The writer very likely derived his information either from personal observation or from a description by an eyewitness, of the mining operations of Sinai. No traces of ancient mines have yet been found in Palestine and Syria … The usual Egyptian method of mining was to follow the vein from the surface as far as it was practicable with tools corresponding to our pick and hoe, hammer and chisel. The shafts frequently extended into the ground a distance of 180 to 200 ft. The rock when too hard to be dug out was first cracked by having fires built on it. The metal-bearing stone was carried in baskets to the surface, where the crushing and separating took place. The mining operations were performed by an army of slaves who were kept at their work day and night, driven with the lash until they died, when their places were taken by others.

What Job does – and does memorably – is to suffuse the kind of technical data suited to an encyclopaedia article such as that quoted above with the emotional colouring of poetry. He draws our attention, for example, to the physical perils and isolation associated with penetrating the subterranean darkness in quest of treasure (28.3-4). Here, in Darby's translation, is his gripping tribute to heroic human endeavour:

> Man putteth an end to the darkness, and exploreth to the utmost limit, the stones of darkness and of the shadow of death. He openeth a shaft far from

the inhabitants of the earth: forgotten of the foot, they hang suspended; away below men they hover (28.3-4, JND).

While other people go about their normal business, the miner daringly burrows into the obscure recesses of the earth's crust. He disperses the darkness with the blaze of his torch, and uncovers costly "stones" (68), a word first used in the Edenic context of precious gems (Gen 2.12). Far from centres of population, in places where no one goes ("forgotten of the foot"), he plies his risky trade, hanging and swinging dangerously in caverns below, suspended from ropes or cages as he works a vertical shaft.

The **marvel** (28.5-8) of divinely endowed human ingenuity is seen in man's capacity to access and appropriate what is both unknown and unappreciated by the animal kingdom:

> As for the earth, out of it cometh bread, and underneath it is turned up as by fire; The stones of it are the place of sapphires, and it hath dust of gold. It is a path no bird of prey knoweth, and the vulture's eye hath not seen it; The proud beasts have not trodden it, nor the fierce lion passed over it (28.5-8, JND).

Although, in God's providential goodness, the earth's surface supplies the cereals needed for the maintenance of human life, deep beneath that fertile exterior lurk treasures beyond the wit of the brute creation. The contrast between the prepositions "out of it" and "underneath" highlights the gulf between what can be seen and what is concealed. It is easy to observe that bread comes from the farmer's toil on the earth's surface, but out of sight and often out of mind the miner negotiates the darkness in his search for invaluable minerals ("sapphires" and "dust of gold"), using fire to blast the rock and separate the precious ore from its encasing stone. Hartley informs us that

> in some mining processes a large fire was built on a platform to heat the wall of the tunnel. When the rock became hot, water was poured on it, causing the stone to crack. The miners would then rake up the fallen stones and carry them to the surface.[313]

Knowledge of these resources was not entrusted to the lower creation; birds of prey, however far sighted, are ignorant of their whereabouts, and animals as majestic as the lion are unaware of their existence. In a world deluded by evolutionary mythology into denigrating the uniqueness of humanity, the book of Job stands as a reminder of the essential difference between man and the beasts. One aspect of the image of God in man is an appreciation of the precious and the beautiful.

The sheer human **mastery** (28.9-11) of the physical creation is emphasised by the verbs Job draws on to sketch out the way the miner delves for riches:

> Man putteth forth his hand upon the flinty rock, he overturneth the mountains by the root. He cutteth out channels in the rocks, and his eye

seeth every precious thing. He bindeth the streams that they drip not, and what is hidden he bringeth forth to light (28.9-11, JND).

He "putteth forth his hand ... overturneth ... cutteth out ... seeth ... bindeth ... bringeth forth". The language speaks of energy and persistence. Solomon's shrewd advice, "Whatsoever thy hand findeth to do, do it with thy might; for there is no work, nor device, nor knowledge, nor wisdom, in the grave, whither thou goest" (Eccl 9.10), is here acted out in the hunt for wealth. The overturning of mountains refers to the rock upheavals involved in mining. The word, an explosive one, describes the destruction of Sodom and Gomorrah (Gen 19.25). Here in Job, according to Delitzsch, it probably alludes to "Blasting in mining which lays bare the roots (the lowest parts) of the mountains" so that the miner can reach the ore. Again, Delitzsch, quoting from another authority but inserting his own explanatory comments in square brackets, helps us understand what is meant by "binding the streams":

> The miner makes ways through the hard rock into his section in which the perpendicular shaft terminates, guides the water which is found in abundance at that depth through it [i.e., the water at the bottom of the pit that hinders the progress of the work], and is able ... to judge of the ore and fragments that are at the bottom, and bring them to the light. This mode of mining by constantly forming one gallery under the other [so that a new gallery is made under the pit that is worked out by extending the shaft, and also freeing this from water by making another outlet below the previous one] is the oldest of all, of which anything certain is known in the history of mining, and the most natural in the days when they had no notion of hydraulics.[314]

Clearly, it is no easy matter to prise out riches from beneath the earth's crust. Yet men do it in their unquenchable thirst for material treasure and personal gain.

At this point Job moves smoothly into the second section of the chapter: the **place of wisdom** (28.12-28):

> But wisdom, where shall it be found? and where is the place of understanding? Man knoweth not the value thereof; and it is not found in the land of the living. The deep saith, It is not in me; and the sea saith, It is not with me. Choice gold cannot be given for it, nor silver be weighed for its price. It is not set in the balance with gold of Ophir, with the precious onyx, and the sapphire. Gold and glass cannot be compared to it, nor vessels of fine gold be its exchange. Corals and crystal are no more remembered; yea, the acquisition of wisdom is above rubies. The topaz of Ethiopia shall not be compared to it, neither shall it be set in the balance with pure gold (28.12-19, JND).

Job's catalogue of the planet's mineral wealth highlights two things: the contrast between what man greedily pursues and what he neglects, and the inability of wisdom to be purchased with money. In the first section of the chapter he listed some of the metals sought by man – silver, gold and sapphires (for value), copper and iron (for strength) – but now he adds others: onyx, glass, coral, crystal, ruby, topaz. The onyx, like gold, was found in Eden (Gen 2.12). Glass (or crystal) is mentioned only here. Coral appears only here and Ezekiel 27.16. The ruby turns up in a few poetic passages. The commentators debate the precise meaning of the Hebrew words (much as they argue about the scientific identification of the decorative stones in the New Jerusalem), but the general point is obvious. Wisdom, the value of which outweighs the world's wealth, is not to be purchased at any price. Job's earlier description of mining endeavour hints that not even hard work can lead to its discovery.

The next few verses again raise the question of wisdom's whereabouts:

Whence then cometh wisdom? and where is the place of understanding? For it is hidden from the eyes of all living, and concealed from the fowl of the heavens. Destruction and death say, We have heard its report with our ears (28.20-22, JND).

It cannot be located in the created universe, and no living creature can trace it. Even the world of the dead seems only to have heard a rumour of it.

The answer to Job's question (and, indeed, the final answer to Job's predicament as the innocent victim of suffering) is to bring in God:

God understandeth the way thereof, and he knoweth its place: For he looketh to the ends of the earth, he seeth under the whole heaven. In making a weight for the wind, and meting out the waters by measure, In appointing a statute for the rain, and a way for the thunder's flash: Then did he see it, and declare it; he established it, yea, and searched it out; And unto man he said, Lo, the fear of the Lord, that is wisdom; and to depart from evil is understanding (28.23-28, JND).

For the first time in the chapter, God is named. Job's wisdom hymn broadly reflects the movement of the whole book. Seeking the solution to his personal trauma, Job finds nothing but disappointment until Jehovah steps in with such a stunning self-disclosure as to still his fears. In the same way, men ransack the globe for financial gain yet cannot answer the riddle of human life – unless, that is, God intervenes. We should take note of the stupendous majesty of this God. Job's words condense an entire body of systematic theology. God is all-knowing (for He "understandeth the way thereof, and he knoweth its place"), everywhere present (because "he looketh to the ends of the earth, he seeth under the whole heaven"), and all-powerful in His government of the natural world ("making a weight for the wind, and meting out the waters by measure, In appointing a statute for the rain, and a way for the thunder's flash"). This summary of divine attributes unconsciously paves the way for the grand manifestation of chapters 38 to 41.

It might be appropriate at this point to attempt some definition of wisdom, the key idea of the chapter. William Shedd's *Dogmatic Theology* informs us that the Hebrew and Greek words for wisdom "primarily signify skilful, expert", and explains wisdom in Scripture as "a particular aspect of the Divine knowledge", namely "the intelligence of God as manifested in the adaptation of means to ends". It is seen in creation, providence and redemption. Shedd goes on to say that

> wisdom implies a final end, to which all secondary ends are subordinate. This end is the glory of God … The glory of God is such a manifestation of the Divine perfections as leads creatures to worship and adore.[315]

Wisdom, then, is an attribute of God. The *Westminster Larger Catechism* of 1647 agrees. In answer to the question "What is God?", it offers the following capsule definition:

> God is a Spirit, in and of himself infinite in being, glory, blessedness, and perfection; all-sufficient, eternal, unchangeable, incomprehensible, everywhere present, almighty, knowing all things, most wise, most holy, most just, most merciful and gracious, longsuffering, and abundant in goodness and truth.[316]

The God of the Bible is eternally and unerringly "most wise" in all His ways. Wisdom, in this context, describes the infallible skill with which He made and governs His universe. It is that same wisdom which is given a voice in the book of Proverbs and sounds, read in the fuller light of New Testament revelation (Lk 11.49; 1 Cor 1.24), like a divine person:

> I was set up from everlasting, from the beginning, or ever the earth was. When there were no depths, I was brought forth; when there were no fountains abounding with water. Before the mountains were settled, before the hills was I brought forth: While as yet he had not made the earth, nor the fields, nor the highest part of the dust of the world. When he prepared the heavens, I was there: when he set a compass upon the face of the depth: When he established the clouds above: when he strengthened the fountains of the deep: When he gave to the sea his decree, that the waters should not pass his commandment: when he appointed the foundations of the earth: Then I was by him, as one brought up with him: and I was daily his delight, rejoicing always before him; Rejoicing in the habitable part of his earth; and my delights were with the sons of men (Prov 8.23-31).

Wisdom is the unfathomable excellence of the living God whereby, with beautiful perfection, He governs His creatures. His sway cannot be resisted nor

His purpose thwarted. The Lord Jesus Christ, Himself Creator, Conserver and Consummator of the universe, is divine wisdom manifest in the flesh.

But there is another kind of wisdom, and it is important in reading chapter 28 that we note the difference. The Hebrew word used in Job 28 (2451) first appears, along with a related term, in connection with the practical expertise needed to construct Israel's tabernacle:

> And thou shalt speak unto all that are wise [2450] hearted, whom I have filled with the spirit of wisdom [2451], that they may make Aaron's garments to consecrate him, that he may minister unto me in the priest's office (Ex 28.3).

Wisdom is therefore not exclusively a divine attribute; the same word can be used to describe God-given human intelligence or skill. This wisdom, we note, is no innate possession of man but a gift from above. Parallel to the noun "wisdom" in Job 28.12 is the synonym "understanding" (998). The two words occur together for the first time in Jehovah's exhortation to Israel to obey His commandments when they enter their promised land, "for this is your wisdom [2451] and your understanding [998] in the sight of the nations, which shall hear all these statutes, and say, Surely this great nation is a wise and understanding people" (Deut 4.6). Wisdom, then, is a gracious gift from God enabling His people to submit to His law, that rule of life given them for their earthly blessing. It might be considered synonymous with reverence and obedience.

As mentioned earlier, Job 28 may be viewed as the book in miniature. In its description of man's search for riches it illustrates the earnest quest for an answer to God's dealings with Job, a quest extending over thirty chapters. How can mortal man comprehend God's ways with him? Human ingenuity may uncover the treasures of the earth but it cannot solve the enigma of Job's trials. Significantly, the answer with which the chapter ends is not the one Job sought, for he seems finally to acknowledge that there are different kinds of wisdom. The first consists of the mysterious plans of God for individual men and women, something they, for all their intelligence, cannot comprehend – and Job of course never learns why he suffered. The second relates to man's responsibility to submit to God's ways with him, and depart from evil. Wisdom embraces two distinct truths: first, the inscrutable divine counsels in the government of the world, including His arrangement of the tiniest details of a man's life; and, second, the conduct He requires of man. God's ways with His people are His personal prerogative which none can share. But our response must be reverent submission and uprightness. In suddenly informing us that God alone "understandeth … and … knoweth" (28.23), Job anticipates the divine intervention of chapter 38.

Not surprisingly, the commentator Elmer B Smick sees chapter 28 as a key moment:

> The chapter as the literary apex of the book anticipates the theophany but does so without creating a climax. God alone has the answer or, better, *is* the answer to the mystery Job and his friends have sought to fathom.[317]

It may help to understand the chapter's crucial lesson if we remind ourselves of Moses's statement in Deuteronomy, with Israel poised on the borders of their land. Although his words relate primarily to God's warnings to the elect nation that disobedience would lead to exile, they establish a basic principle of submission which transcends all dispensational distinctions:

> The secret things belong unto the Lord our God: but those things which are revealed belong unto us and to our children for ever, that we may do all the words of this law (Deut 29.29).

"The secret things" include God's wise administration of His creation, His often perplexing dealings with individual men, and the unfolding of His gracious purpose. These things are essentially beyond our ken. However, God has chosen to reveal a great deal – including the way we should live in His world. If the phrase "The secret things" casts the spotlight on His sovereignty, the "things which are revealed" relates to human responsibility. Man cannot peer into the secrets of God's ways with His saints, for the creaturely mind is too small and too damaged by sin to comprehend. What man *can* – and indeed *must* – do, is exhibit the second kind of wisdom: the wisdom of godly behaviour, which reverently surrenders to God, seeking to steer a righteous path in the world.

What practical lessons may we draw from Job's great hymn to wisdom? Three spring to mind.

First of all, we are reminded that **creation** stands as a glorious testimony to God's generous provision of raw materials for man's resourcefulness to discover and work. It was never intended that man should be idle: even in his innocence God placed him in Eden to "dress it and to keep it" (Gen 2.15). The two words sum up his duties. The first (5647) basically means to work or labour (and is translated "till" in Genesis 2.5); the second (8104) means to guard or preserve (and is used that way in Job 10.12 and 29.2). It is God's purpose that "Man goeth forth unto his work and to his labour until the evening" (Ps 104.23). Absence of employment robs men of dignity, meaning and structure in life. For the believer, work is essential, as Paul points out: "even when we were with you, this we commanded you, that if any would not work, neither should he eat" (2 Thess 3.10). The earth has been amazingly fashioned by God to offer innumerable opportunities for exciting and productive industry. Doubtless this will be seen in its perfection during the kingdom reign of the Lord Jesus Christ.

Second, man's **exploitation** of the riches of nature demonstrates a God-given drive to probe and harness his environment. Vishal Mangalwadi's fascinating study, *The Book that Made your World*, argues that it was an acceptance of biblical teaching which led, particularly in the western hemisphere, to the wide-scale development of technology (which he defines as "integrating mind and muscles"[318]), arts and sciences for the betterment of mankind. These advancements took place in the west rather than the fatalistic east because – in the past, at least – the west took seriously the scriptural view that man has been given by God both the power and the right to explore and exploit his world. "Technology", he writes, "is a fruit of a biblical worldview". He goes on to assert further that "only one culture has promoted technology for general welfare and for liberating and empowering the weak – slaves, women, children, the handicapped, and the poor".[319]

Of course, Adam's original authority over the created world was to be exercised primarily for the glory of God. Sin has compromised all human activities so that selfishness, rather than godliness, now characterizes the arts, sciences and technologies. Man's fallen tendency to elevate the material above the spiritual is especially seen in his desperate deification of wealth, fame, and pleasure. To paraphrase the well-known remark of G K Chesterton, when men cease to worship the living God of creation they don't worship nothing at all, they worship anything. The terrible downhill slide into idolatry is charted in Romans 1. Job's tribute to human technological innovation in the quest for earthly fortune is simultaneously a sad acknowledgement of fallen man's obsession with the temporal. Men are clever, but rarely wise.

Yet the chapter's graphic portrayal of heroic human endeavour in the realm of the physical may, paradoxically, act as a positive **stimulation** to the believer. It hints at the resolve needed to dig out the riches of God's written Word. The resourcefulness of human ingenuity in extracting precious minerals out of the earth illustrates the spiritual diligence necessary to uncover the far more durable treasures in the Scriptures, the source of true wisdom:

> My son, if thou wilt receive my words, and hide my commandments with thee; So that thou incline thine ear unto wisdom, and apply thine heart to understanding; Yea, if thou criest after knowledge, and liftest up thy voice for understanding; If thou seekest her as silver, and searchest for her as for hid treasures; Then shalt thou understand the fear of the Lord, and find the knowledge of God. For the Lord giveth wisdom: out of his mouth cometh knowledge and understanding (Prov 2.1-6).

Temporal riches picture imperishable riches. In the KJV, the phrase "gold and silver" appears seven times throughout the historical books of the Old Testament in a purely literal sense to describe the amassing of material wealth (2 Kings 14.14; 1 Chr 18.10; 29.3; 2 Chr 9.14; 24.14; Ezra 5.14; Esth 1.6). However, it reappears in the Psalms to speak of the incomparable value of God's Word: "The law of thy mouth is better unto me than thousands of gold and silver" (Ps 119.72). But, like gold and silver ore, the written Word needs to be worked at to access its marvellous resources of wisdom, comfort and strength. Scripture will only yield its blessings to those who study it regularly, seriously, systematically, contextually and – above all – thoughtfully. Someone has said that we should read the Scriptures to get the facts, study to get the meaning, and meditate to get the benefit.

The final verse of the chapter presents the attainment of wisdom as the great goal of human endeavour. It takes us back to the beginning of the book, where Job was described as one who "feared God, and eschewed evil" (1.1). As if to cement the connection even more emphatically, the terminology is identical; the

Hebrew word translated "eschewed" (1.1) is the same as that rendered "depart from" (28.28). Chapter 29 will go on to catalogue detailed evidence that Job truly feared God, while chapter 31 will prove that he departed from evil. From the very start of his story Job is presented as a wise man marked by reverence and obedience. That was his essential character – and yet possessing such an outstanding testimony neither sheltered him from distress nor enabled him to account for that distress. It does not seem to answer the question of why God should deal with him as though he were one of the wicked. But the book is not yet over. Chapter 28 faintly hints at a resolution: Job's burdened heart will only be satisfied when God Himself breaks the silence.

For the Christian believer, of course, genuine spiritual wisdom is found in the pages of the Bible. It is there that the living Word (the Lord Jesus Christ), "In whom are hid all the treasures of wisdom and knowledge" (Col 2.3), is mediated to His people. True wisdom – heaven's recipe for living a blessed life in this world – still consists in fearing the Lord (reverence) and departing from evil (righteousness). Genuine God-fearingness can never be out of date. As the psalmist puts it, "The fear of the Lord is the beginning of wisdom: a good understanding have all they that do his commandments" (Ps 111.10). Those who cannot understand His ways with them – and that includes not just Job but all of us – can still bow to His will for them, knowing (in the reassuring light of Calvary) that it is always right.

> Men search for wisdom: they scour through the skies,
> Vainly pursuing the way to be wise;
> Down in the depths they go grubbing for gold,
> Hoping to gain from it riches untold;
> Money and industry, learning and zeal,
> None of these efforts can wisdom reveal.
> Where is its origin, where does it live?
> How can I find it, and what must I give?
> This is the answer the Scriptures afford:
> "Wisdom consists in the fear of the Lord!"

SECTION 21
Dialogue: Job 4 – 42.6
Contest: Round 3: Job 22-31
Job's 8th and Final Speech: Job 26-31
Part Three: Job 29-31

At long last we are now on the home stretch of Job's concluding speech of self-defence. In chapter 26 he delivered a master class on divine greatness which completely eclipsed Bildad's orthodox but uninspired summary. He then moved on to a more detailed response to the charge that man cannot be just with God. This paved the way for an honest acknowledgement in chapter 27 that God will indeed eventually judge wickedness. But the problem of why He currently afflicts the righteous remains insoluble. God-given wisdom, as presented in chapter 28, offers a recipe of humble submission but does not in itself afford an answer to personal calamity.

This concluding section, which makes no direct mention of the friends, consists of three chapters in which Job pens his autobiography. His presentation is carefully structured. Chapter 29 recounts his prosperous past ("Oh that I were as in months past", 29.2), while chapter 30 laments his miserable present ("But now", 30.1,9,16). Chapter 31 ends by offering a final, solemn protestation of innocence ("I made a covenant with mine eyes", 31.1) in the face of all the unjust charges his friends, explicitly or implicitly, have laid against him. The section can be broken down as follows:

>   1. Job's Prosperous Past: 29
>   2. Job's Pitiful Present: 30
>   3. Job's Pious Protestation: 31

Job's Prosperous Past: Chapter 29

After a brief introduction, the chapter subdivides into two main paragraphs. The first summarises Job's **personal affluence** (29.1-6), while the second elaborates in some detail on his **social influence** (29.7-25).

We start then with his **personal affluence** (29.1-6):

The introductory verse suggests that Job has momentarily halted in his flow to see if any of his friends is willing to reply to what he has said so far. This narrative prelude reminds us that he is continuing with his "parable" (29.1), a carefully measured and crafted poetic discourse which brings his verbal testimony to a formal closure. Spontaneity and casualness, so overrated in twenty-first century western society, are completely out of place here. Judging his words by modern fashions of oratory or eloquence is entirely irrelevant. With an almost operatic stylisation, lifting everything he says above the commonplace, Job proceeds to offer a series of selected glimpses into his past life which foreground its external success and esteem. The whole speech is deliberately stately in its rhetoric. One fact we must not miss is that Job first and foremost credits all his blessings to the gracious hand of God in his life.

His **personal affluence** is categorised in terms of a three-fold generous divine provision. This consists of protection from harm, a sense of God's presence, and the enjoyment of material prosperity.

As he looks back to happier days we learn that he was always deeply conscious of God's **protection** from calamity (29.2-3): "Oh that I were as in months past, as in the days when God preserved me; When his lamp shone over my head, and by his light I walked through darkness" (29.2-3, JND).

"Months" may offer some insight into the length of time Job has been suffering, or it may simply allude to a past contentment which seems now but a distant memory. Yet its reality was a certainty, because God kept him for "days", discrete units of time in which he bathed in the sunshine of heaven's favour. "Preserve" (8104) translates a word that appears twelve times in Job. It is rendered in the KJV "save" (2.6), "preserve" (10.12), "mark" (10.14; 22.15; 33.11; 39.1), "look narrowly" (13.27), "watch" (14.16), "keep" (23.11), "wait" (24.15), and "take heed" (36.21). Appropriately, its first and last occurrences are in the framework speeches of Jehovah (2.6; 39.1). Even when Job was least conscious of it, his God was watching over him in love. How much every child of God owes to unseen daily divine protection! Whether enduring storm or sunshine, the believer can know that "The eternal God is thy refuge, and underneath are the everlasting arms" (Deut 33.27).

It was heaven's favour which guided him safely through previous seasons of potential catastrophe when, as he admits, "I walked through darkness". The noun is common in Job, appearing twenty-three times, and referring sometimes to literal darkness (3.4), sometimes to ignorance (5.14), sometimes to disaster (15.22-23; 23.17). Job is thinking of light as an emblem of God's special goodwill toward him and his household, but the two nouns ("lamp" and "light") are the same as those used by the psalmist to testify to the power of the word to direct the believer's steps. We can be thankful that it is still true that God's word *is* "a lamp unto my feet, and a light unto my path" (Ps 119.105). In a world of uncertainty and anxiety, where every step is a potential pitfall, the Scriptures alone are our reliable source of guidance.

He was also fully aware of the intimate **presence** of the Almighty in his life: "As I was in the days of my youth, when the secret counsel of God was over my tent, When the Almighty was yet with me, my young men round about me" (29.4-5, JND).

Good times recollected are often suffused with the rosy glow of nostalgia. On the other hand, they may also be wiped from the mind by the miseries of the present. Spurgeon says somewhere that "too many people write their blessings in the sand but engrave their sorrows in marble".[320] Job, however, has a lively appreciation of God's goodness. He describes his heyday as his "youth". The word literally refers to autumn or winter (it first appears in Genesis 8.22 as part of the post-diluvian promise that the natural cycle of the seasons would continue for the duration of the present universe), but Job uses it metaphorically of what we might call the prime of life. The Jamieson, Fausset and Brown note is helpful: "the time of the ripe fruits of my prosperity. Applied to *youth,* as the Orientalists *began* their year with autumn, the most temperate season in the East". More significant, though, is the specific nature of his blessing: "the secret of God was upon my tabernacle" (29.4). "Secret" (5475) is first used of Simeon and Levi's vile conspiracy to slaughter their pagan neighbours, a plot fertilized by "anger" and "selfwill", which brought Jacob into real danger (Gen 49.6). It suggests close consultation and solidarity, here in the context of appalling brutality (Ps 64.2; 83.3). But the same word is used positively by David to describe times of spiritual fellowship, when "we took sweet counsel [5475] together, and walked unto the house of God in company" (Ps 55.14). Eliphaz earlier inquired sarcastically about Job's source of information: "Hast thou heard the secret [5475] of God? and dost thou restrain wisdom to thyself?" (15.8). Job has used the word of his most intimate companions, "my inward [5475] friends ... they whom I loved are turned against me" (19.19). But he now looks back longingly to moments when he consciously savoured the companionate nearness of his God. This is yet another testimony to his moral rectitude for, as the psalmist says, "the secret of the Lord is with them that fear him; and he will shew them his covenant" (Ps 25.14). As an upright man, Job genuinely lived in the good of the proverb that "the froward is abomination to the Lord: but his secret is with the righteous" (Prov 3.32). Whatever external miseries he might be suffering there is no question that Job knew far more than his friends about God.

His words sketch a brief, idealised scene of spiritual and familial contentment. Godly Job enjoyed insight into something of the divine counsels, knew the Almighty's nearness, and revelled in the cherished companionship of his children. The prepositions indicate how the goodness of God surrounded him on all sides, "over" his tent, "with" him, and his family "round about" him. The reference to his children, however, pointedly reminds the reader of how far poor Job has been removed from those halcyon days. Nevertheless, as Hartley writes, "his conviction about God's blessing keeps his lament focused on the real cause of his pain, a ruptured relationship with God".[321] What breaks Job's heart is that he has been deprived of what he valued most.

By contrast, the New Testament believer, blessed with the complete revelation of God's mind in Christ, can rejoice that nothing has the ability to separate him "from the love of God, which is in Christ Jesus our Lord" (Rom 8.39), or from the benevolent company of a dependable Saviour who has pledged that "I will never leave thee, nor forsake thee" (Heb 13.5b). More, that promise is presented not as some theoretical dogma but as a practical incentive to godly behaviour: "Let your conversation be without covetousness; and be content with such things as ye have" (Heb 13.5a). To know the presence of Christ puts everything else into true perspective.

Along with all this spiritual fellowship went that outward **prosperity** which so often accompanied godliness in Old Testament days: "When my steps were bathed in milk, and the rock poured out beside me rivers of oil!" (29.6, JND).

Job's word picture conjures up a world of unconstrained abundance and luxury: wherever he went ("my steps") Job lived in the enjoyment of the best milk and oil, materials suggestive of eastern wealth. It was with such rich dairy produce that Abram entertained his heavenly visitors (Gen 18.8), Jael dined Sisera (Judg 5.25), and loyal friends supported the outcast David (2 Sam 17.29). From olive trees among the rocks, noted for yielding the finest fruits, Job was supplied with oil beyond measure. "Olive oil was a vital product for the ancients. They used it for cooking, for fuel in their lamps, and as an ointment for the body".[322] The hyperbole underlines his wealth.

All material benefits are ultimately traceable to God's grace and may indeed testify to divine pleasure, but – and this is important to grasp, for it lies at the heart of the book of Job – their presence is in itself no guarantee of heavenly approval any more than their absence betokens censure. The Lord Jesus taught His disciples about God's impartial benevolence, saying that "your Father which is in heaven … maketh his sun to rise on the evil and on the good, and sendeth rain on the just and on the unjust" (Mt 5.45). Even in the Old Testament the wicked could be wealthy and the godly comparatively poor, otherwise David's contrast is meaningless: "A little that a righteous man hath is better than the riches of many wicked" (Ps 37.16). Today, when there is little or no correlation between a man's faith and his finances, impoverished saints may take heart from the knowledge that they are heirs to imperishable riches in Christ. As the Saviour says to the messenger from the Smyrnan assembly, "I know thy works, and tribulation, and poverty, (but thou art rich)" (Rev 2.9). How cheering is that parenthesis!

Job, then, was rich. However, the number of verses devoted to it suggest that even more significant to him than his wealth was his remarkable **social influence** in the world of his day (29.7-25).

Job presents us with a series of verbal tableaux illustrating the admiration in which he was held. It is rather like one of those old Pathé newsreels. We witness him moving slowly from his house down the city street towards the gate in which all major business transactions and judicial hearings took place. Along the route he is greeted with the deepest veneration by his fellow-citizens. His stately **advance** to the centre of civic life is depicted as a kind of solemn ceremonial procession (29.7-10). Then follows a condensed description of his **activities** as an ideal magistrate, upholding right and punishing wrong (29.11-17), After this comes an unusual if brief glimpse into his thinking processes in those days, a kind of mini-soliloquy of **anticipation** in which (with an irony all too painfully obvious to the reader) he looks forward to a long continuation of these outward blessings (29.18-20), Finally, the judicial session comes to its end with Job acclaimed as the last word in legal wisdom. He stands as the ultimate **authority** before whom all others bow in submission (29.21-25). But let us examine this narrative in greater depth.

Job's **advance** from his home to the hub of city life (29.7-10) clearly makes the point that he was esteemed by all, regardless of their age ("the young … the aged") or status ("the princes … the nobles"). Davidson comments that "as a rich landowner [he] would not live in the city but on his estate that adjoined it. He took part, however, in all the life of the city, and sat in the council that guided its affairs".[323] Job enjoyed universal respect:

When I went out to the gate by the city, when I prepared my seat on the broadway, The young men saw me, and hid themselves; and the aged arose and stood up; Princes refrained from talking, and laid the hand on their mouth; The voice of the nobles was hushed, and their tongue cleaved to their palate (29.7-10, JND).

In an eastern city, the gate was the site of commercial and legal transactions, the place where the elders gathered to debate matters of common concern. According to Keil and Delitzsch, it was

generally an arched entrance with deep recesses and seats on either side ... a place of meeting in the ancient towns of the East, where the inhabitants assembled either for social intercourse or to transact public business.[324]

It was "business centre, town hall, and courthouse combined".[325] Lot's tragedy was that he "sat in the gate of Sodom" (Gen 19.1), implicitly endorsing a society where the divine standards instituted at creation had been shamelessly abandoned. Abraham, however, lawfully purchased land from the Hittites for Sarah's burial, appropriately completing the formal business in the presence of witnesses "at the gate of [the] city" (Gen 23.10). Job was evidently a man of immense distinction with his own honourable seat not so much in the street (as the KJV, perhaps slightly misleadingly, translates) as "on the broadway" (JND) or "in the plaza" (ISV). So highly esteemed was he that young men deferentially drew back as he approached, while his fellow elders rose in respectful greeting, remaining standing until he was seated. The most prestigious men of his society, princes and nobles, immediately ceased their conversation as though in awe of his proven wisdom. Just as Ezekiel was for a time struck dumb as a sign to recalcitrant Judah (Ezek 3.26), so Job's peers found themselves tongue-tied in his presence.

But Job was far more than a mere object of esteem revered by great and small. As we read about his **activities** (29.11-17) we learn that the needy were profoundly – and rightly – grateful for his energetic exertions on their behalf. Whatever judicial verdict he pronounced people applauded, for he worked tirelessly in support of the disadvantaged. This passage consists of a detailed account of his benevolent ministry as a local magistrate (29.11-13,15-17), in the middle of which stands a verse which sums up his activities (29.14).

First, then, we see him in action as "the champion of the underdog":[326]

For I delivered the afflicted that cried, and the fatherless who had no helper. The blessing of him that was perishing came upon me, and I caused the widow's heart to sing for joy ... I was eyes to the blind, and feet was I to the lame; I was a father to the needy, and the cause which I knew not I searched out; And I broke the jaws of the unrighteous, and plucked the spoil out of his teeth (29.12-13,15-17, JND).

Job initially catalogues four kinds of vulnerable people: the afflicted, the fatherless, those on the verge of perishing, and the widows. The first word (6041) is often translated "poor", and describes any general condition of destitution and distress. However, it is also, amazingly, used of Israel's Messiah entering Jerusalem "lowly [6041], and riding upon an ass, and upon a colt the foal of an ass" (Zech 9.9). This lowly Messiah would, in grace, provide true deliverance for the needy. The psalmist looks ahead to a righteous reign in which Jehovah's promised king would

> judge thy people with righteousness, and thy poor [6041] with judgment. The mountains shall bring peace to the people, and the little hills, by righteousness. He shall judge the poor [6041] of the people, he shall save the children of the needy, and shall break in pieces the oppressor (Ps 72.2-4).

From Exodus 22.22 onwards, the Lord made clear that the fatherless and the widow were to be the special objects of Israel's care. Where Israel, alas, so often failed in its duty, Job was outstandingly faithful. The Hebrew word in 29.13 rendered "perish" (6) has a range of English equivalents of which "perish" and "destroy" are the commonest. It is first used in Exodus 10.17 of the devastating effects of divine judgment on the land of Egypt. Job saw it as his responsibility to afford practical assistance, financial aid, and protection for the helpless.

But not only did Job rescue the materially disadvantaged, he exercised himself on behalf of the physically disabled ("the blind … the lame"), making up for their incapacity. To such needy people he was like a father in his stalwart aid, and even those who had no claims upon him at all – the outsiders, the strangers, the foreigners – were sure of his support because he vigorously investigated the "cause of him that I knew not" (29.16, RV). In Job judicial conscientiousness reached its apogee.

Nor is that all. He tells us that while the needy blessed him, the wicked feared him, for he exposed their lawless schemes and delivered their victims. The language likens them to ravening wild animals eager to seize on their quarry. In Job, however, they met their match, for he smashed their jaws, causing them to drop their prey, just as David later battled with lion and bear to save his father's flock (1 Sam 17.34-35).

It is very clear that Job's righteousness was not some esoteric ritual divorced from the realities of daily life; rather, it was a practical hands-on involvement in the affairs of men, especially in response to the sufferings of the marginalised. In answer to Eliphaz's earlier and wholly unsubstantiated charge of dereliction of social duty (22.5-9), Job counters with an account of his life which fleshes out in detail the divine estimate recorded at the start of the book (1.1). In an Old Testament context he abundantly fulfilled the teaching of James that "Pure religion and undefiled before God and the Father is this, To visit the fatherless and widows in their affliction, and to keep himself unspotted from the world" (James 1.27).

At the same time, because of the idealised language employed in this description,

Job seems to anticipate something of the just but compassionate administration of the Lord Jesus when He rules the earth. A glimpse of this was seen at the first advent, when the Saviour fulfilled much of Isaiah's messianic prediction that "the eyes of the blind shall be opened, and the ears of the deaf shall be unstopped. Then shall the lame man leap as an hart" (Is 35.5-6). His consideration for the needy was boundless and His power incalculable. This was evidence sufficient to quash all John the Baptist's doubts as to the Lord's identity (Mt 11.1-6), for such gracious miracles proved Him capable of introducing those kingdom conditions of righteousness and well-being which the Old Testament led Israel to expect. If the beneficiaries of Job's ministry could not contain their delight (for Job tells us he was showered with the plaudits and songs of those he rescued), how much more should those redeemed from eternal destruction by the infinite value of Calvary express their gratitude in glad hymns of praise!

Nestling at the heart of this section is a key verse summing up Job's ministrations: "I put on [3847] righteousness [6664], and it clothed me: my judgment was as a robe [4598] and a diadem" (29.14). Davidson's comment, that "Job clothed himself with righteousness, so that as a man he was lost in the justice that clothed him",[327] usefully draws out the implication of the metaphor: Job became justice personified. But such extravagant language must remind us of another who will, without the slightest exaggeration, be arrayed with all the attributes of justice. When Isaiah looks ahead to the glorious coming of Messiah to deliver Israel and destroy His enemies, he pictures Him as One who

> put on [3847] righteousness [6666] as a breastplate, and an helmet of salvation upon his head; and he put on the garments of vengeance for clothing, and was clad with zeal as a cloke [4598] (Is 59.17).

Righteousness, salvation, vengeance and zeal – these features will characterise the perfect reign of Christ over the earth. It is not difficult to see the verbal parallels with Job's self-description. Once again we have to acknowledge that in Job's indisputable moral and spiritual excellence, as in his innocent sufferings, we have fleeting glimpses of the Lord Jesus. What, however, could be true of a mere man only in the heavily qualified terms of poetic hyperbole is absolutely and uniquely true of Christ, who is "made unto us wisdom, and righteousness, and sanctification, and redemption" (1 Cor 1.30). It is in seeing this that we can in part answer the question that plagued Job: why are such terrible things overtaking me? In the secret counsels of the Godhead it was determined that upright Job, unbeknown to himself, should figure forth something of the excellences and the afflictions of a greater One who would come after him.

In view of this, Job's soliloquising **anticipation** of a peaceful, prosperous future (29.18-20) seems wholly reasonable. This is not the idle daydream of a selfish worldling (such as that recorded in Luke 12.16-20), but the justifiable hope of one whose life has been both blessed and approved of God. After all, he had known heaven's favour and, in his capacity as magistrate, sought to maintain heaven's standards on earth. But, reading his confession of confidence in the light of his current misery, the language sounds painfully ironic: "And I said, I shall die in my nest, and multiply my days as the sand;[328] My root shall be spread out to the waters, and the dew will lie all night on my branch; My glory shall be fresh in me, and my bow be renewed in my hand" (29.18-20, JND). Job's expectation was that of the psalmist: "in my prosperity I said, I shall never be moved" (Ps 30.6).

But in a fallen world life is precarious at best, and no man can guarantee length of days. Job draws on the imagery of birds ("nest"), trees ("root", "branch") and human physical prowess ("my bow"). He speculated that he would die comfortably in the bosom of his family (the implication of "in my nest") after a long and fulfilled life of days innumerable as the sand. His root (a popular word in Job, appearing nine times) would stretch out to tap an abundant supply of nourishment, while the dew (which often speaks of the blessing of heaven, as in Genesis 27.28) would invigorate his branch. The imagery of a robust, long-lived tree describes the blessed man of Psalm 1 and the man of Jeremiah 17 who rests his confidence not in himself or other men but in Jehovah:

> Blessed is the man that trusteth in the Lord, and whose hope the Lord is. For he shall be as a tree planted by the waters, and that spreadeth out her roots by the river, and shall not see when heat cometh, but her leaf shall be green; and shall not be careful in the year of drought, neither shall cease from yielding fruit (Jer 17.7-8).

The picture is one of radiant health. Job is certain that his glory (which probably refers to his manly vigour) would remain fresh (everywhere else this word appears in the Old Testament, including Job 32.19, it is translated "new") and his ability to wield the battle bow would be unimpaired with age. We may be reminded of Jacob's blessing on his favourite son Joseph, which announced that "his bow abode in strength, and the arms of his hands were made strong by the hands of the mighty God of Jacob" (Gen 49.24). At the height of his favour, Job looked forward to an old age untainted by mental or physical decline.

As he recounts his past musings in all their naïvety, Job must be bitterly conscious of the catastrophic failure of his expectations. All his fondest hopes have come to nothing. Family, wealth, honour, and his valued relationship with God, lie in ruins. There awaits him nothing but an ignominious death. And yet (as we have constantly to bear in mind as we read through this long book) the narrative is not finished. If we fast-forward to the close of the story we shall see that those earlier hopes were, in the final analysis, no illusion at all. With the termination of his afflictions, length of days, prosperity, family comfort and – best of all – a publicly restored fellowship with his God are all restored.

After this brief pause, Job returns to factual autobiography in order to confirm his **authority** as a figure of paramount wisdom and justice (29.21-25). This is the scene with which he winds up his bitter-sweet remembrance of things past:

> Unto me they listened, and waited, and kept silence for my counsel: After my words they spoke not again, and my speech dropped upon them; And

they waited for me as for the rain, and they opened their mouth wide as for the latter rain. If I laughed on them, they believed it not; and they troubled not the serenity of my countenance. I chose their way, and sat as chief, and dwelt as a king in the army, as one that comforteth mourners (29.21-25, JND).

The account of his deferential reception at the court of justice (29.7-10) and his indefatigable exertions on behalf of the defenceless (29.11-17), suspended for three verses while Job disclosed his innermost thoughts, is now continued to its grand conclusion. Those who were silenced by his arrival respectfully waited for his legal decisions. "Counsel" (6098), which appears nine times in Job, is used of God's wisdom (12.13), "the counsel of the wicked" (21.16; 22.18), and – ironically – of the limitations of Job's boasted intelligence. It is God who, at the conclusion of the debate, asks "Who is this that darkeneth counsel [6098] by words without knowledge?" (38.2), while Job humbly accepts the divine verdict on him: "therefore have I uttered that I understood not; things too wonderful for me, which I knew not" (42.3). The man whose wisdom awed his peers is eventually reduced to nothingness in the presence of God.

Job's judicial actions met with rapt attention and universal approbation. No one dared to challenge his legal rulings. He uses the verb "drop" (5197) to describe the way his statements were received like gently distilling rain. The same term is used occasionally of prophetic utterances (Ezek 20.46; 21.2; Amos 7.16; Micah 2.6), offering a hint of the weightiness of Job's words. The metaphor continues into the next verse, where his audience is compared to the parched soil of the Middle East longing for refreshing showers. God had promised Israel that, conditional upon obedience to His word, He would enrich them with "the rain of your land in his due season, the first rain and the latter rain, that thou mayest gather in thy corn, and thy wine, and thine oil" (Deut 11.14). The *Jamieson, Fausset and Brown Commentary* informs us that

The "early rain" is in autumn and onwards, while the seed is being sown. The "latter rain" is in March, and brings forward the harvest, which ripens in May or June. Between the early and latter rains, some rain falls, but not in such quantities as those rains. Between March and October no rain falls.

Solomon compares a king's favour to the latter rain (Prov 16.15), while the prophets liken God's future blessings on repentant Israel to the arrival of long-awaited showers (Hosea 6.3; Joel 2.23). The song of Moses uses related imagery when speaking of the impact of God's word: "Give ear, O ye heavens, and I will speak; and hear, O earth, the words of my mouth. My doctrine shall drop as the rain, my speech shall distil as the dew, as the small rain upon the tender herb, and as the showers upon the grass" (Deut 32.1-2). There is still nothing like God's Word to refresh and revitalise the thirsty soul.

Just as God graciously provided for Israel's blessing so Job's compassionate wisdom brought good to the people of his society. Verse 24 is a little difficult to understand. The Hebrew verb "laugh" (7832) is rendered by the KJV in a variety of ways (such as "play", "make sport", "make merry", "deride"). We must bear in mind that the whole passage concerns Job's role as a magistrate dealing skilfully with tricky law cases. It may therefore refer to the genial smile of favour with which he looked on those in distress, a smile of condescending and benevolent kindness which they scarcely believed possible from so exalted a justice. Alternatively it could mean (as proposed by the ESV) that when they thought their case completely hopeless Job beamed encouragingly on them: "I smiled on them when they had no confidence". Whatever the circumstances and however grave the difficulty, Job retained a cheerful countenance which nothing could dissipate. As Davidson comments, "Job, with broader insight and more capable counsel, smiled on those who were perplexed and despondent".[329] What we have is a sketch of the ideal legal counsel, expert, sensitive and undaunted.

The summary conclusion (29.25) is deliberately impressive. In his happier days Job was endowed with unquestioned authority. He was the decider of the correct procedure (in legal tangles); he sat enthroned as the foremost person in the court of justice, almost like a king at the centre of his troops; he offered comfort to those who mourned. We may imagine, in passing, that the group of silent friends listening to him might have cringed somewhat at that last remark. They had conspicuously failed to provide comfort for the bereaved. But three features especially should attract our notice: Job was wise, strong, and compassionate. In such attributes he faintly anticipates the wonderful excellences of the Lord Jesus Christ. These perfections were uniquely displayed in the Saviour's earthly life as He dealt with intractable problems, delivered those trapped in Satanic bondage, and responded sensitively to the heart-break of human misery. He was marked by wisdom (Mt 13.54), power (Lk 4.36) and gentle consideration (Lk 7.13). Yes, Job certainly makes us think a little about Christ.

And yet … We have to acknowledge a strange paradox in Job. His speech of self-defence is no swaggering parade of personal virtue but a justifiable response to the outrageous charges of misconduct which his friends have laid against him. In the process of asserting his innocence, Job momentarily even becomes a type of the persecuted Messiah. Further, wise, authoritative and pitiful, he anticipates in his judicial role aspects of the "wonderful counsellor" whose perfect understanding will be universally manifest when He takes the reins of world government. However, at the same time we may have the uneasy feeling that there is something distastefully self-promoting and self-absorbed about Job's pious autobiography. It is never good for a man to speak (let alone write) about himself, lest he slip into cosy self-congratulation. This may be one of the reasons that Solomon advises his son to "Let another man praise thee, and not thine own mouth; a stranger, and not thine own lips" (Prov 27.2). Even the apostle Paul wrote about himself with the greatest reluctance, and only then because the genuineness of his apostleship – and therefore the truth of God – was at stake. The language he employs in the last few chapters of 2 Corinthians clearly reveals how repugnant he finds the entire business of self-commendation.

In the chapter we are considering, God is mentioned by name but thrice, whereas Job uses first person singular pronouns ("I", "my", "me") nearly fifty times. Agreed, the circumstances of his case required him to foreground his own actions. Agreed, too, that Job is an exceptionally good man. Nevertheless, a sense of disquiet lingers. One would not go so far as to liken him to John Bold in Anthony Trollope's Victorian novel *The Warden*, a man who, faced with opposition to his reforming zeal, was able (in the author's memorable phrase) "to comfort himself in the warmth of his own virtue".[330] The cases are entirely different. Still, it has to be admitted that Job plants himself squarely centre-stage, taking unconcealed delight in his social prestige.

The coexistence in the same man of typological anticipation and a measure of personal failure should not surprise us. The prophet Jonah only became a picture of the Saviour's future death and resurrection because of his deliberate attempt to escape the unsavoury task of ministering to Gentiles. Strange that a disobedient servant should prefigure the perfect servant of Jehovah! But when we stop to think about it, all typical characters, even at their best, are of necessity fallen humans. Aaron the high priest needed garments of glory and beauty to conceal his personal blemishes; Moses collapsed in the very sphere that Scripture records as his greatest strength; the man "after [God's] own heart" was guilty of adultery, conspiracy and murder. The often striking contrast between type and antitype is one of the ways scripture spotlights the stand-alone glories of Christ Jesus. There can be no one on a par with Him.

> "Oh that I were as in the past,
> When God my life maintained!"
> Thus Job, now stricken and outcast,
> Of blessings lost complained.
>
> He hankered after early days
> When all revered his name,
> When people sounded out his praise –
> Before his troubles came.
>
> He catalogued his kindly deeds,
> His wisdom and renown;
> He'd met the helpless victim's needs,
> His counsel awed the town.
>
> Self-satisfaction is a sin
> From which no man is free;
> It goads the saints to gaze within,
> Approving what they see.
>
> But better far to look above
> And gaze upon the Lord
> Where He, the object of our love,
> Is rightfully adored.

And when with Him we're taken up
We shall the less contest
The contents of our earthly cup,
Knowing He knows what's best.

Job's Pitiful Present: Chapter 30

The contrast between chapter 29 and chapter 30 could scarcely be greater. In chapter 29 Job, in his dazzling prosperity, domestic happiness, and social esteem, was the cynosure of every eye. "But now", as chapter 30 ominously begins, the scene changes with a vengeance. In chapter 29 Job was the possessor of blessing from God (29.2-6), honour from men (29.7-11), and practised admirable benevolence in his public actions (29.12-17). Each of these positives is negated in chapter 30, although not in the same order: first he loses his honour among men (30.1-15), then his sense of divine favour (30.16-23), and finally all his previous good deeds seem of no account (30.24-31). If chapter 29 tells us what God gave, its successor tells us what He took away.

Bitterly, Job describes the kind of people who have combined against him in his misery. They have eagerly seized the opportunity afforded by his startling reversals to heap on him the opprobrium they never dared display during his affluence. The chapter is a stunning indictment of that human vindictiveness which longs to vaunt over those it has long and secretly envied. Job's persecutors behave much in the manner of the descendants of Esau when confronted with the overthrow of their neighbours, Israel. Enemies of many years, they could not conceal a gloating delight when the chosen people came under God's disciplinary judgments, meted out savagely by barbaric Gentiles. The prophet Obadiah was commissioned to analyse their sin and pronounce their retribution:

> For thy violence against thy brother Jacob shame shall cover thee, and thou shalt be cut off for ever. In the day that thou stoodest on the other side, in the day that the strangers carried away captive his forces, and foreigners entered into his gates, and cast lots upon Jerusalem, even thou wast as one of them. But thou shouldest not have looked on the day of thy brother in the day that he became a stranger; neither shouldest thou have rejoiced over the children of Judah in the day of their destruction; neither shouldest thou have spoken proudly in the day of distress. Thou shouldest not have entered into the gate of my people in the day of their calamity; yea, thou shouldest not have looked on their affliction in the day of their calamity, nor have laid hands on their substance in the day of their calamity; Neither shouldest thou have stood in the crossway, to cut off those of his that did escape; neither shouldest thou have delivered up those of his that did remain in the day of distress (Obad vv.10-14).

The parallel is all the more telling when we recall that the story of Job is probably set in the vicinity of Edom, a culture noted, amongst other things, for worldly wisdom and overweening pride. But there can be no excuse for the malignancy with which the Edomites smacked their lips over the sufferings of their relatives. Envy is one of the nastiest of sins because it covertly resents the blessings of others, while spitefulness is even worse, openly rejoicing in their troubles. Can we imagine anything more opposed to the spirit of Christ, who commanded His disciples to "Love your enemies, bless them that curse you, do good to them that hate you, and pray for them which despitefully use you, and persecute you" (Mt 5.44)?

Perhaps the best way to break up this hefty chapter is to divide it into two parallel sections, each of which concentrates on one of Job's two opponents. First, he considers the **antagonism of men** (30.1-14), following this with a brief account of the personal **anguish** it brings him (30.15-18). Second, he turns to a far more painful subject, the **antagonism of God** (30.19-24), which again leads into a narrative of his consequent **anguish** (30.25-31). Most important to note is the key verse which joins together his two great causes of grief: "Because he hath loosed my cord, and afflicted me, they have also let loose the bridle before me" (30.11). The construction is crucial: "because he … they also". It is only because God has suddenly withdrawn His support, exposing Job to the hostility of malicious foes, that anyone is able to touch him. Previously there was, in Satan's words, a "hedge about him, and about his house, and about all that he hath" (1.10). But now, because God has turned against him, his fellow men can freely abuse him. As we have seen in the past, Job is not ashamed to trace all his circumstances, good or ill, to the hand of God.

First he details the **antagonism of men** (30.1-14).

The passage recounts the humiliation showered on Job by certain members of his society. It starts with an extended parenthesis which takes the wraps off the nature of those who principally rejoiced in his fall. The introductory "But now" (30.1) is repeated in verse 9, signalling the fact that Job digresses slightly from his main topic to pen a detailed sketch of his foes. We are initially confronted with the base **character** of his persecutors (30.1-8): "But now they that are younger than I have me in derision, whose fathers I would have disdained to have set with the dogs of my flock" (30.1, JND).

The man who in chapter 29 was venerated by young and old alike, the man whose words of wisdom held his peers spellbound, is now publicly mocked by his juniors and social inferiors. "Younger than I" distinguishes this group from the three friends. The latter may have failed abysmally in their aim of comforting Job, but at least they have not stooped to the crude insolence of the mob. To a man of Job's intellectual refinement and moral sensitivity, the mindless jeering and jostling of the rabble must have been a torment not to be borne. In the words of Delitzsch,

> Bereft of the protection of his children and servants, become an object of disgust to his wife, and an abhorrence to his brethren, forsaken by every attention of true affection … Job lies out of doors … abandoned to the hideous malignant joy of these gypsy hordes.[331]

It was a humiliation in itself to be despised by the very scum of society, men of such base parentage that Job would have refused to employ them even with the dogs that guarded his flocks.

Job spares no efforts in highlighting their depravity. Smick makes a telling comment on the notably extravagant quality of his poetic language:

> The modern Western mind prefers understatement; so when Semitic literature indulges in overstatement, such hyperbole becomes a mystery to the average Western reader.[332]

Repetition, parallelism, exaggeration – these are the distinguishing features of Job's language as he draws attention to his deep sense of shame at the hands of the riffraff. Not for him the stiff upper-lip reserve which represses pain and suffers in silence – rather, he pours out the anguish of his heart, and in so doing provides God's people with encouragement in their own lesser afflictions. In reading his words we realise that, by the grace of God, not one of us will ever approach his unique experience of misery.

We learn three facts about this malicious rabble. First, they are **physically emaciated**:

> Yea, whereto should the strength of their hands profit me, men in whom vigour hath perished? Withered up through want and hunger, they flee into waste places long since desolate and desert: They gather the salt-wort among the bushes, and the roots of the broom for their food (30.2-4, JND).

Job has already said that he would have disdained to put their fathers into the meanest employment; now, by way of justification, he offers a close-up of their condition. Their physical debility must be viewed as an external signal of internal worthlessness. It is as if hidden corruption is reflected in outer repulsiveness. Such men have no mental or manual skills and, as a consequence, suffer extreme poverty and famine. The word for "want" (2639) only occurs twice in Scripture; its other appearance is in Proverbs 28.22 where it describes the fate of the selfish man who, eager to be rich, comes instead to penury. "Famine" (3720) also occurs but twice; here and Job 5.22. More recent translations of verse 3 bring out the unbelievably desperate lengths to which these people go in order to sustain life: "Through want and hard hunger they gnaw the dry ground by night in waste and desolation" (ESV). Delitzsch's paraphrase sharply etches the degradation involved: "they gnaw the sunburnt parched ground of the steppe, stretched out there more like beasts than men … and derive from it their scanty food".[333]

Their pitiful diet consists of "saltwort" (the word appears only here) and juniper roots. According to Delitzsch, the former refers to "the tall shrubby orach, the so-called sea-purslain, the buds and young leaves of which are gathered and eaten by the poor".[334] How far Job has fallen! Once the man who received the acclaim of the social and intellectual elite, he is now subjected to the scorn of the half-starved degenerate masses.

Second, we discover that they are **socially excluded**:

> They are driven forth from among men – they cry after them as after a thief – To dwell in gloomy gorges, in caves of the earth and the rocks: They bray among the bushes; under the brambles they are gathered together (30.5-7, JND).

Like Adam and Eve in Genesis 3.24 these vagabonds are driven out from protection and security into the wilds of the desert. Job sketches a scene of hue and cry in which a thief is hounded out of town by the law-abiding population. The word for "cry" (7321) covers a range of loud, clamorous shouts. It is used, for example, of the urgent trumpet blast which gathered Israel's congregation together for military action:

> But when the congregation is to be gathered together, ye shall blow, but ye shall not sound an alarm [7321] … And if ye go to war in your land against the enemy that oppresseth you, then ye shall blow an alarm [7321] with the trumpets (Num 10.7-9).

Although the word "thief" appears here as part of a comparative expression ("as after a thief"), the suggestion is direct: these people are no more than lawless vagrants who merit the revulsion with which they are treated. Job's diction paints a deliberately repellent picture: "gloomy gorges", "caves of the earth", "they bray among the bushes … under the brambles". It is a landscape of desolation and waste, indicative of the debased nature of the men who inhabit it. Like inarticulate animals they "bray" (the word appears only here and in Job 6.5, where it describes the wild ass desperately seeking food) and huddle together for shelter among thorn bushes.

In some ways the language reminds us of the company mentioned in chapter 24.5-8, the significant difference being that those people were described as "the poor of the earth" (24.4), innocent victims of human oppression and injustice. Here, however, Job makes it clear that these men – who eagerly seek to aggravate his sorrows – have been driven out from respectable society because of their innate villainy. They are in no sense the deserving poor, but suffer want because of their own folly. The Old Testament recognises that – contrary to much modern thinking – material poverty is not always the product of misfortune or social negligence. The comprehensive catalogue of miseries to befall Israel recorded in Deuteronomy 28 (including famine, defeat, illness and exile) is carefully signalled as the inevitable consequence of persistent disobedience to God's law. The men who gang up against Job are what the New Testament might call, in the delicious language of the KJV, "lewd fellows of the baser sort" (Acts 17.5). Their physical degradation is not to be viewed as a reason for sympathetic pity but is simply the built-in fruit of personal wickedness. As Romans chapter 1 teaches us, even in this life sin may carry its own penalty.

Third, and most significantly, we learn the reason for their exile, which is that they are **morally evil**: "Sons of fools, and sons of nameless sires, they are driven out of the land" (30.8, JND).

Hinted at in earlier verses, this is now brought to the fore. As we have noted before, "fool" is trenchant biblical terminology for the ungodly man. The noun used here (5036) appears eighteen times in the Old Testament and is related to the personal name of Nabal, Abigail's sottish husband, a historical example of the nature of folly. He is described as a "man of Belial, even Nabal: for as his name is, so is he; Nabal is his name, and folly is with him" (1 Sam 25.25). The idea of foolishness therefore encompasses wilful impiety, senseless conduct, and obtuse stubbornness. Job's enemies are "sons of fools"; that is to say, they perpetuate the obnoxious ungodliness of their ancestors. Base-born and detestable, they are fittingly expelled from human habitation.

Job, by contrast, is a man with the ability and compassion to relieve those in distress, a man with the highest social connections, one of impeccably upright character. This man is forced to endure the vilification of godless outcasts. We cannot help but think a little of the sufferings of the spotless Son of God at the hands of men.

Having exposed the degraded nature of his opponents, Job now records their despicable **conduct** towards him (30.9-14): "And now I am their song, yea, I am their byword. They abhor me, they stand aloof from me, yea, they spare not to spit in my face" (30.9-10, JND).

The introductory "And now" takes us back to the beginning of the chapter as Job returns to his main theme: once respected, he is now reviled by the most disreputable of men. In Hartley's words, "the noblest elder has become the byword of the scum of society".[335] "Song" (5058) translates a word which first appears here, but for most of its occurrences in the Psalms is transliterated *neginoth* (modern versions usually replace the Hebrew with "stringed instruments"). On at least two occasions it clearly connotes contempt, as in the messianic Psalm 69: "They that sit in the gate speak against me; and I was the song [5058] of the drunkards" (Ps 69.12). Jeremiah's painful experience is equally suggestive of Messiah's rejection: "I was a derision to all my people; and their song [5058] all the day" (Lam 3.14). The parallel term "byword" (the Hebrew, meaning a word or speech, is found thirty-four times in Job) is infected by the sour mood of its context and takes on the colour of sneering, offensive jibes. The mob make Job's miseries the theme of their sing-song taunts, aiming, as they pass by, to wound him with deliberately humiliating remarks. On the one hand they shun him, refraining from showing the least sympathy; on the other, they draw near only to spit at him (the same word is used of the sufferings of Jehovah's servant in Isaiah 50.6). Delitzsch assumes, perhaps with justification, that these people have in the past been the object of Job's judicial activities (as recorded in chapter 29), and that their judge's reversal fills them with glee:

> This rabble, constitutionally as well as morally degraded, when it comes upon Job's domain in its marauding expeditions, makes sport of the sufferer, whose former earnest admonitions, given from sympathizing anxiety for them, seemed to them as insults for which they revenge themselves.[336]

Job now formulates a key statement in which he traces all his ills – even the distinctively human antipathy just described – to God: "For he hath loosed my cord and afflicted me; so they cast off the bridle before me" (30.11, JND).

The imagery of the cord could refer to a slackened tent rope which causes the entire structure to collapse, or (ironically negating the language of 29.20) to a relaxed bowstring which impedes an archer's efficiency. Delitzsch opts for the first, expanding the idea with the paraphrase, "He has untied (loosened) my cord of life, i.e., the cord which stretched out and held up my tent (the body)".[337] Whichever way we interpret the metaphor, it is evident Job is acknowledging that his lamentable condition is God's handiwork. Because God has suddenly turned against him, men have followed suit, taking the opportunity to add to his griefs. Much the same occurred in Israel's history. The Gentile nations around, used by God to discipline His erring people, incurred His ire because they sought to go beyond the limits of divine chastisement. To satisfy their blood lust they attempted to exterminate the chosen seed. As a result, Jehovah announces through the prophet Zechariah, "I am very sore displeased with the heathen that are at ease: for I was but a little displeased, and they helped forward the affliction" (Zech 1.15). In a similar way, David's prophetic Psalm 69 exposes the motives of those who eagerly added their pennyworth of hatred to one who was suffering under God's hand: "they persecute him whom thou hast smitten; and they talk to the grief of those whom thou hast wounded" (Ps 69.26). But it is not man's prerogative to intensify God's judgment.

What are the mean actions with which Job's foes seek to increase his pain?

At my right hand rise the young brood; they push away my feet, and raise up against me their pernicious ways; They mar my path, they set forward my calamity, without any to help them; They come in as through a wide breach: amid the confusion they roll themselves onward (30.12-14, JND).

The vivid physical diction hints at the indignities Job has to endure from the local ragamuffins: they "let loose the bridle", "push away my feet", "mar my path", they "rolled themselves upon me" (KJV). "Bridle" (7448) only appears four times (Job 30.11; 41.13; Ps 32.9; Is 30.28), and reduces Job's enemies to brute beasts who have abandoned all restraint to vent their malice on him. The idea seems to include kicking and jostling, not surprising when we recall that they have even descended to spitting in his face. Thereafter Job moves into the imagery of siege warfare. Like an army encircling a defenceless town, they "raise up against me their pernicious ways", constructing mounds and ramparts from which to assault their hapless victim. Further, they "mar my path", ruining the roadways along which assistance might reach him. They require no support from others, for Job is wholly without helpers. As the walls of Job's fortress crumble, his enemies surge in "as through a wide breach", overwhelming him with sheer weight of numbers. The prolonged military metaphor underlines the remorseless deliberation with which they proceed against him.

This leads into a deeply personal lament. Job shifts attention away from the surrounding mob to offer a poignant close-up of his **anguish** (30.15-18). Darby's translation helps us appreciate what he is saying:

> Terrors are turned against me; they pursue mine honour as the wind; and my welfare is passed away like a cloud. And now my soul is poured out in me; days of affliction have taken hold upon me. The night pierceth through my bones and detacheth them from me, and my gnawing pains take no rest: By their great force they have become my raiment; they bind me about as the collar of my coat (30.15-18, JND).

Four times the word "terrors" (1091) has appeared in Job (18.11,14; 24.17; 27.20); on each occasion it described the terrible fate of the wicked. Here Job uses the same word of his own experience as he is hounded by dread. His metaphor changes from the military to the meteorological as he pictures himself engulfed by stormy winds which blow away the possessions in which he boasted – his social status and his wealth. What the KJV and Darby render "welfare" (3444) is most frequently translated "salvation" in the Old Testament. It first appears in Jacob's benediction, "I have waited for thy salvation [3444], O Lord" (Gen 49.18), and is the word Jonah uses in his great expression of thanksgiving, "Salvation [3444] is of the Lord" (Jonah 2.9). Job is thinking primarily of his vanished earthly prosperity. Nevertheless, other associations of the word influence our reading of Job; material blessings may come and go, but spiritual salvation, which it is the special prerogative of the Lord to bestow, is infinitely durable. Indeed, Job himself uses the word of far more than material security when claiming that "this also shall be my salvation, that a profane man shall not come before his face" (13.16, JND). For him, convinced – and rightly so – of his own integrity, salvation involves restoration to an enjoyment of God's presence.

But this cannot dilute the tragedy of Job's present situation. His soul is "poured out" (8210), just as the blood of a murderer had to be shed (Gen 9.6), just as the blood of the sin offering had to be splattered at the foot of the brazen altar in Israel's tabernacle (Lev 4.7), just as the psalmist likens his exhaustion to being "poured out like water" (Ps 22.14). It suggests both the terrible lassitude of Job's spirit and his unanswered cries to God.

The "days of affliction" which have seized him make us think of the protracted though unspecified period of his sufferings. "Affliction" (6040) appears six times in Job (in fact he will use the same "days of affliction" phrase again in verse 27 of this chapter) and thirty-seven times as a whole in the Old Testament. A great many of its uses are connected with the assurance of divine deliverance. Here are the first six occurrences:

The Lord hath heard thy affliction (Gen 16.11).

The Lord hath looked upon my affliction (Gen 29.32).

God hath seen mine affliction (Gen 31.42).

God hath caused me to be fruitful in the land of my affliction (Gen 41.52).

I have surely seen the affliction of my people which are in Egypt (Ex 3.7).

I will bring you up out of the affliction of Egypt (Ex 3.17).

The combined testimony of the angel of the Lord, Leah, Jacob, Joseph, and Jehovah is immensely powerful. How gracious of God to combine the reality of affliction with promises of relief! So too with Job – the man who endured such wearisome days of distress will yet live to see God moving in mercy on his behalf. James's New Testament commentary on Job is written, of course, from the perspective of an accomplished event:

> Behold, we count them happy which endure. Ye have heard of the patience of Job, and have seen the end of the Lord; that the Lord is very pitiful, and of tender mercy (James 5.11).

Because we are reading chronologically through the book we have not yet "seen the end of the Lord", but we soon shall. Every affliction is in His hands.

Pain and misery are at their worst at night time, when there is nothing to distract the sufferer's mind from their presence. This was Asaph's experience: "In the day of my trouble I sought the Lord: my sore ran in the night, and ceased not: my soul refused to be comforted" (Ps 77.2). Job is no different. The night season, far from offering release from daily toil, seems to him like an enemy stabbing his bones, almost (in Darby's rendering) detaching them from him, so acute are the gnawing pains racking his frame. Delitzsch understands the language of verse 18 as referring to the distorting effect of Job's bodily diseases, which ruin the shapeliness of his outer apparel:

> If the body is wasted away to a skeleton, there is an end to the rich appearance and beautiful flow which the outer garment gains by the full and rounded forms of the limbs: it falls down straight and in perpendicular folds upon the wasted body, and contributes in no small degree to make him whom one formerly saw in all the fulness of health still less recognisable than he otherwise is.[338]

The translation of the ESV follows suit: "With great force my garment is disfigured; it binds me about like the collar of my tunic". Other commentators take Job to be using metaphorical language to express the idea that his overwhelming pangs have become the very garment he wears. This would contrast with the imagery of chapter 29, making the point that we have come a long way from the time when Job could say "I put on righteousness, and it clothed me; my justice was as a mantle and a turban" (29.14, JND). Instead of honour, Job's clothing is now constant humiliation; instead of outward prestige, pain. Constable suggests that "verse 18 probably means he felt that God was grabbing him by the lapels, so to speak, or perhaps that his sickness had discoloured, rather than dishevelled, his clothing".[339] Whatever the case, Job's extreme discomfort is evident.

But now we move into the second major section of the chapter. Far more acutely distressing to Job is his consciousness of **the antagonism of God** (30.19-24). He has already mentioned this in verse 11 as the fundamental reason for the human hatred he has to endure. Now he elaborates on divine enmity, alternating between statement and direct address. The paragraph forms a sandwich beginning and ending with a comment on God's actions against him (30.19,24), in between which comes a direct complaint to God about His cruelty (30.20-23). It follows in Darby's translation:

(a) He hath cast me into the mire, and I have become like dust and ashes.

(b) I cry unto thee, and thou answerest me not; I stand up, and thou lookest at me. Thou art changed to a cruel one to me; with the strength of thy hand thou pursuest me. Thou liftest me up to the wind; thou causest me to be borne away, and dissolvest my substance. For I know that thou wilt bring me to death, and into the house of assemblage for all living.

(a) Indeed, no prayer availeth when he stretcheth out his hand: though they cry when he destroyeth (30.19-24, JND).

Interestingly, the text does not specifically name the one who has cast Job into the mud but, as we read on, there can be no doubt that he is referring to the Almighty. "Cast" translates a word (3384) found nine times in Job but usually rendered "teach" (as in 6.24; 8.10; 12.7,8; 27.11). According to Strong it means basically "to *lay* or *throw* (especially an arrow, that is, to *shoot*); figuratively to *point* out (as if by *aiming* the finger), to *teach*". Bearing in mind the book's conclusion, would it be far-fetched to suggest that, in throwing him into the mire, God is in reality teaching Job a lesson about himself and Jehovah? The consistent message of Scripture as a whole is that the sovereign God who brings calamity on His people does so with a view to their instruction. The psalmist is able to acknowledge that his afflictions, which he frankly traces to God, are ultimately beneficial. As he writes, "I know, O Lord … that thou in faithfulness hast afflicted me" (Ps 119.75), and "It is good for me that I have been afflicted; that I might learn thy statutes" (Ps 119.71). So too Job will come eventually to assent to God's ways, although, as far as the book is concerned, he will not be informed of their original function in giving the lie to Satan's accusations. That knowledge is the privilege of the reader. It gives us yet another reason for submitting to God's dealings with us, however unbearable we currently find them: they may conceal a hidden purpose, one higher than we can ever guess.

Not only has Job been hurled into the mud, he has become identified with the very ash-heap on which he sits. The book uses the word "dust" (6083) twenty-six times (often as a synonym for death), but "ashes" (665) turns up on only four occasions. The first refers to the city refuse tip which forms the dismal setting of Job's conversations (2.8), but the last repeats the collocation used here as part of Job's final confession of repentance "in dust and ashes" (42.6). At the moment, Job considers himself unjustly tossed aside into ignominy and shame; in the presence of God, however, he will voluntarily bow in acknowledgment of personal unworthiness. In this he will echo the language of Abraham interceding on behalf of Sodom (Gen 18.27); in fact, Job will himself engage in earnest prayer for his now shame-faced accusers.

But at this stage he does not shrink from speaking directly to the God who, in his estimation, has grievously mistreated him. Job is always candid in his indignation. The reader might consider such honesty almost embarrassing in its forthrightness; yet it is faithfully recorded in Scripture. He reproaches God for refusing to answer his cries, for staring at him with implacable hostility, for unjustifiably reversing His former benevolence (just as in 1 Samuel 10.6 Saul was "turned [2015 – the same word for "changed" in Job 30.21] into another man"), for lifting His mighty hand against him. The word Darby translates "pursuest" (7852 – "opposest thyself against", is the KJV rendering), appears only six times in the Old Testament and, apart from this instance, is each time rendered "hated" in the KJV. Its first appearance sets the tone: "And Esau hated [7852] Jacob because of the blessing wherewith his father blessed him: and Esau said in his heart, The days of mourning for my father are at hand; then will I slay my brother Jacob" (Gen 27.41).

Job, we are bound to feel, is treading on the brink of irreverence in daring to charge God with hatred. Delitzsch's translation brings out the implications:

> Thou changest Thyself to a cruel being towards me,
> With the strength of Thy hand Thou makest war upon me.[340]

The language of verse 22 reaches a level of poetic hyperbole which may be hard for the reader to appreciate. In Psalm 18 the ability to ride upon the wind imaginatively describes the unique majesty and swiftness of Jehovah as "he rode upon a cherub, and did fly: yea, he did fly upon the wings of the wind" (Ps 18.10). Human speech is inevitably crippled when attempting to communicate the grandeur of God, but the psalmist captures something of the divine authority over the natural world. Job's experience, by contrast, is one of terrifying helplessness. Like a dead leaf, or like swirling grains of sand caught up in a savage desert storm, he is swept away from peaceful stability into a bewildering spiral of agitation over which he has no control. Like a traveller trapped and battered by a sudden tempest, he feels himself melting away, bereft of everything that offered him a firm foothold in the world. But perhaps this is unnecessarily to literalise the poetry. Job is almost incapable of articulating his misery and despair, and the volatility of his diction hints at dreadful confusion of soul.

This is his great fear: that God has destined him for imminent death, so that he will leave the world unvindicated before the men who have accused him of misconduct. Job is right in recognising that God brings men into death. Whoever or whatever may be providentially used to deprive any particular individual of his breath, it is ultimately the Lord who "killeth, and maketh alive: he bringeth down to the grave, and bringeth up" (1 Sam 2.6). As Jehovah announced to Moses: "I, even I, am he, and there is no god with me: I kill, and I make alive; I wound, and I heal: neither is there any that can deliver out of my hand" (Deut 32.39). The New Testament sums up the situation: "it is appointed unto men once to die, but after this the judgment" (Heb 9.27). What Job calls the "house" appointed for all living men is either the grave (where the body rests) or *sheol*, the place of departed spirits, where the dead are confined until resurrection and final assizes.

The language of verse 24 is particularly difficult and has led to a variety of translations. As usual, for those who wish to explore the technical details, Delitzsch summarises and assesses the relative merits of the different options. As it stands, the KJV does not make immediate sense, but Darby takes the verse as describing God's entrenched animosity despite the pleas of those against whom His hand has been raised. Conversely, the ESV considers the verse to be referring to those who are enduring affliction and who nevertheless, though convinced of imminent death, instinctively call out for aid. Both versions, though unlike, have the virtue of intelligibility. Here they are, for the sake of contrast:

> Indeed, no prayer availeth when he stretcheth out his hand: though they cry when he destroyeth (30.24, JND).

> Yet does not one in a heap of ruins stretch out his hand, and in his disaster cry for help? (30.24, ESV).

Darby makes Job sound resigned to his fate: God is implacable when executing His purpose of judgment. The ESV, on the other hand, connects the stretched out hand to the one in distress (that is to say, Job), even though his world is tumbling around him and his case hopeless. Darby's understanding of the verse fits well with the language of the preceding section (30.20-23) in which Job has charged God with merciless cruelty. The ESV, however, fits better with what follows – which is tantamount to an appeal to divine sympathy, as Job reminds God of his own compassion on the needy (30.25-26). Since I have behaved kindly toward the distressed, why should not God show mercy to me? Both approaches can be justified doctrinally: God's determinative will is inflexible (because He is God), yet at the same time it is wonderfully true that those in the direst straits may still appeal to Him for mercy.

Since it is almost impossible for the layman to arbitrate between these different viewpoints (and there are other possible renderings), for the sake of consistency I am going to adhere to Darby's wording. This means that verse 24 concludes the section in which Job deplores God's antagonism (man is helpless before His sovereign purpose), rather than starting the section which follows, in which he expresses the depth of his misery in order to provoke heaven's sympathy. In brief, we may understand the verse like this. It is because Job fears death is inevitable that, reverting to detached statement rather than direct address, he confesses that no prayers can deflect God from His purpose once He has stretched out His omnipotent hand.

The concluding section of the chapter is the second of Job's great outpourings of personal **anguish** (30.25-31). His lament comprises a recapitulation of his outgoing sympathy for the disadvantaged, along with his reasonable expectations of continued blessing, matters recorded in detail in chapter 29. Darby's translation is again worthy of attention:

> Did not I weep for him whose days were hard? was not my soul grieved for the needy? For I expected good, and there came evil; and I waited for light, but there came darkness. My bowels well up, and rest not; days of affliction have confronted me. I go about blackened, but not by the sun; I stand up, I cry in the congregation. I am become a brother to jackals, and a companion of ostriches. My skin is become black and falleth off me, and my bones are parched with heat. My harp also is turned to mourning, and my pipe into the voice of weepers (30.25-31, JND).

The paragraph is bookended by weeping. It occurs in verse 25 as an evidence of Job's empathy with the afflicted (as narrated in 29.15-17), and in verse 31 as a testimony to the complete withdrawal of all blessings so that he is now himself a helpless, tearful victim of adversity. His initial questions are more than rhetorical: they are a final moving entreaty to God. There is no suggestion that his statements are untrue. Job genuinely knew what it was to "weep with them that weep" (Rom 12.15), entering into the sorrows of others. Such sensitive large-heartedness is a necessary qualification for any who seek to minister to believers in distress. The Lord Jesus Christ, we may remember with wonderment, wept silent tears with Mary and Martha before He miraculously raised Lazarus from the dead. His power to do the second in no way compromised the touching pity He displayed in the first.

Bearing in mind his piety, it is hardly surprising that Job looked forward to a continuance of earthly blessing. This makes the sharp contrast between what he expected and what he received all the more shocking: he looked for good and met with evil, for light and was blanketed in darkness. The word "expected" (6960) is used in his original complaint, when he wished that the light of his birth day had been extinguished: "Let the stars of the twilight thereof be dark; let it look for [6960] light, but have none; neither let it see the dawning of the day" (3.9). Instead of reaping the rewards of his righteousness, Job faced distress. The Old Testament word "evil" (7451) has a range of meanings; it may refer to moral evil (as in Genesis 6.5, where its two appearances are translated in the KJV by "evil" and "wickedness"), or to outward calamity, as in statements like the following. In each case the ESV translation is printed after the KJV:

> I form the light, and create darkness: I make peace, and create evil: I the Lord do all these things (Is 45.7, KJV).

> I form light and create darkness, I make well-being and create calamity, I am the Lord, who does all these things (Is 45.7, ESV).

> Shall a trumpet be blown in the city, and the people not be afraid? shall there be evil in a city, and the Lord hath not done it? (Amos 3.6, KJV).

> Is a trumpet blown in a city, and the people are not afraid? Does disaster come to a city, unless the Lord has done it? (Amos 3.6, ESV).

The ESV's choice of the words "calamity" and "disaster" removes any possible confusion. The God of the Bible does not originate moral evil, for He is infinitely and eternally holy; nevertheless, for the accomplishment of His gracious though often mysterious sovereign purposes, He does bring about and superintend the adverse circumstances which befall men. Never are they outside the sphere of His control.

Job has gone through a series of tragic events encompassing every conceivable grief which can afflict men. The final five verses methodically categorize the wholesale disintegration of his life. He has been ravaged emotionally (30.27-28), socially (30.29), physically (30.30) and vocally (30.31).

Emotionally he has been dragged through unimaginable turmoil (30.27-28). In biblical physiology the bowels are the seat of the feelings. The prophet Isaiah tells us that "my bowels shall sound like an harp for Moab, and mine inward parts for Kirharesh" (Is 16.11). Awareness of the doom awaiting an inveterate enemy of Israel like Moab wrung the prophet's compassionate heartstrings. Job's emotions are so agitated that they are said in the KJV to "boil", a verb used only on two other occasions, both literal. Towards the end of the book, Jehovah refers to the sea churning like a boiling cauldron as the monstrous leviathan trails his wake across the ocean (41.31), and Ezekiel's parable about Jerusalem pictures a cooking pot bubbling up as it seethes the rebellious citizens (Ezek 24.5). The language is almost tactile: Job's soul is restless, writhing under the pain God has showered on him. Far from being kindly diverted away, days of affliction have met him head on.

Moreover, this acute distress has caused him to wander about like a man in mourning, looking as though he has been scorched by the sun. What the KJV translates here as "mourning" (6937) it elsewhere mainly renders "black(ish)" or "dark(ened)". Its first appearance describes the heaven as "black [6937] with clouds and wind" (1 Kings 18.45). The imagery is dramatically paradoxical: Job has been seared and blackened – not by the sun's heat but by the ferocity of God's anger. His disease-ravaged skin bears what look like symptoms of intense scorching, as he will explain further in verse 30. Delitzsch argues persuasively that Job is literally wearing black mourning apparel,[341] but although plausible in view of his multiple bereavements it does not fit so well with the allusion to the sun. Like the widow in the parable who insistently pestered an unjust magistrate for redress (Lk 18.1-8), Job has been crying out in public for justice and relief. Of the twenty-one uses of the verb "cry" (7768), eight are found in Job: it sums up his clamorous protest in the face of an implacable heaven (for example, 19.7; 24.12; 29.12; 30.20). The terrible contrast is this: while Job has responded in mercy to the needy and "delivered the poor that cried [7768]" (29.12), God has not heeded him. How different was David's experience:

In my distress I called upon the Lord, and cried [7768] unto my God: he heard my voice out of his temple, and my cry came before him, even into his ears. Then the earth shook and trembled; the foundations also of the hills moved and were shaken (Ps 18.6-7).

Still, David is writing from the viewpoint of an accomplished deliverance, not out of the midst of peril. Job is for most of the book stuck in that middle ground, uncomfortably sandwiched between the prosperity of the past and the as-yet unknown blessings of the future. Believers enduring times of trauma need to cherish the stabilizing truth that they are currently only in the middle of the action. The end is not yet. The Lord's words promise long-term benefits: "and shall not God avenge his own elect, which cry day and night unto him, though he bear long with them? I tell you that he will avenge them speedily" (Lk 18.7-8).

Socially, Job has been ostracised by his household and his peers. The language of the KJV is wonderfully atmospheric: "I am a brother to dragons, and a companion to owls" (30.29). It memorably expresses Job's abandonment to a waste world of desolation, deprived of all living company save that of wild creatures both sinister and strange. The Hebrew words are, however, problematic. Of the first, *tannin* (8577), the *Theological Wordbook of the Old Testament* offers the following explanation:

The word denotes "any large reptile" ... Referring to anything from large snakes (Ex 7.9-10,12; Deut 32.33; Ps 91.13) to enormous sea creatures (Gen 1.21; Ps 148.7), *tannin/m* is also often used in a figurative sense to denote God's most powerful opponents, whether natural (Job 7.12) or national (Babylon: Jer 51.34; Egypt: Is 51.9; Ezek 29.3; 32.2 ...).[342]

What complicates matters is that there is a very similar word which modern versions from the RV onwards almost uniformly render "jackal". This certainly seems to fit the context of Job 30. Comments *TWOT* again:

The jackal ... a scavenger that feeds on carrion, was often observed in the OT period as roaming about in the ruins of abandoned cities and so was almost always used as a symbol of desolation and divine judgment against sinful nations and individuals.

The second creature (the KJV's "owl", 1323 and 3284) is equally resistant to easy classification. Here is Cansdale's comment:

The owls have always been a translator's problem. The AV uses the name sixteen times, from five different Hebrew words; two of these appear only once each ... and their meaning is very uncertain.[343]

Nevertheless, somewhat surprisingly, he opts for the KJV's "owl" as opposed to the "ostrich", which is favoured by most modern translations (with the significant exception of the NIV). He identifies the bird with the huge but rarely seen eagle owl which, he claims, is one of the world's largest. Its haunt is desert places, which fits the setting of Job's complaint. An online account of the Pharaoh or Desert Eagle Owl (*Bubo ascalaphus*) provides this description of its habitat:

> Rocky deserts and semi-deserts, mountains with gorges and cliffs, dry, rocky mountain slopes with scattered trees or shrubs, outcrops of oases, occasionally in dry savannas.[344]

This certainly sounds like the bleak landscape of abandonment in which, despite the presence of his visitors, Job finds himself. Bereft of any genuine human friendship, he feels cast out into a metaphorical wasteland where the creatures of the wild are his sole company.

Physically, he continues to bear the gruesome evidences of illness (30.30). Delitzsch brings out the distasteful specificity of the symptoms which make Job so repulsive:

> My skin having become black, peels off from me,
> And my bones are parched with dryness.[345]

He goes on to describe the effects of elephantiasis, which he considers a viable diagnosis of Job's condition:

> the skin of the sufferer ... becomes first an intense red, then assumes a black colour; scales like fishes' scales are formed upon it, and the brittle, dark-coloured surface of the body is like a lump of earth.[346]

Vocally, even the simple ability to speak has been damaged, probably by his constant cries for relief and the cumulative effects of his various ailments (30.31). Harp and pipe (the latter is the usual emendation for the KJV's "organ") are instruments often associated with festivity and gladness. They appear together in connection with the prototypical musician, Jubal (Gen 4.21), and in Job's earlier description of the unalloyed merriment of the godless (21.12). They are used in the context of mirth (Gen 31.27) and worship (2 Sam 6.5; 1 Chr 16.5; 25.1; 2 Chr 20.28; Neh 12.27). The harp is mentioned fourteen times in the Psalter as an accompaniment of Israel's praise, while the pipe joins it in the concluding Psalm, where the entire creation unites aloud in the honour of God:

> Praise him with the sound of the trumpet: praise him with the psaltery and harp. Praise him with the timbrel and dance: praise him with stringed instruments and organs [pipe]. Praise him upon the loud cymbals: praise him upon the high sounding cymbals (Ps 150.3-5).

But for Job, joy and celebration have been muted by his current distress. The most majestic and versatile of all instruments – the human voice – hitherto tuned for the glory of God, is now reduced to the plaintive wailing of the mourner. Job, whose earlier testimony to the rightness of God's ways with him has gone down in history (1.21), has become the mouthpiece of misery.

It is a painful chapter to read. We cannot but be touched by Job's terrible sufferings, and even more by his steely-eyed awareness of the source of it all, even though, of course, he remains wholly ignorant of the purpose. Perhaps most frightening is his forthright charge that God has become gratuitously vindictive. It is a kind of nightmare scenario in which the God of infinite goodness has, in Job's fevered thought processes, become transformed into a monster of tyranny: "I cry unto thee, and thou dost not hear me: I stand up, and thou regardest me not. Thou art become cruel to me: with thy strong hand thou opposest thyself against me" (30.20-21). Robinson comments that

> Job, under the misleading suggestions of the flesh, views God as sporting with his sufferings while in reality [He is] glorying in him before principalities and powers as His faithful servant who had not his like upon the earth.[347]

But Job knows nothing of this. He cannot make sense of his circumstances in the light of what he knows about God. "Trouble of soul", Robinson remarks, "is the soul of all trouble". Job was spiritually troubled that the God who had blessed him so abundantly in the past and whom he faithfully honoured and worshipped should now without explanation cast him off. Worse still, Job's strident challenge to heaven remains unanswered. It is comparatively easy for believers living in the good of the Lord's resurrection to turn to the completed Scriptures (incorporating the book of Job) for encouragement amidst inexplicable trials. We have so many texts on which to lean. Even then we may slip into depression or dark thoughts about God as we wonder how long our present affliction will last. Paul tells us it is "light" and merely "for a moment" in contrast with a long and blissful eternity, but sometimes that glorious future seems all too distant and unreal. If we today struggle to surrender to God's plans for us, how much more did Job, with far less information on which to rest his soul.

In all this we can hardly miss the pre-echoes of the suffering Messiah, who bore both men's hatred and God's wrath. Several verses suggest parallels, and the thoughtful reader will uncover more, for the following examples are only representative.

- First, there is the degradation of spitting: "They abhor me, they flee far from me, and spare not to spit in my face" (30.10). The language looks ahead to Isaiah's prophetic foreview of Messiah's humiliation as One who "gave [his] back to the smiters, and [his] cheeks to them that plucked off the hair", who "hid not [his] face from shame and spitting" (Is 50.6). Without any trace of emotional extravagance the historical fulfilment is recorded in Matthew 27.30.

- Second is man's wilful supplementing of God's verdict: "Because he hath loosed my cord, and afflicted me, they have also let loose the bridle before me" (30.11). Job is aware that men have seized the opportunity to add their own store of malice to what they see as God's disapproval. It paves the way for the summary Isaiah offers of Israel's ignorant assessment of Messiah: "we did esteem him stricken, smitten of God, and afflicted" (Is 53.4).

- Third is the language with which Job describes his pain: "And now my soul is poured out upon me; the days of affliction have taken hold upon me" (30.16). The imagery hints at the terrible agony of One who "poured out his soul unto death: and … was numbered with the transgressors; and … bare the sin of many" (Is 53.12).

- Fourth, we note the ominous silence of heaven: "I cry unto thee, and thou dost not hear me: I stand up, and thou regardest me not" (30.20). This reminds us of the psalmist's prophetic cry of abandonment: "O my God, I cry in the daytime, but thou hearest not; and in the night season, and am not silent" (Ps 22.2).

There is at the same time a significant dissimilarity. To remind us of the incomparable excellence of Christ there is always a discrepancy in Scripture between shadow and substance, as there is between parable and meaning. While Job groans long and loud under his yoke, the perfectly innocent man was "oppressed, and … afflicted, yet he opened not his mouth: he is brought as a lamb to the slaughter, and as a sheep before her shearers is dumb, so he openeth not his mouth" (Is 53.7).

Job's Pious Protestation: Chapter 31
The change in mood at this point brings us up with a start. Although forming the climactic part of Job's final speech, chapter 31 stands entirely apart from anything he has uttered in the course of the long and acrimonious argument with his friends. In what ways is this chapter distinct? It is unique in its character, its construction and its challenge.

It is distinct in its **character**, because it constitutes a solemn legal avowal of innocence. Throughout the book Job has steadfastly rejected the increasingly detailed allegations levelled against him by men who cannot believe that a good man could ever be called upon to suffer as he did. But this is as comprehensive and coherent a refutation as we could imagine. It is, in effect, his "final effort to extricate himself from the false accusations made by his assailants and from his injustice at God's hand".[348] If chapter 29 was devoted mainly to demonstrating his righteousness in the public arena, this chapter includes every area of life.

It is also unique in its **construction**, presenting a lengthy "series of protestations on the one hand, accompanied on the other by curses on himself if these protestations of innocence are not true".[349] It consists of a sequence of what might be called "if … then" conditional clauses, in which Job avers that, were he to be guilty of specific sins, then it would be only right that various calamities fell on his head. This formula is not uncommon in the Old Testament. The following examples come respectively from the lips of Judah, Absalom and David (the last responding directly to the slanders of Cush the Benjamite):

> I will be surety for him; of my hand shalt thou require him: **if** I bring him not unto thee, and set him before thee, **then let me bear the blame** for ever (Gen 43.9).

> And Absalom answered Joab, Behold, I sent unto thee, saying, Come hither, that I may send thee to the king, to say, Wherefore am I come from Geshur? it had been good for me to have been there still: now therefore let me see the king's face; and **if** there be any iniquity in me, **let him kill me** (2 Sam 14.32).

> O Lord my God, **if** I have done this; **if** there be iniquity in my hands; **If** I have rewarded evil unto him that was at peace with me; (yea, I have delivered him that without cause is mine enemy:) **Let the enemy persecute my soul, and take it**; yea, let him tread down my life upon the earth, and lay mine honour in the dust (Ps 7.3-5).

Of course, in all human utterances there are varying degrees of candour. Not everyone who claims innocence can be believed. Judah and David are earnest in their protestations, the former looking to the future, the latter to the past, while the scoundrelly Absalom is outrageously brazen in his insincerity.

There are some fourteen "if" statements (in the KJV translation of chapter 31) in which Job catalogues the sins of which he is innocent. These include sins of thought as well as deed, for it is his intention to "demonstrate that he has maintained right relationships on all levels." There are four imperatives ("let" in 31.8,10,22,40), in which he "specifies the curses that should befall him if he be guilty".[350] The language echoes the penalties with which God threatened Israel were they to rebel against the terms of His covenant. Moses tells us about a solemn scene which was to be enacted on Mount Ebal, when

> the Levites shall speak, and say unto all the men of Israel with a loud voice, Cursed be the man that maketh any graven or molten image, an abomination unto the Lord, the work of the hands of the craftsman, and putteth it in a secret place. And all the people shall answer and say, Amen (Deut 27.14-15).

There is a crucial distinction, however. Whereas God arranged for the Levites to pronounce these curses on Israel the moment they entered the land as a reminder that practical enjoyment of their inheritance was conditional upon obedience, in his final speech Job initiates the entire procedure. Here is a man so boldly convinced of his innocence that he is prepared to invoke on his own person the terrible earthly consequences of sin.

Again, the chapter is different in its **challenge** to the reader, for it itemises sins which have blighted the human race ever since Adam fell. It reminds us of those great biblical x-rays which expose the spiritually diseased condition of the human heart:

> The heart is deceitful above all things, and desperately wicked: who can know it? I the Lord search the heart, I try the reins, even to give every man according to his ways, and according to the fruit of his doings (Jer 17.9-10).

> From within, out of the heart of men, proceed evil thoughts, adulteries, fornications, murders, Thefts, covetousness, wickedness, deceit, lasciviousness, an evil eye, blasphemy, pride, foolishness: All these evil things come from within, and defile the man (Mk 7.21-23).

Job, however, claims to be not guilty. His uprightness (and we must keep in mind the prologue's insistence, whatever may have befallen him, that he was a good, God-fearing man) is a standing rebuke to the failure of men in general. One might feel that it also reproaches New Testament saints in particular. Here was a man living before the giving of Israel's law (God's special rule of life for a nation set apart from others that, in their inevitable failure, they might demonstrate the sinfulness of all), before the completion of the Old Testament canon, before the entrance into humanity of the eternal Son as God's final self-disclosure. We today bask in the full glow of God's revelation in Christ, yet how many of us could claim to live up to Job's high standard of conduct?

The chapter divides into five main sections, each dealing with a different aspect of Job's life: the personal (31.1-12), the social (31.13-23), the spiritual (31.24-28), the general (31.29-34), and the agricultural (31.38-40). Warren Wiersbe offers the following handy topical headings: Job the man (31.1-12), Job the employer (31.13-15), Job the neighbour (31.16-23, 29-32), Job the worshipper (31.24-28), and Job the steward (31.38-40). Before the final section, however, comes a sudden and unexpected outburst of emotion (31.35-37) which momentarily disturbs the detached legal coolness of the language. It is only with difficulty that Job is keeping his feelings in check. Each section is itself subdivided, by the repeated "if ... let" formula, into distinct sins, which may be listed as follows:

> The personal life (31.1-12) comprehends insincerity (31.5-6), iniquity (31.7-8) and immorality (31.9-12).

> The social life (31.13-23) comprehends injustice (31.13-15) and inhumanity (31.16-23).

> The spiritual life (31.24-28) concentrates on idolatry.

The general life (31.29-34) includes malicious glee (31.29-30) and inhospitality (31.31-32), as well as that tendency to conceal errors through fear of the majority.

The agricultural life (31.38-40) mentions the dangers of overworking the land and robbing workers of their hire.

First of all Job takes the covers off his **personal life** (31.1-12). Evidently his personal behaviour was governed by the highest principles. The first four verses act as a general preamble, setting the tone of the whole: Job's conduct in every sphere was influenced by his knowledge of God.

> I made a covenant with mine eyes; and how should I fix my regard upon a maid? For what would have been my portion of God from above, and what the heritage of the Almighty from on high? Is not calamity for the unrighteous? and misfortune for the workers of iniquity? Doth not he see my ways, and number all my steps? (31.1-4, JND).

From the start Job employs the language of legal obligation. Conscious of the inbuilt weakness of the flesh, and perhaps recollecting the way Eve was misled in Genesis 3.6, he entered into a binding contract with his eyes not to look with desire at any woman other than his wife. Delitzsch underlines this implicit testimony to marital fidelity:

> With the confession of having [kept] this marriage ... sacred, and restrained himself not only from every adulterous act, but also from adulterous desires, his confessions begin.[351]

The word the KJV renders "maid" (1330) occurs fifty times in the Old Testament and, from Genesis 24.16 onwards, is usually translated "virgin". Not only did Job respect the marriage union, he had the highest regard for virginity. Writes Delitzsch,

> virginity is ever to be revered, a most sacred thing, the holy purity of which Job acknowledges himself to have guarded against profanation from any lascivious gaze by keeping a strict watch over his eyes.[352]

Adultery has colossal and lasting repercussions. It attacks both the wife it despises and the young woman it violates, as well as the God whose commands it disobeys.

What governed Job's behaviour, we note, was his knowledge that the Almighty faithfully recompenses evil. He lived his life, both private and public, in the light of an all-powerful God whose gaze was unblinkingly fixed upon his pathway. In the western world today the concept of God-fearingness is reviled, but Job showed the utmost wisdom in recognising that the Creator of heaven and earth is no absentee landlord who has withdrawn from interest in His creatures.

Like Abraham, he knew that "the Judge of all the earth" (Gen 18.25) will deal righteously with men.

The words "portion" and "inheritance" are paralleled to indicate the idea of recompense. They first appear together in the words of the sisters Rachel and Leah speaking to Jacob about their negative expectations from their father: "Is there yet any portion or inheritance for us in our father"s house?" (Gen 31.14). The difference is that God's awards are certain and come "from above", "from on high". Being a God of scrupulous justice and infallible accuracy, His judgment on the wicked will be devastating. Verse 3 therefore answers the questions of verse 2. "Destruction" (343) translates a word usually rendered "calamity" in the KJV. It turns up five other times in Job (18.12; 21.17; 21.30; 30.12; 31.23), each time in relation to the terrible distresses awaiting the godless. "Strange punishment" is the KJV's handling of a word from a Hebrew root describing knowledge, discernment and understanding. The idea seems to be that God metes out extraordinary but appropriate retribution on those who practise iniquity. He, the omniscient One, watches man's lifestyle ("ways [1870]") and registers every movement ("steps [6806]") of his pathway. Job has used similar language before, and Elihu will pick it up in a subsequent chapter. Here is Job: "For now thou numberest my steps [6806]: dost thou not watch over my sin?" (14.16). Here is Elihu: "For his eyes are upon the ways [1870] of man, and he seeth all his goings [6806]" (34.21). In his currently disillusioned state of soul Job can only think of God scrutinizing him like an unsympathetic supervisor, ever on the lookout for mistakes. We might recall the terrible testimony of the previous chapter where Job confesses that "I cry unto thee, and thou dost not hear me: I stand up, and thou regardest me *not*" (30.20). The KJV chooses to negate the second clause by analogy with the first (hence the italicised "*not*"), but in fact the Hebrew simply reads "thou regardest me". The impression is of a stern, fixed stare without the slightest flicker of compassion or understanding.

But this is Job's misunderstanding, brought about by unbearable grief. Theology, no matter how robust, can go to pieces under the weight of personal trial. For the reader, however, the entire book enlarges our knowledge of God's omniscience: truly, He sees everything (including our sins), but He also watched over His loyal servant Job with such delight as to point him out to Satan as a model of rectitude. The abiding truth that "Thou God seest me" (Gen 16.13), properly understood, brings terror to the unbeliever but sweet comfort to the saint.

Job elaborates further on his personal life by repudiating the practice of three specific sins: insincerity (31.5-6), iniquity (31.7-8) and immorality (31.9-12). He rejects any charge of disingenuousness or deception, inviting God to subject his claim to the fullest investigation:

> If I have walked with falsehood, and my foot hath hasted to deceit, (Let me be weighed in an even balance, and God will take knowledge of my blamelessness) (31.5-6, JND).

Artful duplicity is all too common. The collocation of "falsehood" ("vanity" in the KJV) and "deceit" recurs in the psalmist's description of the man with the right to ascend into the hill of the Lord: "He that hath clean hands, and a pure heart; who hath not lifted up his soul unto vanity, nor sworn deceitfully" (Ps 24.3-4). The only one to fulfil such a stringent requirement was the Lord Jesus Christ. But Job speaks as a man of genuine integrity, even if it could never measure up to the spotlessness of the incarnate Son. The "Let" parenthesis in verse 6 is not one of his curses (as in verse 8) but rather a plea that God would search him thoroughly, much as David prays, "Search me, O God, and know my heart: try me, and know my thoughts" (Ps 139.23). Job maintains that his life is an open book. The verb "weigh" (8254) seems always to be used in literal contexts (for example, Genesis 23.16) except in Job, where it appears in the patriarch's request that his miseries be measured so that his friends might sympathise: "Oh that my grief were throughly weighed, and my calamity laid in the balances together!" (6.2). Job emphatically refutes any charge of deception.

Further, he is innocent of the kind of iniquity which encourages deviation from the pathway of uprightness:

> If my step hath turned out of the way, and mine heart walked after mine eyes, and if any spot hath cleaved to mine hands: Then let me sow, and let another eat; yea, let the produce of my field be rooted out (31.7-8, RV).

His anatomical language makes the conceptual concrete: Job's feet, heart, eyes and hands are free from error. To use the words of the psalmist, he has not "turn[ed] aside to lies" (Ps 40.4) or, like Israel in its idolatry, "turned aside quickly out of the way which I commanded them" (Ex 32.8). Nor, like Achan in Joshua 7.21, has his heart coveted what his eyes beheld. He is reiterating the claim of verse 1, with the addition that he has not sullied his hands with any wicked action. The word "blot" is usually translated "blemish" when used of animal sacrifices, but Job is obviously thinking in terms of moral defilement.

He now pronounces his first curse: "Then let me sow, and let another eat; yea, let my offspring be rooted out" (31.8). It is likely that in this context "offspring", as an example of synonymous parallelism, alludes to the fruit of the ground rather than children. Comments Delitzsch:

> In so far as he may have acted thus, Job calls down upon himself the curse of [Deut 28.33,51]: what he sows, let strangers reap and eat; and even when that which is sown does not fall into the hands of strangers, let it be uprooted.[353]

But his most emphatic denial (and his most staggering curse) concerns sexual immorality:

> If mine heart have been enticed unto a woman, and I have laid wait at my neighbour's door: Then let my wife grind unto another, and let others bow down upon her. For that were an heinous crime; yea, it were an iniquity to

be punished by the judges: For it is a fire that consumeth unto Destruction [*abaddon*], and would root out all mine increase (31.9-12, RV).

"Enticed" (6601) renders a word used sometimes in the context of sexual dalliance. It appears in Israel's law: "if a man entice a maid that is not betrothed, and lie with her, he shall surely endow her to be his wife" (Ex 22.16). It is also used of Delilah's seduction of Samson (Judg 14.15; 16.5), and of Jehovah's tender appeal to backsliding Israel (Hosea 2.14). Again the language is direct and graphic. Job speaks of laying wait, or lurking secretly near his neighbour's door, waiting until he goes out so as to be able to sneak inside for the purpose of illicit pleasure. It is much the same world as that of the strange woman of the Proverbs, a woman quick to assure her naïve victim that there is no fear of discovery:

> Come, let us take our fill of love until the morning: let us solace ourselves with loves. For the goodman is not at home, he is gone a long journey: He hath taken a bag of money with him, and will come home at the day appointed (Prov 7.18-20).

Zuck's comment on Job's words is worth reproducing:

> Adultery is denied in strong words … considered a disgustingly lewd crime, punishable by man in court. In addition, the sin brought its own punishment … it consumes a man's soul, destroying his reputation, his conscience, his body, his family relationships, his future, and even his increase.[354]

Adultery – the sin Job places at the head of his list of possible crimes – is seen as treachery, theft, covetousness, blasphemy, and appalling self-harm. This is why he denounces it as "an heinous crime" (the word first appears in Leviticus 18.17 and is translated "wickedness" in the KJV) and "iniquity" deserving to be brought to court. As in the cases recorded in Genesis 38.24 and Deuteronomy 22.22, such acts of immorality were seen as dire offenses against the community as a whole. Job's concluding word is therefore solemn: "it is a fire that consumeth to destruction, and would root out all mine increase" (31.12). The imagery anticipates the language of the book of Proverbs:

> Can a man take fire in his bosom, and his clothes not be burned? Can one go upon hot coals, and his feet not be burned? So he that goeth in to his neighbour's wife; whosoever toucheth her shall not be innocent … whoso committeth adultery with a woman lacketh understanding: he that doeth it destroyeth his own soul. A wound and dishonour shall he get; and his reproach shall not be wiped away. For jealousy is the rage of a man: therefore he will not spare in the day of vengeance (Prov 6.27-34).

The adulterer, says Job, is playing with a flame which will eventually consume him in "destruction". The word is *abaddon* (11), which appears just six times in the Old Testament, only in the poetical books (Job 26.6; 28.22; 31.12; Ps 88.11; Prov 15.11; 27.70) and always coupled with death, *sheol* or the grave. Far from offering pleasure or profit, adultery is self-destructive. Even if he escapes censure by the local magistrates the adulterer cannot flee from the judgment of God.

Bearing in mind those comments in the book indicating that his wife has not shown the sympathy he might have expected (2.9; 19.17), Job – all the more remarkably – maintains the highest view of marriage. As instituted at creation it involved the joining together of one man and one woman so that "they shall be one flesh" (Gen 2.24), thus forming a life-long union which, having been brought about by God, was not to be shattered by man. It was to this key passage that the Lord Jesus returned, deliberately bypassing the temporary allowances of the law, to teach in the starkest terms the indissolubility of the marriage bond:

> And he saith unto them, Whosoever shall put away his wife, and marry another, committeth adultery against her. And if a woman shall put away her husband, and be married to another, she committeth adultery (Mk 10.11-12).

Though living outside the commonwealth of Israel, Job recognised the sacredness of the marriage relationship with such fervent intensity that we may justifiably use of him the language of the New Testament when laying down the qualifications of an assembly elder. He was "a man of irreproachable character, true to his one wife" (1 Tim 3.2, Weymouth).

So vehement is his disavowal of adulterous activity that the associated curse is startling: "Then let my wife grind unto another, and let others bow down upon her" (31.10). This presumably means that, were he guilty of adultery, he should be punished by the shame of seeing another man take his wife. Parallel to the ugly sexual implication is the idea of social degradation: his wife would be reduced to the level of the lowest slave, grinding the family corn. In a similar way, Isaiah pictures the misery awaiting the proud daughter of Babylon, who was commanded to "Take the millstones, and grind meal: uncover thy locks, make bare the leg, uncover the thigh" (Is 47.2).

Job now turns to his **social life** as a wealthy employer of labour (31.13-23). There too he was governed by a deep consciousness of God. Had he been guilty of injustice in dealing with any servants who had a complaint against him?

> If I have despised the cause of my bondman or of my bondmaid, when they contended with me, What then should I do when God riseth up? and if he visited, what should I answer him? Did not he that made me in the womb make him? and did not One fashion us in the womb? (31.13-15, JND).

He treated his servants "not as possessions but as persons, who had rights as well as himself".[355] His language constitutes what Zuck calls "a lofty statement about the equality of the human race",[356] a statement which follows logically from his knowledge that all men are descended from Adam rather than being the chance products of random evolutionary processes. The biblical narrative of creation endows mankind with the utmost dignity – made uniquely in the image of God – while accounting for his present misery because of inherited sin. Social or intellectual snobbery and workplace injustice, no less than racism, find no support in Scripture.

New Testament instruction about labour relations is crystal clear:

> Servants, obey in all things your masters according to the flesh; not with eyeservice, as menpleasers; but in singleness of heart, fearing God: And whatsoever ye do, do it heartily, as to the Lord, and not unto men ... for ye serve the Lord Christ ... Masters, give unto your servants that which is just and equal; knowing that ye also have a Master in heaven (Col 3.22 – 4.1).

Believing employees are to work loyally for their secular employers, knowing that in so doing they show themselves to be the Lord's servants; while believing employers are to treat their workers with justice, knowing that they in their turn are responsible to a heavenly Master. Job seems to have been practising this long before Paul wrote from a Roman prison, even though his reasons were grounded on the truth of creation rather than, as in Paul's case, the blessings of redemption.

Not only has he acted as a godly man towards his workers, he has been generous in his concern for the needy of the wider community. Job comprehensively denies the charge of inhumanity, his denial consisting of two parts, each prefaced by "If" (31.16-23). The first part exemplifies his concern for the nourishment of the poor, the widow, and the orphan:

> If I have withheld the poor from their desire, or caused the eyes of the widow to fail; Or have eaten my morsel alone, so that the fatherless ate not thereof, (For from my youth he grew up with me as with a father, and I have guided the widow from my mother's womb) (31.16-18, JND).

Job has kept open house, not primarily for wealthy associates (though doubtless he enjoyed feasting affluent friends), but for the poor. His hospitality fulfils the standards of the New Testament:

> When thou makest a dinner or a supper, call not thy friends, nor thy brethren, neither thy kinsmen, nor thy rich neighbours; lest they also bid thee again, and a recompence be made thee. But when thou makest a feast, call the poor, the maimed, the lame, the blind: And thou shalt be blessed; for they cannot recompense thee: for thou shalt be recompensed at the resurrection of the just (Lk 14.12-14).

When Paul encourages believers to be "given to hospitality" (Rom 12.13) he uses a verb which is translated differently but illuminatingly in Hebrews: "Be not forgetful to entertain strangers: for thereby some have entertained angels unawares" (Heb 13.2). Hospitality involves catering for strangers. Unlike most of the inhabitants of the lawless town of Gibeah (Judg 19.15), Job faithfully discharged his duty as a rich man able to extend generous provision to the needy.

This habit seems to have been long established. As he says, by way of explanation: "from my youth the fatherless grew up with me as with a father, and from my mother's womb I guided the widow" (31.18, ESV). Delitzsch paraphrases thus: "From earliest youth, so far back as he can remember, he was wont to behave like a father to the orphan, and like a child to the widow".[357] On the basis of this testimony it is reasonable to assume that Job learned about practical kindness from his parents, who had set him a pattern of godly charity which he continued on reaching maturity. We cannot overestimate the lasting impact on the young of impressions gained from the simple observation of parental conduct. Actions speak far louder than instructions. The Lord Jesus encouraged His disciples to submit to the authority of Israel's leaders, while at the same time exposing their hypocritical failure: "whatsoever they bid you observe, that observe and do; but do not ye after their works: for they say, and do not" (Mt 23.3). But Job was raised in a home where godly values were not only preached but practised. Like father, like son, is the worldly adage; and Job reflects well upon his upbringing.

Job's second answer to the charge of inhumanity (31.19-23) elaborates further upon what he has already said, this time with a focus on clothing:

> If I have seen any perishing for want of clothing, or any needy without covering; If his loins have not blessed me, and if he were not warmed with the fleece of my lambs; If I have lifted up my hand against an orphan, because I saw my help in the gate: Then let my shoulder fall from the shoulder-blade, and mine arm be broken from the bone! For calamity from God was a terror to me, and by reason of his excellency I was powerless (31.19-23, JND).

Not only has he fed the poor, he has clothed them, using the products of his extensive flocks and herds. Again we think of New Testament instructions:

> If a brother or sister be naked, and destitute of daily food, And one of you say unto them, Depart in peace, be ye warmed and filled; notwithstanding ye give them not those things which are needful to the body; what doth it profit? (James 2.15-16).

Whereas James writes to encourage believers to exercise practical kindness amongst their own number ("a brother or sister"), Job's generosity of spirit seems to have spilled beyond his immediate circle to society at large. Here is a man who put into effect the spirit of Paul's exhortation to the rich to "do good ... be rich in good works, ready to distribute, willing to communicate" (1 Tim 6.18).

Job rejects any charge that he has used his power against the fatherless and the helpless, even when knowing he had plenty of support among the judiciary ("my help in the gate") and could have got away with oppressive measures. His curse is again impressive in its severity: "let mine arm fall from my shoulder blade, and mine arm be broken from the bone" (31.22). If I have lifted my hand unjustly against the poor, says Job, let me be fittingly punished by literally losing the strength of my arm. The words may be taken at face value. The apostate King Jeroboam must have been terrified to discover himself suddenly crippled by a divine miracle when he dared to move against God's prophet:

> And it came to pass, when king Jeroboam heard the saying of the man of God, which had cried against the altar in Bethel, that he put forth his hand from the altar, saying, Lay hold on him. And his hand, which he put forth against him, dried up, so that he could not pull it in again to him (1 Kings 13.4).

Job's language is deliberately extravagant to emphasise his absolute conviction of innocence. The governing reason behind his scrupulously just conduct is spelled out in verse 23: "For calamity from God was a terror to me, and by reason of his excellency I was powerless" (31.23, JND). Job feared God's anger, which might erupt in some dreadful calamity against anyone who misused his power. In comparison with such divine majesty Job knew he was impotent. The word Darby translates "excellency" (7613) means an elevation, whether literal, as in the case of a leprous eruption in the skin (Lev 13.2,10,19), or metaphorical, as in the case of kingly loftiness (Job 13.11; Ps 62.4). Job was so conscious of the living God that he trembled to flout His commands. The bald statement of the prologue that Job "feared God" (1.1) is here borne out in detail.

We probably remember Eliphaz's allegation that "thou hast sent widows away empty, and the arms of the fatherless have been broken" (22.9). When people become angry, and especially when they realise they are losing the argument, they often resort to casting groundless accusations as wildly as small boys throw stones. The venerable Eliphaz descended to such an unjust and unsupported charge.

But wait. How can the modern reader arbitrate between Eliphaz's accusation and Job's response? Our instinctive sympathies are all with the suffering Job, of course, but that does not in itself prove that his claims are correct. After all, both he and Eliphaz are mature men of repute and wisdom. Is it possible to tell who is speaking the truth? Students writing a research paper are often advised to keep asking themselves the question, "How do I know this?", so that they carefully register the sources and evidences for everything they assert. Eliphaz maintains that Job did not fulfil his duty to the disadvantaged; Job replies, to the contrary, that he did. It has to be admitted that Job's calm and serious demeanour does not sound like the blusterings of a guilty man; but that alone is no guarantee of genuineness. We have only to read 1 Kings 21.13 and Matthew 26.60-61 to realise that it is possible for wicked men to swear to the most atrocious lies in a judicial hearing. Where then do we turn? Our final court of appeal has to be the overall testimony of the book of Job. There we find – in both prologue and epilogue – Job's reliability fully endorsed by the approbation of the narrator (1.1) and Jehovah Himself (1.8; 2.3). We can therefore accept Job's claims as completely trustworthy.

If the more apparently secular aspects of Job's life were shaped by his relationship with God, how much more was his **spiritual life** (31.24-28)? In this passage Job repudiates the practice of idolatry:

The three "If" clauses give a driving energy to this affirmation. The first two concern the danger of trusting wealth, always a temptation to men and women whether rich or poor. Gold is a lure in itself, although in Old Testament times it was also associated with idolatry, being the material of which the best gods were constructed (Ps 115.4; 135.15; Is 2.20). But Job denies being ensnared by love of money. He would have concurred with Paul's instruction to Timothy: "Charge them that are rich in this world, that they be not highminded, nor trust in uncertain riches, but in the living God" (1 Tim 6.17). Since, all too often, "riches … make themselves wings; [and] fly away as an eagle toward heaven" (Prov 23.4-5), the advice is sound: "Labour not to be rich". Rather, "In the fear of the Lord is strong confidence: and his children shall have a place of refuge" (Prov 14.26). Job had much wealth, as "the greatest of all the men of the east" (1.3), but wealth was not his god. In J R R Tolkien's fantasy story *The Lord of the Rings*, a prophecy is uttered over the head of Gimli the dwarf: "your hands shall flow with gold, and yet over you gold shall have no dominion".[358] Far more fittingly may such words be used of Job.

Job firmly repudiates placing his trust in his affluence. But nor did he secretly indulge in the contemporary folly of worshipping the sun and moon, along with the host of heaven. Israel was warned against this gross error before they entered Canaan, a land immersed in idolatry:

> lest thou lift up thine eyes unto heaven, and when thou seest the sun, and the moon, and the stars, even all the host of heaven, shouldest be driven to worship them, and serve them, which the Lord thy God hath divided unto all nations under the whole heaven (Deut 4.19).

That the God of the Bible is repeatedly called the "Lord of hosts" (the name first occurs in 1 Samuel 1.3) emphatically places Him far above the "host of heaven", which He made on the fourth day of the Genesis creation record. The heavens are liberally speckled with His marvellous handiwork, so much so as to baffle human computation. Writes Sarfati:

> The observable universe is so huge – 46 billion light-years radius – that it is estimated to contain about 10^{22} stars. This number is so vast that even using a computer that could count a trillion of these every second, it would take over 300 years to count this high. It's notable that the Bible says that it is impossible for any man to number the stars … It took science millennia to catch up with the Bible on this. Before Galileo trained his telescope on the skies, astronomers could see only 3,000 stars in each hemisphere. And

even Galileo could see only about 30,000 stars. But modern telescopes have affirmed that indeed we can't count all the stars.[359]

No wonder the Lord of hosts is infinitely superior to the universe He created, however massive it may seem to men on earth. Job, therefore, would not countenance even a covert gesture towards idolatry (such as kissing his hand at the heavens as a token of loyalty and affection), a sin deserving of judicial retribution. In the righteous theocratic rule of the millennial era, any refusal to worship the God of Israel will involve instant catastrophic penalties (Zech 14.16-19).

Any form of idolatry is a flat denial of the living God because it involves substituting the creature for the Creator. The various trendy isms which proliferate in the western world (led by materialism, evolutionism and environmentalism) are a testimony to man's continuing rebellion against God. Paul exposes the culpable stupidity of idolaters by describing them as those who "changed the truth of God into a lie, and worshipped and served the creature more than the Creator, who is blessed for ever" (Rom 1.25). We are not allowed to overlook the crass folly of their bargain: they exchanged truth for a lie. That the elect nation tragically succumbed to the practice while paying lip service to Jehovah is demonstrated in Ezekiel's shocking investigation into temple activities at Jerusalem (Ezek 8.14-18). Job, by contrast, exemplifies the highest respect for the Creator of the universe.

After this unequivocal stand against idolatry, which forms the spiritual heart of the chapter, Job reverts to scrutinising his life in **general** (31.29-34).

Because verse 31 may be easily misunderstood in the KJV the following is the rendering provided by the RV:

> If I rejoiced at the destruction of him that hated me, or lifted up myself when evil found him; (Yea, I suffered not my mouth to sin by asking his life with a curse;) If the men of my tent said not, Who can find one that hath not been satisfied with his flesh? The stranger did not lodge in the street; but I opened my doors to the traveller; If like Adam I covered my transgressions, by hiding mine iniquity in my bosom; Because I feared the great multitude, and the contempt of families terrified me, so that I kept silence, and went not out of the door (31.29-34, RV).

Job is, we notice, realistic. He acknowledges that there were men in his society who hated him (for whatever reason), yet repudiates any delight in their downfall or spiteful entreaty for their distress. He exemplifies the advice of the writer of Proverbs: "Rejoice not when thine enemy falleth, and let not thine heart be glad when he stumbleth" (Prov 24.17). Secret (and sometimes not-so-secret – many of us remember the undisguised jubilation in certain parts of the world at the terrible disaster of the Twin Towers) inner joy at the misfortune of one's enemies must be one of the commonest as well as the meanest of sins. The Lord Jesus went further than Old Testament instruction in exhorting His disciples to "Love your enemies, bless them that curse you, do good to them that hate you, and pray for them which despitefully use you, and persecute you" (Mt 5.44). The reason He gave was that in so doing they would express something of the gracious character of God Himself. Since "when we were enemies, we were reconciled to God by the death of his Son" (Rom 5.10), it behoves us to reflect His mercy in our dealings with human antagonists.

If Job was innocent of such malevolence, he was also free from any accusation of miserly inhospitality either towards his dependants ("the men of my tent") or strangers. In the KJV verse 31 sounds initially like a criticism of Job: his servants were so starved and ill-treated that they longed to devour his flesh. But other translations make clear that this is a ringing endorsement of his practical generosity in sharing the best foodstuffs. No one left Job's table with hunger pangs. One of the great features of the Lord's earthly miracles was that He provided sufficient to satisfy all. John's eyewitness language at the feeding of the five thousand leaves no room for doubt:

> Two hundred pennyworth of bread is not sufficient for them, that every one of them may take a little … Jesus took the loaves; and … distributed to the disciples, and the disciples to them that were set down; and likewise of the fishes as much as they would. When they were filled, he said unto his disciples, Gather up the fragments that remain, that nothing be lost (Jn 6.7-12).

The difference between Philip's expectation ("a little") and the Saviour's provision ("as much as they would") is a proof of the Lord's divine power as Creator and Sustainer of His people. All who come to Him find their needs met, and more.

Job goes further. Looking back to the archetypal sin of Adam – about which he was obviously well informed – He disclaims any effort to cover his "transgressions" (the word means an act of rebellion, which perfectly describes the first man's deliberate disobedience) or his "iniquity" (a word suggesting moral perversity). "Hiding" his sin from God was what Adam unsuccessfully attempted to do (Gen 3.8,10); but, as David announced, a special blessedness is enjoyed by the man whose "transgression is forgiven, whose sin is covered" (Ps 32.1). This covering is not the desperate expedient of a guilty man but a work of God which in no sense compromises His righteous standards because, as Paul makes clear in Romans, it is grounded on a propitiatory sacrifice (Rom 3.24-26).

If verse 33 speaks of Job's transparency before God (he had no need to conceal his sin, as Adam tried to do, for his conscience was clear), the following verse speaks of his innocence before men. He had done nothing which might cause him to shun the glare of publicity and keep him cowering in his house.

It is at this point that he seems, suddenly and unexpectedly, to shatter the calm structure of his formal asseveration with a passionate outburst (31.35-37).

This is what Job has long been seeking – that God would speak to him directly and explain the reasons for His animosity so that he (Job) might respond. We have to look back to what he said in chapters 13 and 19:

Then call thou, and I will answer: or let me speak, and answer thou me (13.22).

Oh that my words were now written! oh that they were printed in a book! (19.23).

The word (8420) the KJV translates "desire" (31.35) only appears three times in Scripture, and refers to the mark of a signature. It is used in Ezekiel's prophecy of the identifying and preserving sign set on the foreheads of those men in Jerusalem who sighed in sorrow at the idolatry which defiled Jehovah's earthly capital (Ezek 9.4,6). The Revised Version helps us understand what Job is saying: "Oh that I had one to hear me! (lo, here is my signature, let the Almighty answer me;) and that I had the indictment which mine adversary hath written!" (31.35, RV). Job is happy to put his name to all he has just avowed: it is his final defence. According to Delitzsch, "it is his ultimatum, as it were, the letter and seal to all that he has hitherto said about his innocence in opposition to the friends and God".[360]

Without any misgivings, he boldly appends his signature to the preceding comprehensive oath of innocence. "Job", writes Zuck, "figuratively attached his signature to his oath of purity ... and then asked that God respond to the oath".[361] We note that he implicitly calls God his "adversary", the one who contends with him in court. What Job regrets is that God has not written down all the things He holds against him in a formal bill of indictment. Had God done so, Job would not have been intimidated or distraught. Rather, he would have taken up the divine charge sheet as a badge of honour and distinction, convinced that he could respond to all accusations with an honest claim of "Not guilty", and thus be cleared before the bar of divine justice. With this charge sheet he would boldly draw near to his Judge. As Fausset rightly comments on verse 37, "A good conscience imparts a princely dignity before man and free assurance in approaching God".

But the speech is not quite over. There remains a brief section in which Job disclaims any misuse of the land or its inhabitants - what I have earlier called an allusion to his **agricultural life** (31.38-40).

But before we examine these final words it may be as well to consider the vexed problem of structure.

Commentators have found it hard to detect any obvious design principle governing this chapter. It is unquestionably comprehensive (most readers find fourteen specific sins mentioned), but does it follow any logically coherent order? Some expositors describe the final three verses as a limp anti-climax after the triumphant peroration of verses 35-37, and propose reconstructing the speech so that the latter verses constitute the concluding, as opposed to the penultimate, section. Surely such a powerful piece of rhetoric should end with a resounding climax? It is, however, a dangerous thing to rewrite or reorganise Scripture according to our fallible predilections. In reality there is no need to tamper with the text at all. Smick notes that Job "has a penchant for anti-climax",[362] citing 3.23-26 and 14.18-22 as earlier examples. But we do not even need to justify the bathetic ending of chapter 31 by viewing it as one of Job's idiosyncracies. It is far more likely that – and how human this is! – having made his grand and all-embracing declaration of integrity, Job suddenly recalls an area of life (in this case his agricultural stewardship) which he has not included in his list, and slips it in at the close. In other words, the last three verses are a kind of postscript to the whole. But even what I have described as a kind of memory lapse is entirely fitting, completing a circle: just as his final curse relates to agriculture, so does his first (31.8).

Darby's translation is a little more vivid than the KJV:

> If my land cry out against me, and its furrows weep together; If I have eaten the fruits thereof without money, and have tormented to death the souls of its owners: Let thistles grow instead of wheat, and tares instead of barley. The words of Job are ended (31.38-40, JND).

Crime against the land may sound strange to us, although the rise of the environmental lobby has placed the impossible and absurd task of "saving the planet" high on the fashionable political agenda. The Old Testament Israelite, however, knew that the very soil he possessed and worked was leased to him by God, who remained the ultimate landlord. Had not Jehovah declared that "The land shall not be sold for ever: for the land is mine; for ye are strangers and sojourners with me" (Lev 25.23)? This truth underlay all the regulations which the Lord laid down for the effective farming of Canaan, and Israel's long-term failure to abide by those instructions – particularly the sabbatical year – led eventually to its forcible exile. The Babylonians may have seen the fall of Judah as simply one more national conquest, but Scripture views it in relation to Israel's persistent disobedience, because the exile was designed "To fulfil the word of the Lord by the mouth of Jeremiah, until the land had enjoyed her sabbaths: for as long as she lay desolate she kept sabbath, to fulfil threescore and ten years" (2 Chr 36.21). For 490 years the people of Israel had failed to put Leviticus 25.2-4 into practice, and therefore fell under the penalty specified in Leviticus 26.34. Farming in ancient Israel was as much a spiritual as a commercial activity.

Job seems to view things in a similar light. Using the literary device of personification, he assures us that he has not so over-exploited his land that it cries aloud in protest against him, or weeps in pain because of his ruthless agricultural methods. The word the KJV translates "complain" (1058) really means (as in Darby) to weep, and is used of Hagar's grief in Genesis 21.16, of Abraham's mourning in Genesis 23.2, and Esau's tearful regret for his lost blessing in Genesis 27.38. It also describes the terrible sorrow of Job's three visitors when they first behold their much-altered and disease-ridden friend (2.12). Job pitches the emotional level high: his soil has neither been wounded nor mistreated. Furthermore, he has not oppressed his workers, failing to pay proper wages or harassing them so hard that they have been driven into an early grave. It is impossible to miss the allusion to this passage about labour relations when reading James 5:

Behold, the hire of the labourers who have reaped down your fields, which is of you kept back by fraud, crieth: and the cries of them which have reaped are entered into the ears of the Lord of sabaoth (James 5.4).

James's solemn words to rich men (James 5.1-6) invite the question of whether he has the whole of Job 31 at the back of his mind, for the patriarch's confession is a sturdy disavowal of all sins commonly laid at the door of the affluent. The advice of Proverbs is not to be forgotten:

Labour not to be rich: cease from thine own wisdom. Wilt thou set thine eyes upon that which is not? for riches certainly make themselves wings; they fly away as an eagle toward heaven (Prov 23.4-5).

Although the book of Job demonstrates that material prosperity is neither undesirable nor incompatible with genuine godliness (for everything is restored twofold at the end), it also underlines wealth's essential transience. That is why every generation of believers needs to be taught that, should they become wealthy, they are not to be "highminded, nor trust in uncertain riches, but in the living God, who giveth us richly all things to enjoy" (1 Tim 6.17).

In the interests of self-advancement or profit Job has mistreated neither his land nor his labourers. If he has (so runs his curse), then let his produce be reduced to worthless thistles and tares. The word translated "thistles" (KJV, RV, JND) is rendered "thorns" in 2 Chronicles 33.11 and Job 41.2. "Cockle" (KJV, RV) translates a word found only here but which, according to Strong's Concordance, refers to "*stink weed* or any other noxious or useless plant". Wheat was the choicest grain, barley the food of the poor; but were Job to be guilty of the charges he denies in verses 38 and 39, his fields should be condemned to grow nothing but useless, harmful weeds.

With this, "the words of Job are ended".

The last three chapters are tied together as an expansive but lucid argument. Looking back over his past life Job has testified to personal uprightness and esteem (Job 29), but now, as a result of God's sudden hostility, everything has changed (Job 30); yet he remains unshakeably conscious of nothing in himself to justify such treatment (Job 31). To all imaginable charges Job replies, "Not guilty!"

What have we learned from Job's lengthy protestation of innocence? First, we learn, if we did not know it before, that Job has a comprehensive knowledge of God's greatness. What does he teach us in this chapter about God? He reminds us that God recompenses men for their behaviour (31.2-3), that He knows every detail about us (31.4,6), that He intervenes in human history as it pleases Him (31.14), that He is the sovereign Creator of all (31.15,33), that He is overwhelmingly excellent in His majesty (31.23), that He is enthroned above all (31.28), that He is Almighty (31.2,35). Second, we can see in Job a picture of what man ought to be in this world: loyal to his Creator, just to his neighbours, faithful to his wife, kindly to the needy, caring to his environment. Third, we note that continued physical and emotional pain causes even the best of mere men to slip intermittently into unworthy thoughts of God.

Having read the first thirty-one chapters of this long book, the unavoidable conclusion is two-fold. First, we have to acknowledge that Job was an innocent man as far as any specific sin is concerned. As the Lord indicated at the start, his personal conduct in every sphere is outstanding. Second, incessant battering by his perplexed visitors has taken its toll: Job has become increasingly subject to "self-confident glorying and self-righteous pride".[363] The man who began the book so well, speaking submissively and reverently of God even in the midst of pain, ends by eulogizing himself.

It is uncomfortable to criticise one whose godliness far outstrips ours, but part of the point of this unique book is to expose the failure of the flesh in the finest man. In his understandable self-absorption, brought about by sufferings both physical and emotional, Job overlooks some key truths. What does Job forget?

- His own innately corrupt nature (to be distinguished from specifically sinful acts of commission or omission). He is still a sinner even if he is not guilty of the particular evils detailed in chapter 31. The oral record of human history would have taught him the sad reality of original sin, for "Adam lived an hundred and thirty years, and begat a son in his own likeness, after his image" (Gen 5.3). Adam and Eve were created in the image of God (untarnished, undimmed), but sinful Adam begat a son in his own fallen image. Job's nature is traceable back to him.

- God's eternal righteousness in all His ways. The record of Noah's flood is prefaced with the divine invitation, "Come thou and all thy house into the ark; for thee have I seen righteous before me" (Gen 7.1). We usually take this as a comment on Noah himself, but with the words "before me" it is first of all a testimony to the righteousness of God, in that He alone is the measure of what is right. There can be no virtue, no goodness outside of Him. Because Job is suffering without apparent reason he jumps to the hasty conclusion that God must be unjust. But if God is unjust He is no longer God.

- The inevitable limitations of his own creaturely knowledge, which might be blind to divine purposes beyond his understanding. Just as even an atheist will reluctantly admit that God may yet exist outside the sphere of his present knowledge, so the believer has to own that there may be divine intentions which God has not seen fit to disclose. Adam was created fresh from God's hand with a marvellous unhindered intellect, but sin has not only damaged man's spirit, it has also corrupted his mental capacity. The post-flood generation which proposed to "build us a city and a tower, whose top may reach unto heaven" (Gen 11.4), perhaps as an attempt to escape any future inundation, only demonstrated its laughable ignorance of divine power. Job is a man of great insight and intelligence, but he is still a damaged creature.

- God's sovereign rights to do as He will with His creatures. Because God is God, He is answerable to no one. Job persists in demanding that God answer him. Though in those early days God did on occasion speak audibly to men (Gen 4.6-7; 6.13-21; 9.1-17; 12.1-3), He was not obligated to do so, nor indeed to explain Himself. As Wiersbe puts it, "the God of the universe is not at the beck and call of His creatures".[364]

I have deliberately tied these points to the knowledge which we may reasonably assume Job would have absorbed from the oral traditions of his time. But to relate them to ourselves is much easier, for we live in the "last days" of divine revelation, a period in which God has said through His Son everything He wishes to say. Because of his terrible sufferings and because of the inevitable limitations of his knowledge, Job may be pardoned for his occasional temerity, but we have no such excuse.

Schaper sums it up like this:

> [Job] has gone out without a whimper. He not only maintains his righteousness, he glories in it. Job is correct in the principle that his trouble did not come because of his sin. But in his headlong rush for vindication he has lost his humility and awe.[365]

Job is speaking of and to God with less than the reverence which is God's due. Robinson is correct to remind us that "the proper place for fallen man before God, even at his best, is the dust".[366] "The fear of God", he writes, is "a good man's preservative against sin".[367] In this good man, at present, that fear seems to be somewhat on the wane. How it is to be rekindled will be the subject of the remaining chapters of the book.

SECTION 22
Dialogue: Job 4 – 42.6
Corrective: Job 32-37
Elihu's Speech: Job 32-37
Part One: Job 32-33

Chapter 32 springs a surprise on readers of the book of Job. By this stage, the formal debate between the patriarch and his peers has ground to a halt in total deadlock. On the one hand, he refuses to surrender to their combined insistence upon the personal guilt which, they are convinced, must lie behind his present suffering. On the other hand, they cannot be persuaded to drop their charges against him; they may be silenced, but they are by no means won over. All this time Job has been engaged in a double address: he has spoken directly to the friends, treating them sometimes individually, sometimes as a group; but he has also appealed over their heads to God, as the final arbiter. His speeches have alternated between belligerent protestation and agonised prayer. He has, we might say, been waging a campaign simultaneously on two fronts. Now that the human opposition appears to be exhausted, the reader probably anticipates a divine verdict to settle the matter once and for all. After all, Job has long prayed that God, his ultimate opponent (as he sees it), would speak.

But this is not the case; at least, not yet. Before Jehovah steps in to terminate the contest we have a six-chapter passage in which an entirely new voice is raised. It is impossible to overemphasize the shock value of this. Chapter 32 suddenly tosses a squib into the ring.

In order to get a sense of the new figure who takes the stage, let us attempt a broad overview of Elihu. His very **presence** in the narrative is startling. Nothing in the earlier chapters has led the reader to anticipate another human participant joining the debate. The introduction gave us what we reasonably assumed to be an exhaustive *dramatis personae* for the major part of the book. Apart from the heavenly prologue, attention is focused entirely on the earth – on Job and his three visitors. There may, of course, be others listening to the to-and-fro battle at the city rubbish tip where Job sits. We know, for example, that as a wealthy man he possessed many household servants (1.3), but probably they, like his wife (19.17), are no longer prepared to identify themselves with one whose fortunes have plunged so low (19.16). There is also the ruffianly mob of young thugs who mock, jeer and spit as they pass (30.10-14). But the text does not inform us of any others. If any bystanders opt to say anything it remains unrecorded. Elihu's intrusion is therefore both unheralded and, to an extent, unexplained. What we are told is that he has listened to the protracted debate (so we may assume he has been there from the beginning) with ever growing frustration. One might suggest that in some ways he represents the ordinary reader of the book. We too, exposed to a tedious and verbose argument, have longed at intervals to press a pause button in order to interview the combatants in quest of clarification, or grasp hold of a truly authoritative word. But Elihu is there on the spot, acutely attentive and increasingly irritated at what he hears.

Before he speaks, Elihu is granted his own **pedigree**, quite a privilege for an admittedly young man. Whereas the three friends were introduced simply with reference to their place of origin (2.11), he is announced as "Elihu the son of Barachel the Buzite, of the kindred of Ram" (32.2). As Robinson notes, he is "the only individual in the poem whose parentage is recorded".[368] Perhaps the point is that, being comparatively obscure, unlike the distinguished men who have hitherto dominated the scene, he requires some background. His name probably means "He is my God", and his ancestry relates him to Abraham's brother Nahor, whose second son was called Buz (Gen 22.20-21). Buz was also an area of the Arabian Desert named after Abraham's nephew (Jer 25.23). Ram may refer to Aram, who in Genesis 22.21 is listed as another descendant of Nahor. Elihu appears to come from a biblically significant stock, yet one more of those scattered clues which lead us to place the entire book in the patriarchal era.

Further, we are told in no uncertain terms about his simmering **passion**. Just as we learned earlier that the three friends were deeply grieved and dumbstruck at their first sight of Job (2.12-13), so we discover that Elihu is overcome not, however, by sorrow but by anger. Four times in this narrative prologue the word "wrath" is used to describe his attitude both to Job and his would-be comforters. This noun (639) appears twenty-one times in the book as a whole, and is occasionally translated "nostrils" and "nose" (4.9; 27.3; 40.24; 41.2) but most of the time is rendered "wrath" or "anger". The first and last references describe God's indignation (4.9; 42.7), the latter significantly identifying the three friends (rather than Job or Elihu) as the objects of His displeasure. Elihu's intemperate outburst places him as a kind of angry young man who has sat back deferentially listening to his elders with an increasing impatience which he can no longer contain. He may be likened to a young believer at an assembly Bible reading who hesitates to intrude upon what he considers the excessively long-winded and circuitous deliberations of more mature expositors, but eventually has to have his say.

Once Elihu begins to speak we discover the distinctive **principles** underlying his comments. These principles set him apart from the others, and may be summarised in two words – citation and correction. Elihu has been listening carefully to what has been said, and proceeds to quote more or less accurately from Job's earlier speeches (33.8-11; 34.9; 35.2-3,14). Unlike the other disputants, he interacts very closely with the patriarch. Further, his effort at correction is focused not upon what Job may have done to deserve his present ills (the inflexible approach taken by the friends) but rather on the self-righteous way Job has responded to adverse circumstances. He is angry because Job "held himself in the right at the expense of God's righteousness",[369] and because, in spite of their prolonged discourses, the three friends failed to expose his error. The wisest of men have been unable to answer Job. Elihu, says Kelly, is "put forward by God, to bring to naught the pride of age and experience, observation and tradition".[370]

What, then, is his **purpose** in the book? The commentators are divided. It cannot be denied that once he gets going young Elihu has a great deal to say. Job's friends were allocated no more than three speeches each, spread out over the course of the debate; Elihu, however, is allowed four speeches on the trot. Even Job, in his long final defence recorded in chapters 26 to 31, has less to say than

Elihu. Is Elihu, then, perhaps nothing more than a windbag? Is he to be viewed as an irrelevant, garrulous buffoon, "self-important and banal",[371] an absurd figure of light relief who serves only to dissipate the leaden atmosphere created by Job's final words? Both the narrative introduction and his own spoken prologue may be misread as announcing a youthful chatterbox who talks much but says little. This idea, far from new, originated (according to Delitzsch) with Jerome in the fourth century. Attractive to those literary scholars who relish finding a subversive figure in a serious text, it fails on two counts: it underestimates, first, the weightiness and, second, the sanity of his contribution. Comic relief is one thing; six chapters of earnest argument are another. His speech consists of four meticulously separated discourses containing marvellous and memorable insights. No, any cheap dismissal of Elihu undermines the value of divine revelation.

Others who find him an irritant sometimes suggest that he must be the invention of a different author, one who succeeds merely in disturbing the careful construction of the original writer of Job. But this presupposes, without any textual evidence, a duality of writers at loggerheads, a notion which sits ill with reverent submission to the inspiration of Scripture, replacing it with confusion and fragmentation. Those who believe that the Bible is God's word will not resort to such desperate expedients, any more than they will carve up the Pentateuch among a plurality of discordant authors or editors. Someone once described the gulf between the conservative and the liberal view of the Pentateuch as the difference between an upper and lower case letter: is it truly Mosaic (as the Lord Jesus affirms) or merely a mosaic? Crediting the Elihu section of Job to another human hand does nothing to elucidate his function and, moreover, betrays a disturbingly inadequate view of the authority of Scripture.

The easiest, and I believe the correct, way to view Elihu's contribution is to see it as a strategically placed bridge passage between the stalemate of the debate and Jehovah's conclusive intervention. What he does is to anticipate the emphasis on God's power which will dominate chapters 38-41, and unconsciously pave the way for Jehovah's arrival by describing the imminent approach of a storm. Elihu's ominous weather forecast in 37.2-5 is the overture to the voice of God.

We may sum up Elihu's distinctiveness with the following points:

- Unlike the other speakers, he refers to and addresses Job by name (32.12; 33.1,31; 34.5,7,35,36; 35.16; 37.14)
- He significantly quotes or paraphrases some of Job's earlier remarks
- He strikes a new note in the argument, blaming Job not for his past iniquities but for his present irreverence. While the others "claimed that Job was suffering because he was sinning … Elihu explained that he was sinning because he was suffering".[372]
- He maintains a higher view of God than the others, confessing that he consciously trembles before the divine majesty (37.1)
- Unlike the three comforters, he receives no response from Job or rebuke from Jehovah.

Elihu's contribution consists of four long, distinct speeches, set apart by narrative breaks (32.1-5; 34.1; 35.1; 36.1). The four speeches are as follows:

(i) 32-33
(ii) 34
(iii) 35
(iv) 36-37.

This dense, four-part discourse is akin in some ways to Job's lengthy concluding defence in the preceding chapters. We may sum up the gist of Elihu's argument like this.

In **chapters 32 and 33** he introduces himself, accounts for his silence hitherto and, addressing the friends, castigates them for their inept attempts to answer Job. Then, turning directly to the patriarch (33.1), he urges him to pay close attention since he (Elihu) is also a mere man made from the clay: Job has no need to feel unduly intimidated. Elihu quotes from Job's words to the effect that he is an innocent victim of gratuitous divine harassment. This, says Elihu, is unjust. God, by definition, is greater than man, and does not have to give account of His actions. Nevertheless, through dreams and chastening circumstances, God graciously communicates with His creatures to draw them back to Himself. God's government, however hard, ultimately has man's good in view.

In **chapter 34** Elihu starts by addressing the friends, perhaps with a degree of irony ("ye wise men ", 34.2,10), but then turns again to Job, accusing him of behaving like the wicked in his rash and irreverent remarks about God.

Chapter 35 further develops the charge that Job's reaction to divine chastisement has been rebellious. Instead of bowing humbly before God's ways, Job has presumed to assert his own righteousness at the expense of God's.

In **chapters 36 and 37** Elihu continues to speak "on God's behalf" (36.2), affirming His power and corrective ministry. Job has forgotten how great He is, for example in His control of the natural world, atmospheric storms in particular. Admitting his own terror at these exhibitions of divine majesty, Elihu describes an approaching tempest which proves to be the very phenomenon out of which Jehovah will speak in chapter 38.

This first section (chapters 32 and 33) consists of a prose narrative prelude, followed by a caustic comment to the friends, and then an address to Job. It may be broken up thus:

1. Elihu's Introduction: 32.1-5
2. Elihu's Impatience – Directed to the Friends: 32.6-22
3. Elihu's Inquiry – Directed to Job: 33.1-33.

Elihu's Introduction: 32.1-5

The first verse of the chapter is of vital importance: right from the start it signals the broad accuracy of Elihu's viewpoint. We have throughout this book taken the position that the narrative is entirely trustworthy in its commentary on Job and his friends. Whereas their dialogue is clearly flawed by ignorance or prejudice, the narrator, guided by divine inspiration, is enabled not only to provide an accurate record of human misunderstandings but also to unveil the truth behind the story. He is therefore as reliable as Moses reporting the journeys of Israel, or the historian chronicling the lives of Judah's kings.

The first verse registers the *impasse* in the debate: "So these three men ceased to answer Job, because he was righteous in his own eyes" (32.1). The friends call a halt, not because they have convinced Job of specific sin, nor because they have accepted his claims of innocence, but because he is entrenched in an impregnable fortress of self-righteousness. All their arguments and objections have completely failed to shatter Job's defences.

The key feature governing biblical character description is how a man stands in the sight of God. When the text tells us that Job was "righteous in his own eyes [5869]", it uses a noun commonly translated either "eyes" or "sight". To trace this formula through Scripture is to discover that the only true assessor of man is Jehovah:

And Er, Judah's firstborn, was wicked in the sight [5869] of the Lord (Gen 38.7).

And the children of Israel did evil in the sight [5869] of the Lord (Judg 3.7).

And Solomon did evil in the sight [5869] of the Lord (1 Kings 11.6).

David did that which was right in the eyes [5869] of the Lord (1 Kings 15.5).

But Omri wrought evil in the eyes [5869] of the Lord (1 Kings 16.25).

Jehoiachin … did that which was evil in the sight [5869] of the Lord (2 Chr 36.9).

From Genesis to the end of the historical books the formula remains the same: however men may measure themselves, in the final analysis the only evaluation that counts is God's. We do not inhabit a random or anarchic universe of relative values, but one governed by an immutable Creator against whose verdict there is no appeal. Remove God from the picture and there can be no absolute standards of right and wrong, merely a smorgasbord of individual preferences. The biblical worldview is sturdily consistent. People who resort to doing what is right in their own judgment (as was the case in Judges 21.25) only betray their folly in disregarding the living God.

When, therefore, the inspired narrator tells us that Job was "righteous in his own eyes" (32.1), we are alerted to the essential weakness of Job's position: his self-assessment is worth little. To be sure, the book asserts through the voice of the same reliable narrator that Job is an upright man of outstanding virtue (1.1), but that of course relates primarily to his life before his testings commenced. By this stage, he has been sorely tried in the furnace of affliction with the result that, under such pressure, "the greatest of all the men of the east" (1.3) has been found lacking in a submissive spirit. Self-righteousness is Job's problem and Elihu calls attention to it.

Four topics are addressed in this prose introduction. **Elihu's vehemence** (32.2), we learn, is in part a consequence of Job's self-satisfaction. Elihu is incensed at the way Job puts his own vindication before God's honour, because he realises that the justification of God is more important than the justification of man. In this he anticipates the argument of Paul's letter to the Romans, where the apostle insists that God must first of all be seen to be right in all He does. Calvary is the great vindication of divine righteousness. There God set forth His Son to be

> a propitiation through faith in his blood, to declare his righteousness for the remission of sins that are past, through the forbearance of God; To declare, I say, at this time his righteousness: that he might be just, and the justifier of him which believeth in Jesus (Rom 3.24-26).

Paul's reiteration of the key words hammers home his message: "righteousness … righteousness … just … justifier". The work of the cross proclaims that God is absolutely just in pardoning the guilty, because the righteous claims of His law have been fully met by a sinless substitute. The gospel of grace, as well as saving sinners, magnifies God's justice. When angels concluded their announcement of the Messiah's birth with the words, "Glory to God in the highest, and on earth peace, good will toward men" (Lk 2.14), they prioritised God's honour over man's blessing. Peter's telling insight into the purpose of Christian service includes everything in the believer's life: "if any man minister, let him do it as of the ability which God giveth: that God in all things may be glorified through Jesus Christ" (1 Pet 4.11). Our entire reason for existing is to glorify Him "in all things". This cannot be cosily restricted to "spiritual" or "assembly" activities. The student who customarily initials his university essays with the letters AMDG (short for *ad majorem Dei gloriam,* "to the greater glory of God", the motto of the Jesuits) may have the right idea, but of course mechanically advertising such an aim is not at all the same as fulfilling it. The believer has to pray regularly and earnestly that the Lord will keep him mindful of the true goal of living.

It is **Job's irreverence** (32.2b), expressed in his passionate outbursts, which has so irritated Elihu; he has put his needs before God's glory. In harping constantly on personal innocence, Job "brings upon God the appearance of injustice" and "condemns God that he may be able to maintain his own righteousness".[373] This is a serious accusation. It is not, we note, the old charge that Job's past life harboured some secret fault to account for his terrible suffering; rather, it is that in his suffering Job has placed himself centre stage.

This is one of the perils of distress. It may serve to cast us upon the Lord (which is good), or it may drive us into thinking ourselves the hub of the universe, and so become self-obsessed, self-absorbed, and self-occupied. The believer's safest course is to follow the example of the psalmist, who tells us that "In my distress I cried unto the Lord, and he heard me" (Ps 120.1).

The friends' incompetence (32.3,5) is the other cause of Elihu's anger. They claim to represent piety (4.7), established wisdom (15.18), and venerable experience (15.10) and yet, despite their combined efforts over the past thirty or so chapters, they have been unable to budge Job from his ground. Indeed, far from shaking his beliefs, they have served only to cement his convictions; his final speech was his strongest yet.

But Elihu has not rushed into speech. His **diffidence** (32.4) and innate respect for age and status have held him back from intruding earlier on the conversation. The meaning of verse 4 is probably better expressed in the RV than in the KJV: "Now Elihu had waited to speak unto Job, because they were elder than he" (32.4, RV). Such self-restraint in young and old alike is commendable. One of Paul's important lessons about the exercise of spiritual enablements in the local assembly is that gifts are at all times under the control of the individual. Writing in an era when biblical tongues speaking was still in operation, he says of the man with such a gift,

> if there be no interpreter, let him keep silence in the church; and let him speak to himself, and to God. Let the prophets speak two or three, and let the other judge. If any thing be revealed to another that sitteth by, let the first hold his peace. For ye may all prophesy one by one, that all may learn, and all may be comforted. And the spirits of the prophets are subject to the prophets. For God is not the author of confusion, but of peace, as in all churches of the saints (1 Cor 14.28-33).

New Testament tongues speakers and New Testament prophets were not prompted to participate by some obscure, involuntary impulse, for "the spirits of the prophets are subject to the prophets". Paul insists that men are in control of their gifts and not *vice-versa*. A man is always personally accountable for his ministry. These principles may be applied to the continuing gift of teaching (the opening up and application of the Scriptures), for each local assembly should possess several men able to minister the word, although not all will necessarily speak at every meeting. Such men are to exercise courtesy towards one another, not monopolising the time to the exclusion of others. Gifts may be divinely granted empowerments for service, but they are certainly not irrational: God never bypasses the mind, for He appeals constantly to our intelligent understanding.

Having explained the cause of Elihu's anger and his sudden intervention, the narrator now records the first of his four speeches.

Elihu's Impatience – Directed to the Friends: 32.6-22

This rather verbose address to Job's friends is not easy to break down into component parts, but may be viewed as consisting of three segments. Elihu's first concern is to note the **contrast** between the other speakers and himself (32.6-9):

And Elihu the son of Barachel the Buzite answered and said, I am young, and ye are aged; wherefore I was timid, and feared to shew you what I know. I said, Let days speak, and multitude of years teach wisdom. But there is a spirit which is in man; and the breath of the Almighty giveth them understanding. It is not the great that are wise; neither do the aged understand judgment (32.6-9, JND).

He sets up two categories: the young and the old. Most of his linguistic energies are devoted to fleshing out the second, describing his immediate audience as "old" (3453), possessed of a "multitude [7230] of years [8141]", "great" (7227) and "aged" (2205). The first word appears exclusively in Job (12.12; 15.10; 29.8; 32.6), while the second is found in this exact collocation only in Leviticus 25.16. "Great", as the parallelism indicates, refers not so much to social importance as seniority, while "aged" is first used to describe Abraham and his wife who were "old [2205] and well stricken in age" (Gen 18.11). Having expressed a natural deference towards age and an awareness of the respect it deserves (although he scarcely sounds like someone who is, in Darby's word, "timid"), Elihu proceeds to qualify his contrast between old and young. This he does by affirming, first, that God's Spirit resides in all men (not just those advanced in years) and, second, that the mere passing of time does not guarantee the attainment of wisdom.

He is right. The young men of Israel were taught to show due respect for age because in so doing they demonstrated reverence for God: "Thou shalt rise up before the hoary head, and honour the face of the old man, and fear thy God" (Lev 19.32). The New Testament teaching is equally direct: "Rebuke not an elder, but intreat him as a father" (1 Tim 5.1). Nevertheless, by its many examples Scripture shows that old age is not automatically accompanied by either wisdom or godliness. The old man in Gibeah who generously offered hospitality to a travelling Levite also betrayed an appalling lack of paternal care for his own daughter and his visitor's concubine (Judg 19.17-21,24); the elderly priest Eli possessed neither the discernment to recognise a genuinely heart-broken woman nor the backbone to discipline his rebellious sons (1 Sam 1.13-14; 2.29). Wisdom may be found with the poor and despised rather than with the affluent and influential (Eccl 9.15). In the local assembly, the mere possession of a pension book is no sufficient qualification for leadership; those who guide God's people are described not only as elders (underlining a maturity which is as much spiritual as physical) but as shepherds and overseers. The right spiritual equipment is essential. A man may have seen many days and yet have learned nothing from any of them.

It is equally true, of course, that inexperience is no sure-fire recipe for astuteness. The younger generation brought up with King Rehoboam offered him disastrous advice, although it obviously appealed to his vanity to pretend that he was a bigger and tougher man than his father (1 Kings 12.6-11).

Elihu's point is simple: considering that all men, young and old, are given breath by the Almighty, even the youthful may have some grasp of truth. His language echoes the Genesis creation narrative, in which "the Lord God formed man of the dust of the ground, and breathed into his nostrils the breath of life" (Gen 2.7). In fact, the word in Job 32.8 translated by the KJV "inspiration" is the same rendered "breath" in Genesis 2.7. Since both life and mental capacity come from God as the birthright of all, they cannot be restricted to those who are advanced in years: "the Lord giveth wisdom: out of his mouth cometh knowledge and understanding" (Prov 2.6). Three times in 1 Samuel 18 we learn that young David "behaved himself wisely" (vv.5,14-15,30) while, presumably in later life, David himself tells us that "The mouth of the righteous speaketh wisdom, and his tongue talketh of judgment" (Ps 37.30). The prime qualification for wisdom, we note, is spiritual: not age or even experience, but righteousness. Understanding is one of the endowments granted those who are right with God and who therefore take the trouble to spend quality time with His Word. Jeremiah's exposure of the failed counsellors of his day is biting: "The wise men are ashamed, they are dismayed and taken: lo, they have rejected the word of the Lord; and what wisdom is in them?" (Jer 8.9) The principle remains true: to bypass God's Word is tragically to miss the main highway to wisdom.

Because he is aware that the elderly do not necessarily have all the answers, and because he knows that true wisdom is uniquely God's gift, Elihu is prepared to put himself forward.

He now focuses on his own **comprehension** (32.10-16) of the reasons why the three friends have failed:

> Therefore I say, Hearken to me; I also will shew what I know. Lo, I waited for your words; I gave ear to your reasonings, until ye searched out what to say. Yea, I gave you mine attention, and behold, there was none of you that confuted Job, that answered his words; That ye may not say, We have found out wisdom; God will make him yield, not man. Now he hath not directed his words against me; and I will not answer him with your speeches. They were amazed, they answered no more; words failed them. And I waited, for they spoke not, but stood still, and answered no more (32.10-16, JND).

His verdict is hardly flattering. Although he gave them every opportunity to convict Job of error, they simply were not up to it. But Elihu does not stop there. He sees past man's failure to recognise a divine purpose behind it: "Lest ye should say, We have found out wisdom: God thrusteth him down, not man" (32.13). The verse is admittedly ambiguous. Delitzsch translates it as follows:

> Lest ye should say: "We found wisdom,
> God is able to smite him, not man!"[374]

Other versions (such as the ESV) take a similar view – that Elihu's analysis of the friends' thought processes takes up the entire verse rather than simply the first part. According to Elihu, they are identifying their arguments with God's voice (rather in the way that Eliphaz, back in 15.11, pretentiously described his own words as "the consolations of God"). Had they silenced Job, they would have trumpeted their success, asserting that God (through them) had demolished his defences.

Nevertheless, the KJV wording makes a powerful point. There is, says Elihu, a reason behind human inadequacy – it is ordained of God to suppress human pride and glorify divine wisdom. In other words, to prevent men becoming smugly gratified by their intellectual and persuasive skills, God reserves the right to deal with Job Himself. It may well be that Elihu is thinking here of the special insight he believes God has given him (unlike the friends, who argued largely on the basis of experience, tradition and convention); or perhaps he is faintly aware that his role is to clear the way for a heavenly intervention. However much he may or may not understand, the principle is correct: man's extremity is God's opportunity.

In looking behind the immediate circumstances to see God's hand at work, Elihu is not unlike Job himself, who has throughout the book insistently traced all his circumstances directly to heaven. Both a man's trials and the failure of his brethren to elucidate those trials may be seen, then, as part of the divine plan to throw God's absolute sovereignty into relief. "Thrusteth down" (5086) is an unexpectedly forceful expression. It translates a word which occurs only eight times in the Bible, and is usually rendered "drive" or "shake". It first appears in a warning to Israel of the perils awaiting the nation should they turn from the Lord:

> And upon them that are left alive of you I will send a faintness into their hearts in the lands of their enemies; and the sound of a shaken [5086] leaf shall chase them; and they shall flee, as fleeing from a sword; and they shall fall when none pursueth (Lev 26.36).

Since men cannot dislodge Job from his citadel of self-righteousness, God will have to shake him out of complacency. In the final analysis, God is both the author of and the answer to Job's sufferings. Not, mind you, that God is obligated to respond to all Job's questions, but rather that He Himself, in all the glories of His person, is the solution. As we shall see, the final chapters of this book do not resolve Job's difficulties; instead, they confront him with Omnipotence.

Having offered a remarkable reason for the friends' failure to defeat Job, Elihu draws attention to his own objectivity. Job's past responses have had the official comforters in their sights, but Elihu is a new voice, coming at the matter from a different angle. Nothing Job has said hitherto has touched him personally, nor will he bother to repeat tired arguments (32.14). He arrives on the scene as a breath of fresh air.

Verses 15 and 16, an acidic commentary on the older men, parallel verses 11 and 12, underlining their discomfiture and perplexity. Their humiliation clears the way for Elihu. There is, one must admit, a self-consciously stylized posturing about his introduction which sits ill with western cultural expectations, but was probably highly esteemed in the east. Standing as he does in the presence of a critical audience of oratorical specialists, we should not be surprised that this young man wants to demonstrate his own rhetorical skills.

Finally, just before speaking directly to Job, he somewhat artlessly describes the inner **compulsion** which made him join the debate (32.17-22):

> I will answer, I also in my turn, I also will shew what I know: For I am full of matter, the spirit within me constraineth me. Behold, my belly is as wine which hath no vent; like new flasks, it is ready to burst. I will speak, that I may find relief; I will open my lips and answer. Let me not, I pray you, accept any man's person; neither will I give flattery to man. For I know not how to flatter; my Maker would soon take me away (32.17-22, JND).

When he says he is "full of matter", Elihu simply means he has plenty to say. The Hebrew term (found more often in Job than anywhere else) is usually rendered "words" in its thirty-four appearances (for example, 4.4; 6.26; 8.10; 38.2). Elihu is so packed with material that he is at bursting point. We must not confuse him with the prattling fool whom Solomon sardonically describes as "full of words" (Eccl 10.14). Both the context and the language are entirely different. Elihu is closer in spirit to Jeremiah who, though tempted to abandon his thankless prophetic ministry to unrepentant Judah, had to confess that God's word "was in mine heart as a burning fire shut up in my bones, and I was weary with forbearing, and I could not stay" (Jer 20.9). For all his reluctance he had to speak. Similarly, though for a different reason, David tells us that "My heart was hot within me, while I was musing the fire burned: then spake I with my tongue" (Ps 39.3).

By "the spirit within me", Elihu may refer back to the human spirit inbreathed by God (32.8), or forward to the Spirit of God whom he will name in the next chapter (33.4). In one sense it matters little: he intends to speak out, utilising the capacity God has granted him. His spirit has so urged him that he has to break the silence. Although the imagery is different from Jeremiah's it makes the same point: pent up thoughts are like new wine which threatens to split its wineskins. The act of speaking brings release from pressure. In the words of Darby's translation: "I will speak, that I may find relief; I will open my lips and answer" (32.20, JND).

One final point Elihu makes before beginning a formal address to Job. This illustrates a characteristic feature of his approach. His retentive memory and sharp mind flash back to some of Job's earlier words accusing the friends of partiality:

> Will ye speak wickedly for God? and talk deceitfully for him? Will ye accept his person? will ye contend for God? Is it good that he should search you out? or as one man mocketh another, do ye so mock him? He will surely reprove you, if ye do secretly accept persons (13.7-10).

According to Job, they were like corrupt magistrates at the law courts. For personal considerations they secretly favoured one party over another and were thus guilty of undermining judicial integrity. Israel's God-given legal code strictly forbad such bias:

Ye shall do no unrighteousness in judgment: thou shalt not respect the person of the poor, nor honour the person of the mighty: but in righteousness shalt thou judge thy neighbour (Lev 19.15).

Remembering this charge against the three older men, Elihu insists that he will stoop neither to partiality nor flattery (32.21-22). To do so would render him liable to judgment: God might "take [him] away" in death. We could do worse than imitate this sturdy commitment to truth, because favouritism and flattery (sheltering perhaps under the guise of family loyalty or extravagant courtesy) are by no means extinct, even in local assemblies.

To sum up, Elihu's introductory words to the older counsellors reveal intelligence, reverence, and the slightly breathless enthusiasm of a youngster suddenly placed in the spotlight. Positive lessons to be drawn from the three failing comforters were catalogued in earlier chapters, and the same may be done for Elihu. What might we learn from his opening remarks?

- The justification of God takes priority over the justification of man (32.2)
- Courtesy permits others to speak first (32.4)
- The young should show respect for the old (32.6)
- True understanding is the gift of God (32.8)
- Wisdom is not automatically acquired with age (32.9)
- Man's failure throws the excellence of God into relief (32.13)
- Bias and flattery should be avoided (32.21-22).

Elihu's youth should not blind us to the doctrinal soundness or the relevance of his words. Envy and position often combine to make it hard for older men to accept instruction from their juniors but, as has been pointed out, wisdom and truth are not the exclusive preserve of the elderly. Those with an appetite to learn can benefit from the most unexpected of teachers.

Elihu's Inquiry – Directed to Job: 33.1-33

Having disposed of the friends, Elihu turns his guns on Job. His inquiry concentrates on why the patriarch has been so resentful about God's ways with him (33.13). After introducing his own **analysis** of Job's situation (33.1-11), he offers a brief two-fold **answer** to Job's complaints (33.12-13), leading into an **amplification** of this answer (33.14-30), followed by an **admonition** (33.31-33).

The initial **analysis** (33.1-11) covers three matters. By way of prologue, Elihu draws attention to his personal sincerity (33.1-3):

Howbeit, Job, I pray thee, hear mine utterances, and hearken to all my words. Behold now, I have opened my mouth, my tongue speaketh in my palate, My words shall be of the uprightness of my heart, and my lips shall utter knowledge purely (33.1-3, JND).

In requesting that Job pay heed to him, Elihu wishes to stress his genuineness.

At first glance, verse 3 may sound presumptuously self-satisfied to the point of arrogance, but in reality it is the kind of statement of individual honesty often found in the Psalms. The "uprightness [3476] of heart" Elihu claims is not sinless perfection any more than it is when David prays "Let integrity and uprightness [3476] preserve me; for I wait on thee" (Ps 25.21), or when he pleads, "judge me, O Lord, according to my righteousness, and according to mine integrity that is in me" (Ps 7.8). The language simply expresses moral honesty: Elihu speaks out of a deep inward conviction. Further, his lips will "utter knowledge clearly". Because of the parallel phrase, "uprightness of my heart", the word seems here to mean not so much lucidity of speech as sincerity of motive. Elsewhere it is translated, for example, "pure" (2 Sam 22.27; Zeph 3.9), "choice" (1 Chr 7.40; Neh 5.18), "polished" (Is 49.2), "clean" (Is 52.11), and "bright" (Jer 51.11). The Revised Version (followed roughly by the ESV) translates "My words shall utter the uprightness of my heart: and that which my lips know they shall speak sincerely" (33.3, RV). Elihu is in earnest.

Second, he establishes the equality of speaker and audience (33.4-7). For all their initial expressions of compassion, the three friends tended to argue from the vantage point of spiritual superiority, with increasingly ungracious condescension. As Parsons puts it, "they came to sympathize with Job, then began to sermonize".[375] Elihu, however, wants to make it clear that he and Job stand on a level footing. Darby's translation brings out the meaning of verse 6:

> The Spirit of God hath made me, and the breath of the Almighty hath given me life. If thou canst, answer me; array thy words before me: take thy stand. Behold, before God I am as thou; I also am formed out of the clay. Behold, my terror shall not make thee afraid, nor my burden be heavy upon thee (33.4-7, JND).

Referring back to creation, when "the Lord God formed man of the dust of the ground, and breathed into his nostrils the breath of life" (Gen 2.7), Elihu reminds Job that they are both the products of God's hand and breath. As Delitzsch renders verse 6:

> Behold, I am like thyself, of God,
> Formed out of clay am I also.[376]

"Formed out of clay" uses a rare verb (7169) elsewhere translated in the KJV "move" and "wink" (as in Proverbs 6.13). Strong's Concordance offers this lexical definition:

> A primitive root; to *pinch*, that is, (partially) to *bite* the lips, *blink* the eyes (as a gesture of malice), or (fully) to *squeeze* off (a piece of clay in order to mould a vessel from it).

With exquisite precision, the language pictures God's delicate skill in shaping man from the dust of the ground. As David reminds us, we are "fearfully and wonderfully made" (Ps 139.14).

Job therefore has no need to dread Elihu's intervention in the argument. There will be none of the "terror" (367) which he feels he has endured from God (9.34; 13.21), nor will an unbearably "heavy" (3513) hand be laid on him (23.2). Although it demands careful reading, Delitzsch's comment is so good as to be worth quoting in full:

> [Elihu] has both in common with Job: the spirituality as well as the earthliness of man's nature; but by virtue of the former he does not, indeed, feel himself exalted above Job's person, but above the present standpoint taken up by Job; and in consideration of this, Job need not fear any unequal contest, nor as before God, Job 9.34; Job 13.21, in order that he may be able to defend himself against Him, make it a stipulation that His majesty may not terrify him. It is man's twofold origin which Elihu, Job 33.4, Job 33.6, gives utterance to in harmony with Gen 2.7: the mode of man's origin, which is exalted above that of all other earthly beings that have life; for the life of the animal is only the individualizing of the breath of the Divine Spirit already existing in matter. The spirit of man, on the contrary … is an inspiration directly coming forth from God the personal being, transferred into the bodily frame, and therefore forming a person.[377]

Properly understood, the foundational biblical doctrine of creation, like the death penalty imposed on the human race because of Adam's sin, is the great universal leveller. The truth that all men are made equally and uniquely in God's image at one stroke disposes of racism, sexism and every form of social snobbery. Paul deflated the pride of the boastful Corinthians with a series of devastating questions: "who maketh thee to differ from another? and what hast thou that thou didst not receive? now if thou didst receive it, why dost thou glory, as if thou hadst not received it?" (1 Cor 4.7). The common blessings of humanity are God's grace gifts for which we are to be thankful, not proud. Elihu stands before Job as a man like himself.

Although we may not wish to go quite as far as Fausset in asserting that "Elihu was designed by the Holy Ghost to be a type of Jesus Christ", we can certainly see in his intervention some glimmerings of anticipation. But what a gulf there is between the man Elihu and Christ Jesus! Elihu's manhood, though real, was no choice of his own. By contrast, our great Mediator voluntarily added to His eternal and untarnishable deity a sinless, genuine humanity that He might fully meet our needs, revealing God's heart and paying the price for our wickedness. In grace He stepped down to where we were.

Third, engaging closely with what the patriarch has been saying, Elihu homes in on Job's audaciousness (33.8-11). It is important to repeat the point that, unlike the other speakers, he has little interest in Job's past life. His focus of attention is the words he has heard Job speak:

Surely thou hast spoken in my hearing, and I have heard the voice of thy words: - I am clean without transgression; I am pure, and there is no iniquity in me; Lo, he findeth occasions of hostility against me, he counteth me for his enemy; He putteth my feet in the stocks, he marketh all my paths (33.8-11, JND).

Elihu offers a record of Job's testimony, dividing it into three parts. Job, he maintains, has been insisting upon his innocence (33.9), accusing God of injustice towards him (33.10), and protesting that he has been subjected to unfair detention (33.11).

We must, of course, check that Elihu's witness is trustworthy. The Bible, the most realistic of books, recognises that men, through human frailty or wickedness, are sadly capable of giving false testimony. Such was the case with Naboth's accusers (1 Kings 21.13), the witnesses at the Saviour's trial (Mt 26.60-61), and even the disciples (Jn 21.23). So what about Elihu? Is he right to say that Job has claimed innocence? Here is a selection of some of the latter's earlier remarks. Generally speaking, Elihu paraphrases Job, but in the second of the quotations below Job uses the very word (here rendered "pure") which Elihu picked up when he cited Job's claim "I am clean [2134]":

Thou knowest that I am not wicked (10.7).

Not for any injustice in mine hands: also my prayer is pure [2134] (16.17).

My foot hath held his steps, his way have I kept, and not declined. Neither have I gone back from the commandment of his lips (23.11-12).

Till I die I will not remove mine integrity from me. My righteousness I hold fast, and will not let it go: my heart shall not reproach me so long as I live (27.5-6).

I put on righteousness, and it clothed me: my judgment was as a robe and a diadem (29.14).

Such statements powerfully suggest a man pleading "Not guilty!" They are not to be confused with a spurious claim to perfection, which Job never makes. On the contrary, he specifically denies being sinless (9.20-21). Rather, he maintains that, as far as he is aware, he has done nothing to merit his sufferings. In that sense he pleads innocence. Some commentators accuse Elihu of mistaking Zophar's words in 11.4 for Job's. Given the scrupulous precision of this young man, the charge seems highly unlikely. Sloppy research and faulty referencing are out of keeping with the biblical presentation of his character. His summary of Job's positive self-assessment needs therefore to be viewed in the context of the latter's constant assertions of blamelessness. Elihu recognises what Job is claiming for himself and – more importantly – he is alert to its insidious dangers. As Darby puts it, the genuine piety of Job did not prevent his turning this consciousness of integrity into a robe of self-righteousness which hid God from him, and even hid him from himself. He declares himself to be more righteous than God.[378]

This is what Elihu points out in the second part of his analysis of Job's testimony.

Job, then, has asserted his own innocence, but has he gone so far as to accuse God of injustice? Here Elihu quotes the patriarch almost verbatim. We only have to look back to chapter 13 where Job inquires of God, "Wherefore hidest thou thy face, and holdest me for thine enemy?" (13.24). The word for "enemy" (341) is the same used by Elihu (33.10). Job uses different words elsewhere (19.11 and 30.21), but they make the same point: God has without warrant treated him as a bitter foe.

The final charge is unfair custody: because of the tragedies which have befallen him and his family he has been robbed of freedom. He has been, we might say, ghettoed into misery. Once again Elihu's language reflects Job's own. Here is Job:

> Thou puttest my feet [7272] also in the stocks [5465], and lookest narrowly [8104] unto all my paths [734]; thou settest a print upon the heels of my feet (13.27).

And here is Elihu:

> He putteth my feet [7272] in the stocks [5465], he marketh [8104] all my paths [734] (33.11).

The link is unmistakable. Elihu deserves top marks for the verbal accuracy of his précis. All too often, even in Christian circles, critical judgments are based on garbled hearsay, unreliable second-hand information, faulty memories, or wilful falsification of the evidence in support of a predetermined conclusion. Elihu may be young, he may even be long-winded, but he is reliable in his handling of the facts.

This, then, is Elihu's analysis of the situation. He does more than simply summarise Job's claims; he directs the spotlight onto the key issues. During the course of the long debate Job has said a great deal – but Elihu has the uncanny ability to cut through peripheral or incidental material to reach the heart of the matter. As Delitzsch sums it up: "It is a principal trait of Job's speeches which Elihu here makes prominent: his maintenance of his own righteousness at the expense of the divine justice".[379]

This leads into his concise **answer** to Job (33.12-13):

> Behold, I will answer thee in this, thou art not right; for God is greater than man. Why dost thou strive against him? for he giveth not account of any of his matters (33.12-13, JND).

God, being greater than man, does not have to explain Himself. Verse 13 has been rendered in different ways. The KJV (followed by the RV and Darby) takes it as a statement of divine inscrutability: there are mysteries about God's dealings with His creatures which are entirely beyond man's ability to grasp. Other versions (notably the ASV and the ESV) add a question mark, turning a statement into a query: Is Job contesting with God because He has not explained His actions? This method of handling the text has the advantage of facilitating a logical progression into the verses that follow, which elaborate on the ways in which God does, indeed, speak to men.

If we take the KJV translation at its face value, Elihu is making two critical comments about Job: he is unjust (not in his life in general, but) in his specific charges against God, and, more, he is engaged in the foolhardy activity of fighting with the Almighty. He therefore needs a remedial course in basic theology: because God is greater than man, He is under no obligation to explain Himself to His creatures. Essentially, then, Elihu is insisting upon the supremacy and inscrutability of God.

The first point should be self-evident. Everything the Scriptures teach about God rests on the assumption that He is infinitely greater than His creatures. Though Job had no written revelation he had the unmuted testimony of the created universe. As Paul tells us,

> the invisible things of him from the creation of the world are clearly seen, being understood by the things that are made, even his eternal power and Godhead; so that they are without excuse (Rom 1.19-20).

Those who call themselves atheists may more properly be described as antitheists or misotheists: it is not that they are intellectually convinced that there is no God – rather, they know in their hearts that He exists, and they hate Him. The passionate frenzy of their opposition all too patently betrays their innate hostility. Such crusading zeal is not cool, objective scientific rationality, but the undisguised malevolence of the fanatic.

Elihu's insistence on the truth of God's supremacy unconsciously paves the way for the divine intervention in chapters 38 to 41, an intervention which will explore in depth the immensity of divine power. In the same way, Jehovah's series of questions to Job in those chapters will follow up Elihu's emphasis on His inscrutability. "He giveth not account of any of his matters" (33.13) summarises the reality – unpalatable as it is to proud man – that God is (in Delitzsch's words) "a ruler who governs according to His own sovereign arbitrary will".[380] Advised by no one, accountable to no one, reliant on no one, "he doeth according to his will in the army of heaven, and among the inhabitants of the earth: and none can stay his hand, or say unto him, What doest thou?" (Dan 4.35).

It is important to understand that divine sovereignty is not arbitrary in the way that this word is commonly used of men. My word-processing programme offers the following synonyms for the adjective "arbitrary": "random, chance, subjective, uninformed, illogical, capricious, indiscriminate, and haphazard". Not one of these applies to the majestic power of the living God. Etymology best explains the English word: it comes from the Latin *arbitrarius*, from *arbiter* meaning "judge, supreme ruler". All human rulers and magistrates are inevitably restricted in both ability and authority. For them, arbitrariness is tainted by innate weakness. God alone is eternal and absolute. As the ultimate ruler of the universe He created, His power is therefore truly arbitrary in the sense that He acts irresistibly in harmony with His own perfect, holy and righteous will. Much of His will remains secret, far beyond the grasp of His creatures. Isaiah's memorable statement is uttered in the context of God's amazing, pardoning grace, but it still applies to the mystery of His movements in general:

> my thoughts are not your thoughts, neither are your ways my ways, saith the Lord. For as the heavens are higher than the earth, so are my ways higher than your ways, and my thoughts than your thoughts (Is 55.8-9).

As if to underline the point, the book of Job concludes with Job still in the dark about the reasons behind his sufferings. We may know, but he does not.

There is, however, a qualification to be made. Elihu is speaking before Scripture was penned. With a completed revelation from Genesis to the Apocalypse (whereby, as Paul argues in 1 Corinthians 13.12, we potentially see "face to face" and "know even as also I am known"), God has seen fit to disclose Himself, unveiling the most astonishing details of His purpose. To read, say, Ephesians is to get an overwhelming sense of the magnitude of God's programme of mercy with this great end in view – to exalt His Son publicly over all. In answer to the question "Can God be known?", we may therefore respond with a resounding "Yes", because in the written Word He has infallibly spoken. In answer to the question, "Can we comprehend all His ways with His people?", the response must be "No". Principles and promises we have (and we can think of outstanding passages of practical comfort, such as Romans 8.28 and 1 Corinthians 10.13), but an explanation of every detail of our human experience is withheld from us. This silence energises faith. As the *Jamieson, Fausset and Brown Commentary* helpfully points out: "Our part is, not to 'strive' with God, but to *submit*. To believe it is right because He does it, not because *we see all the reasons* for His doing it."

Having said this, it is worth looking at the alternative translation which reads verse 13 as a question: "Why dost thou strive against him, For that he giveth not account of any of his matters?" (33.13, ASV) In this case, Elihu is not so much stating that God's ways are unknowable as challenging Job by asking if he is piqued because God has not explained His purpose. This makes a smooth connection with the following verses, where Elihu argues that, contrary to Job's complaints, God does indeed speak to men, although they are often loath to hear His voice: "For God speaketh once, yea twice, yet man perceiveth it not" (33.14).

Elihu therefore proceeds to give an **amplification** of his brief response (33.14-30). Job has complained that God does not talk to him; nevertheless, God does graciously make Himself known to men in a variety of ways. Of course, as Robinson points out, "He employs sufficient means of instruction to supply man's necessity though not to gratify his curiosity".[381] That is to say, divine inscrutability remains intact. Still, He communicates with His creatures for their good. Elihu specifies three methods: dreams (33.15-18), diseases (33.19-22) and deliverances (33.23-30).

First, God warns men through terrifying dreams (33.15-18):

> In a dream, in a vision of the night, when deep sleep falleth upon men, in slumberings upon the bed; Then he openeth men's ears, and sealeth their instruction, That he may withdraw man from his work, and hide pride from man. He keepeth back his soul from the pit, and his life from passing away by the sword (33.15-18, JND).

As always, we must keep in mind that the book of Job predates the written law. The Old Testament testifies to God's use of dreams as a means of disclosing His will before the completion of the canon of Scripture. It was, for example, through a dream that He warned Abimelech off Sarah (Gen 20.3-6); by means of a dream He counselled Jacob, victimised by Laban's duplicity (Gen 31.10-13); in a dream He curbed Laban's vengeful intentions (Gen 31.24); by means of a dream He predicted Joseph's advancement (Gen 37.5-7). Even in the days after the law was given God occasionally communicated in this manner, as He made clear to Moses's envious siblings:

> And he said, Hear now my words: If there be a prophet among you, I the Lord will make myself known unto him in a vision, and will speak unto him in a dream. My servant Moses is not so, who is faithful in all mine house. With him will I speak mouth to mouth, even apparently, and not in dark speeches; and the similitude of the Lord shall he behold (Num 12.6-8).

This passage carefully distinguishes between more ordinary means of revelation and God's special intimacy with Moses. With him God spoke face to face: not through the "dark speeches" of dream or vision, but with the clarity of plain words. The innate difficulties associated with interpreting divinely-given dreams are illustrated in the histories of Joseph and Daniel: both were used by God to make known His will to Gentile monarchs, but both required divine assistance in decoding their benefactors' nightmares.

We may reasonably presume that Elihu, so attentive to Job's words, has also remembered Eliphaz's creepy story of his night vision (4.13-16), as well as Job's own claim that God scared him with dreams (7.14). Was God acting gratuitously, or did these visionary communications – supposing them to be real – have a purpose? Elihu argues that they did. They were intended as preventative medicine, to "withdraw man from his purpose, and hide pride from man" (33.17). Scripture illustrates both. Laban's dream in Genesis 31 had the first aim in view ("to withdraw man from his purpose"), Nebuchadnezzar's in Daniel 4 the second (to "hide pride from man"). Laban heeded his dream; Nebuchadnezzar, alas, did not. With great longsuffering and kindness, God intervenes to deter people from self-destructive folly. Elihu leaves no doubt that danger lies ahead for the wicked and proud: "He keepeth back his soul from the pit, and his life from perishing by the sword" (33.18). The pit (representing the grave) and the sword (picturing a violent death) speak of the grim destiny awaiting those who pay no heed to God's gracious warnings. The first word, "the pit" (7845), is much on Elihu's lips: he uses it five times in this chapter (33.18,22,24,28,30).

What, then, is the function of divinely-given dreams? Davidson sums it up:

> The object of this intervention of God is the gracious one of anticipating the sinner in the evil which he meditates, and hindering it, and withdrawing him from his sinful purpose.[382]

Let us be clear. God no longer makes known His will through night-time visitations. The canon of Scripture being completed, we now see truth in the unambiguous way in which the Lord spoke to Moses – "face to face". In 1 Corinthians 13 Paul makes a deliberate reference to the Numbers 12 episode:

> For now we see through a glass, darkly; but then face to face: now I know in part; but then shall I know even as also I am known (1 Cor 13.12).

This citation makes it plain that 1 Corinthians 13.10, with its mention of "that which is perfect [or, more properly, the complete thing]", is not (as some people insist) about the believer's glorification in heaven but about God's revelation on earth. The contrast is between the gradual, bit by bit disclosure of truth in the Old Testament and the apostolic era ("now"), and the final communication of "the faith which was once for all delivered unto the saints" (Jude v.3, RV) in the finished Scriptures ("then"). Our responsibility today is not to wait for dreams but to search the Word.

Second, says Elihu, God can get man's attention through disease (33.19-22):

> He is chastened also with pain upon his bed, and with constant strife in his bones; And his life abhorreth bread, and his soul dainty food; His flesh is consumed away from view, and his bones that were not seen stick out; And his soul draweth near to the pit, and his life to the destroyers (33.19-22, JND).

Sometimes extreme measures are necessary to arrest us in our tracks. Only when a man is laid flat on his back is he forced to look upwards. Elihu's explicit description of an illness heading towards inevitable death is uncomfortable to read. The helpless victim is bed-ridden, racked with bodily pain, suffering from debilitating appetite and weight loss. "Consumed" (3615) in verse 21 appears eleven times in Job and is translated variously "consumed, spent, destroyed, fail". Here is a man wasting away to nothing. We are made to recall, uneasily, the earlier descriptions of Job in the grip of his multiple diseases. The picture Elihu paints is reminiscent of the man he is addressing.

The key word, however, is "chastened" (3198), a word hinting at a positive and ultimately benign purpose behind suffering. In the Old Testament it is translated by a range of terms: reprove, rebuke, plead, appoint, correct. It first occurs in the episode where Sarah (who had connived in Abraham's self-protective lie) is "reproved" by Abimelech (Gen 20.16). It therefore supposes failure requiring a sharp reprimand to bring the culprit to a right frame of mind. It is used of Laban in the story mentioned earlier in relation to warning dreams:

> Except the God of my father, the God of Abraham, and the fear of Isaac, had been with me, surely thou hadst sent me away now empty. God hath seen mine affliction and the labour of my hands, and rebuked [3198] thee yesternight (Gen 31.42).

It appears again in the Davidic Covenant, where it is promised of David's descendant who transgresses against the Lord that "I will chasten [3198] him with the rod of men" (2 Sam 7.14). Earlier in the debate – so long ago that we have almost forgotten – it was Eliphaz who said to Job, "happy is the man whom God correcteth [3198]: therefore despise not thou the chastening of the Almighty" (5.17).

There is plenty of biblical evidence that, in the fulfilment of His gracious plans, God uses the physical consequences of sin in the human race. The death penalty imposed on Adam and his descendants inevitably includes all lesser pains. Since, as Hannah tells us, "The Lord killeth, and maketh alive: he bringeth down to the grave, and bringeth up" (1 Sam 2.6), we may be certain that He is equally in control of everything in between those extremes. Sickness may be a discipline designed to stimulate repentance for a particular sin or sins. Built into God's contract with Israel, for example, was the warning of physical illness as a penalty for national disobedience (Deut 28.58-59; 29.22). King Asa started well but ended badly. His serious foot trouble was designed to lead him to contrition:

> Then Asa was wroth with the seer, and put him in a prison house; for he was in a rage with him because of this thing. And Asa oppressed some of the people the same time … And Asa in the thirty and ninth year of his reign was diseased in his feet, until his disease was exceeding great: yet in his disease he sought not to the Lord, but to the physicians (2 Chr 16.10-12).

The inspired historian's language implies that in his sickness Asa *ought* to have sought the Lord. David's psalms occasionally suggest he knew he was suffering bodily ailments as a result of personal error. Psalm 30 may relate to a terrible disease which overtook him in response to his sin of numbering the people:

> O Lord my God, I cried unto thee, and thou hast healed me. O Lord, thou hast brought up my soul from the grave: thou hast kept me alive, that I should not go down to the pit (Ps 30.2-3).

Psalm 32, referring to a different occasion, recounts the deep sense of spiritual and physical malaise he experienced before turning to the Lord for forgiveness:

> When I kept silence, my bones waxed old through my roaring all the day long. For day and night thy hand was heavy upon me: my moisture is turned into the drought of summer (Ps 32.3-4).

Even though Christians are not under the covenant of the law, the same principle (that God may elect to discipline His children through sickness) holds true in the New Testament. The saints at Corinth were suffering an epidemic of illness for a particular reason:

> He that eateth and drinketh unworthily, eateth and drinketh damnation [better, "judgment", as in RV, JND, ESV] to himself, not discerning the Lord's body. For this cause many are weak and sickly among you, and many sleep (1 Cor 11.29-30).

"Many" of the Corinthian believers were unwell – "many" had even died – because of a cavalier attitude towards the holy seriousness of the Lord's Supper. The letter of James even envisages a situation where an individual Christian might call for local assembly elders to pray and administer medication with a view to his recovery from a disciplinary illness (James 5.14-15).

Yes, God uses sickness among the armoury of weapons calculated to awaken His people to their need and cast them on Him. As C S Lewis famously remarks in *The Problem of Pain*, "God whispers to us in our pleasures, speaks in our consciences, but shouts in our pains; it is His megaphone to rouse a deaf world".[383] Lewis is thinking of mankind in general, but God always has a special concern for His people.

It was mentioned above that, as far back as chapter 5, Eliphaz, the most senior of the friends, had raised a similar point about God's benevolent chastisements. Does this call into question what has been suggested about the novelty of Elihu's approach to Job? Is the young man simply parroting someone else's argument? Not necessarily. In attitude and emphasis there is a subtle but crucial difference between Elihu and Eliphaz. Delitzsch, always sensitive to biblical nuance, comments on the first:

> It is true one must listen very closely to discover the difference between the tone which Elihu takes and the tone in which Eliphaz began his first speech. But there is a difference notwithstanding: both designate Job's affliction as a chastisement ... which will end gloriously, if he receives it without murmuring; but Eliphaz at once demands of him humiliation under the mighty hand of God; Elihu, on the contrary, makes this humiliation lighter to him, by setting over against his longing for God to answer him, the pleasing teaching that his affliction in itself is already the speech of God to him - a speech designed to educate him, and to bring about his spiritual well-being.[384]

Jamieson, Fausset and Brown draw attention to the second:

> Eliphaz does not give due prominence to this truth, but rather to *Job's sin*. It is Elihu alone (Job 32.1 – 37.24) who fully dwells upon the truth, that affliction is mercy and justice in disguise, for the good of the sufferer.

Although the elderly and experienced Eliphaz is well aware in theory of God's disciplinary ways, unlike Elihu he fails to emphasise the reality that this father-like concern is God's gracious means of making Himself known. Elihu's handling of the matter is far more developed and persuasive.

Finally Elihu comes to the third of God's communication methods: remarkable deliverances (33.23-28). Darby's version is worth quoting because it helpfully clarifies verses 23 and 27:

> If there be a messenger with him, an interpreter, one among a thousand, to shew unto man his duty; Then he will be gracious unto him, and say, Deliver him from going down to the pit: I have found a ransom. His flesh shall be fresher than in childhood; he shall return to the days of his youth. He shall pray unto God, and he will receive him with favour; and he shall see his face with shoutings, and he will render unto man his righteousness. He will sing before men, and say, I have sinned, and perverted what was right, and it hath not been requited to me; He hath delivered my soul from going into the pit, and my life shall see the light (33.23-28, JND).

Elihu's three examples of divine revelation form a connected sequence. When men fail to take notice of warning dreams, God may then move into a more rigorous disciplinary mode, inflicting painful illness. However, a divinely-commissioned "messenger" (4397) or "interpreter" (3887) is required to point out the right course of action for the man languishing under God's hand. The correct action being taken, God then responds with gracious deliverance. The word "messenger" is often rendered "angel" (as in Genesis 16.7) while the "interpreter" is first used when Joseph spoke to his brethren by means of a translator (Gen 42.23). Because of the damage done by Adam's sin to humanity's in-built spiritual receptors, God's voice is not always immediately or intuitively understood by men. An accurate interpreter is therefore essential.

Who does Elihu have in mind when he speaks of a messenger? He may be thinking back to the remarkable revelatory appearances of "the angel of the Lord" in early Pentateuchal times (for example, Genesis 16 and 22). Then again, he may be thinking of himself as an interpreter provided by God to instruct Job in the way he should view his circumstances. After all, Job has been a recipient of both dreams and sicknesses, and needs an exegete to explain their meaning. But even if Elihu is, in some small measure, an elucidator of these divine providences, the Christian reader will detect a hint of the ultimate expounder of God, the incarnate Son. Those Old Testament theophanies already mentioned (preincarnate manifestations of God the Son) were simply foretastes of the

New Testament ministry of Christ. Just as Job longed for a "daysman" (9.33) to mediate between him and God, so Elihu's intimation of a gracious but rare ("one among a thousand") spokesman who can unfold God's ways, looks ahead to the coming of Christ. John lays down the basic principle: "No man hath seen God at any time; the only begotten Son, which is in the bosom of the Father, he hath declared him" (Jn 1.18). In declaring the Father, the Son is uniquely able "to shew unto man his [God's] uprightness" (33.23, KJV) as well as holding forth what man's right behaviour (or duty) ought to be. Remarkably, a book dating back to the patriarchal era contains scattered previews of God's final answer in Christ to man's sin, man's ignorance, and the deepest yearnings of his heart.

As a result of the ministry of this messenger, God would extend deliverance to the now-instructed and suitably repentant sufferer. This divine announcement of pardon is a marvellous adumbration of what God says, in effect, to each sinner who today pleads the value of the atoning work of Christ: "Deliver him from going down to the pit: I have found a ransom" (33.24, JND). "Ransom" (3724), a word used seventeen times in the Hebrew Scriptures, is most often rendered (in the KJV) by "ransom" and "satisfaction". It first appears as the "pitch" which covered the ark (Gen 6.14), and is closely related to the word normally translated "atone" (3722). Every Old Testament ransom (whether blood sacrifice or atonement money) only satisfied God temporarily on behalf of guilty sinners, but pointed forward to the one currency recognised in heaven – "the precious blood of Christ, as of a lamb without blemish and without spot" (1 Pet 1.19). The work of Christ has always been before God's eye.

Because of his early position in the scheme of redemption, Elihu cannot state exactly what the ransom is that enables God to go out in saving grace. The Christian believer, by contrast, can appropriate the language of verse 24 with the greatest confidence and joy. Why? Because he knows that there is "one God, and one mediator between God and men, the man Christ Jesus; Who gave himself a ransom for all, to be testified in due time" (1 Tim 2.5-6). In Christ, all God's claims are fully met and the sinner's debt fully paid.

There follows in verses 25 to 28 a glowing description of the ransomed sinner newly restored to physical health, spiritual vitality, and public testimony. The man so lately ravaged by deadly disease will be able to boast "flesh … fresher than in childhood" (which makes us think of the cleansed leper Naaman) and "return to the days of his youth" (perhaps hinting at the blessing of new birth). But physical restoration is only the start. He will be enabled to "pray unto God", who will "receive him with favour", so that "he shall see his face with shoutings". The word Darby translates "shoutings" (8643) is used in many occasions of celebration: of the "blowing of trumpets" in the feast of the seventh month (Lev 23.24), of the "shout of a king" in Israel (Num 23.21), of the great cry that demolished Jericho's walls (Josh 6.5), of the jubilation accompanying the bringing up of the ark to Jerusalem (2 Sam 6.15), and of the audible delight when the post-exilic temple foundations were laid (Ezra 3.12). David chooses it to describe his own "sacrifices of joy [8643]" (Ps 27.6), and the "loud noise" associated with praise (Ps 33.3). For Ethan it is the "joyful sound" (Ps 89.15) of God's worshipping people. It is as if Elihu's language looks far ahead, past the immediate matter of Job's prospective recovery, past the earthly delight of renewed spiritual fellowship with God, past the enjoyment of heaven's favour even while living in this world, to the climactic moment when all God's saints will see His face with unalloyed pleasure. It is almost impossible to read this passage without thinking back to David's great anticipation and forward to the Saviour's request:

> As for me, I will behold thy face in righteousness: I shall be satisfied, when I awake, with thy likeness (Ps 17.15).

> Father, I will that they also, whom thou hast given me, be with me where I am; that they may behold my glory, which thou hast given me: for thou lovedst me before the foundation of the world (Jn 17.24).

Elihu sums it up like this: "he will render unto man his righteousness" (33.26). That is to say (applying the words to the immediate audience) Job's innocence, so hotly contested by his friends and so stoutly defended by himself, will finally be endorsed before all.

As a last consequence, the restored penitent will be able to bear grateful testimony to God's grace in the presence of his fellow men:

> He will sing before men, and say, I have sinned, and perverted what was right, and it hath not been requited to me; He hath delivered my soul from going into the pit, and my life shall see the light (33.27-28, JND).

These beautiful words of thanksgiving constitute a miniature psalm of confession and praise to God for His goodness. Elihu unconsciously looks ahead to the patriarch's restoration when he will admit to uttering things "that I understood not; things too wonderful for me, which I knew not" (42.3). By no means a wicked man deserving of punishment, Job will nevertheless acknowledge that, though his life was blameless, his words were irreverent. He had sinned in his shrill accusations against the Almighty, misrepresenting and maligning God's justice, making crooked what was in reality straight. Yet "it hath not been requited to me"; that is to say, God had not rendered to him what his outspokenness merited. Rather, He had delivered him from the pit, the dread destiny which, in its five appearances (33.18,22,24,28,30), hovers over the entire passage (33.15-28). The verb "deliver" (6299) occurs three times in Job. Eliphaz had promised that "in famine he shall redeem [6299] thee from death" (5.20), while Job denied ever having implored his friends to "redeem [6299] me from the hand of the mighty" (6.23). But at the close Job would know in experience that God, and God alone, truly redeems His people.

The language of verses 27 and 28 is well suited to the Christian believer who, through the work of Christ, basks in the sunshine of divine favour. Every child of God can freely confess that, though he has sinned, his sins have not been laid to his charge because they have been borne by Another. Delivered from the terrible fate of the godless, he has been "called ... out of darkness into his marvellous light" (1 Pet 2.9).

In closing, Elihu recapitulates the ways of God in restoring an erring creature:

> Lo, all these things worketh God twice, thrice, with man, To bring back his soul from the pit, that he may be enlightened with the light of the living (33.29-30, JND).

The KJV's "oftentimes" in verse 29 is more literally "twice, thrice", which ties up neatly with the three modes of dealing with men specified in verses 14 to 28. "All these things" refers back to the dreams, diseases, and miraculous deliverances God uses to accomplish His amazing plans. What Elihu particularly underlines – significantly missing from Eliphaz's allusion to beneficial chastisement – is the tender purpose of God to rescue from destruction ("the pit") and to enlighten. "The light of the living" suggests not simply the continuation of earthly existence, where "the light is sweet, and a pleasant thing it is for the eyes to behold the sun" (Eccl 11.7), but the enjoyment of spiritual blessing. David seems to aspire to such a condition when he says "thou hast delivered my soul from death: wilt not thou deliver my feet from falling, that I may walk before God in the light of the living?" (Ps 56.13) A future generation of redeemed Israelites will be thrilled by their new spiritual zest: "O house of Jacob, come ye, and let us walk in the light of the Lord" (Is 2.5). To live in the light of the Lord's favour is living indeed.

This long first address terminates with a brief **admonition** (33.31-33) to the one-man audience. Job should quietly pay attention, because Elihu's basic desire is only to do him justice. If he has any question, let him raise it now; otherwise, he should silently continue listening to the speaker. It might seem precocious for the youthful Elihu to instruct his elder in wisdom, but it is difficult to resist the conclusion that he has successfully steered the discussion away from rancorous stalemate into a fruitful reminder of God's compassionate purposes. He has, significantly, introduced the adjective "gracious" (33.24). This word (2603) appears only six times in the book of Job. It is used by Bildad and Job in the sense of human supplication or intreaty (8.5; 9.15; 19.16-17), it is used twice by Job in imploring pity (19.21), but it is used uniquely by Elihu to speak of divine kindness. Strong defines the word as meaning "properly to *bend* or *stoop* in kindness to an inferior". In the Bible as a whole it appears first in the mouth of Jacob when confessing to his estranged brother Esau that "God hath dealt graciously with me" (Gen 33.5,11). Grace is one truth about the living God which seems oddly missing from the theology of the three friends. But Elihu brings it the fore.

Ever seeking our good and nurturing our spiritual growth, God moves in grace to promote a closer enjoyment of Himself. Living in the light of Calvary, it is much easier to comprehend the idea that God uses pain, suffering and distress to accomplish benevolent ends. Theory, however, is one thing; practice is quite another. In the middle of personal grief and affliction we often need to make a conscious effort to look back to the great historical demonstration of divine love, that fixed point of certainty around which all our circumstances, however painful and inexplicable, revolve. Paul sums it up: "God commendeth his love toward us, in that, while we were yet sinners, Christ died for us" (Rom 5.8). To grasp this is to enjoy true stability, so that even amidst weakness we may "glory in tribulations also: knowing that tribulation worketh patience; And patience, experience; and experience, hope" (Rom 5.3-4).

Even the most upright of men – and Job *was* the most upright of men – needed such an education, if only to discover the deceitfulness of his own heart. In pointing out Job's tendency to self-congratulation at the expense of divine justice, Elihu paves the way for Jehovah's voice. He does this, Delitzsch argues,

> by directing Job to regard his affliction, not indeed as a punishment from the angry God, but as a chastisement of the God who desires his highest good, as disciplinary affliction which is intended to secure him against hurtful temptation to sin, especially to pride.[385]

In an understandably groping and incomplete way, Elihu is stumbling towards the reality, best expressed by Paul, that "all things work together for good to them that love God, to them who are the called according to his purpose" (Rom 8.28). In doing this he sets the scene for the entrance of Jehovah to complete Job's education.

SECTION 23
Dialogue: Job 4 – 42.6
Corrective: Job 32-37
Elihu's Speech: Job 32-37
Part Two: Job 34

The second part of Elihu's four-part speech builds on what he has argued so far. Though Job is not being chastened for specific sins, he has rushed headlong into criticism of God's dealings with him, and in so doing has both exalted himself and demeaned the Almighty. We may feel that Elihu – like the three friends – does not make adequate allowance for the terrible pressures on Job. Bodily pain and mental perplexity can needle even the most self-controlled man into exasperated speech. Yet Elihu is correct to highlight what Jehovah will demonstrate later: that we all have a fleshly propensity to murmur against God.

The second stage of Elihu's discourse is headed by one of the brief narrative signals which punctuate his response: "Furthermore Elihu answered and said" (34.1). In keeping with his offer for Job to respond to his comments, he has momentarily paused in his flow (33.32). There being no answer, he presses on. The speech falls into four paragraphs. First, Elihu directs himself (we may presume) to the silent friends, calling them, both at the start and end of this chapter, "wise men " (34.2), and "men of understanding" (34.10,34). How far his description is to be read ironically is not evident in context, but the previous chapter was not exactly a resounding endorsement of their spiritual intelligence. They had failed to convince Job, and their arguments had been flawed. His **challenge** is that they learn to distinguish between good words and bad (34.1-4). The reason is found in what follows, which is another précis of Job's **claims** (implicitly bad words) about his righteousness and God's unfairness (34.5-9). Because of this verbal assault on the Almighty, Elihu reasserts the excellence of God's **character** (34.10-33), a defence of the divine majesty which forms the major part of the chapter. That completed, he lays out his **conclusion** (34.34-37).

In the previous chapters Elihu addressed himself to the friends (Job 32) and then to Job (Job 33). On this occasion his intended audience is less clear-cut. As noted above, he appeals initially to an audience with a reputation for wisdom and understanding, but Job as an individual is directly addressed only in verses 16-17 and 33 ("thou"), though he is named in verses 5 and 7, 35 and 36. While the grammatical shape of the chapter largely avoids direct address to anyone in particular, it is evident that Job is the target. The four paragraphs may be captioned as follows:

> 1. Elihu's Challenge: 34.1-4
> 2. Job's Claims: 34.5-9
> 3. God's Character: 34.10-33
> 4. Elihu's Conclusion: 34.34-37.

Elihu's Challenge: 34.1-4

The introduction is a lesson to every believer in every era. We are to make sure that we pay careful attention to what we hear so as to distinguish truth from error:

> Hear my words, ye wise men; and give ear unto me, ye that have knowledge. For the ear trieth words, as the palate tasteth food. Let us choose for ourselves what is right; let us know among ourselves what is good! (34.2-4, JND).

Elihu is echoing Job's imagery from an earlier speech ("Doth not the ear try words, as the palate tasteth food?" 12.11, JND). Fausset explains the meaning:

> As the mouth by tasting meats selects what pleases it, so the ear tries the words of others and retains what is convincing. Each chooses according to his taste.

According to Strong, the word translated "mouth" in the KJV properly refers to "the *palate* or inside of the mouth". Elihu is saying that all Job's claims, along with the responses offered during the course of the debate, need to be assessed with due care. As the Lord Jesus taught, "by thy words thou shalt be justified, and by thy words thou shalt be condemned" (Mt 12.37). That a man is able to say a great deal does not mean that his words are automatically "right" or "good". Fluency of speech is no substitute for accuracy of teaching. Which of the many assertions made in the long contest between Job and his friends can stand up to a rigorous test?

A New Testament parallel to Elihu's challenge is found in 1 Thessalonians, where the apostle advocates the exercise of quality control over everything we hear: "Despise not prophesyings. Prove all things; hold fast that which is good" (1 Thess 5.20-21). These two verses constitute a balanced whole: the early believers at Thessalonica were not to undervalue messages emanating from the genuine New Testament gift of prophecy, but nor were they to swallow everything they heard without thinking. All purporting to come directly from God was to be measured against the standard of what had already been made known, for only on the basis of previously disclosed truth could they recognise what was "good". No true prophet would ever contradict earlier revelation. That is the solemn principle laid down in Deuteronomy 13. No matter whether the new prophet came backed by impressive supporting miracles, no matter whether he was a beloved relative, or whether his teaching proved so popular as to win over an entire city – if he attempted to lead God's people away from God's law he was to be put to death. Now that the New Testament is complete there are no more prophets (save false ones), but the principle still applies in the sense that everything taught from the platform (or published or broadcast by any other method) is to be tested carefully against Scripture. Truth, not tradition, is the yardstick. Paul's exhortation is a direct encouragement to all who teach the Lord's people to make sure that what they say is grounded clearly on specific scriptures. This greatly facilitates the assessment process. A congregation ought always to be encouraged to follow the passage under consideration in their open Bibles. Ministry which is so nebulous that it cannot be tied down to the text of God's Word is likely to be erroneous.

Job's Claims: 34.5-9

The second paragraph is enclosed by a reference to Job's claims: "For Job hath said ... For he hath said" (34.5,9). This is important, because it makes clear the precise subject under investigation. Why must wise men test the words they hear and distinguish between good and bad? It is because, over the past thirty or so chapters, Job has been goaded into saying a great deal, and his arguments require sober investigation in order to sort the wheat from the chaff.

Once again Elihu applies his technique of specific speech citation:

> For Job hath said, I am righteous, and God hath taken away my right: Notwithstanding my right I am accounted a liar; my wound is incurable, though I am without transgression (34.5-6, RV).

Job has maintained his personal righteousness while simultaneously accusing God of injustice. This sounds very much like a paraphrase of earlier remarks:

> My righteousness I hold fast, and will not let it go: my heart shall not reproach me so long as I live (27.6).

> As God liveth, who hath taken away my judgment; and the Almighty, who hath vexed my soul (27.2).

Further, Job maintains that he is the victim of divine assault. "Wound" is the word (2671) translated "arrows" in 6.4, when Job protested that he had been injured by poisoned shafts from God's bow. His wound is "incurable" (interestingly the same epithet rendered "wicked" in the archetypal analysis of the human heart in Jeremiah 17.9), because it is so deep and lacerating. This reminds us of his complaints about what he daringly describes as God's barbarity:

> He teareth me in his wrath, who hateth me: he gnasheth upon me with his teeth; mine enemy sharpeneth his eyes upon me (16.9).

> He hath also kindled his wrath against me, and he counteth me unto him as one of his enemies (19.11).

Elihu's analysis sounds distinctly unsympathetic:

> What man is like Job? he drinketh up scorning like water, And goeth in company with workers of iniquity, and walketh with wicked men. For he hath said, It profiteth not a man if he delight himself in God (34.7-9, JND).

On the basis of these verses, it is sometimes suggested that Elihu has suddenly changed tack; he is now siding with the older friends in charging Job with some personal sin which identifies him with "workers of iniquity" and "wicked men". But this is to misunderstand the context. The evidence for Elihu's stricture is still Job's spoken words ("for he hath said"), not his past conduct. It is because he has been so publicly outspoken in his criticism of God that Elihu accuses him of saturating himself with derision, almost as a thirsty man gulps down water. The idea is, according to Delitzsch, "to give one's self up to mockery with delight, and to find satisfaction in it".[386] Eliphaz introduced the imagery earlier when speaking of the way sinful men drink "iniquity like water" (15.16). In questioning God's government of His universe, Job is in danger of aligning himself with the crowd who love to arraign God and "set their mouth against the heavens" (Ps 73.9). It is not that he walks *with* them in practical fellowship (in his lifestyle Job is a living example of Psalm 1.1) but that, in his hysterical complaints, he is beginning to sound *like* them.

Every believer going through tough times needs to pray, like the psalmist, "Set a watch, O Lord, before my mouth; keep the door of my lips" (Ps 141.3), lest he slip into irreverence. In the ease with which we fall into it, sin in speech is second only to sin in thought. As James points out, "the tongue can no man tame; it is an unruly evil, full of deadly poison" (James 3.8). How solemn, then, to hear that "every idle word that men shall speak, they shall give account thereof in the day of judgment" (Mt 12.36). The word "idle" suggests what is lazy, slow, barren and fruitless (it is translated "barren" in 2 Peter 1.8). The believer's words should be active and lively, bearing good fruit for the glory of the God whose great salvation redeems not only our lives but also our lips.

The particular statement Elihu finds so offensive is this: "It profiteth a man nothing that he should delight himself with God" (34.9). In this case it is not easy to find an exact parallel in Job's recorded words. Perhaps the closest we get is the charge that God treats good and bad alike so that, it may be inferred, there is no practical benefit in being upright. In Job's words, "This is one thing, therefore I said it, He destroyeth the perfect and the wicked" (9.22). Israel, with nothing like the same excuse for its cynicism, fell into such sentiments in the dark days of Malachi:

> Ye have said, It is vain to serve God: and what profit is it that we have kept his ordinance, and that we have walked mournfully before the Lord of hosts? (Mal 3.14).

Whatever the accuracy of the quotation, Elihu's paraphrase in 34.9 is arresting. To delight oneself in God is a wonderful expression. The word rendered "delight" appears fifty-seven times in the Old Testament, translated in a variety of ways (accept, pleasure, favourable). It speaks of Esau's goodwill towards Jacob (Gen 33.10), the acceptability of a burnt offering (Lev 1.4; Ps 51.16), God's favour to Israel (Ps 44.3), and Jehovah's delight in His perfect servant (Is 42.1). If we combine with this expression Elihu's rhetorical question, "What man is like Job" (34.7), we have, remarkably enough, an accurate description of Job as he is presented at the start of the book. Did not God ask Satan, "Hast thou considered my servant Job, that there is none like him in the earth, a perfect and an upright man, one that feareth God, and escheweth evil?" (1.8). Job was therefore unique in his reverence. There was no one like him, for he found his pleasure in God. Yet for all his piety Job is only a faint suggestion of someone far greater. If it may be said of him that he stood out from others because he delighted in God, how much more may such language be used without reservation of the incarnate Son? Psalm 40 offers a preview of the Son's faithful service on earth, giving us a privileged glimpse into His mind: "I delight to do thy will, O my God: yea, thy law is within my heart" (Ps 40.8). While even Job eventually gave way to hard thoughts and harsh words, the Lord Jesus Christ never failed.

To find delight in the living God should be the constant aim of every believer. Only as we make the effort to focus on Him, deliberately savouring His kindness to us in Christ Jesus, can life in a sin-damaged world make sense. When we reach the New Jerusalem it will be obvious, beyond any possibility of demur, that to delight in Him is abundantly worthwhile:

> And there shall be no more curse: but the throne of God and of the Lamb shall be in it; and his servants shall serve him: And they shall see his face; and his name shall be in their foreheads. And there shall be no night there; and they need no candle, neither light of the sun; for the Lord God giveth them light: and they shall reign for ever and ever (Rev 22.3-5).

But in the midst of his terrible misery and festering anxiety about a sweet fellowship with God which seems for ever shattered, Job gives voice to serious doubts and fears. And who among us – even with our far greater knowledge of God since Calvary – dare guarantee that we would have done better?

God's Character: 34.10-33

Elihu starts his detailed response to Job with an **assertion** about God (34.10-12): the living God of the universe is inexorably just. This terse doctrinal statement consists of two negatives (a) which frame a positive (b):

Therefore hearken unto me, ye men of understanding:
(a) far be it from God, that he should do wickedness; and from the Almighty, that he should commit iniquity.
    (b) For the work of a man shall he render unto him, and cause every man to find according to his ways.
(a) Yea, surely God will not do wickedly, neither will the Almighty pervert judgment (34.10-12).

Negative statements predominate because Elihu feels compelled to emphasise in the strongest terms the impropriety of any suggestion that God is unjust.

God, being God, will not do wrong: He does not commit wickedness (7562) or iniquity (5766), nor will He pervert justice. The first word ("wickedness") only appears on the lips of Elihu (34.8,10; 35.8). The second ("iniquity"), which occurs more frequently in the book, is used in Deuteronomy to describe Jehovah's essential uprightness: "He is the Rock, his work is perfect: for all his ways are judgment: a God of truth and without iniquity [5766], just and right is he" (Deut 32.4). Elihu's repetition in verse 12 of this denial of divine injustice uses again a version of the same basic word for wickedness (7561), but introduces a new term: "pervert" (5791). Found only eleven times in the Old Testament, it is translated by a range of English words such as "crooked" (Eccl 1.15; 7.13), "subvert" (Lam 3.36) and "falsify" (Amos 8.5). The idea is to twist or wrest. Bildad had earlier asked, working on the faulty assumption that Job was being punished for wickedness, "Doth God pervert [5791] judgment? or doth the Almighty pervert justice?" (8.3). In response (though somewhat later) Job had insisted that "God hath overthrown [5791] me, and hath compassed me with his net" (19.6). But Elihu bases his answer on the nature of God: He cannot bend the truth, He cannot be unjust. "Surely" (meaning it is true beyond any possibility of doubt) is his way of underlining the point.

In between the negative framework verses (God cannot be unjust) stands a positive example of His active righteousness: "For the work of a man shall he render unto him, and cause every man to find according to his ways" (34.11). The judge of all the earth, says Elihu, must do right, giving to man what is his due. It is the teaching of Romans that God will ultimately "render to every man according to his deeds" (Rom 2.6), but Paul significantly distinguishes between present and future consequences of sin. There is a "wrath of God" revealed right now (Rom 1.18), in the sense that even in this life God penalises sin with more sin; but there is also a stockpile of eternal wrath awaiting a future "revelation of the righteous judgment of God" (Rom 2.5). Elihu makes no such sharp distinction, simply stating the bare principle of divine justice, much as Jeremiah does in one of his earnest prayers: "thine eyes are open upon all the ways of the sons of men: to give every one according to his ways, and according to the fruit of his doings" (Jer 32.19). There is no escaping the final judgment of God. Even Christians, the eternal penalty of whose sins has been fully borne by their sinless substitute, will be manifested in their true character "before the judgment seat of Christ; that every one may receive the things done in his body, according to that he hath done, whether it be good or bad" (2 Cor 5.10). It is a sobering thought.

Having baldly affirmed God's immutable justice, Elihu goes on to construct an **argument** for it (34.13-15) on the grounds of God's creatorial supremacy. He is, after all, the Almighty (34.10,12):

> Who hath entrusted to him the earth? and who hath disposed the whole world? If he only thought of himself, and gathered unto him his spirit and his breath, All flesh would expire together, and man would return to the dust (34.13-15, JND).

The answer to the rhetorical questions of verse 13 is obviously "no one". Isaiah and Paul employ a similar strategy to testify to divine solitariness:

> Who hath directed the Spirit of the Lord, or being his counsellor hath taught him? With whom took he counsel, and who instructed him, and taught him in the path of judgment, and taught him knowledge, and shewed to him the way of understanding? (Is 40.13-14).

> For who hath known the mind of the Lord? or who hath been his counsellor? Or who hath first given to him, and it shall be recompensed unto him again? (Rom 11.34-35).

Elihu's argument seems to go something like this. Since God is the ultimate, the Creator, the first cause and owner of all, there can be no higher authority to whom He is accountable. As the originator of everything, He is the source of the very concept of righteousness. In the words of Wiersbe, "an unjust God would be as unthinkable as a square circle or a round triangle".[387] A world without God would be a world without absolutes. Fausset puts it slightly differently, but arrives at the same conclusion:

> If the world were not God's property, as having been made by Him, but committed to His charge by some superior, it might be possible for Him to act unjustly, as He would not thereby be injuring Himself; but as it is, for God to act unjustly would undermine the whole order of the world, and so would injure God's own property.

Indeed, so caring is He of His creation that, moment by moment, He graciously sustains it. Daniel reminds the blasphemous Belshazzar of "the God in whose hand thy breath is, and whose are all thy ways" (Dan 5.23). Were He but to withdraw His ever-active preserving mercy the universe would collapse. Elihu is perhaps thinking along the lines of Solomon, who describes death as the time when "the dust [shall] return to the earth as it was: and the spirit shall return unto God who gave it" (Eccl 12.7). Psalm 104, the great poetic celebration of God's providence, uses similar terminology about creaturely dissolution: "Thou hidest thy face, they are troubled: thou takest away their breath, they die, and return to their dust" (Ps 104.29). God gives and removes life as it pleases Him. The very continuance of the created world around us is an evidence of His tender concern for the products of His hand for, as the Hebrew writer teaches us, the Lord Jesus is constantly "upholding all things by the word of his power" (Heb 1.3).

Twice Elihu has described God as the "Almighty" (34.10,12). This title appears thirty-one times in the book of Job as a whole. The word (7706), found elsewhere in the Old Testament mainly in the Pentateuch, has provoked debate about its exact meaning. *The Theological Wordbook of the Old Testament* offers the following information:

The translation "Almighty" goes back to ancient times, at least as far back as the LXX, which translates *shadday* as *pantokrator* "all-powerful". This is also reflected in the Vulgate, *omnipotens*. The rabbinic analysis of this word is that it is a compound word composed of the relative *she*, "who" and the word *day*, "enough": *she-day*, "the one who is (self-) sufficient".[388]

The combination of power and sufficiency suggests One who is not only infinitely strong but also fully willing to meet the needs of others. He is enough for every situation. This is important, because Elihu's account of God's being does more than announce His unopposable power. He creates, He sustains – and therefore, implicitly, He cares. Divine justice is not some cold, impersonal standard of rectitude but the character of a God who has a compassionate interest in His creation.

The second person singular pronoun ("thou") indicates that Elihu is now addressing Job directly (34.17). He draws attention to the instinctive human recognition that government should ideally be righteous. He is arguing, we might say, on the basis of **appropriateness** (34.16-19). It is only fitting that the absolute Lord of creation should be just. Hartley puts the matter in its cultural context:

> In the OT it is assumed that justice is the foundation of God's rule … It is logically impossible in Elihu's reasoning for one who hates justice to govern … This argument had much more weight in ancient times than today … for the philosophy behind Western democracies requires the separation of the judicial system from the executive branch of government. But in ancient thought justice and power were believed to be united in the ideal ruler.[389]

Even in the modern world of human politics the most anarchic of opposition parties usually appeals to some abstract notion of what is right – hence (ostensibly) its objection to the current government. Only in Scripture are we assured that, in the sovereign purpose of God, this world will one day be securely ruled in perfect righteousness. In Christ might and right join in harmony.

But here is Elihu's question to Job:

> If now thou hast understanding, hear this: give ear to the voice of my words! Should he that hateth right indeed govern? and wilt thou condemn the All-just? Shall one say to a king, Belial? to nobles, Wicked? How then to him that accepteth not the persons of princes, nor regardeth the rich man more than the poor? for they are all the work of his hands (34.16-19, JND).

If injustice brings a human administration into disrepute, how much more is it fatal to the divine administration of the universe? The very fact of God's sovereign rule means He must be just. As far as Elihu is concerned, this is a truth almost as unnecessary of proof as the existence of God. David thought the same way:

The God of Israel said, the Rock of Israel spake to me, He that ruleth over men must be just, ruling in the fear of God. And he shall be as the light of the morning, when the sun riseth, even a morning without clouds; as the tender grass springing out of the earth by clear shining after rain (2 Sam 23.3-4).

The expectation that human governors uphold righteousness derives from God's essential being, for they constitute a faint reflection of Him. That mortal rulers have historically been far from upright is not a denial of this truth but a sad testimony to the impact of sin in the human race. Nevertheless, absolute justice will always detest not what is right but what is wrong. Psalm 45 bears witness to the divine repudiation of imperfection. The language, as we know from its quotation in Hebrews 1, goes beyond the immediate context of Israel's Old Testament rulers to address the Messiah Himself: "Thou lovest righteousness, and hatest [8130] wickedness" (Ps 45.7). The same verb which in Job refers to the impossibility of the supreme ruler hating (8130) right is here used to affirm Messiah's utter abhorrence of evil.

In verse 17 Elihu uses an unexpected word for "govern" (2280). Thirteen of its thirty-three appearances in the Old Testament are rendered by the verb "to saddle"; it first occurs in the description of Abraham loading his ass for the journey to Moriah (Gen 22.3). It seems to have the idea of binding and controlling. Eliphaz uses it of God, who "bindeth up" those He chastises (5.18), Job of mining engineers who dam up underground waterways to facilitate their excavations (28.11), while Jehovah uses it later to emphasise Job's inability to restrain global wickedness (40.13). It is as though Elihu is thinking of humanity in the same terms as the psalmist who advises his readers, "Be ye not as the horse, or as the mule, which have no understanding: whose mouth must be held in with bit and bridle, lest they come near unto thee" (Ps 32.9). Because sinful man is, according to Zophar, "born like a wild ass's colt" (11.12), it is hardly surprising that he needs to be firmly bound, saddled, or governed. The all-powerful God constantly pulls the reins in the affairs of headstrong men to work His sovereign will.

Job, says Elihu, dares to condemn God, who is by definition "most just". The charge is not without foundation. Jehovah repeats it in chapter 40 when He asks Job, "Wilt thou also disannul my judgment? wilt thou condemn me, that thou mayest be righteous?" (40.8). God is not only "most just" (as the KJV puts it); He is "just and mighty" (RV), uniting perfectly in Himself all power and all righteousness. In taking it on him to question the moral government of the universe Job has trespassed onto the treacherous ground of irreverence. Robinson pithily sums up the lesson for the believer:

God's ways [are] to be believed to be just and right, simply because they are His, and because they cannot be otherwise. The thought of injustice and wrong in God [is] to be repelled with loathing and execration, as profane and abominable.[390]

Verses 18 and 19 seem, in the KJV (supported by the RV and Darby), to set up a simple but effective argument from the lesser to the greater. The Old Testament Israelite was instructed that "thou shalt not revile the gods, nor curse the ruler of thy people" (Ex 22.28). If, therefore, it is unseemly (and, bearing in mind the culture of the day, probably extremely risky) to charge an earthly ruler with wickedness, how much more improper is it to accuse God of evil? The language is designed to underline the gravity of Job's folly. But not all translators agree. The ASV takes verses 18 and 19 to be a continuation of verse 17's description of God as "most just". God is Himself the One who

> saith to a king, Thou art vile, Or to nobles, Ye are wicked; That respecteth not the persons of princes, Nor regardeth the rich more than the poor; For they all are the work of his hands (34.18-19, ASV).

In other words, God alone has both right and power to condemn the failures of men, be they rich or poor. In his apocalyptic vision, John explicitly sees "the dead, small and great, stand before God" (Rev 20.12). Little sinners and big sinners alike will be judged impartially by God.

Whatever way these verses are translated, the essential point is the same: the mighty God, not feeble man, is the ultimate source and dispenser of justice. He has the authority and the ability, for men are but "the work of his hands".

Elihu's next step is to bring forward some of God's judicial **actions** towards His creatures (34.20-30). This he does in two stages, by introducing the attributes of divine omniscience (34.20-23), followed by omnipotence (34.24-30). First comes the truth of God's infallible knowledge:

> In a moment they die, even at midnight the people are convulsed and pass away; and the strong are taken away without hand. For his eyes are upon the ways of man, and he seeth all his steps. There is no darkness, nor shadow of death, where the workers of iniquity may hide themselves. For he doth not long consider a man, to bring him before God in judgment (34.20-23, JND).

Though it often appears that wicked men flourish with impunity, they are all – without exception – eventually swept away in death, the divine sentence imposed on human sin. The "they" mentioned in verse 20 must refer back to the people of the previous verses (the king, the princes, the rich, the poor). In an instant, oftentimes in the dead of night when man is at his weakest, they face disaster and are "taken away without hand". The language describes judgment falling without human agency. However "mighty" a man might seem in comparison with his fellows, he is helpless before the God of all the earth. Nebuchadnezzar, we may remember, dreamed about a tiny stone "cut out without hands" (Dan 2.34) which struck the emblem of earthly greatness, toppling the entire structure of human government just prior to the establishment of the messianic Kingdom. Whether a man die peacefully in his bed or agonisingly in the field of battle, he receives his death sentence from God.

The God who removes men from this world has "his eyes ... upon the ways of man, and he seeth all his goings" (34.21). The noun "goings" (6806) is normally rendered "steps". It first occurs in the literal context of David bringing up the ark: "And it was so, that when they that bare the ark of the Lord had gone six paces [6806], he sacrificed oxen and fatlings" (2 Sam 6.13). By the time we reach the poetic books, however, it is being used metaphorically to picture the pathway of life:

> Thou hast enlarged my steps [6806] under me, that my feet did not slip (Ps 18.36).

> When thou goest, thy steps [6806] shall not be straitened; and when thou runnest, thou shalt not stumble (Prov 4.12).

> A man's heart deviseth his way: but the Lord directeth his steps [6806] (Prov 16.9).

> O Lord, I know that the way of man is not in himself: it is not in man that walketh to direct his steps [6806] (Jer 10.23).

Although the living God specially directs His people's walk, He is privy to the lifestyle of all, and will act judicially in harmony with this perfect knowledge.

Lest any attempt foolishly to hide from God, Elihu makes clear that this is not a viable possibility. Adam and Eve were the first to try, and failed. Neither darkness nor death can shelter men from God's all-seeing eye. Whereas the guilty vainly seek to conceal themselves to avoid justice, David gladly rejoices in a divine omniscience which guarantees the continual safety of His people:

> If I say, Surely the darkness shall cover me; even the night shall be light about me. Yea, the darkness hideth not from thee; but the night shineth as the day: the darkness and the light are both alike to thee (Ps 139.11-12).

Unlike human law enforcement agencies and judicial systems, God requires no painstaking investigation to unravel a man's true character, for His knowledge is both instantaneous and infallible. Verse 23 makes better sense in the RV translation: "For he needeth not further to consider a man, that he should go before God in judgment" (34.23, RV). His understanding being both perfect and complete, He can mete out what is due to man whenever He chooses.

Elihu continues his lesson in basic theology by moving on to consider God's omnipotence (34.24-30). There can be no doubt about His power to accomplish His will:

> He breaketh in pieces mighty men without inquiry, and setteth others in their stead; Since he knoweth their actions; and he overthroweth them in the night, and they are crushed. He striketh them as wicked men in

the open sight of others, Because they have turned back from him, and would consider none of his ways; So that they cause the cry of the poor to come unto him, and he heareth the cry of the afflicted. When he giveth quietness, who then will disturb? and when he hideth his face, who shall behold him? and this towards a nation, or towards a man alike; That the ungodly man reign not, that the people be not ensnared (34.24-30, JND).

Because there is nothing outside the scope of God's knowledge, He has the ability to judge accurately; because He possesses all power, He is able to execute His sentence regardless of opposition. Elihu uses several words indicative of the energy with which God accomplishes His will: He breaks in pieces (34.24), overturns (34.25), and strikes (34.26).

The word for "break in pieces" (7489) is translated in a variety of ways in the Old Testament: do evil, displease, hurt, afflict, harm, punish. Perhaps most relevant for our purpose is its messianic use in Psalm 2: "Thou shalt break [7489] them with a rod of iron; thou shalt dash them in pieces like a potter's vessel" (Ps 2.9). It is through the Lord Jesus Christ that God will mete out final justice to men, for "the Father judgeth no man, but hath committed all judgment unto the Son" (Jn 5.22). He whom men dared to judge and condemn will have the last word in the final assizes.

The word (2015) in verse 25 translated "overturn" (KJV) or "overthrow" (Darby) is used of the destruction of Sodom and Gomorrah, when God "overthrew [2015] those cities, and all the plain, and all the inhabitants of the cities, and that which grew upon the ground" (Gen 19.25). The point is reiterated when, at the close of the Pentateuch, Moses predicts the devastation of the countryside should Israel turn away from the Lord:

the whole land thereof is brimstone, and salt, and burning, that it is not sown, nor beareth, nor any grass groweth therein, like the overthrow of Sodom, and Gomorrah, Admah, and Zeboim, which the Lord overthrew [2015] in his anger, and in his wrath (Deut 29.23).

When, because of the terrible sins of King Manasseh, the Lord pronounced irreversible judgment on Judah, He used the same word:

And I will stretch over Jerusalem the line of Samaria, and the plummet of the house of Ahab: and I will wipe Jerusalem as a man wipeth a dish, wiping it, and turning [2015] it upside down (2 Kings 21.13).

Twelve times it appears in Job, sometimes of a change of mind or an alteration of attitude (19.19; 20.14; 30.15,21), sometimes of physical transformation or upheaval (9.5; 12.15; 28.5,9; 37.12). The book of Revelation offers a terrifying preview of the global upheavals to take place during the coming tribulation. When God determines to overthrow the works of men, none can halt Him.

The word "strike" (5606) is less common. It describes Balak involuntarily smiting his hands together in exasperation at Balaam's failure to curse Israel (Num 24.10), and is variously used to depict a physical exhibition of derision or grief (Job 27.23; Jer 31.19; Lam 2.15; Ezek 21.12). In Elihu's speech, however, it plainly pictures a divine outpouring of wrath upon the wicked.

There is nothing ambiguous about what Elihu is saying. The God to whom all men are accountable has the power to award just retribution as and when it pleases Him. Although the emphasis of the argument may have shifted to divine omnipotence, the attribute of omniscience (which crucially ensures accurate assessment) is not forgotten. Whereas the KJV rendering of verse 24 speaks of vast multitudes whom God judges when He breaks in pieces "mighty men without number", more recent translations take the Hebrew to continue from the previous verse an allusion to divine knowledge. Thus Darby (in company with the ESV) puts it like this: "He breaketh in pieces mighty men without inquiry" (34.24, JND). This agrees with the other appearances of the word. Elsewhere in Job it is translated, for example, "unsearchable" (5.9), and "past finding out" (9.10). As we learned in verse 23, God requires none of the tedious investigative procedures necessary to the administration of human justice. He instantaneously plumbs the depths of actions and motives.

Not only does He remove, He also replaces (34.24). This was what Nebuchadnezzar discovered, when confronted with a visionary sequence of human empires constituting what the New Testament calls "the times of the Gentiles" (Lk 21.24). During this period, when Israel has been set aside as the prime instrument of divine government in the world, rulers come and go in accordance with God's purpose. As Daniel puts it, He "removeth kings, and setteth up kings" (Dan 2.21), for "God is the judge: he putteth down one, and setteth up another" (Ps 75.7). The succession of political power may most of the time seem purely arbitrary, but it is all controlled by God for the accomplishment of His will. The removal of particularly evil rulers is simply the imposition of His judicial government, for "he knoweth their actions; and he overthroweth them in the night, and they are crushed. He striketh them as wicked men in the open sight of others, Because they have turned back from him, and would consider none of his ways" (34.25-27, JND).

The reason for their destruction, we are told, is that "they have turned back from him, and would consider none of his ways". But not only are such men guilty of disregarding God, they have also treated their fellow men with brutality, in that they "cause the cry of the poor to come unto him, and he heareth the cry of the afflicted" (34.28). It is the same sequence as Paul specifies in Romans when he tells us that even in the present age "the wrath of God is revealed from heaven against all ungodliness and unrighteousness of men" (Rom 1.18). If "ungodliness" is sin against God, then "unrighteousness" suggests sin against man. Failure in the first table of the law leads inexorably to failure in the second, for as men abandon their responsibility of worship and submission to God they slide into inhumanity. After all, if man was not specially created in the image of God as His earthly vice-regent, then he is simply the result of blind amoral chance, accountable to no one and governed only by his own unstable preferences.

Nevertheless, God still heeds the cry of the distressed. Elihu's list of the divine excellences goes beyond what are sometimes called the attributes of God's greatness (such as omniscience, omnipotence, omnipresence) to include what may be described as the attributes of His goodness (such as love and mercy). The living God responds with sensitive concern to the sighs of His creatures. The reason is given in verse 30: "That the godless man reign not, that there be none to ensnare the people" (34.30, RV). A wicked ruler abuses his people as a hunter traps animals. Israel's bitter experience in Egypt perfectly illustrates the truth that God is not deaf to men's sorrows:

> And it came to pass in process of time, that the king of Egypt died: and the children of Israel sighed by reason of the bondage, and they cried, and their cry came up unto God by reason of the bondage. And God heard their groaning, and God remembered his covenant with Abraham, with Isaac, and with Jacob (Ex 2.23-24).

God graciously responds to the groaning of the miserable.

But Elihu has not finished his outline of God's ways. He is as aware as Job that God does not always step instantly and predictably into human affairs to strike down the bad or deliver the innocent. He has listened with care to Job's complaints that he has been treated unfairly. Verse 29 confronts the issue. Because there are some difficulties in understanding the language, I quote the KJV, followed by the ESV translation:

> When he giveth quietness, who then can make trouble? and when he hideth his face, who then can behold him? whether it be done against a nation, or against a man only (34.29).

> When he is quiet, who can condemn? When he hides his face, who can behold him, whether it be a nation or a man? (34.29, ESV).

The verse needs to be read carefully in the context of the argument, which is designed to answer Job's charge that God has been unjust to him. "Quietness" means rest or stillness. Elihu has just spoken of God's right to intervene and remove wicked rulers so that those who have been harmed by their tyranny might have relief; he will return to the same idea in verse 30. The KJV therefore, quite reasonably, offers this meaning: when God provides quietness (that is to say, peace after sufferings endured at the hands of evil governors) who can possibly make trouble or disrupt this serenity? When in hot displeasure He hides His face from the evildoer, who has the ability to overturn His verdict? This principle comprehends His dealings both with nations and with individuals. As far as general biblical doctrine is concerned, the idea conveyed by the KJV is both accurate and positively encouraging. That unique tranquillity of soul which God alone can grant His people is like an impregnable military garrison for, as Paul tells the praying Philippians, "the peace of God, which passeth all understanding, shall keep your hearts and minds through Christ Jesus" (Phil 4.7). The real problem is, however, does such an interpretation harmonise with Elihu's broad purpose to refute Job's defamatory assault upon God?

The ESV offers a different account of what he is saying, one which better fits the general context. The word the KJV renders "make trouble" (7561) first appears in relation to Israel's judiciary: "whom the judges shall condemn [7561], he shall pay double unto his neighbour" (Ex 22.9). Its uses in the Old Testament seem to divide almost equally between the idea of judicial condemnation and that of evil behaviour, but the thrust of Elihu's argument favours the first. Job, we must keep in mind, has been critical of God's ways. The ESV translators therefore posit a contrast between, on the one hand, God's direct interventions in men's affairs to remove the wicked and relieve the oppressed (as described in verses 24-28,30) and, on the other, His unaccountable silences. Verse 29 forms a crucial but parenthetical statement falling between the allusion to the cause and the effect of divine judgment (34.28,30). If God elects to remain quiet in the face of human provocation and wickedness, how can anyone possibly condemn Him for His behaviour? When He withdraws Himself and seems deaf to the cries of the distressed, who can search Him out? It matters not whether the oppressed are an entire nation or just one man. The mention of an individual brings us back to Job's own case. Job, we remember, has been calling on God to defend him against his accusers. The root of his grievance is that he is the victim of false charges and that God has attacked him with unwarranted ferocity. In his mind there has never been any doubt that from the first chapter onwards all his adverse circumstances are directly traceable to God. And he is right.

Hartley's excellent exposition of verse 29 follows a similar view of the text, relating it directly to Job's bitter complaints:

> Though God remains silent, i.e., He lets affairs on earth take their ordinary course so that a tyrant rises to rule over a nation, who among mankind would ever be in a position to condemn Him as Job has (e.g., 24.1-17)? When God hides His face (i.e., Himself) or seems to withdraw His influence from the course of events on earth, no one can behold Him. Then evil appears to reign supreme. Nevertheless, God is still in control … God's slowness to act does not deny His sovereignty.[391]

Whichever view of the text we take, we have to assent to Delitzsch's conclusion: "exalted above human controversy and defiance, God rules both over the mass and over individuals alike".[392] Both translations quoted above offer cheer to the believer. When God grants quietness, none can disturb it. This is true right now in relation to the blessings of salvation, and it will be true in the coming millennial Kingdom when Christ will usher in universal peace grounded upon righteousness. It is equally true that when God withholds His hand, there is no higher court which can force Him to take action in compliance with human wishes. Whether He moves immediately in judgment or bears long with human sin He is still sovereign.

When God does act in direct judgment, it is so that a wicked ruler cannot permanently continue in power, bringing prolonged misery on his subjects (34.30). Biblical history records examples: Pharaoh, given every opportunity to submit to God, was penalized where it hurt him most (his heir); Belshazzar's impiety was answered in the sudden fall of his city to the Medo-Persian forces; Herod's blasphemy was rewarded with a fatal disease. At the same time we should recognise that, even in the flow of the biblical narrative, wickedness is not always countered by instant retribution. Secular history follows the same pattern. Many live out a long life of terrible crime, dying in relative peace (Mao Zedong); others are removed through suicide (Hitler), illness (Stalin), or human agency (Gaddafi). Rarely does God step supernaturally into man's affairs in manifest power. The flood and the destruction of Sodom were exceptional cases, and even then unbelievers could credit the catastrophes to the impersonal forces of nature. Only when Christ returns in His glorious and visible military procession from the heavens will it become plain to all – beyond any possibility of misinterpretation – that the Creator of the universe is invading rebel planet earth.

After this summary of God's judgmental dealings, Elihu again addresses Job with the second person singular pronoun ("thou", 34.33), offering practical **advice** (34.31-33). Rather like the prophets who put words of contrition into the mouth of Israel (as, for example, Isaiah 64.5 and Jeremiah 3.25), Elihu constructs a confession suitable for one who has foolishly challenged God's justice. The man accused of speaking without wisdom (34.35) is here given good words to say. Job is encouraged to take three steps. First, he must recognise that he has borne discipline from God's hand: "I have borne *chastisement*". "Borne" (5375) is first used when Cain admits "My punishment is greater than I can bear [5375]" (Gen 4.13). Second, he must promise to sin no longer: "I will not offend any more ... if I have done iniquity, I will do no more". "Offend" (2254) is the word used when Nehemiah acknowledges "We have dealt very corruptly [2254] against thee" (Neh 1.7). "Iniquity" (5766) is sometimes translated "unrighteousness" (Lev 19.15). Job is to make full and frank confession. Third, he must request instruction: "That which I see not teach thou me". "Teach" (3384) is the term the Lord uses with Moses and Aaron after the former pleads his incapacity: "I will be with thy mouth, and teach [3384] thee what thou shalt say ... and I will be with thy mouth, and with his mouth, and will teach [3384] you what ye shall do" (Ex 4.12-15). Elihu is encouraging Job to ask the Lord to point out the failures of which he is ignorant. As Matthew Henry puts it:

> A good man is willing to know the worst of himself, and particularly, under affliction, desires to be told wherefore God contends with him and what God designs in correcting him.[393]

These lessons are eminently practical. God's people undergoing incomprehensible circumstances of trial may take such language on their lips (for as Solomon reminds us, "there is no man which sinneth not"), tracing everything to God, admitting personal failure, and requesting illumination. It can never be wrong to pray, with the psalmist, "Search me, O God, and know my heart: try me, and know my thoughts: And see if there be any wicked way in me, and lead me in the way everlasting" (Ps 139.23-24). The rebel sinner flees as far from God as he can, but the believer loves to draw near.

But wait a moment. Is not Job a man "perfect and upright, and one that feared God, and eschewed evil" (1.1)? What has just been said does not contradict this record of uprightness, nor does it deny that his trials have descended on him because of his outstanding godliness. Rather it recognises – as Elihu does – that some of his words subsequent to that bitter testing have betrayed a rash and hasty spirit. Fausset takes the point further:

> Though no hypocrite, Job, like all, had sin; therefore through affliction he was to be brought to humble himself under God. All sorrow is a proof of the common heritage of sin, in which the godly shares; and therefore he ought to regard it as a merciful correction.

Almost as if to justify Elihu's advice, Job's response to Jehovah's intervention at the end of the book will be to cast himself in lowly submission before One whose ways he cannot fathom but who must be trusted. These are his last recorded words:

> Then Job answered the Lord, and said, I know that thou canst do every thing, and that no thought can be withholden from thee. Who is he that hideth counsel without knowledge? therefore have I uttered that I understood not; things too wonderful for me, which I knew not. Hear, I beseech thee, and I will speak: I will demand of thee, and declare thou unto me. I have heard of thee by the hearing of the ear: but now mine eye seeth thee. Wherefore I abhor myself, and repent in dust and ashes (42.1-6).

But we are moving ahead of the argument.

Verse 33 is another difficult passage, largely because the language is so terse, although the general drift seems plain enough. The ASV offers the following translation: "Shall his recompense be as thou wilt, that thou refusest it? For thou must choose, and not I: Therefore speak what thou knowest" (34.33, ASV). With cutting irony, Elihu challenges Job in words which may be roughly paraphrased as follows: must God be compelled to treat men in accordance with your wishes, just because you are so resentful of His present dealings with you? And if you alone have the right to decree how the world ought to be governed, then you had better make your choice and start laying down the law. Obviously you are the only one whose opinion counts! Come on then, let's hear what's in store for us all.

The sharp tone of voice serves its turn. Not even Job, good man though he is, has the right, the wisdom, or the power to manage the universe. To His creatures, God's ways may often be mysterious and opaque, but our place is to trust and obey.

Let us consider Elihu's tactics in this section. Essentially, his answer to Job's feverish murmurings is to restate cardinal aspects of the doctrine of God. God is righteous, all-knowing, all-powerful, and tenderly moved by the sufferings of His creatures, yet over all He remains absolutely sovereign. This is a good way to respond to the fears and perplexities which dog the pathway of the saints. When plagued with doubts, we can only turn back to the clear teaching of Scripture. Job and his comforters, of course, had no written revelation to which they could appeal, but Elihu draws on what we must take to be the knowledge of God accessible to men in those far off days. Truth is always the answer to internal turmoil. Bunyan illustrates the amazing power of the written word to bring us through distress when he writes of Christian and Hopeful crossing the river of death. Surprisingly, it is the older and more mature pilgrim who suddenly becomes downcast:

> Then they addressed themselves to the water, and entering, Christian began to sink, and crying out to his good friend Hopeful, he said, I sink in deep waters; the billows go over my head; all his waves go over me. Selah.

> Then said the other, Be of good cheer, my brother: I feel the bottom, and it is good. Then said Christian, Ah! my friend, the sorrows of death have compassed me about, I shall not see the land that flows with milk and honey. And with that a great darkness and horror fell upon Christian, so that he could not see before him. Also here he in a great measure lost his senses, so that he could neither remember nor orderly talk of any of those sweet refreshments that he had met with in the way of his pilgrimage. But all the words that he spoke still tended to discover that he had horror of mind, and heart-fears that he should die in that river, and never obtain entrance in at the gate. Here also, as they that stood by perceived, he was much in the troublesome thoughts of the sins that he had committed, both since and before he began to be a pilgrim. It was also observed that he was troubled with apparitions of hobgoblins and evil spirits; for ever and anon he would intimate so much by words.

> Hopeful therefore here had much ado to keep his brother's head above water; yea, sometimes he would be quite gone down, and then, ere a while, he would rise up again half dead. Hopeful did also endeavor to comfort him, saying, Brother, I see the gate, and men standing by to receive us; but Christian would answer, It is you, it is you they wait for; for you have been hopeful ever since I knew you. And so have you, said he to Christian. Ah, brother, (said he,) surely if I was right he would now arise to help me; but for my sins he hath brought me into the snare, and hath left me. Then said Hopeful, My brother, you have quite forgot the text where it is said of the wicked, "There are no bands in their death, but their strength is firm; they are not troubled as other men, neither are they plagued like other men." Ps 73.4,5. These troubles and distresses that you go through

in these waters, are no sign that God hath forsaken you; but are sent to try you, whether you will call to mind that which heretofore you have received of his goodness, and live upon him in your distresses. Then I saw in my dream, that Christian was in a muse a while. To whom also Hopeful added these words, Be of good cheer, Jesus Christ maketh thee whole. And with that Christian brake out with a loud voice, Oh, I see him again; and he tells me, "When thou passest through the waters, I will be with thee; and through the rivers, they shall not overflow thee." Is 43.2. Then they both took courage, and the enemy was after that as still as a stone until they were gone over. Christian, therefore, presently found ground to stand upon, and so it followed that the rest of the river was but shallow. Thus they got over.[394]

How did they get over? By laying fast hold on the promises of Scripture. That is still the recipe for all who, in the mysterious providence of God, have to endure unexplained trials and interminable pains. In this present age "we walk by faith, not by sight" (2 Cor 5.7) – and true faith is grounded upon and nourished by God's written Word. Nothing else can satisfy.

Elihu's Conclusion: 34.34-37

As he brings his second speech to a close, we can imagine Elihu beckoning to the three friends standing near at hand, to draw them, as "men of understanding", into his concluding words.

Elihu charges Job with speaking "without knowledge", "without wisdom", of answering "for wicked men" (which means, as Darby translates it, "after the manner of evil men"), and of energetically multiplying "words against God". Basically the criticisms are three: Job's words are ignorant, they sound disturbingly like the complaints of the ungodly, and they are fired at God. Can we disagree? Since chapter 3 Job has been speaking without a real understanding of what is going on (Jehovah accuses him of that in 38.2); his attack on the government of the universe approximates at times to the standard objections of the atheist; his target is God, as the Lord reiterates in 40.2, describing Job as "he that contendeth with the Almighty", and "he that reproveth God".

Perhaps, in his zeal for God's honour, Elihu goes somewhat beyond the truth in painting Job as a man who adds "rebellion unto his sin", and "clappeth his hands among us". The first phrase presumably means that, in his persistent avowals of innocence and his aggressive complaints about the way God is handling him, he has slithered into open defiance. To clap the hands is not, as in the modern west, a sign of approval, but an eastern expression of scornful derision (as seen in Job 27.23 and possibly Ezekiel 21.17). Whatever he may have blurted out in his anguish of soul, however, Job cannot be tarred with the same brush as the God-hater. Scripture, we should bear in mind, can be tenderly gracious towards saints who fall prey to sudden sins and errors. David was guilty of adultery, conspiracy and murder; yet the Lord, who foreknew every one of his faults, still speaks of him as "a man after my heart, who shall do all my will" (Acts 13.22 JND).

It is common in human interactions to exaggerate our own rightness and intensify the errors of our opponents beyond what the facts would justify. Elihu, we have learned, is young and a trifle hot-headed. With age, one would hope, come mellowness and the enlargement of a sympathetic heart. Nevertheless, the desire he expresses in verse 36 sounds, initially at least, almost vindictive: "Would that Job may be tried unto the end, because of his answers after the manner of evil men!" (34.36, JND). What does he mean? Perhaps the word "end" (5331) offers a clue. In its forty-three appearances in the Old Testament, it is variously translated in the KJV. In its first three occurrences it is rendered respectively "Strength" (1 Sam 15.29), "for ever" (2 Sam 2.26), and "victory" (1 Chr 29.11). In the vast majority of cases it is rendered "for ever", but the choice of "victory" in 1 Chronicles (it appears again in Isaiah 25.8) is intriguing. According to Strong, the Hebrew word means "properly a *goal*, that is, the bright object at a distance travelled towards". If this is the case, it is possible to read Elihu's words not so much as a malicious desire that Job suffer even more, but rather as an aspiration that he will reach the glorious destination God has in mind for him. The Christian reader is bound to think of James's commentary:

> Behold, we count them happy which endure. Ye have heard of the patience of Job, and have seen the end of the Lord; that the Lord is very pitiful, and of tender mercy (James 5.11).

God's great end for Job was his eventual blessing, his restoration, and his invaluable function for all future saints as a model of endurance under adversity. Elihu could not possibly be aware of this, but he seems to have realised that God's final goal for His servant was so good that it must on no account be missed.

If that is his meaning, then his second speech concludes by blending trenchant criticism ("his answers for wicked men") with gracious encouragement ("that Job may be tried unto the end"). By the time we reach the close of the book, Job will no longer be speaking in a tone which aligns him, if only momentarily, with the ungodly. Rather, he will gladly honour Jehovah. Whatever we may think of his youthful impetuousness, Elihu commendably maintains that God is right in all His ways, however incomprehensible, and holds out the hope that He has a good end in view. Paul puts it in language coloured by his knowledge of the incarnation and the atonement:

> we know that all things work together for good to them that love God, to them who are the called according to his purpose. For whom he did foreknow, he also did predestinate to be conformed to the image of his Son, that he might be the firstborn among many brethren (Rom 8.28-29).

What Job could not know, we know: that "all things" (and how much that expression covers!) cooperate for the astonishing purpose of making saved sinners in measure like the Lord Jesus Christ Himself, without in the slightest compromising His eternal pre-eminence. That, we may be certain, is a divine goal which will not be missed.

SECTION 24
Dialogue: Job 4 – 42.6
Corrective: Job 32-37
Elihu's Speech: Job 32-37
Part Three: Job 35

This, the third and briefest of Elihu's four responses to Job, is his most condensed. In sixteen verses he continues a direct challenge to the older man's self-assessment and his censorious view of the divine government of the world. The focus on Job is unwavering: second person singular pronouns cluster at the beginning of the speech (35.2-8) and reappear in verse 14, whereas "thy companions" are awarded only a passing mention in verse 4. It is, in fact, likely that Elihu refers there not to the three friends (who in any case have been in constant disagreement with Job, though unable to confute his arguments) but rather to all who hold similar opinions to the patriarch.

The chapter may be broken down as follows:

> 1. The Profit of Piety: 35.1-4
> 2. The Height of the Heavens: 35.5-8
> 3. The Voice of the Victim: 35.9-13
> 4. The Wisdom of Waiting: 35.14-16.

The Profit of Piety: 35.1-4

As before, Elihu's tactic is to question Job's words. Can it be right to assert that his righteousness exceeds God's? Of course, neither Job nor Elihu is thinking in absolute terms; they are not debating systematic theology or the doctrine of the divine attributes. Both would instantly agree that God is immutably righteous in His being, whereas fallen Adamic man is innately stained by sin. There is no disagreement about that. Their focus is the localised problem of Job's bitter experiences. The charge against God – if we may put it like that – relates to the present controversy, which is whether He is acting fairly inflicting misery on the innocent. Some of Job's earlier language certainly questions God's ways. Take, for example, the following statements:

> He breaketh me with a tempest, and multiplieth my wounds without cause (9.17).

> He hath broken me asunder: he hath also taken me by my neck, and shaken me to pieces, and set me up for his mark … Not for any injustice in mine hands: also my prayer is pure (16.12-17).

> As God liveth, who hath taken away my judgment; and the Almighty, who hath vexed my soul (27.2).

The key phrases are "without cause" (9.17), "not for any injustice in mine hands" (16.17), and "taken away my judgment" (27.2). In cataloguing the ills he has endured Job carefully washes his hands of personal culpability. His griefs come from God, he knows, but he is without fault: no specific error can be found in him to justify his punishment. It follows (at least, as far as Job is concerned) that in persecuting him God is behaving inappropriately. In the case of God versus the man from Uz, however astonishing it may seem, Job appears to be just and God unjust.

A second challenge follows from this. If God behaves so unfairly in His dealings with men, treating good and bad alike, what then is the value of being good at all? As we have seen in the previous chapter, because of the torment of his soul Job has toyed with such ideas (9.22). Furthermore, he has paraphrased the thoughts of wicked men who, despite their blasphemous attitude, appear to get away with their effrontery. It could be argued that, in giving voice to these errors, Job has teetered on the brink of sanctioning their sentiments. This is what he said back in chapter 21:

> They spend their days in wealth, and in a moment go down to the grave. Therefore they say unto God, Depart from us; for we desire not the knowledge of thy ways. What is the Almighty, that we should serve him? and what profit should we have, if we pray unto him? (21.13-15).

Elihu has already given this topic some attention. This time, however, he tackles the issue with greater rigour, seeking to demonstrate that man's behaviour (be it bad or good) neither lessens nor increases the eternal blessedness of the everlasting God. Eliphaz touched on the matter back in chapter 22, but Elihu takes it further.

Scripture as a whole informs us that godliness is both right and profitable. For the Old Testament Israelite it ensured a prolonged and prosperous stay in the land which God had freely given His people. The first commandment with a promise attached makes that clear:

> Honour thy father and thy mother: that thy days may be long upon the land which the Lord thy God giveth thee (Ex 20.12).

The New Testament Christian, by contrast, has been given no plot of land on earth as an essential element of his blessings in Christ; nevertheless he may still rest assured that godly living carries its own rewards both now and hereafter. Bodily exercise may have only limited value, says Paul, but "godliness is profitable unto all things, having promise of the life that now is, and of that which is to come" (1 Tim 4.8). Our western culture which, in abandoning its biblical heritage, has reverted to a pagan glorification of the physical, needs to be reminded that there is temporal and eternal value in living for God.

The reason Job asks whether godliness is worthwhile is because he knows he is a pious man, and yet he suffers. As we read Elihu's expansive response, ranging as it does over several chapters, we may feel that this young man (like the older men whose contributions he dismissed) is often reduced to repeating himself. After all, he has touched these stops before (33.9-11; 34.5-6). But even if this is the case, it is only because throughout the debate Job has rung constant variations on the single theme of his innocence. If a man reiterates a particular point, it is probably because this is the very kernel of his grievance. Elihu has therefore isolated the epicentre of Job's argument, directing all his artillery at it, just as a shrewd military general concentrates his fire on the enemy's command and control centre. If he is crippled there, his entire defence is liable to crumble.

What, then, is Elihu's response to the man who asserts his uprightness yet, because of his appalling circumstances, wonders whether godliness makes sense? Is virtue simply its own reward?

The Height of the Heavens: 35.5-8

Elihu's answer is a startling one. He urges Job to look away from himself, for once, into the wider regions of space. It has already been suggested that his intrusion into the debate (unbeknown to himself, of course) clears the stage for Jehovah's final intervention, and here is one of the lines of evidence. In exhorting the patriarch to look to the heavens and behold the infinite vastness of the sky, Elihu is only doing on a small scale what God will do magisterially in chapter 38 onwards. The advice is scarcely surprising when we remember the psalmist's revelation that "The heavens declare the glory of God; and the firmament sheweth his handywork" (Ps 19.1). Just as the visible atmospheric clouds are "higher [1361] than thou", so too is the outworking of Gods purposes for His creatures, for "as the heavens are higher [1361] than the earth, so are my ways higher [1361] than your ways, and my thoughts than your thoughts" (Is 55.9).

Elihu's exhortation shows a perceptive knowledge of men. We are all apt to get things out of proportion when we simply look inside, concentrating on ourselves. This was Job's habit. For example, even in his great testimony to personal integrity in chapter 31 he felt compelled to keep employing the risky first person pronoun. But the more we foreground self the less likely we are to maintain the stand-alone majesty of God. To look away to One who is infinitely greater than we are is the counsel of both Testaments:

> When I consider thy heavens, the work of thy fingers, the moon and the stars, which thou hast ordained; What is man, that thou art mindful of him? and the son of man, that thou visitest him? (Ps 8.3-4).

> Looking unto Jesus the author and finisher of our faith; who for the joy that was set before him endured the cross, despising the shame, and is set down at the right hand of the throne of God (Heb 12.2).

The Old Testament psalmist marvels as he feasts his eyes on the immensity of the created universe; the New Testament writer goes further, fixing his gaze on One who died, rose again, and is now seated triumphantly above the stellar heavens in the highest heights. To be taken up with a Saviour in glory is a great antidote to self-occupation.

Interestingly, the first time we find the combination of "look" (5027) and "heavens" (8064) is in God's command to Abram to "Look [5027] now toward heaven [8064], and tell the stars, if thou be able to number them" (Gen 15.5). The purpose, however, is entirely different. God wished Abram to realise how innumerable would be his descendants, even though at that time he was still childless: "he said unto him, So shall thy seed be". Elihu, on the other hand, intends to remind Job of the inaccessible awesomeness of God: since he can scarcely penetrate the depths of the sky he is in no position to peer into God's throne room and pass judgment on His governmental policies. The word "Look" implies a steady, careful gaze. It is used of the dying Israelites in the desert who had to stare fixedly at the brazen serpent so that, "if a serpent had bitten any man, when he beheld [5027] the serpent of brass, he lived" (Num 21.9). At the other end of the Old Testament it describes repentant Israel looking in earnest faith on their returning Messiah: "they shall look [5027] upon me whom they have pierced" (Zech 12.10). The word for "clouds" (7834) is explained by Strong as meaning primarily "a *powder* (as *beaten* small); by analogy a thin *vapor*; by extension the *firmament*". In the KJV it is generally translated "clouds" or "sky", but is once rendered "dust" in the phrase, "the small dust [7834] of the balance" (Is 40.15). Elihu points Job to the fine vapoury wisps of cloud trailing through the skies above him. So much lies beyond the reach of the natural eye, and yet even the little we can see highlights our comparative insignificance measured against the backcloth of space. If the universe is greater than man, how much more is God?

How can mere man, therefore, dare to presume that his conduct on this tiny earth interferes with God in the heights of the heavens? Elihu's vocabulary distinguishes carefully between evil behaviour ("sin", "transgression", "wickedness", 35.6,8) and good ("righteousness", 35.7-8). Nonetheless, he finally lumps them both together in a devastating series of queries: "what doest thou against him? … what doest thou unto him? … what givest thou him? or what receiveth he of thine hand?" (35.6-7). Whether man is good or evil, the God who made the universe remains eternally untainted, unindebted, unimproved and undiminished. He is too immutably glorious to be enriched by man's virtue or impoverished by man's sin.

Tersely but effectively, Delitzsch sums up the meaning of Elihu's words. Because of God's supreme exaltation,

> it is impossible to exercise any human influence upon Him, by which He might suffer … Human wrong or right doing neither diminishes nor increases His blessedness; injury or advantage is only on the side of man, from whom it proceeds.[395]

Zuck's comment is equally helpful:

> God's actions (of justice and benevolence) towards man are self-determined, not man-centred. God is not under man's control or subject to man's bribes (35.8) … God's standards of justice are not flexible or partial. If He shows mercy, it is not because He has been induced by man's goodness; and if He inflicts judgment, it is not because He has been injured and fears man.[396]

The lesson is a painful but necessary one because it puts proud man in his place. Believers are sometimes guilty of giving the impression that their little sphere of service is essential to the accomplishment of God's programme; but the God of the Bible is not dependent on His creatures. He has no needs of any kind whatsoever. As Paul explained to the Athenian philosophers, God is not "worshipped with men's hands, as though he needed any thing, seeing he giveth to all life, and breath, and all things" (Acts 17.25). Rather, He is the One who supplies all His people's needs "according to his riches in glory by Christ Jesus" (Phil 4.19). God is neither gratified by our obedience nor perturbed by our failure, any more than the opposition of Satan ruffles the perfect contentment He has in Himself. This, of course, is not to condone human sin or minimise the importance of submission to His revealed will. It is only to acknowledge that, in the final analysis, we neither give to nor take from His majesty. Being His creatures, simple obedience is mandatory, but obedience does not of itself merit a round of applause or a pat on the back. The Lord Jesus told a parable to guard His disciples against the temptation to smugness:

> But which of you, having a servant plowing or feeding cattle, will say unto him by and by, when he is come from the field, Go and sit down to meat? And will not rather say unto him, Make ready wherewith I may sup, and gird thyself, and serve me, till I have eaten and drunken; and afterward thou shalt eat and drink? Doth he thank that servant because he did the things that were commanded him? I trow not. So likewise ye, when ye shall have done all those things which are commanded you, say, We are unprofitable servants: we have done that which was our duty to do (Lk 17.7-10).

The lesson is a salutary one: we can never place God under any obligation to us, nor can we ever be legitimately self-satisfied about our service. Hartley puts it well:

> No amount of good works benefits God or puts Him under any obligation to anybody … there is nothing that God wants or needs from human hands. Since God is not dependent on human beings for anything, a person has no leverage with God.[397]

What, then, we might ask Elihu, is the point of being good at all? If it does not help God, who *does* it help? His answer is direct: "Thy wickedness may hurt a man as thou art; and thy righteousness may profit the son of man" (35.8). The way we behave in this world neither harms nor profits God, but it does have a real impact on ourselves and our fellow men. A man's sin will eventually meet with divine judgment, but in the meantime it often damages his neighbour. That is one reason why the New Testament urges God's people to "do good unto all men, especially unto them who are of the household of faith" (Gal 6.10). Obedience to the divine commands is, of course, our responsibility as creatures and as believers, but although such obedience in no sense conveys a benefit on God it does bring genuine joy to the believer's heart (Jn 13.17) and often improves the lot of our fellows. Conversely, sin spreads misery to perpetrator and victim alike.

An important corollary is concealed behind Elihu's assertion. F B Meyer teases it out for us:

God is so exalted above man in His nature that He is altogether independent of him. When men sin against Him, they hurt not Him but themselves. There is no motive, therefore, of retaliation or revenge in His chastisements.

If, as Elihu argues, God is altogether beyond man's reach, then it is impossible to accuse Him of retaliatory action. There must therefore be other motives lying behind His involvement with humanity. The mistake made by both Job and his friends, says Robinson, consists of "judging of God's justice from His present dealings". They seem unaware that God "for special reasons, may allow a godly man to be very severely tried".[398] Some of those other reasons are spelled out for us in the Scriptures as a whole. Solomon urges his son, "despise not the chastening of the Lord; neither be weary of his correction: For whom the Lord loveth he correcteth; even as a father the son in whom he delighteth" (Prov 3.11-12). God's treatment of men may have wise long-term purposes other than the simple doling out of retribution for sin or reward for piety. His ways, as Paul tells us in an outburst of adoring wonderment, are beyond human comprehension: "O the depth of the riches both of the wisdom and knowledge of God! how unsearchable are his judgments, and his ways past finding out!" (Rom 11.33).

The Voice of the Victim: 35.9-13

Having subtly undermined the contention that there is no profit in godliness, Elihu goes on to focus on those who find themselves the victims of oppression and injustice. He has admitted that though man's wickedness cannot damage God it can certainly hurt other men. He therefore draws attention to those who have been injured. And, inevitably, in addressing the question of human suffering, he has in mind the man who throughout the book has loudly protested his innocence and called on God for vindication.

Earlier, Job had regretted the unaccountable silence of God in the face of human wretchedness. For example, he tells us that "Men groan from out of the city, and the soul of the wounded crieth out: yet God layeth not folly to them" (24.12). Then, casting the spotlight on himself and adopting the language of prayer, he confesses that "I cry unto thee, and thou dost not hear me: I stand up, and thou regardest me not" (30.20). Job knows that human wickedness is under overall divine supervision, for nothing happens outside the scope of His power. Nevertheless, in the face of men's pleading, God remains silent.

In a sin-dominated world tyrannical bullies cause their victims to cry out (35.9,12), yet God appears remote and indifferent. No one "giveth answer" (35.12); God "will not hear" or "regard" (35.13). Why does He not step in promptly to halt human wickedness? Here is one reason, says Elihu. Not every petition or prayer is a genuine appeal to God in reverent and humble dependence. This unexpected answer is disturbing, but is not without support elsewhere in Scripture. Not all prayer is real. Far from God being indifferent to man (as Job has hinted), the problem is that man, in his ingrained self-centeredness, is indifferent to God. It is all too possible that cries for aid may be subtly contaminated by human "pride" (35.12) and "vanity" (35.13). The first word (1347) is mainly used to describe the arrogance of men (as, for example, in Leviticus 26.19; Psalm 59.12; Proverbs 8.13; Isaiah 13.11) but its initial appearance refers to God Himself who, in the destruction of Egypt, manifested His consummate majesty:

> in the greatness of thine excellency [1347] thou hast overthrown them that rose up against thee: thou sentest forth thy wrath, which consumed them as stubble (Ex 15.7).

Creaturely pride, as well as being absurd (for man has nothing in himself of which to boast), is an insult to the God who alone possesses true excellence. The second word, "vanity" (7723), describes emptiness and falsehood. It is used, for example, of taking Jehovah's name in vain (Ex 20.7), of bearing "false [7723] witness against thy neighbour" (Deut 5.20), of the folly of those who engage in idolatry and "regard lying [7723] vanities" (Ps 31.6). We know from the teaching of the Lord Jesus that long and eloquent prayers, however impressive, may in reality be barren of genuine meaning. Did He not expose the hypocrisy of Israel's religious leadership who "devour widows' houses, and for a pretence make long prayers" (Mk 12.40)?

James's letter, admonishing professing believers, similarly insists that motivation in prayer is just as important as articulation: "Ye ask, and receive not, because ye ask amiss, that ye may consume it upon your lusts" (James 4.3). In every spiritual exercise, outward expression, though scrupulously correct theologically, must harmonise with a right condition of heart. Those who plead for deliverance from extremity or peril may simply hanker after a selfish liberty to revert to their sinful ways. It may well be, indeed, that their cries are not so much *to* God as *against* God, whose dealings with them have run counter to the grain of their preferences and stirred up bitter resentment.

There is evidence for Elihu's viewpoint. The first use of the verb "cry" (2199) in Job 35.9 comes in the account of the Israelites' Egyptian bondage:

> And it came to pass in process of time, that the king of Egypt died: and the children of Israel sighed by reason of the bondage, and they cried [2199], and their cry came up unto God by reason of the bondage (Ex 2.23).

The language is interesting. We are not told that the Israelites called directly upon the Lord (which, by contrast, is clearly what they did in Judges 3.9,15; 6.6-7; 10.10), but rather that their groanings, the result of intense sufferings, rose up to heaven. This at least allows for the possibility that it was not so much a conscious prayer to Jehovah as a loud self-pitying lament provoked by extreme pain. Revelation 16 records the defiance of men who endure divine judgment upon the earth during the future tribulation era. Their pains do not provoke prayers but blasphemies. In His omniscience God hears everything, not merely those supplications specifically addressed to His throne. But the spiritual exercise of genuine prayer involves a serious recognition of who God is in the overwhelming majesty of His person, and therefore approaches Him with due humility and submissiveness. Those who swagger jauntily into the presence of the Almighty, whistling in blithe self-assurance, only betray their ignorance.

We see the same principle in the Gospels. There we find multitudes ardently pursuing the Lord Jesus for entirely the wrong reasons. John 6 records the aftermath of the feeding of the five thousand:

> When the people therefore saw that Jesus was not there, neither his disciples, they also took shipping, and came to Capernaum, seeking for Jesus. And when they had found him on the other side of the sea, they said unto him, Rabbi, when camest thou hither? Jesus answered them and said, Verily, verily, I say unto you, Ye seek me, not because ye saw the miracles, but because ye did eat of the loaves, and were filled. Labour not for the meat which perisheth, but for that meat which endureth unto everlasting life, which the Son of man shall give unto you: for him hath God the Father sealed (Jn 6.24-27).

The positive language of the narrative ("seeking for Jesus") is suddenly dismantled as the Lord stripped their motivation to the bone. Why did they seek Him? Not because they had truly perceived the meaning of the miracle (designed to point them to His wonderful person as the long-promised Messiah of Israel) but because they had enjoyed a free meal, and wanted a repeat performance. Their superficiality was clearly exposed during the rest of the chapter in their hostile response to Christ's unfolding of His divine person and purpose.

Those who truly call on the name of the Lord must therefore come before Him with a deep sense of their own inadequacy and of His glory. Abraham sets the pattern: "Behold now, I have taken upon me to speak unto the Lord, which am but dust and ashes" (Gen 18.27). Appeals to heaven, writes Davidson, "should not be the mere instinctive cry of suffering, but the voice of trust and submission".[399] The supplicant's real thirst should be for God Himself, rather than for some quick fix. He should confess with the psalmist, "As the hart panteth after the water brooks, so panteth my soul after thee, O God. My soul thirsteth for God, for the living God" (Ps 42.1-2). In Elihu's words, he ought to sigh for "God my maker [6213]". This word appears for the first time in the creation narrative, when we are told that "God made [6213] the firmament" (Gen 1.7). In their prayers, says Elihu, true seekers for God will acknowledge both His creatorial dignity ("my maker"), and His overflowing bounty, for "he giveth songs in the night" and "teacheth us more than the beasts". From the living God alone comes that astonishing spiritual resilience which empowers the sufferer to sing amidst his sorrows, because (unlike the lower creation) he has been taught intelligently to comprehend something of God's wise purposes. "The beasts of the earth, and … the fowls of heaven" are supplied by God's tender care, but they know nothing of His mind; man, on the other hand, made uniquely in His image, was created to have pleasurable fellowship with his Creator. To encourage His disciples' confidence, the Lord Jesus revealed who it was who superintended the animal kingdom: "your heavenly Father feedeth them" (Mt 6.26). Not, we notice, "*their* heavenly Father". Even in His practical concern for the birds and the beasts God remains uniquely the Father of His redeemed.

"Songs in the night", delicious as they may sound, come of course at considerable cost. The word for "song" is uncommon. It is found a mere six times in the Hebrew Bible, describing David as the "sweet psalmist [2158] of Israel" (2 Sam 23.1), those who approach the Lord "with thanksgiving, and make a joyful noise unto him with psalms [2158]" (Ps 95.2), and the "songs [2158] in the house of my pilgrimage" (Ps 119.54) which the poet composed as a result of contemplating God's statutes. Solomon uses it of "the singing [2158] of birds" (Song 2.12), while for Isaiah it captures the hymns of Jewish exiles: "From the uttermost part of the earth have we heard songs [2158], even glory to the righteous" (Is 24.16). It speaks of a heart uplifted in melodious gratitude.

The qualifying expression "in the night" might reasonably be paraphrased "in calamity". It was one thing for Israel to sing on the far bank of the Red Sea, basking in the visible evidences of redemption by power (Ex 14.30-31; 15.1). The wreckage of the Egyptian military elite strewn on the sea shore trumpeted news of a glorious deliverance. It was quite a different situation when they faced the trials of the wilderness; then the same choir changed its hymn of victory into a sour lament (Ex 15.23-24; 16.2-3). Many years ago a Christian calendar printed Elihu's words in Job 35.10 alongside the sobering comment, "if God would make manifest that He "giveth songs in the night", He must first make it night". Both the suffering and the songs come from Him. As the hymn writer Frances Ridley Havergal correctly tells us,

> Every joy or trial falleth from above,
> Traced upon our dial by the Sun of Love;
> We may trust Him fully all for us to do;
> They who trust Him wholly find Him wholly true.

Not just the delights but the disappointments of life are of God's wise giving. It is a faulty theology which credits the bad things to Satan and the good things to God. Our God is gloriously sovereign in all His ways, leading His people through sunshine and shadow as it pleases Him.

> Night is the time of deep distress,
> Of pain, of fear, of loneliness,
> For every burden that we bear
> Seems heavier, more hopeless, there.
> Yet though the night be lone and long
> It also may be full of song,
> For suffering saints have strength to raise
> To God a voice of thankful praise.
> "God giveth songs" - a proof that He
> Is greater than adversity;
> And just to underline His power
> To keep us in the darkest hour,
> Our God, who gives those songs so bright,

Is also He who makes it night.
Our trials and triumphs both we trace
To God's amazing, sovereign grace!

Elihu's trenchant comment on prayer is a challenge to the believer. It raises serious questions. First, in our own times of adversity, whatever their immediate cause, do we instinctively ask "Where is God my maker?", looking to detect His hand in our circumstances? Do we flee for refuge to Him who not only created us but also wonderfully redeemed us through the work of the Lord Jesus Christ? Second, do we turn to Him in the right state of soul? Elihu's negative language ("none saith") suggests, sadly, that in his day few came before God with the required humility of spirit.

Yet suffering has always been the lot of God's people in a fallen world. So often in the spiritual pathway we discover that character-building is a rough and tough business. Do I need patience? Then it is more than likely that God will plunge me into testings of various shapes and sizes, because "tribulation worketh patience" (Rom 5.3). Do I long for a deep personal encounter with the "God of all comfort", so that I might minister solace to others? Then it is probable that I shall find myself enduring bitter distresses, since that is God's appointed means of equipping His people "to comfort them which are in any trouble, by the comfort wherewith we ourselves are comforted of God" (2 Cor 1.4). Do I aspire to the privilege of honouring the Lord even in the darkest hour? Then God will surely hasten the night-time of calamity to demonstrate conclusively that He alone has the ability to give His people songs of praise on beds of pain.

As we might expect, Spurgeon squeezes the juice out of verse 10. Here is an extract from one of his sermons:

> Usually in the night of a Christian's experience, God is his only song. If it be daylight in my heart, I can sing songs touching my graces, songs touching my sweet experiences, songs touching my duties, songs touching my labours; but let the night come, my graces appear to have withered; my evidences, though they are there, are hidden; now I have nothing left to sing of but my God. It is strange that, when God gives His children mercies, they generally set their hearts more on the mercies than on the Giver of them; but when the night comes, and He sweeps all the mercies away, then at once they each say, "Now, my God, I have nothing to sing of but Thee".[400]

Many Christian graces are nurtured under the pressures of sorrow and privation. Both the psalmist and the apostles rose above their immediate distresses to speak well of God in circumstances of extreme hardship. Their experiences are faithfully recorded for our encouragement:

> The Lord will command his lovingkindness in the daytime, and in the night his song shall be with me, and my prayer unto the God of my life (Ps 42.8).

I call to remembrance my song in the night: I commune with mine own heart: and my spirit made diligent search (Ps 77.6).

And at midnight Paul and Silas prayed, and sang praises unto God: and the prisoners heard them (Acts 16.25).

The poetic language of the psalmist ("in the night" and "my song") is transmuted into the down-to-earth literal squalor of a first-century Philippian jail ("at midnight"), and in such a place and at such a time two bruised servants of Christ lifted their voices in praise. As Robinson aptly reminds us, "no night of trouble [is] too dark for God to give songs in it".[401]

The Wisdom of Waiting: 35.14-16

The final verses of this chapter are acknowledged by all commentators to be difficult to understand. Darby's translation (which broadly follows the KJV) makes good sense of verse 14, even if the remainder of the section is not quite so plain:

Although thou sayest thou dost not see him, judgment is before him, therefore wait for him. But now, because he hath not visited in his anger, doth not Job know his great arrogancy? For Job hath opened his mouth in vanity, and made words abundant without knowledge (35.14-16, JND).

What does Elihu mean? Let us take verse 14 first of all. Job claims that God has not intervened to vindicate him or undertake his cause. That may be the case, admits Elihu, but Job must keep in mind that judgment is God's prerogative: He moves at His own pace, not man's. Job's part is to endure and "wait for him". Men demand instant action (by which they usually mean a prompt and favourable outcome for themselves), but for His own inscrutable reasons God bides His time; He will not be hurried or delayed by anybody.

The word rendered "trust" (2342) by the KJV is translated "wait" by Darby (and by most recent biblical versions). It describes the patience of Noah who "stayed [2342] yet other seven days" in the ark (Gen 8.10), and the embarrassed delay of Eglon's servants who "tarried [2342] till they were ashamed" (Judg 3.25). Nevertheless the Hebrew seems to comprehend a bewildering range of meanings. The KJV draws on a raft of apparently unrelated words to make sense of its sixty-eight appearances in the Old Testament, using words such as "pain", "form", "grieve", "travail", "tremble", "fear", "dance". The context, however, supports the translation "wait". Job has complained that God is unresponsive to his petitions; but Job must surrender to God's timing. The essence of trust is that sturdy endurance which confidently clings to God's promises despite the absence of any supporting evidence, because "faith is the assurance of things hoped for, the conviction of things not seen" (Heb 11.1, ESV). Such confidence enabled Paul to announce, in the teeth of a howling storm, "sirs, be of good cheer: for I believe God, that it shall be even as it was told me" (Acts 27.25).

The importance of waiting on the Lord, assured that He will accomplish His programme, is the special theme of the poetic and prophetic portions of the Old Testament. Here are samples of the testimony and exhortation they contain:

I have waited for thy salvation, O Lord (Gen 49.18).

Yea, let none that wait on thee be ashamed: let them be ashamed which transgress without cause (Ps 25.3).

Wait on the Lord: be of good courage, and he shall strengthen thine heart: wait, I say, on the Lord (Ps 27.14).

Rest in the Lord, and wait patiently for him: fret not thyself because of him who prospereth in his way, because of the man who bringeth wicked devices to pass (Ps 37.7).

I waited patiently for the Lord; and he inclined unto me, and heard my cry (Ps 40.1).

I wait for the Lord, my soul doth wait, and in his word do I hope (Ps 130.5).

And it shall be said in that day, Lo, this is our God; we have waited for him, and he will save us: this is the Lord; we have waited for him, we will be glad and rejoice in his salvation (Is 25.9).

The New Testament believer is similarly instructed to wait, though never in slothful indolence. Paul's summary of the Thessalonians' conversion puts it like this:

ye turned to God from idols to serve the living and true God; And to wait for his Son from heaven, whom he raised from the dead, even Jesus, which delivered us from the wrath to come (1 Thess 1.9-10).

They "turned" (their act of conversion – to God, from idols – in the past), they continued "to serve" (their present occupation in worship and witness), while their outlook was "to wait" for a returning deliverer. What, however, if some were laid aside through illness, unable to serve as once they did? Then they would continue to live in the expectation of the coming of God's Son to snatch them from the outpouring of His wrath on a rebel planet, granting them sin-free bodies for eternity. That is why, in his second letter to the Thessalonians, Paul prays that "the Lord direct your hearts into the love of God, and into the patient waiting for Christ" (2 Thess 3.5). However, the KJV fails to represent accurately what the original language is saying. Here is Darby's translation: "the Lord direct your hearts into the love of God, and into the patience of the Christ" (2 Thess 3.5, JND). The Lord Jesus on earth was the grand example of steadfast endurance, blazing the trail for His people (Heb 12.1-2). He teaches us to wait without repining. The ultimate goal of the believer's waiting is not some short-term relief from oppression (which God in grace may from time to time grant us in measure) but the return of Christ for His own.

When there is nothing else we can do, we rest on God to fulfil His word. Indeed, sometimes simply to cling on and wait is the most difficult thing in the world. That is why it requires patient endurance. Activity, however futile, is so much easier because it occupies mind and body, distracting our attention from current ills. Notwithstanding, the Saviour's current spiritual provision for His people is not tied to the present enjoyment of physical health or social liberty. He came "that they might have life, and that they might have it more abundantly" (Jn 10.10); and the child of God paralysed by pain, blinded by tears, or bed-ridden because of infirmity is not thereby deprived of that glorious blessing. The language of abundant life is but short-hand for "all spiritual blessings in heavenly places in Christ" (Eph 1.3). Because they are heavenly they cannot be put at risk by earthly circumstances; because they are in Him they cannot be forfeited by our own failures.

Elihu therefore counsels Job to wait patiently. This, admittedly, is not what Job has been doing for most of the book. True, he displayed amazing fortitude in the first two chapters; but thereafter, goaded into prolonged self-justification by the injudicious consolations offered by his friends, he has lapsed into testy criticism of God. How then does Elihu conclude his third speech? Below are two different translations of the final verses:

> But now, because he hath not visited in his anger, doth not Job know his great arrogancy? For Job hath opened his mouth in vanity, and made words abundant without knowledge (35.15-16, JND)

> And now, because his anger does not punish, and he does not take much note of transgression, Job opens his mouth in empty talk; he multiplies words without knowledge (35.15-16, ESV).

Darby's version appears to be interpreting Elihu's words thus: because God has not angrily intervened directly to reprove his irreverent words, Job has continued to pour forth a torrent of outrageous remarks without understanding what he is saying. The word rendered "arrogancy" ("extremity" in the KJV) appears nowhere else, so we have no sure guide to its meaning. By translating it as "transgression" the ESV seems to refer it to the wickedness of men whom God leaves unpunished, adding fuel to the fire of Job's discontent: God victimises an innocent man but lets rank sinners get away with their evil deeds. Therefore Job complains, not fully realising what he says.

Although the detail is obscure, the drift of the passage is clear enough. Job has used God's silence as a stick with which to beat the Almighty. The accusation, that Job is guilty of speaking "words without knowledge", is Elihu's repeated charge, one later picked up by Jehovah and finally admitted by Job himself:

> Job hath spoken without knowledge, and his words were without wisdom (34.35).

Then the Lord answered Job out of the whirlwind, and said, Who is this that darkeneth counsel by words without knowledge? (38.1-2).

Who is he that hideth counsel without knowledge? therefore have I uttered that I understood not; things too wonderful for me, which I knew not (42.3).

In retrospect we can see that young Elihu anticipates the very charge the Lord will shortly lay at Job's door. The end of the book is in sight.

Delitzsch sums up the contents of this third speech as follows:

> The chief thought of the speech we have also heard already from the three friends and Job himself. That the piety of the pious profits himself without involving God in any obligation to him, Eliphaz has already said, Job 22.2; and that prayer that is heard in time of need and the unanswered cry of the godly and the ungodly are distinct, Job said, Job 27.9. Elihu, however, deprives these thoughts of their hitherto erroneous application. If piety gives nothing to God which He ought to reward, Job dare not regard his affliction, mysterious as it is to him, as unjust; and if the godly do not directly experience the avenging wrath of God on the haughtiness of their oppressors, the question, whether then their prayer for help is of the right kind, is more natural than the complaint of a want of justice in God's government of the world. Job is silent also after this speech. It does not contain the right consolation; it contains, however, censure which he ought humbly to receive.[402]

The key teaching for the believer is found in verses 10 and 14. In perplexity we must wait on the Lord, and in suffering we should sing about Him. Neither duty is easy, but nor is it impossible. Paul is the New Testament model. He could last out a Mediterranean tempest by resting in God's word; he could sing in prison, conscious of His grace in Christ Jesus. Lest, forgetting our own constant weakness, we are tempted to look down on Job, who vented his irritation in angry words, let us keep in mind the vast dispensational gulf between the patriarch and the apostle. On board his storm-tossed ship Paul had a spoken message from the Lord; and every believer today possesses the complete canon of Scripture on which to draw for daily nourishment. To the best of our knowledge, Job had neither written revelation nor audible word from heaven. All he could hang on to as his spiritual lifebelt was that inherited truth about the living God passed down by his ancestors. In the light of his position before the dawn of written revelation we can hardly wonder at his confusion. Rather, we should marvel at the confidence and reverence so often displayed in his statements. That seems to be James's point as he exhorts his readers to fortitude despite difficulties:

> Be ye also patient; stablish your hearts: for the coming of the Lord draweth nigh. Grudge not one against another, brethren, lest ye be condemned: behold, the judge standeth before the door. Take, my brethren, the

prophets, who have spoken in the name of the Lord, for an example of suffering affliction, and of patience. Behold, we count them happy which endure. Ye have heard of the patience of Job, and have seen the end of the Lord; that the Lord is very pitiful, and of tender mercy (James 5.8-11).

Job, we note, is his classic example of patience. The idea is continuing endurance and persistence. Perhaps James is thinking primarily of Job's behaviour in the prologue, but even if we consider him in the heat of the dialogue we can still recognise one clinging like a drowning man to what he knew about God. When we long for divine intervention to rescue us from our current ills, let us remember the steadfastness of Job. He was but a man, therefore he occasionally vacillated, needing encouragement to endure; but endure he did.

Unlike Job, Christian believers know exactly for whom they are waiting and why they have every reason to sing. Listen to Paul's authoritative disclosure of God's grand purpose:

if we believe that Jesus died and rose again, even so them also which sleep in Jesus will God bring with him. For this we say unto you by the word of the Lord, that we which are alive and remain unto the coming of the Lord shall not prevent them which are asleep. For the Lord himself shall descend from heaven with a shout, with the voice of the archangel, and with the trump of God: and the dead in Christ shall rise first: Then we which are alive and remain shall be caught up together with them in the clouds, to meet the Lord in the air: and so shall we ever be with the Lord (1 Thess 4.14-17).

If Job, with all his disadvantages, persisted in cleaving to his God, how much more should we, having such clear promises grounded on the facts of history, endure with heads uplifted and hearts aflame!

SECTION 25
Dialogue: Job 4 – 42.6
Corrective: Job 32-37
Elihu's Speech: Job 32-37
Part Four: Job 36-37

The grand culmination of Elihu's response to Job and the three friends pulls out all the stops, poetically, emotionally, theologically. Most commentators – even those least sympathetic to this young interloper – acknowledge that these two chapters rise to a magnificent hymn in praise of divine grandeur. Here, for example, is Andersen's grudging admission:

> This concluding statement contains Elihu's best and most distinctive ideas. Up until now he has been treading on familiar and conventional ground, repeating largely the ideas which Job and his friends have already expressed. The harsh tone that Elihu had adopted in his second and third speeches is here softened. Job 36.1-21 is a more mature and engaging statement of orthodox theology than anything found elsewhere in the book.[403]

One suspects that the word "orthodox" in this context is subtly designed to rob Elihu of any credit for his doctrinal acuteness, but nothing can muffle the resonance of his poetry. Chapters 36 and 37 contain a compelling amalgam of theology and meteorology. Keen to underline for Job's benefit the key attributes of God (power, righteousness, wisdom), Elihu focusses particular attention on the wise omnipotence displayed in, for example, control of global weather systems. But his words are much more than a textbook catalogue, however accurate, of God's ways in providence: they intimate the build-up of a colossal storm, a storm heralding the dramatic intervention in the debate of Jehovah Himself. Although in his references to atmospheric conditions as tokens of divine power Elihu may seem to be drawing at random on all the seasons, it becomes apparent that his language is no scientific abstraction but genuinely pictures a fast-approaching tempest. Even Elihu confesses that he is afraid (37.1).

As we enter the last stage of his speech (the final human voice raised before God takes over in chapter 38) it is fitting to summarise the situation as it stands. Job's three venerable friends, shocked to the core by his terrible sufferings, have found the only way they can account for his troubles is to assume that, despite everything they know about him, he must all the time have been a secret sinner who is now receiving his just deserts. Over three rounds of debate they insist on this explanation, although Job robustly and consistently denies their accusations. Both sides become increasingly entrenched in their positions. The quarrel having reached deadlock, Elihu steps in with a subtly new voice. His view is that, while Job may not have been guilty of sinful deeds, he has fallen into the trap of uttering indefensible words. In saying this, he aligns himself with the increasing unease felt by the reader. The Job of the first two chapters was triumphantly guiltless in life and lip. There can be no question about that. But the Job of the debate begins to say things about God which are best left unsaid, betraying a hasty and unbecoming bitterness of spirit. Elihu, it may be argued, is the reader's spokesman, acting as our representative when he puts these niggling worries into words. Eliphaz earlier suggested that Job's trials were divine chastisements because of Job's actions; Elihu relates them instead to Job's attitude. The proper response to God, he maintains, is not defiant, self-righteous criticism but humble submission.

Before examining these chapters in depth, let us foreground the focus of Elihu's **theology** (36.1-23). Interestingly, four critical moments in the speech are signalled with the attention-grabbing exhortation, "Behold!" (36.5,22,26,30). It is tempting to see these imperatives as paragraph markers, offering the reader a thread through the labyrinth of the argument, but in reality they are simply peremptory commands to Job to be aware of God's power. Nevertheless they are worthy of notice:

> Behold, God is mighty, and despiseth not any: he is mighty in strength and wisdom (36.5).

> Behold, God exalteth by his power: who teacheth like him? (36.22).

> Behold, God is great, and we know him not, neither can the number of his years be searched out (36.26).

> Behold, he spreadeth his light upon it, and covereth the bottom of the sea (36.30).

The living God is immeasurable in His omnipotence, of course, but we should observe the ways in which that strength is manifested, for Elihu's language is carefully nuanced not to condemn but to offer Job encouragement.

First, we learn that God, though mighty, "despiseth not any" (36.5). The word "despiseth" (3988), initially used of Israel's wilful disobedience (Lev 26.15), is also employed to affirm God's longsuffering towards His chronically faithless people:

> when they be in the land of their enemies, I will not cast them away [3988], neither will I abhor them, to destroy them utterly, and to break my covenant with them: for I am the Lord their God (Lev 26.44).

The chosen nation might ungratefully reject His word, but – astonishingly – He would not respond in kind and wash His hands of them. Alongside divine power in all its terrifying energy stands commensurate pity. It is essential to read Job with an eye on James's pertinent lesson from the story, that "the Lord is very pitiful, and of tender mercy" (James 5.11). If He disciplines, it is in love; behind His correction lies compassion.

Second, the One who is "exalted in his power" (36.22, JND) is simultaneously the great educator: "who teacheth [3384] like him?" The verb is used, for example, of God's promise to be with Moses and "teach thee what thou shalt say" (Ex 4.12), of the Levites whose special responsibility was to "teach

Jacob thy judgments" (Deut 33.10), of Samuel who pledged, despite Israel's rebellion, "I will teach you the good and the right way" (1 Sam 12.23). Its nine appearances in Job are mainly rendered "teach", although two of them (30.19, translated "cast"; and 38.6, translated "laid") more literally represent the physical action of pointing or aiming which appears to be embedded in the Hebrew word – hence in military contexts it describes the shooting of arrows. The almighty God of whom Elihu speaks has not left His creatures blundering in the darkness of spiritual ignorance, but is willing to point out what they need to know. The believer's life on earth is shaped in accordance with God's educational programme for him.

Third, God's unique greatness renders Him sublimely inscrutable. "We know him not", confesses Elihu, "neither can the number of his years be searched out" (36.26). The word "searched out" (2714) turns up twelve times in the Old Testament, half of which describe directly or indirectly Jehovah's impenetrability (Job 5.9; 9.10; 11.7; Ps 145.3; Prov 25.3; Is 40.28). The God of infinite power is One who, in the glorious mysteries of His being, cannot be probed or analysed by men. This sets the great Gospel revelation of the Son in its true light:

> All things are delivered unto me of my Father: and no man knoweth the
> Son, but the Father; neither knoweth any man the Father, save the Son,
> and he to whomsoever the Son will reveal him (Mt 11.27).

This fascinatingly asymmetrical verse informs us that, although the incarnate Son makes the Father known to those who, in His sovereign will, He chooses to illuminate, the Son Himself remains transparent only to the Father. It is a paradox: He through whom we come to know God is in His personal excellences beyond our grasp. That is why Christians should make every effort to speak about the Lord Jesus Christ with the utmost reverence. It is impossible to think too highly of Him.

Fourth – and by this stage Elihu is homing in on up-to-the-minute local details – divine power is specifically exhibited in the electrifying energy of atmospheric storms. Or, more to the point, at that very moment divine power is being displayed in the tempest rumbling threateningly on the horizon, a tempest which shakes the heavens with thunder and irradiates sky and ocean with terrific flashes of lightning (36.30). What God in grace elects to reveal of Himself in the created universe we do well to ponder. The hymn writer Stuart K Hine has summed it up masterfully in a well-loved verse and chorus:

> O Lord my God! When I in awesome wonder
> Consider all the works Thy hand hath made,
> I see the stars, I hear the mighty thunder,
> Thy power throughout the universe displayed;
>
> Then sings my soul, my Saviour God, to Thee,
> How great Thou art, how great Thou art!

How, then, should Job find encouragement in listening to Elihu? He should rejoice that God is compassionate as well as powerful, able to instruct His creatures in the wisdom of His ways, while remaining, in His eternal glory, beyond their comprehension. In the sheer overwhelming thunder of His majesty He is worthy of humble adoration and worship. One of the notable things about this final speech is that Elihu no longer casts the spotlight on Job the sufferer, but on God the sovereign. That is why the keynote, which rises in chapter 37 to a great crescendo, is praise.

Elihu's fourth exhortation to "Behold", which points to the lightning flashes probably crackling across the sky even as he speaks, leads us neatly into his **meteorology** (36.24 – 37.24). This takes up the rest of chapter 36 and the whole of chapter 37, and will be addressed when we reach it in the exposition.

In summary, this fourth speech is an exceptionally meaty, mind-stretching climax to Elihu's contribution. It foregrounds the supreme glories of God and, with a view to illustrating His omnipotence, paints an awe-inspiring picture of His control over natural phenomena. The storm brewing in the background provides a fitting gateway through which Jehovah will make Himself known to Job. Even a cursory reading of Elihu's words should alert us to the pre-echoes of the greater voice to come. His questions, "Dost thou know" (37.15-16), anticipate the Lord's ironic queries (38.33; 39.1-2), just as his challenge to Job's ability (37.18) hints at the Lord's insistent "Canst thou" (38.31,32,34,35). If an operatic overture consists of a potpourri of themes from arias yet to be heard, then Elihu's last speech constitutes a curtain-raiser to the book's finale – the arrival of the living God Himself.

All this, however, is merely by way of introduction. The speech as a whole is not easy to break down into logical components. As has been indicated above, in the broadest terms it concerns **theology** (36.1-23) and **meteorology** (36.24 – 37.24). Crumbling it into five unequal sections may offer a pathway through it:

1. Elihu's Aim: 36.1-4
2. God's Attributes: 36.5
3. God's Actions: 36.6-15
4. Elihu's Application to Job: 36.16-23
5. Elihu's Adoration: 36.24 – 37.24.

Elihu's Aim: 36.1-4

This brief introduction again allows a courteous hiatus in which Job, if he wishes, may respond to what has been said so far. But whether Job replies or not, it is obvious that Eihu intends to carry on. He tells us three things: that he is speaking on God's behalf, that his great aim is to uphold divine righteousness, and that his words are genuine. His first claim is a reiteration of the earlier comment that "before God I am as thou; I also am formed out of the clay" (33.6, JND). Because Elihu is merely a man, he can engage with Job on God's behalf without undue intimidation. Notwithstanding, his priority is to refute the charges of injustice which Job has levelled against the Almighty. Like the apostle Paul's epistle to the Romans, Elihu aims to vindicate God's rightness. The great lesson to be learned by the end of the book of Job is that God is invariably just in all His ways; it is one thing to agree with the doctrine of divine righteousness in the abstract, but another to assent to it in the tangled affairs of daily life. Further, Elihu's words will not be "false". The term he employs (8267) was used earlier by Job, accusing his friends of being "forgers of lies [8267] … physicians of no value" (13.4). Unlike them, Elihu will employ no verbal trickery, nor will he attempt to defend God with unsound reasoning.

The reader may be a little taken aback by the speaker's self-assessment. Surely Elihu is insufferably arrogant to say that "he that is perfect in knowledge is with thee" (36.4b)? The claim is the more startling when we discover identical words used later to describe God, when Elihu asks if Job knows "the wondrous works of him which is perfect in knowledge?" (37.16). In an absolute sense such language can only apply to Jehovah. It is probable, however, that the expression in chapter 36 needs to be read in the light of the explanatory parallel phrase, "truly my words shall not be false" (36.4a); that is to say, Elihu's answer will not be flawed by the same unsympathetic misunderstandings and theological oversimplifications which compromised the counsel of the friends.

One further comment may be offered. Elihu maintains that he will fetch his knowledge "from afar" (36.3). This does not imply abstruse logic or a dependence on esoteric examples; rather, he draws on the evidences for God's greatness in the vast universe all around. Lest any respond that Job is well aware of this, and has touched on it several times in his own speeches, it is enough to note that when Jehovah closes up the debate He draws attention to the same area of truth. Job needs to recognise the practical implications of God's infinite greatness, one of which is a complete and unconditional self-humbling in His presence, a consciousness of his own littleness. Those sensitive to their own comparative insignificance will not stand on their dignity or dare accuse the Almighty of mismanaging His universe.

God's Attributes: 36.5

Verse 5 deserves emphasis as a capsule summary of what Elihu considers the most pertinent of God's attributes. He has touched on divine righteousness as the heart of his argument (36.3), but he supplements this with power, mercy, and wisdom. The adjective "mighty" (3524) is used seven times in Job, appearing first in Bildad's contemptuous dismissal of Job's words as the bluster of a "strong [3524] wind" (8.2). The living God, however, is of unquantifiable strength. Elihu will use other significant synonyms later:

> Behold, God exalteth by his power [3581] (36.22).

> Behold, God is great [7689] (36.26).

> He is excellent [7689] in power [3581] (37.23).

This truth must not be kicked into the long grass. In our struggles and stresses we should never forget God's infinite greatness. The God of creation stands alone in His omnipotence, and Elihu will shortly adduce appropriate examples of His power. But alongside power he adds the important corollary, that he "despiseth not any". This is vital. Human history tragically demonstrates that power is usually accompanied by contempt for the weak. Without compunction, military might tramples on the defenceless and the feeble. When in 1887 Lord Acton framed one of the best known aphorisms, "Power tends to corrupt, and absolute power corrupts absolutely. Great men are almost always bad men",[404] he was merely putting into words a long-held axiom. But with God incontestable power is combined with goodness. With Him, might and mercy go wonderfully hand in hand. As far as his overall argument is concerned, Elihu has concentrated on divine righteousness, but this can never be divorced from the equally significant attributes of power, mercy and wisdom. Because He is the One who "despiseth not any", we may be sure that the righteous God will not misuse His power.

Further, in Darby's rendering of the verse, He is "mighty in strength of understanding" (36.5, JND). That is to say, His divine energy is especially manifested in the expansiveness of a wisdom fully able to comprehend without fail all people, all circumstances, and all conditions. "Understanding" here translates the important Old Testament word normally rendered "heart" (3820): the headquarters of the individual, the place where a man thinks, feels, and decides. God is magnificent in the capacities of His heart. Though so far exalted above His creatures, yet He condescends to the lowly because He understands them completely.

God's Actions: 36.6-15

Having summarised those attributes of the Deity which are particularly important to his thesis, Elihu now illustrates them in action.

> He preserveth not the life of the wicked: but giveth to the afflicted their right. He withdraweth not his eyes from the righteous: but with kings upon the throne he setteth them for ever, and they are exalted (36.6-7, RV).

How does God exercise His righteousness, power and wisdom in the government of the world? It seems initially that four categories of people are considered: the wicked, the afflicted, the righteous, and the exalted. God does not sustain those who merit judgment, but rather moves in justice on behalf of their victims. The word the RV and other versions translate "afflicted" (6041) frequently refers to the materially impoverished. Its first appearance comes in Jehovah's ban on high interest money-lending in the nation of Israel: "If thou lend money to any of my people that is poor [6041] by thee, thou shalt not be to him as an usurer, neither shalt thou lay upon him usury" (Ex 22.25). However, although the term may include financial destitution, the context in Job suggests that it refers to those who, poor or not, are denied their rights. The idea will return in verse 15. God's preserving eye is fixed favourably on the righteous: whatever Job may have insinuated in earlier speeches, He does not forsake them. Further, it is by His doing that earthly monarchs are settled in their positions of power.

Rereading these verses, however, may cause us to refine our understanding of Elihu's categories. Instead of four, there are more likely only two: the wicked and the righteous (identified with those who are rescued from misery and raised up into unlooked-for positions of privilege). With an eye on the New Testament, we may read Elihu's words as a miniature pen-portrait of the believer's blessings in Christ. Delivered by God's grace from the dominion of sin, he is granted a standing of righteousness on the grounds of the atoning death of the Lord Jesus. More, the sunshine of God's favour perpetually rests on him, safeguarding him from ultimate harm. From the condition of a worthless outcast he is elevated to the highest honours as a child of God and a joint-heir with Christ. Hannah beautifully expresses the idea in Old Testament imagery:

> He raiseth up the poor out of the dust, and lifteth up the beggar from the dunghill, to set them among princes, and to make them inherit the throne of glory: for the pillars of the earth are the Lord's, and he hath set the world upon them (1 Sam 2.8).

The New Testament equivalent may be found in Ephesians:

> God, who is rich in mercy, for his great love wherewith he loved us, Even when we were dead in sins, hath quickened us together with Christ, (by grace ye are saved;) And hath raised us up together, and made us sit together in heavenly places in Christ Jesus (Eph 2.4-6).

But Elihu goes further in his analysis of divine activity, tracing God's continuing dealings with the righteous. We last saw them securely installed on thrones of kingly dignity. Yet human life on planet earth is fraught with unexpected changes of circumstance:

> And if they be bound in fetters, and be taken in the cords of affliction; Then he sheweth them their work, and their transgressions, that they have behaved themselves proudly. He openeth also their ear to instruction, and commandeth that they return from iniquity. If they hearken and serve him, they shall spend their days in prosperity, and their years in pleasures (36.8-11, RV).

In verse 7 such people were established and ennobled; now they are "bound in fetters". Why the sudden reversal? The answer is that God's concern with His people does not terminate with salvation; when they go astray He exercises firm fatherly discipline. The "fetters" (2131) speak of literal captivity. The psalmist uses similar language when he looks ahead to restored Israel fulfilling its role in the millennial Kingdom as the instrument of God's righteous government on earth:

> To execute vengeance upon the heathen, and punishments upon the

people; To bind their kings with chains [2131], and their nobles with fetters of iron; To execute upon them the judgment written (Ps 149.7-9).

King Manasseh exemplifies the beneficial value of trials. Beyond all expectation, that most atrocious of Judah's later monarchs was drawn to the Lord whom he had defied by means of the grievous sufferings the Assyrians inflicted on him:

And the Lord spake to Manasseh, and to his people: but they would not hearken. Wherefore the Lord brought upon them the captains of the host of the king of Assyria, which took Manasseh among the thorns, and bound him with fetters, and carried him to Babylon. And when he was in affliction, he besought the Lord his God, and humbled himself greatly before the God of his fathers, And prayed unto him: and he was intreated of him, and heard his supplication, and brought him again to Jerusalem into his kingdom. Then Manasseh knew that the Lord he was God (2 Chr 33.10-13).

This must be one of the most outstanding examples of God's ability to bring a rebel to heel that he might be saved. Robinson, skilled at formulating biblical axioms, writes that "affliction of the body [is] one of God's remedial measures for the welfare of the soul". Certainly, we must agree with him that "Manasseh's iron chain [was] better for him than his golden crown".[405] If men will not heed when God speaks gently, through His Word or through His servants, then He may resort to sterner measures.

Elihu, however, is thinking primarily of God's treatment of the godly. Why would those who are already positionally righteous have to endure slavery, whether literal or metaphorical? The reason is spelled out: even though enjoying a right relationship with God they have been guilty of "transgressions", they have "behaved themselves proudly", and committed "iniquity". Since transgression and iniquity are non-specific words, it may be that the middle description of their misdemeanour is the key: they have become full of themselves. How easily we fall prey to this folly! While scrupulously avoiding the grosser sins of the flesh and steering a pathway of commendable uprightness in daily life, we may become smugly self-satisfied with our own piety. The vital principle Elihu establishes is that there are always good and sufficient reasons lying behind God's dealings with men, for – as this book constantly demonstrates – all their circumstances are disposed by His hand. Heaven's movements are never arbitrary. Those in a genuine relationship with God come under the scope of His serious but gracious correction if they drift into error, for

whom the Lord loveth he correcteth; even as a father the son in whom he delighteth. Happy is the man that findeth wisdom, and the man that getteth understanding (Prov 3.12-13).

Affliction is therefore no infallible sign of hypocrisy (as the friends suggest), nor does it prove that God has turned away His face in displeasure (as Job fears).

Rather, it is for the believer a distinct mark of divine affection. Delitzsch is good at drawing out the application:

> The fundamental thought of Elihu here once again comes unmistakeably to view: the sufferings of the righteous are well-meant chastisements, which are to wean them from the sins into which through carnal security they have fallen – a warning from God to penitence, designed to work their good.[406]

To respond to correction with contrition and submission is to come into the brightness of restored blessing. This is the Hebrew writer's inspired New Testament commentary on Solomon's advice:

> Now no chastening for the present seemeth to be joyous, but grievous: nevertheless afterward it yieldeth the peaceable fruit of righteousness unto them which are exercised thereby (Heb 12.11).

The "afterward" in Job's experience is now not far off. Once the Lord has spoken to him directly he will be fully equipped as a champion spiritual athlete, discarding the weight of self-obsession which impedes his progress, and instead clinging humbly to his God. Chapter 42 fulfils the pledge of 36.11 by documenting Job's abundant restoration to prosperity. It is the message of both Testaments that practical obedience to divine commands guarantees blessing. As Jehovah said to Israel through the prophet Isaiah,

> If ye be willing and obedient, ye shall eat the good of the land: But if ye refuse and rebel, ye shall be devoured with the sword: for the mouth of the Lord hath spoken it (Is 1.19-20).

For Israel, blessing was normally associated with earthly affluence and security in the land God had given them; for the New Testament believer it is linked with the present enjoyment of our spiritual benefits in Christ (Eph 1.3-4). Our responsibility is to "lay hold on eternal life, whereunto thou art also called" (1 Tim 6.12), to enter practically into the personal appreciation of what is ours because of the person and work of the Lord Jesus. That means reading, enjoying, assimilating, storing away, pondering, and spending time with God's Word.

On the other hand, Elihu is realistic enough to allow for the tragic possibility that some might stubbornly resist God's kindly overtures of mercy:

> But if they hearken not, they shall perish by the sword, and they shall die without knowledge. But they that are godless in heart lay up anger: they cry not for help when he bindeth them. They die in youth, and their life perisheth among the unclean (36.12-14, RV).

A refusal to heed God's voice speaking through distress would lead to violent death, says Elihu, a death in which the victim forfeits the blessing of spiritual insight which illuminates those who submit to divine discipline.

Behind Elihu's words lies a principle. The way a man reacts to affliction discloses his true condition before God. Though he may for many years kick against the pricks, a genuine believer will eventually acknowledge God's hand in his trials and God's heart in his spiritual education. David, guilty of serious sins and on many occasions profoundly downcast, always turned back to the Lord who had smitten him. Jeremiah goes further, reminding us that even the very act of turning back to God in repentance is the result of a prior divine movement in the heart. Broken, dispersed, diminished Judah would need to pray "Turn thou us unto thee, O Lord, and we shall be turned; renew our days as of old" (Lam 5.21). Unaided, feeble man is of himself incapable of doing anything good.

After this solemn warning, Elihu's overview of God's corrective measures closes on a positive note as he reverts to the encouraging point made in verse 10. Suffering is a divine alarm clock to wake us up to reality:

> He delivereth the afflicted by his affliction, and openeth their ear in oppression (36.15, RV).

Translations differ slightly. While the KJV and Darby tell us that God delivers the poor man "in his affliction", which means that He intervenes in the midst of suffering to rescue the godly individual who has learned from its inbuilt message, others (notably the RV and the ESV) stress the fact that it is "by his affliction" that God instructs. Both ideas are true. Adversity is commonly God's means of getting His people's attention and weaning them away from the follies which mar their lives. As Davidson puts it, "afflictions are but instances of His gracious wisdom, for by them He opens the ears of men to instruction".[407] Further, He eventually snatches them out of the very hardship itself. Since our pathway through this world is potholed with snares and traps, adversity of one kind or another will be the believer's experience until removed from this scene altogether by the Lord's return or by death.

Elihu's Application to Job: 36.16-23

Elihu makes a direct application of these principles to the solitary audience – for, as we note from the second person singular pronouns in verses 16-19, 21 and 24, he is by now addressing no one but Job. Darby, unlike the KJV, brings out the imagery. Here is the difference between the translations:

> Even so would he have removed thee out of the strait into a broad place, where there is no straitness; and that which should be set on thy table should be full of fatness (36.16, KJV).

> Even so would he have allured thee out of the jaws of distress into a broad place, where there is no straitness; and the supply of thy table would be full of fatness (36.16, JND).

The KJV's rather bland "removed" (5496) does not do justice to a verb which most often appears in the context of subtle enticement (as in Deuteronomy 13.6). Nor does "strait" have the vivid impact of "the jaws of distress" (a rendering followed by Delitzsch). The adversities God lays on His people are designed lovingly to lure them away from peril into a sphere of safety ("a broad place") and plenty ("full of fatness"). Elihu winsomely sketches a picture of the benefits awaiting the man who bows to God's correcting hand. Abundantly unrestricted living space is one of the psalmist's illustrations of salvation:

> He brought me forth also into a large place; he delivered me, because he delighted in me (Ps 18.19).

> I called upon the Lord in distress: the Lord answered me, and set me in a large place (Ps 118.5).

If oppression is like imprisonment in a cramped cell, release comes as a breath of fresh air. Churchill's famous Battle of Britain speech in 1940 used a similar metaphor to embolden the heart of a nation in desperate peril. Deliverance from the tyranny of Nazi Germany would usher the world into joyous liberty:

> If we can stand up to him [Hitler], all Europe may be freed and the life of the world may move forward into broad, sunlit uplands.[408]

The attractions of such an idyllic scene are obvious. Along with spacious, rolling hills bathed in mellow sunlight goes the promise of limitless provision. A richly furnished table is the imagery used by psalmist and prophet alike to picture divine blessing (Ps 23.5; Is 25.6). Every sinner who has cast himself upon Christ for salvation has been brought by grace into the enjoyment of a landscape of spiritual blessing too vast to be fully explored or mapped out. There is always more to discover and enjoy.

Readers privy to the story of Job will by now be looking ahead to the reversal of fortunes in chapter 42. Released from misery he will be showered with restored prosperity on a scale far exceeding the past. Of this neither Job nor Elihu knows anything. But the basic principle is correct: whatever our circumstances, submission to God's hand is the recipe for blessing, even though the blessing be delayed, or arrive in unexpected ways.

But Job, alas, has not responded in such a spirit. Hence Elihu's shift into admonitory mode:

> But thou art full of the judgment of the wicked: judgment and justice take hold on thee. Because there is wrath, beware lest thou be led away by thy sufficiency; neither let the greatness of the ransom turn thee aside. Will thy riches suffice, that thou be not in distress, or all the forces of thy strength? (36.17-19, RV).

According to Smick, "there are few verses in the entire Old Testament that are more difficult to translate than 17-20"[409] of this chapter. What is Elihu saying? Job is "full of the judgment of the wicked", not because he is guilty of great sins, for Elihu has never charged him with that, but because his sufferings have goaded him into uttering improper words about God (34.5-7,36). He has judged God as sinners do. In speaking like this, he has implicitly sided with the godless who "set their mouth against the heavens" (Ps 73.9). Such outspokenness, asserting his righteousness at the expense of God's, has placed him in a dangerous position. Delitzsch offers the following useful explanation of verse 18:

> Elihu admonishes Job not to allow himself to be drawn by the heat of passion into derision, or to deride; nor to be allured from the right way by the ransom which is required of him as the price of restoration to happiness, viz., humble submission to the divine chastisement, as though this ransom were exceeding great.[410]

The word the KJV renders "stroke" (36.18) appears only here and Job 20.22, where almost all translators take it to mean "sufficiency". If this is also the case in chapter 36, then Elihu is warning Job against allowing his anger to side-track him into vain self-reliance. Not even the exemplary Job can be self-sufficient in the presence of God. Robinson helpfully defines the word "ransom" in this context: "the ransom, in reference to men, [is] whatever God may please in His wisdom and goodness to appoint".[411] The "greatness of the ransom", in this case, refers to the lesson Elihu has been insisting upon throughout the chapter: that Job – like all others in distress – must bow to the divine discipline. In Peter's words, "Humble yourselves therefore under the mighty hand of God, that he may exalt you in due time" (1 Pet 5.6). For one of Job's genuine integrity, such a course of action is a bitter pill to swallow. Pious men can sometimes find it very tough to take a lowly place and confess personal inadequacy. Yet it is the only pathway to follow. Neither Job's one-time fabulous wealth (some, like Delitzsch, translate this as "thy crying") nor all the resources of his hitherto undeniable strength (of character, of godliness, of influence, of reputation) can relieve him. Only in submission is there safety.

In context, "the greatness of the ransom" refers to what Job requires to be restored to favour. The Christian reader, however, will inevitably think beyond Job's circumstances to "the greatness of the ransom" provided by the Lord Jesus Christ to secure the eternal salvation of His people, for "the Son of man came not to be ministered unto, but to minister, and to give his life a ransom for many" (Mt 20.28). Unconditional surrender to God's chastising hand may be a costly business, but how much costlier was the price paid by the Saviour for the rescue of helpless sinners!

Elihu's warning continues:

> Desire not the night, when peoples are cut off from their place. Take heed, turn not to iniquity; for this hast thou chosen rather than affliction. Lo,

God is exalted in his power: who teacheth as he? Who hath appointed him
his way? or who hath said, Thou hast wrought unrighteousness? (36.20-
23, JND).

Job's longing for death, though understandable in the light of his sufferings,
cannot be commended. Elihu's reference to "the night" looks back to the
patriarch's earlier wistful aspirations, recorded from chapter 3 onwards. We
recollect his deeply embittered words, asking "Wherefore is light given to him
that is in misery, and life unto the bitter in soul; Which long for death, but
it cometh not; and dig for it more than for hid treasures?" (3.20-21). He has
pictured the end of his earthly life as an escape into "A land of darkness, as
darkness itself; and of the shadow of death, without any order, and where the
light is as darkness" (10.22). In his constant clamour to appear in a divine
courtroom and plead his case before the Almighty, says Elihu, Job is treading
treacherous ground. The God with whom he dares to contend is One of greater
power and grandeur than he yet grasps. Delitzsch paraphrases Elihu's entreaty
like this:

> And yet Job presses forward on to the tribunal of the terrible Judge, instead
> of humbling himself under His mighty hand. Oh that in time he would
> shrink back from this absolute wickedness.[412]

Moving towards the long peroration of his speech, Elihu reminds Job of
the doctrinal truths which should make a man pause before challenging God's
rights to deal with him as He pleases. Rather than attempting to probe into the
why and wherefore of His actions, men should praise Him. In verses 22 and 23
Elihu adduces four facts. First, God is exalted through the sheer immensity of
His power – in the final analysis, no one has the ability to resist Him. Second, in
His concern for His creatures He is the greatest of instructors although, being
also in sovereign control over creation, He is under no obligation to explain
the reasons behind His actions. Dare Job presume to teach God how to rule
His own universe? Third, He stands gloriously solitary in His wisdom, needing
advice from no one in the conduct of His affairs. Fourth, being in Himself
the absolute, immutable standard of what is right, He cannot be accused of
injustice (as Job has been doing), for there is no external measure against which
to assess Him.

Since injustice has long been Job's theme, it is worth noting that the Hebrew
word (5766) Elihu uses (translated "iniquity" in the KJV, but "unrighteousness"
in both the RV and Darby) appears in the judicial setting of Moses's law:

> Ye shall do no unrighteousness [5766] in judgment: thou shalt not respect
> the person of the poor, nor honour the person of the mighty: but in
> righteousness shalt thou judge thy neighbour (Lev 19.15).

Further, it is used to describe God Himself:

He is the Rock, his work is perfect: for all his ways are judgment: a God of truth and without iniquity [5766], just and right is he (Deut 32.4).

King Jehoshaphat affirmed that "there is no iniquity [5766] with the Lord our God, nor respect of persons, nor taking of gifts" (2 Chr 19.7). All this is of crucial significance. Job has argued for his own righteousness (not sinless perfection, but a relative uprightness of conduct meriting divine approval) while insinuating that God has treated him unfairly. But, says Elihu, no one can charge God with injustice, for without Him there would be no concept of justice. Simply to cast the mind upon Him should stimulate not resentment but adoration.

Paul treads a similar pathway when, at the close of his lengthy exposition of the rightness of God's ways with Israel, he rises to a memorable expression of awestruck worship. Having argued from the evidence of the Old Testament that God cannot be accused of partiality in His dealings with men (especially in His mysterious purposes of election), he erupts into this doxology:

> O the depth of the riches both of the wisdom and knowledge of God! how unsearchable are his judgments, and his ways past finding out! For who hath known the mind of the Lord? or who hath been his counsellor? Or who hath first given to him, and it shall be recompensed unto him again? For of him, and through him, and to him, are all things: to whom be glory for ever. Amen (Rom 11.33-36).

Although lacking the full revelation granted Paul, Elihu is engaged in a similar exercise – seeking to shepherd Job away from whinging into worship, from self-assertion into self-abnegation, from protest into praise. He may be short on tact, and he is certainly ignorant of God's secret purpose in Job's trials, but his counsel is, broadly speaking, right. We are better on our knees than on our high horse.

Elihu's Adoration: 36.24 – 37.24

This brings us appropriately to the final section of the speech, which I have entitled "Elihu's Adoration". It is a massive climax, running all the way to the close of chapter 37, largely because the speaker becomes so absorbed in his theme that he finds it almost impossible to terminate what is essentially a psalm of praise. Although still addressing Job (by name in 37.14, and in the second person singular pronouns in 36.24; 37.15-18), for much of the time Elihu loses sight of his immediate audience in his wonderment at the astonishing grandeur, variety and complexity of the created world.

He starts with a stirring affirmation of man's responsibility to praise his Creator:

> Remember that thou magnify his work, whereof men have sung. All men have looked thereon; man beholdeth it afar off (36.24-25, RV).

The Hebrew word translated "magnify" (7679) appears only twice in Scripture.

The other occasion is Job 12.23, where it describes the way God "increaseth [7679] the nations, and destroyeth them", multiplying or diminishing populations as it pleases Him. Although man cannot in any sense increase God's glory, he can speak well of Him so that others become more conscious of His excellence. Job's duty, then, is not to derogate from God's greatness but proclaim it loudly to the world. More recent versions (RV, Darby, Delitzsch, ESV) reject the KJV's "which men behold" for language suggestive of audible celebration: men not only see God's work, they gladly sing about it in praise and worship. The word in verse 25 all versions render "behold" (5027) is the one with which the Lord instructs Abram to "look [5027] now toward heaven" (Gen 15.5) and count the stars. It is used of Lot's wife looking back at the doomed city of Sodom, thus betraying how her life had become inextricably linked with a wicked world (Gen 19.26). It therefore suggests an intense, close, desiring gaze rather than a passing glance. The more intently we scrutinise God's works in creation and redemption – or for that matter, His written Word – the more fuel we shall garner for praise.

Elihu's teaching harmonises perfectly with the psalmist's worship:

> The works of the Lord are great, sought out of all them that have pleasure therein. His work is honourable and glorious: and his righteousness endureth for ever. He hath made his wonderful works to be remembered: the Lord is gracious and full of compassion (Ps 111.2-4).

A similar principle underlies Paul's demolition job on the foolish concept of atheism:

> that which may be known of God is manifest in them; for God hath shewed it unto them. For the invisible things of him from the creation of the world are clearly seen, being understood by the things that are made, even his eternal power and Godhead; so that they are without excuse: Because that, when they knew God, they glorified him not as God, neither were thankful; but became vain in their imaginations, and their foolish heart was darkened (Rom 1.19-21).

The visible evidences of divine handiwork in the universe bear testimony to the existence and power of an invisible Creator. If what we can see is so stupendous in its witness to God, it is only reasonable to infer that He who so fittingly framed the world governs it with equal wisdom. It is not a shortage of evidence which produces so-called atheism (better described as anti-theism or misotheism), but a stubborn refusal to bow to the Creator.

Elihu's exhortation to Job is, we must remember, not abstract theory. Worship is not simply man's duty, it is his practical blessing. When Job eventually turns to praise, he will leave off his complaint. As has been said, "That man should sing praises in the deepest darkness does not explain suffering, but it negates its poison".[413]

No human ignorance or antipathy, however, can obscure the majesty of God. Elihu sums this up in another of his neat capsule statements:

Behold, God is great, and we know him not, neither can the number of his years be searched out (36.26).

Divine greatness is the more overwhelming because God is ultimately unknowable. Creation may be observed and investigated (36.25), but the Creator remains perpetually beyond the creature's comprehension. Even the number of His years is immeasurable for, as Moses says, "Before the mountains were brought forth, or ever thou hadst formed the earth and the world, even from everlasting to everlasting, thou art God" (Ps 90.2). Elihu is of course speaking before the incarnation. With the coming of Christ, however, God is revealed as never before. As John tells us, making a clear distinction between the Old and the New Testament, "No man hath seen God at any time; the only begotten Son, which is in the bosom of the Father, he hath declared him" (Jn 1.18). And in Him, the Son, "dwelleth all the fulness of the Godhead bodily" (Col 2.9). But not even the redeemed of this age, blessed as they are with an unsurpassed disclosure of God in Christ, will ever plumb the depths of deity. One of the wonders of eternity will be the constantly new and satisfying discovery of fresh beauties in the living God.

A well-known children's tale illustrates the point. When C S Lewis's Narnia stories finally reach their conclusion with *The Last Battle*, the children find themselves in a splendid new world where everything appears more real and more beautiful than anything they have seen before. They are told that "the further up and the further in you go, the bigger everything gets. The inside is larger than the outside". The narrator closes up the saga with these words:

All their life in this world and their adventures in Narnia had only been the cover and the title page: now at last they were beginning Chapter One of the Great Story which no one on earth has read: which goes on for ever: in which every chapter is better than the one before.[414]

For the believer there will be no let-downs in eternity.

Elihu's awe-struck affirmation of divine splendour (36.26) leads naturally into an examination of the stunning works of God in providence. Because his song of praise continues over so many verses it is not easy to detect an evident structure. Wiersbe[415] suggests that he is systematically tracing God's creatorial superintendence of the seasons, starting with autumn (36.27 – 37.5), moving into winter (37.6-10), spring (37.11-13), and concluding with summer (37.14-18). There is good sense in this: snow and ice are mentioned in 37.6-10, while 37.11-13 hints at the plentiful spring rainfall which refreshes the soil. Whether, however, we see a clear progression in thought or not, Elihu's testimony revolves around storms and the various forms of precipitation God employs to sustain His creation.

Before examining the text in detail it may be helpful to consider the vocabulary of this section. Elihu's language is remarkably wide-ranging and technical. The following table lists some of the key words and their occurrences.

KJV	Strong's No	Meaning (from Strong's Concordance)	First Occurrence in the Bible	Occurrences in Job
Rain	4306		Ex 9.33	5.10; 28.26; 29.23; 36.27; 37.6; 38.28
Rain	1653		Gen 7.12	37.6 (twice)
Vapour	108	a *fog*: - mist, vapor	Gen 2.6 ("mist")	36.27
Clouds	7834	*a powder* (as beaten small); by analogy a thin *vapor*; by extension the *firmament*: - cloud, small dust, heaven, sky	Deut 33.26 ("sky")	35.5; 36.28; 37.18 ("sky"); 37.21; 38.37
Clouds	5645	properly an envelope, that is, *darkness* (or *density*; specifically a (scud) *cloud*; also a *copse*: - clay, (thick) cloud	Ex 19.9 ("thick")	20.6; 22.14; 26.8; 30.15; 36.29; 37.11,16; 38.34
Clouds	6051	a *cloud* (as *covering* the sky), that is, the *nimbus* or thunder cloud	Gen 9.13	7.9; 26.8,9; 37.11,15; 38.9
Light	216	*illumination* or (concretely) *luminary* (in every sense, including *lightning*, *happiness*, etc.): - bright, clear, + day, light (-ning), morning, sun	Gen 1.3	32 times between 3.9 and 41.18 (rendered both "light" and "lightning")

Thunder	7481	to *tumble*, that is, be violently *agitated*; specifically to *crash* (of thunder); figuratively to *irritate* (with anger): - make to fret, roar, thunder, trouble	1 Sam 1.6 ("fret"); 2.10 ("thunder")	37.4,5; 40.9
Snow	7950	*snow* (probably from its *whiteness*): - snow (-y)	Ex 4.6	6.16; 9.30; 24.19; 37.6; 38.22
Frost/ice	7140	*ice* (as if bald, that is, *smooth*); hence, *hail*; by resemblance, rock *crystal*: - crystal, frost, ice	Gen 31.40	6.16; 37.10; 38.29
Wind	7307	*wind*; by resemblance *breath*, that is, a sensible (or even violent) exhalation; figuratively *life*, *anger*, *unsubstantiality*; by extension a *region* of the sky; by resemblance *spirit*, but only of a rational being (including its expression and functions): - air, anger, blast, breath	Gen 1.2 ("Spirit"); 3.8 ("cool")	1.19; 6.26; 7.7; 8.2; 21.18; 28.25; 30.15,22; 37.21 ("wind"); 4.9; 9.18; 12;10; 15.30; 17.1; 19.17 ("breath"); 4.15; 6.4; 7.11; 10.12; 15.13; 20.3; 21.4; 26.13; 27.3; 32.8,18; 33.4,14 ("spirit"); 15.2; 16.3 ("vain"); 41.16 ("air")
Whirlwind	5492	*a hurricane*: - Red Sea, storm, tempest, whirlwind	Num 21.14 ("Red Sea"); Ps 83.15 ("storm")	21.18; 27.20; 37.9 ("storm", "tempest, "whirlwind")

Simply to glance at this list is to remind ourselves that Elihu is not the first person in the book to note how atmospheric conditions manifest divine power and benevolence. The weather systems of planet earth constitute an abiding testimony to God's authority and gracious provision for men. Elihu's acute perspective on the weather accords with the invariable Old Testament acknowledgment of God's hand in the day to day affairs of His universe. We do not live in a world that is out of control: our God superintends natural phenomena. Indeed, on several Old Testament occasions, God chose to reveal Himself in the terrible grandeur of a storm. We might think, for example, of His descent upon Mount Sinai, His appearance to the dejected Elijah, the divine display granted to David, and Habakkuk's overpowering vision of Jehovah's majesty. The four descriptions are worth quoting.

> And it came to pass on the third day in the morning, that there were thunders and lightnings, and a thick cloud upon the mount, and the voice of the trumpet exceeding loud; so that all the people that was in the camp trembled. And Moses brought forth the people out of the camp to meet with God; and they stood at the nether part of the mount. And mount Sinai was altogether on a smoke, because the Lord descended upon it in fire: and the smoke thereof ascended as the smoke of a furnace, and the whole mount quaked greatly (Ex 19.16-18).

> And he said, Go forth, and stand upon the mount before the Lord. And, behold, the Lord passed by, and a great and strong wind rent the mountains, and brake in pieces the rocks before the Lord; but the Lord was not in the wind: and after the wind an earthquake; but the Lord was not in the earthquake: And after the earthquake a fire; but the Lord was not in the fire: and after the fire a still small voice (1 Kings 19.11-12).

> In my distress I called upon the Lord, and cried to my God: and he did hear my voice out of his temple, and my cry did enter into his ears. Then the earth shook and trembled; the foundations of heaven moved and shook, because he was wroth. There went up a smoke out of his nostrils, and fire out of his mouth devoured: coals were kindled by it. He bowed the heavens also, and came down; and darkness was under his feet. And he rode upon a cherub, and did fly: and he was seen upon the wings of the wind. And he made darkness pavilions round about him, dark waters, and thick clouds of the skies. Through the brightness before him were coals of fire kindled. The Lord thundered from heaven, and the most High uttered his voice. And he sent out arrows, and scattered them; lightning, and discomfited them. And the channels of the sea appeared, the foundations of the world were discovered, at the rebuking of the Lord, at the blast of the breath of his nostrils (2 Sam 22.7-16).

> God came from Teman, and the Holy One from mount Paran. Selah.

His glory covered the heavens, and the earth was full of his praise. And his brightness was as the light; he had horns coming out of his hand: and there *was* the hiding of his power. Before him went the pestilence, and burning coals went forth at his feet. He stood, and measured the earth: he beheld, and drove asunder the nations; and the everlasting mountains were scattered, the perpetual hills did bow: his ways are everlasting (Hab 3.3-6).

The differences between the four accounts quoted above are in part the result of four distinct historical incidents, but also relate to the essential contrast between Hebrew prose narrative (Exodus and 1 Kings) and poetry (David's psalm and Habakkuk's prophecy). The historical narratives mention meteorological phenomena (wind, cloud, thunder, lightning, earthquake), while the poetic descriptions enhance these features by tracing them directly to divine activity (the wind is God's chariot, the clouds His pavilion, the thunder His voice, the lightning His arrows). Behind the poetry is a theological reality: every activity of the natural world, whatever its cold scientific analysis, is traceable to the God who created it. Hebrew thinking, undistracted by second causes, recognized that Jehovah was ever supreme, and that man's rebellion had in no sense dethroned Him from the government of His universe. The New Testament takes this further, identifying the Lord Jesus as the grand Superintendent of everything, "upholding all things by the word of his power" (Heb 1.3). He is the One in whom "all things hold together" (Col 1.17, ESV).

But let us return to Elihu's speech. With what Wiersbe fittingly calls "the mind of a scientist but the heart of a poet",[416] he first draws attention to **rainfall** (36.27-29). If anyone should question what evidences we have that "God is great", here is one worth pondering:

For he draweth up the drops of water, which distil in rain from his vapour: Which the skies pour down and drop upon man abundantly. Yea, can any understand the spreadings of the clouds, the thunderings of his pavilion? (36.27-29, RV).

Back in 5.9-10 Eliphaz touched briefly on the water cycle, but Elihu dwells lingeringly and lovingly on God's gracious provision for His creation. He shows a keen observation of atmospheric conditions and their impact. With its abundant water supply, planet earth has been uniquely designed for comfortable habitation. Sarfati reminds us of water's remarkable properties:

We drink it, wash in it, cook with it, swim in it and generally take it for granted. This clear, tasteless and odorless liquid is so much part of our lives that we hardly ever think about its amazing properties. We would die in a few days without water—and our bodies are 65% water. Water is necessary to dissolve essential minerals and oxygen, flush our bodies of waste products, and transport nutrients around the body where needed. Water is the only substance that has these properties. And as we shall see, it has many more fascinating features that suggest that it has been designed "just right" for life.[417]

Elihu's vocabulary is rich and diverse: water, rain, vapour, clouds, thunderings (the KJV "noise" translates a word suggestive of a tremendous clamour), and light (probably here lightning, as in 37.3).

It is passages like this which undermine any notion that the book of Job is a naïve, primitive document. Readers can hardly fail to register the speakers' impressive understanding of the natural world – and this long before the rise of modern science. Barfield's useful and enthralling *Why the Bible is Number 1* puts it all into context, and a relevant paragraph from his book was quoted above in the commentary on Job 26.

Focusing particularly on Job 28.24-27; 36.27-28 and 37.16, the hydraulics engineer Henry Morris comments that "there are several significant references in Job that are remarkably consistent with modern hydrology and meteorology". He goes on to elaborate in detail on the book's extraordinary scientific precision:

We now know that the global weights of air and water must be in critical relationship to each other, and to the earth as a whole, to maintain life on earth ... But how is all this accomplished? Water weighs much more than air, so how is it retained in the sky at all? Here is how: "He maketh small the drops of water: they pour down rain according to the vapour thereof: Which the clouds do drop and distil upon man abundantly" (Job 36.27-28).

Water is converted by solar energy into the vapour state. Since water vapour is lighter than air, the winds can first elevate, then transport the water from the oceans to the lands where it is needed. There, under the right conditions, the vapour can condense around dust particles, salt particles, or other nuclei of condensation.

When this happens, clouds are formed. Water vapour is invisible, whereas clouds are aggregations of liquid water droplets. But then the question again must be raised: how do the clouds stay aloft? Job [actually Elihu] rightly stressed the remarkable nature of this phenomenon. "Dost thou know the balancing of the clouds?" (Job 37.16). They did *not* know in his day ... The secret, however, is ... in the fact that "He maketh small the drops of water". The water droplets are indeed very small, and their weight is sustained by the drag force of the uprushing winds, as the air is pushed skyward due to temperature decrease with elevation.

How is this "balancing of the clouds" finally overcome, so that they can "pour down rain according to the vapour thereof?" The answer is given in Job 37.11. "By watering he wearieth the thick cloud." That is, the water droplets coalesce to form larger and larger drops, which finally become so large that their weight is greater than the drag forces of the uprushing atmospheric turbulence, causing them to fall to the ground as rain or snow.[418]

A recent article on the hydrologic cycle and Scripture concludes with this interesting series of questions:

> After 2,000 years of pondering, observing, and measuring, do we now fully understand how this global hydrologic system works? If we do, why then are rainfall predictions still estimates only? And why aren't scientists able to predict the severity of the next flood or drought? We still need to ask the question — will we ever *fully* understand this cycle? Perhaps we have already been given the answer to that question in Job: "Indeed, can anyone understand the spreading of clouds, the thunder from His canopy?" (Job 36.29)[419]

"Can any understand?" is Elihu's challenge to proud man in general and Job in particular. Behind it lies the unspoken corollary that, if God's ways with water are past finding out, how much more are His ways with men. How can anyone possibly complain about God's special providences when he cannot even fathom His day to day management of the natural world? On what basis dare Job object to God's dealings with him when he is ignorant of what we might call His ordinary marvels?

Continuing with his witness to divine power, Elihu turns from the wonders of the water cycle to the more overtly dramatic splendours of the **thunderstorm** (36.30-33):

> Behold, he spreadeth his light around him; and he covereth the bottom of the sea. For by these he judgeth the peoples; he giveth meat in abundance. He covereth his hands with the lightning; and giveth it a charge that it strike the mark. The noise thereof telleth concerning him, the cattle also concerning the storm that cometh up (36.30-33, RV).

So dazzling is the lightning flash that it seems to lay bare the bottoms of the ocean, for nothing can be hidden from God's gaze. It is by means of these natural phenomena – rains and tempests – that "he judgeth the peoples" and "giveth meat in abundance". God uses the weather systems He has built into His world both to punish sin and to provide for His creatures. Examples of judgment are not hard to find. The global flood of Noah's day stands out, but there have been lesser interventions: hail devastated both the Egyptians (Ex 9.23) and the Canaanites (Josh 10.11), while thunderstorms scattered the Philistines (1 Sam 7.10). Even in the benign conditions of the millennial earth the threat of drought will effectively keep in order any nations who foolishly consider rebellion (Zech 14.17-19). As for His beneficence, Paul informed the ignorant pagans of Lystra that God "left not himself without witness, in that he did good, and gave us rain from heaven, and fruitful seasons, filling our hearts with food and gladness" (Acts 14.17).

Not surprisingly, the lightning is catalogued among God's armoury of weapons. Delitzsch's comment on verse 32 paraphrases and clarifies the meaning:

> With both hands He seizes the substance of the lightning, fills them with it so that they are completely covered by it, and gives it the command (appoints it its goal), a sure aimer![420]

The final verse of this chapter heralds the even greater unfolding of magisterial divine works to follow. Reading it in the ESV brings out the underlying sense of breathless anticipation and stupefaction: "Its crashing declares his presence; the cattle also declare that he rises" (36.33, ESV). Claps of thunder announce the nearness of God; even the brute creation seems instinctively to scent the approach of a distant storm before ever it breaks.

If the beasts of the field respond to the seasonal provisions God has built into the natural world, how much more should man, gifted with the capacity to acknowledge and adore his Creator! Chapter 37 begins, then, with a fitting though unexpected confession by Elihu of personal trepidation:

> Aye, my heart trembleth at this also, and leapeth up out of its place (37.1, JND).

"This" refers to the gathering storm which is beginning to sweep over the sky even as he speaks. "Trembleth" (2729) is first used of old Isaac's physical perturbation on realising that he had blessed the wrong son (Gen 27.33). It is also used of Joseph's brothers' anxiety on discovering their money unaccountably returned in their sacks (Gen 42.28), and of Israel's terror on hearing the loud trumpet blast at Sinai (Ex 19.16). In the KJV Elihu admits that his heart is "moved" (5425). The word, according to Strong, means "to *jump*, that is, *be* violently *agitated*", and is first used of creeping insects in Leviticus 11.21. As the tempest approaches, Elihu's dread becomes palpable. Much earlier in the book Eliphaz referred to a visionary experience when "fear came upon me, and trembling, which made all my bones to shake" (4.14). It sounds highly dramatic, but we have only his word for the historicity of that eerie dream. Elihu, however, is quivering with fright at the approach of a genuine whirlwind which will break over Job's head in chapter 38. Lest anyone think that, because of New Testament revelation, God has diminished His ineffable majesty, the writer to the Hebrews puts us right. Believers are to "have grace, whereby we may serve God acceptably with reverence and godly fear: For our God is a consuming fire" (Heb 12.28-29). In all dispensations reverential awe is the correct response to God.

In verses 2 to 5 of chapter 37, Elihu, having pulled himself together, concentrates his attention on **God's voice in the storm** (37.2-5), urging Job to

> Hear attentively the roar of his voice, and the murmur going forth from

his mouth. He sendeth it forth under the whole heaven, and his lightning unto the ends of the earth. After it a voice roareth: he thundereth with the voice of his excellency, and holdeth not back the flashes when his voice is heard. God thundereth marvellously with his voice, doing great things which we do not comprehend (37.2-5, JND).

This is both a powerful description of atmospheric disturbance, with flashes of lightning and subsequent rumbles of thunder (note "after it" in verse 4), and a testimony to a God who deigns to make Himself known. The key word is "voice" (6963), which turns up five times in this brief passage. The Hebrew term appears twenty-one times in Job. It is used first of the friends who, on seeing Job, "lifted up their voice, and wept" (2.12), and last in Jehovah's challenge, "canst thou thunder with a voice like him?" (40.9). The ostensible subject matter may be the thunder which increasingly drowns out Elihu's speech, but behind it all is the voice of God. Though possessing no vocal chords, creation has much to say:

Day unto day uttereth speech, and night unto night sheweth knowledge. There is no speech and there are no words, yet their voice is heard. Their line is gone out through all the earth, and their language to the extremity of the world (Ps 19.2-4, JND).

The message of creation, nevertheless, is limited. The natural world testifies to its Maker's power. Inbuilt human conscience takes us further, bearing witness to man's damaged condition, while the specific code of conduct given to Israel spells out the wholesale guilt of the entire human race. Only in the Lord Jesus Christ, however, is there a comprehensive and conclusive disclosure of God. Job and his contemporaries lived before Israel received its law, before the Son entered the world, and yet they possessed a sharp awareness of God handed down by oral tradition and supplemented by the witness of creation. The Hebrew psalmist had no doubt that God's voice in nature was deafening:

The voice of the Lord is upon the waters: the God of glory thundereth: the Lord is upon many waters. The voice of the Lord is powerful; the voice of the Lord is full of majesty. The voice of the Lord breaketh the cedars; yea, the Lord breaketh the cedars of Lebanon. He maketh them also to skip like a calf; Lebanon and Sirion like a young unicorn. The voice of the Lord divideth the flames of fire. The voice of the Lord shaketh the wilderness; the Lord shaketh the wilderness of Kadesh. The voice of the Lord maketh the hinds to calve, and discovereth the forests: and in his temple doth every one speak of his glory. The Lord sitteth upon the flood; yea, the Lord sitteth King for ever (Ps 29.3-10).

David's epic description of a savage storm sweeping through the land from Lebanon to Kadesh perhaps sounds more academic and contrived than Elihu's, but the import is the same. In the universe He made and daily sustains, God still speaks. Only the wilfully deaf fail to hear His voice.

The testimony of Scripture is that God is not a silent, hidden God. Yet at the same time it has to be admitted that His public works – even in the visible sphere of creation – remain beyond the full understanding of men. As Delitzsch rightly remarks:

> God's mighty acts, with respect to the connection between cause and effect and the employment of means, transcend our comprehension.[421]

This is the God who does "great things" (37.5). The psalmist uses the same word to describe Jehovah's miraculous historical interventions on behalf of His people:

> The works of the Lord are great, sought out of all them that have pleasure therein. His work is honourable and glorious: and his righteousness endureth for ever. He hath made his wonderful works to be remembered: the Lord is gracious and full of compassion (Ps 111.2-4).

Elihu tells us that God does "great things which we do not comprehend" (37.5, JND), but the psalmist maintains that they are "sought out" and "remembered". There is no contradiction. It is possible to ponder the works of God without in any sense fathoming them; those who have benefited from His marvels will keep them in mind, even though what they have experienced is but the tip of the iceberg of divine greatness. It was Job who, having listed some natural wonders earlier in the book, had to conclude that

> these are but the outskirts of his ways, and how small a whisper do we hear of him! But the thunder of his power who can understand? (26.14, ESV).

Elihu moves on to **wintery storms** which batter the landscape (37.6-10):

> For he saith to the snow, Fall on the earth! and to the pouring rain, even the pouring rains of his might. He sealeth up the hand of every man; that all men may know his work. And the wild beast goeth into its lair, and they remain in their dens. From the chamber of the south cometh the whirlwind; and cold from the winds of the north. By the breath of God ice is given; and the breadth of the waters is straitened (37.6-10, JND).

The "treasures of the snow" (to be taken up later in 38.22) exemplify some of the many things "we cannot comprehend" (37.5). Comments Hartley:

> Sometimes in the hills of Palestine the winter rains turn into falling snow. The downpour is a marvel, and the seldom seen snow is even more wondrous. God commands the snow to fall to the ground just as his word orders the rain to descend in torrents.[422]

As the snowfall demonstrates God's power, so it highlights human vulnerability, bringing man's normal activities to a halt. There is nothing like a heavy overnight blizzard to transform the countryside, terminating human business and confronting people with a phenomenon over which they have no control. The all-embracing blanket of snow which has interfered with their plans should cause men to acknowledge God's hand. Animals instinctively recognise the need to shelter from these inhospitable elements, and "remain in their dens", sometimes preserved in a state of hibernation. Out of what Elihu poetically describes as God's chambers come freezing winds, themselves imagined as divine breath, bringing frost and ice, so that stretches of water become suddenly "straitened" or "frozen fast" (ESV). Fausset notes that the word is "physically accurate; frost *compresses* or *contracts* the expanded liquid into a congealed mass".

This survey of various modes of precipitation concludes with a passage about Gods **power and purpose** (37.11-13):

> Also with plentiful moisture he loadeth the thick clouds, his light dispels the cloud; And they are turned every way by his guidance, that they may do whatsoever he commandeth them upon the face of the circuit of the earth, Whether he cause it to come as a rod, or for his land, or in mercy (37.11-13, JND).

Elihu's fascinating insight into the mysterious way the clouds bear moisture across the face of the earth should not divert us from his more important theological lesson: whatever the clouds do, they do at God's bidding. Divine orders to the elements and the lower creation are heeded without fail. The book of Jonah records Jehovah's use of "a great wind" and "a mighty tempest" (Jonah 1.4), "a great fish" (Jonah 1.17; 2.10), "a gourd" (Jonah 4.6), "a worm" (Jonah 4.7), and "a vehement east wind" (Jonah 4.8) in the infallible accomplishment of His will – yet the book as a whole places centre-stage a wilfully disobedient, disgruntled servant. Man alone, it seems, is capable of flagrant insubordination. The clouds do God's bidding in fulfilling His purpose. Elihu lists three reasons for the coming (or, presumably, the withholding) of rain: "as a rod, or for his land, or in mercy". Taken at face value, the three reasons tell us that God uses rain as a rod of correction against sinful people (in Isaiah 10.5 the word describes Assyria as "the rod of mine anger"), as a means of blessing for the thirsty land itself, or as a merciful provision for man's needs. "Mercy" translates that lovely Hebrew word (2617) which is variously rendered in the KJV "kindness" (Gen 20.13), "goodness" (Ex 34.6), "favour" (Esth 2.17), "pity" (Job 6.14), and "lovingkindness" (Ps 17.7). God's regular marvels for the maintenance of the earth are expressions of His tender mercy.

It is the middle reason for rainfall which is perhaps the most unexpected: "for his land". Zuck comments:

> All those phenomena of nature in autumn and winter are purposeful and causal, not haphazard. God may use them for various purposes (37.13):

to bring judgment on some … or to benefit the earth, or as a means of showing His loyalty-love to man … The second reason has no relationship to man; God often does in nature things that man knows nothing about (sending rain on the desert is only one example).[423]

"The earth is the Lord's", therefore He does with it and to it as He will. This is important. There is a connection between God's rule over the natural world and His personal dealings with men. Smick remarks pointedly that "some things that God does have no other explanation than that they please Him".[424] This is a truth Job will eventually come to acknowledge.

Much about our marvellously habitable planet, stocked with a rich diversity of life and dazzling kinds of beauty, must be simply for God's own delight. The ocean depths are beyond the normal man's reach, but they are nonetheless packed with fascinating life. The *Answers in Genesis* website offers the following example:

Before modern cameras and technology, the inky blackness of the deep barred its mysteries from human eyes. But now these wonders are coming to light. For the first time, our generation is privileged to behold this alien world, teeming with life.

As the *Johnson Sea-Link* submersible plows through the dark water, hundreds of feet below the surface, lights flash constantly all over the front of the camera. Surprised by the alien craft, tiny creatures spark and flash in protest. Ninety percent of deep-sea creatures may produce some sort of light.

This light amazes scientists. On land only a few creatures, such as fireflies and glowworms, possess this miraculous ability. But in the deep, where sunlight never penetrates, God has designed a variety of alternative light sources.[425]

The deeper we dig into God's handiwork the more we uncover. As a young man, the seventeenth-century poet George Herbert wrote a sonnet deploring the wasted labours commonly spent celebrating human charms. Instead of hymning their female paramours, poets should concentrate upon God, whose unsullied loveliness shines out of His works. Whereas human good looks are ultimately a washout, God never disappoints:

> Sure Lord, there is enough in thee to dry
> Oceans of ink; for, as the Deluge did
> Cover the earth, so doth thy Majesty:
> Each cloud distills thy praise, and doth forbid
> Poets to turn it to another use.
> Roses and lilies speak thee; and to make
> A pair of cheeks of them, is thy abuse.
> Why should I women's eyes for crystal take?
> Such poor invention burns in their low mind

> Whose fire is wild, and doth not upward go
> To praise, and on thee, Lord, some ink bestow.
> Open the bones, and you shall nothing find
> In the best face but filth; when Lord, in thee
> The beauty lies in the discovery.[426]

Those who have been redeemed by the precious blood of Christ will agree that the more we probe the work of Calvary, the more reasons we find for glad thanksgiving.

By now, Elihu is approaching the close of his speech. But first, for Job's benefit, he pauses to draw together the threads of his argument:

> Hearken unto this, Job; stand still and discern the wondrous works of God. Dost thou know how God hath disposed them, and how he causeth the lightning of his cloud to flash? Dost thou know about the balancings of the clouds, the wondrous works of him that is perfect in knowledge? How thy garments become warm when he quieteth the earth by the south wind? Hast thou with him spread out the sky, firm, like a molten mirror? Teach us what we shall say unto him! We cannot order our words by reason of darkness. Shall it be told him if I would speak? if a man so say, surely he shall be swallowed up (37.14-20, JND).

His earnest exhortation looks back over the past two chapters in which he has scanned God's control over nature. What Elihu is saying is this: just to pause and ponder God's created universe is to confront mysteries far beyond our imagination. "Consider" translates a Hebrew word (995) associated with wisdom, understanding and knowledge. It is used of Joseph, a man "discreet [995] and wise" (Gen 41.39), of Israel as an "understanding [995] people" (Deut 4.6), of Eli who "perceived [995] that the Lord had called the child" (1 Sam 3.8). But to fathom even the outer fringes of creation requires a mental capacity beyond the scope of fallen man. To "consider" is a serious business.

In order to demolish Job's self-confidence, Elihu bombards him with questions which he cannot answer – an interrogation which will continue in earnest when Jehovah takes over: "Dost thou know ... Dost thou know ... Hast thou?" (37.15-16,18). The challenges are very specific. Can Job understand how God arranges for the lightning to flash out of the dark cloud (37.15)? Does Job comprehend how clouds are so poised in the heavens that they carry their load of moisture great distances, to discharge it at the appropriate time (37.16)? Coming down to more mundane matters, does he even know why his clothes warm up as his body is heated by sultry southern winds (37.17)? Has he the ability to spread out the lustrous shining sky, so firmly secured like a metal mirror above him (37.18)? In ancient times mirrors were made not of glass but of brightly polished metal (Ex 38.8). "Spread out" (7554) translates a verb used elsewhere of beating out gold leaf for the high priest's ephod (Ex 39.3), and of the "broad plates" covering the altar, plates made from the two hundred and fifty brazen censers of Korah's abortive rebellion (Num 16.39). It also appears, in a creation context, of God who "stretched out [7554] the earth above the waters" (Ps 136.6). Elihu's carefully chosen language reminds us of the exquisite divine handiwork which so perfectly, so skilfully, so unerringly, fitted every component of the cosmos.

However, supposing for one moment that Job possessed the brainpower to master the mysteries of the universe, then (a piece of blistering irony, this), let him "Teach us what we shall say unto him; for we cannot order our speech by reason of darkness" (37.19). Man cannot peer unblinkingly into the glory of the sun, which dazzles and disorientates all who attempt to gaze on it. How much less can he contemplate the glory of the almighty Creator Himself? How then can God's creatures dispute His ways with them? What can man possibly say to such a God? Job, we remember, has been agitating for an interview with his Maker, at times seeming confident that he could hold his own:

> Surely I would speak to the Almighty, and I desire to reason with God (13.3).

> Then call thou, and I will answer: or let me speak, and answer thou me (13.22).

> I would declare unto him the number of my steps; as a prince would I go near unto him (31.37).

But presuming to debate with God, says Elihu, places one in deadly peril of being "swallowed up" (37.20). It is a vivid word with plenty of associations. It makes us think of the fat ears of corn in Pharaoh's dream which were devoured by the thin ears (Gen 41.7), Pharaoh's magicians' rods swallowed up by Aaron's (Ex 7.12), Korah and his supporters engulfed by the earth (Num 16.30ff), and Jonah gobbled down by a great fish (Jonah 1.17). The examples are not encouraging. Elihu's message is this: "to attempt to argue a case with God in self-defence would only result in self-destruction".[427] The only possible response to the great Creator is wonder and worship.

The coda of Elihu's paean of praise announces – with intensifying consternation – the evidently visible progress of the Lord of the universe as He draws near to Job. That glitteringly radiant cloud approaching from the north is now almost overhead:

> And now men see not the light which is bright in the skies: but the wind passeth, and cleanseth them. Out of the north cometh golden splendour: God hath upon him terrible majesty. Touching the Almighty, we can not find him out; he is excellent in power: and in judgment and plenteous justice he will not afflict. Men do therefore fear him: he regardeth not any that are wise of heart (37.21-24, RV).

When clouds cover the sun its brilliance is veiled; but once the winds scatter these obstructions it shines out all the more impressively. This is both an observation and a parable. The analogy to Job's situation is unmistakable. His adverse circumstances have clouded his judgment so that he has come to doubt the rightness of God's dealings with him; but when the mists have rolled away he will see clearly. For believers of the church age the obscuring clouds of anxiety and uncertainty, which often darken our pathway, will be dispersed with the coming of the Lord Jesus for His people. Then will "the day dawn, and the day star arise in [our] hearts" (2 Pet 1.19), bringing a fullness of joy never known before. By contrast, Job will shortly enjoy the blessing of restored earthly prosperity, which is neither the expectation nor the desire of those whose citizenship is in heaven.

At this point Elihu's parable suddenly becomes reality, because his language registers the terrifying approach of a theophany. The very God about whom Job and his friends have been speaking for the past thirty-seven chapters is intruding on the scene in person. The word the KJV renders "fair weather" appears nearly four hundred times in the Old Testament and is everywhere translated in the KJV "gold" or "golden" – except here. It depicts the glittering royal pageantry of Jehovah's glory-filled presence, hence the aptness of the RV's phrase "golden splendour" (taken up by the ASV and the ESV). God's majesty is truly "terrible" (3372), inspiring tremulous awe in all who behold it. The Hebrew word first appears in fallen Adam's confession, "I heard thy voice in the garden, and I was afraid [3372]" (Gen 3.10), and last in Malachi's prophecy of "the great and dreadful [3372] day of the Lord" (Mal 4.5). As Job well knows (6.4), the terrors of God are no flights of poetic fancy but hard fact. So overwhelming is His presence that Elihu is forced hastily to curtail his conclusion, condensing into a mere two verses a summary of what Job needs to know about God.

What then is his final appeal to Job? It is a reminder of what he argued at the beginning (36.3-5) when foregrounding certain divine attributes:

> The Almighty, we cannot find him out: excellent in power, and in judgment, and in abundance of justice, he doth not afflict. Men do therefore fear him: he respecteth not any that are wise of heart (37.23-24, JND).

It is imperative that Job realise these great facts about the God with whom he has to do. He is the Almighty (a name of infinite sufficiency), and in Himself beyond human understanding. We should not be surprised when we cannot make sense of His dealings with individual men. His power is excellent (the word is rendered "great" in 36.26), but so too is His commitment to judgment and righteousness; as a consequence, it is inconceivable that He should ever oppress His creatures. Jeremiah uses the same word ("afflict") in Lamentations. Admitting that God has brought Jerusalem low, he goes on to reassure the reader that "he does not willingly afflict or grieve the children of men" (Lam 3.33, ESV). That is to say, if God brings hardship it is not for the pleasure of causing misery but with the end in view that His people be led to a proper state of soul. The conclusion is that He is to be feared (the same word as "terrible" in verse 22). Those who boast in their wisdom count for nothing with Him. This may be Elihu's ironic doff of the cap to the three friends who so pitifully failed to help Job, or it may be a final tilt at Job himself. Possibly it is both. After all, the entire book has been, in a manner of speaking, a battle of wits between pious representatives of ancient and traditional wisdom. If, however, human wisdom at its best cannot comprehend God, how then should man behave towards his Creator? Isaiah offers the answer, passing on to men the wonderful promise of Jehovah: "to this man will I look, even to him that is poor and of a contrite spirit, and trembleth at my word" (Is 66.2). Poor, contrite, trembling – Job has not yet been reduced to this extremity of self-abasement. But after the next few chapters he will be. And that, for him, will be the gateway into blessing.

Over the years Elihu has had many critics. Henry Morris becomes so incensed as to charge him with distortion, deception and Satanically-inspired delusion.[428] Yet, allowing for his admitted youth and undeniable long-windedness, he has much to say that is relevant to Job's situation. Instead of positing terrible past sins for which Job is being punished, he concentrates on the rash utterances to which Job has given voice. Instead of constantly rubbing in the truth of divine retribution on the wicked, he has offered a fuller and more balanced account of a God who is both just and gracious, mighty and merciful. Instead of going round in circles like the friends, he has – unconsciously of course – steadily paved the way for the entrance of Jehovah, who will implicitly endorse the young man's strategy by continuing a similar line of interrogation.

Kelly, in his very best account of the book of Job, passes this superb comment:

> Elihu brings in, as far as man could in that day, the light of God. He shows that, instead of there being mere judicial dealing, there is a righteous and gracious discipline on God's part, which, as it deals with the unconverted to break him down, and save his soul, so also it addresses itself to the converted for his correction where he has slipped aside, and encourages him where he needs to be quickened in his pace while following the Lord. And so he spreads out before him and vindicates the worthy ways of God, reproving Job's self-righteousness and impatience and irreverence, but eschewing any such imputations on Job as his friends had allowed; for we have seen Job in the agony of grief, again and again giving way to the sense of desertion by God, and then uttering words rash and violent, but soon again asking pardon after each fresh outbreak, when stung to the quick by the deeply cutting words of his friends — the more cutting because they seemed quiet, but not the less severely wounding to his open and generous spirit. In Elihu we have had quite another tone and judgment — a man who does not spare impropriety, or conceal its heinous consequences; but who can see in the darkest troubles the gracious end of God in His ways, even with the unconverted, and particularly so with His saints.[429]

Since this is the last appearance of Elihu (for he is excluded from the epilogue), perhaps it is appropriate to listen once more to his final word, as it stands in Delitzsch's translation:

> Therefore men regard Him with reverence,
> He hath no regard for all the wise of heart.[430]

How right it is, whatever our circumstances, to hold the living God in the utmost awe, knowing that human intelligence is incapable of passing judgment on His actions or entering into the purposes of His heart. Godly fear is not the dread which forces a slave to grovel before a stern master but the confident respect of a child in the presence of a loving Father. Every believer faces situations when all he can do is wait in humble submission, and worship. As the Lord said to Peter – whose instinctive zeal for His Master's honour shrank from accepting such lowly service as Christ was about to perform – "What I do thou knowest not now; but thou shalt know hereafter" (Jn 13.7). "Hereafter" we shall doubtless be able to comprehend much that is currently hidden, and rejoice in the all-embracing wisdom of God. As Delitzsch rightly observes,

> since by His nature God can never do wrong, all human wrangling before God is a sinful advance against the mystery of divine guidance, under which he should rather humbly bow.[431]

Practical as always, Robinson notes that

> the tendency of suffering and trial [is] to draw our attention to ourselves [rather] than our Maker. In dwelling on our own griefs we are apt to forget His glory.[432]

This has been Job's problem: his sorrows have lured him into understandable but inappropriate self-absorption. Over the last chapter, Elihu's restorative theme has been the magnificence of God's glory displayed in the created universe. The New Testament believer, however, has fuller information than that available to Elihu and Job, because the same "God, who commanded the light to shine out of darkness, hath shined in our hearts, to give the light of the knowledge of the glory of God in the face of Jesus Christ" (2 Cor 4.6). When the child of God feels bewildered and battered, when there seems no light in the gloom, when all explanations fail, then is the time to remember the story of Job – but even more to marvel at the completeness of divine glory radiating from the person of the Lord Jesus Christ.

SECTION 26
Dialogue: Job 4 – 42.6
Climax: Job 38 – 42.6
Jehovah's Speech: Job 38.1 – 42.6
Part One: Job 38.1 – 40.5

This is the great heart-stopping moment in the book of Job. The God about whom so much has been said, who has stood silently in the shadows behind the arguments which have raged to and fro, and on whom Job has persistently and sometimes petulantly called, at last comes forward to speak.

We should take particular note that the One who now takes the stage is specifically announced as "the LORD", that is to say, Jehovah. This personal name of God is found thirty-two times in the book of Job, but (apart from 12.9) only in the first two and the final five chapters. It is a name of supreme authority, identifying God as eternally immutable, self-existent and self-sufficient. It is appropriate that such a glorious name dominates the book's narrative framework, for it testifies to inflexible divine control. Whatever Job may have feared, the Lord has always had His hand firmly on the tiller.

The exact meaning of this ineffable name is spelled out in Exodus, when the Lord responds to Moses's anxious query about how he is to introduce God to the enslaved and demoralized Israelites: "God said unto Moses, I AM THAT I AM: and he said, Thus shalt thou say unto the children of Israel, I AM hath sent me unto you" (Ex 3.14). This is the special name of covenant faithfulness towards the elect nation, a name which threads its way through the Old Testament, witnessing to God's reliability despite His people's failures. However, Christians hearing that name are reminded of One who announced to scandalised Jews, "Verily, verily, I say unto you, Before Abraham was, I am" (Jn 8.58). John 1.18 teaches that all disclosures of God have been revelations of the Son; therefore we pause to marvel that the God who now makes Himself known to His much maligned and bewildered servant Job is none other than our Lord Jesus. The Creator whom Job revered, the Judge from whom he sought vindication, the Mediator for whom he instinctively yearned, the Redeemer in whom he trusted – they all unite in the one person of Christ. Job, of course, did not realise this; he was living in advance of the incarnation. But Christians delight to hear in the voice of Jehovah the well-loved tones of the Son.

Though Job has long pleaded for such a supernatural response from heaven (9.14-16; 10.2; 13.3,20-22; 19.7; 23.3-7; 30.20), and though Elihu's recent words have unconsciously paved the way for it, when it comes – heralded by a monumental tempest – the intervention is nonetheless electrifying. That the book has in one sense anticipated this moment should not blind us to the stupendous condescension of the living God in conversing personally with one of His creatures. If that be true, how much more amazing it is to consider that, when the fullness of time was come, the Son of God took on Himself manhood as the final expositor of God's heart.

Let us first of all approach this climactic section of Job in the broadest terms, using five headings: its outline, its omissions, its object, its outcome, and its operation.

As to its **outline,** this grand culminating speech falls naturally into two substantial parts (38.2 – 40.2; and 40.6 – 41.34), the first of which is framed by a brief narration (38.1 and 40.1) while the second is introduced by a terse prologue (40.6). In between the two parts, and after the second, comes a short response by Job (40.3-5; 42.1-6). Each part of Jehovah's speech subdivides into two major components. The first part comprises an overview of God's inanimate creation (38.4-38), followed by an investigation of specific examples of the animate creation (38.39 – 39.30). The second, after an ironic challenge to Job's ability to manage this vast universe, devotes itself entirely to a close-quarters consideration of two great specimens of God's handiwork, behemoth on the land (40.15-24) and leviathan in the sea (41.1-34). These are selected for their terrifying size and magnificence, as "the chief of the ways of God" (40.19) and "king over all the children of pride" (41.34). The language throughout is spectacularly concrete and vivid, gripping the reader with its sharp attention to detail.

As we might expect from the Creator of an orderly universe, the speech is both methodical and compelling. Perhaps, however, the most immediately surprising feature is its **omissions**. We are bound to notice what Jehovah conspicuously does *not* say. For a start, He neither addresses nor even mentions Job's friends. He does not answer any of Job's anxious questions or explain why all the disasters of the book have befallen him. He does not pull back the veil from the unseen world to give an account of the counsel in heaven which led to his sufferings. He does not console Job with the knowledge that he was being held up as an exemplar of such outstanding righteousness that God trusted him to endure Satan's worst assaults. Nor does He soothe the patriarch's wounds by offering a comforting reminder of His love and tender mercy. He does not say to Job, "Look, just as I gave you abundant blessings in the past so, for My own wise purposes, I also handed out the bruises you have had to bear". No – what He does is bring Job down to earth with a shattering sequence of questions about His own infinite creatorial might and majesty.

The irony is evident in the first two verses: "Then the Lord answered Job … and said, Who is this that darkeneth counsel by words without knowledge?" (38.1-2). In other words, contrary to all expectation, God's answer is itself a question – the first, in reality, of a series of almost eighty questions, all aimed primarily at Job (not his friends) and all designed to test him in the very doctrine of divine creative power about which he has so often spoken. Textbook theology is suddenly confronted with solid and staggering reality.

It is important to keep these omissions in mind. Too often in our reading we fail to register what Scripture actually says because we are so obsessed with our own ideas of what it ought to say. Let us take just one example. The book of the Acts, the only inspired historical account of New Testament gospel preaching we possess, does not exactly endorse some of the formulaic notions often propounded about the necessary ingredients of an evangelistic message. For a start, no one preaches specifically about God's love (the word does not appear in the book, save in reference to "our beloved Barnabas and Paul" in Acts 15.25). Further, no one mentions the blood of Christ in a gospel context (Acts

20.28 is Paul speaking to believers). Even more startling is the fact that, as far as the recorded messages are concerned, the exact way the death of Christ deals with sins is never explained. Of course, His death is regularly alluded to as the prelude to His historical resurrection, which stands as the stupendous testimony to divine satisfaction with His person (Acts 2.24; 3.15; 4.2,10; 10.41; 13.30,34; 17.3,31; 25.19; 26.23), while His crucifixion is adduced as an evidence of human wickedness (Acts 2.23,36; 4.10; 7.52; 13.28). Furthermore, it is through Him and Him alone that "forgiveness of sins" is made available to those who believe (Acts 5.31; 13.38; 26.18). But where do any of the apostolic preachers disclose precisely how the work of Calvary, in the language of Paul, enables God to be "just, and the justifier of him which believeth in Jesus" (Rom 3.26)? Perhaps they did indeed include these matters, but the Spirit of God has not elected to record their words. The Acts provides a selective account of gospel preaching from the outside, as it were, from the point of view of the unsaved listener, whereas Paul's Roman epistle examines it from the inside, from the point of view of those who have already come into the good of God's great salvation. And it is in that context and to that audience that the great doctrine of the atoning death of the Lord Jesus Christ is fully explored. This of course is not to say that today's preaching must be restricted to exactly the kind of presentation found in the Acts, but simply to make the point that we need to be cautious about dogmatism. Inherited traditions need constantly to be measured against the infallible Word.

Returning, then, to God's personal interview with Job, it is imperative to allow Him to say precisely what He says – no more and no less. This highlights another unlooked-for feature of the following chapters: Jehovah announces nothing new. He adds no profound novelty to the debate, contributes no startling revelation, fills in no gaps, injects no new argument. Rather, He carries on, albeit on a far grander level, from where Elihu left off – and even Elihu has been treading in the well-worn footsteps of Job and his friends. All of them, to a greater or lesser extent, have touched on the greatness of God as seen in the created universe (9.4-10; 12.7-10,13-25; 26.5-14; 28.23-27). But have they the faintest idea in practice of what that greatness entails? Davidson puts it very well when he claims that God's design is "to make [Job] feel the truth which he knows".[433] The tantalisingly brief glimpses Scripture affords of God's creative power in, say, the first chapter of Genesis and Psalm 104, are – to say the least – amazingly restrained. An intellectual awareness of the glory of God is by no means the same as a personal encounter with the God of glory.

What, then, is the great **object** of the speech? It is, initially, to point out Job's ignorance and impudence. His ignorance is addressed with the stinging rhetorical question, "Who is this that darkeneth counsel by words without knowledge?" (38.2); his impudence is exposed with the challenge, "Wilt thou also disannul my judgment? wilt thou condemn me, that thou mayest be righteous?" (40.8). Job has not only dared to contend with God; in a hasty zeal to defend his cherished innocence against the multiple accusations of his friends, he has even charged Him with injustice. A personal examination of Job is therefore the supreme object of God's intervention – but it is not the sole object. Although the pronouns are singular ("thou") rather than plural, it is, I think, worth bearing in mind that Jehovah speaks to Job in the audience of his companions. There seems little doubt that they hear something of the voice from heaven and the response of Job on the earth – otherwise the Lord's special words to three of them in chapter 42 lack any clear connection with what has preceded. Job responds correctly to Jehovah's interrogation; they, too, must learn to submit to His ways in requesting the much-abused patriarch to intercede with God on their behalf. This is both for their blessing and, significantly, to bring about the triumphant termination of Job's ordeal.

Although God speaks to Job from out of a mighty whirlwind, this is not to destroy him, as he feared earlier in the debate. "He breaketh me with a tempest, and multiplieth my wounds without cause" (9.17) is the complaint of a man who sees himself like a tree stripped bare of its foliage by the devastating force of a hurricane. That, of course, was picture language; when the real tempest bursts upon Job it is designed to bring him to a proper state of soul before God.

That is exactly what it achieves. The eventual **outcome** of the speech is tersely recorded. Job, the most vociferous of speakers, is first of all reduced to comparative silence (40.3-5), and then to total submission in the presence of God (42.1-6). This scene perfectly illustrates the unfailing ability of God's spoken word to accomplish its end. Isaiah's language springs to mind:

> as the rain cometh down, and the snow from heaven, and returneth not thither, but watereth the earth, and maketh it bring forth and bud, that it may give seed to the sower, and bread to the eater: So shall my word be that goeth forth out of my mouth: it shall not return unto me void, but it shall accomplish that which I please, and it shall prosper in the thing whereto I sent it (Is 55.10-11).

"As the rain cometh down … So shall my word". The analogy is particularly apt when we consider the storm raging in the background and the Lord's later allusions to the unceasing providential care with which He meets the needs of His creation.

The **operation** of the speech (that is to say, the precise way it works) is to confront Job with sharply specific realities in the natural world, realities of which he already has some knowledge but the final meaning of which he has never properly fathomed. All testify to the incomprehensible power and wisdom of God. If Job does not have the capacity to understand the basic principles underlying what we call natural phenomena, how can he possibly dare to pass judgment on the reasons behind God's moral government? In Kelly's words, "did he who could not explain God's least things presume to judge the deepest part of His ways and designs?"[434] Creation, properly understood, silences our complaints. A contributor to a symposium entitled *Transformed by the Evidence* puts it like this: "We are imperfect, sinful, limited human beings with a short life span, and we have no business challenging God and telling Him how to run His universe".[435]

The lesson is short and sharp – and accomplishes its end. Jehovah's intervention is not what Job anticipated, but it fully meets his need and soothes his soul. Indeed, it brings the best out of him. When we request the God who is "able to do exceeding abundantly above all that we ask or think" (Eph 3.20) to move on our behalf, He may elect to do so in ways far beyond our feeble imaginings.

> **The Request and the Response**
> "I desire the Almighty to answer"
> Was what Job in his misery said;
> But God's voice overturned his requirement
> By insisting *he* answer instead.
>
> All his difficulties and misgivings
> Were reduced to inconsequence now,
> For Jehovah's astonishing challenge
> Was the question to Job, "Where wast *thou*?"
>
> When God laid the earth's solid foundations,
> When He opened the gates of the sea,
> When the day spring arose in the morning
> And light dawned - as for Job, where was *he*?
>
> It reduces our gripes and our grumbles,
> It gives strength to continue to plod,
> If we learn, whatsoever befall us,
> To submit to the greatness of God.

The first part of Jehovah's response (38.1 – 40.5) may be divided into four sections as follows:

> 1. Introduction: 38.1-3
> 2. Interrogation (i) – God's Inanimate Creation: 38.4-38
> 3. Interrogation (ii) – God's Animal Creation: 38.39 – 39.30
> 4. Interchange: 40.1-5.

Introduction: 38.1-3

In Exodus 19 the piercing sound of a trumpet long and loud preceded Jehovah's voice on Mount Sinai; at the same location years later there was (one presumes) a thrilling silence eventually broken by that unexpectedly "still small voice" (1 Kings 19.12). But here the Lord publicly signals His royal approach with a whirlwind, out of which He speaks. The term "whirlwind" (591) appears only twice in Job (38.1; 40.1), but elsewhere in the Old Testament twenty-two times. It is first used of the extraordinary means by which God took Elijah bodily up into heaven (2 Kings 2.1), and thereafter turns up in the Psalms and prophetic books as, for instance, an external evidence of divine power (Ps 107.25,29; 148.8) or judgment on the ungodly (Ps 83.15; Is 29.6; 40.24). It is only appropriate that the God who is about to exhibit something of His majesty to Job should introduce Himself in so impressive a fashion.

The fact that the Lord addresses Job directly ("the Lord answered Job") should scotch any notion (such as that proposed by the Elihu-phobic Henry Morris) that His first words allude to the last speaker. It is not Elihu who is in the spotlight, but Job. Certainly Job is in no doubt that he is being singled out as one who has obscured God's counsels by uttering ignorant words, because in 42.3 he fully acknowledges this description of himself. His touchy and ill-informed accusations have created a smoke screen hindering any real appreciation of the wisdom of God's ways with His universe. "Counsel" (6098) refers in the broadest manner to the divine purposes. The word appears in the poetic and prophetic books, describing Jehovah's programme:

The counsel of the Lord standeth for ever, the thoughts of his heart to all generations (Ps 33.11).

Counsel is mine, and sound wisdom: I am understanding; I have strength (Prov 8.14).

There are many devices in a man's heart; nevertheless the counsel of the Lord, that shall stand (Prov 19.21).

This is the purpose [6098] that is purposed upon the whole earth: and this is the hand that is stretched out upon all the nations (Is 14.26).

It is something of a shock to discover that our unguarded words may either highlight or obscure the glory of God's plans for His people. The book of Job, like the letter of James, majors on the potential of the tongue for good and ill. The particular focus of Jehovah's interest in this speech is thus clearly defined from the start: Job is not being accused of sinful actions but of an improper attitude towards God betrayed in his conversation. Elihu's analysis was correct.

The man who has long pleaded with God to answer him now finds himself at the receiving end of a colossal cosmic quiz. He must prepare himself, like the sturdy man he is, to take Jehovah's test on creation truth. The Lord gives him credit for being a battle-hardened veteran by using, not the word associating man with the dust from which he was made (120, as in Genesis 1.26), nor the term suggestive of human frailty (582 – translated "mortal man" in Job 4.17), but that word (1397) which means "properly a *valiant* man or *warrior*" (Strong's Concordance).

But this *viva voce* challenge is not simply an examination of bald facts. As we have already seen, Job is well versed in the evidences of God's universal power (9.5-10; 12.7-10; 26.7-14). But it is one thing to recite a catalogue of miracles and quite another to realise their personal significance in daily life. The word "answer" (3045) appears seventy times in Job, predominantly translated in the KJV by "know". In Jehovah's speech it is rendered "understanding" (38.4), and turns up frequently in the reiterated challenges, "knowest thou" (38.5,18,21,33; 39.1,2). Job is being probed on how much he has really taken to heart about the astonishing created universe in which he lives.

God parades the marvels of His omnipotence in a systematic way, dealing first with inanimate nature. He mentions aspects of **creation,** specifically the earth and the sea (38.4-11), before passing on to miracles of daily **conservation** (38.12-21) whereby the planet is sustained, and the various means of **precipitation** (38.22-30), including snow and rain, which keep it refreshed. He concludes with a glance at the **constellations** (38.31-38).

Interrogation (i) – God's Inanimate Creation: 38.4-38

How can any creature pretend to understand the universe when he was not there at its inception? It is here that Bible believers possess a singular advantage over all others who seek to grapple with the problem of origins: we have the infallible word of the One who created it all. The answer to the first question, "Where wast thou?" is, of course, "Nowhere". The Puritan who encouraged humility by reminding his congregation that "our father was Adam; our grandfather, dust; and our great-grandfather, nothing" was biblically informed. As the hymn writer J John Young has put it

> In the beginning God –
> Sovereign – Supreme – Alone –
> Even before creation had
> His power and glory shown;
> Long e'er an angel stood
> Before His holy throne,
> From all eternity "He is" –
> The ever Living One.
>
> All things are of Thy will,
> In answer to Thy call,
> Things seen and things invisible,
> For Thou hast made them all;
> Snow, hail and rain are Thine,
> And every ocean stream,
> Sun, moon and all the stars that shine,
> Thy wisdom still proclaim.[436]

Jehovah first draws attention to the **earth**, describing its creation as though it were a vast building project complete with foundation, measuring lines, and corner stone. The same word for laying foundations in verse 4 appears in the description of Solomon's temple (1 Kings 5.17), while a different term in verse 6 is used of the silver "sockets" on which the tabernacle boards rested (Ex 26.19). The "line" stretched out in verse 6 is used to describe the circumference of Solomon's molten sea (1 Kings 7.23). The colocation of "corner" and "stone" is later employed metaphorically to describe the coming Messiah as the one who alone can fulfil God's programme (Ps 118.22; Is 28.16). Jehovah chooses terminology which relates literally to Israel's later temple and typically to Israel's Messiah, but here suggests the complexity, grandeur, and design excellence of the massive creation project.

The fitting accompaniment of that activity, we discover, was jubilation, for "the morning stars sang together, and all the sons of God shouted for joy" (38.7). When the foundation of the post-exilic temple was laid there was a mingling of joy and sadness as the older generation looked back wistfully to the glory that had departed. But the sight of God's pristine handiwork produced nothing but unalloyed delight. The morning stars rejoiced to perform their function in the universe, hence the picture language of the psalmist: "Praise ye him, sun and moon: praise him, all ye stars of light" (Ps 148.3). If inanimate heavenly bodies find satisfaction in God's work of creation, how much more should intelligent sinners of Adam's race revel in the fullness of salvation they have received in Christ? In faithfully fulfilling their role, the sun, moon and stars are an example to us.

The poetic parallelism of verse 7 perhaps suggests that the morning stars are also symbols for angelic beings. We first met these sons of God in chapter 1 when Satan came among them into Jehovah's presence. The language descriptive of their hymn of praise may remind us that Job's generosity in earlier days had "caused the widow's heart to sing for joy" (29.13). The two verbs, "sang" (7442) and "shout" (7321), recur in Isaiah, describing the global celebrations to accompany Israel's future restoration:

> Sing [7442], O ye heavens; for the Lord hath done it: shout [7321], ye lower parts of the earth: break forth into singing, ye mountains, O forest, and every tree therein: for the Lord hath redeemed Jacob, and glorified himself in Israel (Is 44.23).

Festivity marked the original untarnished creation; festivity will dignify God's end-times revival of Israel.

After the solid earth, the focus shifts to the **waters:**

> And who shut up the sea with doors, when it burst forth, issuing out of the womb? When I made the cloud its garment, and thick darkness a swaddling band for it; When I cut out for it my boundary, and set bars and doors, And said, Hitherto shalt thou come and no further, and here shall thy proud waves be stayed? (38.8-11, JND).

Although it is possible, as Henry Morris argues, that this is an allusion to the Noahic Flood, coming as it does immediately after a description of the earth's formation it is more likely a reference to the origin of the oceans. If the creation of the solid, material earth is portrayed as a building site, the origin of the sea is likened to a birth. "Brake forth" (1518) is used in the context of literal and metaphorical childbirth (Ps 22.9; Micah 4.10). The sea is brought into existence complete with suitable baby clothes ("garment … swaddlingband"), echoing the language of Ezekiel's parable about Israel's lowly beginnings (Ezek 16.4-6). The clouds and the thick darkness accompanying the sea's creation suggest both the sublime mystery of divine manufacture and the current storm engulfing Job as he listens to God's voice.

Perhaps most important, for Job's personal encouragement, is the sturdy affirmation of absolute divine control: "Hitherto shalt thou come, but no further: and here shall thy proud waves be stayed" (38.11). Delitzsch observes: "that the sea, in spite of the flatness of its banks, does not flow over the land, is a work of omnipotence".[437] God, who set the boundaries of the waters, equally superintends all the conditions of His people. In the ancient world the sea was often viewed as an emblem of unrestrained and threatening disorder. The Bible, however, presents the Creator as simultaneously the hands-on Sustainer and Governor of His universe. He has never abdicated His position of supreme authority. Job – like believers today – needed to be reminded that he was not living in an anarchic environment. Back in the narrative prologue God had made plain the strict limitations of Satan's power (1.12; 2.6). Nothing stands outside the sphere of divine supervision: what may appear random is in reality the outworking of a perfect design.

Jehovah now draws Job's gaze away from the one-off work of creation as recorded in Genesis to the mundane marvels that facilitate the smooth running of His world. What, for instance, can Job contribute to the regular miracle of a new **dawn**? Hartley nicely sums up the divine authority evidenced in this passage: "Like a master builder He laid the earth's foundation … like a midwife He brought forth the sea … and like a general He commanded the light to shine".[438]

> Hast thou since thy days commanded the morning? hast thou caused the dawn to know its place, That it might take hold of the ends of the earth, and the wicked might be shaken out of it? It is changed like the signet-clay; and all things stand forth as in a garment: And from the wicked their light is withholden, and the uplifted arm is broken (38.12-15, JND).

Job had never in the whole of his life ("since thy days") given the order to the morning to sweep aside the shadowy veil of night, scattering wicked men whose plots tend to be hatched under cover of darkness. "Shaken out" is the language used to describe the fate of the Egyptian army overthrown in the Red Sea (Ex 14.27; Ps 136.15), Samson shaking himself free from the Philistines (Judg 16.20), and Nehemiah's pictorial malediction against those who refused to abandon usurious practices (Neh 5.13). This last best parallels the situation in Job. Just as Nehemiah threatened recalcitrant Jews with judgment, so the Lord speaks of the way the coming of light exposes wickedness. Delitzsch opens up the way the picture language works:

The dawn of the morning, spreading out from one point, takes hold of the carpet of the earth as it were by the edges, and shakes off from it the evil-doers, who had laid themselves to rest upon it the night before.[439]

This kind of imagery recurs in John's Gospel as a testimony to the innate depravity of the human heart. Into a gloomy world of sin came the spotless Son of God, radiating the light of divine holiness, and yet

light is come into the world, and men loved darkness rather than light, because their deeds were evil. For every one that doeth evil hateth the light, neither cometh to the light, lest his deeds should be reproved (Jn 3.19-20).

Job has been claiming on and off (for he has not been consistent) that the wicked, who are especially rampant at night (24.13-17), get away with their wickedness. Far from it, says the Lord. The time will come when everything is brought into the penetrating holy light of God's public scrutiny.

Jehovah's imagery of the seal vividly pictures the way the gradually spreading light of dawn brings into distinct shape the many and varied details of the earth's chequered surface. Fausset explains the analogy:

As the plastic clay presents various figures impressed on it by the revolving cylinder seal *(one to three inches long, of terra cotta or precious stone, such as is found in Assyria)*, as "it is turned," so the morning light rolling on over the earth, previously void of form through the darkness, brings out to view hills, valleys, etc.[440]

Our planet's geographical features, in their astonishingly beautiful diversity, are likened to a colourful robe worn by the earth. But all this aesthetic wonder is lost on the wicked, for whom the coming of daylight is the removal of the very condition in which they love to operate – that is to say, darkness. Jehovah speaks with irony when He says "from the wicked their light is withholden" (38.15), for what is light to them is in reality the obscurity of night-time. Isaiah pronounces woe on those who, in their moral perversity, confound opposites and "call evil good, and good evil; that put darkness for light, and light for darkness" (Is 5.20). But at the close of Job the Lord previews the final uncovering and discomfiture of such people. Though they might brag about their strength, they are no match for the living God. When Christ comes in His manifest glory then, once and for all, "the high arm shall be broken" (38.15).

The next paragraph offers a compact tour of some of the **mysteries of the universe** in a rapid-fire sequence of challenges:

Hast thou entered as far as the springs of the sea? and hast thou walked in the recesses of the deep? Have the gates of death been revealed unto thee? and hast thou seen the gates of the shadow of death? Hath thine understanding compassed the breadths of the earth? Declare if thou knowest it all. Where is the way to where light dwelleth? and the darkness, where is its place, That thou shouldest take it to its bound, and that thou shouldest know the paths to its house? Thou knowest, for thou wast then born, and the number of thy days is great! (38.16-21, JND).

If Job has no power over things visible to mortal sight, like the earth, the sea and the dawn, what hope has he of understanding matters beyond his gaze? Has he entered, has he walked, has he seen, has he understood, does he know? The questions come thick and fast. We first descend into the ocean depths to explore the fountains and springs on the sea bed. These may be the very fountains which erupted at the time of the Flood (Gen 7.11), producing gigantic tsunami waves that inundated the land, contributing to the destructive impact of a prolonged cataclysmic downpour. But has Job even seen them, let alone searched them? In earlier chapters he has spoken familiarly and confidently about the world of the dead (3.21; 10.21-22), the place called *sheol* (7.9; 14.13; 17.13) – but has he ever visited it? The answer is obvious: he has not. From the depths we travel up through the "breadth of the earth". What does Job know about that? And, passing higher still, what about the wonders of the stellar heavens? Can he locate the dwelling places of light and darkness? It was God who originally commanded "Let there be light: and there was light" (Gen 1.3), but where was Job at that time? He was not even born. Job lived in the days of the patriarchs, when the human life span was far greater than it is now, but even Methuselah's years are insufficient to compare with the eternity of One who possesses "neither beginning of days, nor end of life" (Heb 7.3).

To be reminded of our finite and transient existence is to be reduced to the right position before God. Job was a giant amongst men, "the greatest of all the men of the east" (1.3). Further, though he never knew it, the Lord affirmed that "there is none like him in the earth" (1.8). In material prosperity and spiritual piety he stood alone – but he was as nothing compared with God. All the questions with which he is being bombarded are Jehovah's appointed means of bringing him to a proper state of mind. If he was unable to respond to any of these challenges, how could he presume to criticise God's rule over the world in general and His purposes with Job in particular?

Jehovah's interrogation continues with an overview of the earth's **weather systems**:

Hast thou entered into the storehouses of the snow, and hast thou seen the treasuries of the hail, Which I have reserved for the time of distress, for the day of battle and war? By what way is the light parted, and the east wind scattered upon the earth? Who hath divided a channel for the rain-flood, and a way for the thunder's flash; To cause it to rain on the earth, where no one is; on the wilderness wherein there is not a man; To satisfy the desolate and waste ground, and to cause the sprout of the grass to spring forth? Hath the rain a father? or who begetteth the drops of dew? Out of

whose womb cometh the ice? and the hoary frost of heaven, who bringeth
it forth? When the waters lie hidden as in stone, and the face of the deep
holdeth fast together (38.22-30, JND).

"Treasures" (214) in verse 22 translates a word which is variously rendered
"treasury" (Josh 6.19, 24), "storehouse" (1 Chr 27.25; Ps 33.7; Mal 3.10), "cellar"
(1 Chr 27.27), and "armoury" (Jer 50.25). The psalmist uses it to express his
wonderment at Jehovah's sovereign authority:

Whatsoever the Lord pleased, that did he in heaven, and in earth, in the
seas, and all deep places. He causeth the vapours to ascend from the ends
of the earth; he maketh lightnings for the rain; he bringeth the wind out
of his treasuries [214] (Ps 135.6-7).

The metaphors are memorable. As Elihu pointed out earlier (37.5-6), every
phenomenon of the natural world is ultimately the work of God. Like an
immeasurably wealthy monarch, He owns vast storehouses of wind, rain, snow
and hail on which to draw as it pleases Him. Biblical history and prophecy testify
to the devastating impact of hail (Ex 9.18; Rev 16.21): Egypt's local experience in
the days of Moses was but a faint foretaste of what will happen on a global scale
in the tribulation period. Haggai tells of the sufferings of the returned Jewish
exiles, when "I [the Lord] smote you with blasting and with mildew and with hail
in all the labours of your hands" (Hag 2.17), because of their failure to prioritise
the things of God. God is never short of weapons with which to chastise the
impenitent.
    But Job has never entered into these cavernous reservoirs of moisture. Nor does
he know how light is distributed across the earth, or how the east wind (which
destroyed Egypt's crops, causing the famine in the time of Joseph) blows over the
face of the land. "Light" (216) could mean either lightning (as it does in 37.3)
or the sun's beams – in either case Job is nonplussed, knowing neither where
lightning will strike next, nor how the sun's rays illuminate the globe.

Darby's translation of the section about rainfall clarifies the meaning:

Who hath divided a channel for the rain-flood, and a way for the thunder's
flash; To cause it to rain on the earth, where no one is; on the wilderness
wherein there is not a man; To satisfy the desolate and waste ground, and
to cause the sprout of the grass to spring forth? (38.25-27, JND).

It is as if God has carved gigantic though invisible channels through the
atmosphere for directing torrents of rain upon the earth. The same word is used of
the "trench" Elijah dug about his altar on Mount Carmel to hold the water which
saturated his offering (1 Kings 18.32,35), and the "conduit" through which
Hezekiah guaranteed Jerusalem's water supply (2 Kings 20.20). But these were
the evident effects of men's labours. God, on the other hand, moves in inimitable

majesty. He even unleashes showers over unoccupied deserts, thus proving that not all His weather patterns are for the good of humans alone. Elihu had raised this point earlier, noting that "He causeth it [the rain] to come, whether for correction, or for his land, or for mercy" (37.13).

Robinson, always alert to practical applications, makes the following comment:

> No stinting with God, neither from want of ability nor willingness to bestow. Enough and to spare with Him. Even the beasts in the solitary waste [are] provided for.[441]

There is in God's generosity a magnificent lavishness – but never a wastefulness – which warms the heart. "Enough and to spare" (Lk 15.17) is the language of the prodigal recollecting what he has lost, and its reality is demonstrated in the feeding of the five thousand, where a meagre provision insufficient that "every one ... may take a little" (Jn 6.7) was transformed into a supply so abundant that all could enjoy "as much as they would" (Jn 6.11). God Himself is the most cheerful of givers.

Reverting to the imagery of childbirth, the Lord tests Job with more questions about the origin of various forms of precipitation.

> Hath the rain a father? or who hath begotten the drops of dew? Out of whose womb came the ice? and the hoary frost of heaven, who hath gendered it? (38.28-29).

Has the rain a father? Who begot the dewdrops? Who (changing the metaphor slightly) gave birth to ice and hoar frost? Jehovah's pictorial language permits us to describe Him reverently as the fatherly and motherly Creator of His universe with all its myriad of wonders. Dew is moisture suspended in the air which becomes condensed on reaching night-cooled objects on the earth. According to the online *Collins English Dictionary*, hoarfrost (sometimes called white frost) is "a deposit of needle-like ice crystals formed on the ground by direct condensation at temperatures below freezing point".[442] The psalmist draws on different similes to celebrate the profusion of God's giving: "He giveth snow like wool: he scattereth the hoarfrost like ashes" (Ps 147.16).

The description of an ice-bound pond or stream illustrates another amazing property of water: "The waters are hidden as with stone, and the face of the deep is frozen" (38.30, RV). The language is very precise: the waters beneath the icy surface are hidden as though by a hard but transparent stony casing, but they are not frozen solid. Writes Sarfati:

> A vital and very unusual property of water is that it expands as it freezes, unlike most other substances. That is why icebergs float. In fact, water contracts normally as it is cooled, until it reaches 4°C (39.2°F), when it starts to expand again. This means that icy-cold water is less dense, so

tends to move upwards. This is very important. Most liquids exposed to cold air would cool, and the cold liquid would sink, forcing more liquid to rise and be cooled by the air. Eventually all the liquid would lose heat to the air and freeze, from the bottom up, till completely frozen. But with water, the cold regions, being less dense, stay on top, allowing the warmer regions to stay below and avoid losing heat to the air. This means that the surface may be frozen, but fish can still live in the water below. But if water were like other substances, large bodies of water, such as North America's Great Lakes, would be frozen solid, with dire effects on life on earth as a whole.[443]

God's gracious arrangements, whether natural phenomena or spiritual blessings in Christ, are always ideal.

This survey of the works of God in creation and preservation has confronted Job with the bankruptcy of his knowledge. He cannot understand even the most trivial of God's marvels; how then can he possibly comprehend the mysterious ways of God with a human soul? As we read this speech we are bound to be reminded once again of the words recorded in Isaiah:

> For my thoughts are not your thoughts, neither are your ways my ways, saith the Lord. For as the heavens are higher than the earth, so are my ways higher than your ways, and my thoughts than your thoughts (Is 55.8-9).

The heavens are indeed higher than the earth, and the final stage of Jehovah's tour of the inanimate creation lifts us up to unimaginable heights in order to consider the **constellations**:

> Canst thou fasten the bands of the Pleiades, or loosen the cords of Orion? Dost thou bring forth the constellations each in its season? or dost thou guide the Bear with her sons? Knowest thou the ordinances of the heavens? dost thou determine their rule over the earth? (38.31-33, JND).

God names three of the impressive star clusters that dominate the night sky: the Pleiades, Orion, and Arcturus (Ursa Major, the Great Bear, with its three smaller attendant stars). The Pleiades (3598) occurs only three times in the Bible: in Job's own words (9.9), here, and in Amos 5.8, where it is translated in the KJV "the seven stars". But the challenge is devastating: can Job fasten or loose these famed groupings of heavenly bodies, as if they were cosmic necklaces of precious gemstones? Can he control their seasonal appearance in the firmament? Darby's "constellations" in verse 32 translates what the KJV transliterates as "Mazzaroth" – a word the Brown, Driver and Briggs Lexicon defines as "the twelve signs of the Zodiac and their 36 associated constellations". Job could see them, but he had no power to guide them. Implicitly, Jehovah looks back to the creation account, with its pithy summary of the function of those many lights that spangle the skies:

> And God said, Let there be lights in the firmament of the heaven to divide

the day from the night; and let them be for signs, and for seasons, and for days, and years: And let them be for lights in the firmament of the heaven to give light upon the earth: and it was so. And God made two great lights; the greater light to rule the day, and the lesser light to rule the night: he made the stars also (Gen 1.14-16).

It was God who made and activated these bodies in the heavens which, though they have been there since the fourth day of creation, remain beyond the full comprehension of man.

As a concluding doff of the cap to all the stupendous wonders over which Job has neither control nor influence, the Lord reminds him of the regular blessing of rainfall, so necessary and so precious in the Middle East:

> Dost thou lift up thy voice to the clouds, that floods of waters may cover thee? Dost thou send forth lightnings that they may go, and say unto thee, Here we are? Who hath put wisdom in the inward parts? or who hath given understanding to the mind? Who numbereth the clouds with wisdom? or who poureth out the bottles of the heavens, When the dust runneth as into a molten mass, and the clods cleave fast together? (38.34-38, JND).

Although, in the will of God, men have prayed for rain and have been answered (1 Kings 18.42; James 5.17-18), they were never themselves the cause of the rain. God alone commands His creation, giving orders to the lightning flash to strike as He pleases. He alone speaks to the clouds (5645) – the word, as in Exodus 19.9 and 2 Samuel 22.12, suggesting thick darkness and density – and enumerates the clouds (7834) – a different noun meaning fine dust, and translated "sky" in Deuteronomy 33.26 and Psalm 77.17. The varieties of beautiful cloud formation are endless, but God shapes, knows and numbers them all.

Verse 38 is ambiguous. It pictures either hardened dry ground just prior to a much-needed downpour (the soil baked by the sun's heat into a solid mass, its clods fused together), or the dramatic effects of a rainstorm (whereby the ground turns into what appears to be a sea of molten metal, all its parched chunks of earth coalescing into slippery, shiny mud). Man is totally dependent on God to bring the rains which transform caked ground into fertile soil.

Two key moments stand out in this brief section. First, God commands every detail of His world. In the same way as He limits the incursions of the sea (38.11) so He orders the excursions of the lightning (38.35). There is nothing on or above the earth that is exempt from divine control, including the terrible circumstances which Job has had to endure. The lightning, of course, has no option but to do as God directs, though the poetic language makes it sound boyishly eager in its enthusiasm, crying out, "Here we are"! Isaiah, by contrast, willingly offered himself to Jehovah's service: "I heard the voice of the Lord, saying, Whom shall I send, and who will go for us? Then said I, Here am I; send me" (Is 6.8). His voluntary submission makes us think of the incarnate Son, who unfailingly did the Father's bidding: "he that sent me is with me: the Father hath not left me alone; for I do always those things that please him" (Jn 8.29).

Second, God uniquely is the One who "put wisdom in the inward parts" and gave "understanding to the mind" (38.36, JND). This verse admittedly has its own difficulties because two of its words are obscure ("inwards parts" and "mind"). Those wanting technical data should consult Hartley, who offers the translation, "Who imparted wisdom to the ibis? Who gave understanding to the cock?"[444] The idea is (perhaps) that God has bestowed amazing intuition on certain species of bird so that they can herald the coming of dawn or the approach of a storm. If, however, we retain the translation adopted not only by the KJV but also the RV, Darby, and the ESV, there is here a further challenge to Job. The fusillade of questions aimed at him all assume a negative answer: Job was *not* there at the commencement of creation, he has *not* entered into the underworld, he did *not* put the stars in place, he *cannot* command the rain. However … should he possess even the slightest insight into any of the natural marvels which have been paraded before him, it is only because God has granted him the ability. All wisdom emanates from God. Man of himself possesses nothing in which he may legitimately boast.

Interrogation (ii) – God's Animal Creation: 38.39 – 39.30

From the inanimate creation Job's attention is transferred to a world around him teeming with life. The book of Job is packed with allusions to zoology. The protagonist and his friends have, in their earlier speeches, referred to various aspects of the wealth of the animal kingdom. To give an impression of the range of allusions, the following table lists the animals mentioned in the book.

Creature (KJV)	Creature (ESV)	Hebrew word (Strong's No)	Reference in Job
General			
Beasts		929	12.7; 18.3; 35.11
Fowls		5775	12.7; 28.21; 35.11
Fishes		1709	12.8; 41.7
Specific			
Sheep		6629	1.3,16; 21.11; 30.1; 42.12
Camel		1581	1.3,17; 42.12
Ox		1241	1.3,14; 40.15; 42.12
She ass	Female donkey	860	1.3,14; 42.12
Lion		738	4.10
Fierce lion		7826	4.10; 10.16; 28.8
Young lion		3715	4.10; 38.39
Old lion		3918	4.11

Stout lion (lioness)		3833	4.11; 38.39
Moth		6211	4.19; 13.28; 27.18
Wild ass	Wild donkey	6501	6.5; 11.12; 24.5; 39.5
Ox, bull		7794	6.5; 21.10; 24.3
Worm	Maggot	7415	7.5; 17.14; 21.26; 24.20; 25.6
Whale, dragon	Sea monster	8577	7.12; 30.29
Spider		5908	8.14
Eagle		5404	9.26; 39.27
Asp	Cobra	6620	20.14,16
Viper		660	20.16
Cow		6510	21.10
Ass	Donkey	2543	24.3
Worm		8438	25.6
Lion		7830	28.8; 41.34
Vulture	Falcon	344	28.7
Dog		3611	30.1
Owl	Ostrich	3284	30.29
Sheep		3532	31.20
Raven		6158	38.41
Wild goat	Mountain goat	3277	39.1
Hind	Doe	355	39.1
Wild ass	Swift donkey	6171	39.5
Unicorn	Wild ox	7214	39.9,10
Ostrich		5133	39.13
Horse		5483	39.18,19
Grasshopper	Locust	697	39.20
Hawk		5322	39.26
Behemoth		930	40.15
Leviathan		3882	3.8; 41.1
Bullock		6499	42.8
Ram		352	42.8

The ten animals selected for scrutiny in chapters 38 and 39 are very different from one another in size, shape, speed, strength and sense. Zuck makes the point that, although they seem to be chosen at random, "they do include the ferocious, the helpless, the shy, the strong, the bizarre, the wild".[445] But, with the significant exception of the warhorse, they all have this in common: they are not tamed by man. It is not domestic animals, such as those which constituted Job's original wealth (1.3), and about which he was well instructed, but the feral creatures of the wilderness which are primarily listed for his consideration. They may be untamed, yet they are each possessed of a marvellous God-given instinct for survival. Further, unlike other passages in Hebrew wisdom literature (such as Proverbs 6.6; 30.24-31), these creatures are not selected for the moral lessons they can teach man. Rather, they testify to the gracious practical provision of God.

George Cansdale's investigation of biblical animals is still a recommended sourcebook for identifying and describing the creatures in this section. Most of the zoological details below rely on his comprehensive and informative study.

First comes the **lion**. Although the Bible does not specifically call him the king of beasts, he is associated directly with kingship in Proverbs 19.12 and 20.2, and it therefore seems appropriate that he heads the list:

> Dost thou hunt the prey for the lioness, and dost thou satisfy the appetite of the young lions, When they crouch in their dens, and abide in the thicket to lie in wait? (38.39-40, JND).

The psalmist uses lions in a similar manner, as evidence of God's care for His whole creation:

> The young lions roar after their prey, and seek their meat from God. The sun ariseth, they gather themselves together, and lay them down in their dens (Ps 104.21-22).

They possess a built-in instinct allowing them, with impressive efficiency, to hunt down their prey. We know from Genesis that they were not originally created as carnivores but, like all other beasts, lived initially on a vegetarian diet: the Lord said that "to every beast of the earth, and to every fowl of the air, and to everything that creepeth upon the earth, wherein there is life, I have given every green herb for meat" (Gen 1.30). Man's rebellion damaged the entire ecosystem. As a consequence, "the whole creation groaneth and travaileth in pain together until now" (Rom 8.22), eagerly anticipating the day of liberation which will accompany the public manifestation of God's saints. This will initiate an extraordinary transformation. In the millennial Kingdom no lion will hunt another creature, for "the lion shall eat straw like the ox" (Is 11.7). But in the book of Job the Lord is looking at conditions in the natural world as they were in Job's day, and as they will continue to be until the Saviour inaugurates His reign. The searching question for Job then is this: can he provide all these wild animals with their daily food? Answer: no. Only their Creator can meet their various needs.

One of Rudyard Kipling's delightful *Just So Stories* ("The Butterfly that Stamped") concerns Suleiman-bin-Daoud, whose wisdom and wealth were proverbial. Kipling describes an occasion when he attempted to feed the world's animal population:

> He very seldom showed off, and when he did he was sorry for it. Once he tried to feed all the animals in all the world in one day, but when the food was ready an Animal came out of the deep sea and ate it up in

three mouthfuls. Suleiman-bin-Daoud was very surprised and said, "O Animal, who are you?" And the Animal said, "O King, live for ever! I am the smallest of thirty thousand brothers, and our home is at the bottom of the sea. We heard that you were going to feed all the animals in all the world, and my brothers sent me to ask when dinner would be ready." Suleiman-bin-Daoud was more surprised than ever and said, "O Animal, you have eaten all the dinner that I made ready for all the animals in the world." And the Animal said, "O King, live for ever, but do you really call that a dinner? Where I come from we each eat twice as much as that between meals." Then Suleiman-bin-Daoud fell flat on his face and said, "O Animal! I gave that dinner to show what a great and rich king I was, and not because I really wanted to be kind to the animals. Now I am ashamed, and it serves me right".[446]

What neither Suleiman-bin-Daoud nor Job could do, God does daily and effortlessly.

The text employs two synonyms for lion, the first (3833) variously translated in the KJV by "old lion", "great lion" and "lioness", the second (3715) normally rendered "young lion". It is interesting to observe that each word appears in messianic passages. The first is introduced in Genesis 49.9 to describe Judah as an "old lion", formidable in its regal dignity. This prophetic verse announces the tribe from which the kingly Messiah would descend. The second is found in Psalm 91, part of which the devil quoted to the Lord Jesus in the wilderness (Mt 4.6). However, he significantly did not cite these words which, addressing the Messiah and looking back to Genesis 3.15, pronounce his own downfall: "Thou shalt tread upon the lion and adder: the young lion [3715] and the dragon shalt thou trample under feet" (Ps 91.13). In this context, the dangerous beasts (lion, adder, dragon) fittingly represent Satan, that "roaring lion … seeking whom he may devour" (1 Pet 5.8), and "the great dragon … that old serpent" (Rev 12.9). That Jehovah's first animal should remind us both of the coming Messiah and His conquered foe is a testimony to the richness of Scripture. It hints, right from the start of this survey of the animal kingdom, that the God who created and controls the fiercest creatures can also handle Satan. Nothing that has happened to Job has been outside the scope of heaven's restraining hand.

After the noble lion, with a swift change from the mammalian to the avian kingdom, comes the **raven**:

Who provideth for the raven his food? when his young ones cry unto God, they wander for lack of meat (38.41).

He who manages the majestic lion also caters for the raven. The word appears ten times in the Old Testament. This was the bird Noah sent out from the ark (Gen 8.7), a bird in the Levitical list of unclean animals (Lev 11.15), yet amazingly used of God, contrary to its nature, to sustain the prophet Elijah (1 Kings 17.4-6). The psalmist includes it in his hymn of praise to a God whose greatness is seen in His ability to give "to the beast his food, and to the young ravens which cry" (Ps 147.9). According to Fausset, "the shrewd and ill visage of the raven, its mourning hue, its solitary haunts, harsh croak, instant scenting of premonitory decomposition even before death, made it be regarded as of ill omen".[447] Nevertheless, the Lord Jesus instructed His disciples to "Consider the ravens: for they neither sow nor reap; which neither have storehouse nor barn; and God feedeth them: how much more are ye better than the fowls?" (Lk 12.24). Job did not have access to this precious truth, but he knew from the handed-down record of creation that man had been entrusted with dominion over the animals. God who supplied the needs of the one was obviously capable of meeting the needs of the other. Like the ravens, Job was wholly dependent on a trustworthy God.

Greater space is devoted to the **wild goats**:

> Knowest thou the time when the wild goats of the rock bring forth? dost thou mark the calving of the hinds? Dost thou number the months that they fulfil? and knowest thou the time when they bring forth? They bow themselves, they give birth to their young ones, they cast out their pains; Their young ones become strong, they grow up in the open field, they go forth, and return not unto them (39.1-4, JND).

The noun "wild goat" (3277) appears only here, in 1 Samuel 24.2 (to describe the bleak landscape where David sought to escape from Saul), and in Psalm 104, where we learn that "The high hills are a refuge for the wild goats" (Ps 104.18).

According to Cansdale, the "wild goat" is in fact the Nubian ibex, "still found in Palestine and known as *Beden* to the Arabs, and it has never been domesticated in any way". He continues:

> The root means "climber" and all passages associate it with mountains ... It is significant that this word does not occur in the sing., for the Nubian ibex is a herd animal and usually lives in small family groups of up to ten ... The Nubian ibex is the same size as the better-known Alpine ibex ... standing about 34 in. at the shoulder, but having rather more slender but more clearly ridged horns, sweeping back in a wide curve to a length of up to 50 in. in the buck, and much less in the doe. The general colour is grey, becoming browner in winter.[448]

The particular interest for Job is how the creature gives birth to its young: "They bow themselves, they bring forth their young ones, they cast out their sorrows" (39.3). Another similar creature appears to be mentioned in passing: "canst thou mark when the hinds do calve?" (39.1). The hind (355) refers in general to any species of deer, animals which select a carefully secluded place to bear their young. It is linked here with the ibex because the subject is the way these shy creatures give birth. The close-up description is finely etched. Men know neither the time nor the secret places where they produce their offspring, but the female's pains are rewarded in the delivery of strong and sturdy kids, which feed on corn (the idea is that they graze in the open fields without the supervision of men) and mature quickly into creatures independent of their parents. Job has no hand in any of this.

Then follows the **wild ass**:

> Who hath sent out the wild ass free? and who hath loosed the bands of the onager, Whose house I made the wilderness, and the salt plain his dwellings? He laugheth at the tumult of the city, and heareth not the shouts of the driver; The range of the mountains is his pasture, and he searcheth after every green thing (39.5-8, JND).

Two synonyms are used. The first (6501) occurs ten times in the Old Testament, initially in the description of Ishmael, stamping him as "a wild-ass of a man" (Gen 16.12, JND). This term is found on four occasions in Job (6.5; 11.12; 24.5; 39.5), and appears twice in Jeremiah, vividly snapshotting the animal's characteristics (2.24; 14.6). The second word (6171) is found only here. According to Cansdale,

> The animal that Job and the Prophets knew was a native of SW Asia whose correct name was Onager, *Equus hemionus*, and classed by zoologists as a "half-ass" ... It was a gregarious animal of the dry grassy plains and Job described its habitat precisely: "the steppe for his home, and the salt land for his dwelling" (Job 39.6, RSV). Its instinct was to escape by running to the open plains ... it is single-hoofed and as such was forbidden food to the Hebrews.[449]

Jehovah underlines the creature's unquenchable thirst for liberty. It loves the open country ("the wilderness ... the barren land ... the mountains") but abhors the city, and cannot be subjected to human control. The delicious comedy sketch of an onager stubbornly deaf to the raucous threatening and cajoling of its irascible owner sums up its inherent intractability (39.7b). The *Jamieson, Fausset and Brown Commentary* pertinently remarks that "Man can rob animals of freedom, but not, as God, give freedom, combined with subordination to fixed laws." And that is the great point here: only God can grant liberty.

The truth applies equally in the spiritual realm. Just as it was God who initially opened the floodgates of Job's trials, so it is God who will turn his captivity, releasing him from the cramped confinement of misery and leading him back to prosperity (42.10). True deliverance from spiritual bondage today is found only in the person of the Lord Jesus Christ, for "If the Son therefore shall make you free, ye shall be free indeed" (Jn 8.36).

After the wild ass comes what the KJV terms the "unicorn", but is generally recognised as the **wild ox**:

> Will the wild-ox be content to serve thee? or will he abide by thy crib? Canst

thou bind the wild-ox with his band in the furrow? or will he harrow the valleys after thee? Wilt thou trust him, because his strength is great? or wilt thou leave to him thy labour? Wilt thou confide in him, that he will bring home thy seed, and gather the corn of thy threshingfloor? (39.9-12, RV).

The Hebrew word (7214) turns up nine times in the Old Testament, from Numbers 23.22 to Isaiah 34.7, and in the KJV is always rendered "unicorn". Other versions generally agree on "wild ox", although Darby suggests "buffalo". According to Cansdale,

the Aurochs, *Bos primigenius*, [is the] ancestor of our domestic cattle. This is the beast that the Hebrews knew as *re'em* [7214] ... the last recorded specimen of aurochs died in AD 1627 in a Polish park north of Warsaw, where a herd had been enclosed for at least a century – possibly even two centuries, for it had disappeared from W Europe generally by about 1400.

He goes on to describe the animal:

the bulls were enormous, over 6 ft. at the shoulder, with long, forward-pointing horns; the coat was very dark brown or black, with a white dorsal line, curly in winter and sleeker in summer. The smaller cows were usually brown; in this the aurochs differed from most modern breeds, in which the sexes are of the same colour. Many of the original characteristics survived, distributed among many breeds of domestic cattle.[450]

Obviously it was an impressively massive and potent creature. "It was not only the most powerful hoofed animal they knew but it was also the largest, apart from the hippopotamus and elephant".[451] In Job 39 it is contrasted with the domesticated oxen with which the farmer ploughed his land and threshed his grain. The questions addressed to the wealthy farmer Job, whose stock had once included five hundred yoke of oxen, raise the impossibility of his ever harnessing the service of the wild ox. Its enormous but unpredictable power was not available for the benefit of man. The unstated comment behind the passage is this: man cannot control or use such a beast, but the Creator can.

Then comes another shift to the avian kingdom with the biggest (and, some might say, the oddest) of living birds, the **ostrich**:

The wing of the ostrich rejoiceth, but are her pinions and feathers kindly? For she leaveth her eggs on the earth, and warmeth them in the dust, And forgetteth that the foot may crush them, or that the wild beast may trample them. She is hardened against her young ones, as if they were not hers: though her labour be in vain, she is without fear; Because God hath deprived her of wisdom, neither hath he imparted to her understanding. What time she lifteth up herself on high, she scorneth the horse and his rider (39.13-18, RV).

The terminology is slightly tricky. Perhaps the problems are best pinpointed by setting the KJV alongside a representative alternative version. Here, first, is the KJV, followed by the ESV, which basically takes the line established by the RV, ASV and Darby:

> Gavest thou the goodly wings unto the peacocks? or wings and feathers unto the ostrich? (39.13, KJV).

> The wings of the ostrich wave proudly, but are they the pinions and plumage of love? (39.13, ESV).

While the KJV alludes to two birds (the peacock and the ostrich), more recent versions find only one, the ostrich. The noun the 1611 translators took to mean "peacock", a word (7443) which appears only here, is now generally accepted as describing the ostrich itself. The word (5133) translated "ostrich" by the KJV is one basically meaning "feathers" (and so rendered in its three other occurrences: Lev 1.16; Ezek 17.3,7). On the other hand, the word the KJV here translates "feathers" (2624) is everywhere else rendered "stork" (Lev 11.19; Deut 14.18; Ps 104.17; Jer 8.7; Zech 5.9). The Hebrew term derives from a root meaning kindly or maternal (the stork was considered an unusually caring bird towards its young), which explains the allusion to love in the ESV. The idea of the verse, then, is this: the ostrich may flap its wings for all it is worth (as in its flamboyant courtship ritual), but does this prove that it is as maternally tender as the stork? Obviously not, for the rest of the passage underlines the poor parenting skills of the ostrich.

Once again Cansdale has done the research:

> Standing between 6 and 8 ft. tall and weighing up to 300 lb. it is approached in size only by the giant flightless birds of the S. hemisphere – rheas, emus, and cassowaries. The wings are tiny and quite useless for flight; the cocks use their wings in their breeding display and these bear the plumes which have long been used for ornamental purposes. Their feet are adapted for fast running, each with only two toes, and they make formidable weapons.[452]

Jehovah points out the ostrich's flashy (if redundant for flying purposes) plumage (39.13), and its sensational speed on land (39.18). Indeed, Cansdale notes that "on its own ground it can leave the horse behind, maintaining fifty m.p.h. for at least the first half-mile".[453] But most of the description is devoted to the bird's apparently callous treatment of its young (39.14-17). It appears carelessly unconcerned about its eggs. Unsurprisingly, there have been objections to the accuracy of the biblical account of the ostrich's character.[454] There have also been ripostes. There follows an extract from an online article on the subject:

Female ostriches will lay eggs in a dirt nest that has been prepared by the male ostrich. Multiple females will use the same nest but typically the last female to lay eggs is the dominant female and she will roll and kick many or all of the prior eggs that were laid out of the nest. The female and male will periodically take turns incubating the remaining eggs with no attention paid to the surrounding eggs. Among the eggs that are incubated many are lost or broken in the dirt nest. Even after hatching it is the male ostrich that will take care of the young of which only 15% typically will survive to reproductive age with most becoming food for a number of predators.[455]

Jehovah's point, we should note, is not that the ostrich is bad; moral categories do not come into play here. Rather, the idea is that He has, of His own good pleasure, deprived it in some areas of the wisdom and understanding which, implicitly, He has given other creatures. Even though the lower creation suffers the consequences of Adam's sin, the Creator still takes accountability for His universe, just as in Exodus 4.11 He assumes hands-on responsibility for human birth defects. There is nothing light-touch about the sovereignty of God!

The ostrich's running skills offer a neat lead-in to what Delitzsch calls "the oldest and most beautiful description"[456] of the **horse**:

Hast thou given strength to the horse? hast thou clothed his neck with the quivering mane? Dost thou make him to leap as a locust? His majestic snorting is terrible. He paweth in the valley, and rejoiceth in his strength; he goeth forth to meet the armed host. He laugheth at fear, and is not affrighted; neither turneth he back from before the sword. The quiver rattleth upon him, the glittering spear and the javelin. He swalloweth the ground with fierceness and rage, and cannot contain himself at the sound of the trumpet: At the noise of the trumpets he saith, Aha! and he smelleth the battle afar off, the thunder of the captains, and the shouting (39.19-25, JND).

The whole passage bristles with pulsating activity and excitement. The charger's delight in the noise, smell and confusion of battle is rendered anthropomorphically ("rejoiceth ... laugheth ... rage ... he saith, Aha!"). But the three prefatory questions (39.19-20) take us back to creation. Job, like other men, might be able to train the horse for warfare, but was he responsible for the creature's distinctive strength, beauty and agility, which made it such a superb mount? The answer is obviously, no; but the Lord does not stop there. He goes on, demonstrating an unmistakable enjoyment in contemplating the horse's exhilarating energy in the clash of battle. The young Winston Churchill was present at what has been called the last successful cavalry charge of the British army, at the Battle of Omdurman in 1898. This is the beginning of his description of the action, contained in his book *The River War*:

The trumpet jerked out a shrill note, heard faintly above the trampling of the horses and the noise of the rifles. On the instant all the sixteen troops swung round and locked up into a long galloping line, and the 21st Lancers were committed to their first charge in war. Two hundred and fifty yards away the dark-blue men were firing madly in a thin film of light-blue smoke. Their bullets struck the hard gravel into the air, and the troopers, to shield their faces from the stinging dust, bowed their helmets forward, like the Cuirassiers at Waterloo. The pace was fast and the distance short.[457]

The archaic spear and javelin may be absent from his description, but the stirring atmosphere is recognisably the same.

This one tameable animal appears in Jehovah's catalogue because, like all the others, it testifies to man's limitations. He may train and ride the warhorse, but he is not in any way responsible for its superb attributes.

We close with two birds. First, the **hawk**:

Doth the hawk soar by thy wisdom, and stretch her wings toward the south? (39.26, RV).

The word for hawk (5322) appears only three other times in Scripture – in the dietary lists (Lev 11.16; Deut 14.5) and in a description of vine buds shooting out their blossoms (Gen 40.10). Cansdale, who helpfully catalogues the birds of prey mentioned in the Bible, places this Hebrew word in the category of hawks and falcons. He adds:

The falcons, with their long pointed wings and long tails, catch most of their prey by sheer speed. Palestine has a wonderful range of them, from the Peregrine and Lanner of 18 in. down to the Merlin and Lesser Kestrel, of about 12 in. ... Kestrels and Lesser Kestrels are very common, breeding right in the towns, often forming small colonies in old ruins and towers. The latter is one of the commonest migratory hawks and is doubtless included in the comment in Job 39.26 RSV, "The hawk spreads his wings towards the south", setting off on the autumn journey to Africa.[458]

Man's wisdom neither made nor maintains this bird, whose mysterious migratory instinct causes it to take its annual flight south. In an informative online article on migration, David Catchpoole writes:

The ability of migratory birds to fly to their destination with such precision requires two abilities: orientation (knowing direction) and navigation (knowing when to change direction). The first requires some kind of compass; the second needs a map. One without the other is useless — it seems migratory birds have both. The mechanism of birds' innate direction-finding capacity has puzzled scientists for years. At various times it has been mooted that birds navigate by the sun, the stars, and geographical landmarks. All of these have been shown to be true *but* these abilities all appear to be learned by experience — e.g. pigeons raised out of sight of the sun and exercised only on overcast days cannot navigate by the sun, but can still easily find their way. Conversely, pigeons that had learned to navigate by "solar compass" have a harder time navigating on cloudy days. So while birds apparently can learn to use a whole range of environmental cues for navigation, there is considerable evidence that birds primarily use some kind of built-in "magnetic compass".[459]

Whatever astonishing facility has been built into the hawk has been placed there by its Creator.

Finally there is the **eagle**, which we may take to be the avian equivalent of the regal lion who started the list:

> Doth the eagle mount up at thy command, and make his nest on high? He inhabiteth the rock and maketh his dwelling on the point of the cliff, and the fastness: From thence he spieth out the prey, his eyes look into the distance; And his young ones suck up blood; and where the slain are, there is he (39.27-30, JND).

Twenty-six times the word for eagle (5404) occurs in the Old Testament, from Exodus 19.4 (illustrating the loving-kindness with which Jehovah carried His redeemed people) to Habakkuk 1.8 (a verse dense with animal imagery, likening the swift horses of the invading Chaldeans to leopards, evening wolves, and eagles). Twice it appears in the lists of prohibited meats (Lev 11.13; Deut 14.12), but elsewhere tends to have a metaphorical function, emphasising speed (Deut 28.49), tender care (Deut 32.11), strength (Ps 103.5), soaring capacity (Prov 23.5), and voraciousness (Prov 30.17). Cansdale informs us that the Hebrew term "covers the large eagles, especially the Imperial Eagle, and the Griffon-Vulture",[460] but concludes that the description in Job most likely relates to the latter. This imposing creature "is between 3 and 4 ft. long, with a wing span of almost 8 ft." A visitor to the Holy Land in the nineteenth century noted that "no landscape was ever without its circling vultures. There were breeding colonies wherever it could find suitable nesting-sites – especially in the rocky gorges in and leading off the Jordan valley, some of which held hundreds of birds".[461]

Jehovah draws attention to the high-placed and precipitous nesting location, alongside the bird's amazing capacity to spot its prey over a vast distance. Cansdale quotes an ancient proverb from the Talmud to the effect that a vulture in Babylon can see a carcase in Palestine. The final comment, about its attraction to carrion, is particularly interesting because it is picked up by the Lord Jesus in the Olivet Discourse.

> For as the lightning cometh out of the east, and shineth even unto the west; so shall also the coming of the Son of man be. For wheresoever the carcase is, there will the eagles be gathered together (Mt 24.27-28).

The graphic allusion to encircling vultures testifies to the wholesale slaughter which will accompany the return of Christ in stupendous power to put down all opposition. This gory scene is described more fully in Revelation 19, where birds of prey *en masse* are summoned to "the supper of the great God" (Rev 19.17). The Lord Jesus also uses the Job passage when, earlier in Luke's Gospel, He intimates the dramatic separating impact of His coming:

> I tell you, in that night there shall be two men in one bed; the one shall be taken, and the other shall be left. Two women shall be grinding together; the one shall be taken, and the other left. Two men shall be in the field; the one shall be taken, and the other left. And they answered and said unto him, Where, Lord? And he said unto them, Wheresoever the body is, thither will the eagles be gathered together (Lk 17.34-37).

His answer to the disciples' question – where will these people be taken? – cites Job's aphorism about the grisly presence of vultures with the slain. Those taken are not raptured away from danger (the distinctive destiny of the church, the body of Christ, is not the subject matter of the synoptic Gospels) but seized for slaughter. Those remaining are preserved so that they can enter the Kingdom in their mortal bodies.

Dizzyingly the vulture soars aloft and speeds to its prey – but not at Job's command.

God's zoological quiz has touched in varying depth on ten creatures great and small. What is the purpose behind it? The repeated questions, each inviting the answer "No", have exposed Job's consistent ignorance ("Knowest thou?", 39.1) and impotence ("Canst thou?", 39.2,10,20). His mind cannot explain the characteristics God has built into His animal kingdom, nor can he cater for this menagerie of diverse creatures. Even though, alone of the ten, the horse may be harnessed for human purposes, its attributes remain uniquely God-given. The chapter begins with birth (39.1) and ends with death (39.30) – with perhaps an ironic backward glance at the range of human life built into Job's opening complaint (3.3,22) – yet Jehovah is supremely in control of it all.

Interchange: 40.1-5

This brief bridging passage records a snatch of dialogue between Jehovah and Job in response to the first part of the Lord's speech (in chapters 38-39).

After the survey of the wonders of the created universe, God pauses to address Job directly and bring him back to the main point: dare the man who finds fault with God offer Him instruction? "Contend" (7378) is a vigorous word. It describes, for example, the strife between Isaac's servants and Abimelech's (Gen 26.20-22), Jacob chiding Laban for his hasty accusations (Gen 31.36), the Israelites complaining against Moses (Ex 17.2; Num 20.3), those who set themselves up as "the adversaries of the Lord" (1 Sam 2.10), and Nehemiah rebuking the returned exiles who oppressed their brethren with exorbitant rates of interest (Neh 5.7). The synonym, "reprove" (3198), is equally forceful. Used seventeen times in Job, it elsewhere describes the rebuke Sarah received for her lie (Gen 20.16), the chastening which would befall David's son for disobedience (2 Sam 7.14), and the discipline which comes on God's people to restore them to Himself (Ps 6.1; 38.1; 94.10). Combined with three great names of God in close conjunction ("the LORD", "the Almighty", and "God"), the choice of such words highlights Job's sheer effrontery. Believers of the present age, exposed to the full revelation of God in His Son, have far less excuse than Job. In times of distress and incomprehension, which are the lot of all God's people in all dispensations, we often need a sobering dose of Paul's Roman epistle:

> Nay but, O man, who art thou that repliest against God? Shall the thing formed say to him that formed it, Why hast thou made me thus? (Rom 9.20).

How has Job taken Jehovah's words? He said nothing in answer to Elihu's lengthy arguments, but now an uncharacteristically muted response bears eloquent testimony to the impact of Jehovah's lesson. His self-assessment sounds far removed from the confident protestations of innocence and rectitude which peppered earlier speeches. The man who claimed that "I put on righteousness, and it clothed me: my judgment was as a robe and a diadem" (29.14), and who boldly asserted that "as a prince" (31.37) he would approach God, now confesses "I am vile". "Vile" (7043) translates a word elsewhere rendered, for example, "despised" (Gen 16.4), "revile" (Ex 22.28), "curse" (Lev 19.14) and "lightly esteemed" (1 Sam 2.30). The KJV only employs "vile" for this Hebrew term in three other places (1 Sam 3.13; 2 Sam 6.22; Nahum 1.14). More recent translations tend to follow the lead of the RV's "I am of small account", or Darby's "I am nought". Job – great man though he was – has been thoroughly convicted of his insignificance in the presence of God. A right view of the created universe and its wonders will provoke praise, not pride; and true praise is only possible where there is genuine self-humbling before God.

To dramatise that he has been reduced to silence, Job claps his hand over his mouth as though to prevent any further impertinent outbursts. We may recall that, in earlier speeches, Job had counselled his friends to do just that: "Mark me, and be astonished, and lay your hand upon your mouth" (21.5). At that stage in the debate, Job the innocent victim saw himself as the centre of attention, causing wonderment to all who beheld him. But things have changed. Overawed by the grandeur of God's handiwork, it is now Job who is stilled. He admits having made persistent accusations against the Almighty ("Once have I spoken … yea, twice"), but there will be no more. His language echoes the description of Jehovah's absolute divine authority over the raging of the sea: "Hitherto shalt thou come, but no further" (38.11). God's power over the tumultuous ocean swell is now mirrored in miniature in Job's abashed self-restraint. His tempest of words has come to an end.

Delitzsch, as we might expect, offers a superb summary of the way Jehovah's intervention works in Job a healthy change of outlook. The sentence is long and cumbersome, but its point is worth grasping:

That God is the almighty and all-wise Creator and Ruler of the world, that the natural world is exalted above human knowledge and power, and is full of marvellous divine creations and arrangements, full of things mysterious and incomprehensible to ignorant and feeble man, Job knows even before God speaks, and yet he must now hear it, because he does not know it rightly; for the nature with which he is acquainted as the herald of the creative and governing power of God, is also the preacher of humility; and exalted as God the Creator and Ruler of the natural world is above Job's censure, so is He also as the Author of his affliction.[462]

Job has to acknowledge that a God of such inexhaustible power, author and sustainer of things inherently breath-taking in their beauty, complexity, size and variety, is One to be adored, not argued with. As Davidson astutely notes, "it is not any attribute of God that is dwelt upon, it is God in all the manifoldness of His being that passes before Job's mind".[463] Still, the lesson is not yet over. Jehovah has two further creatures to introduce to His servant.

SECTION 27
Dialogue: Job 4 – 42.6
Climax: Job 38 – 42.6
Jehovah's Speech: Job 38.1 – 42.6
Part Two: Job 40.6 – 42.6

The English writer Saki (Hector Hugh Munro) published in 1914 a collection of witty short stories under the title *Beasts and Super-Beasts*. It might be argued that the final chapters of the book of Job better deserve that name. We have already met a parade of beasts (ten of them) in Jehovah's first speech, which quizzed Job on two areas of the created universe: things inanimate and things animate. His second and concluding speech now focuses attention on a pair of gigantic creatures which we might without exaggeration call "super beasts": behemoth and leviathan. There seems, roughly speaking, to be a correlation in Jehovah's carnival of the animals between the size of the animals and the space allocated to them: the raven receives one verse (38.41), while behemoth and leviathan have ten and thirty-four respectively. Yet the God who supplies food for the one (38.41) equally shaped the others (40.19; 41.33). We are about to be overwhelmed by an extended close-up of beings monstrous in bulk and strength.

Job has by now been reduced to silence in God's presence; but he has not yet been brought to complete and unconditional submission. This is the purpose of Jehovah's final words. The speech is held together by one of the glories of divine omnipotence: the inimitable power of God to do what no one else can do – deflate the proud and the wicked. The topic is introduced near the start and repeated at the close:

> Cast abroad the rage of thy wrath: and behold every one that is proud, and abase him. Look on every one that is proud, and bring him low; and tread down the wicked in their place (40.11-12).

> He [leviathan] beholdeth all high things: he is a king over all the children of pride (41.34).

The first two verses (40.11-12) dare Job to suppress all the arrogant and evil things in the world; the third (41.34) sets up leviathan as the great emblem of terrifying self-conceit. Only God can humble pride. That sin was the condemnation of the devil (1 Tim 3.6) and is the attitude of heart which underlies all human rebellion against God (Gen 3.5), constituting the first of the things He hates (Prov 6.16-17). For all his self-esteem and vocal fluency Job, in common with other men, has neither the right nor the might to administer final justice in the world, and must defer to the superior majesty of Jehovah. In so doing he will, for the first time, come to acknowledge the foolishness of his hasty words.

The speech falls into four unequal sections, clearing the ground for Job's response. After a brief introduction comes a direct test of Job's competence to criticise God's management of His universe, followed by two stunning examples of God's handiwork which, in their proportions and their potency, tower over the greatest of mere men. If Job can successfully tame *them*, then God will take seriously his claims to personal significance.

      1. Connection: 40.6-7
      2. Challenging Job: 40.8-14
      3. Case Study (i) – Behemoth: 40.15-24
      4. Case Study (ii) – Leviathan: 41.1-34
      5. Comprehension: 42.1-6.

Connection: 40.6-7

The lead-in, connecting with the preceding speech, directly echoes the beginning of Jehovah's intervention back in chapter 38. The storm is obviously still rumbling overhead as fitting background music to the voice of God which, as we learned in 37.4-5, is thunder-like in its energy. Although Job is going to be pointed to the animal world, he is never permitted to forget the all-pervasive power of God in the atmospheric heavens. There is to be no let-up in the divine examination until he is thoroughly convinced of his own inadequacies.

If the first speech cast the spotlight on Job's ignorance by bombarding him with questions he could not answer, this (though continuing with a rigorous interrogation) emphasises his insolence in presuming to object to God's ways. It does so by raising the matter of governmental authority.

Challenging Job: 40.8-14

The language of the initial challenge is deliberately striking. "Disannul" (6565) translates a word meaning to break or violate. It is used of breaking a covenant (Gen 17.14; Lev 26.15) or a command (Num 15.31), making a vow "of none effect" (Num 30.8), defeating another's counsel (2 Sam 15.34), frustrating someone's plans (Ezra 4.5), and dividing the sea (Ps 74.13). In the book of Job it is used by Eliphaz of God who "disappointeth [6565] the devices of the crafty" (5.12), and of Job as one who casts off fear (15.4). Job himself employs the word to picture God smashing him in pieces (16.12). To disannul God's judgment is therefore a very serious charge. It means essentially to declare null and void God's right to administer His own world. The parallel word, "condemn" (7561), appears eleven times in Job, frequently on his own lips (9.20,29; 10.2,7,15), but significantly in Elihu's pointed question, "wilt thou condemn him that is most just?" (34.17).

This is the crux of Job's problem. In loudly maintaining his innocence (in which he is correct) he has implicitly undermined God's rights and righteousness (in which he is wrong). As is so often the case, Delitzsch gets to the heart of the matter:

> Job contended not alone with God, which is in itself wrong, let it be whatsoever it may; he went so far as to lose sight of the divine justice in the government of the world, and in order not to be obliged to give up his own righteousness, so far as to doubt the divine.[464]

In order to convict Job of his temerity, the Lord sardonically asks him if he possesses the attributes of deity, in particular that power by which the created universe is constantly and fittingly managed. The passage moves swiftly from questions to a sequence of ironic commands:

> Hast thou an arm like God? or canst thou thunder with a voice like him? Deck thyself now with glory and excellency, and clothe thyself with majesty and splendour. Cast abroad the ragings of thine anger, and look on every one that is proud, and abase him: Look on every one that is proud, bring him low, and tread down the wicked in their place: Hide them in the dust together; bind their faces in secret. Then will I also praise thee, because thy right hand saveth thee (40.9-14, JND).

In asking if Job is "like God", Jehovah lists some of His outstanding attributes as rightful judge of all the earth: His power ("arm"), His voice ("thunder"), His intrinsic splendour ("majesty ... excellency ... glory ... beauty", KJV), His anger ("wrath", KJV), His omniscience ("behold every one", KJV), His incomparable ability to mete out justice ("tread down the wicked"), and His control over the death sentence ("Hide them in the dust").

Shakespeare's Macbeth, having murdered his way to the throne of Scotland, is likened to a little man uncomfortably wearing clothes far too big for him. He may bear the name of king but he has no right to the position. As one of the minor characters in the play says,

> Now does he feel his title
> Hang loose about him, like a giant's robe
> Upon a dwarfish thief.[465]

It is as though Jehovah, with pointed irony, invites Job to don the robes of divine office and become king for a day. The object in view is to bring Job to a practical realisation of his own littleness. Let us consider the challenges one by one.

Does Job possess the **power** of God's arm? Scripture is packed with practical exhibitions of omnipotence. By His stretched out arm the Lord miraculously rescued Israel from Egyptian slavery (Ex 6.6), an event which stands as the grand Old Testament example of Jehovah's power. However, by the time we reach Isaiah 53 we discover that God's arm is a metaphor for His perfect servant: "Who hath believed our report? and to whom is the arm of the Lord revealed?" (Is 53.1). It is the eternal Son who manifests divine strength and implements the divine will. He, not Job, is the infallible executor of God's purposes in grace and in government.

Is Job's **voice** like a deafening clap of thunder? His friends have accused him of being somewhat blustery in his speeches (8.2; 15.2), but never of rivalling a tempest. In scriptural history we read of God's thunder devastating the Philistines (1 Sam 7.10), and discomfiting David's enemies (Ps 18.13). Elihu earlier anticipated the language of 40.9 when he said "God thundereth marvellously with his voice; great things doeth he, which we cannot comprehend" (37.5). In the book of Revelation, heaven's dramatic intrusion into the affairs of men during the coming tribulation will be accompanied by tremendous and terrifying thunderings (Rev 4.5; 6.1; 8.5; 10.3-4; 11.19; 14.2; 16.18; 19.6). Once again what might be dismissed as graphic picture language is made disturbingly real in Job's experience: at this very moment he is engulfed by a mighty whirlwind where thunder is far more than just a figure of speech.

Can Job array himself in God-like **splendour**? Although the four synonyms in verse 10 mean much the same thing, in combination they give an impression of the weighty and inexhaustible glory of the divine majesty. Scripture frequently piles word upon word to suggest the inadequacy of human language to do justice to God's greatness:

> Thine, O Lord, is the greatness, and the power, and the glory, and the victory, and the majesty: for all that is in the heaven and in the earth is thine; thine is the kingdom, O Lord, and thou art exalted as head above all (1 Chr 29.11).

> Honour and majesty are before him: strength and beauty are in his sanctuary (Ps 96.6).

> Worthy is the Lamb that was slain to receive power, and riches, and wisdom, and strength, and honour, and glory, and blessing ... Blessing, and honour, and glory, and power, be unto him that sitteth upon the throne, and unto the Lamb for ever and ever (Rev 5.12-13).

One word alone is insufficient to register Jehovah's supremacy, just as one Gospel narrative falls short of the many-faceted glories of the Saviour's earthly ministry, and one Old Testament messianic type fails to reflect the wonders of the ultimate reality in Christ Jesus. But Job possesses none of these qualities of uniquely divine majesty.

Can Job effectively exhibit righteous **anger** against human sin? Unlike much of twenty-first century Christendom, the Bible is consistently unembarrassed about disclosing the solemn reality of God's wrath. It does not soft-pedal the disturbing message of judgment. A God of infinite holiness cannot fail to be incensed by the fact and the fruits of sin, the fullest outpouring of His indignation being reserved for the future tribulation. From its very beginning, the New Testament warns of "the wrath to come" (Mt 3.7). While this was previewed in a limited way at the fall of Jerusalem, when there was "great distress in the land, and wrath upon this people" (Lk 21.23), it will be conclusively revealed in the period just preceding the Lord's coming in glory. The book of Revelation repeatedly describes the tribulation as the manifestation of God's "wrath" (Rev 6.16-17; 11.18; 14.10,19; 15.1,7; 16.1,19; 19.15). This suggests that we may legitimately read the word not primarily as a reference to the eternal lake of fire but rather as a technical term describing the unleashing of terrible judgments on the earth in preparation for the millennial Kingdom. The promise that believers of the present era are "not appointed … to wrath, but to obtain salvation by our Lord Jesus Christ" (1 Thess 5.9) is therefore a firm pledge that they will not pass through the future tribulation; instead, church saints will be removed by means of a special divine deliverance. Job, of course, is uninformed about a coming day of the Lord, and about the unique status of the church, the body of Christ. For all his genuine distress at the prevalence of sin around him, he simply has not the resources to exhibit God's fiery anger in dealing with wickedness.

Has Job the **omniscience** to assess everything that goes on in the universe? The God whose holy ire is yet to be fully released against rebellion is, mercifully, also a God of infallible knowledge. This guarantees that His judgment falls, without any possibility of mistake, upon those who deserve it. Job may be invited to "behold" and "Look on" the wicked as though he had taken on the role of judge, but in reality only the living God has the capacity to evaluate actions and motives. At the dedication of Israel's temple King Solomon, under inspiration, looked ahead to a situation when the individual Israelite or the nation as a whole, conscious of personal failure, would pray toward God's dwelling place in genuine repentance of heart:

> What prayer and supplication soever be made by any man, or by all thy people Israel, which shall know every man the plague of his own heart, and spread forth his hands toward this house: Then hear thou in heaven thy dwelling place, and forgive, and do, and give to every man according to his ways, whose heart thou knowest; (for thou, even thou only, knowest the hearts of all the children of men;) (1 Kings 8.38-39).

"Thou only knowest the hearts". The Lord Jesus proved His deity in the Gospels not just by miraculously healing a paralysed man but by reading the unspoken objections of His critics (Mk 2.6-8). If men possess some, admittedly feeble and sin-damaged, insight into the plague of their own hearts, how much more does God know perfectly both a man's actions and his deepest thoughts? But what could Job know, aware at best of some of the external deeds of a few people, while being blind to the innermost secrets of their hearts? Only an all-knowing, unfailing God has the rights and resources to evaluate men.

Has Job the authority to **mete out justice** or put down wickedness? Sin springs from the absurd pretensions of human conceit, hence the paralleling of pride and wickedness in verse 12. "Proud" (1343) is always used in a negative context, such as those prophetic passages which announce the abasing of pride (Ps 94.2; Prov 15.25; Is 2.12). Three synonyms combine here to describe God's power to topple the self-satisfied: "abase", "bring him low", and "tread down". Only He can "abase" (8213) the lofty for, writes David, "thine eyes are upon the haughty, that thou mayest bring them down [8213]" (2 Sam 22.28); only God can "bring down high looks" (Ps 18.27), for "he casteth the wicked down [8213] to the ground" (Ps 147.6). One of the devastating effects of Jehovah's coming intervention in the affairs of men will be that "the day of the Lord of hosts shall be upon every one that is proud and lofty, and upon every one that is lifted up; and he shall be brought low [8213]" (Is 2.12). Yet – marvellously – the same word which is used mainly to describe God's overturning of human pretensions is also used of God Himself:

> The Lord is high above all nations, and his glory above the heavens. Who is like unto the Lord our God, who dwelleth on high, Who humbleth himself [8213] to behold the things that are in heaven, and in the earth! (Ps 113.4-6).

The first two verses quoted above are unsurprising, but the third is a real stunner. The same God who dwells on high does not disdain to humble Himself in order to probe in depth the doings of His earthly creatures. As so often is the case, Old Testament picture language finds its literal fulfilment in the person of the incarnate Son of God, who

> made himself of no reputation, and took upon him the form of a servant, and was made in the likeness of men: And being found in fashion as a man, he humbled himself, and became obedient unto death, even the death of the cross (Phil 2.7-8).

Even as we learn about Jehovah's unique power to put down the proud, we are reminded of the One who voluntarily stepped down into manhood that He might graciously lift up "the beggar from the dunghill, to set them among princes, and to make them inherit the throne of glory" (1 Sam 2.8). How much we owe to the matchless condescension of Christ!

The word rendered "bring him low" (3665) is frequently translated "subdue", or "humble", while the third synonym, "tread down", is found only here. The three together underline the irresistible power of God to demolish all the high towers of human vanity. The context suggests that it takes the merest glance ("Look") from Jehovah to crumble inflated men into the dust: "Look on every one that is proud, and bring him low; and tread down the wicked in their place" (40.12). When we recall that simply a glimpse of the countenance of the Judge of all the earth will send the present universe packing (Rev 20.11), we can well believe that it requires no greater exercise of power to smash human pretensions.

Can Job, of his own energy, implement the **death sentence**? Doubtless, as a respected magistrate, he pronounced judgment on gross offenders (29.17), but ultimately it is "The Lord [who] killeth, and maketh alive: he bringeth down to the grave, and bringeth up" (1 Sam 2.6). Just as man's physical body was originally formed out of the dust and returns to it in death (Gen 2.7; 3.19), so it is God who brings him down to that depth. "Hide their faces" may allude to the practice (as recorded in Esther 7.8) of covering the face of a man about to be executed, or it may simply describe the removal of the guilty from the light of day as they enter the dark world of the dead. Whatever the case, Job is clearly not up to it. He shares none of these unique divine attributes. If he did, says the Lord, "Then will I also praise thee, because thy right hand saveth thee" (40.14, JND). The irony is unmistakable. God alone is worthy of praise, not Job; and it is God alone who saves, not Job. Both Testaments agree:

> Let them praise the name of the Lord: for his name alone is excellent; his glory is above the earth and heaven (Ps 148.13).

> To the only wise God our Saviour, be glory and majesty, dominion and power, both now and ever. Amen (Jude v.25).

The answer to each question in Jehovah's catechism is an emphatic "No". Job has neither the authority nor the ability to wear the insignia of divine office, for he cannot perform any of the glorious works of deity, let alone deliver himself – from his friends' false accusations, from disaster and death, from the righteous judgment of God. In spite of all his piety he is unworthy of the adoration that is rightfully God's alone.

We do not know how much Job understood about the great deliverance to be accomplished by the promised seed of the woman, but he must have realised that only God was able to save, and only God was worthy of praise. This truth is all the more evident to those who live in the light of Calvary's finished work. Because we can deliver neither ourselves nor anyone else (Ps 49.7-8), we are cast on the infinite value of the Saviour's atoning death. As a consequence, we delight to lift our praises to His name, an exercise which starts down here but continues into eternity. The great exhortation that John hears, coming out of the throne, is to "Praise our God, all ye his servants, and ye that fear him, both small and great" (Rev 19.5). Praising God is the believer's privilege and delight.

Case Study (i) – Behemoth: 40.15-24

Jehovah now turns from what we might call an abstract doctrinal challenge (involving a selective catalogue of divine attributes) to confront Job with physical objects – two great creatures He has made, which defy human strength.

Two vexed matters need immediate attention before we embark on a textual consideration of behemoth and leviathan: the historical reality and the zoological identity of these monster beings. The questions are closely connected. Commentators have traditionally related behemoth to the elephant or hippopotamus, and leviathan to the crocodile or whale. For example, the note on Job 40.15 in the Geneva Bible of 1587, a version much favoured by the English Puritans, reads "this beast is thought to be the elephant, or some other, which is unknown", while the comment on 40.1 says simply, "meaning the whale". The original King James Bible of 1611 preserves similar identifications. Thus the margin alongside behemoth reads "the Elephant, as some think", while leviathan is associated with "a whale or a whirlpool".

But because the language of colossal grandeur used to describe these creatures seems to surpass any simple identification with still living animals, some have therefore proposed that they are purely imaginary, fabulous depictions of magnificence. Let us first, then, consider the question of their **reality**. Is Jehovah tantalising Job with invented beasts from contemporary Middle Eastern mythology, or is He continuing to deal with factual animals which the patriarch would have known? That both behemoth and leviathan are presented to us in the text as genuine creatures is, I would argue, indisputable.

First, they follow hard on the sequence of ten unquestionably literal animals selected in chapters 38 and 39 to teach Job a lesson. At least one of those animals may now be extinct (the wild ox or aurochs), but that does not deny the existence of all ten in Job's day. The Lord is drawing His servant's attention to what he already knows in the natural world around him. Fantasy creatures are hardly a fitting testimony to God's creatorial power.

Second, Job is specifically instructed to "Behold now behemoth, which I made with thee" (40.15). "With thee" is crucial. It signals that this great creature was constructed, just as man was made, by God: "which I made as I made you" (ESV). It also strongly suggests that the making occurred at the same time: that is to say, on the sixth of the twenty-four hour days of the creation week (Gen 1.24-30). This was the day which commenced with God commanding the earth to "bring forth the living creature after his kind, cattle, and creeping thing, and beast of the earth after his kind" (Gen 1.24), and which ended with the making of man. The word behemoth (930), a transliteration of the Hebrew, appears only in this one verse in Job, but in its form it is a plural (presumably the plural of majesty) of the common word rendered "cattle" (929) in Genesis 1.24. Behemoth is, we might say, in its size and strength the beast of all beasts.

Third, both these creatures are described in such precise and plausible anatomical detail that it is hard to relegate them comfortably to the realms of myth or legend. Just consider the terminology. We learn (using the words of Darby's translation) about behemoth's loins, belly, tail, thighs, bones, members (limbs), mouth and nose (40.15-24). Leviathan receives even greater close scrutiny, for the Lord says "I will not be silent as to his parts, the story of his power, and the beauty of his structure" (41.12, JND). We find highlighted his jaws, teeth, scales, mouth, nostrils, neck, and flanks. These are real animals whose superb design features honour their Creator.

Fourth, Job is challenged as to his practical ability to hunt or subdue such creatures. He is invited to "Behold", that is, to gaze at behemoth (40.15) – which takes it for granted that an example of behemoth was available to him, though Job might be expected, wisely, to keep his distance. He is also asked if he is able to capture leviathan in the way that he might hook up a fish from the sea (41.1-2). Can he train him as a pet (41.3-4), or keep him as one keeps a caged bird (41.5), or sell him as fishermen trade their catch (41.6-7)? The expected answer to all these questions is "No", but the language again presupposes a genuine marine creature with which Job was familiar. Even Cansdale, who takes the popular view that leviathan is a crocodile, has to admit that though "the whole of Job 41 is poetic and full of imagery; nevertheless … it seems impossible for such a passage to be written without personal knowledge".[466]

One of the reasons people have questioned the historicity of leviathan in particular is, I suspect, because the word is used elsewhere in a symbolic or metaphorical sense to describe opponents of the living God. The Hebrew word (3882), which according to Gesenius's lexicon means "wreathed, twisted in folds", appears six times in the Old Testament: Job 3.8; 41.1; Psalm 74.14; 104.26; Isaiah 27.1 (twice). The occurrences may be divided into two groups. One group (Job 3.8; Ps 74.14; Is 27.1) uses the term metaphorically. In the bitter complaint of Job 3, those who are "ready to rouse up Leviathan" (3.8, JND) are those local necromancers who pretend to raise the devil or pronounce curses upon their enemies. It is an evidence of Job's tortured soul that he is prepared even to mention such grotesque pagan practices. In Psalm 74 the context is God's mighty work in devastating the Egyptian armies who pursued Israel after the exodus. It seems reasonable, then, that leviathan symbolically represents the power of the Egyptians which was abruptly terminated at the Red Sea, where "Thou brakest the heads of leviathan in pieces" (Ps 74.14). The same appears to be true in Isaiah 27, except that the context is eschatological rather than historical, looking ahead to the final destruction of Satan and his anti-God hordes:

> In that day the Lord with his sore and great and strong sword shall punish leviathan the piercing serpent, even leviathan that crooked serpent; and he shall slay the dragon that is in the sea (Is 27.1).

The second group (Job 41.1; Ps 104. 26), on the other hand, describes a genuine creature. The contexts are quite distinct. Psalm 104 is a stirring poetic celebration of God's creative works, exhibiting remarkable parallels with the six-day creation narrative of Genesis 1.[467] Thus we read this about the ocean: "There go the ships: there is that leviathan, whom thou hast made to play therein" (Ps 104.26). Likewise, the context of Job 41 is a series of questions about the visible grandeur of Jehovah's marvellous handiwork in all its rich variety.

Studying its uses in the Bible leads to the conclusion that, although the Hebrew word leviathan may at times be used in a figurative way, context is the ultimate guide to meaning. Job 41 is an entirely different kind of writing from Psalm 74 and Isaiah 27. Here is Lita Cosner's useful comment:

> How can Leviathan have a symbolic, poetic meaning in these passages [Ps 74.14 and Isa 27.1], but represent a real creature in Job 41? It's important to note that just because two passages use the same word, it doesn't mean the word is representing the same thing.

> So perhaps the answer is to recognize that while Job's Leviathan was a real aquatic creature, Leviathan in [Psalm 74] and Isaiah is something different altogether. So when Job talks about an animal that scorns fish hooks, it is referring to an actual fearsome, water-based creature. By contrast, when Isaiah and the Psalms talk about a multi-headed monster in the context

of foreign nations and gods, it is probably talking about the false god, depicted as a sea monster ….

The next question is *when* did Yahweh destroy Leviathan in a watery judgment? A prime candidate for this would be imagery of the parting of the Red Sea; if this is the case, then Leviathan is embodied by the Egyptian army who were destroyed when the waters came crashing down on them. Such exalted poetic imagery is appropriate for this event because the Exodus throughout the Old Testament is depicted as a prime example of God's power and majesty, second only to creation.

The Exodus imagery is also supported by the Old Testament use of the word Rahab. In Job 26.12, we have Rahab, who is apparently a sea creature destroyed in a watery judgment. However, in Psalm 87.4, 89.10, and Isaiah 30.7, we see Rahab used as a name for Egypt … It is possible, then, that Rahab and Leviathan may have overlapping semantic ranges, and both of them could be used poetically to refer to Egypt.[468]

The evidence, then, weighs heavily in favour of the physical reality of both behemoth and leviathan in Job 40 and 41.

What, however, about the precise **identity** of these beasts? Creatures like the elephant or hippopotamus, whale or crocodile, seem inadequate when compared with the deliberately mind-blowing language Jehovah uses. Behemoth, for example, is said to be "the chief of the ways of God" (40.19), and therefore unapproachable, while leviathan is so terrifying that Jehovah asks "shall not one be cast down even at the sight of him?" (41.9). More significantly, the standard identifications fail the test of a point-by-point examination. The *NKJV Study Bible*, which disappointingly opts for the hippopotamus in its note on Job 40.15, noticeably fails to address the problem of his tail, which alone highlights the unsuitability of either of the traditional candidates for behemoth.[469]

In an interesting article, Mart-Jan Paul argues persuasively that behemoth and leviathan were real creatures which cannot be identified with hippopotamus or crocodile. His conclusion is both temperate and judicious:

Behemoth and leviathan may well be now extinct species that were still living in Job's day. While what is known about several species of dinosaurs may appear to fit some aspects of God's description of behemoth and leviathan, the most we can say with confidence is that the descriptions do not match any known living species today. At the same time, to call them "mythological" creatures is to do violence to the text and context of Job; therefore, we affirm that these were actual creatures of which Job had knowledge (although we cannot state whether Job had direct or indirect knowledge of them). They symbolize the power of evil, connected with Satan, who is mentioned in the first chapters of the book. The words of God humbled Job and showed him that God is above all powers in this world.[470]

The unsatisfactory nature of elephant and hippopotamus as the originals of behemoth is also highlighted in an article by Allan K Steel. Having foregrounded the most striking difference – the cedar-like tail – he sums up the evidence as follows:

> The elephant is outstanding for its trunk, its great size (especially its feet), its enormous appetite and its ears. None of these unique features are mentioned in our passage, but they ought to have been, if Behemoth was the elephant. Also, the elephant retreats to the depths of the forest during the hot part of the day. This does not seem to fit with Job 40.21, which suggests that Behemoth spends his time in marshy areas.

> The hippopotamus is noted for its weight, its large and strong mouth, with its deadly tusks, its thick skin, its pink sweat and its ability to walk on the bed of a river for long periods. It spends most of the day in the water, as its skin dries out very quickly in the sun. Again, none of these unique features are mentioned in our passage! Similarly, the hippopotamus stays in the deeper water, and this does not seem to fit with Job 40.22, where we are told that Behemoth stays under the trees on the bank.[471]

He concludes:

> the most reasonable interpretation (which also takes the whole passage into account) is that Behemoth was a large animal, now extinct, which had a large tail. Thus some type of extinct dinosaur should still be considered a perfectly reasonable possibility according to our present state of knowledge.

Certainly, taken at its face value, the description of behemoth sounds far more like a massive land dinosaur than anything we can currently observe in the local zoo.[472]

Is it possible, then, to identify leviathan? Here is the answer offered by Tim Clarey:

> Could the leviathan described in Job 41 be a description of a semiaquatic dinosaur like the *Spinosaurus*? "Who can open the doors of his face, with his terrible teeth all around?" (v.14). "Darts are regarded as straw; he laughs at the threat of javelins. His undersides are like sharp potsherds; he spreads pointed marks in the mire" (vv.29-30). "He leaves a shining wake behind him; one would think the deep had white hair. On earth there is nothing like him, which is made without fear" (vv.32-33).

> These descriptive words indicate a large, ferocious animal that crawled or walked on the bottom of a river or shallow body of water, similar to the suggested behaviour of *Spinosaurus*. The "wake [or path] behind him" may refer to the trail the bony sail left in the water as it swam.[473]

Clarey goes on to describe spinosaurs thus:

> Spinosaurs were designed with a bony sail on their backs, up to seven feet high. Its exact purpose is unclear. Recent research indicates that spinosaurs spent a considerable part of their lives in water, eating fish and other aquatic prey. They had long, narrow jaws with round, reptile-like teeth in the lower jaw and larger, more dinosaur-like teeth in their upper jaw. And unlike most theropod dinosaurs, they had solid limb bones for better buoyancy and shorter hind legs - a feature common to semiaquatic vertebrates like crocodiles. The flexible tail and the shape of the tail bones suggest they used their tail for swimming. Spinosaurs seem perfectly designed to live in aquatic settings like modern crocodiles, possibly possessing webbed, paddle-like hind feet and nostrils placed high on their skulls.

Lita Cosner has an alternative suggestion:

> The best explanation seems to be that the Leviathan in Job was a giant crocodile known as *Sarcosuchus*, which grew to 11.2–12.2 metres and weighed up to 8 tonnes. This huge crocodile dwarfs today's largest - the saltwater crocodile (the largest confirmed individual was only 6.3m long and only 1,200kg). Furthermore, its back had a row of bony plates, called osteoderms, which fits the description in Job 41.15, "His back is made of rows of shields".[474]

Whichever creature it may have been – and, because it may be assumed by now to be extinct, all suggestions can only be provisional – it was obviously a beast of colossal grandeur. More importantly, as we shall see later, in the course of its elaborate description it becomes a symbol of the cosmic pride and lawlessness which finds its ultimate expression in Satan.

But let us return to the account of behemoth as it stands in the Revised Version:

> Behold now behemoth, which I made with thee; he eateth grass as an ox. Lo now, his strength is in his loins, and his force is in the muscles of his belly. He moveth his tail like a cedar: the sinews of his thighs are knit together. His bones are as tubes of brass; his limbs are like bars of iron. He is the chief of the ways of God: he only that made him can make his sword to approach unto him. Surely the mountains bring him forth food; where all the beasts of the field do play. He lieth under the lotus trees, in the covert of the reed, and the fen. The lotus trees cover him with their shadow; the willows of the brook compass him about. Behold, if a river overflow, he trembleth not: he is confident, though Jordan swell even to his mouth. Shall any take him when he is on the watch, or pierce through his nose with a snare? (40.15-24, RV).

The description deals with five aspects of the creature: its creation ("which I made"), its diet ("he eateth grass"), its size and strength ("his strength is in his loins"), its habitat ("he lieth under the lotus trees"), and its invulnerability ("shall any take him?"). Let us look at these one by one.

Two key verses treat the beast's **creation** (40.15,19). God made it "with thee", which suggests both "equally with" and "in conjunction with". God made behemoth as surely as He also made the first man (just as behemoth is representative of God's animal kingdom so is Job of humanity), and He made it at the same time, on the sixth day of the creation week. But in verse 19 we are told that behemoth is "the chief [the word literally means the first or beginning, and is so translated in Genesis 1.1] of the ways of God". Clearly behemoth was not the first living thing to be made (marine creatures and birds appeared on the fifth day), but in sheer size and power he stands as the masterpiece of the beast kingdom. This alone calls into question any identification of behemoth with the elephant or hippopotamus, since the fossil evidence shows that these were by no means the largest of land animals. "The ways of God" in this context presumably refers to Jehovah's amazing works in forming the animals. That said, it is interesting that the same collocation of words ("beginning" and "ways") appears again only in Proverbs 8.22. Behemoth is the product of eternal divine wisdom, but behemoth is not the culmination of God's creation programme. We know from Genesis 1 that Adam and Eve jointly formed the pinnacle of divine industry, because they are placed at the end as both the climax and the responsible caretakers of God's handiwork. Further, unlike all others – angels included – man was created in God's image, made uniquely to relate to Him by bearing something of His likeness. The image of God in man stretches even beyond the possession of personality and moral consciousness with which it is normally identified to include the design of the human body itself, because Adam was shaped with the incarnation in view. Man is therefore the ideal physical vehicle for the expression of the invisible God.

But we must not miss the key point: behemoth was made, not by Job, but by God, who therefore has the right and the power to control this massive creature. This is the teaching of verse 19, where "sword" refers not to the animal's incisors but to God's supreme power over it. He alone can approach it unafraid. Job would have more sense than to get close to behemoth – has he not therefore been a little presumptuous in his desire to swagger "as a prince" (31.37) into the presence of God?

For such a huge and frightening being, behemoth's **diet** seems strangely bland. Like the smaller cattle from which he gets his name, and like Job's own lost oxen (1.3,14-15), behemoth is herbivorous. In contrast to the lion, behemoth obviously did not change his eating habits as a result of Adam's fall. Accompanied by other wild animals who sport ("play") in the environment God has provided for them, he grazes on the lush herbage growing on the uplands and the hillsides (40.20).

His **size and strength** are suggested by the extended physical description in verses 16 to 19. There we learn about the muscular strength of his loins and belly, the length of his tremendous tail, and his sinewy thighs, wreathed or twisted together like thick rope. The same word for "knit together" appears in Lamentations 1.14, where Jerusalem complains about the heavy yoke of transgression the Lord has laid on it. His bones are like great bronze or copper tubes, or solid bars of iron. Unlike the earlier exhilarating sketch of the horse (39.19-25), the emphasis is not on speed or beauty but sheer massive strength. After such a description the assertion in verse 19 is wholly understandable: "he only that made him can make his sword to approach unto him".

The creature's **habitat** is specified as hillside and marshland. Hartley writes (although assuming the animal is the hippopotamus) that

> a favourite habit of this splendid beast is to lie on the river bank, shading itself under the lotus ... a thorny tree which grows in the hot, damp areas of Israel and Africa. Satisfied with food, it finds safety in a swampy area thick with reeds or on the bank, concealed by lotuses and poplars.[475]

His account is superb although, after the close-up of behemoth's formidable body, the suggestion that this magnificent creature needs to seek safety rings rather hollow. Behemoth is not alarmed when a river overflows, for he can outswim the floods. In this context "Jordan" probably refers generally to any swelling river (Delitzsch renders the verse, "He remaineth cheerful, if a Jordan breaketh forth upon his mouth").[476]

Last of all we are made aware of his **invulnerability**. He is not to be trapped or taken unawares. Those who view behemoth as the hippopotamus agree that its capture, though difficult, was certainly not impossible. Mart-Jan Paul informs us that

> in Egypt the hippopotamus was hunted. A favourite tactic was to pierce the nose, forcing the animal to breathe through its opened mouth. Following this the fatal blow could be inflicted in the mouth. Egyptian pharaohs were proud of being able to kill a hippopotamus, since this contributed to the praise of their power as an incarnated god.[477]

However, in the light of the clear affirmation of verse 19 that only He who made behemoth can conquer him, it seems best to read this concluding statement as clinching evidence of the creature's complete unassailability. The whole point is that neither Job nor any other man has the power to overcome behemoth. And if Job cannot control just one of God's creatures, how dare he presume to dictate to the governor of the universe how He should deal with His world in general – and with Job in particular?

Case Study (ii) – Leviathan: 41.1-34

The immediate connection between behemoth and leviathan is their similar ability to resist all human attempts at capture. Jehovah raised the question about the former – which may only be answered by a negative – "Shall any take him when he is on the watch, or pierce through his nose with a snare?" (40.24, RV).

He now passes on to a creature even more terrifying than behemoth. Behemoth may be big, but leviathan is lethal ferocity embodied.

This lengthy descriptive section may be divided into three major portions. The first eight verses of chapter 41 constitute a direct **challenge** to Job (41.1-8), after which comes, unexpectedly, the vital **conclusion** to be drawn from the entire leviathan episode (41.9-11). There follows a detailed **consideration** of the animal's structure, power and magnificence (41.12-34).

First comes the **challenge**, consisting of a sequence of fourteen questions addressed to Job. Because the Revised Version helpfully clarifies several matters, we shall reproduce it:

> Canst thou draw out leviathan with a fish hook? or press down his tongue with a cord? Canst thou put a rope into his nose? or pierce his jaw through with a hook? Will he make many supplications unto thee? or will he speak soft words unto thee? Will he make a covenant with thee, that thou shouldest take him for a servant for ever? Wilt thou play with him as with a bird? or wilt thou bind him for thy maidens? Shall the bands of fishermen make traffic of him? shall they part him among the merchants? Canst thou fill his skin with barbed irons, or his head with fish spears? Lay thine hand upon him; remember the battle, and do so no more (41.1-8, RV).

While behemoth inhabits the marshy country, leviathan is a monster of the waters. Before he is described we are made aware of his invulnerability. The questions fired at Job are remarkably practical, alluding in detail to the kinds of weaponry used by his contemporaries in their hunting and fishing expeditions (41.1-2,7). "Fish hook" (2443) appears only here and two other places (Is 19.8; Hab 1.15) where the context is fishing and where the KJV translates the word "angle". "Cord" is the word used for the rope by which Rahab smuggled the spies out of Jericho (Josh 2.15) and the siege cables with which a city might be dragged down (2 Sam 17.13). It suggests the sturdy equipment required in any theoretical assault on leviathan. The "rope" of verse 2 denotes a line made of twisted rushes or spun out of rush fibre (the KJV translates the same word as "rush" in Isaiah 9.14-15, and "bulrush" in Isaiah 58.5). What the RV renders "hook" in verse 2 is a word meaning thorn or thistle (as in Job 31.40 and Proverbs 26.9), but in the context of Job 41 appears to refer to some kind of ring forced through a wild animal's pierced nose so that it might be dragged away.

This was also often the fate of prisoners of war. One of the barbaric practices of the ancient Assyrians was to insert hooks through the lips or nose of their captives in order to degrade and dominate them. The following describes a picture found on an Assyrian relief:

> This relief represents part of a scene from a marble slab discovered at Khorsabad. The Assyrian king is using a spear to blind one of his many prisoners. In his left hand he holds a cord with a hook attached at the

opposite end which is inserted into the prisoner's lips. The Assyrians would thrust the point of a dagger or spear into the eye.[478]

The ESV translation of 2 Chronicles 33 usefully highlights this practice in connection with the capture of King Manasseh:

> The Lord brought upon them the commanders of the army of the king of Assyria, who captured Manasseh with hooks and bound him with chains of bronze and brought him to Babylon (2 Chr 33.11, ESV).

Jehovah's metaphors in verses 2 to 4 of Job 41 therefore liken leviathan to a hostile monarch who has been subdued, led captive, forced to sue for peace and enter into a treaty with the victors, recognising their authority over his territory. This was the case with the later kings of Judah, who found themselves under the rule of foreign powers like Assyria, Egypt, and Babylon. Leviathan, however, will not so easily be cowed. The creature's implacable savagery is emphasised with comic irony (41.3-5). He neither begs for mercy nor docilely submits to being tamed for domestic use or entertainment. Small birds (the same word is translated "sparrow" in Psalm 84.3 and 102.7) might be caught and caged for amusement, but not leviathan.

Verse 7 continues with a reference to two other contemporary hunting tools: "barbed irons" (only found here, and best understood as a kind of harpoon) and "fish spears". It is apparent that the tackle and techniques successfully used in securing most species of fish make no impression on leviathan. As well as an insight into the weapons used in hunting, we are given an idea of what might be the normal fate of a captured marine animal. Fish and other sea creatures were caught, cut up and traded by Canaanite merchants. But the snapshot of the fish market is notable for the conspicuous absence of any leviathan steaks or slices (41.6).

As if to cement the solemn lesson about leviathan's unassailability, Jehovah ends with an ominous aphorism: "Lay thine hand upon him; remember the battle, and do so no more" (41.8, RV). The language is highly condensed but the meaning is clear enough: anyone who is so foolhardy as to mess with leviathan will have cause to remember that deadly tussle for the rest of his life – certainly he will never attempt it again.

This extended challenge to Job is designed to produce the inevitable answer, "No". None of these things can Job do with such a formidable opponent.

It is at this point, to the reader's surprise, that we are presented with the **conclusion** (41.9-11), that is to say (using the word as it appears in Ecclesiastes 12.13), the spiritual lesson to be adduced from the whole leviathan passage. Instead of waiting until the end, Jehovah summarises the key message near the start. The reason for bringing it forward is probably because behemoth and leviathan together unite as one grand testimony to man's inability in a fallen world to control even the animal kingdom. The final verses of chapter 40 and the first few of chapter 41 combine to foreground these amazing creatures' immunity to subjugation. Together they pave the way for Jehovah's exposition of the spiritual lesson:

> Behold, the hope of him is in vain: shall not one be cast down even at the sight of him? None is so fierce that he dare stir him up: who then is he that can stand before me? Who hath first given unto me, that I should repay him? whatsoever is under the whole heaven is mine (41.9-11, RV).

The meaning is beautifully clear. We might paraphrase it like this. There is no hope whatever of successfully capturing leviathan – indeed, the mere sight of this monster is enough to chill the blood, causing hunters to drop their weapons and flee in terror. Therefore, since no one has the ferocity or courage to rouse such a creature into fury, who can possibly stand in the presence of the living God who made it? If the creature is grand, how much grander is the Creator?

Three related truths are emphasised: divine omnipotence, divine obligation, and divine ownership. Leviathan may be large and powerful (the pen picture taking up the rest of the chapter makes that abundantly evident) but the One who created him is infinitely greater. Who dares to stand before Him? "Stand" (3320) appears in the prologue, used of the sons of God who came to "present themselves [3320] before the Lord" (1.6; 2.1). The example is not irrelevant. What mere man, created from the dust of the ground, would have the impudence to come boldly into the presence of the almighty God, as though he were an angelic being? Job has been pleading for a hearing in God's courtroom, but he does not know what he is asking. Of course, the New Testament casts new light on this. Believers today possess a privilege unknown to Job, or indeed to any Old Testament saint. Because in Christ we have a Great High Priest, we are entitled to "come boldly unto the throne of grace, that we may obtain mercy, and find grace to help in time of need" (Heb 4.16). This boldness rests not on personal merit or might but on the finished work of Calvary. The omnipotent God is now by grace gloriously accessible to the feeblest of His children.

But if God is omnipotent so is He, unsurprisingly, self-sufficient. Since He is the giver of "life, and breath, and all things" (Acts 17.25), He is under obligation to no one. No one can do God a favour; no one can perform a service so as to place Him in debt. Merely to articulate the idea exposes its absurdity. We cannot give to Him; rather, He gives to us. God was under no compulsion either to create man or, having created him, to move gratuitously in salvation towards any of His disobedient creatures. Deliverance in Christ from the eternal consequences of sin is from first to last a work of matchless free grace. Paul rounds off his classic exploration of the divine programme of salvation with a doxology incorporating this verse from Job:

> O the depth of the riches both of the wisdom and knowledge of God! how unsearchable are his judgments, and his ways past finding out! For who hath known the mind of the Lord? or who hath been his counsellor? Or who hath first given to him, and it shall be recompensed unto him again?

For of him, and through him, and to him, are all things: to whom be glory
for ever. Amen (Rom 11.33-36).

One other matter, highly relevant to the argument of the book of Job,
is touched on in Jehovah's allusion to restitution. The word "repay" (7999) is
elsewhere translated, for example, "reward" (Gen 44.4), "restore" (Ex 22.1),
"make restitution" (Ex 22.3), and "recompense" (Ruth 2.12). The idea is that of
paying a debt or making good something that has been lost or stolen. In raising
the question, "Who hath first given unto me, that I should repay him?" (41.11),
the Lord exposes the error of any theology which maintains that He is required
to reward piety with prosperity. Elihu mentioned the matter when he asked Job,
"If thou be righteous, what givest thou him? or what receiveth he of thine hand?"
(35.7). Eliphaz also acknowledged that man can never add to the sum of God's
blessedness: "Is it any pleasure to the Almighty, that thou art righteous? or is it
gain to him, that thou makest thy ways perfect?" (22.3). Jehovah now confirms
the doctrinal accuracy of those earlier comments. He is not compelled to reward
men for their good works either with exemption from eternal judgment or with
temporal blessing. Everything we receive from Him comes on the basis of free
sovereign grace, not personal merit. This, of course, is crucial to any appreciation
of salvation from sin's penalty: it springs purely from undeserved divine favour
and is received through faith without the addition of any human works.

The principle lies behind much of the debate which has waged through the
book. Job's friends have assumed his outward prosperity was the reward of
personal goodness and that therefore the removal of the former proves the decline
of the latter. Jehovah collapses the entire theory by asserting that man can never
place God in his debt. It is always the other way around. And our debt can never
be repaid. As the Lord Jesus taught His disciples, "when ye shall have done all
those things which are commanded you, say, We are unprofitable servants: we
have done that which was our duty to do" (Lk 17.10).

The final point, expanding on the impossibility of God being obligated to
anyone, is the reality of divine ownership. Everything under the heavens (and,
for that matter, above them) is His. David recognised this when, gazing at the
abundance of raw materials amassed for the temple his son would build, he burst
into praise: "But who am I ... that we should be able to offer so willingly after
this sort? for all things come of thee, and of thine own have we given thee" (1 Chr
29.14). When, in worship, believers present to God their appreciation of His Son,
they are simply giving back to Him what He has first given them. He who gave
us His Son also grants the ability to appreciate Him.

Once we get these truths engraved on our hearts – that God is the all-powerful,
self-sufficient, lawful possessor of heaven and earth – we shall approach Him in
the right spirit. None of us has glimpsed leviathan, save, of course, in the vivid
language of Jehovah's pen picture; but we have all gazed into a night sky, sensing
something of its overwhelming splendour. The more men probe, the vaster
seems the universe. And behind that immensity of space, with its innumerable
constellations, is the God who made it all. If His works are big, He is so much

bigger. To be confronted with such mind-staggering greatness puts us in our place. As sinful creatures we are weak, we are debtors, and we have no intrinsic claim on such a God. Job will feel this deeply at the close of Jehovah's speech. But what a transformation takes place when the weakest, frailest sinner trusts in Christ! In Him we gain everything: unfailing strength (Eph 6.10), undiminishing wealth (Rev 2.9), and an unalienable relationship to God of sons (Gal 3.26).

This brief hiatus in the description (41.9-11) is designed to sum up for Job the core message of the whole leviathan episode. Yet the prolonged **consideration** of the creature which follows (41.12-34) is still needed to give the reader an unforgettable sense of its monumental size and power. Unlike behemoth, no attention is devoted to its diet. Rather, the focus is on his impregnable body armour and his ferociousness. Special attention is devoted to head (41.14,18-22), skin and scales (41.13,15-17,23), obduracy (41.24-29), physical presence on land or water (41.30-32), and unique dauntlessness (41.33-34).

Jehovah resumes His in-depth overview of leviathan with the evident satisfaction of a master designer unveiling a *pièce de résistance*:

> I will not keep silence concerning his limbs, nor his mighty strength, nor his comely proportion (41.12, RV).

God has no reason to be ashamed of His handiwork; indeed, He takes obvious delight in exhibiting what He has made, drawing careful attention to the creature's limbs, superlative power, and beauty of structure. Unlike sinful human beings, God never produces a botched job. The creation week was crowned with the testimony that "God saw every thing that he had made, and, behold, it was very good" (Gen 1.31), and even after the entrance of sin the God who does all things well can still rejoice in His works. Yet leviathan is not His greatest source of pleasure. The following verses indicate what gratifies God:

> Hath the Lord as great delight in burnt offerings and sacrifices, as in obeying the voice of the Lord? Behold, to obey is better than sacrifice, and to hearken than the fat of rams (1 Sam 15.22).

> They that are of a froward heart are abomination to the Lord: but such as are upright in their way are his delight (Prov 11.20).

> The sacrifice of the wicked is an abomination to the Lord: but the prayer of the upright is his delight (Prov 15.8).

> But let him that glorieth glory in this, that he understandeth and knoweth me, that I am the Lord which exercise lovingkindness, judgment, and righteousness, in the earth: for in these things I delight, saith the Lord (Jer 9.24).

Obedience, uprightness, prayer, and the reflection of His own moral character in His people – all these cheer the heart of God. Such features have only been displayed perfectly in one person – the incarnate Son, whose life elicited heaven's joyful commendation, "This is my beloved Son, in whom I have found my delight" (Mt 3.17, JND). If God could not keep silence about the superlative design of leviathan, how much more must He give public voice to His pleasure in His Son? In the Gospel narratives God, so to speak, puts the Lord Jesus on show before the eyes of men, demonstrating His inability to fail even under the most strenuous of tests.

Returning to leviathan, the details we are invited to ponder are, first, his **skin, head and scales**:

> Who can strip off his outer garment? who shall come within his double bridle? Who can open the doors of his face? round about his teeth is terror. His strong scales are his pride, shut up together as with a close seal. One is so near to another, that no air can come between them. They are joined one to another; they stick together, that they cannot be sundered (41.13-17, RV).

Three questions start us off. Once again they all invite the answer, "Nobody". Who can uncover leviathan so as to lay him bare before his enemies? The word the RV translates "strip off" ("discover" in the KJV) first appears in the Old Testament of Noah "uncovered" in his drunken stupor (Gen 9.21). Leviathan is securely protected by a hard outer covering, here likened to clothing. "Bridle" (7448) is used only three other times in the Bible (Job 30.11; Ps 32.9; Is 30.28). It may refer to a literal bridle with which hunters attempt to muzzle their victim, but more likely describes poetically leviathan's great jaws. Darby's rendering makes good sense: "who can come within his double jaws?" (41.13, JND) Jehovah's language permits us to do what none would dare do in practice – creep up close to peer into the creature's terrifying mouth, filled with sharp, menacing teeth. The "terror" (367) is therefore very real. The same word is used of the "horror [367] of great darkness" which descended on Abram (Gen 15.12), the "fear" which overcame the Canaanites who heard about Israel's great deliverance from Egypt (Ex 15.16), the "terror" which swept over the inhabitants of Jericho (Josh 2.9), and the "dread" of God which came upon Job (Job 13.21). It is hardly surprising that Bunyan drew on this description of leviathan when creating the monster Apollyon who battles with Christian in the Valley of Humiliation.

We move suddenly from leviathan's threatening jaws to his impressively snug body armour (41.15-17). The creature is clad with what are metaphorically described as rows of shields (scales) to protect his hide. So closely are they fitted together on his body that no air can come between them. They are locked in place with such precision that it is impossible to prise them apart. The word for "joined" (1692) is, intriguingly, first used in Scripture of marriage: "Therefore shall a man … cleave [1692] unto his wife: and they shall be one flesh" (Gen 2.24). One is tempted to comment that married couples should be equally inseparable. This minute close-up of the creature's scaly body again bears witness to its historical genuineness and reaffirms its invincibility. More important, however, is the passing allusion to pride (1346). This is not the same Hebrew word used in 40.11-12 to describe human arrogance, although it carries a similar freight of meaning. It is used positively of Jehovah's "excellency" (Deut 33.26,29; Ps 68.34), but negatively of the wicked (Ps 10.2; 31.18,23; 36.11; 73.6). The ground is being prepared for seeing leviathan as an emblem of satanic assertiveness and overweening hauteur.

Next, we view his **terrifying head**:

> His sneezings flash light, and his eyes are like the eyelids of the morning. Out of his mouth go forth flames; sparks of fire leap out: Out of his nostrils goeth smoke, as out of a boiling pot and cauldron. His breath kindleth coals, and a flame goeth out of his mouth (41.18-21, JND).

No one sneezes like leviathan. The exact word appears only here. Fausset's comment, doubtless accurate insofar as it describes the crocodile, sounds very pedestrian compared with the sparkle of the Hebrew poetry:

> Amphibious animals, emerging after having long held their breath under water, respire by violently expelling the breath like one sneezing: in the effort the *eyes* which are usually directed towards the sun, seem to flash fire; or it is the expelled *breath* that, in the sun, seems to emit light.

Fausset also informs us that "Egyptian hieroglyphics paint the *eyes of the crocodile* as the symbol for *morning*, because the eyes appear the first thing, before the whole body emerges from the deep". But the same may well have been true of some ancient sea-going dinosaur or extinct giant crocodile.

At first reading, the flames and smoke emitted from leviathan's mouth sound purely fanciful, an exaggerated poetic suggestion of the panic aroused by the sight of this fearsome creature. "Flames" is Darby's alternative to the KJV's "burning lamps". The word (3940) is used, for example, of the "burning lamp" of God's presence which passed between the pieces of Abraham's sacrifice (Gen 15.17), the "lightnings" which illuminated Mount Sinai (Ex 20.18), the "lamps" concealed in Gideon's pitchers (Judg 7.16), and the "lamp" of radiant testimony associated with Israel's future salvation (Is 62.1). The picture in Job is, to say the least, extraordinary: leviathan is accompanied by belching fire and noisome smoke. But need this be pure hyperbole? Russell Grigg suggests that leviathan was

> some sort of large fire-breathing animal. Just as the small bombardier beetle has an explosion-producing mechanism, so the great sea-dragon may have had an explosion-producing mechanism to enable it to be a real fire breathing dragon.[479]

The present state of knowledge does not permit us to dismiss such a proposal out of hand.

The next verses celebrate leviathan's **power**:

In his neck abideth strength, and terror danceth before him. The flakes of his flesh are joined together: they are firm upon him; they cannot be moved. His heart is as firm as a stone; yea, firm as the nether millstone (41.22-24, RV).

Obviously leviathan is not all sound and fury, smoke and fire; he is possessed of a resilient toughness which embraces his physical structure, his material composition, and his brute instincts. The personification in verse 22 is perhaps not easy to paraphrase, but the idea seems to be that wherever he goes he brings fear and dread. His flesh does not consist of yieldingly flabby folds or tyres but is firm and muscular. Delitzsch's rendering is felicitous:

> The flanks of his flesh are thickly set,
> Fitting tightly to him, immoveable.[480]

His heart – the core of his being – is stony in its obdurate hardness and insensitivity. Leviathan will give way neither to pity nor fear. He is built like a machine primed for destruction.

The combination of "heart" and "stone" appears in only four Bible verses. On learning of his imminent peril, the sottish Nabal had what sounds like a stroke, so that "his heart died within him, and he became as a stone" (1 Sam 25.37). More significantly, the Lord predicts of Israel's future spiritual revival that

> I will give them one heart, and I will put a new spirit within you; and I will take the stony heart out of their flesh, and will give them an heart of flesh (Ezek 11.19; 36.26).

A "stony heart" in this context is one which is unregenerate, unresponsive to God's mercy, untouched by God's Word; a "heart of flesh", on the other hand, is tender, sensitive to the voice of Jehovah, and eminently teachable. The latter should describe every believer. The miracle of new birth brings about such a genuine internal revolution that we become – for the first time in our lives – attuned to God, with an unquenchable thirst for the Scriptures of truth.

But leviathan cannot change: he is resolutely fixed in his instinctive savagery. Appropriately, then, we read next about his ability to **laugh at danger**:

> When he raiseth himself up, the mighty are afraid: they are beside themselves with consternation. If any reach him with a sword, it cannot hold; neither spear, nor dart, nor harpoon. He esteemeth iron as straw, bronze as rotten wood. The arrow will not make him flee; slingstones are turned with him into stubble. Clubs are counted as stubble; he laugheth at the shaking of a javelin (41.25-29, JND).

The scene, condensing in a few words a battle between the monster and its would-be hunters, is memorable for its zesty combination of jubilation and terror. The language echoes the ironic challenge of 41.1-8, where the armoury of fisherman and warrior is found totally inadequate to overcome leviathan. Nothing will suffice to bring him to heel. Nonetheless, the arsenal is extensive: sword, spear, dart, harpoon (whether made of iron or bronze), arrow, slingstone, club, javelin. Trouble is, nothing avails, for this creature inspires fear in the greatest of men. "The mighty" translates the word *el* (410), used in the Pentateuch mainly of God Himself (Gen 14.18-20,22 onwards). It appears fifty-six times in Job and is translated "God" in the KJV on every occasion but this. The idea is that even the most successful warriors, men who consider themselves almost god-like in their strength, turn to flee from leviathan.

The account now offers a graphic close-up of **the imprint he leaves** on land and on sea:

> His under parts are sharp potsherds: he spreadeth a threshing-sledge upon the mire. He maketh the deep to boil like a pot; he maketh the sea like a pot of ointment; He maketh the path to shine after him: one would think the deep to be hoary (41.30-32, JND).

Because of the rough, spikey scales on his belly, which are like broken pieces of pottery, he leaves a visible trail over the surface of the mud, just as though a threshing sledge – a stage with three iron-teethed rollers, which cut the straw for fodder while crushing out the grain – had been dragged over it. The word which the KJV translates "sharp pointed things" (2742) is occasionally rendered "threshing instrument" (Is 28.27; Amos 1.3), although some commentators believe the language describes the litter of broken arrows and spears lying around the undefeated monster. But when he thrashes about in the water, his preferred environment, he makes the sea bubble up like a boiling cauldron, or like a pot of ointment so vigorously stirred that it resembles a seething mixture. Carving his way through the waters he leaves a shining, luminescent wake behind him, so that one might think the ocean's surface sported the white hair of an old man. Just as leviathan churns up a wake when he ploughs through the sea, so this powerful poetry leaves a picture indelibly etched on the mind.

Finally comes a **summary of his prowess**, beautifully captured in the words of the KJV:

> Upon earth there is not his like, who is made without fear. He beholdeth all high things: he is a king over all the children of pride (41.33-34).

Although not as crucial as the brief explanatory paragraph in verses 9-11, this is nevertheless a significant comment. Jehovah's last words to Job remind us that leviathan is a created being ("made"), that his habitat is the material world in which we live ("upon earth"), that he is unique in his audacity ("without fear"), that he is able to outstare every other mighty creature while defiantly standing his ground ("beholdeth all high things"), and that he is the king of all proud beasts. The earlier zoological catalogue stretched from the lion (38.39) to the eagle (39.27), traditional monarchs of land and air respectively, but leviathan outclasses them all. The word for "pride" (7830) appears only twice in the Bible: in Job 28.8 (where it is translated "lion") and here in 41.34. The lion's innate haughtiness, we might say, is as nothing compared with leviathan's. If behemoth, "chief of the ways of God" (40.19), is the beast of all beasts, then leviathan is the colossal embodiment of creaturely pride.

The lessons are transparent. No one can control leviathan, save God his Creator. If such a creature, huge in bulk and bravado, provokes due respect, how much more should we reverence the living God who made him? Further, since God alone is able to humble this animal's conceit, He can without effort put men in their place, abasing that overweening human arrogance which presumes to dictate to the Lord of the universe how He should run His creation. As has been suggested earlier, leviathan's serpentine pride inevitably reminds us of Job's unseen enemy in the prologue, the malign spiritual intelligence later revealed as "the great dragon ... that old serpent, called the Devil, and Satan, which deceiveth the whole world" (Rev 12.9). Though unmentioned since chapter 2, Satan's animosity unleashed the initial tornado of trials which battered the patriarch. Yet he, the great enemy of mankind from Genesis 3 onwards, is nonetheless a created being under the ultimate sway of God. In Jehovah's sovereign purpose, Satan is permitted for a while to have his fling, before he is eternally disposed of. What is more, in having his way he unconsciously fulfils God's secret programme of grace. Far from proving Job's piety to be a fraud, Satan's attacks have cast him all the more upon his God. He may at times have spoken mistakenly, angrily, bitterly – but he has always called on the Lord. The case with Peter in Luke 22 is similar. Shaken up in Satan's sieve, the apostle discovered he could place no confidence in self but must find his resources only in the grace of an all-knowing Saviour.

In brief, over the past four chapters Jehovah has fired three major salvos at Job:

- Can he comprehend God's ways in the created universe? 38.1-38
- Can he cater for the needs of God's world? 38.39 – 39.30
- Can he control the most impressive of God's created works? 40.6 – 41.34.

In each case the answer is a resounding "No". Job has neither the knowledge nor the ability to run the world. In coming face to face with his own puniness he has learned more about God. Though he had an intellectual grasp of truth before, he now knows – personally and dynamically – far more about God's power (in making a universe packed with fathomless marvels) and providence (in compassionately meeting the daily needs of creatures as small as the raven, whose "young ones cry unto God"). Such a God is always in complete control.

Readers will wonder why so much space in God's revelation to Job is devoted to the graphic description of two creatures which, if the commentary above is correct, are long extinct and therefore inaccessible to scrutiny. Two answers may be offered. First, since we may assume that, as a result of the earth's more rigorous climate and depleted resources after the Noahic Flood, the survival of dinosaurs was comparatively brief, the language of the text unsurprisingly hints that behemoth and leviathan were unique specimens even in Job's day. Such an in-depth account of their design features was therefore God's gracious provision for later generations, so that future readers of Scripture might have a privileged insight into some of the past wonders of His universe. Second, His works act as an analogy for His Word. If created marvels deserve such a prolonged investigation, how much more does His Word? Robinson comments appropriately that God's "works ... bear to be taken to pieces and viewed in detail. The better known the more admired",[481] but the same language could easily be applied to the Scriptures. It is the psalmist who most obviously points out the parallel. In Psalm 19, David draws attention to the harmony between the created world and the written Word, while the author of Psalm 33 unites the two in one verse: "the word of the Lord is right; and all his works are done in truth" (Ps 33.4). Close investigation of Scripture is a sure-fire recipe for an intellectual and spiritual delight which will inevitably express itself in worship. If leviathan deserves so much attention, how much more should we pay to Leviticus, Lamentations and Luke? We can never spend too much time with the Word.

Comprehension: 42.1-6

The patriarch's final words, though brief, demonstrate that he has at last come to a proper state of mind. His response to Jehovah is magnificent, not least because he is prepared, without argument or protest, to confess his error. In the world it is considered courageous to go down fighting – but not before God. Before Him all we can rightly do is submit in total surrender. All criticisms and complaints have been silenced. The fact that Job, hitherto so garrulous, is now so terse, testifies to the impact of God's intervention. Robinson makes the point that although "Job's repentance [is] expressed in few words" – and certainly, compared with his erstwhile eloquence, his contrition sounds brief – "God requires not many words, but much faith".[482]

His first affirmation is "I know". It is not that he knows the why and wherefore of his terrible circumstances, but rather that he has been led into a right perception of God. As Wood superbly puts it, "Job does not find the answer he was seeking, but he loses the question he was asking".[483] What he discovers is far better than any intellectual solution to the riddle of his life: he finds God. The God of infinite majesty is bigger than His people's circumstances, and that alone should promote worship. Even when we cannot understand, we can trust.

Here, then, after the false termination of 31.40, are Job's final words as they appear in the Revised Version:

> Then Job answered the Lord, and said, I know that thou canst do all things, and that no purpose of thine can be restrained. Who is this that hideth counsel without knowledge? therefore have I uttered that which I understood not, things too wonderful for me, which I knew not. Hear, I beseech thee, and I will speak; I will demand of thee, and declare thou unto me. I had heard of thee by the hearing of the ear; but now mine eye seeth

thee, Wherefore I abhor myself, and repent in dust and ashes (42.1-6, RV).

God's omnipotence ("thou canst do all things") and His infallible programme ("no purpose of thine can be restrained"), which Job now freely acknowledges, are not, of course, new discoveries. He has long possessed a shrewd and reverent appreciation of the divine majesty, as we have seen in his earlier speeches. But his sense of God's attributes has been immeasurably vitalised by his recent conducted tour of the vastness, beauty, variety and complexity of creation, culminating in behemoth and leviathan. Just as Elihu quoted extensively from Job, so Job cites the precise words of Jehovah (38.3-4) as a demonstration that he has listened carefully and learned his lesson.

His words constitute, first, a moment of profound **realisation** which merges into worship: "I know that thou canst do all things, and that no purpose of thine can be restrained" (42.2, RV). Divine omnipotence is no abstract textbook doctrine, but the sure guarantee that God's plan for His universe in general and for His people in particular will be unfailingly fulfilled. In speaking of God's "purpose", Job is conceding that, in spite of appearances to the contrary, the world is governed by a divine order: nothing takes place by accident. The word (4209) translated "thought" (KJV, JND) or "purpose" (RV, ESV) is an unusual one. It first appears in Job's accusation against his friends: "Behold, I know your thoughts, and the devices [4209] which ye wrongfully imagine against me" (21.27). In many of its twenty or so Old Testament uses it refers to men's evil plans (Ps 10.2; 21.11; 37.7; Prov 12.2; 14.17). The comment about it in the *Jamieson, Fausset and Brown Commentary* is worth citing:

> the ambiguous word is designedly chosen to express that, while to Job's finite view, God's plans seem bad, to the All-wise One they continue unhindered in their development, and will at last be seen to be as good as they are infinitely wise. No evil can emanate from the Parent of good … but it is His prerogative to overrule evil to good.

What seemed in the past to be God's implacable animus against him is now viewed in a very different light. The God who, behind the scenes, superintended every one of his steps had a wise strategy in it all. Those trudging along a rough pathway towards an unseen destination may at times wonder why the road is so long and arduous, but once they reach the goal the reasons for the twists and turns become apparent. The pattern is only fully visible in retrospect. Joseph's words to his brothers may be adapted thus for the reader of Job: "[Satan] thought evil against [Job]; but God meant it unto good" (Gen 50.20).

He also confesses personal **regret**: "therefore have I uttered that which I understood not, things too wonderful for me, which I knew not" (42.3, RV). In so doing he first quotes from Jehovah's words to him in chapter 38, admitting the folly of his unguarded speeches. The ironic contrast between his present knowledge ("I know", 42.2) and his former ignorance ("I knew not", 42.3) is important. The man who in chapters 29 and 31 basked in his social and religious esteem is now brought to the self-evaluation which only comes when we forget ourselves in the dazzling splendour of the Almighty. It was R A Torrey who (rightly) said that the man who thinks well of himself has never met God. But Job is meeting Him now. The patriarch's experience is a reminder to us all to set a guard on our lips, for "every idle word that men shall speak, they shall give account thereof in the day of judgment" (Mt 12.36).

Finally, he demonstrates genuine **repentance**: "I had heard of thee by the hearing of the ear; but now mine eye seeth thee, Wherefore I abhor myself, and repent in dust and ashes" (42.5-6, RV). Immediately before making this statement, however, he again quotes, this time from his own words (which he now finds deeply embarrassing) as well as from God's. To understand what Job is doing in this highly condensed double citation, we need to divide the verse into its two halves:

(a) Hear, I beseech thee, and I will speak;
(b) I will demand of thee, and declare thou unto me (42.4, RV).

The first half (a) looks back to chapter 13 when the embittered Job of the debate petulantly summoned God to take part in a court case to decide on his innocence: "call thou, and I will answer: or let me speak, and answer thou me" (13.22). The second half (b), however, echoes Jehovah's challenge in chapter 38 which made plain that God, not Job, has the right to make demands: "I will demand of thee, and answer thou me" (38.3). The juxtaposition of the two voices is deliberately startling: to highlight his folly, Job lays his own words alongside God's. No elaborate explanation or footnote is necessary. How dare a man quarrel with Jehovah? The seventeenth century poet John Donne wrote a number of spiritual sonnets which explore man's relationship with God, often shifting in the course of a few lines from loud and angry protest into quiet submission. One poem in particular pesters God with an incessant "why" before collapsing, with this line, into the glad surrender of resignation:

But who am I, that dare dispute with Thee?[484]

Such language sums up Job's new self-knowledge. As if to prove that he has completely abandoned all previous requests and complaints, Job owns that he has now encountered God in a way he never imagined possible. It is as though all his prior knowledge had only been received at second-hand ("I had heard of thee by the hearing of the ear"), whereas now his spiritual understanding has been revolutionised ("now mine eye seeth thee"). Instead of seeing with the aid of a low-wattage torch, Job has suddenly beheld the breaking of the dawn. The language contrasting hearing and sight is primarily metaphorical. Job is not really seeing a theophany in exactly the way that Abraham did in Genesis 17.1, for the Lord is still hidden in the thick darkness of the engulfing whirlwind. Nevertheless, the encounter is both real and life-changing. Job confesses that all his boasted spiritual wisdom and theological learning are eclipsed in the light of what Jehovah has now revealed. Spurgeon has a good comment:

> The Lord had taken everything away from Job, and this paved the way to
> His giving him more of Himself. In the absence of other goods the good
> God is the better seen. In prosperity God is *heard*, and that is a blessing;
> but in adversity God is *seen*, and that is a greater blessing.[485]

Such a remark helpfully ties the close of the book to its beginning. God had,
from the very start, a great project in view – to bless saintly, suffering Job with a
grander appreciation of Himself than he could ever have imagined possible. This
is what James calls "the end of the Lord" (James 5.11); not, of course, the mere
restoration of material prosperity, but an enlarged grasp of God. It is only when
we are brought to an end of self-absorption that we find our everything in the
One who created, redeemed, and daily sustains us. This God is inexhaustible in
His glories. Even those living in the last days, when God has "spoken unto us by
his Son" (Heb 1.2), do well to remember, in the words of Schaper, "that what we
do not understand is greater than what we do understand".[486]

Two lessons follow. The first is practical. It is disturbingly easy to have an
intellectual acquaintance with the doctrines of Scripture without any genuine
sense of their wonder or power. We may inherit from our parents much that is
good, but all that they teach us about spiritual reality has to be validated personally
from the Scriptures. It is possible to be raised in a godly home, to sit regularly
under the preaching of the Word, even to mouth the conventional formulae
of pious orthodoxy, and yet be a stranger to God's grace. If Job's grasp of God
needed to be expanded – and we must never forget the unique commendation
of the prologue (1.1,8; 2.3) – how much more does ours? Though in terms of
dispensational privilege we are streets ahead of him, we fall far short of him in
personal godliness.

The second lesson is eschatological. Although in context Job's language may be
purely figurative, there is a time coming when all His redeemed people will truly
see the Lord as He is, and the Son's prayer of John 17 will be answered in full:

> Father, I will that they also, whom thou hast given me, be with me where
> I am; that they may behold my glory, which thou hast given me: for thou
> lovedst me before the foundation of the world (Jn 17.24).

If it is currently true of God's saints that "though now ye see him not, yet
believing, ye rejoice with joy unspeakable and full of glory" (1 Pet 1.8), how much
greater will be the delight "when he shall appear, [and] we shall be like him; for we
shall see him as he is" (1 Jn 3.2)? John's language may be concise but his meaning
opens up into the bliss of eternity, where "his servants shall serve him: And they
shall see his face" (Rev 22.3-4).

The consequence of Job's new understanding is total self-abasement:
"Wherefore I abhor myself, and repent in dust and ashes" (42.6). Although most
versions retain this form of words, "abhor myself" may not be the best way to

render the sense. The Hebrew word (3988) means to reject, despise, refuse. It is used of Israel despising God's word (Lev 26.15,43), of God casting away Israel (Lev 26.44), and of Israel rejecting the Lord (1 Sam 8.7). It appears twelve times in Job (5.17; 7.5,16; 8.20; 9.21; 10.3; 19.18; 30.1; 31.13; 34.33; 36.5; 42.6). What is particularly interesting is that the precise object of Job's abhorrence is not specified: "*myself*" is italicised in the KJV (as well as in the RV and Darby), indicating that it was supplied by the translators. The Jewish Publication Society Bible of 1917 offers this rendering: "Wherefore I abhor my words, and repent, seeing I am dust and ashes" (42.6, JPS). Such an expansion of the text at least brings out the idea that what Job now rejects is not himself, which was the burden of his first response – "I am of small account" (40.4, RV) – but his earlier spoken words. This fits the context, in which Job agrees with God that he has been guilty of faulty speech (42.3-4). This was the Lord's double charge against him (38.2; 40.2). Although Job never perpetrated the sins of behaviour of which his friends accused him, he has – under the extreme pressure of their constant badgering – slipped into rash statements about his own piety and God's righteousness. These words he now retracts.

His repentance, therefore, involves a genuine sorrow of mind for that self-satisfaction which caused him, on the one hand, to accuse God of having "taken away my judgment" (27.2) and, on the other, to boast that he would approach God boldly "as a prince" (31.37). The collocation of "dust and ashes", appearing only four times in the Old Testament, is the emblem of prostration before Jehovah. Abraham thus styled himself as he dared to draw near God on behalf of his nephew (Gen 18.27). Job, sitting enthroned in shame on the city ash heap (2.8), similarly described what God had done to him: "He hath cast me into the mire, and I am become like dust and ashes" (30.19). Ezekiel uses the terminology when prophesying proud Tyre's defeat and degradation (Ezek 27.30). It is a staggering reversal: the man, who for most of the book has been seated in a place of public humiliation while unblushingly glorying in his own righteousness, is now brought to mourn his foolish words, humbling himself before the God of all the earth.

What we have just read is not the conversion of a reprobate, but the experience of the godliest man of his day on discovering that God is greater than he ever realised. Just as the prophet Isaiah, on seeing an exalted vision of divine holiness, was convicted of personal defilement, so righteous Job is brought to low thoughts about himself in the light of Jehovah's immensity. Pride and self-satisfaction are among the greatest temptations faced by believers. We become obsessed with our ministry, puffed up by our knowledge, enamoured of the sound of our own voices on the platform, and perhaps even smug about our carefully cultivated modesty. But in the light of God's holy majesty everything comes tumbling down into the dust for, as the apostle tells us twice, "He that glorieth, let him glory in the Lord" (1 Cor 1.31; 2 Cor 10.17). There is no one else in whom we can rejoice without fear of disappointment.

SECTION 28
Epilogue
Conclusion
Job 42.7–17

The prose epilogue to the book of Job balances the two-chapter prologue in subject matter if not in length. At the start we were introduced to the patriarch in all his material prosperity and spiritual piety, before being swiftly transported into an unseen heavenly realm where his indisputable godliness was applauded by Jehovah but contested by Satan. Thereafter there followed wave upon wave of temporal disasters, putting to the test Satan's claim that Job only worshipped God for personal gain. The prologue ended with the arrival of three friends to offer consolation for his terrible losses. Here, in the epilogue, the interest is again centred on Job, this time finally to confirm the reality of that uprightness which so offended Satan and confounded his friends, and to record the abundant restoration of his physical blessings. However, the narrative sequence inverts that of the prologue: the three friends who terminated the one are disposed of first of all in the other.

Yet some things which we might expect to be included are strangely missing. Nothing is said about Satan, nor is there any direct reappearance of Job's wife, both of whom are important figures in the prologue. No mention is made of Elihu, that young late-comer to the debate whose speeches formed a powerful culmination to the argument between Job and his peers. No explanation is offered for Job's calamities, either to him or to his friends.

The total exclusion of Satan from the concluding narrative is the final testimony to his utter impotence. For all his jeering mockery of Job's righteousness, it was in reality not Satan but God who initiated the book's action, deliberately singling out the patriarch for praise and measuring out the limits of interference permitted to the adversary. "Hitherto shalt thou come, but no further: and here shall thy proud waves be stayed" (38.11): it is almost impossible not to view the divine control of the raging sea as an analogy for His superintendence of Satan. Though our "adversary the devil, as a roaring lion, walketh about, seeking whom he may devour" (1 Pet 5.8), both his movements and his victims are under the authority of God. Even leviathan, whose frightening hostility mirrors satanic pride, is seen to be but a tool of Jehovah, for "whatsoever is under the whole heaven is mine" (41.11). Satan's hatred, though he did not know it, was accommodated within the grand scheme of God, serving only to bring to the surface Job's spiritual stamina and highlight God's wisdom for the practical encouragement of saints ever since. God uniquely brings good out of evil. He overruled the dastardly Moabite plan to cripple Israel, and instead "turned the curse into a blessing" (Neh 13.2); He used Joseph's brothers' envy to ensure the survival of the chosen seed; with equal ease He rerouted Satan's wickedness to a good end.

Once the devil is finally consigned to the lake of fire prepared for him and his angels (Mt 25.41), his malignity will be for ever removed so that the new heavens and earth, wherein dwell righteousness, will be a place of inviolable security. The unsullied earthly blessedness awarded Job at the end of the book looks ahead in measure to that everlastingly joyful condition.

Job's wife, so ill-used of the commentators, but perhaps with good reason, remains unmentioned, although the replacement of the children so tragically killed in the prologue assumes either her continuing existence or the introduction of a second wife. There is, however, no indication in the text that she died or was supplanted. We may therefore charitably assume that, just as her husband's sudden reversals brought about in her an uncharacteristic mental breakdown, so his recovery enabled her to resume her proper place at his side. But then of course the attention of the inspired narrative is primarily on Job, not on his wife or his children: they are simply adjuncts to his story. Speculation, however attractive, is not exposition. What God wishes us to learn from His Word usually floats clearly on the surface.

The absence of Elihu is perhaps rather more surprising, considering that he acted (albeit unconsciously) as the herald of Jehovah's royal entry into the story, drawing Job's notice in advance to the areas of doctrinal truth which would dominate God's interview with the patriarch. Nevertheless, rather like John the Baptist, once his work is done he uncomplainingly retreats into the side-lines to allow Jehovah the centre stage. In this he is a pattern of godly service: having discharged his responsibility he steps aside. That his contribution to the debate was in no way erroneous or improper, despite the attempts of some commentators to trivialise his role, is proved by the exclusion of his name from the list of offenders. It is Eliphaz and his two colleagues who are called to account for their injudicious words, not Elihu.

Jehovah's silence as to the reasons for Job's suffering leaves us with the principle of simple faith: like Job, we have to learn to trust our God even when explanations are missing. He has, we may be sure, wise purposes in all His ways with us which will perhaps never be disclosed down here.

The epilogue may be divided into three brief paragraphs as follows:

> 1. The Reprimand: 42.7-9
> 2. The Reversal: 42.10-11
> 3. The Restoration: 42.12-17.

The Reprimand: 42.7-9

Although they make no comment, presumably because they are dumb-struck, I think we may reasonably infer that the friends have been aware of the Lord's conversation with Job. How much they understood is not revealed. Perhaps, like Saul's colleagues on the Damascus Road, they were conscious of a sound rather than intelligible words (Acts 9.7; 22.9). But now Jehovah turns from Job to them. Eliphaz is specifically named, as he is the oldest and the prime spokesman of the three. In each round of the contest he has taken the lead, and his two associates, while preserving their own distinctive voices, have simply followed in his wake. The Lord is seriously displeased with them because, despite their boasted wisdom and knowledge, they have not spoken what is "right" about Him. The Hebrew word (3559) is first used by Joseph to describe the certainty of a pre-announced Middle-Eastern famine: "the thing is established [3559] by God, and God will shortly bring it to pass" (Gen 41.32). The idea therefore is of solidity, firmness, and absolute assurance. For all their poise and polish, Eliphaz's words about God have been decidedly shaky.

The discomfiture of Eliphaz and his colleagues is a pertinent reminder that we should never mistake assurance of manner and fluency of speech for a guarantee that the message is accurate. Sennacherib's field commander sounded dogmatically self-confident when he threatened the besieged Hezekiah, yet he was spouting nonsense (Is 36.4-20). Earlier in the debate Job rounded on his glib opponents with the challenge, "Will ye speak wickedly for God? and talk deceitfully for him?" (13.7), warning them that "He will surely reprove you" (13.10). This He now does.

In what way were their words not right? Primarily because they never abandoned the fundamentally false premise that outward circumstances are a reliable guide to a man's spiritual condition. Wedded to their theory, they persisted with the accusation that Job's sufferings were divinely-awarded retribution for sins which he was stubbornly unwilling to confess. But it is a fallacy to maintain that God's dealings with people in this world are always a direct response to their behaviour. God has the right to treat His creatures as He pleases, simply because He is God. After all, it is evident that the present era in which we live is marked by His gracious longsuffering: He does not instantly strike down those who publicly vilify His name. The biblical answer to people who scoff at the unaccountable silence of heaven is this:

> The Lord is not slack concerning his promise, as some men count slackness; but is longsuffering to us-ward, not willing that any should perish, but that all should come to repentance (2 Pet 3.9).

No slick formula governs His ways with men, for there will always be mysteries beyond our understanding. Moses's well-known words to Israel relate in context to the terms under which the nation would occupy the Promised Land, but the principle has a wider application:

> The secret things belong unto the Lord our God: but those things which are revealed belong unto us and to our children for ever, that we may do all the words of this law (Deut 29.29).

God's secrets are His own, while His instructions for living have been entrusted to His people. For any man to claim to be privy to His hidden counsels is not only supreme arrogance; it is a recipe for personal disaster. That is why the three friends are accused of "folly". The English word has been contaminated by the cultural concept of the good-natured jester who coats his acerbic wisdom with the sugar of wit and clowning. Readers of Shakespeare will think immediately of Touchstone and Feste. But the Hebrew word (5039) is decidedly severe. Its thirteen occurrences in the Old Testament (but never in Proverbs) lay bare its meaning. Translated in the KJV by "folly" or "villainy", it describes Shechem's violation of Jacob's daughter Dinah (Gen 34.7), sexual immorality (Deut 22.21), Achan's sin (Josh 7.15), the gang rapists of Gibeah (Judg 19.23-24; 20.6,10), the moral character of Abigail's husband (1 Sam 25.25), Amnon's incest with Tamar (2 Sam 13.12), the character of sinful Israel (Is 9.17; 32.6), and the wickedness of false prophets (Jer 29.23). The list constitutes a catalogue of the grossest evil. When, then, Jehovah uses this word to describe dignified Eastern wise men He is spelling out in emphatic terms His abhorrence of their behaviour. To misrepresent God – as they have done – is a serious sin. It was A W Tozer who wrote that "the essence of idolatry is the entertainment of thoughts about God that are unworthy of Him".[487] This has been the crime of the three highly religious friends. How carefully and reverently we should speak about the living God of the universe!

Even more important, however, than the exposure of their sin, is the Lord's forthright commendation of Job. First, he is four times honoured as "my servant Job", exactly the same way God twice described him in the original conversation with Satan (1.8; 2.3). But now, like everything else in Job's life, the approval is doubled. While His personal interaction with Job addressed the matter of Job's verbal indiscretions, with outsiders Jehovah has nothing but good to say about His servant. It is sometimes not in a man's best interests to hear how much he means to the Lord. John the Baptist's disciples were already leaving the scene with a reassuring message for the anxious prisoner when the Lord Jesus, addressing the crowd, embarked upon His most resounding endorsement of that great man's ministry (Mt 11.1-14).

Second, Job's words about God, in contrast to those of his friends, are assessed as "right". This is where some readers understandably have problems. After all, the previous four chapters, with their celebration of divine creatorial wisdom and power, were initiated by the questions, "Who is this that darkeneth counsel by words without knowledge?" (38.2), and "Shall he that contendeth with the Almighty instruct him?" (40.2). That is to say, Job has been charged with levelling ignorant criticisms and improper complaints against God. Quite clearly, therefore, the Lord's approval of his words is not a blanket endorsement of everything he has said throughout the book. Job has himself recognised his errors, for he has humbly accepted Jehovah's strictures without demur: "therefore have I uttered that I understood not; things too wonderful for me, which I knew not" (42.3). In what sense, then, has he spoken what is "right"? There are two answers. He has, first, in the course of the long debate, correctly repudiated the over-simplified theology of the friends (who argued back from suffering to personal sin) and, second, in response to Jehovah's intervention, he has penitently confessed the justice of His censure. The *Jamieson, Fausset and Brown Commentary* sums it up admirably:

> Job had spoken rightly in relation to [the friends] and their argument, denying their *theory*, and the *fact* which they alleged, that he was peculiarly

guilty and a hypocrite; but wrongly in relation to *God,* when he fell into the opposite extreme of almost denying *all* guilt. This extreme *he* has now repented of, and therefore God speaks of him as now altogether "right."

Robinson aptly differentiates between Job and his friends in these words:

> Job's cause [was] essentially good, though marred by many unbecoming utterances; the friends' cause [was] essentially bad, though supported by many precious and excellent truths.[488]

It is sadly possible to contend for truth with specious arguments; and to maintain an unbiblical doctrine with persuasive and pious orthodoxy.

But we must never forget that, in the long course of the debate, Job spoke not as some detached theologian or biblical commentator but as the bruised victim of extreme distress. The friends argued about him from the outside, but Job's words were uttered out of the very depths of personal misery. This God recognised, in the gentleness and tenderness with which He spoke of Job. Kelly puts it well:

> On the surface of the book one might think that Job had been saying as many wrong things about God as the rest. Indeed it would appear to a superficial reader that Job had spoken more rashly than either Eliphaz or his two friends. But the truth is that the grace of God bears much more tenderly than men suppose with the random words that men utter under the pressure of so terrible a trial as that of Job.[489]

One other token of God's esteem remains to be considered. Not only is Job acknowledged as "my servant", not only has he spoken "right", he is the only one through whom the erring sages can now find acceptance with God. The story started with a man who daily offered sacrifices on behalf of his family; it ends with the same man praying to God on behalf of friends whose heavy-handed accusations of wrong-doing have, for thirty or so chapters, increased his misery. If anything were needed to convince us of the genuineness of Job's gracious spirit despite all he has endured, this astonishingly uncomplaining act of intercession on behalf of transgressors wipes away any remaining doubts. It also hints once again – like other moments in the story – at the degree to which he becomes an unofficial type of Christ, the innocent sufferer at the hands of Satan and men who willingly took up the cause of His enemies.

The burnt offering of verse 8, the earliest and most all-embracing of Old Testament sacrifices, reminds us that we are in a pre-Israelite setting where the specifics of the Levitical system were unknown. Eliphaz and his friends were to stand the substantial cost of the offerings, but Job was to make oral supplication for them. The word used here (6419), generally rendered "pray", is first employed of Abraham interceding for Abimelech (Gen 20.7,17), and later of Moses repeatedly pleading with God on behalf of guilty Israel (Num 11.2; 21.7; Deut 9.20,26). The reason that Job must intercede for the others is simple: "him will

I accept". The wonderful irony that Job, of all people, should become mediator for his abashed friends must not be missed. The same man they had assumed to be the object of divine disapproval was in reality the only one whose guaranteed acceptance with God could ensure their pardon.

The instant and unquestioning obedience of the downcast comforters is passed over without comment. How could they possibly refuse audible divine instructions from heaven? Whatever people may now say *about* God in the current era of His merciful longsuffering, they will be unable to say anything *to* Him when they stand, trembling and dismayed, before His judgment throne. One of the Lord's parables offers an insight into the guilty silence that will descend on men. The king spots an ill-attired guest at his feast and challenges him: "Friend, how camest thou in hither not having a wedding garment? And he was speechless" (Mt 22.12). The strident atheism which, in the west in particular, loudly parades its contempt for the living God of the universe, will then be struck dumb. Man-made religion, whatever its form – whether fanatical or superstitious or rational – will be brought crashing down in ruins.

But at least we may rejoice that Job's friends "did according as the Lord commanded them". Simple, prompt, and glad submission to the face-value teaching of God's Word, however much it may fly in the face of our preconceptions, traditions or fashions, is the hallmark of the genuine child of God. The final part of the verse is terse but touching: "the Lord also accepted Job". The KJV's unnecessary "also" dilutes the impact of the phrase. Darby is much snappier: "and Jehovah accepted Job". Yes – that is the point. The man everyone had despised and abhorred because of his serial calamities is now the one whom Jehovah publicly honours as His servant. Of course, we know from verse 10 that he contributes his own part in praying for those annoying friends, but the fact remains that it is first of all the man himself whom God accepts. The ESV misses the point by paraphrasing the text: "and the Lord accepted Job's prayer". Although we know that he genuinely prayed (42.10), in verse 9 there is no mention of the action, only of the man.

The lessons are beautiful. Like the coming Messiah, whose pathway he prefigures, the despised Job is found to be the only one acceptable to God. Because Christ is God's delight, all His people find their heavenly standing in Him, "accepted in the beloved" (Eph 1.6). Then again, can we think of an earlier Old Testament example of the Saviour's teaching that His people should "Love your enemies, bless them that curse you, do good to them that hate you, and pray for them which despitefully use you, and persecute you" (Mt 5.44)? The model is not even an Israelite, one of the chosen seed, but an outsider. Job's gracious spirit of forgiveness is bound to make us think of the Lord Jesus Himself who, despite all the suffering He endured at the hands of His own people, "made intercession for the transgressors" (Is 53.12). While Job had no model of pardon on which to pattern his behaviour, Christians do. When our brethren grieve, offend or injure us – and, because of the evil propensities of the flesh, this will always be the case until the Lord returns – we have a clear course of action:

be ye kind one to another, tenderhearted, forgiving one another, even as
God for Christ's sake hath forgiven you (Eph 4.32).

The Reversal: 42.10-11

It is significant that the reversal of Job's fortunes is inseparably tied to his
intercession on behalf of his detractors. Though it is true that they needed his
mediation, it is equally true that he needed to demonstrate a forgiving spirit
before he could come fully into the blessedness of complete recovery. The language
makes the link: "the Lord turned the captivity of Job, when he prayed". Matthew
Henry offers one of his memorable comments:

> Mercy did not return when he was disputing with his friends, no, not
> though he had right on his side, but when he was praying for them; for
> God is better served and pleased with our warm devotions than with our
> warm disputations.[490]

There is a profit in prayer for the one who prays as much as for those who
are the objects of his intercession. We little realise what it means to God when
we take time to pray for our brethren or for our enemies: in either case, God
takes pleasure in the faintest reminder of His Son's self-sacrificing concern for the
undeserving. We see glimpses of it in Moses's entreaties on behalf of disobedient
Israel (Ex 32.32) and Paul's deep burden for his apostate kinsfolk (Rom 9.3). As
the book of Proverbs reminds us, "The Lord is far from the wicked: but he heareth
the prayer of the righteous" (Prov 15.29).

As a result, "the Lord turned the captivity of Job". To turn someone's captivity
is a linguistic idiom threading through the Old Testament, largely in relation to
the final prosperity of Israel although, perhaps to our surprise, we discover that
other nations are also to be restored (Jer 48.47; 49.6). The collocation appears
in passages stretching from Deuteronomy 30.3 ("then the Lord thy God will
turn thy captivity, and have compassion upon thee, and will return and gather
thee from all the nations, whither the Lord thy God hath scattered thee") to
Zephaniah 3.20 ("I will make you a name and a praise among all people of the
earth, when I turn back your captivity before your eyes, saith the Lord"). The glad
testimony of the prophets is that Jehovah has promised to restore His people to
their land and to Himself (Jer 29.14; Joel 3.1); the earnest prayer of the psalmist
is that He will honour that wonderful pledge (Ps 14.7; 126.4).

Job, however, stands alone in Scripture as an individual whose captivity God
reversed; that is to say, whose terrible afflictions God removed and recompensed.
The outstanding difference between the situation of Job and that of Israel is that
the nation fully deserved the captivity into which it was brought, because of its
flagrant disobedience to the terms by which it occupied the Promised Land. Job,
by contrast, was a man as upright and faithful as Israel was unrighteous and fickle.
Israel merited everything that happened to it; Job did not. Again our attention
is drawn to the undeniable fact that God, being God, has the right to do with
His creatures as He pleases. If He wished to use Job as a test case with which to

confound Satan, we cannot dispute His will. Nevertheless, in approaching the glorious end of this daunting book, we can begin to glimpse a little more of the divine purpose behind the pain. God moves both for His own glory and for His people's good. James's inspired précis of the action cannot be bettered:

> Behold, we call them blessed who have endured. Ye have heard of the endurance of Job, and seen the end of the Lord; that the Lord is full of tender compassion and pitiful (James 5.11, JND).

And what a blessed recompense Job receives! It is a token demonstration of God's tender-heartedness. The unlooked-for doubling of divine benefits will be elaborated in verse 12 onwards, but first of all verse 11 catalogues a radical improvement in his human circumstances.

Here again there are some oddities. The prologue made no mention of Job's siblings, but now he is suddenly joined by a congregation of brothers, sisters and acquaintances. It sounds almost as though they are gathering for a large celebratory family photograph. Job earlier described his friends, with some obvious irony, as "my brethren" (6.15), but later made reference to a wider circle of relations:

> He hath put my brethren far from me, and mine acquaintance are verily estranged from me. My kinsfolk have failed, and my familiar friends have forgotten me (19.13-14).

Assuming that "brethren" and "kinsfolk" stand in contrast to "acquaintance" and "familiar friends", we can distinguish between two groups: those related to Job by family connection, and those who are his special associates or comrades. The impression we get from this sad insight into the behind-the-scenes consequences of his tragedy is that, just as his wife abandoned him (19.17), so his brothers and sisters turned their back on one whom the Lord had rejected. Both family and friends forsook him. So utterly cut off has he become that he bitterly describes himself as "a brother to dragons, and a companion to owls" (30.29), so distanced from normal social intercourse that he has even "said to corruption, Thou art my father: to the worm, Thou art my mother, and my sister" (17.14). It is as if he no longer had any consciousness of intimate human companionship or warmth. The book, one has to admit, certainly does not award Job's immediate family any merit points for loyalty. Like the prodigal's fly-by-night acquaintances in the far country, once the resources for the good life evaporated, so did they.

Whatever the reasons for their invisibility in the past, the siblings "all" (three times the word appears in verse 11 in this context) crawl out of the woodwork at the end to bask in the sunshine of Job's restoration to divine favour. What exactly has happened to draw them out into the open? God has announced His approval of Job; God has repudiated the three doubting friends; God has honoured Job's prayer; God has turned his captivity and conspicuously doubled his earthly assets. It is now evident that Job is a man of consequence with whom it makes sense to be on good terms. Some of Solomon's more sardonic proverbs come to mind:

The poor is hated even of his own neighbour: but the rich hath many friends (Prov 14.20).

All the brethren of the poor do hate him: how much more do his friends go far from him? he pursueth them with words, yet they are wanting to him (Prov 19.7).

It is a sad but accurate reflection upon sinful human nature that everyone loves a winner. Losers get short shrift. Built implicitly into the candid but unelaborated account of Job's surviving family is a gentle nudge to the reader: we should aspire, by God's grace, to remain faithful to friends and kin even in their times of distress. We may be grateful that Solomon records other proverbs advocating fidelity:

A friend loveth at all times, and a brother is born for adversity (Prov 17.17).

A man of many friends will come to ruin, but there is a friend that sticketh closer than a brother (Prov 18.24, JND).

Deceived by a smooth-talking rogue, King David fell into the hasty mistake of thinking Mephibosheth a fair-weather friend who had basely deserted him during Absalom's rebellion, but the inspired narrative unveils the touching truth:

Mephibosheth the son of Saul came down to meet the king, and had neither dressed his feet, nor trimmed his beard, nor washed his clothes, from the day the king departed until the day he came again in peace (2 Sam 19.24).

Faithfulness, reliability and continued lovingkindness through thick and thin are rare qualities. As Solomon puts it, "Most men will proclaim every one his own goodness: but a faithful man who can find?" (Prov 20.6). It is easy to brag glibly of constancy, but how few live up to such claims. Delitzsch comments, drily, that

Prosperity now brought those together again whom calamity had frightened away; for the love of men is scarcely anything but a number of coarse or delicate shades of selfishness.[491]

When men let us down, we can turn with relief to the unfailing Christ whose name is announced significantly at the start of Revelation as "the faithful witness" (Rev 1.5), and at the close as "Faithful and True" (Rev 19.11). In Him we see displayed the truth of Jeremiah's testimony amidst Jerusalem's ruin: "great is thy faithfulness" (Lam 3.23). In the Lord Jesus we have that friend who sticks closer than a brother.

Now the dark days have ended, Job's family's actions are, to say the least, intriguing: they ate his food in his house, "they bemoaned [5110] him, and comforted [5162] him … every man also gave him a piece of money, and every one an earring of gold"

(42.11). They not only offer belated consolation; they also bring gifts. The language specifically echoes that of the prologue, where we read that

> when Job's three friends heard of all this evil that was come upon him, they came every one from his own place ... to mourn [5110] with him and to comfort [5162] him (2.11).

The contrast shows Eliphaz, Bildad and Zophar in a kinder light: they took the trouble to visit and condole with their old friend, however unsuccessful they may have been in their ministrations. They at least did it in his time of trial; his family only offer consolation after the testing is over. Whether the gifts of gold were a kind of collection to provide practical support for Job's material recovery, or whether they were simply marks of esteem, is not clear. Gold pieces and gold rings could, one feels, in no way add to Job's restored wealth, but they testify to a reunited family (however much we may suspect their motivation) and a return to public regard.

If nothing else, the behaviour of the patriarch's kinsfolk is a lesson that sympathy and support are best offered when most required. The Lord Jesus, in expressing appreciation for the acts of mercy bestowed, probably at great personal risk, by godly Gentiles on persecuted Jews in the future tribulation period, makes clear that their relief was timely:

> For I was an hungred, and ye gave me meat: I was thirsty, and ye gave me drink: I was a stranger, and ye took me in: Naked, and ye clothed me: I was sick, and ye visited me: I was in prison, and ye came unto me (Mt 25.35-36).

Food and drink, hospitality and clothing, humane fellowship in infirmary or prison are of little value once the emergency has passed.

Further, in a stark but easily overlooked phrase, the narrator reminds us of a fundamental spiritual principle pervading the whole book: "all the evil that the Lord had brought upon him". Not even in the final chapter is there any wavering of viewpoint. The language echoes the great confessions of chapters 1 and 2: "the Lord gave, and the Lord hath taken away" (1.21), and "shall we receive good at the hand of God, and shall we not receive evil?" (2.10). Whether in prosperity or adversity, Job's circumstances were organised by God. Yes, Satan was the malevolent instrument behind his ordeal; yes, the Chaldeans, the Sabeans and the weather were secondary causes; but once we trace the chain of events back to their ultimate origin so that we can go no further, we come to a halt in worship before the throne of God. No one is higher than Him. We may not understand all that our God does with His people, but we can be confident that, because He is infinitely wise, He knows what He is doing, and because He is infinitely loving, He has our final blessing in view.

The Restoration: 42.12-17

This concluding paragraph offers fuller information about Job's restored blessings. The same God who inaugurated his trial now increases his wealth. Both livestock and lifespan are doubled. The caption phrase is telling: "So the Lord blessed the latter end of Job more than his beginning". We must not, however, read this as some kind of material reward for piety; although God may elect to bless the righteous, the principle (as the story of Job proves) is by no means invariable. The entire book is a lesson in the sovereign rights of God to do as He will with His creatures – granting, withholding, removing or replacing temporal benefits as He chooses. He acts according to the secret counsels of His own inscrutable wisdom – and it is the believer's place to bow to His ways, however enigmatic they may appear. All God's gifts to men, whether spiritual or material, are of His grace.

Nevertheless, the narrative ends with Job wonderfully blessed. As Smick writes, "Since Job had successfully endured the test and proved that his righteousness was not rooted in his own selfishness, there was no reason for Job to continue to be tested".[492] His prosperity is therefore renewed, in fulfilment of Bildad's prediction in chapter 8: "Though thy beginning was small, yet thy latter end should greatly increase" (8.7). Among the inducements to repentance offered by the friends during their efforts to coax Job into confession are several ironic foretastes of the book's conclusion. This is no credit to them: they had no special spiritual insight. Indeed, they were working under the delusion that Job was being judged for his sins. Rather, the conclusion is a gracious vindication of his genuine uprightness, and a reminder to hasty people like us that God's wise purposes often take time to reach fruition. Bildad had argued that, were Job really what he claimed to be, God would immediately awake on his behalf to restore his blessings. In this he betrayed a common human failure to comprehend the strategy of heaven. Because God works with a view to the long-term, His people have to learn to wait, and wait patiently. Writing about the time it seemed to take for God to fulfil His amazing covenant promises to Abraham, Davis refers to one of his Bible College students who, despite a Jewish background, was obviously reading the Old Testament for the first time:

> One day he summed up his impression from the biblical accounts: "God is never in a hurry". The unhurriedness of God seems strange – and unwelcome – to us. The passage of time with no noticeable moves towards promise fulfilment poses a problem for faith; it can wear on faith. We prefer a deity with high blood pressure who is on the move, whose promises are delivered with microwavable instructions.[493]

At least Abraham had firm, reiterated promises from God – about a son, about a land, about universal blessing. Job and his friends, however, as far as we are aware, had nothing of the sort; nothing but handed-down information from Adam and Eve and their immediate descendants. Though they knew a good deal about divine attributes, they had a tendency to assume that God was obliged to operate according to their timetable. That is why Bildad counselled repentance. This, he assured the patriarch, would guarantee instant recovery. Even Job at times worried that God let the wicked get away with their wickedness because He did not immediately step in to judge them. Both parties – though so different in so many ways – made the assumption that God has to work at once.

However, He does not. God moves at His own pace. Two of the many lessons to be gleaned from John chapter 11 are that the Lord's delays are not denials, and that God acts for His own glory as well as His people's benefit. Yet in the meantime things can seem so hard. Believers suffer for their faith; saints endure the trying conditions of living in a world wrecked by Adam's sin; godlessness thrives down here. Jeremiah discovered this as he found himself a victim simultaneously of the bitter hatred of his own people and of the deprivations associated with living in a besieged city. Nevertheless, amidst his trials he rose to this sublime expression of confidence in God:

> The Lord is my portion, saith my soul; therefore will I hope in him. The Lord is good unto them that wait for him, to the soul that seeketh him. It is good that a man should both hope and quietly wait for the salvation of the Lord (Lam 3.24-26).

For nearly forty chapters Job has waited. We have little real idea of the timescale involved, but to him it must have seemed an eternity. Eventually, however, in His gracious intervention it is made abundantly clear that "The Lord is good unto them that wait for him". The believer who groans, longing for the redemption of the body, may take heart from the assurance that "all things work together for good to them that love God, to them who are the called according to his purpose" (Rom 8.28). The great good God has in view is that His people might be eternally conformed to the image of His Son. When He returns for His own, the Lord Jesus will fully accomplish that purpose, "[so] that he might be the firstborn among many brethren" (Rom 8.29). The believer who feels weary because of the way would do well to remember Job.

The precise nature of Job's increase is carefully calculated, so that we can rejoice in his restoration. He had prayed earlier, "Oh that I were as in months past, as in the days when God preserved me" (29.2), but God did far better than that. He now received double the cattle he had lost, he gained more children, and he was blessed with an extension of life. We are given no information about the immediate source of his new **cattle** stocks (42.12). Since his family presumably enlarged over a period of time by the processes of natural generation, the same is likely true of his livestock. In other words, he did not awake one morning to discover that all his fields were suddenly and supernaturally full of sheep, camels, oxen and asses. The prologue specified the way in which he lost his original herds, but said little about how he acquired them in the first place. We may assume that, without the involvement of the miraculous, God had blessed His servant's intelligent industry with success, just as Abram, through various means, became "very rich in cattle, in silver, and in gold" (Gen 13.2). It may be that Job's assets at the end were provided partly through the intervention of generous friends. Some commentators have even proposed that the brigands of the prologue had a divinely-prompted change of heart which led them to restore what they had stolen. In reality, however, all we can be certain about is that Job now possessed double what he had before. In keeping with the general (but not invariable) outlook of the Old Testament, faithfulness is rewarded with earthly prosperity, for "them that honour me I will honour, and they that despise me shall be lightly esteemed" (1 Sam 2.30).

Greater attention, however, is devoted to his **children** (42.13-15). Readers may be struck by the apparent discrepancy between the restoration of possessions and the restoration of progeny. The former are clearly doubled in number, while the latter are not. Job used to have seven sons and three daughters (1.2); at the end he has, once more, exactly seven sons and three daughters (42.13). However, if we bear in mind that throughout the Old Testament there is a clear hint of life beyond the temporal, then we may assume that his children were ultimately doubled in number because the original ten were awaiting their father in the place of departed spirits. That, it seems, was the belief of David. When his new-born baby died he said,

I shall go to him, but he shall not return to me (2 Sam 12.23).

The death of Abraham is recorded in a similar way:

Then Abraham gave up the ghost, and died in a good old age, an old man, and full of years; and was gathered to his people (Gen 25.8).

In contrast to the prologue, where his original sons and daughters were anonymous, we now learn some names. So ebullient is Job's delight in his renewed family that, like Eve rejoicing in the birth of Seth as a replacement for the murdered Abel (Gen 4.25), he gives appropriate names to his three daughters. Jemima, it seems, means "daylight", "day by day", or perhaps "dove". Certainly she may be said to have brought into his life a glad dawn after the darkness of calamity (17.13; 19.8). Perhaps, like the bride in Song of Solomon, she possessed beautiful "dove's eyes" (Song 4.1). Kezia appears to refer to the fragrant, aromatic bark cassia, which in Psalm 45.8 is associated with the splendours of the righteous king who will yet rule the earth. The delightfully soothing odour her name implies contrasts dramatically with the foetid breath which so offended Job's wife (17.1; 19.17), and the foul stench of his ulcerous sores (2.7; 7.5). Kerenhappuch means "horn of antimony". According to the Royal Society of Chemistry website,

Antimony and its compounds were known to the ancients and there is a 5,000-year old antimony vase in the Louvre in Paris. Antimony sulfide (Sb_2S_3) is mentioned in an Egyptian papyrus of the 16th century BC. The black form of this pigment, which occurs naturally as the mineral stibnite, was used as mascara and known as *khol*. The most famous user was the temptress Jezebel whose exploits are recorded in the Bible [2 Kings 9.30].[494]

The name probably suggests that Job's third daughter possessed by nature all the beauty which many women have to acquire artificially through cosmetics.

Not all children live up to their names; but verse 15 indicates that Job's daughters were remarkable for their loveliness. That their father gave them an inheritance with their brothers testifies to his special delight. To read Numbers 27 is to see how unusual it was in the Near East for family inheritance to pass to females; in the particular case of Zelophehad's daughters, special provision was made by Jehovah only because there were no sons living to perpetuate the family name. Job, on the other hand, awarded his three daughters an inheritance "among their brethren". The language seems to hint at equality of benefit. If so, it looks forward to the New Testament principle that, as far as spiritual blessing is concerned, "there is neither male nor female: for ye are all one in Christ Jesus" (Gal 3.28). There are no first and second class citizens in grace, for the lavish generosity of God goes out equally and impartially to all who trust in His Son.

The book closes with a glance at Job's personal **continuance** after the closure of his sufferings (42.16-17). If he lived on for another hundred and forty years, and if the principle of double recompense includes his lifespan, then we may reasonably assume that he was seventy in chapter 1. He therefore attained the ripe age of 210. Abraham's father Terah died at 205 (Gen 11.32), so Job's age was within the expected range of his contemporaries (assuming the book places him roughly in the patriarchal era). Even more remarkable than mere length of life, however, is the deep pleasure afforded him in seeing the fruitful growth of his family, for he lived to rejoice in four generations. As Solomon tells us, "Children's children are the crown of old men; and the glory of children are their fathers" (Prov 17.6). It is not too much to infer that, just as Job took delight in his many descendants, so they benefitted spiritually from his unique experience of God.

The book closes with Job's death. But it is far removed from the agonized death he alternately desired and dreaded in the days of his affliction:

> now shall I sleep in the dust; and thou shalt seek me in the morning, but I shall not be (7.21).

> I go whence I shall not return, even to the land of darkness and the shadow of death; A land of darkness, as darkness itself; and of the shadow of death, without any order, and where the light is as darkness (10.21-22).

> Thou prevailest for ever against him, and he passeth: thou changest his countenance, and sendest him away (14.20).

Rather, he died a mellow, grateful old man, "full of days". Similar language is used of Abraham (Gen 25.8), Jacob (Gen 35.29), and David (1 Chr 29.28). The word "full" implies spiritual satisfaction and contentment of soul. Amazingly, Job's final blessing was anticipated earlier by one of the friends who, despite doubting his innocence, predicted the eventual restoration of his property, the abundance of his progeny, and a sense of achievement at death:

And thou shalt know that thy tent is in peace; and thou wilt survey thy fold, and miss nothing. And thou shalt know that thy seed is numerous, and thine offspring as the herb of the earth. Thou shalt come to the grave in a ripe age, as a shock of corn is brought in in its season (5.24-26, JND).

That truly is the case with Job. In God's good time his earthly life is brought to a fulfilled conclusion. Because this is an early patriarchal narrative, its horizon is restricted to the earth. According to the *Jamieson, Fausset and Brown Commentary*, the Septuagint translation of the Old Testament adds a postscript absent from the Hebrew text: "It is written, that he will rise again with those whom the Lord will raise up". But although the doctrine of resurrection is discreetly intimated in the Old Testament, we really have to wait until the New Testament before our expectations are clearly lifted beyond the current world to "an inheritance incorruptible, and undefiled, and that fadeth not away, reserved in heaven for you" (1 Pet 1.4). The book of Job ends with temporary earthly blessing; the Bible ends with the eternal bliss of a new heaven and new earth.

Now that Job has reached the termination of his earthly pilgrimage, what ought we to remember most about him? At this stage the reader might find it useful to revisit the introduction, which attempts to summarise the key features of this fascinating book. But in two ways Job should carve himself on our memories: he stands as a faint picture of the Saviour, and a marvellous pattern for saints.

As a **picture of the Saviour**, like all other types and shadows, of course, he falls far short of the reality. Nevertheless, we cannot overlook his total innocence of all the charges his friends laid at his door. His integrity is affirmed by the inspired narrator and by God at the beginning and end of the story (1.1,8; 2.3; 42.7-8). Job's personal innocence, however, was only relative; that of the Lord Jesus Christ was absolute and unimpeachable sinlessness (1 Pet 2.22). Not only did He do no wrong; He devoted His life to doing everything that was right (Acts 10.38). More, Job engages in intercession on behalf of those who have injured him. Our minds are drawn to the superior advocacy of the Lord Jesus who, without any prompting, continues in heaven to speak up for all who come to Him (1 Jn 2.1). We might also notice Job's personal approval by God, and his position as the book's final centre of attention. The Lord Jesus Christ's eternal acceptance with the Father brings all His people into blessing, in that they are "accepted in the beloved" (Eph 1.6). Further, it is Christ who, by being lifted up, draws all to Himself (Jn 12.32). To read about Job is – at times, certainly – to think about the Lord Jesus.

Yet Job was also "a man subject to like passions as we are" (James 5.17). Despite his tempestuous vacillations of mood in the course of the acrimonious debate, he remains a **pattern for saints**. He is an outstanding model of resignation to God's will, of endurance under adversity, and – wonderfully – of eventual glory after terrible trial. The pathway for God's people in this world is, broadly speaking, suffering down here (because of the hostility of the world, the flesh and the devil) and glory afterwards. But there can be no comparison between the one and the other; as Paul says, "our light affliction, which is but for a moment, worketh for

us a far more exceeding and eternal weight of glory" (2 Cor 4.17). Job's glory days
– as far as the Old Testament narrative is concerned – find their fulfilment in this
present world; ours stretch into the endless splendours of a new universe.

Job is a profoundly difficult book to read and at times a puzzle to understand.
Nonetheless it is packed with practical lessons. The American Presbyterian Albert
Barnes lists some reasons for studying Job:

> The theologian should study it as an invaluable introduction to the volume
> of inspired truth; the humble Christian, to obtain elevated views of God;
> the philosopher, to see how little the human mind can accomplish on the
> most important of all subjects without the aid of revelation; the child of
> sorrow, to learn the lessons of patient submission; the man of science, to
> know what was understood in the far distant periods of the past; the man
> of taste, as an incomparable specimen of poetic beauty and sublimity. It
> will teach invaluable lessons to each advancing generation; and to the end
> of time true piety and taste will find consolation and pleasure in the study
> of the Book of Job.

One of the great consolations found in Job is put into words by Robinson,
pithy as always. It is, he says,

> the part of piety and faith to trust God without seeking to trace Him; and
> to be assured that He does all things well.[495]

But the pathway to such an attitude of godly acquiescence is not easy. Robinson
continues:

> Spiritual knowledge [is] often one of the most blessed fruits of sanctified
> affliction. Often more knowledge of divine things [is] gained in one month
> or one week on a sick bed than in many years of previous experience.

Paul lays down the principle that "tribulation works endurance" (Rom 5.3,
JND); but Job offers the great biblical pattern. One of the practical benefits of
this gritty book is that every reader will go away with a renewed thankfulness
for God's present blessings, and a resolution not to give way to the complaints
which so often mar our testimony. In the light of Job's trials, how many of us
have much to grumble about? Indeed, the Christian believer, because he lives in
the good of the death and resurrection of Christ, has far better reason for hope
and endurance. He can take to himself the words of Fanny Crosby, with special
emphasis on the final two lines:

> All the way my Saviour leads me,
> What have I to ask beside?
> Can I doubt His tender mercy,
> Who through life has been my Guide?

> Heav'nly peace, divinest comfort,
> Here by faith in Him to dwell!
> For I know, whate'er befall me,
> Jesus doeth all things well.

How do we know that "Jesus doeth all things well"? We know it from the infallible record of Scripture; we know it from the infinite value of His death; we know it from the unbreakable promises of God; we know it from the New Testament commentary on the story of Job, which reveals that "the Lord is very pitiful, and of tender mercy" (James 5.11).

The seventeenth-century poet John Milton ends his dramatic poem about the life and death of Samson with these lines, which may, without too much difficulty, be applied to Job:

> ALL is best, though we oft doubt,
> What th'unsearchable dispose
> Of highest wisdom brings about,
> And ever best found in the close.
> Oft he seems to hide his face,
> But unexpectedly returns
> And to his faithful Champion hath in place
> Bore witness gloriously; whence Gaza mourns
> And all that band them to resist
> His uncontrollable intent.
> His servants he with new acquist
> Of true experience from this great event
> With peace and consolation hath dismist,
> And calm of mind all passion spent.[496]

If, in our reading of Job, we learn to recognise the sovereign prerogative of divine wisdom, the need to wait until the end of the journey to see God's purpose, the practical benefit of the experiences He leads us through, and the blessing of peace and consolation found uniquely in Him, then we shall have done well.

APPENDIX 1
Job and the Intermediate State

Lightner's *Handbook of Evangelical Theology* includes an overview of the Old Testament word *sheol*:

> Sheol is [sometimes] translated "hell" in the Authorised Version, but does not refer to the place of eternal punishment. Instead, it means the gloomy place where the good and the evil exist after death. Job has both of these existing together (Job 3.17-19), but Isaiah describes different levels of existence there (Is 14.15-20). The Old Testament [using the word *sheol* coupled with various Hebrew synonyms] presents Sheol as a place of darkness (Job 10.21-22), of silence (Ps 94.17), of forgetfulness (Ps 88.12) … and a place without awareness of what takes place on earth (Eccl 9.5-6,10). Alongside the Old Testament descriptions of the shadowy and gloomy side of Sheol there are passages that reveal a bright and joyful life after death for the people of God. Most of these are found in the poetic literature … (Ps 16.9-11; 17.15; 49.12-15).[497]

As we might expect, truth is unveiled gradually. Full light on these matters has come with "the appearing of our Saviour Jesus Christ, who hath abolished death, and hath brought life and immortality to light through the gospel" (2 Tim 1.10). However, before Christ things were comparatively obscure. About the intermediate state (the whereabouts of the soul between death and resurrection) as it affected Old Testament people in particular, believers have generally taken one of two positions. Both positions agree that at death the body goes to the grave to await resurrection while the soul consciously exists either in blessedness or in torment. The difference, by no means substantive, concerns the precise location of the godly in the unseen world.

(1) The Two-Compartments View

On the basis of the narrative about the rich man and Lazarus in Luke 16, some have posited the existence of two distinct and separate compartments within *sheol/hades* (the place of departed spirits) in which the godly and the ungodly were kept until resurrection. At the Saviour's resurrection, however, the spirits of the godly were removed to the third heaven (or paradise) to be with the Lord. The argument is based largely upon the following scriptures: Luke 16.19-31; Luke 23.43; Ephesians 4.8-9; 2 Corinthians 12.2-4. This is the viewpoint offered above in the commentary on Job chapter 3. It is a line of teaching popularised by the *Scofield Reference Bible* of 1917, supported by a good few teachers (such as Lewis Sperry Chafer, E H Bancroft, Henry Thiessen), and expounded in some detail by Herman Hoyt in *The End Times* (Moody Press, 1969). William Hoste defends it in response to a question about "Paradise" reprinted in *Bible Problems and Answers* (Ritchie, 1957).

The following is Thiessen's summary:

> The NT indicates that there were two compartments in Hades: one for
> the wicked and one for the good. The one for the righteous was called
> Paradise. The one for the wicked is not named, but it is described as a place
> of torment … After the resurrection of Christ there seems to have come
> a change. From that time on believers are represented as going into the
> presence of Christ at death. Thus Paul represented his embodied condition
> as one in which he was "absent from the Lord", and his disembodied
> condition as one in which he would be "at home with the Lord" (2 Cor
> 5.6-9). He expressed his desire to "depart and be with Christ, for it is very
> far better" (Phil 1.23). We also see the "souls of them that had been slain"
> under the altar and conscious (Rev 6.9-11). They still go to Paradise, but
> Paradise is now above (2 Cor 12.2-4). It is possible that when Christ arose,
> he took with him not only a first-fruit of men whom He raised bodily (Mt
> 27.52,53), but also the souls of all the righteous in Hades (Eph 4.8; Ps
> 68.18). Henceforth all believers go into Christ's presence at death, while
> the unbelievers continue to go to Hades, as in OT times.[498]

Thiessen adopts the language of caution: "there seems to have come a change",
"It is possible". Hammond's astute and incisive *In Understanding Be Men* refers in
equally nuanced terms to a "barely possible hint that a difference was effected in
the lot of the faithful departed by the Resurrection and Ascension of our Lord".[499]
We are not in an area of rock-solid certainty. For a start, only with difficulty can
Ephesians 4 be pressed into service for this theory.

(2) The Progress of Revelation View
Others maintain that at death the Old Testament godly (as today) went
immediately into the presence of the Lord (a location perhaps known to
Jewish saints as "Abraham's bosom"), while the ungodly were confined to
the torments of *sheol*. In other words, the separation between the place of
torment and "Abraham's bosom" taught in Luke 16 was not a horizontal
division within *sheol* (as proposed in the first theory), but a vertical one.
The coming of Christ initiated not so much an actual shift in the location
of the saved as a fuller unveiling of an existing reality. Charles Ryrie,
Paul Enns, and Robert Culver are among those who take this line. The
answer[500] to a question about *sheol/hades* in William Kelly's *Bible Treasury*
is of a similar mind.

The arguments may be explored in the following books:

(1) The two-compartment view:

E H Bancroft	*Elemental Theology*, Zondervan, 1977, 390-391
L S Chafer	*Systematic Theology*, Dallas Seminary, 1948, vol 4, 413-14
Herman Hoyt	*The End Times*, Moody Press, 1969, 34-48

| C I Scofield | *The Scofield Reference Bible*, OUP, 1917 (note to Luke 16.23; the equivalent note in the *New Scofield Reference Bible* of 1967 is less dogmatic) |
| Henry C Thiessen | *Lectures in Systematic Theology*, Eerdmans, 1949, 488-489. |

(2) The progress of revelation view:

Robert D Culver	*Systematic Theology*, Mentor, 2005, 1030-1042 (a detailed academic discussion)
Paul Enns	*The Moody Handbook of Theology*, Moody, 1989, 374-5
Charles Ryrie	*Basic Theology*, Victor Books, 1987, 518-20.

Culver offers a series of five propositions with which it would be hard to disagree. They are as follows: (1) "Both Old Testament and New Testament represent the state of mankind after death to be a disembodied state"; (2) "Both Testaments of scripture teach that the intermediate state for the believer is one of conscious blessedness"; (3) "The Bible teaches that the intermediate state of the impenitent and unbelieving is one of misery in hell (or hades). In the Old Testament Sheol, the pit or lowest *sheol*, is a place (or condition) to which the wicked, in distinction to the righteous, are sent at death"; (4) "The condition of the unsaved in their present disembodied state is one of conscious torment"; (5) "The condition of the righteous dead in their present, disembodied, intermediate state, while not one of complete blessedness, is nevertheless "far better" than that of living saints".[501]

Because the book of Job comes from an early period of divine revelation, we must not expect from its speakers the clarity and confidence of the apostle in Philippians 1.23 or 2 Corinthians 5.8. Indeed, the paucity of Old Testament information about the situation after death and before resurrection means that it is impossible to speak dogmatically. Culver makes the excellent point that "a sharp distinction should be made between the expressed opinions of the people who appear on the pages and in the narratives on the one hand and revealed biblical truth on the other".[502] That Job mentions pagan magicians does not endorse their practices (3.8); that he fondly imagines *sheol* as a place of release and rest does not guarantee that it was (3.13-19). Further, a man under inconceivable pressure is liable to blurt out things he might not say in different circumstances.

Even the truth of a future bodily resurrection was not unambiguously revealed until later in the Old Testament (Dan 12.1-3), although we ought to bear in mind that more may have been understood by believers than was specifically disclosed in the written Word. The following passages certainly offer hints of resurrection: Exodus 3.6; 1 Samuel 2.6; Psalm 16.8-11; Psalm 49.14-15; Isaiah 26.19. In the New Testament, Hebrews 11.10,14-16 provides a remarkable retrospective insight into the mind of earlier saints which we might not have detected in the Old Testament record. Furthermore, the covenant promises made to Abraham (Gen 13.15-17; 15.7; 17.8) required that he be eventually raised up to enjoy the land he never actually possessed while alive (Heb 11.8,13). He will be resurrected to enter into millennial glory, along with "many [who] shall come from the east and west, and shall sit down with

Abraham, and Isaac, and Jacob, in the kingdom of heaven" (Mt 8.11). As we read through the Old Testament, then, we begin to realise that resurrection is a necessity if God's pledges are to be honoured.

Job inevitably lacked the assurance of those in the good of clear disclosures given in audible or written form from heaven. We should not expect from him a fixed, authoritative pronouncement about the state of the soul after death, or the hope of resurrection.

APPENDIX 2
Job and Jeremiah

The parallels between the experience and words of Job and those of the prophet Jeremiah have long been noted by commentators. But they extend beyond the personal passages found in the book of Jeremiah to include the poetic complaints which make up the book of Lamentations. There the prophet is inspired to describe in graphic detail the external and internal sufferings of the city of Jerusalem as it endures God's wrath meted out through the Babylonian invaders. Chapter 3 is one of the sections which most obviously remind us of Job. The resemblances are perhaps best examined through tracing some of the close verbal parallels (noted below in the references, in square brackets, to Strong's numbering code for Hebrew words).

Job and Jeremiah both endured God's rod:

"I am the man [1397] that hath seen affliction by the rod [7626] of his wrath" (Lam 3.1). Jeremiah uses the word for "man" which emphasis strength and valour. Job uses the same word in looking back ruefully to the announcement of his birth: "Let the day perish wherein I was born, and the night in which it was said, There is a man child [1397] conceived" (Job 3.3). Like Jeremiah, Job refers to God's rod as the ultimate source of his misery: "Let him take his rod [7626] away from me, and let not his fear terrify me" (Job 9.34).

Job and Jeremiah both experienced darkness:

"He hath led me, and brought me into darkness [2822], but not into light" (Lam 3.2). Job, too, found his pathway obscured so that he had no idea where he was going: "He hath fenced up my way that I cannot pass, and he hath set darkness [2822] in my paths" (Job 19.8).

Job and Jeremiah both saw themselves as victims of God's hand:

"Surely against me is he turned; he turneth his hand [3027] against me all the day" (Lam 3.3). Job also saw himself as the individual target of God's hostility: "Thou knowest that I am not wicked; and there is none that can deliver out of thine hand [3027]" (Job 10.7); "Have pity upon me, have pity upon me, O ye my friends; for the hand [3027] of God hath touched me" (Job 19.21); "Even to day is my complaint bitter: my stroke [3027] is heavier than my groaning" (Job 23.2); "Thou art become cruel to me: with thy strong hand [3027] thou opposest thyself against me" (Job 30.21).

Job and Jeremiah both suffered physical and emotional pain:

"My flesh [1320] and my skin [5785] hath he made old; he hath broken my bones [6106]" (Lam 3.4). Job's physical condition was equally deplorable: "My flesh [1320] is clothed with worms and clods of dust; my skin [5785] is broken, and become loathsome" (Job 7.5); "My bone [6106] cleaveth to my skin [5785] and to my flesh [1320], and I am escaped with the skin of my teeth" (Job 19.20); "My bones [6106] are pierced in me in the night season: and my sinews take no rest" (Job 30.17); "My skin [5785] is black upon me, and my bones [6016] are burned with heat" (Job 30.30).

Job and Jeremiah both considered themselves trapped:
"He hath hedged [1443] me about, that I cannot get out: he hath made my chain heavy" (Lam 3.7); "He hath inclosed [1443] my ways with hewn stone, he hath made my paths crooked" (Lam 3.9). Job felt similarly ensnared: "He hath fenced [1443] up my way that I cannot pass, and he hath set darkness in my paths" (Job 19.8).

Job and Jeremiah both received no answers to their prayers:
"Also when I cry and shout, he shutteth out my prayer" (Lam 3.8). "I cry unto thee, and thou dost not hear me: I stand up, and thou regardest me not" (Job 30.20).

Job and Jeremiah both described God as a wild animal in His ferocity towards them:
"He was unto me as a bear lying in wait, and as a lion in secret places" (Lam 3.10). "Thou huntest me as a fierce lion: and again thou shewest thyself marvellous upon me" (Job 10.16).

Job and Jeremiah both felt desolated and deprived of support:
"He hath turned aside my ways, and pulled me in pieces: he hath made me desolate [8074]" (Lam 3.11). "But now he hath made me weary: thou hast made desolate [8074] all my company" (Job 16.7).

Job and Jeremiah both saw themselves as a target for God's arrows:
"He hath bent his bow, and set me as a mark for the arrow [2671]. He hath caused the arrows of his quiver to enter into my reins" (Lam 3.12-13). "For the arrows [2671] of the Almighty are within me, the poison whereof drinketh up my spirit: the terrors of God do set themselves in array against me" (Job 6.4).

Job and Jeremiah both experienced the humiliation of social rejection:
"I was a derision [7184] to all my people; and their song [5058] all the day" (Lam 3.14). "I am as one mocked [7184] of his neighbour, who calleth upon God, and he answereth him: the just upright man is laughed to scorn" (Job 12.4); "And now am I their song [5058], yea, I am their byword" (Job 30.9).

Job and Jeremiah both associated their grief with ashes:
"He hath also broken my teeth with gravel stones, he hath covered me with ashes [665]" (Lam 3.16). "And he took him a potsherd to scrape himself withal; and he sat down among the ashes [665]" (Job 2.8); "He hath cast me into the mire, and I am become like dust and ashes [665]" (Job 30.19).

Job and Jeremiah both despaired of seeing good:
"And thou hast removed my soul far off from peace: I forgat prosperity [2896]"

(Lam 3.17). "Now my days are swifter than a post: they flee away, they see no good [2896]" (Job 9.25); "When I looked for good [2896], then evil came unto me: and when I waited for light, there came darkness" (Job 30.26).

Job and Jeremiah both bore severe affliction:

"Remembering mine affliction [6040] and my misery, the wormwood and the gall" (Lam 3.19). "And now my soul is poured out upon me; the days of affliction [6040] have taken hold upon me" (Job 30.16).

Job and Jeremiah both spoke about hope:

"This I recall to my mind, therefore have I hope [3176]" (Lam 3.21). "What is my strength, that I should hope [3176]? and what is mine end, that I should prolong my life?" (Job 6.11); "When I looked for good, then evil came unto me: and when I waited [3176] for light, there came darkness" (Job 30.26).

These are but some of the parallels. More may be discovered with the aid of systematic concordance study. But as the last one listed above indicates, the differences between these two faithful men of God are as great as the similarities. In the midst of his distresses the recollection of God's past mercies to Israel gave Jeremiah hope. Job, however, had no such historical treasure house of national blessings from which to draw comfort.

Jeremiah was entrusted with the painful responsibility of informing disobedient Judah of God's impending judgment upon the nation because of its impenitence. It was, as the prologue to his prophecy indicates, a ministry more of demolition than construction:

> But the Lord said unto me, Say not, I am a child: for thou shalt go to all that I shall send thee, and whatsoever I command thee thou shalt speak. Be not afraid of their faces: for I am with thee to deliver thee, saith the Lord. Then the Lord put forth his hand, and touched my mouth. And the Lord said unto me, Behold, I have put my words in thy mouth. See, I have this day set thee over the nations and over the kingdoms, to root out, and to pull down, and to destroy, and to throw down, to build, and to plant (Jer 1.7-10).

Regardless of his understandable reluctance, Jeremiah was commissioned to proclaim an unpalatable message of coming disaster, frankly informed of the hostility he would face, promised the gracious presence of God in his service, and told that his preaching would be four parts negative (solemn warnings about the Babylonian capture of Jerusalem and the collapse of the Davidic monarchy) and two parts positive (wonderful previews of coming blessing with the arrival of the future Messiah). His faithful discharge of this onerous duty gave Jeremiah no personal pleasure, for it involved being accused of treason, being hated by his own people, and living to see his beloved nation fall to a cruel enemy amidst terrible suffering. In Lamentations he becomes the voice of besieged and afflicted Jerusalem in its pain and sorrow. Tender, earnest, loving, prayerful and patriotic by nature, Jeremiah had to proclaim catastrophic judgment upon those he loved best, and he found it heart-breaking. It is no wonder he is called the weeping prophet. As Jensen expresses it, "he wept not for his own trials, grievous as they were. It was the sins of the nation and the fearful destruction these sins were bringing upon them that broke Jeremiah's heart".[503]

Nevertheless, for all his deep distress of soul, Jeremiah knew from the beginning that Judah fully deserved its afflictions because of its faithlessness. As a member of the nation's priesthood, He could see that God's ways with His people were fully in harmony with the terms of His covenant. Obedience would bring blessing; rebellion would bring punishment. Because he had access to the law given to Israel, with all its principles and promises, he could not be in the dark about God's programme. The divine dealings with Judah might seem hard, but they were by no means bewildering. On the other hand, Job lived before the law was given, and had no knowledge of God's special relationship with the nation of Israel. Nor was he a prophet commissioned to bring a message to his people. He was a lone godly man suffering incalculable calamity without the slightest comprehension of why this was happening to him. That is the reason why, even in the middle of Jeremiah's complaints, the tone can suddenly change. Right at the centre of Lamentations stands a marvellous oasis of confidence, where the prophet turns from his misery to rest in what he knows of God:

> It is of the Lord's mercies that we are not consumed, because his compassions fail not. They are new every morning: great is thy faithfulness. The Lord is my portion, saith my soul; therefore will I hope in him. The Lord is good unto them that wait for him, to the soul that seeketh him. It is good that a man should both hope and quietly wait for the salvation of the Lord (Lam 3.22-26).

Job could not speak like that simply because he lived prior to such an extensive and heartening disclosure of God's gracious purposes.

Nonetheless, he has his own remarkable sanctuaries of insight, of hope, of unexpectedly renewed faith as he reasons that the God he knows cannot behave unjustly and must therefore eventually rise to his defence. That these havens of rest are so brief and so rare in no way lessens their impact. For the reader, they are refreshing tables in the wilderness to fortify us as we make our way through a seemingly interminable wasteland of words towards the great moment when Jehovah intervenes personally in the conflict to talk directly with His much-maligned servant.

Jeremiah recognised that God's dealings with Jerusalem were just; and yet the God who disciplines is also the God who delivers, for "though he cause grief, yet will he have compassion according to the multitude of his mercies. For he doth not afflict willingly nor grieve the children of men" (Lam 3.32-33). Failing Jerusalem would eventually be restored to blessing, just as faithful Job, afflicted not because of his sins but because of his uprightness, would finally bask in the renewed sunshine of divine favour.

One final parallel should be added to the list of similarities between these great Old Testament men. Both of them, in their measure, remind us of the Lord Jesus Christ, the One who on Calvary uniquely bore God's wrath against His people. In their consciousness that all their painful circumstances were traceable to God, and especially in Jeremiah's unjust sufferings at the hands of his fellow-countrymen, they anticipate the Messiah's sorrows. Neither seems conscious that he prefigures God's long-promised Saviour, but it cannot be coincidental that one of the answers to the Lord's query, "Whom do men say that I the Son of man am?" (Mt 16.13), was "Some say that thou art … Jeremias" (Mt 16.14). In his tender-hearted grief at the rebellious stubbornness of Judah, the prophet certainly pre-echoes the Saviour's tears over a Jerusalem defiantly resistant to His call. Whether they knew it or not, both Job and Jeremiah had the privilege of being used in God's providential ways to make believers today think about God's Son.

APPENDIX 3
Job and James

Just as there are fascinating parallels between Job and Jeremiah, so there are extensive links between Job and the only New Testament writer to mention him. James's summary has been much quoted in this commentary:

> Take, my brethren, the prophets, who have spoken in the name of the Lord, for an example of suffering affliction, and of patience. Behold, we count them happy which endure. Ye have heard of the patience of Job, and have seen the end of the Lord; that the Lord is very pitiful, and of tender mercy (James 5.10-11).

The well-known reference to Job at the close of the letter, however, should not be taken as a last-minute postscript. Rather, it signals a clue to the subject matter and structure of the letter as a whole. Without embarking on an in-depth comparison between the book of Job and the epistle of James, the following points of connection seem worthy of consideration.

James starts with a reference to the various **trials** which befall believers (James 1.2-4), exhorting them to joy and endurance. His great exemplar of endurance under trial is Job, whom he names, in company with unspecified Old Testament prophets, in his concluding chapter (James 5.10-11). In that sense the topic of faith under fire forms the framework of his letter. The book of Job is the ideal Old Testament example, recounting in graphic detail one man's extreme testing and its results.

James recognises that to respond rightly to trial requires a **wisdom** God alone can provide (James 1.5; 3.17-18). Job is equally alert to the need for spiritual understanding, penning a hymn in praise of the wisdom which consists in the fear of the Lord (Job 28.28).

James encourages readers going through testings to converse with God in **prayer**, confidently seeking in Him what they lack (James 1.5-6; 5.13). Throughout his terrible distresses Job persistently calls upon God (Job 6.8; 30.20; 31.35).

James underlines the **transience** of earthly prosperity, noticing that the rich may be abased and the lowly exalted (James 1.9-11). Job's testing commences with the sudden and inexplicable removal of all his material affluence (Job 1.13-19).

James promises a special **blessing** to the believer who steadfastly endures trials (James 1.12). The book of Job records the double restoration awarded the patriarch at the close (Job 42.12).

James distinguishes carefully between external trials which befall the believer and those solicitations to evil which spring from within. God never prompts men to sin (James 1.13-16). Job's trials came ultimately from God, though mediated by Satan, yet his propensity to complain and accuse God was the reaction of a fleshly heart inherited from Adam (Job 31.33).

James encourages caution and self-control in **speech** (James 1.19,26; 3.2-10). Job illustrates the power of the tongue to offer relief (Job 4.4; 16.5) or to speak inadvisedly (Job 8.2; 11.2; 15.13; 16.3; 29.22; 34.35; 42.3).

James tells us that "pure **religion**" is demonstrated in kindness to the needy and in holiness of living (James 1.27). Job exhibited this in practice (Job 1.1; 29.12-16; 31.16-22).

James urges **impartiality** (James 2.1-9). Job was a model of disinterestedness in his judicial dealings (Job 31.13-15).

James mentions the prohibition against **adultery** as an example of God's law (James 2.11). Job specifically repudiated adultery in his own life (Job 31.9-12).

James warns **teachers** that they will be assessed by a higher standard than others (James 3.1). Eliphaz (wrongly) accuses Job the instructor of failing to live up to his teaching (Job 4.3-6).

James emphasises the benefits of **self-humbling** before God (James 4.6-10). Under the teaching of Jehovah, Job is brought to an acknowledgment of his own lowliness (Job 42.6).

James recognises the activity of the **devil** and counsels resistance (James 4.7). Although Job appears to be unaware of the satanic instrumentality behind his sufferings, his faithful submission to God's hand (Job 1.21; 2.10) means that, from the end of chapter 2, the devil is effectively written out of the book.

James reminds his readers of the **brevity of life** (James 4.14). In his multiple afflictions, Job is deeply conscious of life's frailty (Job 7.7; 8.9; 9.25; 14.2; 20.8).

James denounces the rich for unjust treatment of their **workers** (James 5.4). Job the householder was an upright and generous employer (Job 31.13,31), while Job the farmer was a model of godly labour relations (Job 31.38-40).

As an incentive to endurance, James encourages his readers to exercise patience **until the Lord comes** (James 5.7-8). Job looks ahead to some kind of divine intervention on his behalf (Job 19.25-27) which, to everyone's surprise, is fulfilled in a special personal appearance of Jehovah. Elihu announces the arrival of this startling theophany with the words, "Out of the north cometh golden splendour: God hath upon him terrible majesty" (Job 37.22, RV). In James, the Lord is coming; in Job, the Lord actually comes.

These examples (and the diligent reader will find others) support the suggestion that James employs Job as a kind of Old Testament template for his letter. Since his topic is the trials believers endure, Job is the perfect model, but James's practical exhortations and warnings also draw on a range of other features found in the Old Testament book. Because Job's afflictions were as intense as his behaviour was exemplary, he provides a timeless pattern for the people of God, while remaining "a man subject to like passions as we are" (James 5.17).

APPENDIX 4
Why do Bad Things Happen to Good People?

Such a question demands a quick definition of what is meant in this context by "good". Scripture teaches that "there is none good but one, that is, God" (Mt 19.17), and that "there is none that doeth good, no, not one" (Rom 3.12). Human beings are good absolutely neither in nature nor in practice. When, then, we talk about "good people" we are referring here to those who by grace have been declared right with God through faith in the finished work of Christ at Calvary. Such people will seek to live in a manner worthy of their Redeemer, although they know that their personal virtue at best will only be relative and limited.

But if such people are right with God, why do bad things happen to them? This, of course, is the essential question which threads its nagging way through the book of Job. So disquieting is it, that experienced philosophers like Eliphaz, Bildad and Zophar feel constrained to adjust their entire view of their old friend Job, denouncing him as a secret sinner whose crimes have caught up with him. For them, the evidence of his present suffering drowns out the consistent testimony of his past life.

What is the biblical answer to what C S Lewis famously called the problem of pain?

The following is an article by James J S Johnson published by ICR's *Acts and Facts* magazine in February 2016 under the title "God's Timing Makes Sense of Adversity". It is so pertinent that I quote it in full:

> "Why do people suffer bad things that they don't deserve?" It was the inquirer rather than the question that was surprising: a seven-year-old boy.
>
> The answer to this child's question is provided in the book of Job. In Job's experience, he questioned why an infinitely wise, good, and powerful God would allow a basically good man to suffer terrible calamities on earth while letting other humans, who behave far worse, escape such calamities. Such inequity confuses child and adult alike, especially if one assumes that total "fairness" is supposed to be achieved during this earthly lifetime. But how do you explain Job — its theology of human suffering, and how God tests human character *in time* for His eternal purposes — to a second grader?
>
> Start by explaining the importance of how temporal needs are followed by timely care, in our own lives, using a "nature sermon" — the same approach God Himself used while He was replying to Job's agonizing questions. God pointed to how He takes care of earthly creatures through His providential timing. Lion and raven babies hunger first, then they eat. Wild goats and deer have designed timeframes for gestation, then birth occurs. Hawks and eagles fly with purposeful timing, synching their flights to thermal air currents and season-timed migrations [Job 38.39-40 (lions); 38.41 (ravens); 39.1 (mountain goats); 39.1-4 (deer); 39.26 (hawks); 39.27-30 (eagles)].

Sequential timing is vital for the important things in this life, even the basics of being born, metabolizing food, and daily movements. Timing contextualizes all of the temporal adversities in human life, too. But eventually, all temporal afflictions end [James 5.10-11].

God was testing Job's moral character. We know this now because we have the entire book and know the entire ordeal, including the happy ending. But if God had told Job about the test in advance, including how God was proving that Satan was an impudent liar, it would have ruined the legitimacy of Job's own trial of faith. What Job learned through his agonizing ordeal was synched to sequenced timing — God's timing — so that Job's sufferings ultimately ended and counted for good.

God delayed some answers, but He did not ignore Job. He provided Job with proof of His wisdom and goodness and power in a sermon about nature (Job 38–41). He gave adequate information to Job, emphasizing that He was Maker and Master of His own creation, orchestrating and operating its synchronized moving parts (including humans and animals) so that, as Paul would later say, "all things work together for good."

Amazing! God has ordained seasons and migrations, fitted deer and goats for pregnancies, and provides food to animals to satisfy their hunger. God's timing is important in our own daily challenges, whether we are seven or 77, reminding us like Job that even amidst life's many confusions and agonies we can trust His all-wise and providential care. God knows what He is doing![504]

That final sentence is crucial. We know so little – even in the context of a completed revelation – but our God always knows exactly what He is doing. Until we are willing to bow to that truth, we shall never comprehend anything of the divine purpose in human pain.

There may be many reasons why a child of God endures adversity of various kinds during his earthly life. Let me bring forward a few which can be supported from Scripture.

Living in a sin-damaged body in a sin-dominated world

Even after conversion every believer inhabits a body which tends to dissolution, contains the seeds of decay, and falls under the death sentence pronounced upon Adam in Genesis 3.19, in fulfilment of the clear warning of Genesis 2.17. That sentence includes within it all lesser ills which often pave the way for physical death: congenital deformity and disability, ill-health, accident, disease. There is therefore a relationship between sin and misery, for all misery is ultimately a result of sin in the human race (Rom 5.12; Gen 3.16-19).

However, we must be cautious. Although all suffering is traceable to Adam's disobedience, not every ailment is necessarily a direct result of an individual's acts of sin. That the presence of some striking disability is in itself no sure sign of parental or personal failure was taught by the Lord Jesus in John 9. In response to the disciples' judgmental question about a man born blind, He answered:

> Neither hath this man sinned, nor his parents: but that the works of God should be made manifest in him (Jn 9.3).

These words should be sufficient to scotch the ungracious whispering which sometimes accompanies birth defects. This is neither a denial of that indwelling sin nature which is the inheritance of every descendant of Adam, nor is it a rejection of the possibility that some illnesses may be the product, direct or indirect, of personal conduct. Some, but not all, afflictions may be the consequence of specific sins (Rom 1.26,27). But the Lord's words stand as a corrective of the contemporary notion (tragically one not without its adherents today) that physical deformities, visible or invisible, prove personal transgression.

Therefore we cannot use affliction as an infallible measuring rod to evaluate a person's sinfulness or spirituality (see Job as a whole, and Luke 13.1-5), lest we mistake God's wise purposes. The blind man in John 9 was a living argument against abortion, for his disability became an occasion for the glorious display of the Son's goodness. Instead, we learn to look at our own afflictions in the knowledge that God permits them for His glory, that He might manifest His works in us. After all, He is the God who, without even mentioning the inherited penalty of Adam's sin in the human race, takes personal responsibility for deformity as well as capability (Ex 4.11).

Living righteously in an unrighteous environment

Under this heading may be included both the hostility which the believer faces in the world and the workplace when he tries to stand for what is right, and the specific persecution he may endure because he is identified with the gospel of Christ.

> Blessed are they which are persecuted for righteousness' sake: for theirs is the kingdom of heaven. Blessed are ye, when men shall revile you, and persecute you, and shall say all manner of evil against you falsely, for my sake. Rejoice, and be exceeding glad: for great is your reward in heaven: for so persecuted they the prophets which were before you (Mt 5.10-12).

Such afflictions were a badge of honour which the early believers wore with joy. Peter, having been beaten by the religious leadership, went his way with his fellow believers "rejoicing that they were counted worthy to suffer shame for his name" (Acts 5.41), and wrote later to other Christians facing the fire:

> if ye suffer for righteousness' sake, happy are ye: and be not afraid of their terror, neither be troubled (1 Pet 3.14).

Later in the same letter he gave additional reasons for deep contentment of soul in such distress:

> rejoice, inasmuch as ye are partakers of Christ's sufferings; that, when his glory shall be revealed, ye may be glad also with exceeding joy. If ye be reproached for the name of Christ, happy are ye; for the spirit of glory and of God resteth upon you: on their part he is evil spoken of, but on your part he is glorified (1 Pet 4.13-14).

The biblical principle is plain. Down here the faithful child of God will not enjoy the favour of a world which rejected God's Son. The seventeenth-century Puritan John Collins observed that "the truth of the gospel gets greater advantage by the humble sufferings of one saint, simply for the Word of righteousness, than by ten thousand arguments against error". Suffering is the believer's inevitable lot in a Christ-rejecting world. But that gives us all the more reason to look ahead with eager anticipation for the coming of the Lord from heaven.

Living inappropriately as a child of God

Behind God's dealings with erring saints lies the principle of divine chastisement as a mark of tender affection. It is not to be viewed as some automatic penalty imposed by an unfeeling authority. God deals punitively (and justly) with His enemies; but familial love colours His ways with His people. Several Old Testament passages introduce the principle and lead towards its great elucidatory statement in Hebrews.

> Behold, happy is the man whom God correcteth: therefore despise not thou the chastening of the Almighty: For he maketh sore, and bindeth up: he woundeth, and his hands make whole (Job 5.17-18).

> Blessed is the man whom thou chastenest O Lord, and teachest him out of thy law; That thou mayest give him rest from the days of adversity, until the pit be digged for the wicked (Ps 94.12-13).

> My son, despise not the chastening of the Lord; neither be weary of his correction: For whom the Lord loveth he correcteth; even as a father the son in whom he delighteth. Happy is the man that findeth wisdom, and the man that getteth understanding (Prov 3.11-13).

> For consider him that endured such contradiction of sinners against himself, lest ye be wearied and faint in your minds. Ye have not yet resisted unto blood, striving against sin. And ye have forgotten the exhortation which speaketh unto you as unto children, My son, despise not thou the chastening of the Lord, nor faint when thou art rebuked of him: For whom the Lord loveth he chasteneth, and scourgeth every son whom he receiveth. If ye endure chastening, God dealeth with you as with sons; for what son

is he whom the father chasteneth not? But if ye be without chastisement, whereof all are partakers, then are ye bastards, and not sons. Furthermore we have had fathers of our flesh which corrected us, and we gave them reverence: shall we not much rather be in subjection unto the Father of spirits, and live? For they verily for a few days chastened us after their own pleasure; but he for our profit, that we might be partakers of his holiness. Now no chastening for the present seemeth to be joyous, but grievous: nevertheless afterward it yieldeth the peaceable fruit of righteousness unto them which are exercised thereby (Heb 12.3-11).

The Old Testament passages gradually build up the teaching which is brought to its climax in Hebrews. The language of the epistle is carefully chosen. There is an in-built benefit in divine chastisement ("happy"), because it has in view eventual restoration ("his hands make whole"), it educates ("teachest"), it is an external proof of spiritual relationship ("whom the Lord loveth he correcteth"), and it requires the active cooperation of the one being disciplined ("exercised thereby"). As has often been said, trials will either make us bitter or better.

God dealt with Israel, His child nation, in this manner. Before ever they entered the Land He said to them, "if ye will not yet for all this hearken unto me, then I will punish ["chasten", as in Ps 94.12] you seven times more for your sins" (Lev 26.18). Again, a few verses later He says, "if ye will not be reformed ["chastened", as in Ps 94.12] by me by these things ... I will bring a sword upon you" (Lev 26.23,25). Israel was Jehovah's son nationally (Ex 4.22), Rehoboam, the ostensible addressee of Proverbs 3, was Solomon's son naturally, and the Christian believer is, because of sovereign grace, God's son by spiritual adoption. Sons are trained and matured by discipline. Amazingly, it is said even of the eternal Son, entering into sinless manhood, that "Though he were a Son, yet learned he obedience by the things which he suffered" (Heb 5.8). He therefore becomes, in Hebrews 12, the grand example of godly endurance, so that the argument starts with the One who "endured such contradiction of sinners against himself" (Heb 12.3) before shifting into instruction about the discipline which intrinsically sinful saints require to go through.

The New Testament includes some specific examples. Many of the saints in the Corinthian assembly had fallen ill or died because of the cavalier way they had been engaging in the solemn spiritual exercise of the Lord's Supper. Paul's words are, to say the least, sobering:

Wherefore whosoever shall eat this bread, and drink this cup of the Lord, unworthily, shall be guilty of the body and blood of the Lord. But let a man examine himself, and so let him eat of that bread, and drink of that cup. For he that eateth and drinketh unworthily, eateth and drinketh damnation to himself, not discerning the Lord's body. For this cause many are weak and sickly among you, and many sleep. For if we would judge ourselves, we should not be judged. But when we are judged, we are chastened of the Lord, that we should not be condemned with the world (1 Cor 11.27-32).

The problem was that believers were taking the bread and cup "unworthily" (v.27), "not discerning" (v.29) its significance. In all spiritual activities, the Lord looks for a real, thoughtful engagement of our hearts with Himself. The penalty (vv.29-32), inflicted we may assume by divine intervention, was an outbreak of sickness and death in the assembly (Acts 5.5,10; 1 Jn 5.16), for God disciplines His people precisely because they *are* His people (1 Pet 4.17), His purpose in chastisement (v.32) being to distinguish His saints (that is, "set apart ones") from the world at large. To treat the things of God casually places us in peril. We have only to think of the strict regulations surrounding tabernacle and temple worship in Old Testament times. And yet how consoling are the apostle's final words! Even the believer enduring divine chastisement is thereby distinguished from a world heading for eternal judgment. The Puritan Thomas Brooks remarks that it is "an ill sign for a man when God will not spend a rod upon him",[505] for chastisement proves divine affection.

Child-training is a long-term, rigorous business, and God employs many and varied instructors in His educational programme. Because saints are nothing but sinners saved by grace they will all undergo God's training regimen to mould them into the perfect image of His sinless Son. The process never comes to an end in this world. But once we have been removed at the rapture we shall be granted sin-free bodies in which failure of any kind will be a blessed impossibility.

Living rightly and becoming God's exemplar of faith

This was Job's particular circumstance, made known to the reader but not to Job or any other human in the narrative. Without the prologue we should have been as much in the dark as the three friends, and possibly just as uncharitable in our assessment. The true facts are these: so outstandingly upright was Job that he was held up to Satan as God's choice exhibit of practical godliness. More, when challenged by Satan that Job's piety was merely pragmatic, a selfish response to external prosperity, God permitted the adversary to put Job to the test. In Job's case – and doubtless the situation is a rare one – it was not wickedness but personal worthiness which lay behind his afflictions.

The same applies in measure to Abraham, tested to see whether he would offer back to God the son in whom all God's promises of global blessing were vested. Of course God knew the result before the test began; yet the angel of the Lord, a marvellous pre-incarnate appearance of the Son of God, was pleased to accommodate Himself to limited human understanding, saying to Abraham,

> Lay not thine hand upon the lad, neither do thou any thing unto him: for now I know that thou fearest God, seeing thou hast not withheld thy son, thine only son from me (Gen 22.12).

Abraham passed his test with flying colours.

The testimony of Scripture suggests that the holier the individual, the greater the testing he may be called upon to endure. The apostle Paul was afflicted with an unspecified bodily ailment which kept him humbly dependent on God despite his amazing privileges. He tells us that lest I should be exalted above measure through the abundance of the revelations, there was given to me a thorn in the flesh, the messenger of Satan to buffet me, lest I should be exalted above measure (2 Cor 12.7).

The language is revealing. Paul's disability was physical ("in the flesh"), brought about by satanic instrumentality ("the messenger of Satan"), painful ("thorn … buffet"), yet spiritually beneficial ("lest I should be exalted above measure"). Its positive effect is spelt out in the next few verses. Though Paul prayed to the Lord earnestly for its removal, the answer he received was unexpected:

And he said unto me, My grace is sufficient for thee: for my strength is made perfect in weakness. Most gladly therefore will I rather glory in my infirmities, that the power of Christ may rest upon me. Therefore I take pleasure in infirmities, in reproaches, in necessities, in persecutions, in distresses for Christ's sake: for when I am weak, then am I strong (2 Cor 12.9-10).

Paul stands therefore as a great example of the believer who has to endure a chronic debilitating condition, not because of personal sins but because of the weight of spiritual privileges. In the wise purposes of God, Paul's thorn was designed to preserve him from pride and self-satisfaction, casting him constantly upon the Lord.

Living rightly but, under continued trial, slipping into hard thoughts about God

In the prologue to his story Job is the great example of faith under trial, maintaining a testimony of steadfast confidence in God despite all his ills. In the first two chapters he puts not a foot wrong; nor does he utter a word out of place. The Christian reader can only marvel at such unflinching faith. But as the book proceeds (and we have no real idea of the time frame of the first two chapters in contrast with the following debate) Job becomes – dare we say it? – increasingly self-satisfied with his integrity and uprightness, to the extent that he occasionally casts doubt on the character of God. It is with this that God seeks to deal in His final intervention. Underneath Job's genuine righteousness lay a propensity to fleshly pride which was only drawn out into the open by the trials and accusations he had to endure. Even the best of mere men is but a man at best.

To read the book of Job is to be reminded in the most forcible manner that God's ways are higher than ours, and that He may have gracious and necessary reasons for His dealings with His saints which He does not see fit to reveal. The lesson is to wait (much may be disclosed in eternity), to worship (for God is God), and to trust. It is of the utmost encouragement for the believer to acknowledge that behind *all* his trials – whatever they may be, and whatever may be their immediate cause (the in-built consequences of personal failure, the hostility of a Christ-rejecting world, the deleterious results of sin in the human race, the hatred of Satan, the fatherly exercise of divine discipline) – is the sure hand of a God whose purposes cannot fail.

The book of Job touches every believer, for afflictions are common to all. Every joy or trial is ultimately traceable to the God who has never abdicated sovereign rule over the affairs of His creation. That is why the Puritan Thomas Watson's words are such an unfailing source of uplift: "Whoever brings an affliction to us, it is God that sends it".[506] The messenger may be Satan, or the Chaldeans, or the weather, but the final source is God. Because He has a special hand in His people's circumstances, we may be sure that every load He bestows He will give us grace to bear. Young's Literal Translation of Psalm 55.22 brings out the point: "Cast on Jehovah that which He hath given thee". Therefore we can, with confidence, gladly entrust it all to Him, knowing that He who sovereignly allocated the trial can give strength to endure it. He may not immediately lift us out, but He will surely bring us through.

> Lord, give me grace to bear what Thou dost give me -
> I need Thy strength to make it through each day;
> Grant me Thy patience in the hour of trial,
> And peace bestow when problems come my way.
>
> Thou art the God of all my circumstances,
> For death and life are in Thy sovereign hands;
> No stormy cloud approaches my horizon
> But in accordance with Thy wise commands.
>
> Whate'er my lot, in Thee is true contentment,
> Thy loving-kindness makes the wounded whole;
> And in Thy Word is nourishment sufficient
> To feed the mind and fortify the soul.
>
> When at the last I reach the heav'nly haven
> Where hidden purposes are brought to light,
> Then shall I praise Thee for my pilgrim journey,
> Knowing that all Thy ways with me were right.

NOTES

SECTION 1

[1] H L Ellison, *From Tragedy to Triumph*, Paternoster Press, 1958, [9]

[2] Thomas Robinson, *Homiletical Commentary on the Book of Job*, Richard D Dickinson, 1876, iii

[3] John E Hartley, *The Book of Job* (NICOT), Grand Rapids, Eerdmans, 1988, 372

[4] Dale Ralph Davis, *1 Kings: The Wisdom and the Folly*, Christian Focus, 2002, 279

[5] Warren W Wiersbe, *The Wiersbe Bible Commentary: Old Testament*, David C Cook, 2007, 824

[6] Robinson, 1

[7] William Kelly, *The Bible Treasury*, new series 7, March 1908, 35

[8] W G Scroggie, *Know Your Bible*, Pickering & Inglis, 1940, 133

[9] John Milton, *Paradise Lost*, Book 1, lines 125-6

[10] Keil and Delitzsch, *Commentary on the Old Testament*, Vol 4: Job, 705

[11] A R Fausset, *Fausset's Bible Dictionary*, Zondervan, 1949, 381

[12] William Kelly, *The Bible Treasury*, ns 7, March 1908, 36

[13] *The English Tanach*, Mesorah Publications Ltd, 2011, 1055

[14] W G Scroggie, *Know Your Bible*, Pickering and Inglis, 1940, 130

[15] Henry M Morris, *The Remarkable Record of Job*, Master Books, 2000, 19

[16] J Sidlow Baxter, *Explore the Book*, Oliphants, 1960, 27

[17] R B Zuck, "Job", in *The Bible Knowledge Commentary: Old Testament*, Victor Press, 1985, 715

[18] Gleason Archer, *Survey of Old Testament Introduction*, Moody Press, 1964, 438

[19] J Sidlow Baxter, 77

[20] Walter Scott, *Bible Handbook: Old Testament*, Bible Truth Publishers, nd, 131

[21] M H Finlay, *The Arrows of the Almighty*, reprinted John Ritchie, 2013, 67

[22] J Sidlow Baxter, 26

[23] Alfred Edersheim, cited in J Sidlow Baxter, 24

[24] A A Milne, *Winnie-the-Pooh*, Methuen, 1926, 36

[25] C H Mackintosh, *Job and his Friends* in The Mackintosh Treasury, Loizeaux, 1976, 358

[26] G Harding Wood, *Bird's Eye View of the Bible*, Marshall, Morgan & Scott, 1957, 104

[27] C S Lewis, *The Complete Chronicles of Narnia*, HarperCollins, 1998, 99

[28] http://library.timelesstruths.org/music/God_Moves_in_a_Mysterious_Way/

SECTION 2

[29] Elmer B Smick, "Job", in *The Expositors' Bible Commentary*, ed Frank E Gabelein, vol 4, Zondervan, 1988, 878

[30] Smick, 879

[31] A B Davidson, *The Book of Job*, Cambridge, 1951, 2

[32] Thomas Robinson, *Homiletical Commentary on the Book of Job*, Richard D Dickenson, 1876, 19

[33] This refers to the numbering system for Hebrew words found in Strong's Concordance

[34] John E Hartley, *The Book of Job* (NICOT), Grand Rapids, Eerdmans, 1988, 67

[35] Roy B Zuck, *Everyman's Bible Commentary: Job*, Chicago, Moody Press, 1978, 14

[36] Hartley, 68

[37] Delitzsch, 271

[38] Davidson, 7

[39] Delitzsch, 272

[40] William Kelly, *The Bible Treasury*, new series 7, April 1908, 52

[41] For an informative discussion of the Genesis passage see Gary Bates, *Alien Intrusion*, CMI, 2006, 380-400

[42] William Kelly, *The Bible Treasury*, new series 7, April 1908, 52-53

[43] Robinson, 12

[44] Francis Bacon, "Of Adversity", *Essays,* http://www.bartleby.com/3/1/5.html

[45] Hartley, 76

[46] Delitzsch, 277

[47] Delitzsch, 277

[48] Hartley, 77

[49] Davidson, 12

[50] Robinson, 15

[51] Hartley, 78

[52] Robinson, 16

[53] C H Spurgeon, *The Suffering of Man and the Sovereignty of God*, Fox River Press, 2001, 31

[54] Smick, 885

[55] Delitzsch, 281

[56] Davidson, 17

[57] Smick, 886

[58] Robinson, 19

[59] Delitzsch, 282

[60] Davidson, 18

[61] Robinson, 20

[62] Delitzsch, 281

[63] Hartley, 85

[64] Delitzsch, 283

[65] Gesenius, *Hebrew-Chaldee Lexicon to the Old Testament*, Baker, 1979, 538

[66] Hartley, 85

[67] Gesenius, 544

[68] Delitzsch, 283

[69] Robinson, 21

[70] http://wordsmith.org/words/jobs_comforter.html

SECTION 3

[71] Joseph Hall, *Contemplations on the Historical Passages of the Old and New Testament*, Soli Deo Gloria, 1995, Vol 3, 84

[72] Delitzsch, 289

[73] Smick, 888

[74] C F Keil, *Commentary on the Old Testament: Jeremiah*, Hendrickson, 1996, 198

[75] J N Darby, *Synopsis of the Books of the Bible*: Vol 2, Stow Hill Bible and Tract Depot, 1965, 27

[76] Wiersbe, 827

[77] Delitzsch, 290

SECTION 4

[78] William Kelly, *Eleven Lectures on Job*, 1919, 185

[79] William Kelly, *Eleven Lectures on Job*, 1919, 146

[80] http://www.brainyquote.com/quotes/authors/w/william_osler.html

[81] Robinson, 29

[82] John Bunyan, *The Pilgrim's Progress*, OUP, 1960, 158

[83] http://www.victorianlondon.org/etexts/dickens/pickwick-0008.shtml

[84] Delitzsch, 296

[85] Delitzsch, 303

SECTION 5

[86] Matthew Henry, 37

[87] Ellison, 32

[88] Ellison, 36

[89] Robinson, 53

[90] Smick, 900

[91] Delitzsch, 305

[92] Delitzsch, 306

[93] Davidson, 56

[94] *Fausset's Bible Dictionary*, Zondervan, 1949, 676

[95] Hartley, 140

[96] Delitzsch, 309
[97] Davidson, 61
[98] Hartley, 145
[99] http://www.online-literature.com/swift/gulliver/26/
[100] Delitzsch, 312
[101] Hartley, 151, note
[102] Davidson, 66
[103] Ellison, 40

SECTION 6
[104] Zuck, 43
[105] Robinson, 54
[106] A H Strong, *Systematic Theology*, 1907, reprinted Pickering & Inglis, 1987, 291
[107] Delitzsch, 318
[108] Hartley, 160
[109] Davidson, 69-70

SECTION 7
[110] Davidson, 75
[111] Hartley, 165
[112] Delitzsch, 335
[113] Douglas Wilson, *Letter from a Christian Citizen*, American Vision, 2007, 62-63
[114] Davidson, 80
[115] Delitzsch, 327
[116] Hartley, 173
[117] Hartley, 178
[118] Smick, 911
[119] Davidson, 84
[120] Robinson, 68
[121] Delitzsch, 331
[122] Zuck, 50
[123] Hartley, 181
[124] www.poetryfoundation.org/poems-and-poets/poems/detail/50694
[125] www.theotherpages.org/poems/2000/l/long52.html
[126] Delitzsch, 335
[127] Hartley, 188
[128] www.poetryfoundation.org/poems-and-poets/poems/detail/44392
[129] Delitzsch, 336
[130] Delitzsch, 265
[131] Percy Parsons, *Studies in the Book of Job*, duplicated notes, 1961, 10

SECTION 8
[132] Dale Ralph Davis, *Slogging Along in the Paths of Righteousness*, Christian Focus, 2014, 71
[133] Hartley, 195
[134] Delitzsch, 343
[135] Hartley, 199
[136] Smick, 917

SECTION 9
[137] Delitzsch, 291
[138] Delitzsch, 352
[139] Delitzsch, 353
[140] Davidson, 104
[141] Henry Morris (ed), *The Defender's Study Bible*, Word Publishing, 1995, 575

[142] Smick, 922

[143] Hartley, 209

[144] Zuck, 59

[145] http://www.cyberussr.com/hcunn/q-cromwell-beseech.html

[146] Spurgeon, 119-120

[147] Zuck, 61

[148] Smick, 925

[149] Thomas Constable, *Job*, 2013, 31

[150] C H Spurgeon, *Autobiography; The Early Years,* Banner of Truth, 1962, vol 1, 103

[151] Hartley, 228

[152] Hartley, 231

[153] Delitzsch, 366

[154] Delitzsch, 369

[155] Hartley, 235

[156] Davidson, 122

[157] Delitzsch, 373

[158] Hartley, 240

SECTION 10

[159] Zuck, 69

[160] Hartley, 244

[161] Davidson, 129

[162] Smick, 929

[163] Erwin W Lutzer. *Ten Lies about God*, Word Publishing, 2000, 15

[164] Hartley, 254

[165] Hartley, 253-4

[166] Spurgeon, *The Suffering of Man and the Sovereignty of God*, 133

SECTION 11

[167] Robinson, 98

[168] Warren W Wiersbe, *The Wiersbe Bible Commentary: Old Testament*, David C Cook, 2007, 838

[169] Robinson, 99

[170] I D E Thomas (ed), *The Golden Treasury of Puritan Quotations*, Moody Press, 1975, 13

[171] Delitzsch, 398

[172] Zuck, 77

[173] Davidson, 143

[174] Robinson, 100

[175] Delitzsch, 402

[176] Hartley, 268

[177] Delitzsch, 405

[178] Delitzsch, 406

[179] Hartley, 269, footnote 27

[180] Delitzsch, 408

[181] http://www.oxforddictionaries.com/definition/english/dust

[182] William Kelly, *Bible Treasury*, ns 7, 1908, 117

SECTION 12

[183] Robinson, 109

[184] Hartley, 272

[185] Bernard Ramm, *Protestant Biblical Interpretation*, 3rd edition, Baker, 1970, 55

[186] Smick, 937

[187] Robinson, 109

[188] Davidson, 156

[189] Delitzsch, 422

[190] Delitzsch, 424

[191] Davidson, 160

[192] Bunyan, *The Whole Works*, Ed George Offor, reprinted Baker, 1971, vol 3, 659

[193] Bunyan, 660

[194] Delitzsch, 425

[195] Robinson, 112

SECTION 13

[196] Zuck, 84

[197] Roger A Bullard, *Messiah: The Gospel according to Handel's Oratorio*, Hodder, 1995, 148

[198] Robinson, 113

[199] Delitzsch, 426

[200] Hartley, 283

[201] Zuck, 87

[202] Davidson, 163

[203] Smick, 640

[204] Delitzsch, 429

[205] Davidson, 165

[206] Delitzsch, 433

[207] Smick, 940

[208] Davidson, 165

[209] Robinson, 117

[210] Hartley, 291

[211] Zuck, 89

[212] C H Spurgeon, *The Suffering of Man and the Sovereignty of God*, Fox River Press, 2001, 159

[213] Zuck, 89

[214] Robinson, 118

[215] Davidson, 169

[216] Gleason L Archer, *Survey of Old Testament Introduction*, Moody, 1964, 449

[217] Matthew Henry, 108

[218] Delitzsch, 439

[219] Ellison, 69

[220] Constable, 41

[221] Davidson, 170

[222] Hartley, 294

[223] Delitzsch, 436

[224] Delitzsch, 442

SECTION 14

[225] Robinson, 123

[226] Delitzsch, 458

[227] Zuck, 93

[228] Delitzsch, 459

SECTION 15

[229] Max Hastings, *Catastrophe: Europe Goes to War, 1914*, Collins, 2013, 496

[230] Hartley, 310

[231] Davidson, 181

[232] www.bibles-online.net/1535/OldTestament/18-Job/

[233] Delitzsch, 464

[234] Hartley, 316

[235] Smick, 950

[236] Hartley, 321

[237] See the excellent account by Leonard Verduin, *The Reformers and their Stepchildren*, Baker, 1964

SECTION 16
[238] Delitzsch, 477
[239] H C Hewlett, *The Companion of the Way*, Ritchie, 2014, 53
[240] Hartley, 323
[241] Charles Dickens, *The Christmas Books*, Nonesuch Press, 1937, 47-48
[242] Robinson, 137
[243] Delitzsch, 481-2
[244] Delitzsch, 483
[245] *Fuller's Worthies*, selected by Richard Barber, Folio Society, 1987, 220
[246] Delitzsch, 486
[247] Delitzsch, 498

SECTION 17
[248] Robinson, 142
[249] Hartley, 338
[250] Spurgeon, 197
[251] Zuck, 108
[252] Robinson, 143
[253] Andersen, 210
[254] Robinson, 143
[255] Wiersbe, 848
[256] Hartley, 340
[257] Spurgeon, 205
[258] Delitzsch, 498
[259] Delitzsch, 499
[260] Davidson, 201
[261] Hartley, 345
[262] Hartley, 347
[263] Delitzsch, 504
[264] Davidson, 204
[265] Hartley, 348
[266] Shakespeare, *King Lear,* Act 3, Scene 4
[267] Dickens, *Oliver Twist*, chapter 48
[268] Delitzsch, 508
[269] P B Shelley, *Peter Bell the Third*
[270] Zuck, 111
[271] Hartley, 349
[272] Davidson, 205
[273] Robinson, 151

SECTION 18
[274] Hartley, 355
[275] Robinson, 152
[276] Delitzsch, 515
[277] Wiersbe, 850
[278] Hartley, 357
[279] Cansdale, 236-7
[280] C S Lewis, *Poems*, 1964, 55-56

SECTION 19
[281] Ellison, 45
[282] Davidson, 212
[283] Zuck, 116
[284] Zuck, 117

285 Delitzsch, 519
286 Kenny Barfield, *Why the Bible is Number 1*, Baker, 1988, 107
287 Davidson, 214
288 Barfield, 176
289 Hartley, 366
290 Smick, 967
291 Delitzsch, 520
292 Davidson, 215
293 Delitzsch, 522
294 www.smallchurchmusic3.com/Lyrics/D00/S00268.php

SECTION 20
295 Spurgeon, 226
296 Hartley, 369
297 Smick, 971
298 Smick, 971
299 Robinson, 163
300 Delitzsch, 529
301 Hamilton Smith (ed), *Gleanings from Thomas Watson*, Soli Deo Gloria, 1995, 53
302 Delitzsch, 531
303 Delitzsch, 531
304 Cansdale, 227
305 Davidson, 221
306 Delitzsch, 533
307 Delitzsch, 533, footnote 1
308 http://studybible.info/MSTC/Job%2027
309 Matthew Henry, *Commentary on the Whole Bible*, Macdonald, nd, Vol 3, 146
310 Delitzsch, 535
311 Robinson, 165
312 Zuck, 123
313 Hartley, 377
314 Delitzsch, 546
315 W G T Shedd, *Dogmatic Theology*, reprinted Thomas Nelson, 1980, vol 1, 356-7
316 http://opc.org/lc.html
317 Smick, 975
318 Vishal Mangalwadi, *The Book that Made your World*, Thomas Nelson, 2011, 108
319 Mangalwadi, 95

SECTION 21
320 Quoted in Wiersbe, 853
321 Hartley, 388
322 Hartley, 389
323 Davidson, 236
324 C F Keil, *Commentary on the Pentateuch*, 148
325 Smick, 981
326 Zuck, 128
327 Davidson, 237
328 Jewish tradition, perhaps influenced by the reference to "nest" in the earlier part of the verse, replaces "sand" with "phoenix", a mythical bird supposed to live for hundreds of years before building its own funeral pyre and then miraculously reviving from its ashes. Delitzsch, who takes it seriously, provides details of the tradition. However, the vast majority of English translations retain "sand".
329 Davidson, 239

[330] Trollope, *The Warden*, chapter 6

[331] Delitzsch, 573

[332] Smick, 985

[333] Delitzsch, 566

[334] Delitzsch, 567

[335] Hartley, 400

[336] Delitzsch, 571

[337] Delitzsch, 572

[338] Delitzsch, 577

[339] Constable, 53

[340] Delitzsch, 577

[341] Delitzsch, 582

[342] *Theological Wordbook of the Old Testament*, Moody Press, 1980, vol 2, 976

[343] Cansdale, 148

[344] http://www.owlpages.com/owls.php?genus=Bubo&species=ascalaphus

[345] Delitzsch, 582

[346] Delitzsch, 577

[347] Robinson, 184

[348] Zuck, 133

[349] Davidson, 247

[350] Hartley, 407

[351] Delitzsch, 585

[352] Delitzsch, 585

[353] Delitzsch, 587

[354] Zuck, 135

[355] Davidson, 250

[356] Zuck, 136

[357] Delitzsch, 590

[358] J R R Tolkien, *The Fellowship of the Ring*, book 2, chapter 8

[359] Jonathan D Sarfati, *The Genesis Account: A Theological, Historical, and Scientific Commentary on Genesis 1-11,* Creation Books Publishers, 2015, 207

[360] Delitzsch, 597

[361] Zuck, 138

[362] Smick, 996

[363] Robinson, 199

[364] Wiersbe, 857

[365] Robert N Schaper, *Why Me God?* Glendale, Regal Books, 1974, 91-92

[366] Robinson, 199

[367] Robinson, 194

SECTION 22

[368] Robinson, 202

[369] Davidson, 256

[370] Kelly, *Eleven Lectures on the Book of Job*, 1919, 212

[371] Smick, 997

[372] Zuck, 141

[373] Delitzsch, 603

[374] Delitzsch, 605

[375] Percy Parsons, *Studies in the Book of Job*, privately printed, 1961, 7

[376] Delitzsch, 608

[377] Delitzsch, 608

[378] J N Darby, *Synopsis of the Books of the Bible,* vol 2, 1965, 29

[379] Delitzsch, 610

[380] Delitzsch, 610
[381] Robinson, 209
[382] Davidson, 265
[383] Quoted in John Blanchard, *The Complete Gathered Gold*, Evangelical Press, 2006, 439
[384] Delitzsch, 621
[385] Delitzsch, 621

SECTION 23
[386] Delitzsch, 625
[387] Wiersbe, 860
[388] Harris, Archer and Waltke (eds), *The Theological Wordbook of the Old Testament*, Moody, 1980, vol 2, 907
[389] Hartley, 456-457
[390] Robinson, 218
[391] Hartley, 459
[392] Delitzsch, 631
[393] Matthew Henry , *Commentary on the Whole Bible*, Volume 3, 190
[394] John Bunyan, *The Pilgrim's Progress*, OUP, 1960, 157-8

SECTION 24
[395] Delitzsch, 637
[396] Zuck, 154
[397] Hartley, 466
[398] Robinson, 222
[399] Davidson, 280
[400] Spurgeon, 319-20
[401] Robinson, 225
[402] Delitzsch, 640-41

SECTION 25
[403] Andersen, 258
[404] http://www.phrases.org.uk/meanings/absolute-power-corrupts-absolutely.html
[405] Robinson, 210-11
[406] Delitzsch, 643
[407] Davidson, 283
[408] http://www.rjgeib.com/thoughts/britain/britain.html
[409] Smick, 1022
[410] Delitzsch, 645
[411] Robinson, 212
[412] Delitzsch, 646
[413] S Terrien, quoted in Hartley, 466
[414] C S Lewis, *The Complete Chronicles of Narnia*, Collins, 1998, 524
[415] Wiersbe, 862
[416] Wiersbe, 862
[417] http://creation.com/the-wonders-of-water
[418] Morris, 37-38
[419] Ron Neller, "Do you know the laws of the heavens?— the Bible and the hydrologic cycle", *Journal of Creation* (28) 2014, 66. See also Ron Neller, "The Water Cycle", in *Creation* (38) 2016, 18-19
[420] Delitzsch, 649
[421] Delitzsch, 651
[422] Hartley, 480
[423] Zuck, 160
[424] Smick, 1024

[425] answersingenesis.org/aquatic-animals/beacons-of-the-deep/
[426] sonnets.org/herbert.htm
[427] Zuck, 161
[428] Morris, 75-82
[429] Kelly, "Three Lectures on the Book of Job", *The Bible Treasury*, November 1908, 168
[430] Delitzsch, 656
[431] Delitzsch, 660
[432] Robinson, 232

SECTION 26
[433] Davidson, 319
[434] Kelly, "Three Lectures on the Book of Job", *The Bible Treasury*, November 1908, 170
[435] Doug Sharp and Jerry Bergman (eds), *Transformed by the Evidence*, Leafcutter Press, 2014, 111
[436] Hymn No 25 in *Glorious Themes*, privately printed, nd
[437] Delitzsch, 663
[438] Hartley, 494
[439] Delitzsch, 663
[440] *Fausset's Bible Dictionary*, 1981, 634
[441] Robinson, 250
[442] http://www.thefreedictionary.com/hoarfrost
[443] http://creation.com/the-wonders-of-water
[444] Hartley, 501
[445] Zuck, 170
[446] http://www.boop.org/jan/justso/butter.htm
[447] *Fausset's Bible Dictionary*, 598
[448] Cansdale, 88
[449] Cansdale, 94-95
[450] Cansdale, 82-83
[451] Cansdale, 84
[452] Cansdale, 191
[453] Cansdale, 193
[454] There is a detailed response at http://www.asa3.org/ASA/PSCF/1963/JASA12-63Howe.html
[455] http://thenaturalhistorian.com/2013/02/04/consider-the-ostrich-book-job-creation-wisdom/
[456] Delitzsch, 677
[457] http://www.gutenberg.org/files/4943/4943-h/4943-h.htm#link2HCH0015
[458] Cansdale, 147
[459] David Catchpoole, http://creation.com/wings-on-the-wind
[460] Cansdale, 142
[461] Cansdale, 144
[462] Delitzsch, 683
[463] Davidson, 318

SECTION 27
[464] Delitzsch, 685
[465] Shakespeare, *Macbeth*, Act 5, Scene 2
[466] Cansdale, 197
[467] Lita Cosner's article is illuminating: http://creation.com/psalms-1
[468] http://creation.com/leviathan-real-or-symbolic
[469] *NKJV Study Bible*, second edition, Nelson, 2007, 814
[470] Mart-Jan Paul, "Behemoth and leviathan in the book of Job", *Journal of Creation*, 24 (3) 2010, 94-100
[471] Allan K Steel, "Could Behemoth have been a Dinosaur?", *Technical Journal*, 15 (2) 2001, 42-45
[472] Chapter 19 of the *Creation Answers Book* is worth consulting. See http://creation.com/images pdfs/cabook/chapter19.pdf

[473] Tim Clarey, "Tracking Down Leviathan", *Acts and Facts,* July 2015 (http://www.icr.org article/8811)

[474] Lita Cosner, http://creation.com/leviathan-real-or-symbolic

[475] Hartley, 526

[476] Delitzsch, 688

[477] Mart-Jan Paul, "Behemoth and leviathan in the book of Job", *Journal of Creation*, 24 (3) 2010, 95

[478] http://www.ancientreplicas.com/assyrian-blinding.html

[479] http://creation.com/dinosaurs-and-dragons-stamping-on-the-legends

[480] Delitzsch, 696

[481] Robinson, 270

[482] Robinson, 271

[483] G Harding Wood, *Bird's Eye View of the Bible*, Marshall, Morgan & Scott, 1957, 104

[484] http://www.gbt.org/Donne%20Holy%20Sonnets.htm

[485] Spurgeon, 351

[486] Robert N Schaper, *Why Me God?,* Gospel Light, 1974,113

SECTION 28

[487] A W Tozer, *The Knowledge of the Holy*, 1961, 10

[488] Robinson, 276

[489] William Kelly, *The Bible Treasury*, December 1908, 181

[490] Matthew Henry, *Commentary on the Whole Bible*, Volume 3, McLean, Virginia, Macdonald, nd, 234

[491] Delitzsch, 703

[492] Smick. 1058

[493] Dale Ralph Davis, *Faith of our Father*, Christian Focus, 2015, 80-81

[494] http://www.rsc.org/periodic-table/element/51/antimony

[495] Robinson, 273

[496] Milton, *Samson Agonistes,* http://www.bartleby.com/101/324.html

[497] Robert P Lightner, *Handbook of Evangelical Theology*, Kregel, 1995, 251-2

[498] Henry C Thiessen, *Lectures in Systematic Theology*, Eerdmans, 1949, 489

[499] T C Hammond, *In Understanding Be Men*, IVP, 1951, 197

[500] *The Bible Treasury*, new series 9, May 1912, 79-80. By that stage the editor was W J Hocking, so one may assume the answer to be his; but he refers approvingly to Kelly's *The Preaching to the Spirits in Prison*, 1910.

[501] Robert Duncan Culver, *Systematic Theology*, Mentor, 2005, 1036-1042

[502] Culver, 1031

[503] I L Jensen, *Survey of the Old Testament*, Moody, 1978, 336

[504] http://www.icr.org/article/9143 (for ease of reading, some of the original footnotes have been incorporated into the text in square brackets).

[505] Cited in Robinson, 215

[506] Hamilton Smith (ed), *Gleanings from Thomas Watson*, Soli Deo Gloria, 1995, 56

"Doth Job fear God ..." **The Boo**

"When there are no rational, or even theological, explanati

•

Job is a unique and problematic book:

- in **size** (one of the longest in the canon of Scripture, containing 42 chapters which, apart from th bookends, require painstaking investigation)

- in **style** (though the prose framework is simple in vocabulary and narrative, the poetic body is bo complex and obscure in its linguistic detail)

- in **setting** (the events cannot be locked securely into any particular moment of OT history, standi outside Israel's time and culture zone, and containing no clear allusions to Israelite distinctives)

1-2	3	4 - 42.6		
Prose		Poetry		
Prologue		Dialogue (between Job and his 3 friends, a		
Intercedes for family (1.5) **Context:** 1.1-5 Job's uniqueness • piety • prosperity • priesthood	Monologue	**Contest:** 4 - 31 ("theorising on the basis of incomplete premises and deficient data" (J S Baxter)		
		Round One: 4 - 14 • Eliphaz: 4-5 • Job: 6-7 • Bildad: 8 • Job: 9-10 • Zophar: 11 • Job: 12-14	**Round Two:** 15 - 21 • Eliphaz: 15 • Job: 16-17 • Bildad: 18 • Job: 19 • Zophar: 20 • Job: 21	**Round Three:** 22 - 31 • Eliphaz: 22 • Job: 23-24 • Bildad: 25 • Job: 26-31 *(Bildad has only 6 verses and Zophar is reduced to silence)*
Challenge: 1.6-12 God's initiative **Calamity:** 1.13-2.13 Satan's malice Removal of Job's • possessions • posterity • personal health • partner's support • peers' sympathy	Complaint: Why was I born?	The theology lying behind the friends' comments is that great suffering always proves great sin (4.7-8; 8:6; 11.6; 13.23-24; 15.4-5; 22.5-7), while Job insists that he is innocent of any sin worthy of such punishment (6.10; 9.17; 13.15; 16.17; 21.16; 23.11-12; 27.5-6; 29.14; 30.25; 31). See Job 2.3; John 9.2; Luke 13.2-3. The book vindicates his innocence (1.8) but exposes his ignorance (38.2). His language is contorted by the extremities of his suffering, his three friends' by the dogmatic vehemence of their entrenched doctrinal position.		
Earth/heaven	Earth			

Job 1.21; 2.10 Ye have heard of the **ENDURANCE** of Job ... (James 5.11 JND)	**Job's Friends:** Eliphaz (sympathy) - 3 speeches Bildad (severity) - 3 speeches Zophar (bigotry) - 2 speeches All become increasingly hostile and negative, accusing Job of wickedness, yet are unable to dent his confidence (which is expressed in 9 speeches)	**3 Key Chapters:** 3: **Why** was I born? (v.11) 28: **Where** is wisdom found? (v.12) 38: **Who** is this? (v.2)
A righteous man (1.1,8; 2.3)		

Chart 655

JOB *"... for nought?" (1.9)*

disaster and pain, trust God" *(Macarthur Study Bible)*.

•

subject (e.g., the reason men worship God, the apparently capricious sufferings of a righteous man, Satan's access to God, the earthly focus of Job's final blessings)

strategy (raising difficult questions, offering unsatisfactory human responses, but providing no authoritative commentary to distinguish between the truth and error which pervade them all)

solution (Job's essential problem remains unanswered until the NT disclosure of (i) resurrection, (ii) the ultimate innocent victim, the Lord Jesus, whose sufferings have unique atoning value, and (iii) God's eternal purpose in a new heaven and earth)

4 - 42.6	42.7-17
Poetry	Prose
young Elihu, culminating in Jehovah's voice)	Epilogue

Corrective: 32 - 37	**Climax: 38.1 - 42.6**	Intercedes for friends (42.10)
Elihu's unexpected intervention: Preamble: 32 Speech 1: 33 Speech 2: 34 Speech 3: 35 Speech 4: 36-37 Stand still and consider the wondrous works of God (37.14) Whereas the friends have argued that Job's woes are proof of past sins, Elihu sounds a new note and argues that Job's present words manifest self-righteousness. ⟶ (40.8)	JEHOVAH speaks: Speech 1: 38-39 Where wast thou? Speech 2: 40-41 Behemoth & Leviathan Who then is able to stand before me? *Storm gathers 37.1-5,22; 38.1* N.B. "Job does not find the answer he was seeking, but he loses the question he was asking" (G H Wood)	Conclusion: Double restoration of Job's possessions except his children (42.10,12)

Job hath spoken words without knowledge (34.35; 35.16; 38.2; 42.3)

Job's Final Defence (26-31):
His friends having run out of breath, Job sums up
his case in his longest speech:
26-27: a reply to his critics
28: a hymn in praise of wisdom
29: Job's past prosperity ("O that I were")
30: Job's present adversity ("But now")
31: Job's personal integrity ("If ... then")

Job 42.10
... and have seen
the **END** of the
Lord; that the
Lord is very
pitiful and of
tender mercy
(James 5.11)

A repentant man (42.6)